Illustrated Series™

Microsoft® 365® Word®

Comprehensive

First Edition

Carol Cram
Jennifer Duffy

Cengage

Australia • Brazil • Canada • Mexico • Singapore • United Kingdom • United States

Cengage

Illustrated Microsoft® 365® Word® Comprehensive, **First Edition**

Carol Cram, Jennifer Duffy

SVP, Product Management: Cheryl Costantini

VP, Product Management & Marketing: Thais Alencar

Senior Product Director, Portfolio Product Management: Mark Santee

Portfolio Product Director: Rita Lombard

Senior Portfolio Product Manager: Amy Savino

Senior Product Assistant: Ciara Boynton

Learning Designer: Zenya Molnar

Senior Content Manager: Samantha Rundle

Digital Project Manager: Jim Vaughey

Developmental Editor: Mary-Terese Cozzola

Senior Director, Product Marketing: Danae April

Senior Marketing Manager: Mackenzie Paine

Portfolio Specialist: Matt Schiesl

Content Acquisition Analyst: Callum Panno

Production Service: Lumina Datamatics Ltd.

Senior Designer: Erin Griffin

Cover Image Source: Novendi Prasetya/Shutterstock.com

Mac Users: If you're working through this product using a Mac, some of the steps may vary. Additional information for Mac users is included with the Data files for this product.

Disclaimer: This text is intended for instructional purposes only; data is fictional and does not belong to any real persons or companies.

Disclaimer: The material in this text was written using Microsoft Windows 11 and Office 365 Professional Plus and was Quality Assurance tested before the publication date. As Microsoft continually updates the Windows operating system and Office 365, your software experience may vary slightly from what is presented in the printed text.

Previous edition(s): © 2023, © 2020, © 2017

For product information and technology assistance, contact us at
Cengage Customer & Sales Support, 1-800-354-9706
or support.cengage.com.

For permission to use material from this text or product, submit all requests online at **www.copyright.com.**

Library of Congress Control Number: 2024915464

Student Edition ISBN: 978-0-357-88275-7

Looseleaf ISBN: 978-0-357-88276-4

Cengage
5191 Natorp Boulevard
Mason, OH 45040
USA

Cengage is a leading provider of customized learning solutions. Our employees reside in nearly 40 different countries and serve digital learners in 165 countries around the world. Find your local representative at **www.cengage.com.**

To learn more about Cengage platforms and services, register or access your online learning solution, or purchase materials for your course, visit **www.cengage.com.**

Notice to the Reader

Publisher does not warrant or guarantee any of the products described herein or perform any independent analysis in connection with any of the product information contained herein. Publisher does not assume, and expressly disclaims, any obligation to obtain and include information other than that provided to it by the manufacturer. The reader is expressly warned to consider and adopt all safety precautions that might be indicated by the activities described herein and to avoid all potential hazards. By following the instructions contained herein, the reader willingly assumes all risks in connection with such instructions. The publisher makes no representations or warranties of any kind, including but not limited to, the warranties of fitness for particular purpose or merchantability, nor are any such representations implied with respect to the material set forth herein, and the publisher takes no responsibility with respect to such material. The publisher shall not be liable for any special, consequential, or exemplary damages resulting, in whole or part, from the readers' use of, or reliance upon, this material.

Printed at CLDPC, USA, 09-24

Brief Contents

Contents

Preface: The Illustrated Series®: Microsoft® 365® and Office®

About the Authors

Access: Robert S. Wilson has a Computer Science degree from the University of Waterloo, holds numerous certifications from CompTIA, Microsoft, and Cisco, and has over 40 years of experience in the computing field. Rob has expertise in many areas including database development and administration. He has built complex applications using Microsoft® Access® as its foundation, including production control and project management systems. He is also the co-founder and chief technical officer of Got Your Six Cybersecurity Solutions, a cybersecurity firm offering services covering the entire cybersecurity spectrum.

Excel: Lynn Wermers is a professor in the Computer Science Department at North Shore Community College in Massachusetts, where she teaches IT, data management, data analysis, and web development courses. She also teaches part-time in the math department for the College of Professional Studies at Northeastern University. Professor Wermers has authored numerous leading Cengage books focusing on Excel.

PowerPoint: David W. Beskeen has authored or co-authored over 65 successful computer books since 1992 for Microsoft Press and other publishers, including more than 40 educational titles for Course Technology, Thomson Learning, and Cengage. Over the years he has guided readers in mastering PowerPoint®, Word®, Excel®, Internet Explorer, Outlook®, Windows®, LiveMotion, and other leading proprietary software packages. An expert in applied technology, Beskeen has extensive teaching and consulting experience in today's computer technology.

Integration and Word: Carol M. Cram is the author of more than 35 textbooks on computer applications, business communications, and Internet-related subjects. Ms. Cram was also a long-time faculty member at Capilano College in North Vancouver, where she served as the Convenor of the Executive Support Program and the Program Consultant for Business and Computers in Continuing Education as well as instructor of business and computer-related courses.

Word: Jennifer Duffy is the author of nine editions of Microsoft® Word® Illustrated and many other textbooks on computer applications for the popular Office series. An award-winning writer and educator, she has worked successfully in the business world as a content creator and communications consultant and in colleges and universities as an effective instructor of writing. She combines her expertise in Word with her strong business and teaching knowledge to create compelling learning tools for students.

Preface for the Instructor

The Illustrated series' concise, student-friendly approach uses a proven two-page layout that enables learners to focus on discrete Office skills as they complete module readings. Each module begins with a brief overview of the principles covered in the lesson while large, full-color screen images reflect what students see on their computers. Distinctive to *Illustrated*, Tips and Clues boxes are incorporated throughout the text, while Trouble elements help students troubleshoot or explain common errors to strengthen their confidence. Module learning objectives are mapped to Microsoft Office Specialist (MOS) certification objectives, preparing students to take the MOS exam, which they can leverage in their careers. In addition, MindTap and updated SAM (Skills Assessment Manager) online resources are available to guide additional studies and ensure successful results.

The Illustrated Series is designed for students at two- and four-year schools as well as in continuing education programs. Skill levels range from experienced—for those with a foundational understanding from prior exposure to technology—to introductory—for those using a computer or technology device for the first time. The Illustrated Series is comprised of three parts: introductory, intermediate, and advanced. The series offers a comprehensive title that includes the four main Microsoft applications (Word, Excel, PowerPoint, and Access) at the introductory level. The MindTap Collection includes additional module coverage, including Outlook, Operating Systems, and Teams.

Market research is conducted semi-annually with both current Cengage users and those who use other learning materials. The focus of our market research is to gain insights into the user experience and overall learner needs so we can continuously evolve our content to exceed user expectations. We survey hundreds of instructors to ensure we gather insights from a large and varied demographic.

New to This Edition

The Illustrated Series provides thoroughly updated coverage that reflects current Microsoft 365 features. Narrative content has been authored using Microsoft 365 Business Standard. Module projects incorporate career topics that apply diversity, equity, and inclusion principles and ensure accessibility. All projects, assignments, and lessons have been refreshed with authentic case scenarios that focus on practical skills and employability.

Access: New features in the Access content include an updated, real-world scenario from a leading industry that illustrates the relevance of Access databases in today's businesses. Completely updated projects use gapped Start and Solution files to ensure students use new, authentic files for each project from one module to the next.

Excel: With the thoroughly updated coverage in the Excel modules, students learn both long-standing Excel functions and tools as well as the most recent innovations. New Microsoft® Excel 365® features include dynamic arrays and related functions such as FILTER, RANDARRAY, SEQUENCE, SORT, SORTBY, TRANSPOSE, and UNIQUE. This edition also introduces new Excel data types and the Analyze Data feature for spotting trends and gaining insight into data. With co-authoring, threaded comments, and Notes, users can collaborate with colleagues on workbooks, annotate data, and have useful discussions about the data.

Integration: Along with understanding how to leverage Microsoft Word, Excel, PowerPoint, and Access individually, the Illustrated Series offers further opportunities for users to learn how these applications work together. This knowledge enables students to leverage the full potential of these applications and create comprehensive, professional, and visually appealing documents, spreadsheets, presentations, and databases. By integrating these tools, students can seamlessly transfer data between applications, analyze and visualize data in Excel, import charts and graphs into Word or PowerPoint, and create interactive databases in Access. This knowledge not only enhances their productivity and communication skills but also prepares them for real-world scenarios where the ability to work with these applications in an integrated manner is highly valued in academic and professional settings.

PowerPoint: The PowerPoint coverage introduces the new commenting experience, which lets users display comments in a contextual view or the Comments pane. The comment anchor helps reviewers identify specific slide elements with comments and place the comment bubble anywhere on the slide. With the revised search feature, users can enter a word or phrase in the Search box to find the definition. Microsoft Search also provides support articles to help perform tasks. Users can record and save a presentation that includes digital inking to capture text, drawings, and annotations, and then play back animated drawings. The Speaker Coach uses artificial intelligence (AI) to improve presentation skills by giving feedback on body language, the use of sensitive and filler words, and perceived mispronounced words.

Word: New features in the Word content include the enhanced Accessibility Checker, which identifies potential accessibility issues and presents suggestions to make documents more inclusive. The Word modules also introduce Focus mode, the updated collaboration experience, Microsoft's expanded search tool, and voice options. The Immersive Reader is covered, as is the ability to create a private document copy and use Word's screen reader.

Organization of the Text

The Illustrated Series: Microsoft 365 & Office, First Edition is a comprehensive introduction to Microsoft applications—Word, Excel, PowerPoint, and Access—and is intended for students in introductory computing courses. Each application is divided into modules within the three levels—introductory, intermediate, and advanced. Each module introduces a topic through a real-world case scenario and presents content that aligns directly with the learning objectives stated at the beginning of the module and the more specific learning objectives in each lesson. Skills are taught progressively in visually rich lessons to encourage student learning as they proceed through the modules.

To enable students to practice and apply skills learned and to assess their mastery of the learning objectives, each module ends with three types of exercises: Skills Review, Independent Challenge, and Visual Workshop. The Skills Review contains hands-on exercises that mirror the progression of the lesson material. Each step matches a lesson title or learning objective and provides practice in the skills learned in the module lessons. To encourage critical and creative thinking, modules include two Independent Challenges, with the second more challenging than the first. Each exercise uses a different case scenario based on a real-life application in a top industry. The Visual Workshop provides a figure or screenshot showing a completed document, worksheet, presentation, or part of a database and asks the student to recreate it independently, without following step-by-step instructions.

Features of the text

The features of the text, which are found consistently throughout all modules, are designed to aid the student in a specific way.

The projects are centered around authentic case scenarios focused on employability and based on research and data to motivate students to perform the steps in the module.

Lesson titles organize topics within a module.

WD 1-8 Module 1 Creating Documents with Word

Save a Document

Numbered steps lead students through the process of completing a task while bullets in a Details section provide a planning lesson or, in the case of a challenging topic, a conceptual lesson.

Numbered steps include the following features:

QuickTips provide shortcuts and hints for using the app more effectively. A QuickTip points to a numbered step and is directly related to the corresponding action.

> **Quick Tip**
> You can also type a font size in the Font Size text box.
>
> **4. Click the Font Size list arrow in the Font group, drag the pointer slowly up and down the Font Size list, then click 18**
> As you drag the pointer over a font size, a preview of the font size is applied to the selected text. Clicking 18 increases the font size of the selected text to 18 points.

Troubles are marginal elements that anticipate common errors or provide troubleshooting advice to fix problems that might occur while completing the steps. The troubleshooting advice is related to the numbered step to which it points.

> **Trouble**
> If the Mini toolbar disappears, right-click the selection to display it again.
>
> **1. Select Fall Career Fair**
> The Mini toolbar appears over the selected text, as shown in **Figure 1-9**. You click a formatting option on the Mini toolbar to apply it to the selected text. **Table 1-5** describes the function of the buttons on the Mini toolbar. Yours may differ. The buttons on the Mini toolbar are also available on the Ribbon.

Clues boxes provide information that either expands on one component of the lesson skill or describes an independent task related to the lesson skill.

> **Planning a document**
>
> Before you create a new document, it's a good idea to spend time planning it. Identify the audience for your document, the message you want to convey, and the elements, such as tables or charts, you want to include. You should also think about the tone and appearance of your document—are you writing a business letter, which should be written in a pleasant, but serious, tone and have a formal appearance, or are you creating a flyer that must be colorful, eye-catching, and fun to read? The purpose and audience for your document determine the appropriate design. Planning the layout and design of a document involves deciding how to organize the text, selecting the fonts to use, identifying the graphics to include, and selecting the formatting elements that will enhance the message and appeal of the document. For longer documents, such as newsletters, it can be useful to sketch the layout and design of each page before you begin.

Other in-text pedagogical elements include the following:

Tables provide a quick summary of features that relate to the lesson task, such as identifying pointer shapes and what they do.

Table 1-1: Common mouse pointers in Word

name	pointer	use to
I-beam pointer		Move the insertion point in a document or to select text
Click and Type pointers, including left-align and center-align		Move the insertion point to a blank area of a document in Print Layout or Web Layout view; double-clicking with a Click and Type pointer automatically applies the Paragraph formatting (alignment and indentation) required to position text or a graphic at that location in the document
Selection pointer		Click a button or other element of the Word program window; appears when you point to elements of the Word program window
Right-pointing arrow pointer		Select a line or lines of text; appears when you point to the left edge of a line of text in the document window
Hand pointer		Open a hyperlink; appears when you point to a hyperlink in a task pane or when you press CTRL and point to a hyperlink in a document
Hide white space pointer		Hide the white space in the top and bottom margins of a document in Print Layout view
Show white space pointer		Show the white space in the top and bottom margins of a document in Print Layout view

Icons are included throughout the steps to show students examples of what buttons look like within the app.

> 8. **Click the Save button on the Quick Access toolbar**
> Your change to the notice is saved. After you save a document for the first time, you must continue to save the changes you make to the document.

Key terms appear in blue and bold font. The bold text appears as a clickable link in MindTap.

> - The **title bar** displays the name of the document and the name of the program. Until you give a new document a different name, its temporary name is Document1. The left side of the title bar contains the **Quick Access toolbar**, which includes buttons for saving a document. The middle of the title bar contains the **Search box**, which you can use to find a command or access the Word Help system. The right side of the title bar contains the resizing buttons and the program Close button.

SAM Upload and Download Icons are for SAM users. A SAM download icon appears next to any step where students download a Data File to begin a SAM Project.

> 1. sam **Start Word, then click Blank document**
> A blank document opens in the **Word program window**, as shown in **Figure 1-2**. The blinking vertical line in the document window is the **insertion point**. It indicates where text appears as you type.

A SAM upload icon appears next to any step where students submit a file to SAM for a completed SAM project.

> 9. sam **Click the File tab, then click Close**
> The document closes, but the Word program window remains open.

Course Solutions

Online Learning Platform: MindTap with SAM

The Illustrated Series MindTap Collection, powered by *SAM* (Skills Assessment Manager), enables proficiency in Microsoft Office and computing concepts for your Introductory Computing courses. With a library of renowned course materials, including ready-to-assign, auto-graded learning modules, you can easily adapt your course to best prepare students for the evolving job market. In addition to an eReader that includes the full content of the printed book, the Illustrated Collection, First Edition MindTap course includes the following:

- SAM Textbook Projects: Follow the steps and scenarios outlined in the textbook readings; enable students to complete projects based on a real-world scenario live in Microsoft Office applications and submit them in SAM for automatic grading and feedback.
- SAM Training and Exam: Trainings teach students to complete specific skills in a simulated Microsoft application environment while exams allow students to demonstrate their proficiency (also in a simulated environment).
- SAM Projects: Students complete projects based on real-world scenarios live in Microsoft applications and submit the projects in SAM for automatic grading and feedback. SAM offers several types of projects, each with a unique purpose: 1A and 1B, critical thinking, end of module, capstone, and integration.

- Microsoft Office Specialist (MOS) resources: Training and exams are based on the Microsoft Office 365 Objective Domains for the MOS Exam and exam simulation that replicates the test-taking environment of the MOS exam for Word, Excel, Access, PowerPoint, and Outlook.

To learn more, go to https://www.cengage.com/mindtap-collections/

Ancillary Package

Additional instructor and student resources for this product are available online. Instructor assets include an Instructor Manual, an Educator Guide, PowerPoint® slides, a Guide to Teaching Online, Solution Files, a test bank powered by Cognero®, and a Transition Guide. Student assets include data files and a glossary. Sign up or sign in at www.cengage.com to search for and access this product and its online resources. The instructor and student companion sites contain ancillary material for the full New Perspectives Series Collection, along with instructions on how to find specific content within the companion site.

- Instructor Manual: This guide provides additional instructional material to assist in class preparation, including module objectives, module outline, discussion questions, and additional activities and assignments. Each outline corresponds directly with the content in each module and additional discussion questions and activities are aligned to headings in the book.
- Educator Guide: The MindTap Educator Guide contains a detailed outline of the corresponding MindTap course, including activity types and time on task. The SAM Educator Guide explains how to use SAM functionality to maximize your course.
- PowerPoint slides: The slides may be used to guide classroom presentations, to provide to students for module review, or to print as classroom handouts. The slides align closely with the book while activities and the self-assessment align with module learning objectives and supplement the content in the book.
- Guide to Teaching Online: This guide presents technological and pedagogical considerations and suggestions for teaching the Introductory Computing course when you can't be in the same room with students.
- Solution Files: These files provide solutions to all textbook projects for instructors to use to grade student work.
    - Instructors using SAM do not need solution files since projects are auto-graded within SAM.
    - Solution files are provided on the instructor companion site for instructors *not* using SAM.
- Data Files: These files are provided for students to complete the projects in each module. Students using SAM to complete the projects download the required data files directly from SAM.
    - Students who are *not* using SAM to complete the projects can find data files on the student companion site and within MindTap.
- Test banks: A comprehensive test bank, offered in Cognero, Word, Blackboard, Moodle, Desire2Learn, Canvas, and SAM formats, contains questions aligned with each module's learning objectives and are written by subject matter experts. Powered by Cognero, Cengage Testing is a flexible, online system that allows you to author, edit, and manage test bank content from multiple Cengage solutions and to create multiple test versions that you can deliver from your LMS, your classroom, or wherever you want.
- Transition Guide: This guide highlights all the changes in the text and the digital offerings from the previous edition to the current one so that instructors know what to expect.

Acknowledgments

Lynn Wermers: I am extremely grateful for the creative talent, good judgment, and editing savvy that Mary-Terese Cozzola brought to the development of this publication. MT, thank you for your support, guidance, good humor and always finding the right words for every situation. Thanks also to Samantha Rundle for bringing her outstanding management skills to this project. Zenya Molnar's comprehensive feedback and suggestions for bringing together the concepts with the best learning experience have improved this edition greatly. Thank you also to Amy Savino for getting this project going and supporting it throughout its duration.

David W. Beskeen: The content of this book has evolved significantly since the first edition was published in 1994 and I am proud to have been given the opportunity since then to write and revise this book for the benefit of students. I want to thank Cengage for the opportunity to write this latest edition and to the whole Cengage team for their hard work on this project. Finally, I want to acknowledge my editor Barbara Clemens for her fine work, her diligence to detail, and her patience with me.

Carol M. Cram: Thank you to the wonderful team at Cengage and my developmental editor Michael Sanford for their expertise, support, and dedication. And, as always, my deepest thanks to my husband Gregg and our daughter Julia who make everything I do possible.

Jennifer Duffy: It is always a pleasure to work with a talented team of professionals to create a book. Thank you to Michael Sanford for his careful editing, and to the Cengage team—Amy Savino, Samantha Rundle, Zenya Molnar, and all the others—for their expertise and guidance.

Getting to Know Microsoft Office Versions

Cengage is proud to bring you the next edition of Microsoft Office. This edition was designed to provide a robust learning experience that is not dependent upon a specific version of Office.

Microsoft supports several versions and editions of Office: (Refer to Table 1 below for more information)

- **Microsoft 365 (formerly known as Office 365):** A service that delivers the most up-to-date, feature-rich, modern Microsoft productivity applications direct to your device. There are several combinations of Microsoft 365 programs for business, educational, and personal use. Microsoft 365 is cloud-based, meaning it is stored, managed, and processed on a network of remote servers hosted on the Internet, rather than on local servers or personal computers. Microsoft 365 offers extra online storage and cloud-connected features, as well as updates with the latest features, fixes, and security updates. Microsoft 365 is purchased for a monthly subscription fee that keeps your software up to date with the latest features.
- **Office 2021:** The Microsoft "on-premises" version of the Office apps, available for both PCs and Macintosh computers, offered as a static, one-time purchase and outside of the subscription model. Unlike Microsoft 365, Office 2021 does not include online product updates with new features.
- **Microsoft 365 Online (formerly known as Office Online):** A free, simplified version of Microsoft web applications (Teams, Access, Word, Excel, PowerPoint, and OneNote) that lets users create and edit files collaboratively.
- **Office 365 Education:** A free subscription including Word, Excel, PowerPoint, OneNote, and now Microsoft Teams, plus additional classroom tools. Only available for students and educators at select institutions.

Table 1 Microsoft Office applications — uses and availability

Application	Use	Availability/Editions
Word	Create documents and improve your writing with intelligent assistance features.	Microsoft 365 Family, Home, Business, Office 2021, Office 365 Education
Excel	Simplify complex data into easy-to-read spreadsheets.	Microsoft 365 Personal, Home, Business, Office 2021, Office 365 Education
PowerPoint	Create presentations that stand out.	Home, Business, Office 2021, Office 365 Education
OneNote	A digital notebook for all your note-taking needs.	Home, Office 365 Education
OneDrive	Save and share your files and photos wherever you are.	Home, Business
Outlook	Manage your email, calendar, tasks, and contacts all in one place.	Home, Business
SharePoint	Create team sites to share information, files, and resources.	Business
Publisher	Create polished, professional layouts without the hassle.	Home, Business, Office 2021 (PC only)
Access	Create your own database apps easily in formats that serve your business best.	Home, Business, Office 2021 (PC only)
Teams	Bring everyone together in one place to meet, chat, call, and collaborate.	Business, Office 365 Education
Exchange	Business-class email and calendaring.	Business

Over time, the Microsoft 365 cloud interface will continuously update using its web connection, offering new application features and functions, while Office 2021 will remain static.

Because Microsoft 365 releases updates continuously, your onscreen experience may differ from what you see in this product. For example, the more advanced features and functionalities covered in this product may not be available in Microsoft 365 Online, may have updated from what you see in Office 2021, or may be from a post-publication update of Microsoft 365.

For up-to-date information on the differences between Microsoft 365, Office 2021, and Microsoft 365 Online, please visit the Microsoft Support website.

Cengage is committed to providing high-quality learning solutions for you to gain the knowledge and skills that will empower you throughout your educational and professional careers.

Thank you for using our product, and we look forward to exploring the future of Microsoft Office with you!

Using SAM Projects and Textbook Projects

SAM (Skills Assessment Manager) **Projects** allow you to actively apply the skills you learned in Microsoft Word, Excel, PowerPoint, or Access. You can also submit your work to SAM for online grading. You can use SAM Projects to become a more productive student and use these skills throughout your career.

To complete SAM Textbook Projects, please follow these steps:

SAM Textbook Projects allow you to complete a project as you follow along with the steps in the textbook. As you read the module, look for icons that indicate when you should download your SAM Start file(s) and when to upload your solution file to SAM for grading.

Everything you need to complete this project is provided within SAM. You can launch the eBook directly from SAM, which will allow you to take notes, highlight, and create a custom study guide, or you can use a print textbook or your mobile app. Download IOS or Download Android.

To get started, launch your SAM Project assignment from SAM, MindTap, or a link within your learning management system.

1. Step 1:
   Download Files
   - Click the "Download All" button or the individual links to download your **Start File** and **Support File(s)** (when available). You must use the SAM Start file.
   - Click the Instructions link to launch the eBook (or use the print textbook or mobile app).
   - Disregard any steps in the textbook that ask you to create a new file or to use a file from a location outside of SAM.
   - Look for the SAM Download icon to begin working with your start file.
   - Follow the module's step-by-step instructions until you reach the SAM Upload icon.
   - Save and close the file.

2. Step 2:
   Save Work to SAM
   - Ensure you rename your project file to match the Expected File Name.
   - Upload your in-progress or completed file to SAM. You can download the file to continue working or submit it for grading in the next step.
3. Step 3:
   Submit for Grading
   - Upload your completed solution file to SAM for immediate feedback and to view the available Reports.
     - The **Graded Summary Report** provides a detailed list of project steps, your score, and feedback to aid you in revising and resubmitting the project.
     - The **Study Guide** provides your score for each project step and links to the associated training and textbook pages.
   - If additional attempts are allowed, use your reports to assist with revising and resubmitting your project.
   - To re-submit your project, download the file you saved in step 2.
   - Edit, save, and close the file, then re-upload and submit it again.

For all other SAM Projects, please follow these steps:

To get started, launch your SAM Project assignment from SAM, MindTap, or a link within your learning management system.

1. Step 1:
   Download Files
   - Click the "Download All" button or the individual links to download your **Instruction File**, **Start File**, and **Support File(s)** (when available). You must use the SAM Start file.
   - Open the Instruction file and follow the step-by-step instructions. Ensure you rename your project file to match the Expected File Name (change _1 to _2 at the end of the file name).

2. Step 2:
   Save Work to SAM
   - Upload your in-progress or completed file to SAM. You can download the file to continue working or submit it for grading in the next step.

3. Step 3:
   Submit for Grading
   - Upload the completed file to SAM for immediate feedback and to view available Reports.
     - The **Graded Summary Report** provides a detailed list of project steps, your score, and feedback to aid you in revising and resubmitting the project.
     - The **Study Guide** provides your score for each project step and links to the associated training and textbook pages.
   - If additional attempts are allowed, use your reports to assist with revising and resubmitting your project.
   - To re-submit the project, download the file saved in step 2.
   - Edit, save, and close the file, then re-upload and submit it again.

For additional tips to successfully complete your SAM Projects, please view our SAM Video Tutorials.

Creating Documents with Word

Case

You have been hired to work at Mountain Springs Institute of Technology, an institute of higher education that offers practical, applied education to both local and international students. Shortly after reporting to your new office, Prasad Anil, Director of Career Services, asks you to use Word to create a notice for students and an info sheet for job seekers.

Module Objectives

After completing this module, you will be able to:

- Use word-processing software
- Start Word
- Enter and revise text
- Save a document
- Select text
- Format text using the Mini toolbar and the Ribbon
- View and navigate a document
- Cut and paste text
- Copy and paste text
- Format with fonts
- Set document margins
- Add bullets and numbering
- Insert a graphic
- Apply a theme

Files You Will Need

IL_WD_1-1.docx
Support_WD_1-2.jpg
IL_WD_1-3.docx
Support_WD_1-4.jpg
IL_WD_1-5.docx
Support_WD_1-6.jpg

Use Word-Processing Software

Case Before beginning your notice, you explore the editing and formatting features available in Word.

Objectives
- Identify the features of Word
- State the benefits of using a word-processing program

A **word-processing program** is a software program that includes tools for entering, editing, and formatting text and graphics. Microsoft Word is a powerful word-processing program that allows you to create and enhance a wide range of documents quickly and easily. **Figure 1-1** shows the first page of a report created using Word and illustrates some of the Word features you can use to enhance your documents. The electronic files you create using Word are called **documents**. One of the benefits of using Word is that document files can be stored on a hard disk, flash drive, or another physical storage device, or to OneDrive or another Cloud storage place, making them easy to transport, share, and revise.

Details

You can use Word to accomplish the following tasks:

- **Type and edit text**
  The Word editing tools make it simple to insert and delete text in a document. You can add text to the middle of an existing paragraph; replace text with other text; undo an editing change; and correct typing, spelling, and grammatical errors with ease.

- **Copy and move text from one location to another**
  Using the more advanced editing features of Word, you can copy or move text from one location and insert it in a different location in a document. You also can copy and move text between documents. This means you don't have to retype text that is already entered in a document.

- **Format text and paragraphs with fonts, colors, and other elements**
  The sophisticated formatting tools in Word allow you to make the text in your documents come alive. You can change the size, style, and color of text; add lines and shading to paragraphs; and enhance lists with bullets and numbers. Creatively formatting text helps to highlight important ideas in your documents.

- **Format and design pages**
  The page-formatting features in Word give you the power to design attractive newsletters, create powerful résumés, and produce documents such as research papers, business cards, brochures, and reports. You can change paper size, organize text in columns, and control the layout of text and graphics on each page of a document. For quick results, Word includes preformatted cover pages, pull quotes, and headers and footers, as well as galleries of coordinated text, table, and graphic styles. If you are writing a research paper, Word makes it easy to manage reference sources and create footnotes, endnotes, and bibliographies.

- **Enhance documents with tables, charts, graphics, screenshots, and videos**
  Using the powerful graphics tools in Word, you can spice up your documents with pictures, videos, photographs, screenshots, lines, preset quick shapes, and diagrams. You also can illustrate your documents with tables and charts to help convey your message in a visually interesting way.

- **Use Mail Merge to create form letters and mailing labels**
  The Word Mail Merge feature allows you to send personalized form letters to many different people. You can also use Mail Merge to create mailing labels, directories, email messages, and other types of documents.

- **Share documents securely**
  The security features in Word make it quick and easy to remove comments, tracked changes, and unwanted personal information from your files before you share them with others. You can also add a password or a digital signature to a document and convert a file to a format suitable for publishing on the web.

Figure 1-1: A report created using Word

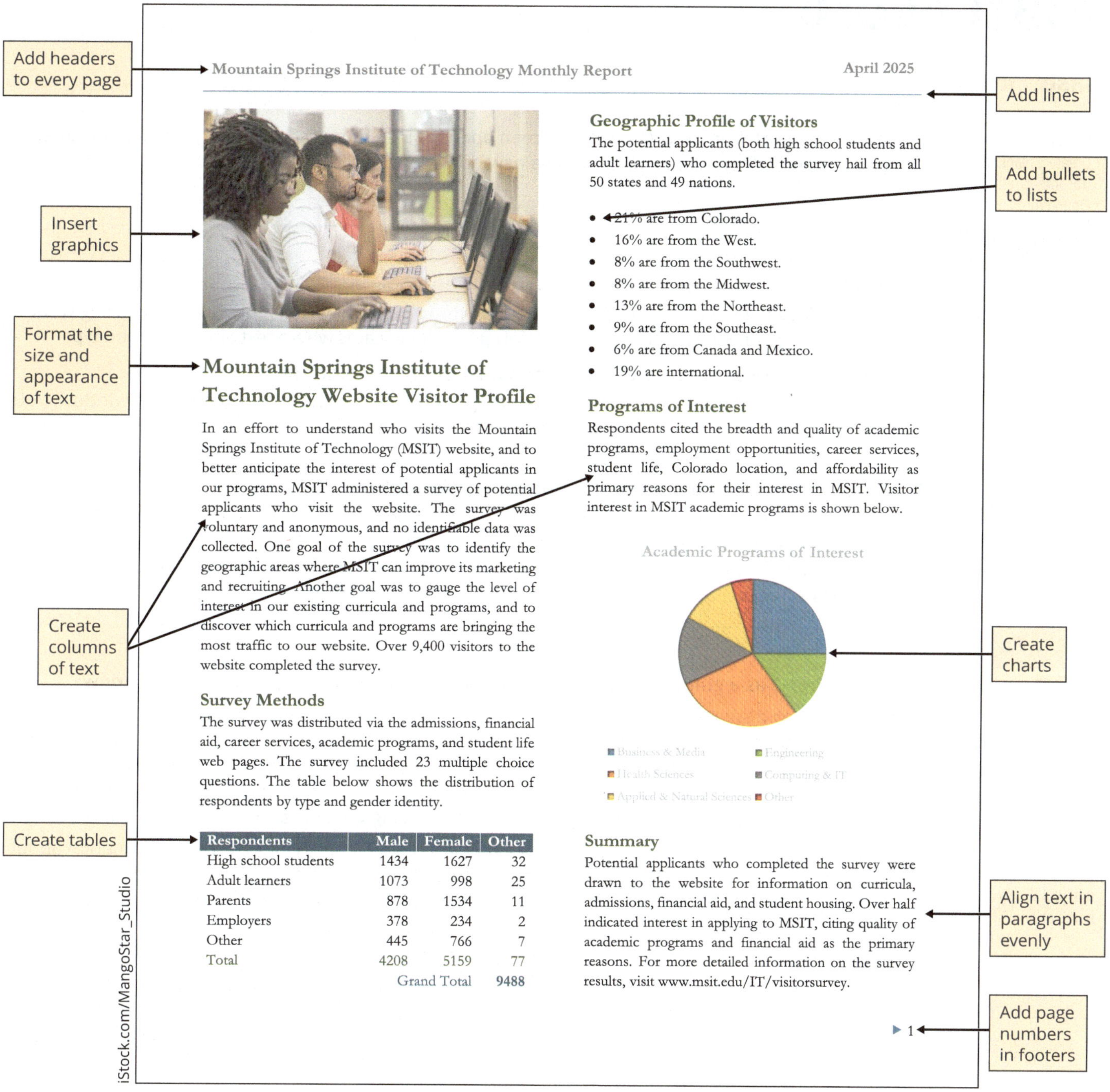

Mountain Springs Institute of Technology Monthly Report April 2025

Mountain Springs Institute of Technology Website Visitor Profile

In an effort to understand who visits the Mountain Springs Institute of Technology (MSIT) website, and to better anticipate the interest of potential applicants in our programs, MSIT administered a survey of potential applicants who visit the website. The survey was voluntary and anonymous, and no identifiable data was collected. One goal of the survey was to identify the geographic areas where MSIT can improve its marketing and recruiting. Another goal was to gauge the level of interest in our existing curricula and programs, and to discover which curricula and programs are bringing the most traffic to our website. Over 9,400 visitors to the website completed the survey.

Survey Methods

The survey was distributed via the admissions, financial aid, career services, academic programs, and student life web pages. The survey included 23 multiple choice questions. The table below shows the distribution of respondents by type and gender identity.

Respondents	Male	Female	Other
High school students	1434	1627	32
Adult learners	1073	998	25
Parents	878	1534	11
Employers	378	234	2
Other	445	766	7
Total	4208	5159	77
		Grand Total	9488

Geographic Profile of Visitors

The potential applicants (both high school students and adult learners) who completed the survey hail from all 50 states and 49 nations.

- 21% are from Colorado.
- 16% are from the West.
- 8% are from the Southwest.
- 8% are from the Midwest.
- 13% are from the Northeast.
- 9% are from the Southeast.
- 6% are from Canada and Mexico.
- 19% are international.

Programs of Interest

Respondents cited the breadth and quality of academic programs, employment opportunities, career services, student life, Colorado location, and affordability as primary reasons for their interest in MSIT. Visitor interest in MSIT academic programs is shown below.

Academic Programs of Interest

Business & Media; Engineering; Health Sciences; Computing & IT; Applied & Natural Sciences; Other

Summary

Potential applicants who completed the survey were drawn to the website for information on curricula, admissions, financial aid, and student housing. Over half indicated interest in applying to MSIT, citing quality of academic programs and financial aid as the primary reasons. For more detailed information on the survey results, visit www.msit.edu/IT/visitorsurvey.

1

Planning a document

Before you create a new document, it's a good idea to spend time planning it. Identify the audience for your document, the message you want to convey, and the elements, such as tables or charts, you want to include. You should also think about the tone and appearance of your document—are you writing a business letter, which should be written in a pleasant, but serious, tone and have a formal appearance, or are you creating a flyer that must be colorful, eye-catching, and fun to read? The purpose and audience for your document determine the appropriate design. Planning the layout and design of a document involves deciding how to organize the text, selecting the fonts to use, identifying the graphics to include, and selecting the formatting elements that will enhance the message and appeal of the document. For longer documents, such as newsletters, it can be useful to sketch the layout and design of each page before you begin.

Start Word

Case You open a blank document and examine the elements of the Word program window.

Objectives
- Create a blank document
- Open Word

When you start Word, the Word start screen opens. It includes a list of recently opened documents and a gallery of templates for creating a new document.

Steps

1. **sam Start Word, then click Blank document**
   A blank document opens in the **Word program window**, as shown in **Figure 1-2**. The blinking vertical line in the document window is the **insertion point**. It indicates where text appears as you type.
2. **Move the mouse pointer around the Word program window**
   The mouse pointer changes shape depending on where it is in the Word program window. You use pointers to move the insertion point or to select text to edit. **Table 1-1** describes common pointers in Word.
3. **Place the mouse pointer over a button on the Ribbon**
   When you place the mouse pointer over a button or some other elements of the Word program window, a ScreenTip appears. A **ScreenTip** is a label that identifies the name of the button or feature, briefly describes its function, conveys any keyboard shortcut for the command, and includes a link to associated help topics, if any.

Trouble
If the full Ribbon is hidden, click the Home tab, click the Ribbon Display Options button in the lower-right corner of the Ribbon, then click Always show Ribbon.

Details

Using Figure 1-2 as a guide, find the elements described below in your program window:

- The **title bar** displays the name of the document and the name of the program. Until you give a new document a different name, its temporary name is Document1. The left side of the title bar contains the **Quick Access toolbar**, which includes buttons for saving a document. The middle of the title bar contains the **Search box**, which you can use to find a command or access the Word Help system. The right side of the title bar contains the resizing buttons and the program Close button.
- The **File tab** provides access to **Backstage view** where you manage files and the information about them. Backstage view includes commands related to working with documents, such as opening, printing, sharing, and saving a document. The File tab also provides access to your account and to the Word Options dialog box, which is used to customize the way you use Word.
- The Ribbon contains the Word tabs. Each **tab** on the Ribbon includes buttons for commands related to editing and formatting documents. The commands are organized in **groups**. For example, the Home tab includes the Undo, Clipboard, Font, Paragraph, Styles, Editing, Voice, and Editor groups. The Ribbon also includes the **Comments button**, which you use to see comments, the Editing button, which is used to switch between editing, reviewing, and viewing modes, and the **Share button**, which you can use to save a document to the Cloud.
- The **document window** displays the current document. You enter text and format your document in the document window.
- The rulers appear in the document window in Print Layout view. The **horizontal ruler** displays left and right document margins as well as the tab settings and paragraph indents, if any, for the paragraph in which the insertion point is located. The **vertical ruler** displays the top and bottom document margins.
- The vertical and **horizontal scroll bars** are used to display different parts of the document in the document window. The scroll bars include **scroll boxes** and **scroll arrows**, which you use to scroll.
- The **status bar** displays the page number of the current page, the total number of pages and words in the document, and the Accessibility checker. It also includes the view buttons, the Zoom slider, and the Zoom level button. You can customize the status bar to display other information.
- The **view buttons** on the status bar allow you to display the document in Focus Mode, Read Mode, Print Layout, or Web Layout view. The **Zoom slider** and the **Zoom level button** provide quick ways to enlarge and decrease the size of the document in the document window, making it easy to zoom in on a detail of a document or to view the layout of the document as a whole.

Quick Tip
The Quick Access toolbar can be customized. Yours might include additional buttons or be located below the ribbon.

Quick Tip
To display a different tab, you simply click its name on the Ribbon.

Trouble
Click the View tab, then click the Ruler check box in the Show group to display the rulers if they are not already displayed.

Figure 1-2: Elements of the Word program window

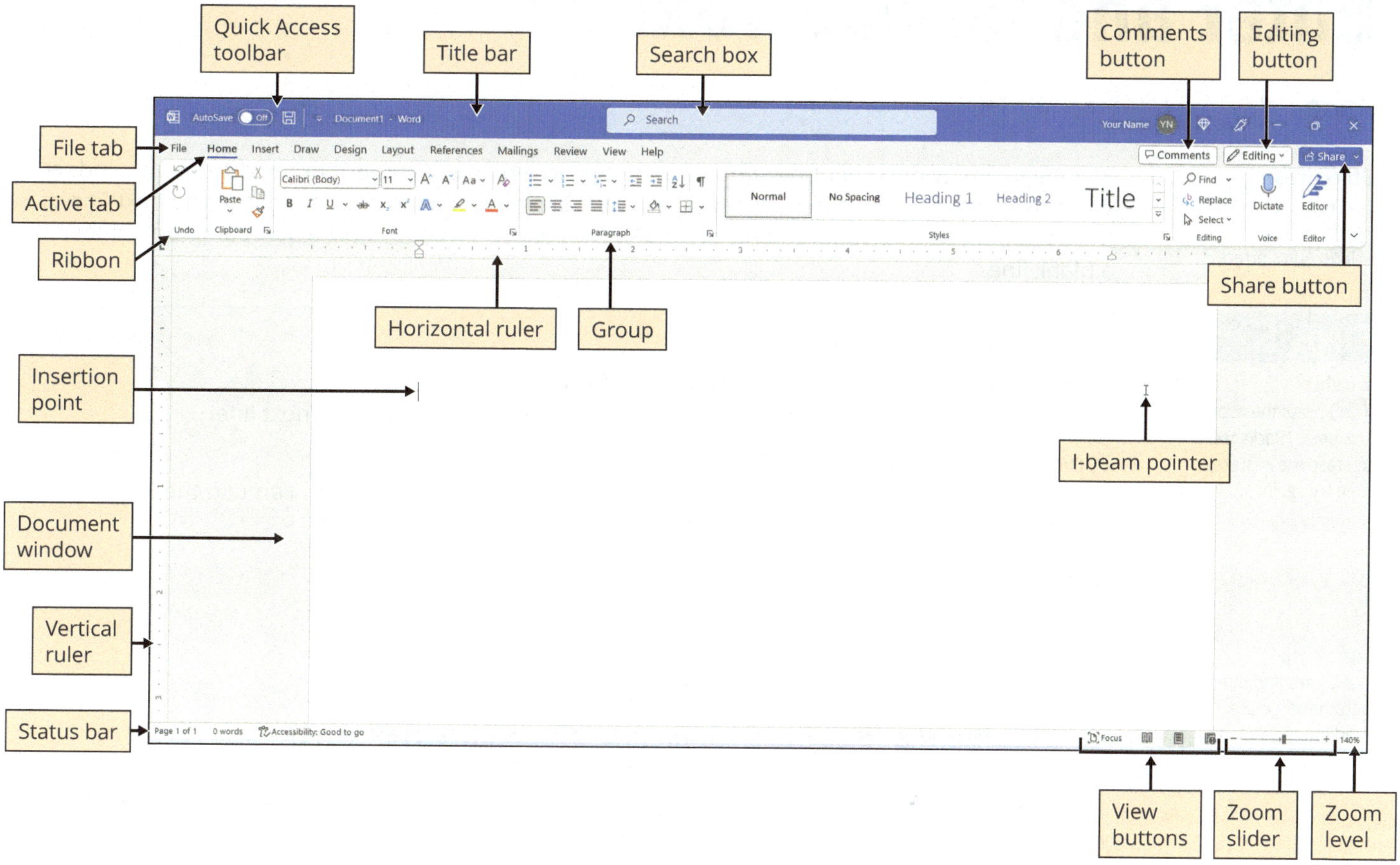

Table 1-1: Common mouse pointers in Word

name	pointer	use to
I-beam pointer	I	Move the insertion point in a document or to select text
Click and Type pointers, including left-align and center-align		Move the insertion point to a blank area of a document in Print Layout or Web Layout view; double-clicking with a Click and Type pointer automatically applies the Paragraph formatting (alignment and indentation) required to position text or a graphic at that location in the document
Selection pointer		Click a button or other element of the Word program window; appears when you point to elements of the Word program window
Right-pointing arrow pointer		Select a line or lines of text; appears when you point to the left edge of a line of text in the document window
Hand pointer		Open a hyperlink; appears when you point to a hyperlink in a task pane or when you press CTRL and point to a hyperlink in a document
Hide white space pointer		Hide the white space in the top and bottom margins of a document in Print Layout view
Show white space pointer		Show the white space in the top and bottom margins of a document in Print Layout view

Enter and Revise Text

Case You type a notice to post on a bulletin board.

Objectives
- Correct spelling and grammar
- Undo AutoCorrect

You begin a new document by simply typing text in a blank document in the document window. Word uses **word wrap**, a feature that automatically moves the insertion point to the next line of the document as you type. You only press ENTER when you want to start a new paragraph or insert a blank line.

Steps

Trouble
If you press the wrong key, press [Backspace] to erase the mistake, then try again.

1. **Type Fall Career Fair, then press ENTER twice**
   Each time you press ENTER, the insertion point moves to the start of the next line.
2. **Type TO:, then press TAB twice**
   Pressing TAB moves the insertion point several spaces to the right. You can use the TAB key to align the text in a notice header or to indent the first line of a paragraph.
3. **Type Volunteers, then press ENTER**
   The insertion point moves to the start of the next line.

Quick Tip
Wavy lines and other automatic feature markers appear on the screen but do not print.

4. **Type: FROM: TAB TAB Prasad Anil ENTER**
   DATE: TAB TAB June 4, 2025 ENTER
   RE: TAB TAB Fall career fair planning meeting ENTER ENTER
   Red wavy or blue double lines may appear under the words you typed, indicating a possible spelling or grammar error. Spelling and grammar checking is one of the many automatic features you will encounter as you type. **Table 1-2** describes several automatic features. You can correct any typing errors you make later.

Trouble
To reverse an AutoCorrect adjustment, immediately click the Undo button in the Undo group on the Home tab.

5. **Type A meeting for senior students interested in volunteering at the fall career fair will be held on the 17th of June at 4 p.m. in the conference room. , then press SPACEBAR**
   As you type, notice that the insertion point moves automatically to the next line of the document. You also might notice that Word automatically changed "17th" to "17th" in the notice. This feature is called **AutoCorrect**. AutoCorrect automatically makes typographical adjustments and detects and adjusts typing errors, certain misspelled words (such as "taht" for "that"), and incorrect capitalization as you type.
6. **Type Volunteering is an excellent opportunity to network with employers. The fall career fair is scheduled for September.**
   When you type the first few characters of "September" and certain other words, the Word text predictions feature displays a complete word in grey type. **Text predictions** suggests text to insert quickly into your documents. You can ignore text predictions for now. Your notice should resemble **Figure 1-3**.

Quick Tip
If you want uniform spacing between lines and paragraphs, apply the No Spacing style to the document by clicking the No Spacing button in the Styles group on the Home tab before you begin to type. Alternatively, select the text and then click the No Spacing button.

7. **Press ENTER, then type Over 100 employers from a wide range of industries will be in attendance. A list is available from Jacinda Zazgra. Employers will be recruiting MSIT talent from all academic programs for jobs, internships, and career opportunities.**
   When you press ENTER and type the new paragraph, notice that Word adds more space between the paragraphs than it does between the lines in each paragraph. This is part of the default style for paragraphs in Word, called the **Normal style**.
8. **Position the I pointer after for (but before the space) in the last sentence of the first paragraph, then click to move the insertion point after for**
9. **Press BACKSPACE three times, then type to take place in**
   Pressing BACKSPACE removes the character before the insertion point.
10. **Move the insertion point before senior in the first sentence, then press DELETE seven times to remove the word "senior" and the space after it**
    Pressing DELETE removes the character after the insertion point. **Figure 1-4** shows the revised notice.

Figure 1-3: Text in the document window

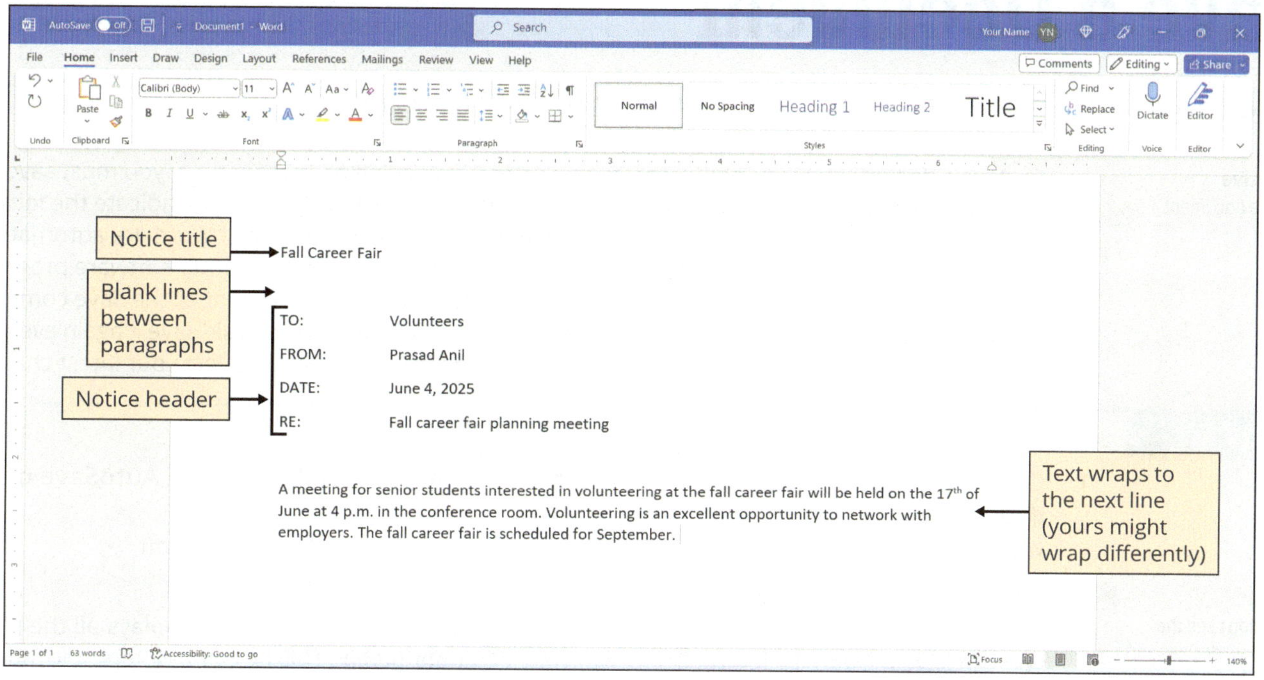

Figure 1-4: Edited document text

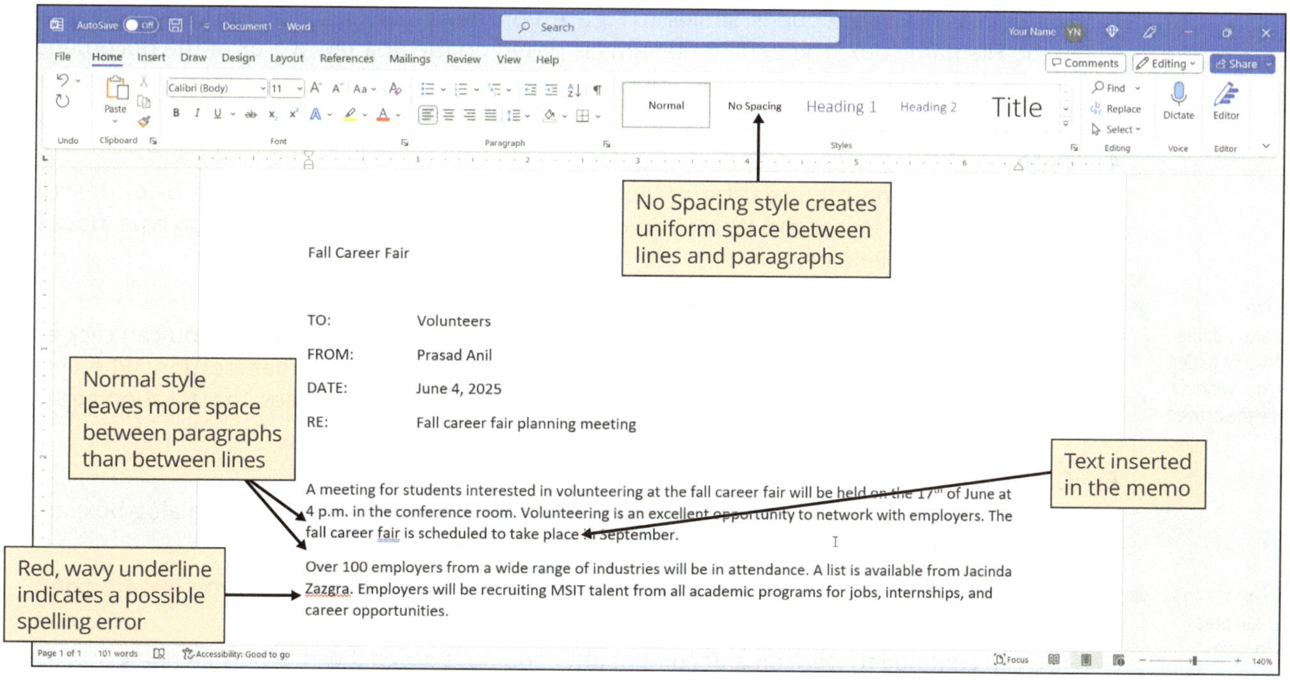

Table 1-2: Automatic features that appear as you type in Word

feature	what appears	to use
Text predications	Grey text suggesting text to insert appears as you type	Press TAB to insert the text suggested by text predictions; continue typing to reject the suggestion
AutoCorrect	A small blue box appears when you place the pointer over text corrected by AutoCorrect; an AutoCorrect Options button appears when you point to the blue box	Word automatically corrects typos, minor spelling errors, and capitalization, and adds typographical symbols (such as © and ™) as you type; to reverse an AutoCorrect adjustment, click the AutoCorrect Options arrow, then click the option that will undo the action
Spelling and Grammar	A red wavy line under a word indicates a possible misspelling or a repeated word; a blue double line under text indicates a possible grammar error	Right-click red- or blue-underlined text to display a shortcut menu of correction options; click a correction option to accept it and remove the colored underline, or click Ignore to leave the text as is

Save a Document

Case You save the notice using a descriptive filename and the default file extension.

Objective
- Save a document

To store a document permanently so you can open it and edit it at another time, you must save it as a **file**. When you **save** a document, you give it a name, called a **filename**, and indicate the location where you want to store the file. Files created in the most recent version of Word are automatically assigned the .docx file extension to distinguish them from files created in other software programs. You can save a document using the Save button on the Quick Access toolbar or the Save command on the File tab. Once you have saved a document for the first time, you should save it again every few minutes and always before printing so that the saved file is updated to reflect your latest changes.

Steps

1. **Click the AutoSave toggle switch on the Quick Access toolbar to turn AutoSave off, if necessary**
   You use the AutoSave toggle switch to turn the AutoSave feature both on and off.

Trouble
If you don't see the extension .docx as part of the filename, the setting in Windows to display file extensions is not active.

2. **Click the File tab on the Ribbon, then click Save As**
   The first time you save a document, the Save As screen opens. The screen displays all the places you can save a file to, including OneDrive, your PC (identified as This PC), or a different location.

3. **Click Browse in the Save As screen**
   The Save As dialog box opens, similar to **Figure 1-5**. The default filename, Fall Career Fair, appears in the File name box. The default filename is based on the first few words of the document. The default file type, Word Document, appears in the Save as type list box. **Table 1-3** describes the functions of some of the buttons in the Save As dialog box.

4. **Type IL_WD_1_Notice in the File name box**
   The new filename replaces the default filename. Giving your documents brief descriptive filenames makes it easier to locate and organize them later. You do not need to type .docx when you type a new filename.

Quick Tip
You can also double-click a drive or folder in the folder window to change the active location.

5. **Navigate to the location where you store your Data Files**
   You can navigate to a different drive or folder in several ways. For example, you can click a drive or folder in the Address bar or the navigation pane to go directly to that location. When you are finished navigating to the drive or folder where you store your Data Files, that location appears in the Address bar. Your Save As dialog box should resemble **Figure 1-6**.

6. **Click Save**
   The document is saved to the drive and folder you specified in the Save As dialog box, and the title bar displays the new filename, IL_WD_1_Notice.docx.

Quick Tip
You also can press CTRL+S to save a document.

7. **Place the insertion point before conference in the first sentence, type green, then press SPACEBAR**
   You can continue to work on a document after you have saved it with a new filename.

8. **Click the Save button on the Quick Access toolbar**
   Your change to the notice is saved. After you save a document for the first time, you must continue to save the changes you make to the document.

Saving with AutoSave

The AutoSave feature saves a file automatically to OneDrive every few seconds for sharing, synching, or backup. AutoSave can be especially useful for live collaboration when multiple users are working on a shared document at once because it allows all users of the document to see the changes others are making in real time. To turn AutoSave on and off, simply click the AutoSave toggle switch on the Quick Access toolbar. AutoSave is enabled by default when a file is stored to OneDrive.

Figure 1-5: Save As dialog box

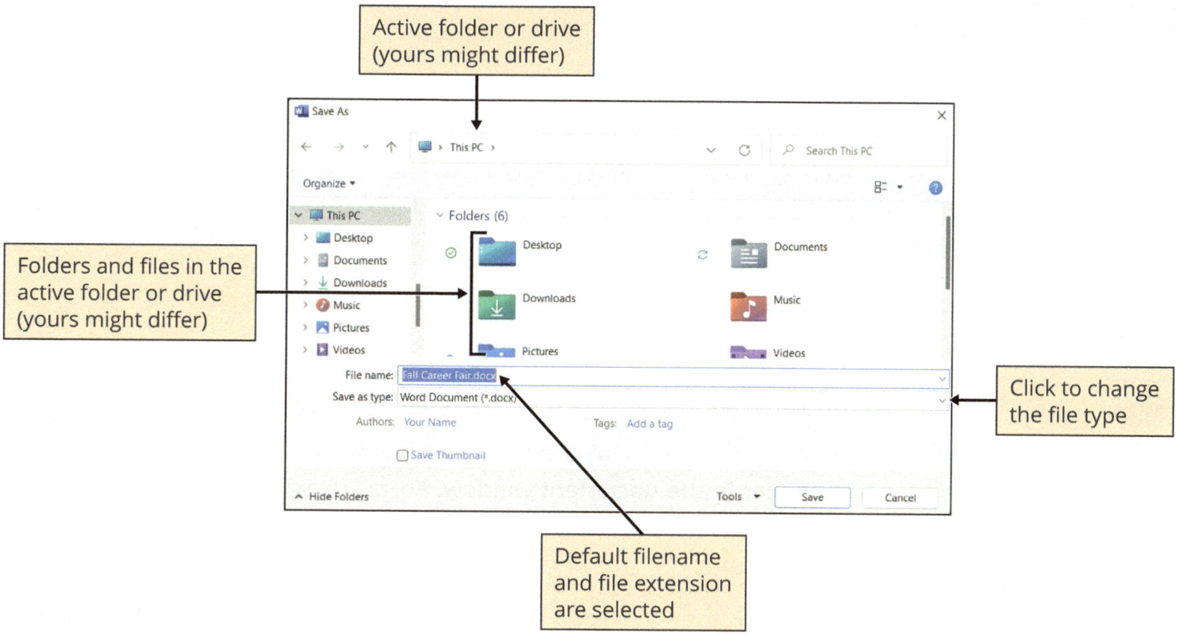

Figure 1-6: File to be saved in the Module 1 folder

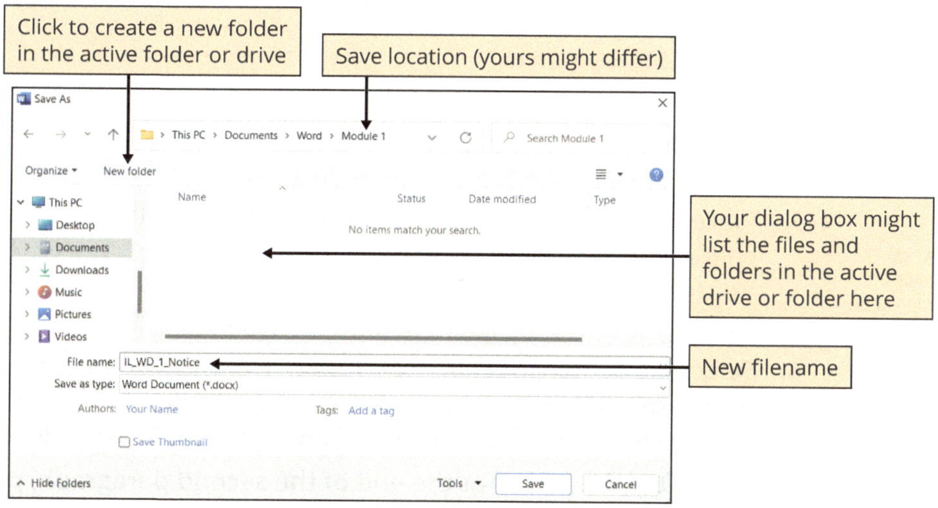

Table 1-3: Save As dialog box buttons

button	use to
Back	Navigate back to the last location shown in the Address bar
Forward	Navigate to the location that was previously shown in the Address bar
Up to	Navigate to the location above the current location in the folder hierarchy
Organize	Open a menu of commands related to organizing the selected file or folder, including Cut, Copy, Delete, Rename, and Properties
New folder	Create a new folder in the current folder or drive
Change your view	Change the way folder and file information is shown in the folder window in the Save As dialog box; click the Change your view button to toggle between views, or click the arrow to open a menu of view options

Select Text

Case You revise the notice by selecting text and replacing it with new text. You also remove a hyperlink from text.

Objectives
- Select text
- Show and hide formatting
- Undo and redo actions
- Remove hyperlinks

Before deleting, editing, or formatting text, you must **select** the text. Selecting text involves clicking and dragging the I-beam pointer across the text to highlight it. You can also select words and paragraphs by double-clicking or triple-clicking text, or you can click or double-click in the margin to the left of text with the pointer to select whole lines or paragraphs. **Table 1-4** describes the many ways to select text.

Steps

1. **Click the Show/Hide ¶ button ¶ in the Paragraph group**
   Formatting marks appear in the document window. **Formatting marks** are special characters that appear on your screen but do not print. Common formatting marks include the paragraph symbol (¶), which shows the end of a paragraph—wherever you press ENTER; the dot symbol (.), which represents a space—wherever you press SPACEBAR; and the arrow symbol (→), which shows the location of a tab stop—wherever you press TAB. Working with formatting marks turned on can help you to select, edit, and format text with precision.

Quick Tip
You deselect text by clicking anywhere in the document window.

2. **Click before Volunteers, then drag the pointer over the text to select it**
   The words are selected, as shown in **Figure 1-7**. For now, you can ignore the floating Mini toolbar that appears over text when you first select it.

3. **Type MSIT Students**
   The text you type replaces the selected text.

4. **Double-click Prasad, type your first name, double-click Anil, then type your last name**
   Double-clicking a word selects the entire word.

Trouble
If you delete text by mistake, immediately click the Undo button in the Undo group on the Home tab to restore the deleted text to the document.

5. **Place the pointer in the margin to the left of the RE: line so that the pointer changes to ↗, click to select the line, then type RE:, press TAB, press TAB, then type Volunteering at the fall career fair**
   Clicking to the left of a line of text with the pointer selects the entire line.

6. **Select the sentence A list is available from Jacinda Zazgra. in the second paragraph, then press DELETE**
   Selecting text and pressing DELETE removes the text from the document.

7. **Click after the period at the end of the second paragraph, press SPACEBAR, then type See www.msit/careerfair.org for more information.**
   When you press SPACEBAR after typing the web address, Word automatically formats the web address as a hyperlink. A **hyperlink** is text that when clicked opens a webpage in a browser window. Text that is formatted as a hyperlink appears as colored, underlined text. You want to remove the hyperlink formatting.

8. **Right-click www.msit/careerfair.org, then click Remove Hyperlink**
   Removing a hyperlink removes the link, but the text remains.

Quick Tip
Always save before and after editing text.

9. **Click ¶, then click the Save button on the Quick Access toolbar**
   Formatting marks are turned off, and your changes to the notice are saved. The Show/Hide ¶ button is a **toggle button**, which means you can use it to turn formatting marks on and off. The edited notice is shown in **Figure 1-8**.

Figure 1-7: Text selected in the document

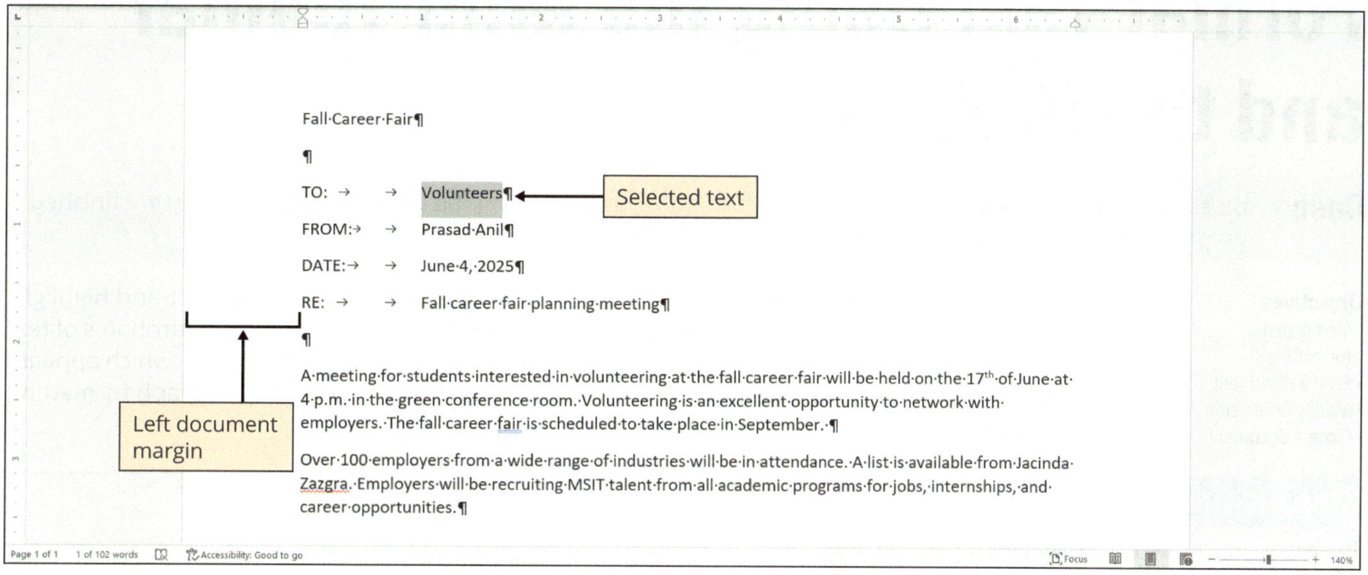

Figure 1-8: Edited document with replacement text

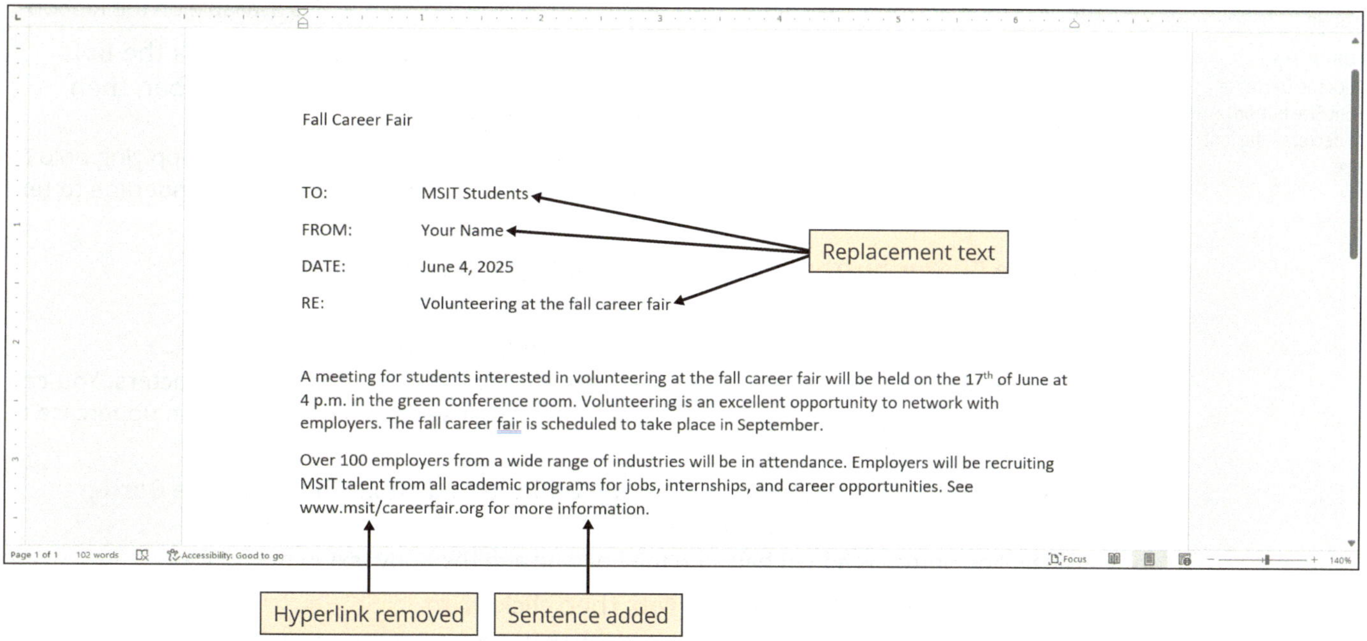

Table 1-4: Methods for selecting text

to select	use the pointer to
Any amount of text	Drag over the text
A word	Double-click the word
A line of text	Move the pointer to the left of the line, then click
A sentence	Press and hold CTRL, then click the sentence
A paragraph	Triple-click the paragraph or double-click with the pointer to the left of the paragraph
A large block of text	Click at the beginning of the selection, press and hold SHIFT, then click at the end of the selection
Multiple nonconsecutive selections	Select the first selection, then press and hold CTRL as you select each additional selection
An entire document	Triple-click with the pointer to the left of any text; press CTRL+A; or click the Select button in the Editing group on the Home tab, and then click Select All

Format Text Using the Mini Toolbar and the Ribbon

Case You enhance the appearance of the notice by formatting the text using the Mini toolbar. When you are finished, you preview the notice for errors and then print it.

Objectives
- Modify text formatting
- Print a document
- Modify print settings
- Close a document

Formatting text is a fast and fun way to improve the appearance of a document and highlight important information. You can easily change the font, color, size, style, and other attributes of text by selecting the text and clicking a command on the Home tab. The **Mini toolbar**, which appears above text when you first select it, also includes commonly used text and paragraph formatting commands.

Steps

Trouble
If the Mini toolbar disappears, right-click the selection to display it again.

Quick Tip
Click the Decrease Font Size button to decrease the font size.

1. **Select Fall Career Fair**
   The Mini toolbar appears over the selected text, as shown in **Figure 1-9**. You click a formatting option on the Mini toolbar to apply it to the selected text. **Table 1-5** describes the function of the buttons on the Mini toolbar. Yours may differ. The buttons on the Mini toolbar are also available on the Ribbon.

2. **Click the Increase Font Size button on the Mini toolbar six times, click the Bold button on the Mini toolbar, click the Italic button on the Mini toolbar, then click the Underline button on the Mini toolbar**
   Each time you click the Increase Font Size button the selected text is enlarged. Applying bold to the text makes it thicker. Applying italic to text makes it slanted. Applying an underline to text adds an underline.

3. **Click the Center button in the Paragraph group on the Home tab**
   The selected text is centered between the left and right margins.

4. **Click the Change Case button in the Font group, then click UPPERCASE**
   The lowercase characters in the selected text are changed to uppercase characters. You can also use the Change Case button to change the case of selected characters from uppercase to lowercase, and vice versa.

5. **Click the blank line between the RE: line and the body text, then click the Borders button in the Paragraph group**
   A single-line border is added between the heading and the body text in the notice.

6. **Save the document, click the File tab, then click Print**
   Information related to printing the document appears on the Print screen in Backstage view. Options for printing the document appear on the left side of the Print screen and a preview of the document as it will look when printed appears on the right side, as shown in **Figure 1-10**. Before you print a document, it's a good habit to examine it closely so you can identify and correct any problems.

7. **Click the Zoom In button on the status bar five times, then proofread your document carefully for errors**
   The document is enlarged in print preview. If you notice errors in your document, you need to correct them before you print. To do this, press ESC or click the Back button in Backstage view, correct any mistakes, save your changes, click the File tab, and then click the Print command again to be ready to print the document.

8. **Click the Print button on the Print screen**
   A copy of the notice prints using the default print settings. To change the current printer, change the number of copies to print, select which pages of a document to print, or modify another print setting, you simply change the appropriate setting on the Print screen before clicking the Print button.

9. **sam Click the File tab, then click Close**
   The document closes, but the Word program window remains open.

Figure 1-9: Mini toolbar

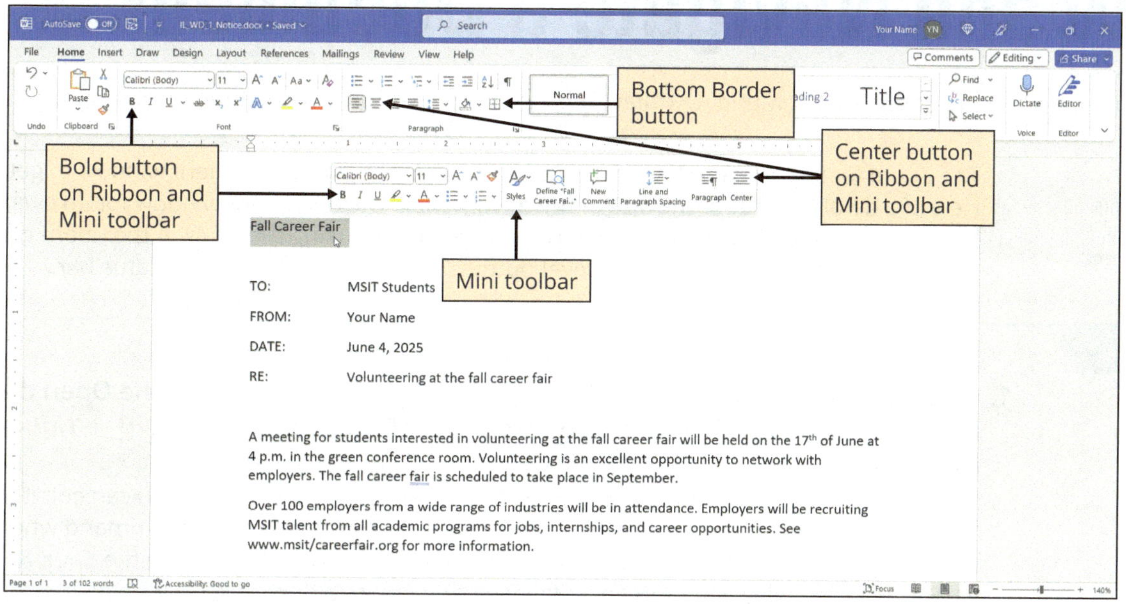

Figure 1-10: Preview of the completed document

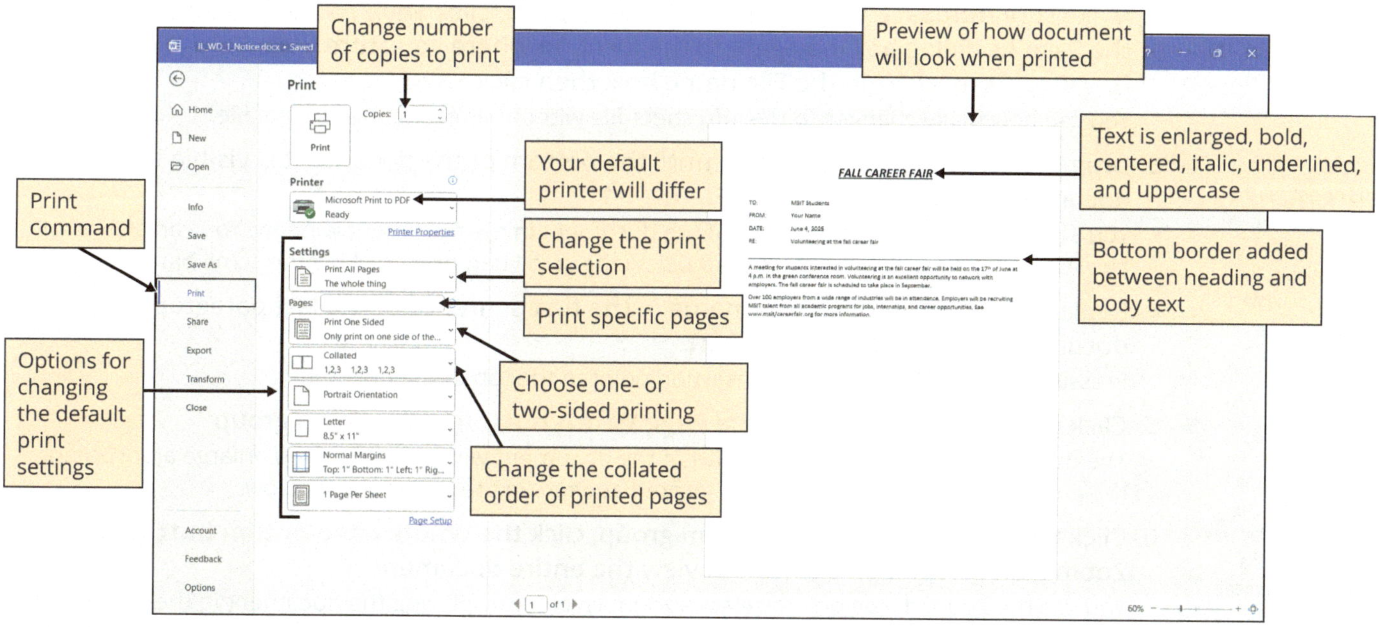

Table 1-5: Buttons on the Mini toolbar

button	use to	button	use to
Calibri (Body)	Change the font of text	B	Apply bold to text
11	Change the font size of text	I	Apply italic to text
A^	Make text larger	U	Apply an underline to text
A˅	Make text smaller	(Highlight)	Apply colored highlighting to text
(Format Painter)	Copy the formats applied to selected text to other text	A (Font Color)	Change the color of text
(Styles)	Apply a style to text	(Bullets)	Apply bullets to paragraphs
(Define)	Look up the definition of a word	(Numbering)	Apply numbering to paragraphs
(New Comment)	Insert a new comment	(Line and Paragraph Spacing)	Change line and paragraph spacing
(Center)	Center text	(Justify)	Align text with both margins

View and Navigate a Document

Case You open the info sheet, save it with a new filename, and then customize a document property for the file.

Objectives
- Open documents
- Zoom in and out
- Change document properties

The Zoom feature in Word lets you enlarge a document in the document window to get a close-up view of a detail, or reduce the size of the document in the document window for an overview of the layout as a whole. You zoom in and out on a document using the tools in the Zoom group on the View tab or you can use the Zoom level buttons and Zoom slider on the status bar.

Steps

1. **Click the File tab, click Open, click This PC, click Browse to open the Open dialog box, navigate to the location where you store your Data Files, click IL_WD_1-1.docx, then click Open**

   The document opens in Print Layout view. Once you have opened a file, you can edit it and use the Save or the Save As command to save your changes. You use the **Save** command when you want to save the changes you make to a file, overwriting the stored file. You use the **Save As** command when you want to leave the original file intact and create a duplicate file with a different filename, file extension, or location.

Trouble
Click the Enable Editing button if necessary.

2. **Make sure AutoSave is set to off, click the File tab, click Save As, click Browse to open the Save As dialog box, navigate to the location where you store your Data Files, type IL_WD_1_CareerFair in the File name box, then click Save**

   You can now make changes to the info sheet file without affecting the original file.

Trouble
If you do not see the vertical scroll box, move the pointer to the right side of the document window to display it.

3. **Drag the vertical scroll box down until the bottom of the document is visible in your document window, as shown in Figure 1-11**

   You **scroll** to display different parts of the document in the document window. You can also scroll by clicking the scroll arrows above and below the scroll bar, or by clicking the scroll bar.

4. **Replace Your Name with your name in the first sentence of the last paragraph in the document, then press CTRL+HOME**

   Pressing CTRL+HOME moves the insertion point to the top of the document.

Quick Tip
Click the Multiple Pages button in the Zoom group on the View tab to display two or more pages of a multi-page document in the document window.

5. **Click the View tab, then click the Page Width button in the Zoom group**

   The document is enlarged to the width of the document window. When you enlarge a document, the area where the insertion point is located appears in the document window.

6. **Click the Zoom button in the Zoom group, click the Whole page option button in the Zoom dialog box, then click OK to view the entire document**

   You use the Zoom dialog box to select a zoom level for displaying the document in the document window.

7. **Move the Zoom slider on the status bar to the right until the Zoom percentage is approximately 200%, then click the Zoom Out button [−] until the zoom level is 140%**

   Dragging the Zoom slider enlarges or reduces a document in the document window. You can also click the Zoom Out and Zoom In buttons to change the zoom level.

8. **Click the File tab, then click Info**

   The right side of the Info screen in Backstage view shows the document properties for the file. **Document properties** are user-defined details about a file that describe its contents and origin, including the name of the author, the title of the document, and keywords that you can assign to help organize and search your files.

9. **Click the Add a title box in the Properties section of the Info screen, type Career Fair, then click outside the box**

   The new Title property for the document appears in Backstage view as shown in **Figure 1-12**

10. **Click Back button to return to the Home tab, then save your changes**

    The document appears at 140% zoom in Print Layout view.

Figure 1-11: Zoom slider

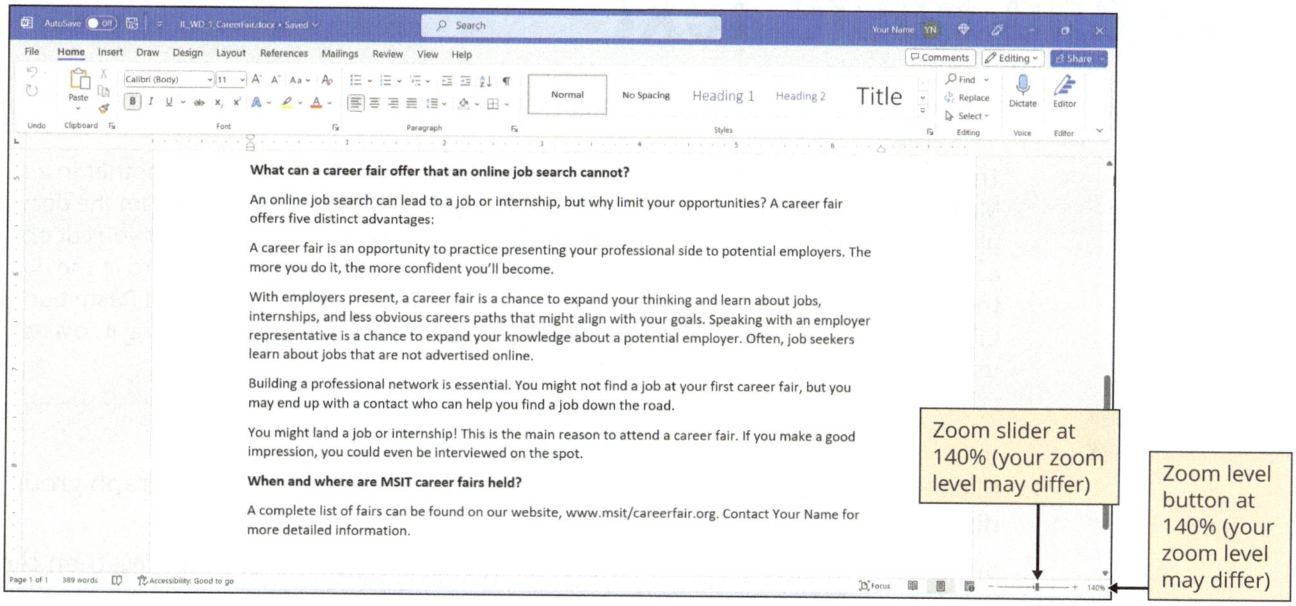

Figure 1-12: Document properties in Backstage view

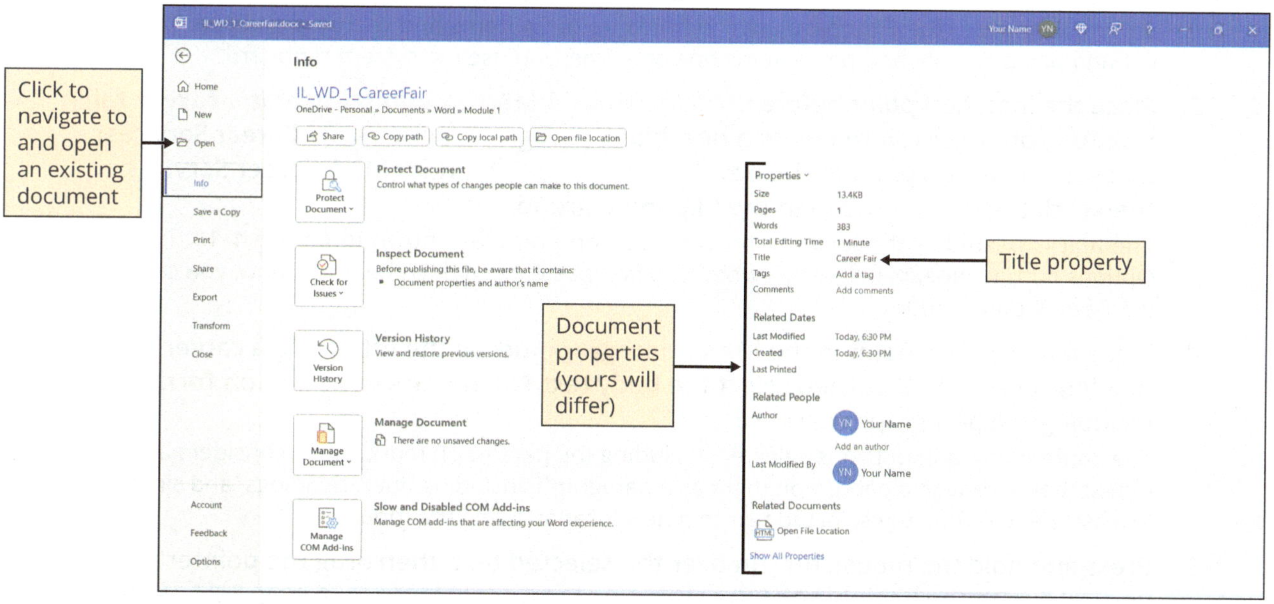

Using Word document views

Document views are different ways of displaying a document in the document window. Each Word view provides features that are useful for working on different types of documents. The default view, **Print Layout view**, displays a document as it will appear on a printed page. Print Layout view is helpful for formatting text and pages, including adjusting document margins, creating columns of text, inserting graphics, and formatting headers and footers. Also useful is **Read Mode view**, which displays document text so that it is easy to read on screen. Other Word views are helpful for performing specialized tasks. **Web Layout view** allows you to format web pages or documents that will be viewed on a computer screen. In Web Layout view, a document appears just as it will when viewed with a web browser. **Outline view** is useful for editing and formatting longer documents that include multiple headings. Outline view allows you to reorganize text by moving the headings. Finally, **Draft view** shows a simplified layout of a document, without margins, headers and footers, or graphics. When you want to quickly type and edit text, it's often easiest to work in Draft view. You switch between views by clicking the view buttons on the status bar or by using the commands on the View tab. Changing views does not affect how the printed document will appear. It simply changes the way you view the document in the document window.

Cut and Paste Text

Case You reorganize the information in the info sheet using the cut-and-paste and drag-and-drop methods.

Objectives
- Cut and paste text
- Undo and redo actions
- Highlight text

The editing features in Word allow you to move text from one location to another in a document. Moving text is often called **cut and paste**. When you **cut** text, it is removed from the document and placed on the **Clipboard**, a temporary storage area for text and graphics that you cut or copy from a document. You can then **paste**, or insert, text that is stored on the Clipboard in the document at the location of the insertion point. You cut and paste text using the Cut and Paste buttons in the Clipboard group on the Home tab. You can also move selected text by dragging it to a new location using the mouse. This is called **drag and drop**.

Steps

1. **Click Home tab, then click the Show/Hide ¶ button ¶ in the Paragraph group to display formatting marks**

2. **Select Attending a career fair (including the paragraph mark after it), then click the Cut button in the Clipboard group**

   The text is removed from the document and placed on the system clipboard. Word uses two different clipboards: the **system clipboard**, which holds just one item and is not visible, and the **Office Clipboard** (the Clipboard), which holds up to 24 items and can be displayed. When you cut-and-paste or copy-and-paste items one at a time, you use the system clipboard.

3. **Place the insertion point before the Why should MSIT students attend a career fair? heading, press ENTER to create a new blank paragraph under MSIT Career Services, place the insertion point in the new blank paragraph under MSIT Career Services, then click the Paste button in the Clipboard group**

   The text is pasted at the location of the insertion point, as shown in **Figure 1-13**. The Paste Options button appears below text when you first paste it in a document. For now, you can ignore the Paste Options button.

4. **Place the insertion point in the blank paragraph below the Attending a career fair heading, press DELETE, then select the body text Fill out the registration form., including the paragraph mark**

   The entire paragraph of text is selected, including the paragraph mark. Word considers any string of text that ends with a paragraph mark as a paragraph, including titles, headings, and single lines in a list. You will drag the selected text to a new location using the mouse.

5. **Press and hold the mouse button over the selected text, then drag the pointer's vertical line to the beginning of the Wear professional clothing. paragraph, as shown in Figure 1-14**

   You drag the insertion point to where you want the text to be inserted when you release the mouse button.

6. **Release the mouse button, click to deselect the text, then save your changes**

   The selected text is moved to the location of the insertion point. Text is not placed on the Clipboard when you drag and drop it.

Quick Tip
As you drag, the pointer changes to , and a black vertical line, which is the insertion point, moves with the pointer.

Quick Tip
If you make a mistake, click the Undo button in the Undo group on the Home tab, then try again.

Highlighting text in a document

The Highlight tool allows you to mark and find important text in a document. **Highlighting** is transparent color that is applied to text using the Highlight pointer . To highlight text, click the Text Highlight Color arrow in the Font group on the Home tab, select a color, then use the I-beam part of the pointer to select the text you want to highlight. Click the Text Highlight Color button to turn off the Highlight pointer. To remove highlighting, select the highlighted text, click the Text Highlight Color arrow then click No Color. Highlighting prints, but it is used most effectively when a document is viewed on screen.

Figure 1-13: Moved text with Paste Options button

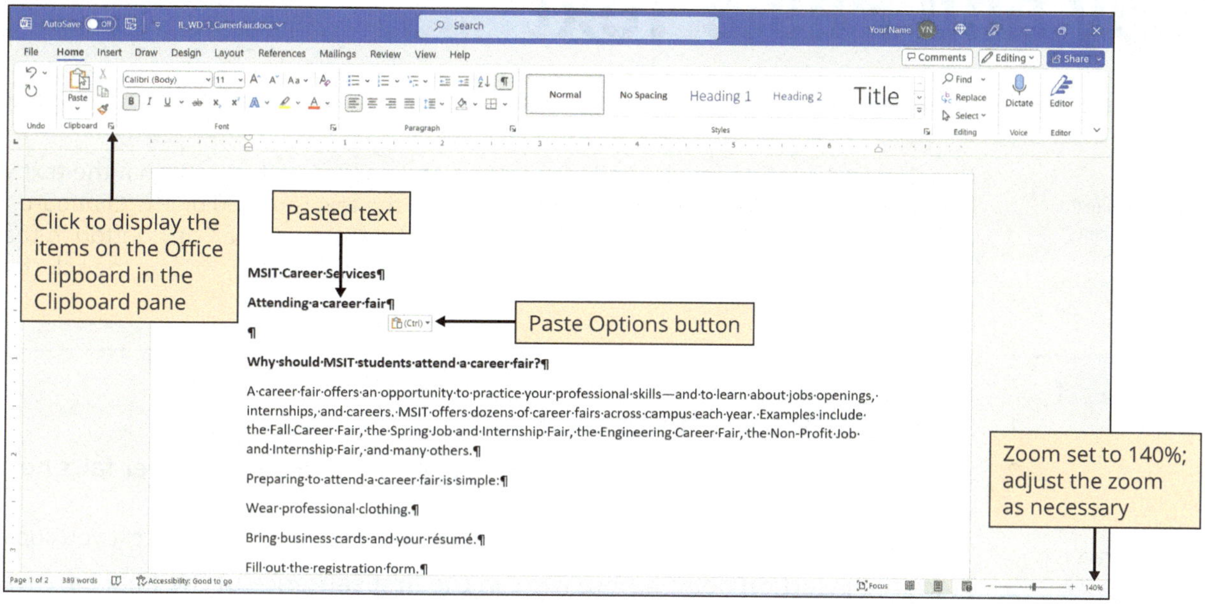

Figure 1-14: Dragging and dropping text in a new location

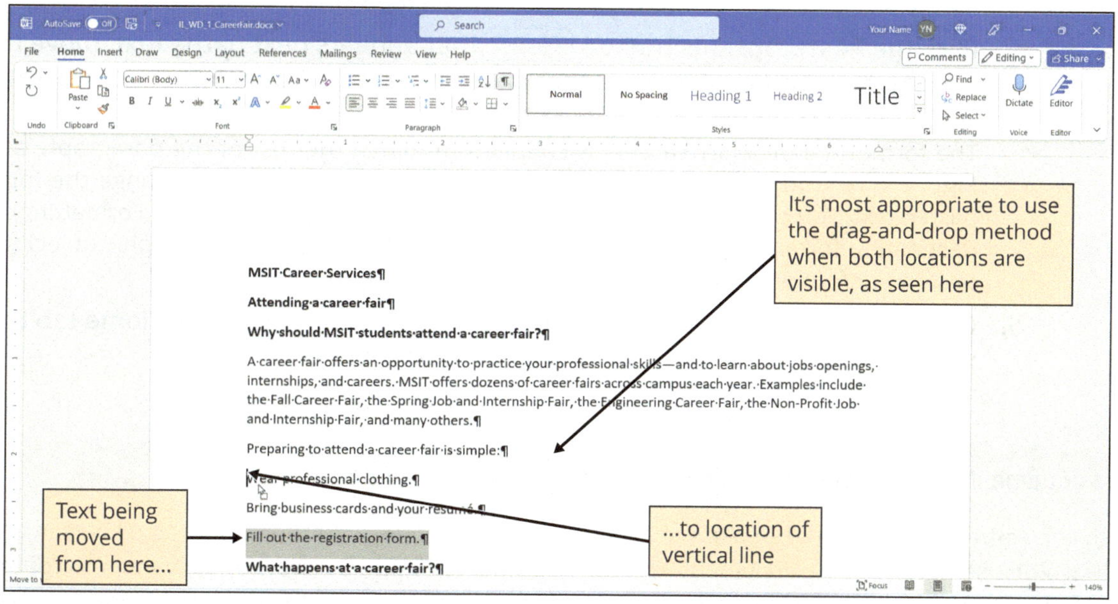

Using the Undo, Redo, and Repeat commands

Word remembers the editing and formatting changes you make so that you can easily reverse or repeat them. You can reverse the last action you took by clicking the Undo button in the Undo group on the Home tab or on the Quick Access toolbar, or you can undo a series of actions by clicking the Undo arrow and selecting the action you want to reverse. When you undo an action using the Undo arrow, you also undo all the actions above it in the list—that is, all actions that were performed after the action you selected. Similarly, you can keep the change you just reversed by using the Redo button in the Undo group on the Home tab or on the Quick Access toolbar. The Redo button appears only immediately after clicking the Undo button to undo a change.

If you want to repeat an action you just completed, you can use the Repeat button in the Undo group on the Home tab or on the Quick Access toolbar. For example, if you just typed "thank you," clicking inserts "thank you" at the location of the insertion point. If you just applied bold, clicking applies bold to the currently selected text. You also can repeat the last action you took by pressing F4.

Copy and Paste Text

Case You continue to edit the info sheet by copying text from one location to another using the copy-and-paste method.

Objectives
- Copy and paste text
- Split the document window
- Display multiple documents

Copying and pasting text is similar to cutting and pasting text, except that the text you **copy** is not removed from the document. Rather, a copy of the text is placed on the Clipboard, leaving the original text in place. You can copy text to the Clipboard using the Copy button in the Clipboard group on the Home tab, or you can copy text by pressing CTRL as you drag the selected text from one location to another.

Steps

Quick Tip
You can also cut or copy text by right-clicking the selected text, and then clicking the Cut or Copy command on the menu that opens.

1. **Scroll to the bottom of the document**
2. **Select MSIT career in the heading When and where are MSIT career fairs held?, then click the Copy button in the Clipboard group**
   A copy of the selected text is placed on the Clipboard, leaving the original text you copied in place.
3. **Place the insertion point before fairs in the first sentence of the final paragraph, then click the Paste button**
   The text "MSIT career" is inserted in the final paragraph, as shown in **Figure 1-15**. Notice that the pasted text is formatted differently than the paragraph in which it was inserted.
4. **Click the Paste Options button (Ctrl) that appears next to the text, move the mouse over each button on the menu that opens to read its ScreenTip, then click the Keep Text Only (T) button**
   The formatting of "MSIT career" is changed to match the rest of the paragraph, as shown in **Figure 1-16**. The buttons on the Paste Options menu allow you to change the formatting of pasted text. You can choose to keep the original formatting (Keep Source Formatting), match the destination formatting (Merge Formatting), paste the selection as a graphic object (Picture), or paste as unformatted text (Keep Text Only).
5. **Click the Show/Hide ¶ button ¶ in the Paragraph group on the Home tab to turn off the display formatting marks, then save your changes.**

Splitting the document window to copy and move items in a long document

If you want to copy or move items between parts of a long document, it can be useful to split the document window into two panes. This allows you to display the item you want to copy or move in one pane and the destination for the item in the other pane. To split a window, click the Split button in the Window group on the View tab, and then drag the horizontal split bar that appears to the location where you want to split the window. Once the document window is split into two panes, you can use the scroll bars in each pane to display different parts of the document. To copy or move an item from one pane to another, you can use the Cut, Copy, and Paste commands, or you can drag the item between the panes. When you are finished editing the document, double-click the split bar to restore the window to a single pane, or click the Remove Split button in the Window group on the View tab.

Figure 1-15: Text pasted in document

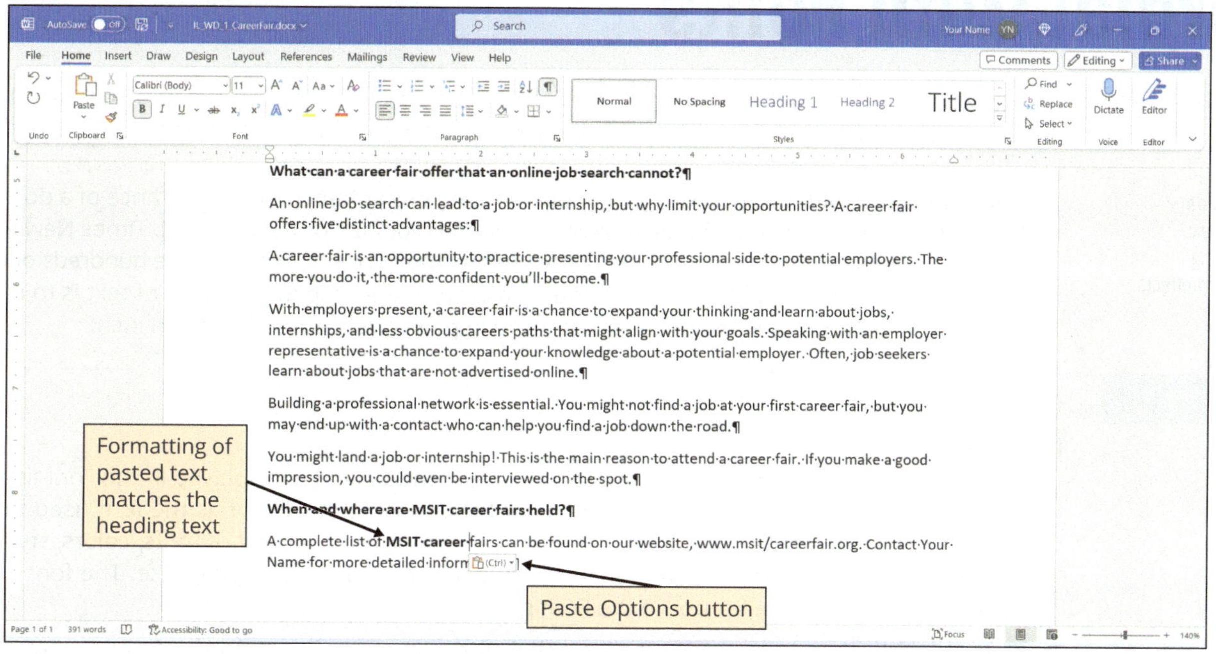

Figure 1-16: Copied text in document

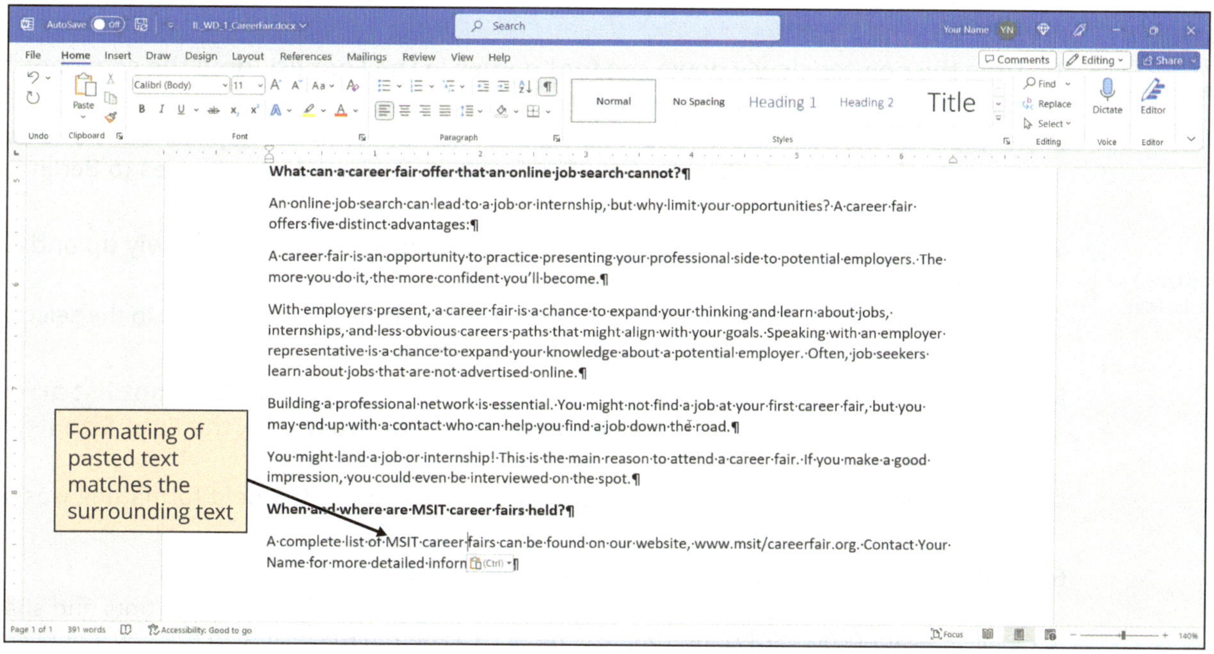

Copying and moving items between documents

You can also use the Clipboard to copy and move items between documents. To do this, open both documents and the Clipboard pane. With multiple documents open, copy or cut an item from one document and then switch to the other document and paste the item. To switch between open documents, point to the Word icon on the taskbar, and then click the document you want to appear in the document window. You can also display more than one document at the same time by clicking the Arrange All button or the View Side by Side button in the Window group on the View tab, or by pointing to the Maximize button on the title bar, and clicking a snap layout.

Format with Fonts

Case You change the font and font size of the headings in the info sheet. You select a font and font sizes that enhance the positive tone of the document and help to structure the info sheet visually for readers.

Objectives
- Modify text formatting
- Apply text effects

Formatting text with fonts is a quick and powerful way to enhance the appearance of a document. A **font** is a complete set of characters with the same typeface or design. Arial, Times New Roman, Courier, Tahoma, and Calibri are some of the more common fonts, but there are hundreds of others, each with a specific design and feel. Another way to change the appearance of text is to increase or decrease its **font size**. Font size is measured in points. A **point** is 1⁄72 of an inch.

Steps

1. **Press CTRL+HOME**
   Notice that the name of the font used in the document, Calibri, is displayed in the Font list box in the Font group. The word "(Body)" in the Font list box indicates Calibri is the font used for body text in the current theme, the default theme. A **theme** is a related set of fonts, colors, styles, and effects that is applied to an entire document to give it a cohesive appearance. The font size, 11, appears in the Font Size list box in the Font group.

Quick Tip
There are two types of fonts: **serif fonts** have a small stroke, called a serif, at the ends of characters; **sans serif fonts** do not have a serif.

2. **Select Attending a career fair, then click the Font list arrow in the Font group**
   The Font list, which shows the fonts available on your computer, opens as shown in **Figure 1-17**. The font names are formatted in the font. Font names can appear in more than one location on the Font list.
3. **Drag the pointer slowly down the font names in the Font list, drag the scroll box to scroll down the Font list, then click Berlin Sans FB Demi**
   As you drag the pointer over a font name, a preview of the font is applied to the selected text. Clicking a font name applies the font. The font of the selected text changes to Berlin Sans FB Demi.

Quick Tip
You can also type a font size in the Font Size text box.

4. **Click the Font Size list arrow in the Font group, drag the pointer slowly up and down the Font Size list, then click 18**
   As you drag the pointer over a font size, a preview of the font size is applied to the selected text. Clicking 18 increases the font size of the selected text to 18 points.
5. **Select Why should MSIT students attend a career fair?, click the Font list arrow, click Berlin Sans FB Demi in the Recently Used Fonts list, click the Font Size list arrow, click 22**
   The title is formatted in 22-point Berlin Sans FB Demi bold. The bold formatting was already applied to the text.
6. **Click the Font Color list arrow in the Font group**
   A gallery of colors opens. It includes the set of theme colors in a range of tints and shades as well as a set of standard colors. You can point to a color in the gallery to preview it applied to the selected text.
7. **Click the Green, Accent 6 color as shown in Figure 1-18, then deselect the text**
   The color of the title text changes to green. The active color on the Font Color button also changes to green.

Trouble
If the mini toolbar closes, select the text again.

8. **Scroll down, select the heading What happens at a career fair?, then, using the Mini toolbar, click the Font list arrow, click Berlin Sans FB Demi, click the Font Size list arrow, click 14, click , then deselect the text**
   The heading is formatted in 14-point Berlin Sans FB Demi bold with a green color.
9. **Repeat step 8 to apply 14-point Berlin Sans FB Demi green to the What can a career fair offer that an online job search cannot? and When and where are MSIT career fairs held? headings, press CTRL+HOME, then save your changes**
   Compare your document to **Figure 1-19**.

Figure 1-17: Font list

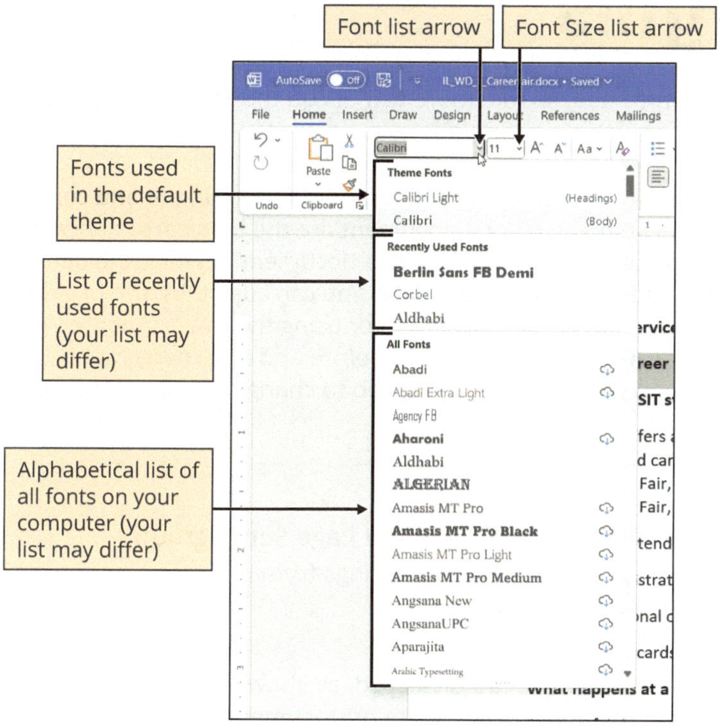

Figure 1-18: Font Color palette

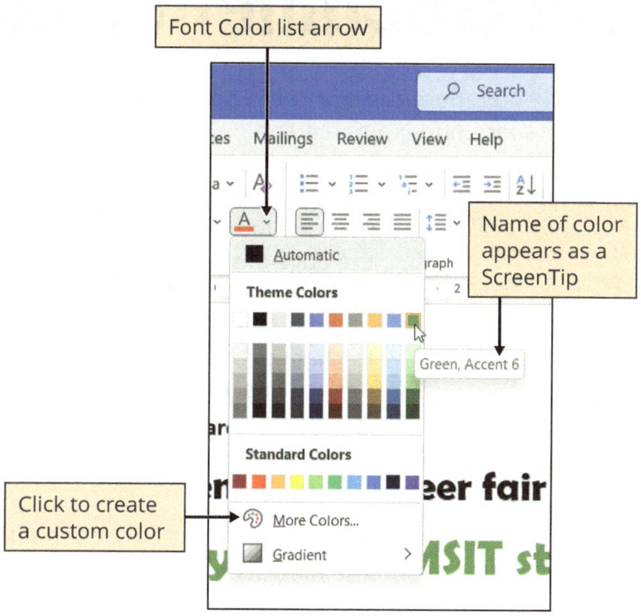

Figure 1-19: Document formatted with fonts

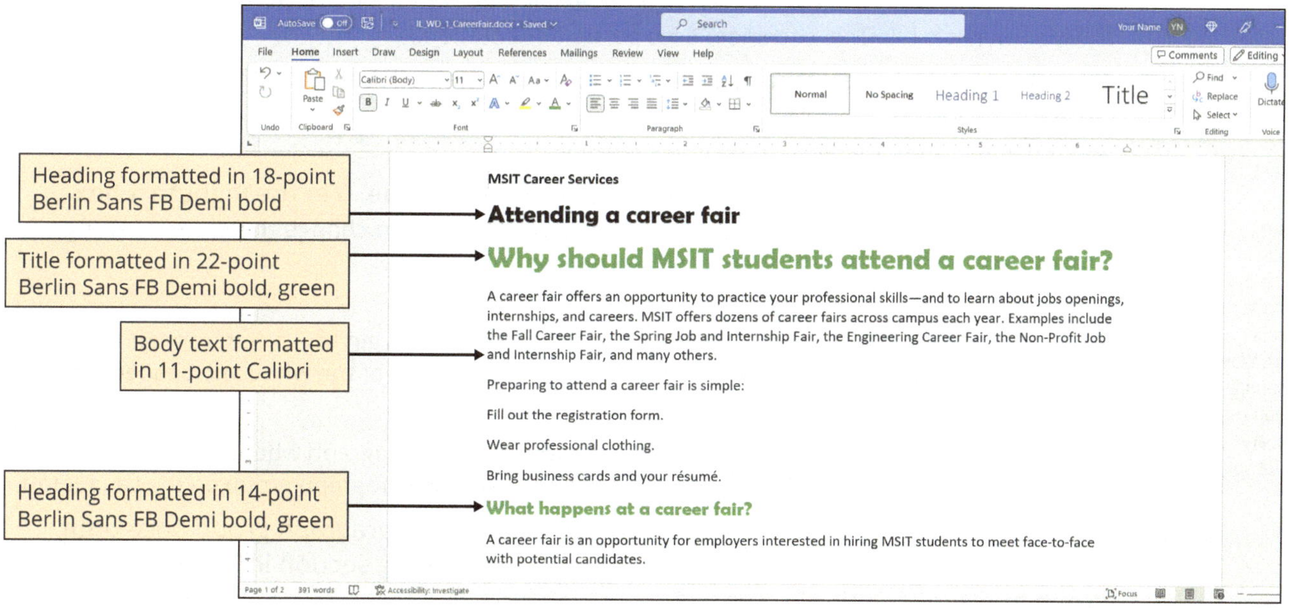

Applying shadows and other text effects to text

The Word Text Effects and Typography feature allows you to add visual appeal to your documents by adding special text effects to text, including outlines, shadows, reflections, and glows. The feature also includes a gallery of preformatted combined text effect styles, called **WordArt**, that you can apply to your text to format it quickly and easily. To apply a WordArt style to text, simply select the text, click the Text Effects and Typography button in the Font group on the Home tab, and select a WordArt style from the gallery. To apply an individual text effect style, such as a shadow, outline, reflection, or glow, select the text, click the Text Effects and Typography button, point to the type of text effect you want to apply, and then select a style from the gallery that opens. Experiment with combining text effect styles to give your text a striking appearance.

If you are unhappy with the way text is formatted, you can use the Clear All Formatting command to return the text to the default format settings—11-point Calibri. Select the text, then click the Clear All Formatting button in the Font group on the Home tab.

Set Document Margins

Case You reduce the size of the document margins in the info sheet so that more text fits on the page. You also add space under a paragraph.

Objectives
- Modify page setup
- Change paragraph spacing

Changing a document's margins is one way to change the appearance of a document and control the amount of text that fits on a page. The **margins** of a document are the blank areas between the edge of the text and the edge of the page. When you create a document in Word, the default margins are 1" at the top, bottom, left, and right sides of the page. You can adjust the size of a document's margins using the Margins command on the Layout tab or using the rulers. Another way to change the amount of open space on a page is to add space before and after paragraphs. You use the Spacing options in the Paragraph group on the Layout tab to change paragraph spacing. Paragraph spacing is measured in points.

Steps

1. **Click the Layout tab, then click the Margins button in the Page Setup group**
   The Margins menu opens. You can select predefined margin settings from this menu, or you can click Custom Margins to create different margin settings.
2. **Click Custom Margins**
   The Page Setup dialog box opens with the Margins tab displayed, as shown in **Figure 1-20**. You can use the Margins tab to change the top, bottom, left, or right document margin, to change the orientation of the pages from portrait to landscape, and to alter other page layout settings. **Portrait orientation** means a page is taller than it is wide; **landscape orientation** means a page is wider than it is tall. This info sheet uses portrait orientation.
3. **Click the Top down four times until 0.6" appears, then click the Bottom down arrow until 0.6" appears**
   The top and bottom margins of the info sheet will be .6".
4. **Press TAB, type .6 in the Left text box, press TAB, then type .6 in the Right text box**
   The left and right margins of the report will also be .6". You can change the margin settings by using the arrows or by typing a value in the appropriate text box.
5. **Click OK**
   The document margins change to .6". The location of each margin (right, left, top, and bottom) is shown on the horizontal and vertical rulers at the intersection of the white and shaded areas.
6. **Place the insertion point in Attending a career fair**
   The paragraph spacing settings for the active paragraph (the paragraph where the insertion point is located) are shown in the Before and After text boxes in the Paragraph group on the Layout tab.
7. **Click the Before up arrow in the Spacing section in the Paragraph group once until 6 pt appears, then click the After up arrow in the Spacing section in the Paragraph group four times until 30 pt appears**
   Six points of space are added before the Attending a career fair paragraph, and thirty points of space are added after, as shown in **Figure 1-21**.

Quick Tip
The minimum allowable margin settings depend on your printer and the size of the paper you are using. Word displays a warning message if you set margins that are too narrow for your printer.

Using keyboard shortcuts

A **shortcut key** is a function key, such as F1, or a combination of keys, such as CTRL+S, that you press to perform a command. For example, instead of using the Cut, Copy, and Paste commands on the Ribbon or the Mini toolbar, you can use the **keyboard shortcuts** CTRL+X to cut text, CTRL+C to copy text, and CTRL+V to paste text. You can also press CTRL+S to save changes to a document instead of clicking the Save button on the Quick Access toolbar. If a keyboard shortcut is available for a command, then it is listed in the ScreenTip for that command.

Figure 1-20: Margins tab in Page Setup dialog box

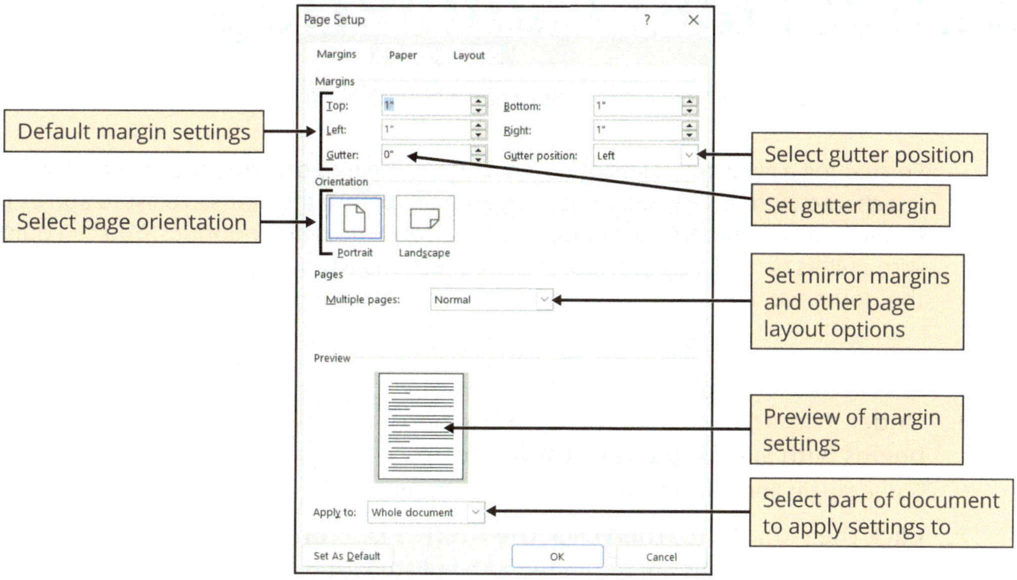

Figure 1-21: Info sheet with smaller margins and space after a paragraph

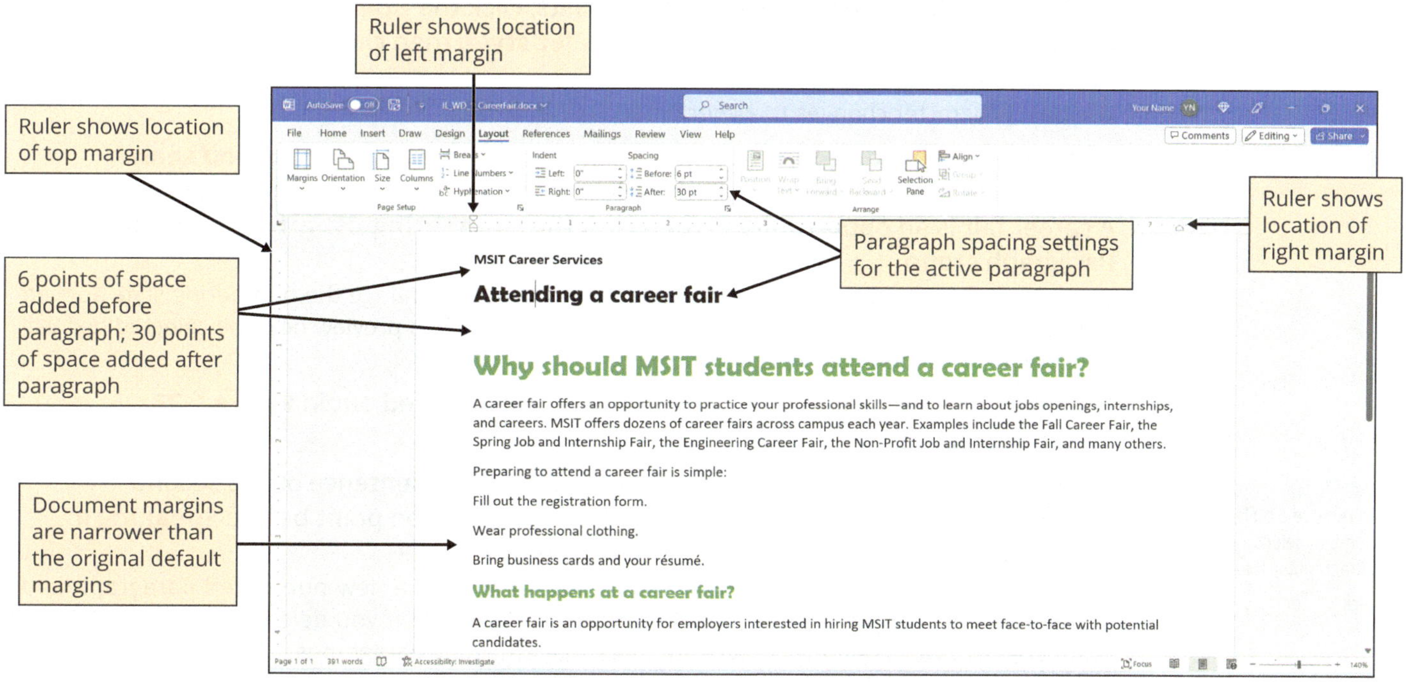

Changing orientation, margin settings, and paper size

By default, the documents you create in Word use an 8 ½" × 11" paper size in portrait orientation with the default margin settings. You can change the orientation, margin settings, and paper size to common settings using the Orientation, Margins, and Size buttons in the Page Setup group on the Layout tab. You can also adjust these settings and others in the Page Setup dialog box. For example, to change the layout of multiple pages, use the Multiple pages arrow on the Margins tab to create pages that use mirror margins, that include two pages per sheet of paper, or that are formatted using a book fold. **Mirror margins** are used in a document with facing pages, such as a magazine, where the margins on the left page of the document are a mirror image of the margins on the right page. Documents with mirror margins have inside and outside margins, rather than right and left margins. Another type of margin is a gutter margin, which is used in documents that are bound, such as books. A gutter adds extra space to the left, top, or inside margin to allow for the binding. Add a gutter to a document by adjusting the setting in the Gutter position box on the Margins tab. To change the size of the paper used, use the Paper size arrow on the Paper tab to select a standard paper size, or enter custom measurements in the Width and Height boxes.

Add Bullets and Numbering

Case You format the lists in your info sheet with numbers and bullets.

Objectives
- Create numbered and bulleted lists

Formatting a list with bullets or numbering can help to organize the ideas in a document. A **bullet** is a character, often a small circle, that appears before the items in a list to add emphasis. Formatting a list as a numbered list helps illustrate sequences and priorities. You can quickly format a list with bullets or numbering by using the Bullets and Numbering buttons in the Paragraph group on the Home tab.

Steps

1. **Under Preparing to attend a career fair is simple:, select the three-line list that begins with Fill out the registration form.**
   Three single-line paragraphs of text are selected.
2. **Click the Home tab, then click the Bullets button in the Paragraph group**
   The three paragraphs are formatted as a bulleted list using the most recently used bullet style as shown in **Figure 1-22**.
3. **Click a bullet in the list to select all the bullets, click the Bullets arrow in the Paragraph group, click the check mark bullet style, then click the document to deselect the text**
   The bullet character changes to a check mark.
4. **Scroll until the heading What can a career fair offer that an online job search cannot? is at the top of your screen, select the four paragraphs that begin with A career fair is an opportunity..., then click the Numbering list arrow in the Paragraph group**
   The Numbering Library opens. You use this list to choose or change the numbering style applied to a list. You can drag the pointer over the numbering styles to preview how the selected text will appear if the numbering style is applied.
5. **Click the Number alignment: Left numbering style called out in Figure 1-23**
   The paragraphs are formatted as a numbered list.
6. **Place the insertion point before employers in the first sentence of the second numbered paragraph, type dozens of, place the insertion point before Speaking in the second sentence of the paragraph, then press ENTER**
   Pressing ENTER in the middle of the numbered list creates a new numbered paragraph and automatically renumbers the remainder of the list. Similarly, if you delete a paragraph from a numbered list, Word automatically renumbers the remaining paragraphs.
7. **Click 1 in the list**
   Clicking a number in a list selects all the numbers, as shown in **Figure 1-24**.
8. **Click the Bold button in the Font group then save your changes**
   The numbers are all formatted in bold. Notice that the formatting of the items in the list does not change when you change the formatting of the numbers. You can also use this technique to change the formatting of bullets in a bulleted list.

Quick Tip
To remove a bullet or number, select the paragraph(s), then click or .

Figure 1-22: Bullets applied to list

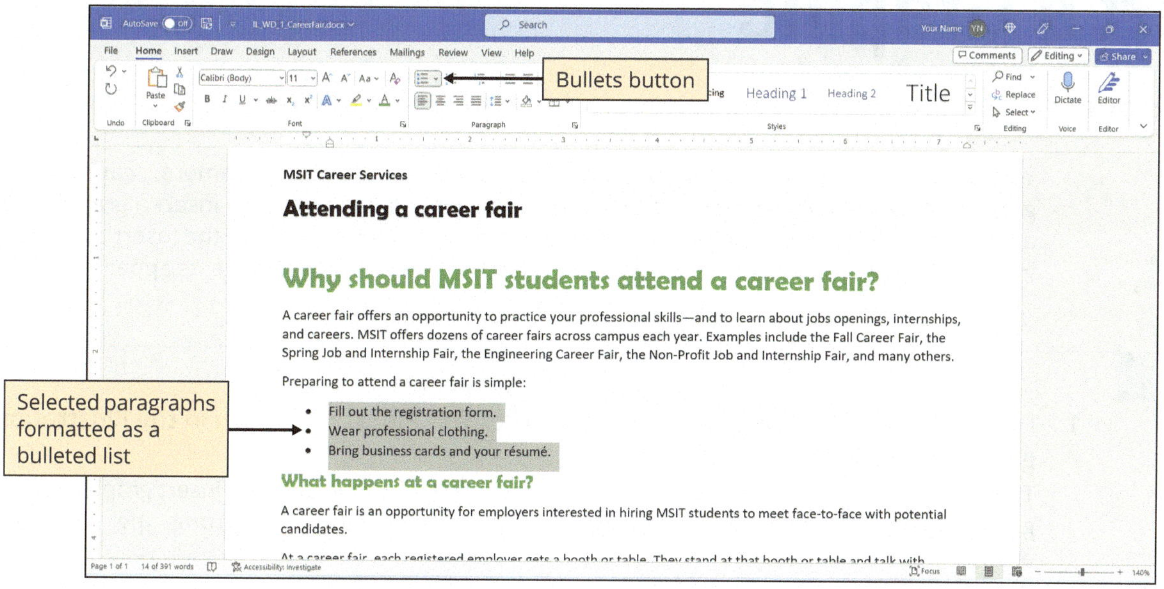

Figure 1-23: Numbering gallery

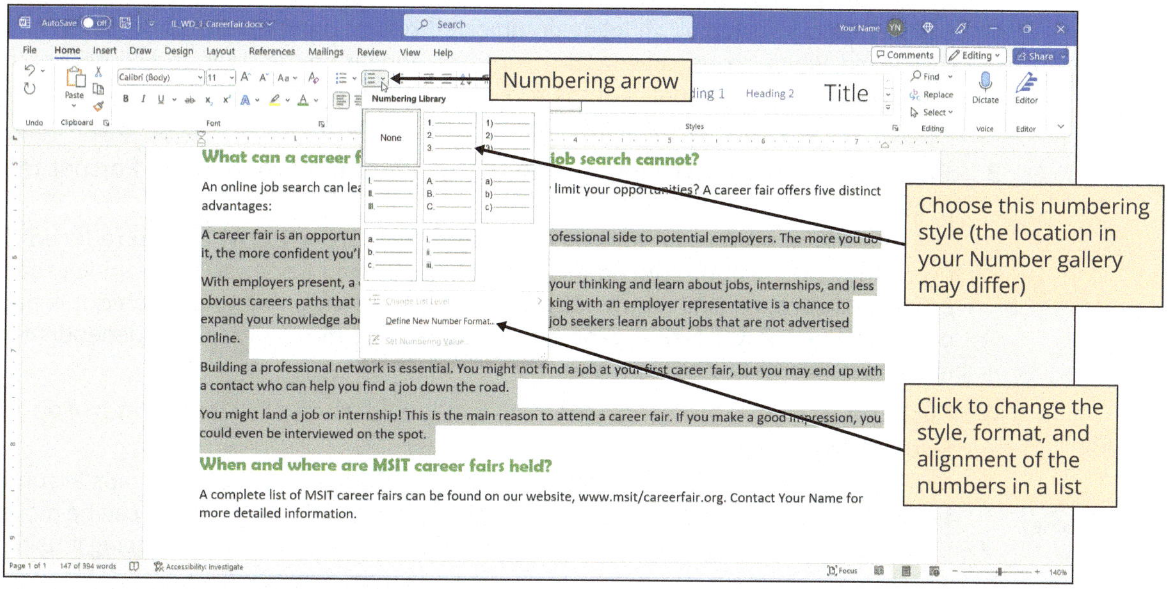

Figure 1-24: Numbered list

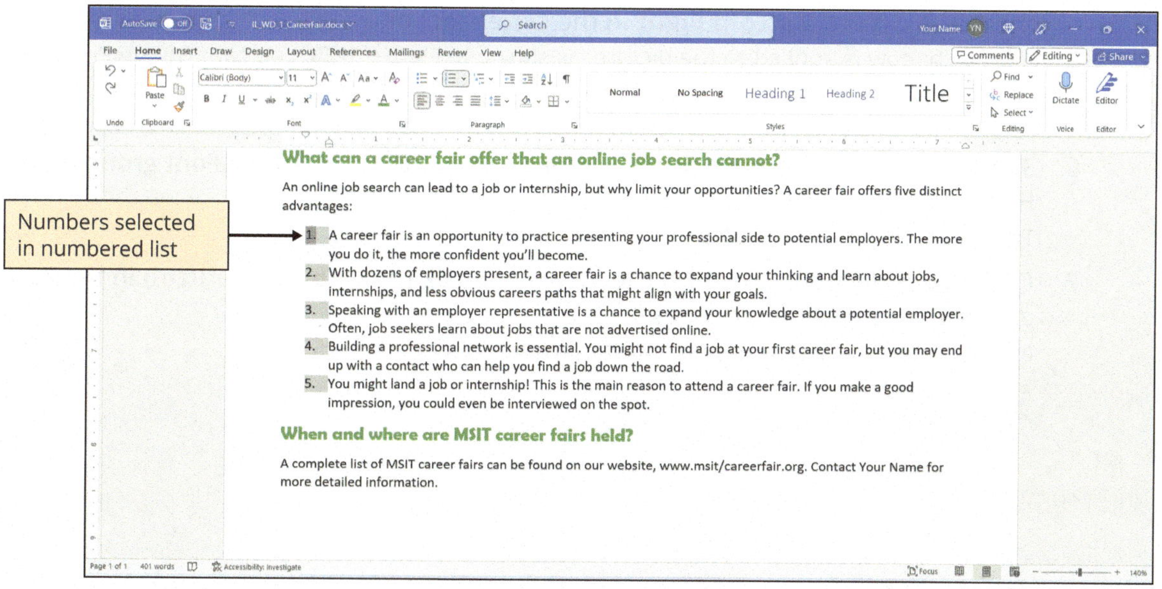

Insert a Graphic

Case You insert a picture in the document, resize it, position it, and then add a shadow.

Objectives
- Insert a picture
- Resize a picture
- Position a picture
- Apply picture styles and effects

You can insert graphic images, including photos taken with a digital camera, scanned art, and graphics created in other graphics programs, into a Word document. To insert a graphic file into a document, you use the Pictures command in the Illustrations group on the Insert tab. Once you insert a graphic, you can resize it and apply a Picture style to it to enhance its appearance.

Steps

1. **Press CTRL+HOME, click the Insert tab, click the Pictures button in the Illustrations group, then click This Device**
   The Insert Picture dialog box opens. You use this dialog box to locate and insert graphic files. Most graphic files are **bitmap graphics**, which are often saved with a .bmp, .png, .jpg, .tif, or .gif file extension.

2. **Navigate to the location where you store your Data Files, click the file Support_WD_1-2.jpg, then click Insert**
   The picture is inserted as an inline graphic at the location of the insertion point. When a graphic is selected, white circles, called **sizing handles**, appear on the sides and corners of the graphic, a white **rotate handle** appears at the top, and the Picture Format tab appears on the Ribbon. You use this tab to size, crop, position, wrap text around, format, and adjust a graphic.

3. **Type 2.1 in the Shape Height box in the Size group on the Picture Format tab, then press ENTER**
   The size of the graphic is reduced, as shown in **Figure 1-25**. When you reduced the height of the graphic, the width reduced proportionally. You can also resize a graphic proportionally by dragging a corner sizing handle. Until you apply text wrapping to a graphic, it is part of the line of text in which it was inserted (an **inline graphic**). To move a graphic independently of text, you must make it a **floating graphic**.

Quick Tip
Change a floating graphic to an inline graphic by changing the text-wrapping style to In Line with Text.

4. **Click the Position button in the Arrange group, then click Position in Top Right with Square Text Wrapping**
   The graphic is moved to the top-right corner of the page and the text wraps around it. Applying text wrapping to the graphic made it a floating graphic. A floating graphic can be moved anywhere on a page. You can also move a floating graphic to a new location by dragging it using the mouse.

5. **Click the Picture Effects button in the Picture Styles group, point to Shadow, move the pointer over the shadow styles in the gallery to preview them in the document, then click Offset: Bottom Right in the Outer section**
   A drop shadow is applied to the picture, as shown in **Figure 1-26**. You can use the Picture Effects button to apply other visual effects to a graphic, such as a glow, soft edge, reflection, bevel, or 3-D rotation.

6. **Select Attending a career fair, click the Font Color arrow in the Font group on the Home tab, then click Gray, Accent 3, Darker 25%**
   The text is formatted in dark gray.

7. **Click to deselect the text, click the View tab, click the One Page button in the Zoom group, then save your changes**
   Next, you will finalize the appearance of the info sheet.

Figure 1-25: Inline graphic in document

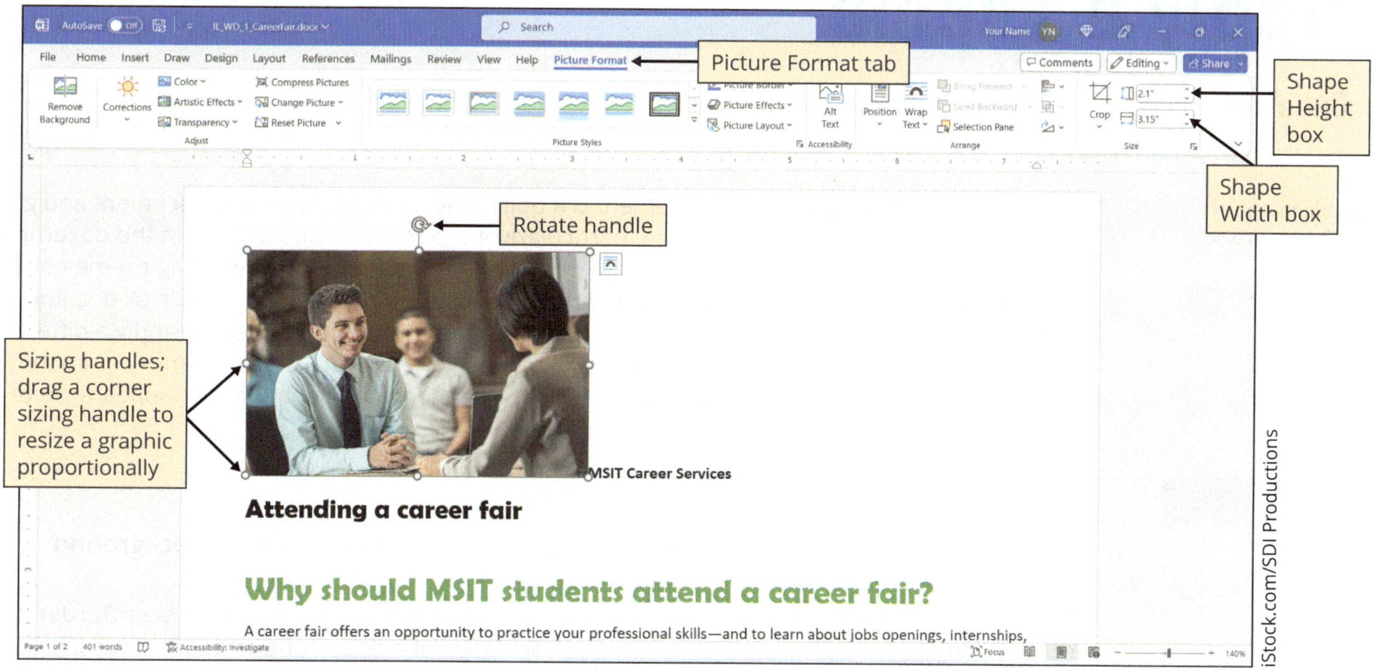

iStock.com/SDI Productions

Figure 1-26: Floating graphic with shadow effect applied

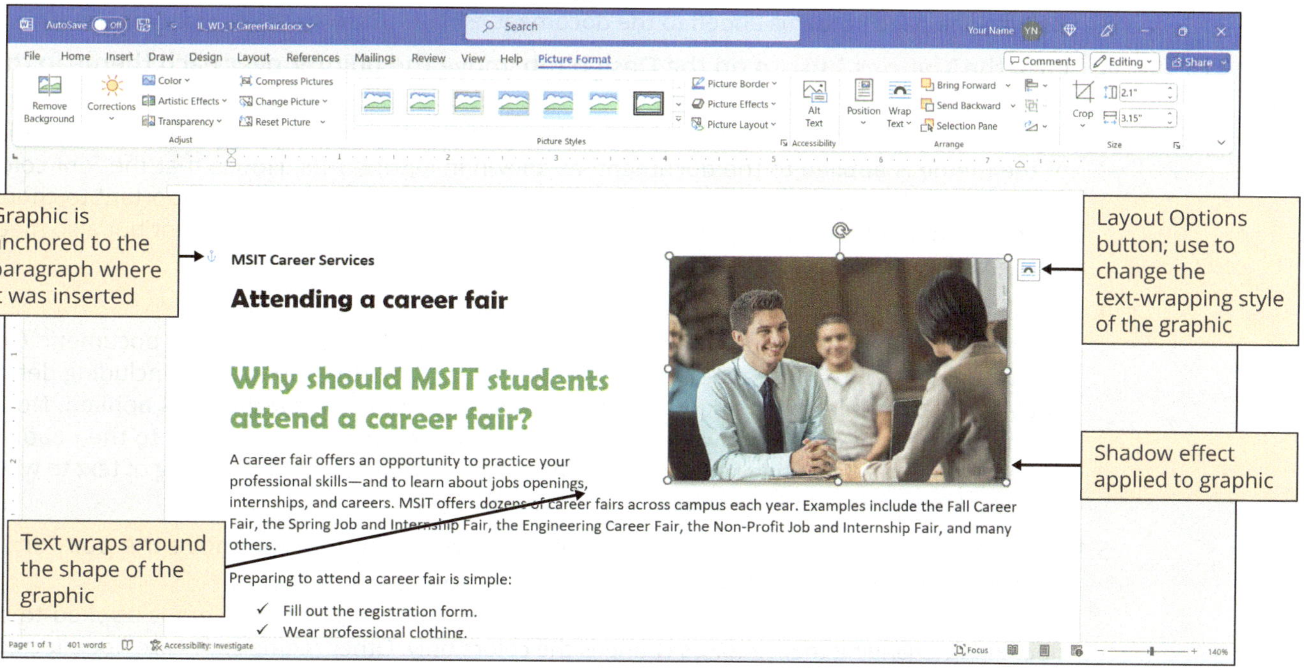

iStock.com/SDI Productions

Enhancing pictures with styles and effects

A fun way to give a document personality and flair is to apply a style or an effect to a picture. To apply a style, select the picture and then choose from the style options in the Styles group on the Picture Format tab. Styles include a preset mixture of effects, such as shading, borders, shadows, and other settings. The Effects command in the Styles group on the Picture Format tab gives you the power to apply a customized variety of effects to an object, including a shadow, bevel, glow, reflection, soft edge, or 3-D rotation. To apply an effect, select the object, click the Picture Effects arrow, point to the type of effect you want to apply, and then select from the options in the gallery that opens. To further customize an effect, click the Options command for that type of effect at the bottom of the gallery to open the Format Picture pane. The best way to learn about styles and effects is to experiment by applying them to a picture and seeing what works. To return a picture to its original settings, click the Reset Picture button in the Adjust group on the Picture Format tab.

Apply a Theme

Case You polish the info sheet by adding a page border to the document, applying a built-in theme, and changing the theme colors.

Objectives
- Change document theme
- Add a page border

Changing the theme applied to a document is a quick way to set the tone of a document and give it a polished and cohesive appearance, particularly if the text and any objects in the document are formatted with styles. A **theme** is a set of unified design elements, including theme colors, theme fonts for body text and headings, and theme effects for graphics. By default, all documents that you create in Word are formatted with the Office theme, but you can easily apply a different built-in theme to a document. To apply a theme to a document, you use the Themes command in the Document Formatting group on the Design tab. Another way to enhance the appearance of a document is to apply a page border.

Steps

1. **Click the Design tab, then click the Page Borders button in the Page Background group**
   The Borders and Shading dialog box opens, as shown in **Figure 1-27**. The Page Border tab includes options for applying a border around each page of a document, and for customizing the appearance of borders.
2. **Click the Box button on the Page Border tab, then click OK**
   A single-line page border is added to the document.
3. **Click the Themes button on the Design tab, move the pointer over each theme in the gallery, then point to Organic**
   A gallery of built-in themes opens. When you point to the Organic theme in the gallery, a preview of the theme is applied to the document, as shown in **Figure 1-28**. Notice that the font colors and the fonts for the body text change when you preview each theme. It's important to choose a theme that not only mirrors the tone, content, and purpose of your document but also meets your goal for document length.
4. **Scroll down, then click Vapor Trail**
   A complete set of new theme colors, fonts, styles, and effects is applied to the document. Only document content that uses theme colors, text that is formatted with a style (including default body text), and table styles and graphic effects change when a new theme is applied. Notice that while the font of the body text changed, the font you previously applied to the headings remains the same. Changing the document theme does not affect the formatting of text to which individual font formatting has already been applied.
5. **Click the Colors button in the Document Formatting group, then move the pointer over each set of theme colors on the menu that opens**
   When you point to a theme color set in the gallery, a preview of the colors is applied to the document. Changing theme colors changes the colors only. Other theme styles are not affected.
6. **Click Blue Green**
   The Blue Green theme colors are applied to the document.
7. **Place the insertion point in What happens at a career fair? heading, click the Layout tab, click the Before up arrow in the Spacing section in the Paragraph group twice until 12 pt appears, then add 12 points of space before the What can a career fair offer that an online job search cannot? and When and where are MSIT career fairs held? headings**
   Twelve points of space are added before the three headings, as shown in **Figure 1-29**.
8. **sam Save the document, submit the document to your instructor, close the file, then exit Word**

Figure 1-27: Page Border tab in Borders and Shading dialog box

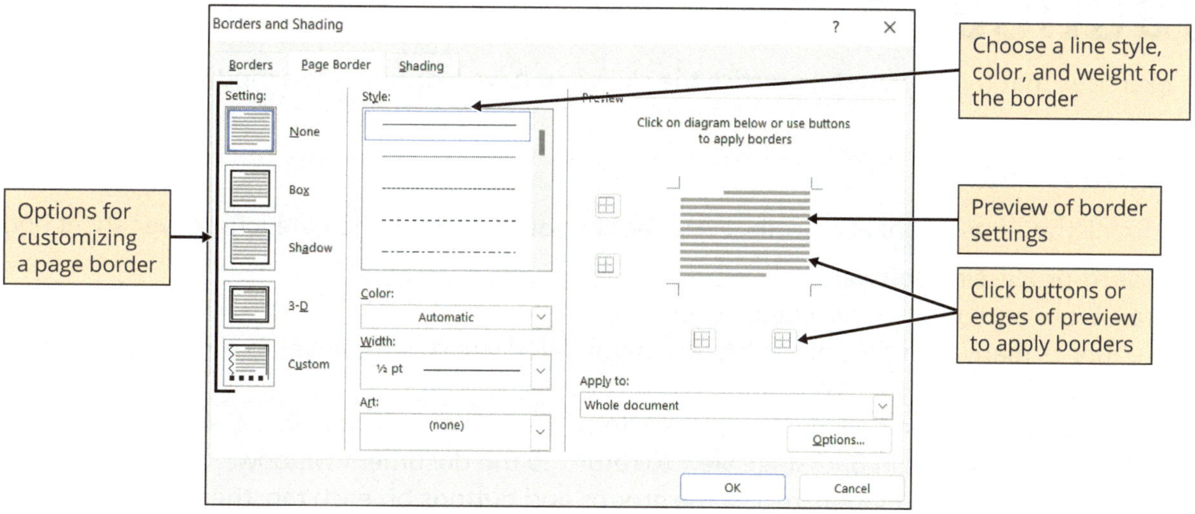

Figure 1-28: Organic theme previewed in document

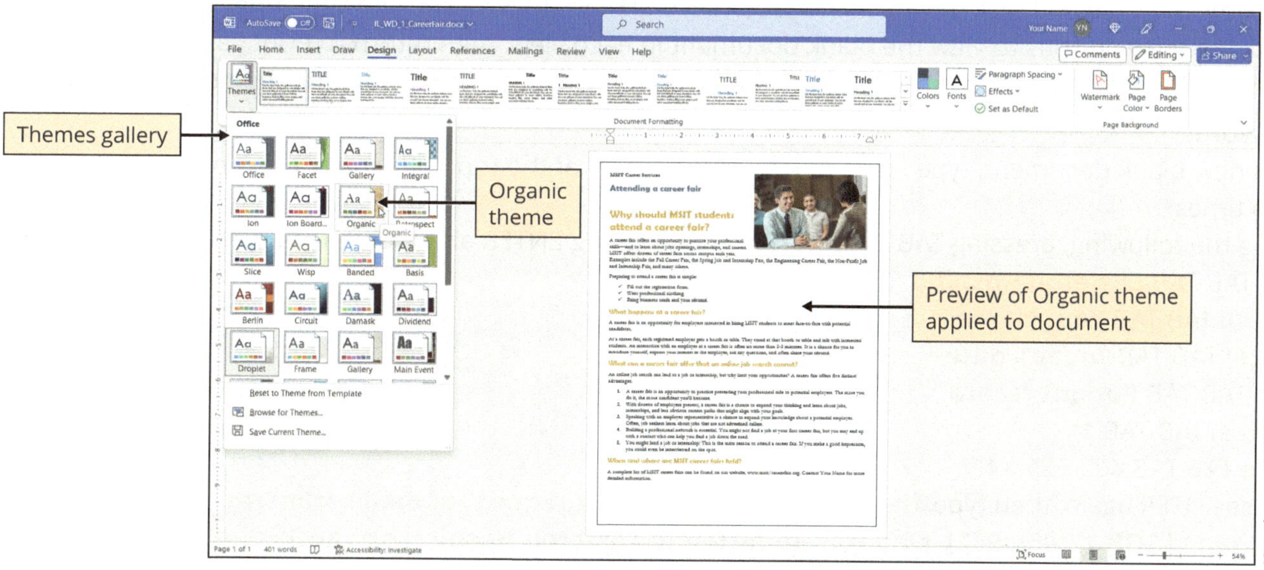

iStock.com/SDI Productions

Figure 1-29: Vapor Trail theme and Blue Green theme colors applied to document

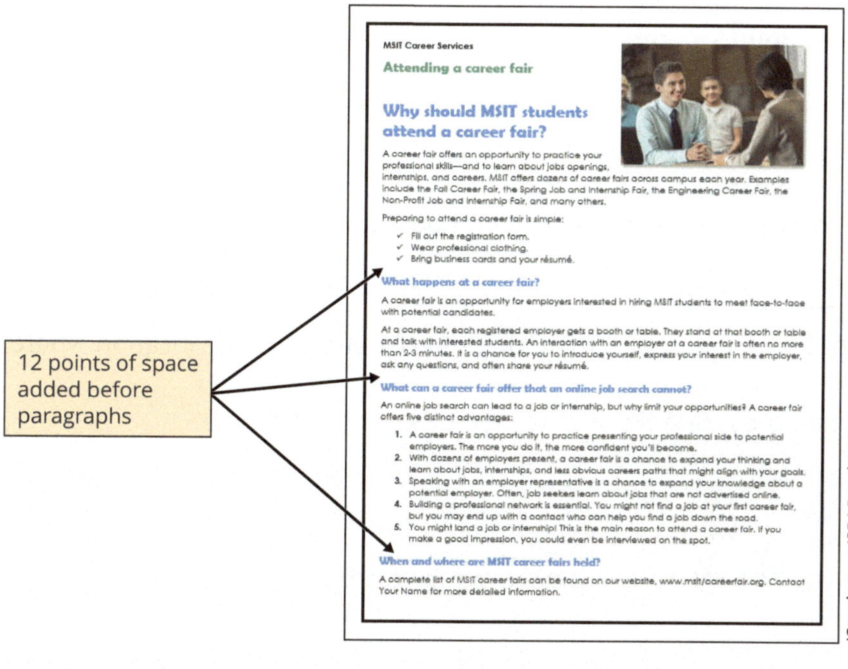

iStock.com/SDI Productions

Practice

In the exercises that follow, you will practice the skills you have learned in this module.

Skills Review

As an administrative assistant at a senior living facility, you use Word to create a fax cover sheet and a flyer.

1. **Use word-processing software.**
   a. Start Word and open a new, blank document.
   b. Identify as many elements of the Word program window as you can without referring to the module material.
   c. Click the File tab, then click the New, Open, Info, Save, Save As, Print, Share, and Export commands.
   d. Click the Back button in Backstage view to return to the document window.
   e. Click each tab on the Ribbon, review the groups and buttons on each tab, then return to the Home tab.
   f. Point to each button on the Home tab and read its ScreenTip.
   g. Click the View tab and click the Ruler check box several times to hide and show the ruler. Show the ruler.
   h. Click the View buttons to view the blank document in each view, then return to Print Layout view.
   i. Use the Zoom slider to zoom all the way in and all the way out on the document, then return to 120%.

2. **Start Word.**
   a. In a new blank document, type **Loon Pond Senior Living** at the top of the page, then press ENTER two times.
   b. Type the following, pressing TAB as indicated and pressing ENTER at the end of each line:
      To: TAB TAB **Littleton Hospital**
      From: TAB TAB **Your Name**
      Date: TAB TAB **Today's date**
      Re: TAB TAB **Patient record**
      Pages: TAB TAB **1**
      Fax: TAB TAB **603-555-8476**
   c. Press ENTER again, then type **Thank you for your recent request of medication records for Li Zhang (DOB 12/08/1942), who was admitted to Littleton Hospital on the 31st of January. With Mr. Zhang's written permission, I am sending you his full medical record. This record includes clinical findings, diagnostic test results, and the patient's progress and prescribed medications.**
   d. Press ENTER, then type **For further information, please call Patient Records at 603-555-4343 or visit our website at www.loonpond/pr.com. All requests will be fulfilled within 24 hours. We are closed on weekends.**
   e. Insert **one of our residents,** before Li Zhang.
   f. Insert **South** before Littleton in the To: line and in the first sentence of the first paragraph.
   g. Use BACKSPACE to delete 1 in the Pages: line, then type **4**.
   h. Use DELETE to delete recent in the first sentence of the first paragraph.

3. **Save a document.**
   a. Click the File tab, then click Save.
   b. Save the document as **IL_WD_1_ZhangFax** with the default file extension to the location where you store your Data Files.
   c. After your name, type a comma, press SPACEBAR, then type **Patient Records**.
   d. Save the document.

4. **Select text.**
   a. Turn on formatting marks.
   b. Select the Re: line, then type **Re:** TAB TAB **Medical Records for Li Zhang**

c. Select prescribed in the third sentence, then type **current**.
d. Select 31st of January in the first sentence of the first paragraph, type **2nd of February**, select medication, then type **medical**.
e. Delete the sentence We are closed on weekends.
f. Turn off the display of formatting marks, then save the document.

5. **Format text using the Mini toolbar and the Ribbon.**
   a. Select Loon Pond Senior Living, click the Increase Font Size button on the Mini toolbar eight times, apply bold, then click the Decrease Font Size button on the Mini toolbar twice.
   b. Center Loon Pond Senior Living on the page.
   c. Change the case of Loon Pond Senior Living to uppercase.
   d. Apply a bottom border under Loon Pond Senior Living.
   e. Apply bold to the following words in the fax heading: To:, From:, Date:, Re:, Pages:, and Fax:.
   f. Apply yellow highlighting to 2nd of February.
   g. Use the Undo, Redo, and Repeat buttons to undo the highlighting, redo the highlighting, undo, repeat, then undo the highlighting again.
   h. Remove the hyperlink from the website address, then underline Li Zhang (DOB 12/08/1942) in the body of the fax.
   i. Italicize the last sentence of the second paragraph.
   j. Read the document using the Read Mode view.
   k. Return to Print Layout view, zoom in on the document, then proofread the fax.
   l. Correct any typing errors in your document, then save the document. Compare your document to **Figure 1-30**.
   m. Preview the document in Print Preview, identify each printing option available to you on the Print screen in Backstage view, then print the document only if required to do so by your instructor.
   n. Return to Print Layout view, save, submit the fax per your instructor's directions, then close the document.

Figure 1-30

LOON POND SENIOR LIVING

To:	South Littleton Hospital
From:	Your Name, Patient Records
Date:	February 3, 2025
Re:	Medical Records for Li Zhang
Pages:	4
Fax:	603-555-8476

Thank you for your request of medical records for one of our residents, Li Zhang (DOB 12/08/1942), who was admitted to South Littleton Hospital on the 2nd of February. With Mr. Zhang's written permission, I am sending you his full medical record. This record includes clinical findings, diagnostic test results, and the patient's progress and current medications.

For further information, please call Patient Records at 603-555-4343 or visit our website at www.loonpond/pr.com. *All requests will be fulfilled within 24 hours.*

6. **View and navigate a document.**
   a. Open the file IL_WD_1-3.docx from the location where you store your Data Files, then save it as **IL_WD_1_LoonPond** in the File name box.
   b. Switch to Page Width view, then scroll through the document to get a feel for its contents.
   c. Use the Zoom dialog box to view the Whole Page.
   d. Use the Zoom slider to set the Zoom percentage at approximately 120%.
   e. Read the document using the Read Mode view. (**Hint**: Press ESC to leave Read Mode view.)
   f. Return to Print Layout view, zoom in, scroll to the bottom of the document, then replace Your Name with your name in the final sentence.
   g. Add the Title property **CCRC** to the document properties in the file, return to Print Layout view, change the zoom level to 140%, then save your changes.

Skills Review (Continued)

7. **Cut and paste text.**
   a. Turn on the display of formatting marks.
   b. Select the first body paragraph that begins We have listened carefully... (including the paragraph mark after it), cut it to the clipboard, then paste the paragraph before the heading Choice in every aspect of life.
   c. In the list of housing options, move the Villa homes... paragraph after the Cottages... paragraph.
   d. Move the One- and two-bedroom apartments... paragraph after the Villa homes... paragraph.
   e. Move the Memory support... paragraph before the Skilled nursing... paragraph.
   f. Delete the heading Housing options, then save your changes.

8. **Copy and paste text.**
   a. Scroll to the bottom of the document, then remove the hyperlink in the final paragraph.
   b. Select the sentence Let the new chapter of your life begin., then copy the sentence to the clipboard.
   c. Scroll to the top of the page, add a blank paragraph under the Loon Pond Senior Living heading, then paste the sentence at the location of the blank paragraph.
   d. Use the Paste Options button to Keep Source formatting.
   e. Format the pasted sentence in italic, turn off formatting marks, then save your changes.

9. **Format with fonts.**
   a. Format the heading Loon Pond Senior Living in 20-point Calibri Light with an Orange, Accent 2, Darker 25% font color.
   b. Format the heading Living at Loon Pond is about choices, security, and lifestyle! in 14-point Calibri Light with a Green, Accent 6, Darker 25% font color.
   c. Format Choice in every aspect of life, Resident-centered care, and Healthy and active lifestyle options in 14-point Calibri Light with an Orange, Accent 2, Darker 25% font color.
   d. Apply bold formatting to the last paragraph in the document, change the font size to 12, then change the font color to Orange, Accent 2, Darker 25%.
   e. Scroll up, select Loon Pond Senior Living, click the Text Effects and Typography arrow, preview several WordArt styles applied to the text, then apply one of the styles.
   f. Click the Undo button, add an Offset: Bottom Right shadow to the title, then save your changes.

10. **Set document margins.**
    a. Change the left and right margins to 2".
    b. View the document in Multiple Pages view.
    c. Change the left and right margins to 1.5".
    d. Change all four document margins to .7".
    e. Change the zoom level to 120%, then add 12 points of space before the heading Living at Loon Pond is about choices, security, and lifestyle!
    f. Save your changes.

11. **Add bullets and numbering.**
    a. Select the six-line list of housing options that begins with Cottages and ends with Skilled nursing, then format it as a bulleted list using the circle bullet symbol.
    b. Change the font color of the bullets to Green, Accent 6, Darker 25%, then deselect the bullets.
    c. Press and hold CTRL to select the headings Choice in every aspect of life, Resident-centered care, and Healthy and active lifestyle options, then apply numbering.
    d. Click 1 in the list, then change the font color of the numbers to Green, Accent 6, Darker 25%.
    e. Save your changes.

12. **Insert a graphic.**
   a. Click in the first body paragraph to move the insertion point to the top of the document, then open the Insert Picture dialog box.
   b. Navigate to the location where you store Data Files, then insert the file **Support_ WD_1-4.jpg**.
   c. Change the height of the graphic to 1.2 using the Shape Height box in the Size group on the Picture Format tab.
   d. Use the Position command to wrap text around the graphic and position it in the Top Left with Square Text Wrapping.
   e. Apply the Double Frame, Black picture style to the graphic.
   f. Click the Reset Picture arrow in the Adjust Group on the Picture Format tab, reset the picture, then apply the Simple Frame, White picture style.
   g. Change the font size of Loon Pond Senior Living to 36 point, then change the font size of Let the new chapter of your life begin. to 14 point.
   h. Click before the Living at Loon Pond is about choices, security, and lifestyle! heading, press ENTER, change the font size of the heading to 20 point, then save your changes.

13. **Apply a theme.**
   a. Change the view to One Page, click the Design tab, click the Page Borders button, then apply a single-line box border to the page.
   b. Use the Themes feature to preview several different themes applied to the document. Apply a theme, zoom in and out on the document to evaluate its suitability, then apply another theme, zoom in and out, and so forth.
   c. Apply the View theme.
   d. Change all four document margins to .6" to better fit the text on the page.
   e. Zoom in on the bottom of the document, then add 24 points of space above the last paragraph.
   f. Change the theme colors to Green.
   g. Zoom in on the top of the document, then change the font color of the Let the new chapter... paragraph to Turquoise, Accent 6, Darker 25%.
   h. Change the font color of the Living at Loon Pond... heading to Lime, Accent 2, Darker 25% and the font color of the last paragraph to Turquoise, Accent 6, Darker 25%. Compare your document to **Figure 1-31**.
   i. Save your changes, preview the document, submit it per your instructors directions, then close the document and exit Word.

Figure 1-31

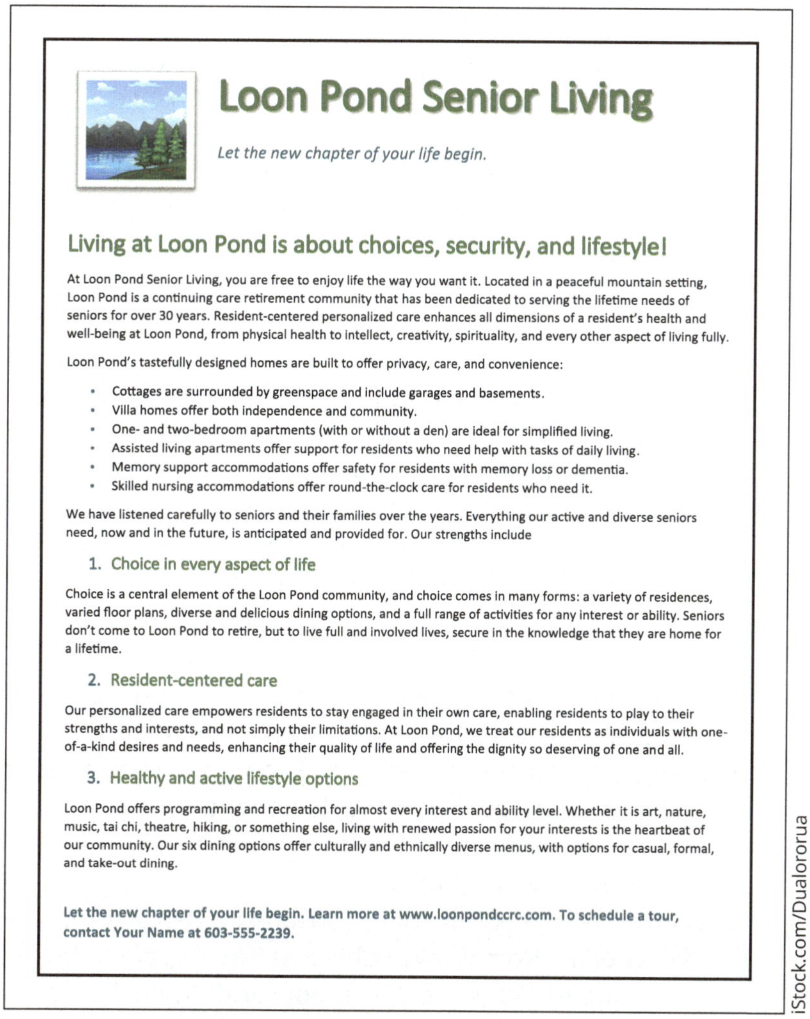

Loon Pond Senior Living

Let the new chapter of your life begin.

Living at Loon Pond is about choices, security, and lifestyle!

At Loon Pond Senior Living, you are free to enjoy life the way you want it. Located in a peaceful mountain setting, Loon Pond is a continuing care retirement community that has been dedicated to serving the lifetime needs of seniors for over 30 years. Resident-centered personalized care enhances all dimensions of a resident's health and well-being at Loon Pond, from physical health to intellect, creativity, spirituality, and every other aspect of living fully.

Loon Pond's tastefully designed homes are built to offer privacy, care, and convenience:

- Cottages are surrounded by greenspace and include garages and basements.
- Villa homes offer both independence and community.
- One- and two-bedroom apartments (with or without a den) are ideal for simplified living.
- Assisted living apartments offer support for residents who need help with tasks of daily living.
- Memory support accommodations offer safety for residents with memory loss or dementia.
- Skilled nursing accommodations offer round-the-clock care for residents who need it.

We have listened carefully to seniors and their families over the years. Everything our active and diverse seniors need, now and in the future, is anticipated and provided for. Our strengths include

1. Choice in every aspect of life

Choice is a central element of the Loon Pond community, and choice comes in many forms: a variety of residences, varied floor plans, diverse and delicious dining options, and a full range of activities for any interest or ability. Seniors don't come to Loon Pond to retire, but to live full and involved lives, secure in the knowledge that they are home for a lifetime.

2. Resident-centered care

Our personalized care empowers residents to stay engaged in their own care, enabling residents to play to their strengths and interests, and not simply their limitations. At Loon Pond, we treat our residents as individuals with one-of-a-kind desires and needs, enhancing their quality of life and offering the dignity so deserving of one and all.

3. Healthy and active lifestyle options

Loon Pond offers programming and recreation for almost every interest and ability level. Whether it is art, nature, music, tai chi, theatre, hiking, or something else, living with renewed passion for your interests is the heartbeat of our community. Our six dining options offer culturally and ethnically diverse menus, with options for casual, formal, and take-out dining.

Let the new chapter of your life begin. Learn more at www.loonpondccrc.com. To schedule a tour, contact Your Name at 603-555-2239.

iStock.com/Dualororua

Independent Challenge 1

You work at Pediatric Health Associates, a large community-based pediatric practice staffed by physicians, specialists, nurses, and other allied health professionals. Your boss has drafted an information sheet to educate parents about influenza and asks you to edit and format it so that it is eye-catching and attractive.

a. Open the file IL_WD_1-5.docx from the drive and folder where you store your Data Files, save it as **IL_WD_1_PediatricFlu**, then read the document to get a feel for the content. **Figure 1-32** shows how you will format the info sheet.

b. Show the rulers in your document window if they are not already visible.

c. Accept or ignore all suggested spelling and grammar changes in the document.

d. Insert the picture file Support_WD_1-6.jpg at the top of the document. Change the height of the image to 2", then position the image in the bottom right with square text wrapping. (**Hint**: Zoom in and out on the document as necessary. If an anchor symbol appears in the margin, you can ignore it.)

e. Center the first two lines of text in the document.

f. Change the font of Pediatric Health Associates to Arial Black. Change the font size to 18 point. Change the font color to Gray, Accent 3, Darker 25%.

g. Format Influenza (Flu) in Children in 28-point Arial Black with a Blue, Accent 1, Darker 25% font color. Apply an Offset: Bottom Left shadow text effect.

Figure 1-32

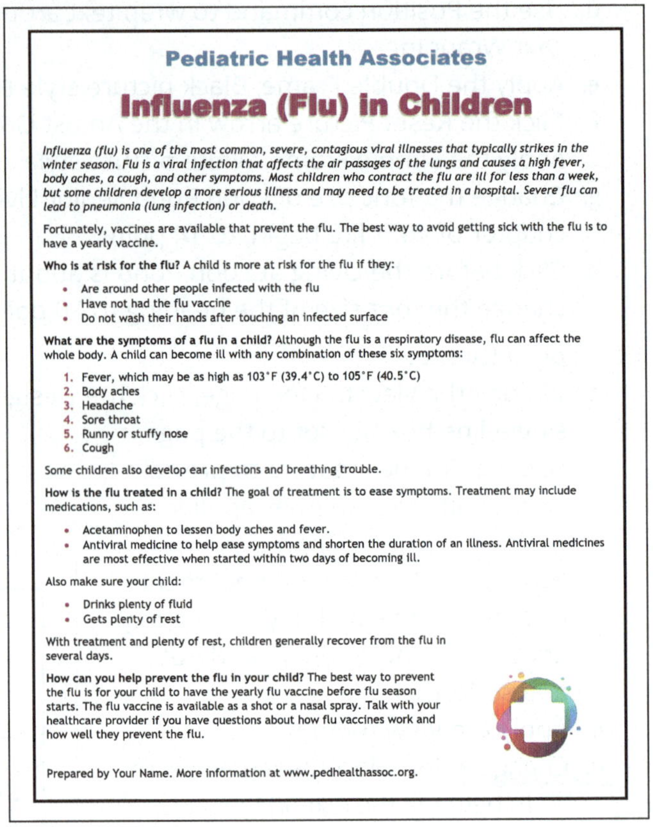

Pediatric Health Associates

Influenza (Flu) in Children

Influenza (flu) is one of the most common, severe, contagious viral illnesses that typically strikes in the winter season. Flu is a viral infection that affects the air passages of the lungs and causes a high fever, body aches, a cough, and other symptoms. Most children who contract the flu are ill for less than a week, but some children develop a more serious illness and may need to be treated in a hospital. Severe flu can lead to pneumonia (lung infection) or death.

Fortunately, vaccines are available that prevent the flu. The best way to avoid getting sick with the flu is to have a yearly vaccine.

Who is at risk for the flu? A child is more at risk for the flu if they:

- Are around other people infected with the flu
- Have not had the flu vaccine
- Do not wash their hands after touching an infected surface

What are the symptoms of a flu in a child? Although the flu is a respiratory disease, flu can affect the whole body. A child can become ill with any combination of these six symptoms:

1. Fever, which may be as high as 103°F (39.4°C) to 105°F (40.5°C)
2. Body aches
3. Headache
4. Sore throat
5. Runny or stuffy nose
6. Cough

Some children also develop ear infections and breathing trouble.

How is the flu treated in a child? The goal of treatment is to ease symptoms. Treatment may include medications, such as:

- Acetaminophen to lessen body aches and fever.
- Antiviral medicine to help ease symptoms and shorten the duration of an illness. Antiviral medicines are most effective when started within two days of becoming ill.

Also make sure your child:

- Drinks plenty of fluid
- Gets plenty of rest

With treatment and plenty of rest, children generally recover from the flu in several days.

How can you help prevent the flu in your child? The best way to prevent the flu is for your child to have the yearly flu vaccine before flu season starts. The flu vaccine is available as a shot or a nasal spray. Talk with your healthcare provider if you have questions about how flu vaccines work and how well they prevent the flu.

Prepared by Your Name. More information at www.pedhealthassoc.org.

iStock.com/Lucky Creative

h. Apply italic to the first body paragraph.

i. Change all four document margins to .5", then reduce the font size of Pediatric Health Associates by 2 points.

j. Format the three-line list of who is at risk (beginning with Are around) as a bulleted list, then apply the Blue, Accent 1, Darker 25% font color to the bullets.

k. Format the Six-line list of common symptoms (beginning with Fever) as a numbered list. (**Hint**: If you make a mistake, click the Undo button and try again.)

l. Format the two-line list of medications (beginning with Acetaminophen) and the two-line list of other tips (beginning with Drinks) as bulleted lists.

m. Apply bold to the numbers in the numbered list, and change the font color of the numbers to Blue, Accent 1, Darker 25%.

n. In the numbered list, select paragraph 3 (Runny or stuffy nose), cut it, place the insertion point before Cough in the new paragraph 5, then paste the text.

o. Change the document theme to Facet, then change the theme colors to Red Violet.

p. Add a Box page border to the document.

q. Increase the font size of **Pediatric Health Associates** to 20, then add 12 points of space after **Influenza (Flu) in Children**.

r. Zoom in on the bottom of the document. Replace Your Name in the final line with your name, remove the hyperlink from www.pedhealthassoc.org, and add 24 points of space before the final line paragraph.

s. Zoom out, examine the document carefully for formatting errors, and make any necessary adjustments so that all the text fits on one page.

t. Save the document, submit it per your instructor's directions, then close the file and exit Word.

Independent Challenge 2

Yesterday you interviewed for a job as a virtual assistant at Valet Business Support Services. You interviewed in person and spoke with several people, including Sabrina Singh, director of human resources, whose business card is shown in **Figure 1-33**. Ms. Singh asked you to send her some physical samples of your work as evidence of your Word skills. You need to write a cover letter to Ms. Singh, thanking her for the interview and expressing your interest in the position.

a. Start Word and save a new blank document as **IL_WD_1_SinghLetter** to the location where you store your Data Files.
b. Begin the letter by clicking the No Spacing button in the Styles group. You use this button to apply the No Spacing style to the document so that your document does not include extra space between paragraphs.
c. Type a personal letterhead for the letter that includes your name, address, telephone number, email address, and webpage or LinkedIn address, if you have one. Remove any hyperlinks. Accept or undo any automatic corrections.
(Note: Format the letterhead after you finish typing the letter.)
d. Four lines below the bottom of the letterhead, type today's date.
e. Four lines below the date, type the inside address, referring to **Figure 1-33** for the information. Include the recipient's title, business name, and full mailing address.
f. Two lines below the inside address, type **Dear Ms. Singh:** for the salutation.
g. Two lines below the salutation, type the body of the letter, leaving a blank space between each paragraph, according to the following guidelines:
   - In the first paragraph, thank her for the interview. Then restate your interest in the position and express your desire to work for the business. Add any specific details you think will enhance the power of your letter.
   - In the second paragraph, note that you are enclosing three samples of your work, and explain something about the samples you are enclosing.
   - Type a short final paragraph.

Figure 1-33

h. Two lines below the last body paragraph, type a closing, then four lines below the closing, type the signature block. Be sure to include your name in the signature block.
i. Two lines below the signature block, type an enclosure notation. (**Hint**: An enclosure notation usually includes the word "Enclosures" or the abbreviation "Enc." followed by the number of enclosures in parentheses.)
j. Edit your letter for clarity and precision. Move sentences if necessary, replace words with more precise words, and correct any spelling or grammar errors.
k. Change the font of the letter to a serif font, such as Times New Roman, Garamond, or something similar. Adjust the font size so the letter can be read easily.
l. Format the letterhead using fonts, font colors, text effects, borders, themes, paragraph spacing, paragraph alignment, change case, and other formatting features. Be sure the design of your letterhead reflects your personality and is suitable for a professional document.
m. Change the Title document property to **Letter**.
n. Save your changes, preview the letter, submit it per your instructor's directions, then close the document and exit Word.

Visual Workshop

Create the letter shown in **Figure 1-34**. Before beginning to type, click the No Spacing button in the Styles group on the Home tab. Type the letter before formatting the letterhead and applying the theme. To format the letterhead, change the font size of the first line of text to 30 point and apply the Fill: Black, Text Color 1; Outline: White, Background color 1; Hard Shadow: Blue, Accent color 5 WordArt style. Change the font color of the address line to Blue, Accent 5. Add the bottom border to the letterhead. When the letterhead is formatted, change the font size of the body text to 12 point, apply the Organic theme, then change the font color of the letterhead text to Red, Accent 4. Save the document as **IL_WD_1_KowalskiBaron** to the location where you store your Data Files, submit the letter to your instructor, then close the document and exit Word.

Figure 1-34

Kowalski-Baron Insurance Agency

3594 Cedar Avenue, Cleveland, OH 44115, www.kowalski-baron.com

August 12. 2025

Ms. Chandra Lakatos
85 Rouse Avenue
Cleveland, OH 44104

Dear Ms. Lakatos:

At Kowalski-Baron Insurance, we have all the protection you need for your home, auto, or business, and all the savings, too. As one of the largest independent, locally owned insurance agencies in the region, we take pride in the value, ease, and quality we offer our customers:

- We compare insurance rates from leading providers to present you with best offer.
- Choose from a range of payment plans, with the ability to pick your payment due date.
- File claims easily through our online system.

Looking for a specific type of coverage? Visit us on the web at www.kowalski-baron.com to explore our products and receive a free quote.

Sincerely,

Your Name
Account Manager

Editing and Formatting Documents

Case

You have been asked to edit and format a research report on expanding the digital media degree program at MSIT. After editing the report and applying styles to format the text, you add page numbers, a header, footnotes, and a bibliography to the document. Finally, before distributing the report electronically, you strip the file of private information.

Module Objectives

After completing this module, you will be able to:

- Insert comments
- Find and replace text
- Check spelling and grammar
- Proofread and revise text
- Change line spacing and indents
- Apply styles to text
- Insert page numbers and page breaks
- Add headers and footers
- Add footnotes and endnotes
- Insert citations
- Create a bibliography
- Inspect a document

Files You Will Need

IL_WD_2-1.docx
IL_WD_2-2.docx
IL_WD_2-3.docx
IL_WD_2-4.docx

Insert Comments

Case Your colleague, Yolanda Ortiz, read the draft of the report and inserted comments. You open the report to review and respond to Yolanda's comments. You add and edit comments.

Objective
- Add comments

You can collaborate on documents with colleagues in different ways. One way is to insert comments into a document when you want to ask questions or provide information to other reviewers. A **comment** is text that appears in a comment box along the right side of a page in Print Layout view. Shading appears in the document at the point where you or another reviewer inserted a comment. A comment icon also appears in the margin to the right of the commented text to indicate the location of a comment. Each reviewer is assigned a unique color automatically, which appears in the comment box.

Steps

Quick Tip
To show all comments in the Comments pane, click the Comments button on the Ribbon.

Quick Tip
When you click the reviewer's initials in the comment box, a person card for the reviewer appears; use this to communicate quickly with reviewers.

Trouble
If a Post comment button does not appear in your comment, click anywhere in the document text.

Trouble
If you don't see the Reply box, click the Reply button, type your reply, then click anywhere in the document text.

1. **sam Start Word, open the file IL_WD_2-1.docx from the location where you store your Data Files, save it as IL_WD_2_DigitalMedia, change the zoom level to 100%, then click the Review tab**

   Simple Markup is the default option in the Display for Review box in the Tracking group on the Review tab. A different markup option may be selected if another user was working on the computer before you. With the Simple Markup option, comments appear along the right side of the page. If you see comment icons and no comment wording, then click the Show Comments button in the Comments group. Alternatively, click a Go to comment icon to show the comments.

2. **Click the Display for Review arrow in the Tracking group, then click All Markup**

   In the first, third, and fourth body paragraphs, some of the text is shaded, indicating the text is associated with a comment.

3. **Select the word MSIT in the title (the first line), then click the New Comment button in the Comments group**

   The word "MSIT" is shaded with color, and a box for a comment appears to the right of the document. Your name or the name assigned to your computer appears in the comment box.

4. **Type This is the working title for the expanded program., then click the Post comment button**

   Your comment appears as shown in **Figure 2-1**. To navigate between comments in a long document, use the Next and Previous buttons in the Comments group.

5. **Click Yolanda's first comment (starts with "Is this…"), click the Reply box in the comment, type I am researching other options., then click the Post comment button**

   When you click in a comment box, it is outlined in color to indicate it is active. The reply you typed is indented under the original comment.

Figure 2-1: New comment in document

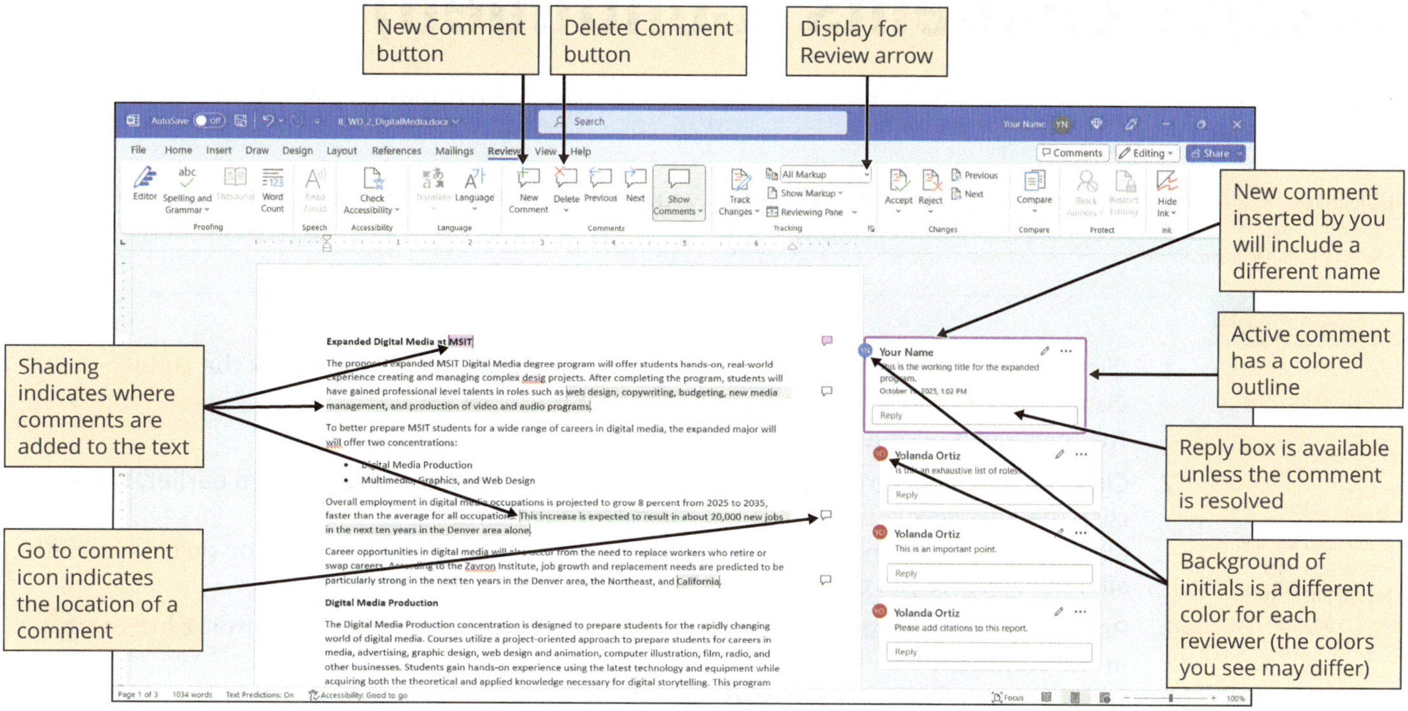

Using modern comments in Word

The "modern comment" experience in Word differs from the "legacy comment" experience. Modern comment boxes include a Post comment button that must be clicked for a comment to "post" or be committed. This allows users to finalize a comment before it becomes visible to collaborators on a shared document. By contrast, legacy comments do not include a Post comment button and are visible to collaborators as they are being typed. Modern comments also include an @mention feature that allows users working in a shared cloud environment to address a specific person in a comment or reply. Eventually, legacy comments will phase out and all Word users will experience modern comments. Until then, it is possible to switch between the modern and legacy comment experiences. To do so, click the File tab, click Options, click General in the Word Options dialog box, and then select or deselect the Enable modern comments check box.

Insert Comments (Continued)

Case You delete a comment, view other comment actions, and then reply to and resolve comments before formatting the document.

Objectives
- Edit comments
- Resolve comments

After inserting and editing comments, you can delete them, reply to them, and resolve them.

Steps

1. **Click Yolanda's second comment ("This is an important…"), then click the Delete Comment button in the Comments group**
   The comment is removed from the document.
2. **Click the "I am researching other options." reply comment you inserted earlier, then click the Edit comment button next to your name**
   Clicking the Edit comment button opens a comment for editing. The insertion point is located after the sentence you typed earlier in the Reply comment box.
3. **Press [Spacebar], type I will send you a list., then click the Post comment button in the comment**
   The edited reply comment is posted.
4. **Click Yolanda's comment containing the text "Please add citations…", click the More thread actions button in the comment, click Resolve thread, then click anywhere in the document text**
   The comment is marked as resolved, as shown in **Figure 2-2**. You can reopen a comment that has been marked as resolved by clicking the Go to resolved comment icon in the document, and then clicking the Reopen button in the comment. You can also see resolved comments in the Comments pane.
5. **Click All Markup in the Tracking group, click No Markup, then save your changes**
   Selecting No Markup hides the comments. Hiding the comments does not remove them from the document. It simply hides them from view on the screen. You will keep the comments hidden while you format the document.

Trouble
If you don't see the Edit button, click in the comment, type your reply, then click anywhere in the document text.

Trouble
If you don't see the More thread actions button, click the Resolve button, then click anywhere in the document text.

Quick Tip
To delete all comments in a document, click the Delete Comment arrow, then click Delete All Comments in Document.

Figure 2-2: Resolved comment in document

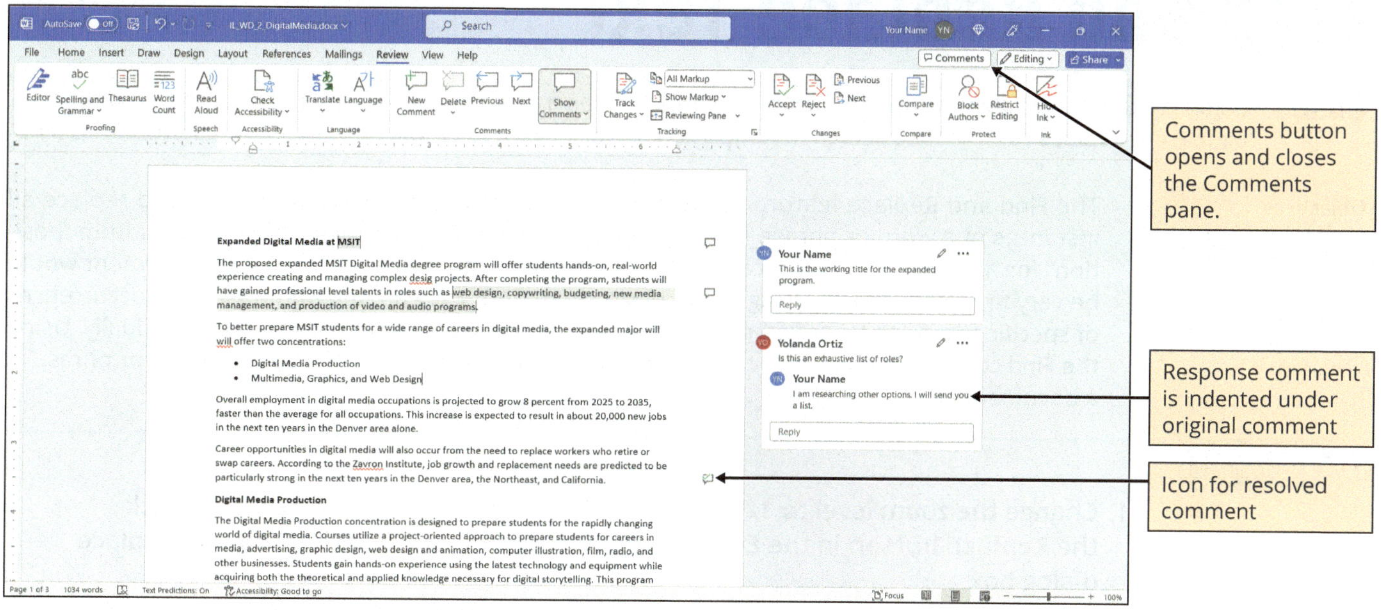

Inking comments in Word

If you are working in Touch mode on a touch-enabled device, you can draw or write comments using your finger, a digital pen, or a mouse. The type of inking features available to you will depend on your device. To begin, click the Draw tab on the Ribbon, click a pen in the Drawing Tools group to create an ink comment, and then use your finger, stylus, or mouse to draw or write in the document. On some devices, you can change the color and type of pen stroke to use for inking by using the Pen button in the Drawing Tools group. You can hide inked comments using the Hide Ink button in the Ink group on the Review tab. When you are finished inking a comment, click anywhere in the document. If you are on a touch-enabled device and want to switch your device to Touch mode and use the full range of inking features available in Word, you can add the Touch/Mouse Mode button to the Quick Access toolbar by clicking the Customize Quick Access Toolbar button on the Quick Access toolbar, and then clicking Touch/Mouse Mode. To use Touch mode, click the Touch/Mouse Mode button, and then click Touch.

Find and Replace Text

Case You notice the word "talent" is used to describe competencies that are actually skills, not talents, in the report. You use the Replace command to search the document for all instances of "talent" and replace them with "skill".

Objectives
- Find and replace text
- Search for text and formatting
- Move to a specific location in a document

The Find and Replace feature in Word allows you to automatically search for and replace all instances of a word or phrase in a document. For example, you might need to substitute "position" for "job". To manually locate and replace each instance of "job" in a long document would be very time-consuming. Using the Replace command, you can find and replace all occurrences of specific text at once, or you can choose to find and review each occurrence individually. Using the Find command, you can locate and highlight every occurrence of a specific word or phrase in a document.

Steps

1. **Change the zoom level to 120%, press CTRL+HOME, click the Home tab, click the Replace button in the Editing group, then click More in the Find and Replace dialog box**
   The Find and Replace dialog box opens and expands, as shown in **Figure 2-3**.

Trouble
If any Search Options check boxes are selected in your Find and Replace dialog box, deselect them. If Format appears under the Find what or Replace with box, click in the box, then click the No Formatting button.

2. **Type talent in the Find what box**
   The text "talent" is the text that will be replaced.

3. **Press TAB, then type skill in the Replace with box**
   The text "skill" will replace the text "talent".

4. **Click the Match case check box in the Search Options section to select it**
   Selecting the Match case check box tells Word to find only exact matches for the uppercase and lowercase characters you entered in the Find what text box. You want to replace all instances of "talent" in the body text of the report. You do not want to replace "Talent" in the proper name "Talent Match Program".

Quick Tip
To find, review, and replace each occurrence individually, click Find Next.

5. **Click Replace All**
   Clicking Replace All changes all occurrences of "talent" to "skill" in the report. A message box reports seven replacements were made.

6. **Click OK to close the message box, then click Close in the Find and Replace dialog box**
   Word replaced "talent" with "skill" in seven locations but did not replace "Talent" in the program name. To find or replace text that is formatted a certain way, click the Find arrow in the Editing group, click Advanced Find, click Format in the Find and Replace dialog box, and then select the appropriate format options. To find or replace special characters such as em dashes and paragraph marks, click Special in the Find and Replace dialog box.

7. **Click the Find button in the Editing group**
   Clicking the Find button opens the Navigation pane, which is used to browse a longer document by headings, pages, or specific text. The Find command allows you to quickly locate all instances of text in a document. You use it to verify that Word did not replace "Talent" in Talent Match Program.

8. **Type Talent in the search box in the Navigation pane**
   The word "Talent" is highlighted and selected in the document, as shown in **Figure 2-4**.

9. **Click the Close button in the Navigation pane**
   The highlighting is removed from the text when you close the Navigation pane.

10. **Press CTRL+HOME, then save the document**

Figure 2-3: Find and Replace dialog box

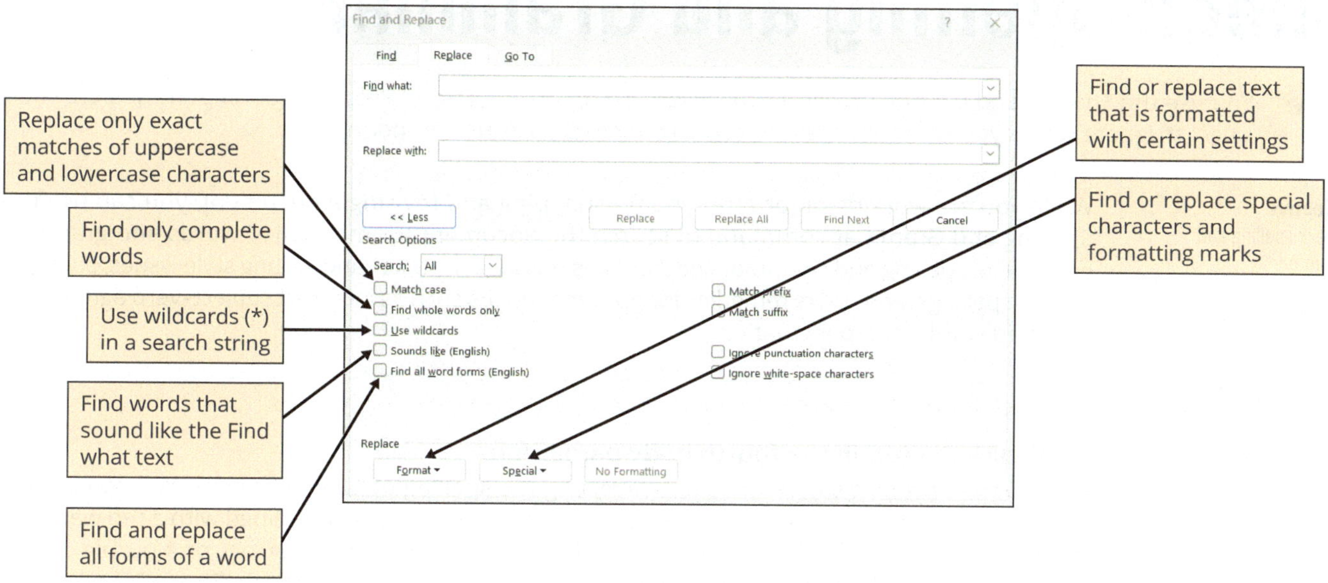

Figure 2-4: Found text highlighted in document

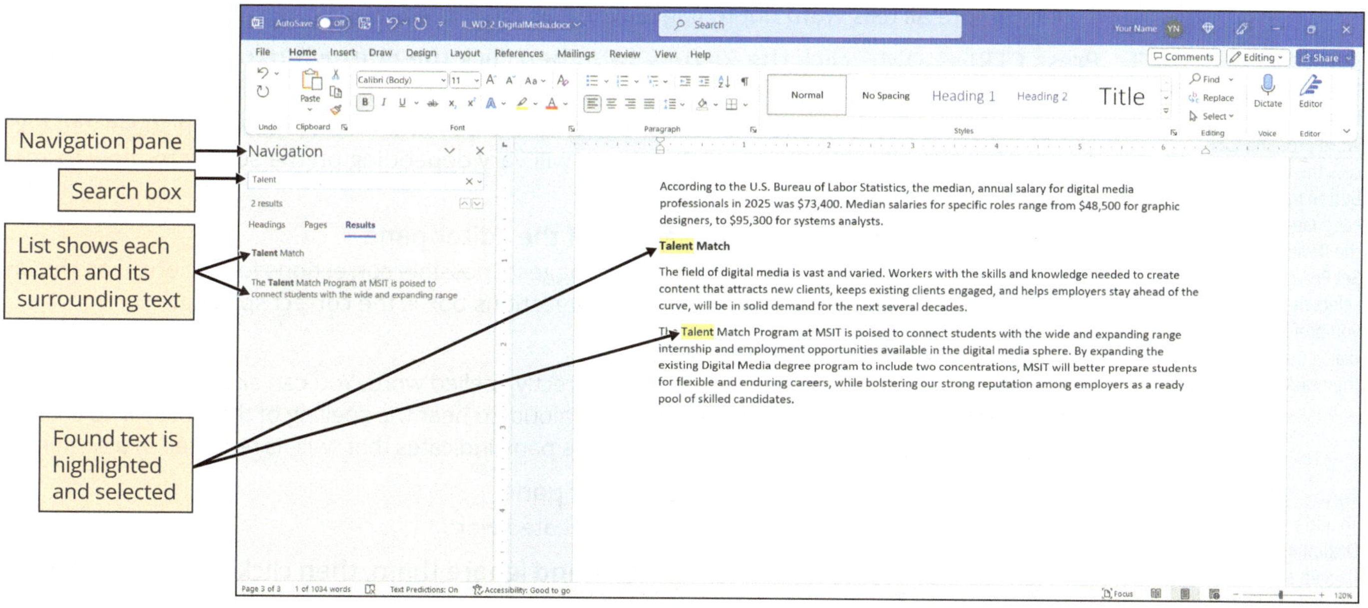

Navigating a document using the Navigation pane and the Go to command

Rather than scrolling to move to a different place in a longer document, you can use the Navigation pane to quickly move the insertion point to a specific page, heading, or text. To open the Navigation pane, click the Page number button on the status bar. In the Navigation pane, click the link for the type of item (headings or pages) you want to use to navigate the document. To navigate by specific text, type the text in the Search document text box, and then click the Results link.

To move to a specific page, section, line, table, graphic, or other item in a document, you use the Go To tab in the Find and Replace dialog box. On the Go To tab in the Find and Replace dialog box, select the type of item you want to find in the Go to what list, enter the relevant information about that item, and then click Next to move the insertion point to the item.

Check Spelling and Grammar

Case You use the Spelling and Grammar checker to search the report for errors. Before beginning the search, you select to ignore words you know are spelled correctly, such as Zavron, a proper noun.

Objective
- Check spelling and grammar

While you are working on or after you finish typing and revising a document, you can use the Spelling and Grammar command to search the document for misspelled words and grammar errors. The Spelling and Grammar checker flags possible mistakes and writing style issues, suggests correct spellings, and offers remedies for grammar errors such as incorrect subject–verb agreement, repeated words, and punctuation.

Steps

1. **Right-click Zavron in the fourth body paragraph**
A menu that includes suggestions for correcting the spelling of "Zavron" opens. You can correct individual spelling and grammar errors by right-clicking text that is underlined with a red wavy line (a possible misspelling), a blue double underline (a possible grammar error), or a purple dotted line (a possible writing style issue), and then selecting a correction. Although "Zavron" is not in the Word dictionary, it is a proper name that is spelled correctly in the document.

Trouble
If Zavron is not flagged as misspelled, skip to Step 3.

2. **Click Ignore All**
Clicking Ignore All tells Word not to flag "Zavron" as misspelled.

Quick Tip
To change the language used by the Word proofing tools, click the Language button in the Language group on the Review tab, click Set Proofing Language, select the language you prefer in the dialog box that opens, then click OK.

3. **Press CTRL+HOME, click the Review tab, then click the Editor button in the Proofing group**
The Editor pane opens. It offers an Editor Score for the document that is based on suggested text corrections and refinements. The Editor Score will vary depending on the setting for how formal the writing is intended to be.

4. **Click Spelling in the Corrections section of the Editor pane**
The pane identifies "desig" as misspelled and suggests possible corrections for the error, as shown in **Figure 2-5**. The first word selected in the Suggestions box is the correct spelling.

5. **Click design in the Suggestions box**
Word replaces the misspelled word with the correctly spelled word. You can also use the arrow next to a suggested correction to hear the word read aloud, to hear the spelling of the word, or to change all instances of the error in a document. Next, the pane indicates that "will" is repeated in a sentence.

Quick Tip
To add a word to the Dictionary so it is not flagged as misspelled, click Add to Dictionary.

6. **Click Delete Repeated Word in the Editor pane**
Word deletes the second occurrence of the repeated word.

7. **If additional errors are identified, review and ignore them, then click OK to complete the spelling and grammar check if necessary**
The Editor identifies many common errors, but you cannot rely on it to find and correct all spelling and grammar errors in your documents, or to always suggest a valid correction. Always proofread your documents carefully.

8. **Click the Close button in the Editor pane, press CTRL+HOME, then save the document**

Searching for information

The Search feature on the References tab gives you quick access to information about document text, including definitions, images, and other material from online sources. For example, you might use Search to see the definition of a word used in a document or to hear the word pronounced. To use Search, select the text you want to look up in your document, right-click it, and then click Search. You can also select text, and then click the Search button in the Research group on the References tab. The Search pane opens and displays images and web links related to the selected text. Click the All button to display only web information, media, help articles files, or other data types.

Figure 2-5: Editor pane

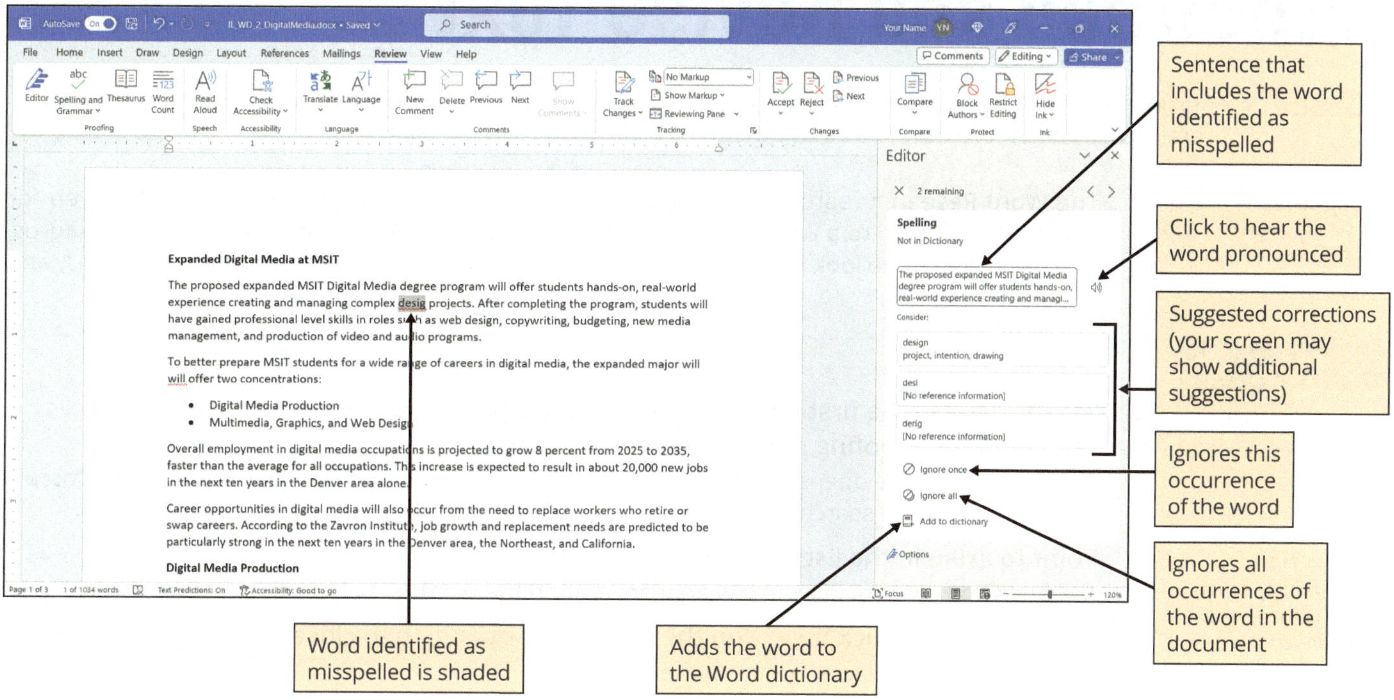

Inserting text with AutoCorrect

As you type, AutoCorrect automatically corrects many commonly misspelled words. By creating your own AutoCorrect entries, you can set Word to insert text that you type often, such as your name or contact information, or to correct words you misspell frequently. For example, you could create an AutoCorrect entry so that the name "Maria T. Weiss" is automatically inserted whenever you type "mtw" followed by a space. You create AutoCorrect entries and customize other AutoCorrect and AutoFormat options using the AutoCorrect dialog box. To open the AutoCorrect dialog box, click the File tab, click Options, click Proofing in the Word Options dialog box that opens, and then click AutoCorrect Options. On the AutoCorrect tab in the AutoCorrect dialog box, type the text you want to be corrected automatically in the Replace box (such as "mtw"), type the text you want to be inserted in its place automatically in the With box (such as "Maria T. Weiss"), and then click Add. The AutoCorrect entry is added to the list. Click OK to close the AutoCorrect dialog box, and then click OK to close the Word Options dialog box. Word inserts an AutoCorrect entry in a document when you press SPACEBAR or a punctuation mark after typing the text you want Word to correct. For example, Word inserts "Maria T. Weiss" when you type "mtw" followed by a space. If you want to remove an AutoCorrect entry, simply open the AutoCorrect dialog box, select the AutoCorrect entry you want to remove in the list, click Delete, click OK, and then click OK to close the Word Options dialog box.

Proofread and Revise Text

Case After proofreading your document for errors, you decide the report would read better for an academic audience if several words were more formal. You use the thesaurus to find synonyms.

Objectives
- Find synonyms
- Check the word count

The Word Research features allow you to quickly search reference sources and the web for information related to a word or phrase. Among the reference sources available is a thesaurus, which you can use to look up synonyms for awkward or repetitive words, as well as dictionary and translation sources.

Steps

1. **Select occur in the first line of the fourth body paragraph, then click the Thesaurus button in the Proofing group on the Review tab**
   The Thesaurus pane opens. "Occur" appears in the search box, and possible synonyms for "occur" are listed under the search box.

Quick Tip
To look up synonyms for a different word, type the word in the search box, then click the search button.

2. **Point to arise in the list of synonyms, as shown in Figure 2-6**
   A shaded box containing an arrow appears around the word.
3. **Click the arrow, click Insert on the menu that opens, then close the Thesaurus pane**
   The word "arise" replaces "occur" in the report.
4. **Right-click swap in the first line of the fourth body paragraph, point to Synonyms on the menu that opens, then click switch**
   The word "switch" replaces "swap" in the report.
5. **Select the four paragraphs of body text under the "Expanded Digital Media..." title (including the bulleted list), then click the Word Count button in the Proofing group**
   The Word Count dialog box opens, as shown in Figure 2-7. The dialog box lists the number of pages, words, characters, paragraphs, and lines included in the selected text. Notice that the status bar also displays the number of words included in the selected text and the total number of words in the entire document. If you want to view the page, character, paragraph, and line count for the entire document, make sure nothing is selected in your document, and then click Word Count in the Proofing group.
6. **Click Close, then save the document**

Reading a document aloud using Word

The Word Read Aloud feature reads a document aloud for you. Listening to a document read aloud can help you hear grammar errors, discover missing words, or notice other writing issues you might not notice when proofreading a document on screen. It can also be useful for multitasking or for increasing your reading comprehension and learning. To read a document aloud using Word, move the insertion point to the beginning of the document, and then click the Read Aloud button in the Speech group on the Review tab. A toolbar of playback controls opens at the top of the document window and Word begins to read aloud. As each word is pronounced, it is highlighted on the screen. You can use the Settings button on the playback controls to change the reading speed or the reading voice. The Previous, Next, Pause, and Play buttons allow you to pause and resume the reading, or to navigate through the document paragraph by paragraph. When you are finished reading the document aloud using Word, click the Stop button on the playback controls.

Figure 2-6: Thesaurus pane

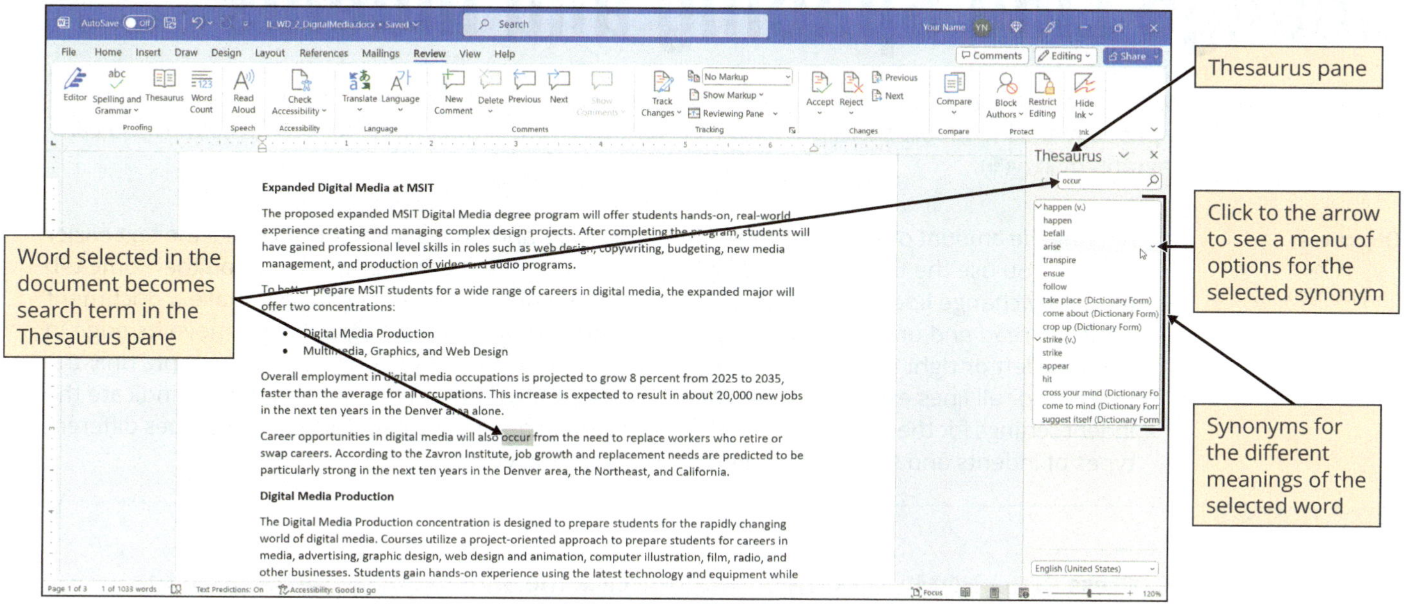

Figure 2-7: Word Count dialog box

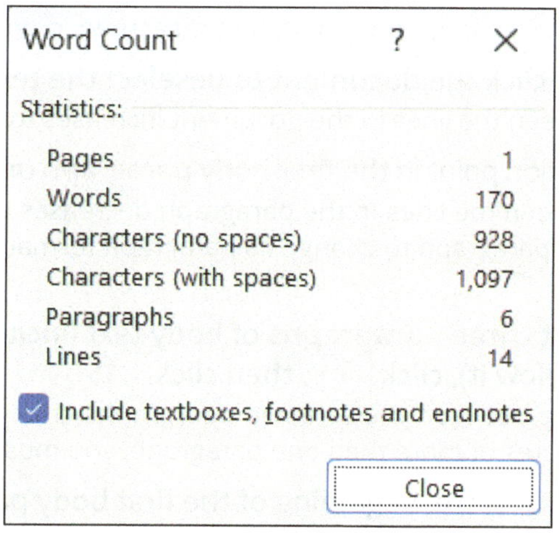

Using an add-in for Word

Add-ins are small programs embedded in Word that allow you to access information on the web without having to leave Word. For example, you can look up something on Wikipedia, insert an online map in one of your documents, or access dictionaries and other reference sources, all from within Word using an add-in. To find and install an add-in, click the Get Add-ins button in the Add-ins group on the Insert tab to open the Office Add-ins gallery. The Store tab in the Office Add-ins gallery includes a searchable list of the add-ins available to you, which you can also browse by category. Some add-ins are free, and some require purchase.

To install an add-in, click the Add button next to it on the Store tab. To use an add-in after you have installed it, click the My Add-ins button on the Insert tab to open the Office Add-ins gallery with the My Add-ins tab displayed. Select the Add-in you want to use on this tab, and then click Add. A new button for the add-in may be added to your ribbon. When you no longer need an add-in you have installed, you can remove it by right-clicking the add-in on the My Add-in tab in the Office Add-ins gallery, and then clicking Remove.

Change Line Spacing and Indents

Case You increase the line spacing of the report, remove space under a paragraph, and create indents for the body text paragraphs to make the report easier to read. You work with formatting marks turned on so that you can see the paragraph marks (¶).

Objectives
- Adjust line spacing
- Adjust indentation

Altering the amount of space between lines and paragraphs in a document can make the text easier to read. You use the Line and Paragraph Spacing button in the Paragraph group on the Home tab to quickly change line and paragraph spacing. Indenting paragraphs can also make a document easier to read and understand at a glance. When you **indent** a paragraph, you move its edge in from the left or right margin. You can indent the entire left or right edge of a paragraph, only the first line, or all lines except the first line. The **indent markers** on the horizontal ruler indicate the indent settings for the paragraph in which the insertion point is located. **Table 2-1** describes different types of indents and some of the methods for creating each.

Steps

1. **Press CTRL+HOME, click the Home tab, click the Show/Hide ¶ button in the Paragraph group, press CTRL+A to select the entire document, then click the Line and Paragraph Spacing button in the Paragraph group**
   The Line Spacing gallery opens. This gallery includes options for increasing the space between lines. Both line and paragraph spacing are measured in points.
2. **Click 2.0, then click the document to deselect the text**
   The space between the lines in the document increases to 2.
3. **Place the insertion point in the first body paragraph under the title, click then click 1.15**
   The space between the lines in the paragraph decreases to 1.15. Notice that you do not need to select an entire paragraph to change its paragraph formatting; simply place the insertion point in the paragraph.

Quick Tip
Word recognizes any string of text that ends with a paragraph mark as a paragraph, including titles, headings, and single lines in a list.

4. **Select the next three paragraphs of body text (including the bulleted list and the two paragraphs below it), click , then click 1.15**
   The line spacing between the selected paragraphs changes to 1.15. To change the paragraph-formatting features of more than one paragraph, you must select the paragraphs.
5. **Click before The at the beginning of the first body paragraph, then press TAB**
   The first line of the paragraph is indented ½", as shown in **Figure 2-8**. Notice the First Line Indent marker is located at the ½" mark on the horizontal ruler. The ruler shows the indent settings for the paragraph in which the insertion point is located. Pressing TAB is a quick way to indent the first line of a paragraph ½".

Quick Tip
If the rulers are not displayed, click the View tab, then click the Ruler check box.

6. **Place the insertion point in the second body paragraph (To better...), then drag the First Line Indent marker right to the ½" mark on the horizontal ruler**
   Figure 2-9 shows the First Line Indent marker being dragged. The first line of the second body paragraph is indented 1/2". Dragging the First Line Indent marker indents only the first line of a paragraph.

Trouble
Take care to drag only the First Line Indent marker. If you make a mistake, click the Undo button , then try again.

7. **Place the insertion point in the third body paragraph (Overall...), then drag the Hanging Indent marker right to the ½" mark on the ruler**
   Take care to drag the Hanging Indent marker and not the Left Indent marker. **Figure 2-10** depicts the Hanging Indent marker being dragged. The lines under the first line of the third body paragraph are indented ½". Dragging the Hanging Indent marker indents the subsequent lines of a paragraph more than the first line.
8. **Place the insertion point in the first body paragraph, click , click Remove Space After Paragraph, then save your changes**
   The space between the first and second body paragraphs is eliminated. Using the Line and Paragraph Spacing button is a quick way to add or remove space between paragraphs. You can also change the paragraph spacing settings for the active paragraph using the Spacing Before and After boxes in the Paragraph group on the Layout tab.

Figure 2-8: First line indent

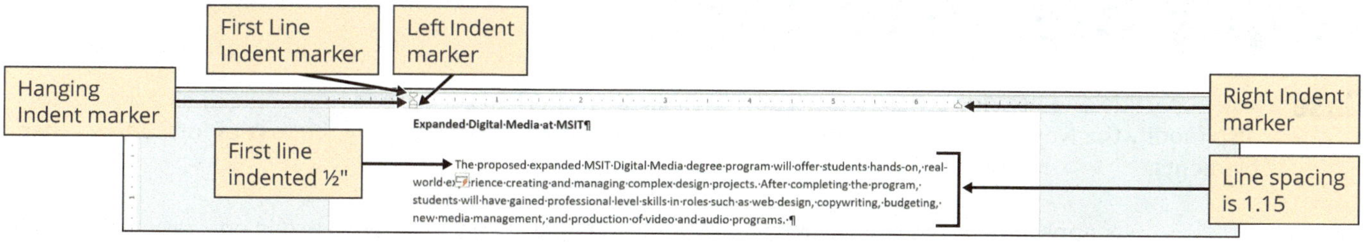

Figure 2-9: Dragging the First Line Indent marker

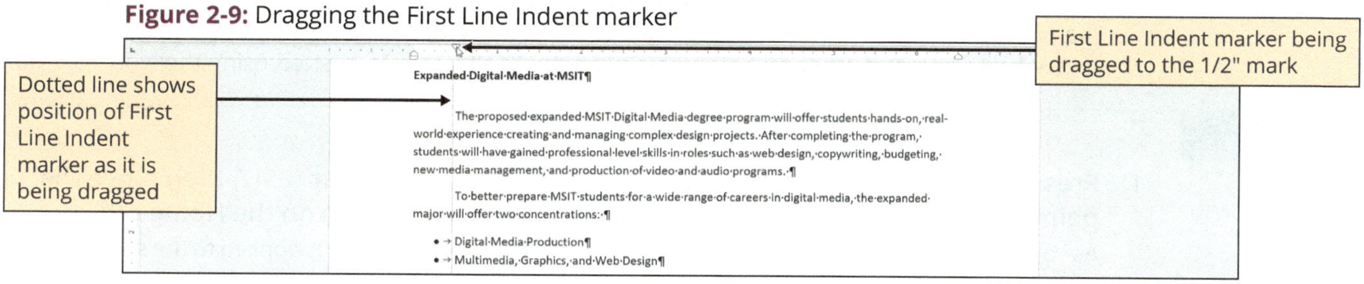

Figure 2-10: Dragging the Hanging Indent marker

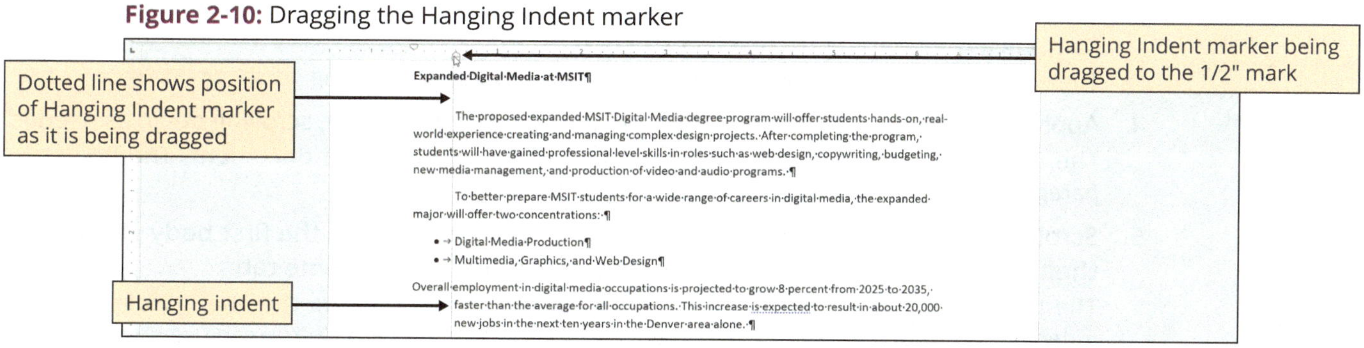

Table 2-1: Types of indents

indent type: description	to create
Left indent: left edge of a paragraph is moved in from the left margin	Drag the Left Indent marker on the ruler to the right to the position where you want the left edge of the paragraph to align; when you drag the left indent marker, all the indent markers move as one
Right indent: right edge of a paragraph is moved in from the right margin	Drag the Right Indent marker on the ruler to the left to the position where you want the right edge of the paragraph to align
First line indent: first line of a paragraph is indented more than the subsequent lines	Drag the First Line Indent marker on the ruler to the right to the position where you want the first line of the paragraph to begin; or activate the First Line Indent marker in the tab indicator, and then click the ruler at the position where you want the first line of the paragraph to begin
Hanging indent: subsequent lines of a paragraph are indented more than the first line	Drag the Hanging Indent marker on the ruler to the right to the position where you want the hanging indent to begin; or activate the Hanging Indent marker in the tab indicator, and then click the ruler at the position where you want the second and remaining lines of the paragraph to begin; when you drag the hanging indent marker, the left indent marker moves with it
Negative indent (or Outdent): left edge of a paragraph is moved to the left of the left margin	Drag the Left Indent marker on the ruler left to the position where you want the negative indent to begin; when you drag the left indent marker, all markers move as one

Apply Styles to Text

Case You apply title and heading styles to the report to make the report easier to read for people of all abilities. You also modify the Normal style that is applied by default to all body text to simplify the task of formatting other elements.

Objectives
- Apply built-in styles to text
- Modify existing styles

Applying a style to text allows you to apply multiple format settings to text in one easy step. A **style** is a set of format settings, such as font, font size, font color, paragraph spacing, and alignment, that are named and stored together. Word includes many **Style sets**—groups of related styles that share common fonts, colors, and formats, and are designed to be used together in a document to give it a polished and cohesive look. Each Style set includes styles for a title, subtitle, several heading levels, body text, and other text elements. By default, all text is formatted using the Normal style.

Steps

1. **Press CTRL+HOME, select the title Expanded Digital Media at MSIT, then move the pointer over the styles in the Styles gallery in the Styles group on the Home tab**
   As you move the pointer over a style in the gallery, a preview of that style is applied to the selected text.

Quick Tip
To change the active Style set, click the Design tab, click the More button in the Document Formatting group, then select a different style set.

2. **Click the More button in the Style gallery, then click Title**
   The Title style is applied to the selected text. All other paragraphs are formatted with the Normal style.
3. **Select the heading Digital Media Production, click Heading 1 in the Styles group, then click the heading to deselect the text**
   The Heading 1 style is applied to the Digital Media Production heading, as shown in **Figure 2-11**.
4. **Apply the Heading 1 style to each bold heading in the document, scrolling down as needed**
   The Heading 1 style is applied to seven headings in total in the document. The body text paragraphs are still formatted with the Normal style.
5. **Scroll to the top of the document, place the insertion point in the first body paragraph, then click the Launcher in the Paragraph group on the Home tab**
   The Indents and Spacing tab in the Paragraph dialog box shows the line, paragraph, and indentation settings for the active paragraph, as shown in **Figure 2-12**. You can use the Paragraph dialog box to check or change any paragraph setting.
6. **Click OK to close the paragraph dialog box, then, with the insertion point in the first body paragraph, right-click Normal in the Styles group, then click Update Normal to Match Selection**
   The format of each paragraph formatted with the Normal style in the document is changed to match the first body paragraph. The title and headings are indented now, too, because the Heading 1 and Title styles are based on the Normal style. When the Normal style changed, the styles based on the Normal style changed, too.

Trouble
If you apply the wrong style, click the Undo button on the Quick Access toolbar, then right-click the style name in the Styles group again.

7. **Right-click Heading 1 in the Styles group, click Modify, click the Style based on arrow in the Modify Style dialog box, click (no style), then click OK**
   The Heading 1 style is now based on no style and the indent is removed from the headings in the document. You can use the Modify Style dialog box to change any format setting in a style.
8. **Right-click Title in the Styles group, click Modify, click the Style based on arrow in the Modify Style dialog box, click (no style), then click OK**
   The Title style is now based on no style and the indent is removed from the title in the document.
9. **Select the Expanded Digital... title, click the Increase Font Size button in the Font group, click the Font Color arrow, click Blue, Accent 1, Darker 25%, click the Line and Paragraph Spacing button in the Paragraph group, click Add Space After Paragraph, deselect the title, then save your changes**
   The font size of the title is increased, the font color changes to dark blue, and extra space is added after the title paragraph, as shown in **Figure 2-13**. You can modify the format of text to which a style has been applied without changing the style itself.

Figure 2-11: Styles applied to the report

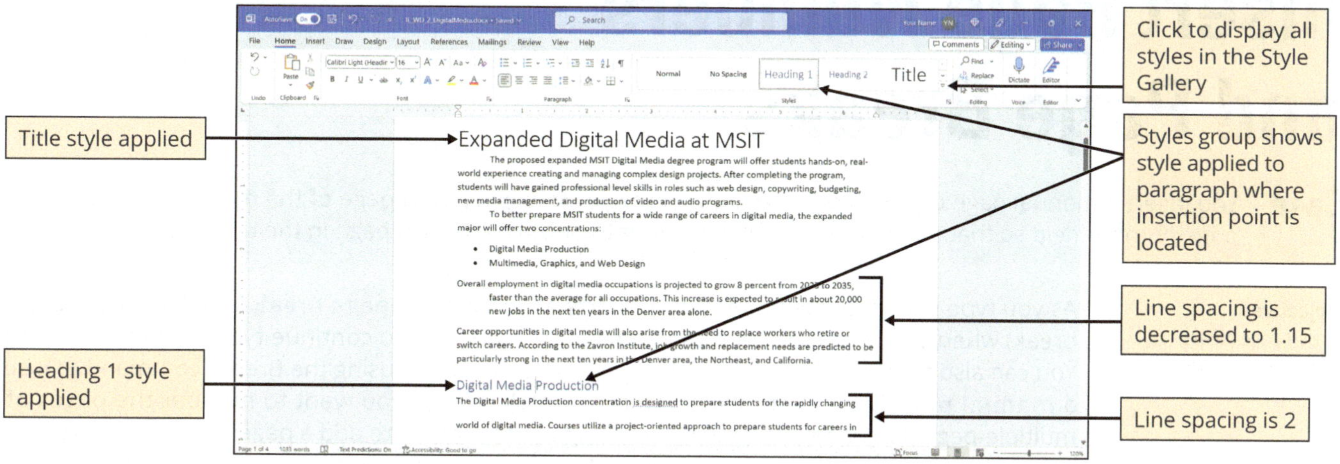

Figure 2-12: Indents and Spacing tab in Paragraph dialog box

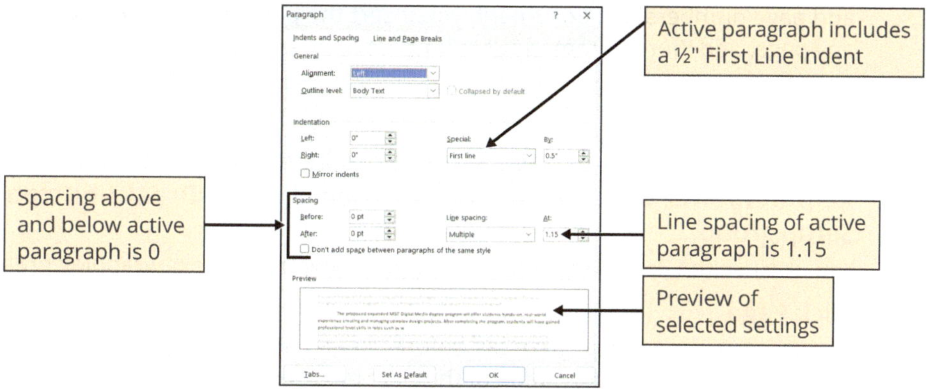

Figure 2-13: Modified styles applied to the document

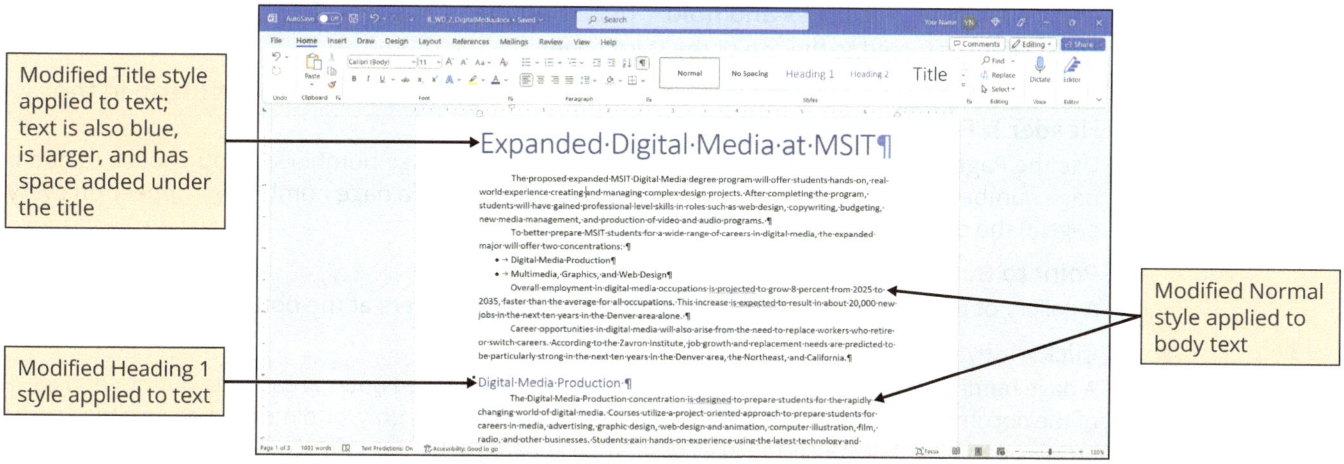

Changing the Style set

Changing the Style set applied to a document is a quick way to give a document a different look and design. Style sets include font and paragraph settings for headings and body text. When you change the Style set, a complete set of new fonts and colors is applied to the entire document. All the body text and all the headings that have been formatted with a style change to the format settings for the active Style set. To change the Style set, you click one of the Style sets available in the Document Formatting group on the Design tab. You can also change the color scheme or font used in the active Style set by clicking the Colors or Fonts buttons in the Document Formatting group and then selecting from the available color schemes or font options.

You can also save a group of font and paragraph settings as a new Style set. To do this, click the More button in the Document Formatting group, and then click Save as a New Style Set. If you want to return a document to its original Style set, click the More button, and then click Reset to the Default Style Set.

Insert Page Numbers and Page Breaks

Case You insert a manual page break where you know you want to begin a new page of the report. You then add a page number field so that page numbers will appear at the bottom of each page in the document.

Objectives
- Insert page breaks
- Insert page numbers

As you type text in a document, Word inserts an **automatic page break** (also called a soft page break) when you reach the bottom of a page, allowing you to continue typing on the next page. You can also force text onto the next page of a document by using the Breaks command to insert a **manual page break** (also called a hard page break). If you want to number the pages of a multiple-page document, you can insert a page number field to add a page number to each page. A **field** is a code that serves as a placeholder for data that changes in a document, such as a page number or the current date. When you use the Page Number button on the Insert tab to add page numbers to a document, you insert the page number field at the top, bottom, or side of any page, and Word automatically numbers all the pages in the document for you.

Steps

Quick Tip
Pressing CTRL+ENTER is a fast way to insert a manual page break.

1. **Scroll to the bottom of page 1, place the insertion point before the heading Degree Requirements, click the Layout tab, then click the Breaks button in the Page Setup group**
   You also use the Breaks menu to insert page, column, and text-wrapping breaks. Refer to **Table 2-2**.

2. **Click Page**
   Word inserts a manual page break before "Degree Requirements" and moves all the text following the page break to the beginning of the next page, as shown in **Figure 2-14**.

Quick Tip
To delete a page break, select it and then press DELETE. Page breaks are only visible when formatting marks are turned on.

3. **Scroll down, place the insertion point before the heading Career Preparation and Outlook on page 2, press and hold CTRL, then press ENTER**
   The heading is forced to the top of the third page.

4. **Press CTRL+HOME, click the Insert tab, then click the Page Number button in the Header & Footer group**
   Use the Page Number menu to select the position for the page numbers. If you choose to add a page number field to the top, bottom, or side of a document, a page number will appear on every page in the document.

5. **Point to Bottom of Page**
   A gallery of formatting and alignment options for page numbers at the bottom of a page opens.

Quick Tip
To change the location or formatting of page numbers, click the Page Number button, point to a page number location, then select a format from the gallery.

6. **Click Plain Number 2 in the Simple section**
   A page number field containing the number 1 is centered in the Footer area at the bottom of page 1 of the document, as shown in **Figure 2-15**. The document text is gray, or dimmed, because the Footer area is open. Text that is inserted in a Footer area appears at the bottom of every page in a document.

7. **Double-click the document text**
   The page number is now dimmed because it is located in the Footer area, which is no longer the active area. When the document is printed, the page numbers appear as normal text.

Quick Tip
To remove page numbers from a document, click the Page Number button, then click Remove Page Numbers.

8. **Press CTRL+HOME, click the View tab, click the Multiple Pages button in the Zoom group, then save the document**
   Word numbered each page of the report automatically, and each page number is centered at the bottom of the page, as shown in **Figure 2-16**.

Figure 2-14: Manual page break in document

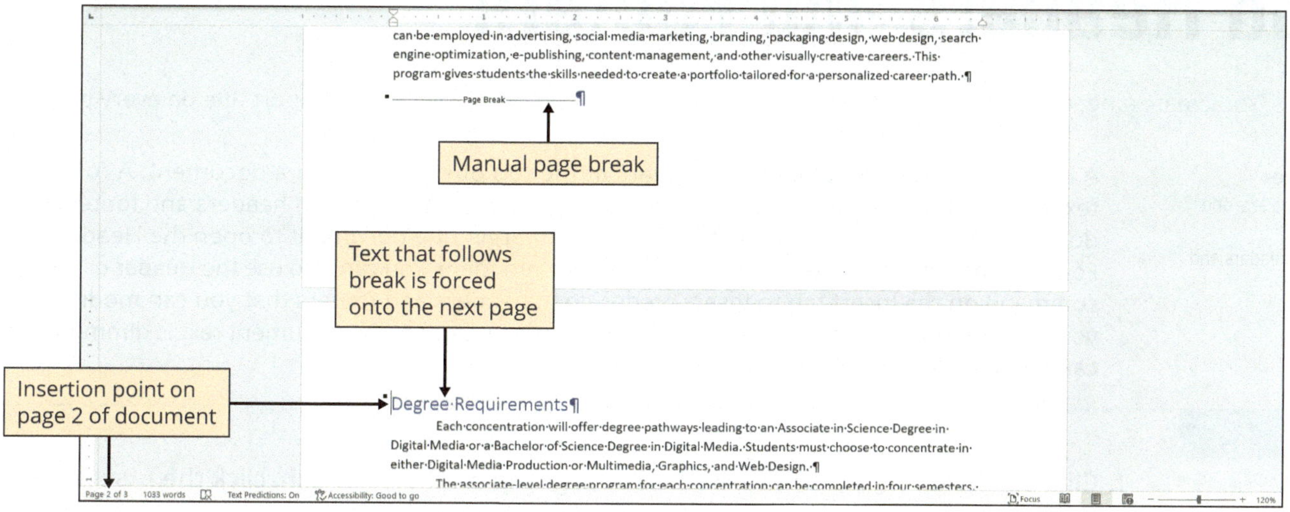

Figure 2-15: Page number in document

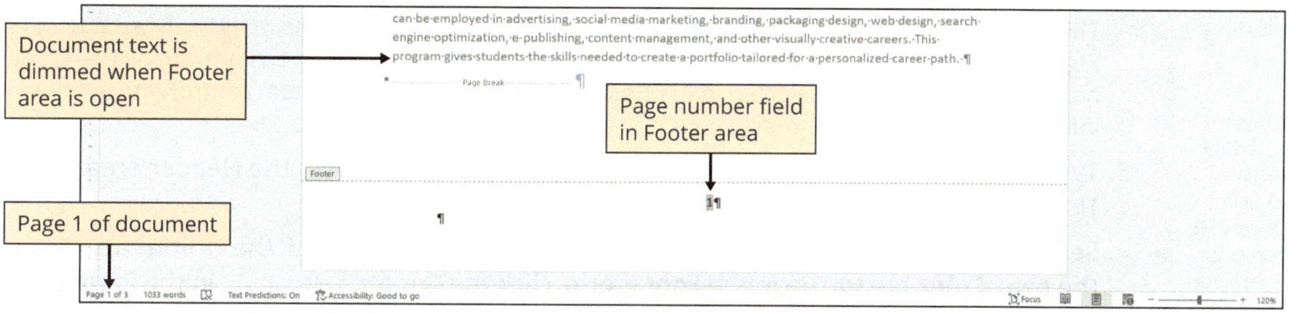

Figure 2-16: Pages 1, 2, and 3

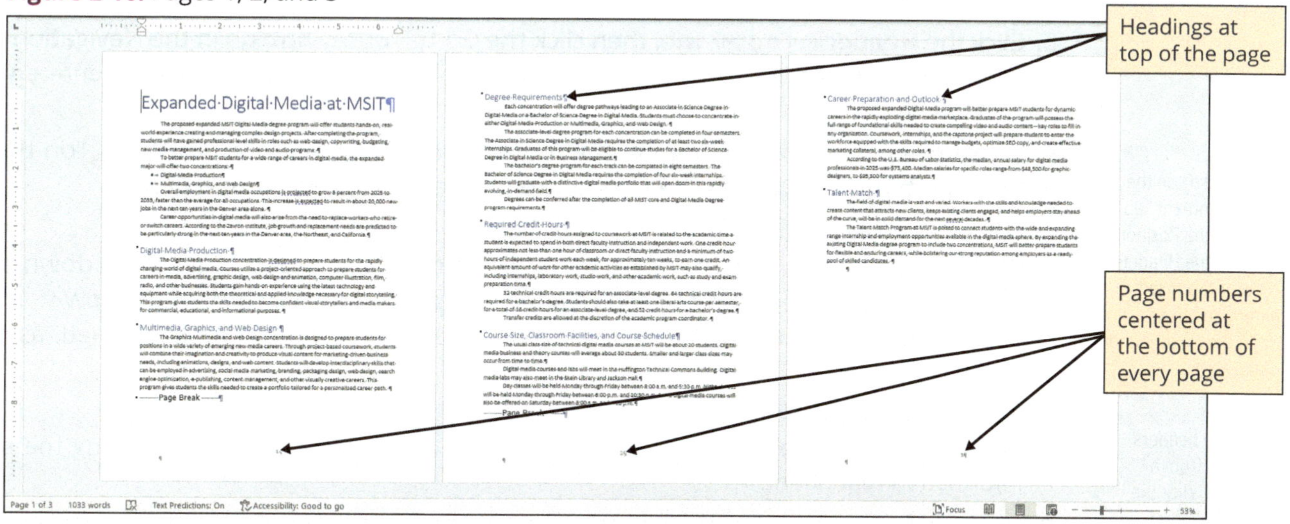

Table 2-2: Types of breaks

break	function
Page	Forces the text following the break to begin at the top of the next page
Column	Forces the text following the break to begin at the top of the next column
Text Wrapping	Forces the text following the break to begin at the beginning of the next line

Add Headers and Footers

Case You create a header that includes the title of the report so that readers can see the report title on every page.

Objectives
- Insert headers and footers
- Format headers and footers

A **header** is text or graphics that appears at the top of every page of a document. A **footer** is text or graphics that appears at the bottom of every page. You can add headers and footers to a document by double-clicking the top or bottom margin of a document to open the Header and Footer areas, and then inserting text and graphics into them. You can also use the Header or Footer command on the Insert tab to insert predesigned headers and footers that you can modify with your information. When the header and footer areas are open, the document text is dimmed and cannot be edited.

Steps

1. **Click the Page Width button in the Zoom group on the View tab, click the Insert tab, then click the Header button in the Header & Footer group**
   A gallery of built-in header designs opens.
2. **Scroll down the gallery to view the header designs, scroll up the gallery, then click Blank**
   The Header area opens and the Header & Footer tab opens and is the active tab, as shown in **Figure 2-17**. This tab is available whenever the Header and Footer areas are open. The [Type here] **content control** is selected in the Header area. You replace a content control with your own information.
3. **Type Expanded Digital Media at MSIT in the content control in the Header area**
   This text will appear at the top of every page in the document.
4. **Select the header text (but not the paragraph mark below it), click the Home tab, click the Font Color button in the Font group, click the Center button in the Paragraph group, click the Borders button, then click in the Header area to deselect the text**
   The text is the same blue used in the document and is centered in the Header area with a bottom border.
5. **Click the Header & Footer tab, then click the Go to Footer button in the Navigation group**
   The insertion point moves to the Footer area, where a page number field is centered in the Footer area.
6. **Select the page number field in the footer, click the Font Color button on the Mini toolbar, then click in the Footer area to deselect the text and field**
   The footer text (the page number) is the same color blue as the headings.
7. **Click the Close Header and Footer button in the Close group, then scroll down until the bottom of page 1 and the top of page 2 appear in the document window**
   The Header and Footer areas close, and the header and footer text is dimmed, as shown in **Figure 2-18**.
8. **Press CTRL+HOME**
   The report already includes the report title at the top of the first page, making the header information redundant.
9. **Position the pointer over the header text at the top of page 1, double-click the header to open the Header area, click the Different First Page check box in the Options group on the Header and Footer tab, then click the Close Header and Footer button**
   The header and footer text is removed from the Header and Footer areas on the first page.
10. **Click the Show/Hide ¶ button in the Paragraph group on the Home tab, click the View tab, click the Multiple Pages button in the Zoom group, then save your changes**
    The headers and footers and all the pages in the document are shown in **Figure 2-19**.

Trouble
If blue is not your active color, click the Font Color arrow, click Blue, Accent 1, Darker 25%. If bottom border is not your active border setting, click the Border arrow, then click Bottom Border.

Quick Tip
You can also use the Insert Alignment Tab button in the Position group on the Header & Footer tab to left-, center-, and right-align text in the Header and Footer areas.

Quick Tip
To remove headers or footers from a document, click the Header or Footer button, and then click Remove Header or Remove Footer.

Figure 2-17: Header area

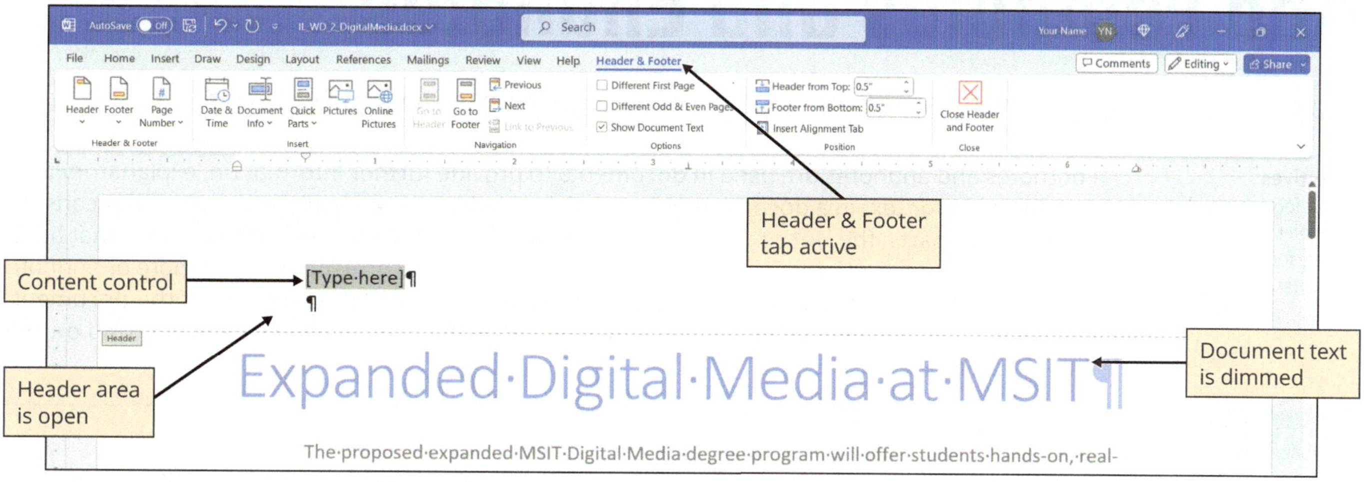

Figure 2-18: Header and footer in document

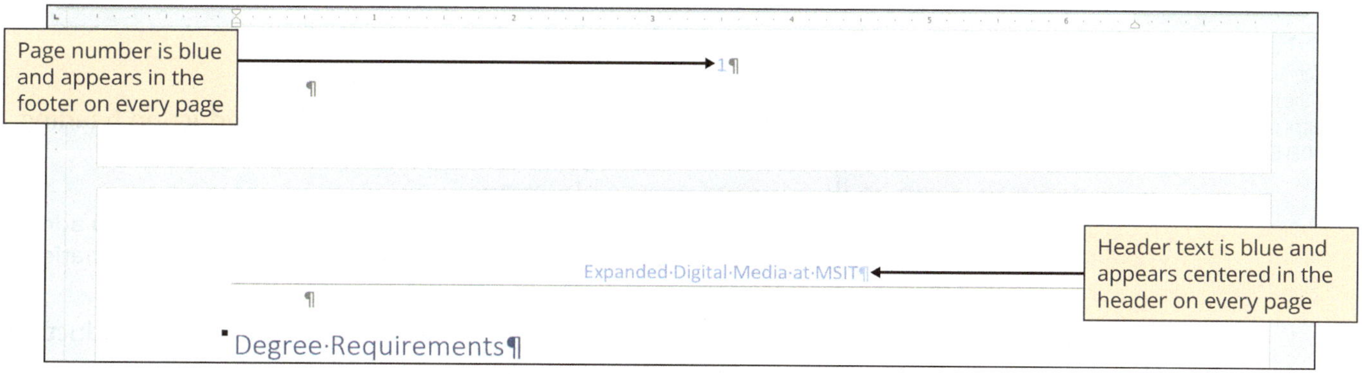

Figure 2-19: Header and footer on pages 2 and 3

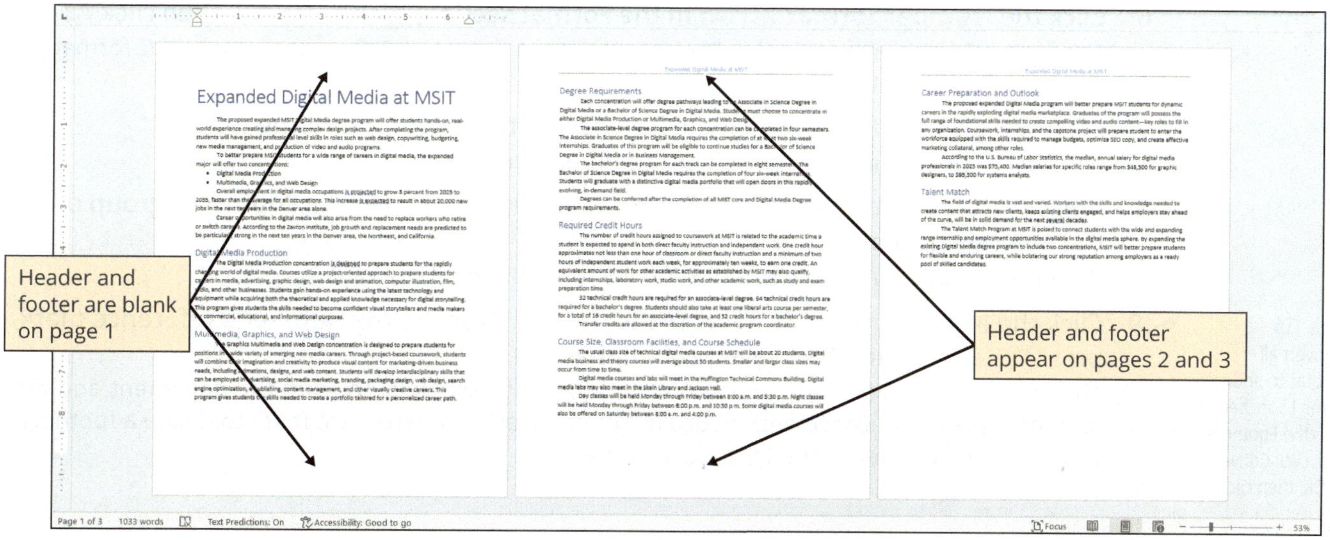

Add Footnotes and Endnotes

Case You add several footnotes to the report that clarify the information in the body of the report for readers.

Objectives
- Insert footnotes and endnotes
- Delete footnotes and endnotes

Footnotes and endnotes are used in documents to provide further information, explanatory text, or references for text in a document. A **footnote** or **endnote** is an explanatory note that consists of two linked parts: the **note reference mark** that appears next to the text to indicate that additional information is offered in a footnote or endnote, and the corresponding footnote or endnote text. Word places footnotes at the end of each page and endnotes at the end of the document. You insert and manage footnotes and endnotes using the tools in the Footnotes group on the References tab.

Steps

1. **Click the 100% button in the Zoom group, scroll until the Multimedia, Graphics, and Web Design heading is at the top of your screen, place the insertion point at the end of the last body paragraph (after "path."), click the References tab, then click the Insert Footnote button in the Footnotes group**
   A note reference mark, in this case a superscript 1, appears after "path.", and the insertion point moves below a separator line at the bottom of the page. A note reference mark can be a number, a symbol, a character, or a combination of characters.

Quick Tip
To delete a footnote, select the note reference mark, then press DELETE.

2. **Type This concentration emphasizes technical skills.**
   The footnote text appears below the separator line at the bottom of page 1.
3. **Scroll up, place the insertion point at the end of the Digital Media Production heading, click the Insert Footnote button, then type Digital media refers to any visual media that can be distributed across platforms.**
   The footnote text appears at the bottom of the first page, above the first footnote you added. Notice that when you inserted a new footnote above an existing footnote, Word automatically renumbered the footnotes, as shown in **Figure 2-20**.
4. **Place the insertion point at the end of the paragraph under the Digital Media Production heading, click the Insert Footnote button, then type Students will specialize.**
   The footnote text appears between the text for footnotes 1 and 3 at the bottom of the page.
5. **Click the Launcher in the Footnotes group**
   The Footnote and Endnote dialog box opens. You can use this dialog box to change the location of footnote and endnote text, convert footnotes to endnotes, and change the formatting of the note reference marks.
6. **Click the Number format arrow in the Format section, click A, B, C,..., then click Apply**
   The note reference marks in the document change from 1, 2, 3 format to an A, B, C format, as shown in **Figure 2-21**.
7. **Click the Undo button on the Quick Access toolbar or the Home tab**
   Clicking the Undo button restores the 1,2,3 numbering format.
8. **Press CTRL+HOME, then click the Next Footnote button in the Footnotes group on the References tab**
   The insertion point moves to the "1" reference mark in the document.

Quick Tip
To convert all footnotes to endnotes, click the Launcher in the Footnotes group, click Convert, click OK, then click Close.

9. **Click the Next Footnote button, press DELETE to select the number 2 reference mark, press DELETE again, then save your changes**
   The second reference mark and associated footnote are deleted from the document and the footnotes are renumbered automatically. You must select a reference mark to delete a footnote; you cannot simply delete the footnote text itself.

Figure 2-20: Renumbered footnotes in the document

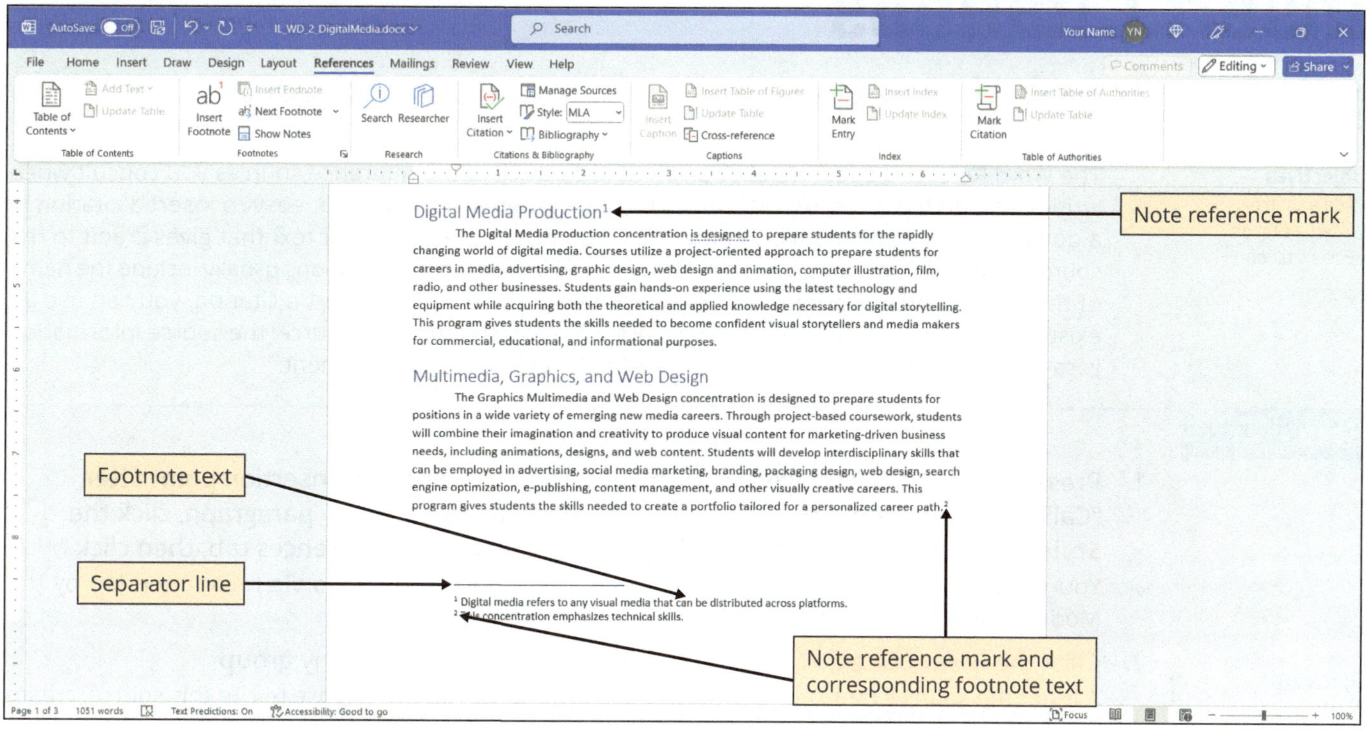

Figure 2-21: Note reference marks in new format

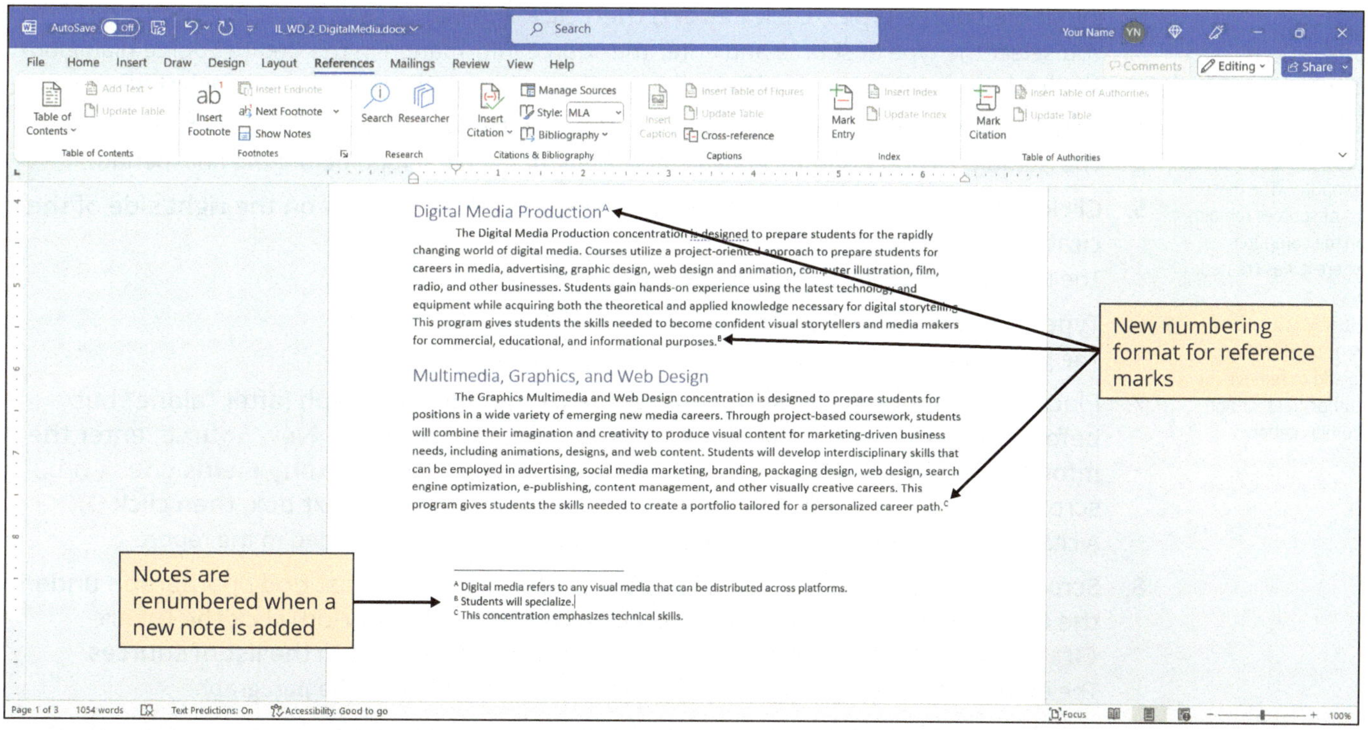

Insert Citations

Case You add several citations to the report that indicate the source of information to readers.

Objectives
- Add a source
- Insert a citation
- Edit a citation

The Word References feature allows you to keep track of the reference sources you consult when writing research papers, reports, and other documents, and makes it easy to insert a citation in a document. A **citation** is a parenthetical reference in the document text that gives credit to the source for a quotation, data, or other content used in a document. Citations usually include the name of the author and, for print sources, a page number. When you insert a citation, you can use an existing source or create a new source. Each time you create a new source, the source information is saved on your computer so that it is available for use in any document.

Steps

1. **Press CTRL+HOME, change the zoom level to 120%, place the insertion point after "California" but before the period at the end of the fourth body paragraph, click the Style arrow in the Citations & Bibliography group on the References tab, then click MLA**
   You will format the sources and citations in the report using the style recommended by the Modern Language Association (MLA).

2. **Click the Insert Citation button in the Citations & Bibliography group**
   A list of the sources (one) already used in the file opens. You can choose to cite this source, create a new source, or add a placeholder for a source. When you add a new citation to a document, the source is added to the list of master sources stored on the computer. The new source is also associated with the document.

Quick Tip
When you create a new source for a document, it appears automatically in the bibliography when you generate it.

3. **Click Add New Source, click the Type of Source arrow, scroll down to view the available source types, click Report, then click the Corporate Author check box**
   You select the type of source and enter the source information in the Create Source dialog box. The fields available in the dialog box change, depending on the type of source selected.

Quick Tip
Only sources that you associate with a document stay with the document when you move it to another computer. The master list of sources remains on the computer where it was created.

4. **Enter the data shown in Figure 2-22 in the Create Source dialog box, then click OK**
   The citation (Zavron Institute) appears at the end of the paragraph before the final period.

5. **Click the citation to select it, click the Citation Options arrow on the right side of the citation, then click Edit Citation**
   The Edit Citation dialog box opens, as shown in **Figure 2-23**.

Quick Tip
You can also choose to add or remove the author, year, or title from a citation.

6. **Type 18 in the Pages box, then click OK**
   The page number 18 is added to the citation.

7. **Place the insertion point at the end of the third body paragraph (after "alone" but before the period), click the Insert Citation button, click Add New Source, enter the information shown in Figure 2-24, click the Show all Bibliography Fields check box, scroll down in the dialog box, type www.bls.gov in the URL text box, then click OK**
   A citation for the Web publication that the data was taken from is added to the report.

8. **Scroll to page 3, place the insertion point at the end of the last body paragraph under the Career Preparation and Outlook heading (before the period) click the Insert Citation button, then click U.S. Bureau of Labor Statistics in the list of sources**
   The citation (U.S. Bureau of Labor Statistics) appears at the end of the paragraph.

9. **Scroll down, place the insertion point at the end of the first body paragraph under the Talent Match heading (before the period) click the Insert Citation button, click Add New Placeholder, type NYT, click OK, then save your changes**
   You added a citation placeholder for a source that you still need to add to the document.

Figure 2-22: Creating a report source

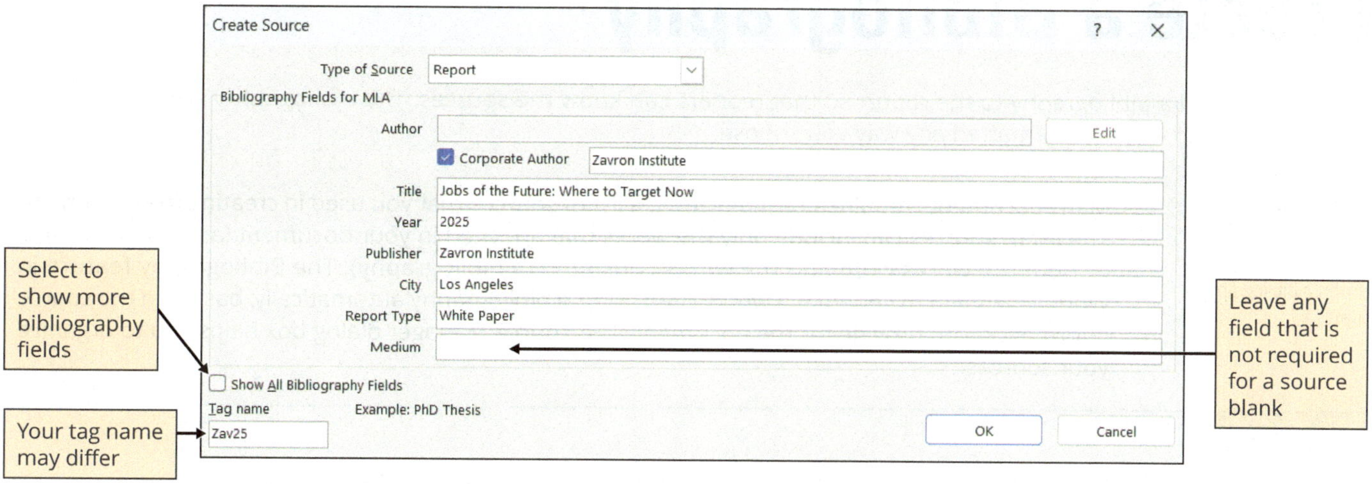

Figure 2-23: Edit Citation dialog box

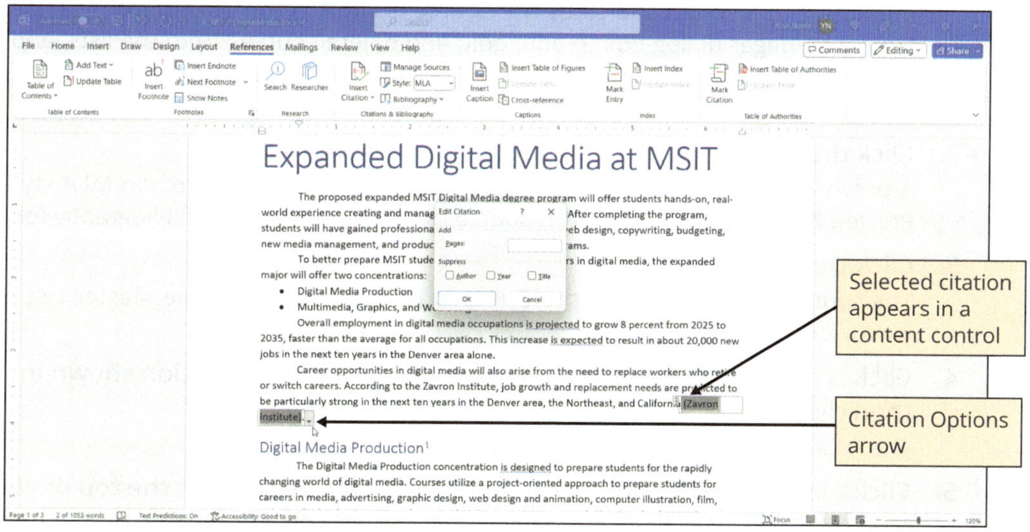

Figure 2-24: Adding a Web publication source

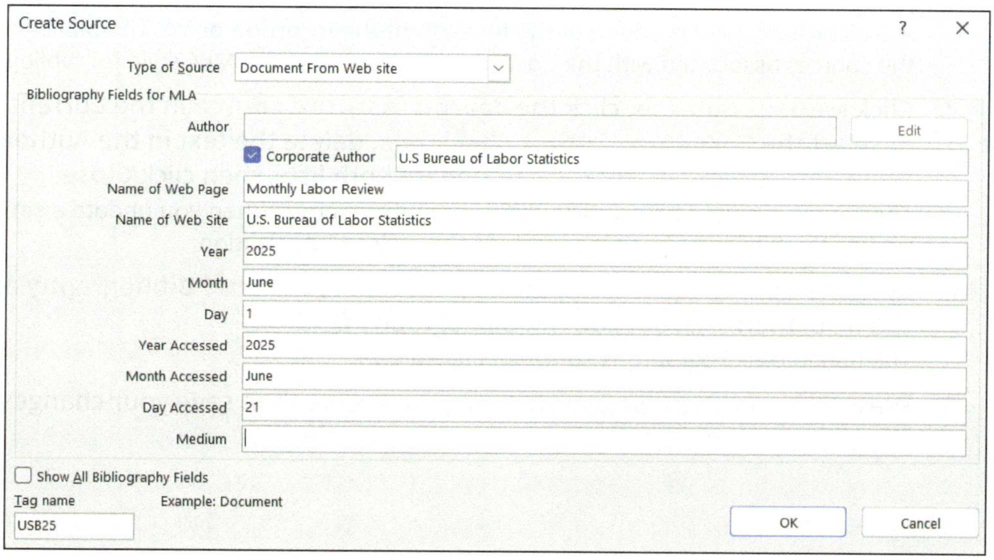

Create a Bibliography

Case You add a bibliography to the report so that readers can know the sources. The bibliography is inserted as a field and it can be formatted any way you choose.

Objectives
- Delete a source
- Edit a source
- Insert a bibliography field

Many documents require a **bibliography**, a list of sources that you used in creating the document. The list of sources can include only the works that are cited in your document (a **works cited** list) or both the works cited and the works consulted (a bibliography). The Bibliography feature in Word allows you to generate a works cited list or a bibliography automatically, based on the source information you provide for the document. The Source Manager dialog box helps you to organize your sources.

Steps

1. **Click the Manage Sources button in the Citations & Bibliography group**
   The Source Manager dialog box opens, as shown in **Figure 2-25**. The Master List shows the two sources you added and any other sources available on your computer. The Current List shows the sources available in the current document, as well as the NYT placeholder you added. A check mark next to a source indicates the source is cited in the document. You use the tools in the Source Manager dialog box to add, edit, and delete sources from the lists, and to copy sources between the Master and Current Lists. The sources that appear in the Current List will appear in the bibliography.

Quick Tip
You must copy sources from the Master List to the Current List for the sources to be available when you open the document on another computer.

2. **Click the Kirtida, Samantha source in the Current List**
   A preview of the citation and bibliographical entry for the source in MLA style appears in the Preview box. You do not want this source to be included in your bibliography for the report.
3. **Click Delete**
   The source is removed from the Current List but remains on the Master List on the computer where it originated.
4. **Click NYT in the Current List, click Edit, enter the information shown in Figure 2-26, then click OK**
   The Anzhela source is added to the Current List.
5. **Click Close, then scroll until the heading Talent Match is at the top of your screen**
   The NYT placeholder citation has been replaced with the information from the "Anzhela" source.

Quick Tip
Click References in the Built-in gallery to insert a References list. Click Works Cited in the Built-in gallery to insert a Works Cited list.

6. **Press CTRL+END to move the insertion point to the end of the document, click the Bibliography button in the Citations & Bibliography group, then click Bibliography in the Built-in gallery**
   A Bibliography field is added at the location of the insertion point. The bibliography includes all the sources associated with the document, formatted in the MLA style for bibliographies.

Quick Tip
To change the style used for citations and the bibliography, click the Style arrow in the Citations & Bibliography group, then select a different style.

7. **Click Manage Sources, click the Zavron Institute source in the Current List, click Edit, deselect the Corporate Author check box, delete the text in the Author text box, type Willa Perlie, click OK, click Yes to update both lists, then click Close**
   The source is edited to include a different author name. When you update a source, you need to update the Bibliography field to include the revised information.
8. **Click the Bibliography field, click Update Citations and Bibliography at the top of the field, then click outside the Bibliography field**
   The updated Bibliography is shown in **Figure 2-27**.
9. **Press CTRL+END, press ENTER, type your name, then save your changes**

Figure 2-25: Source Manager dialog box

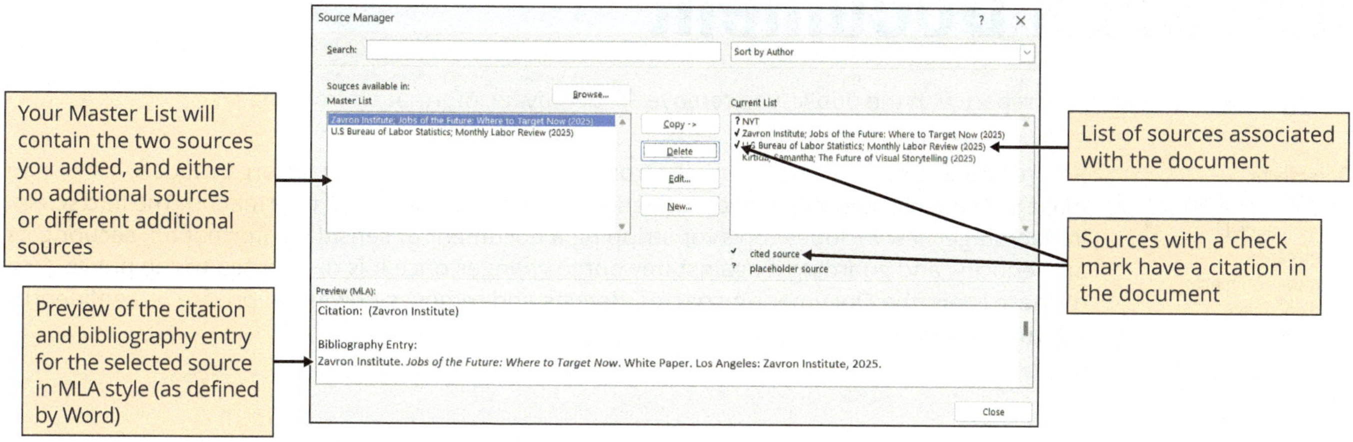

Figure 2-26: Adding a periodical source

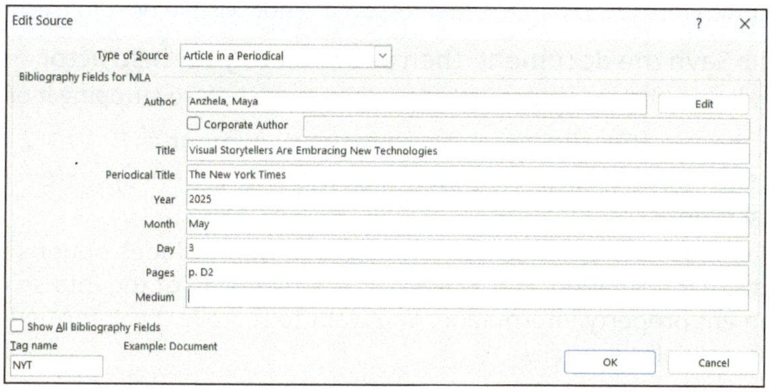

Figure 2-27: Bibliography field in document

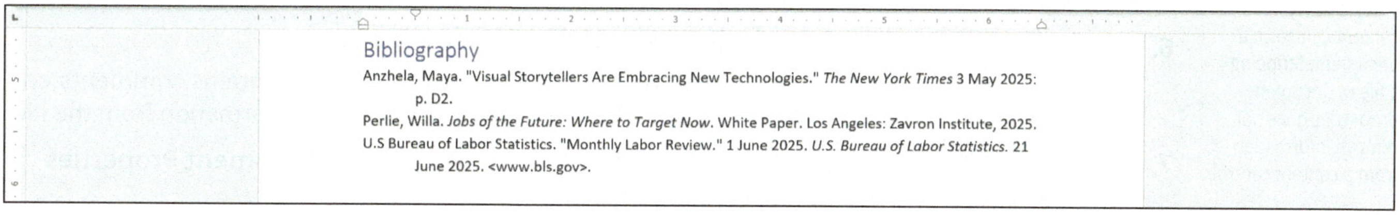

Finding and citing sources with the Word Researcher

The Word Researcher tool helps you find citable sources, quotations, images, and other material for a research paper. Using Researcher, you can search for journal articles and websites that relate to a topic, add information from those sources into a document, automatically create a citation for the source, and automatically create and update a bibliography—all without having to manually enter the source information. To begin, click the Researcher button in the Research group on the References tab to open the Researcher pane. Type a keyword for your topic in the search box, press ENTER, and then explore the list of sources related to your topic. When you find a source that is useful to you, you can select text (or an image) from it and add the selection to your document, choosing to add text only, or to add the text and a citation. When you add a citation, Word automatically creates a bibliography that is updated each time you add additional material to the document. To avoid plagiarism, be sure to paraphrase text that is not a quote, and always include citations giving credit for any content that is not your original work. Also, always verify that the bibliographies you create using Word are formatted in the most up-to-date MLA, APA, Chicago, or other style.

Inspect a Document

Case Before sharing the report with the public, you remove all identifying information from the file.

Objectives
- Inspect a document for embedded information
- Remove comments and document properties

Before you distribute a document electronically to people outside your organization, it's wise to make sure the file does not include embedded private or confidential information. The Info screen in Backstage view includes tools for stripping a document of sensitive information, securing its authenticity, and guarding it against unwanted changes once it is distributed to the public. One of these tools, the Document Inspector, detects and removes unwanted private or confidential information from a document.

Steps

1. **Press CTRL+HOME, click the View tab, then click the Multiple Pages button**
   The completed document is shown in **Figure 2-28**.
2. **Click the Review tab, click No Markup, then click All Markup**
   The comments you hid in the first lesson are now visible next to the document.
3. **sam Save the document, then submit it to your instructor**
   You will save the document with a new file name before stripping it of all identifying information.
4. **Click the File tab, click Save As, save the document as IL_WD_2_DigitalMedia_Inspected, click the File tab, click Info, then click the Show All Properties link at the bottom of the Info screen**
   The left side of the Info screen in Backstage view includes options related to stripping the file of private information. See **Table 2-3**. The right side of the Info screen displays the expanded document property information. You want to remove this information from the file before you distribute it electronically.
5. **Click the Check for Issues button on the Info screen, then click Inspect Document, clicking Yes if prompted to save changes**
   The Document Inspector dialog box opens. You use this dialog box to indicate which private or identifying information you want to search for and remove from the document.
6. **Make sure all the check boxes are selected, then click Inspect**
   After a moment, the Document Inspector dialog box indicates the file contains comments and document properties, as shown in **Figure 2-29**. You want to remove this information from the file.
7. **Click Remove All next to Comments, click Remove All next to Document Properties and Personal Information, then click Close**
   The comments and document property information are removed from the report file, but the change will not be reflected on the Info screen until you reopen it.
8. **Click the Back button on the Info screen, save your changes to the document, click the File tab, then click Info**
   The comments have been removed from the file. The Info screen shows the document properties have been removed from the file.
9. **Submit the document to your instructor, close the file, then exit Word**

Quick Tip
To recover unsaved changes to a file, click Manage Document on the Info screen, then click Recover Unsaved Documents.

Quick Tip
A document property, such as author name, might appear automatically in a content control in a document. Stripping a file of document properties does not remove information from a content control.

Figure 2-28: Formatted document

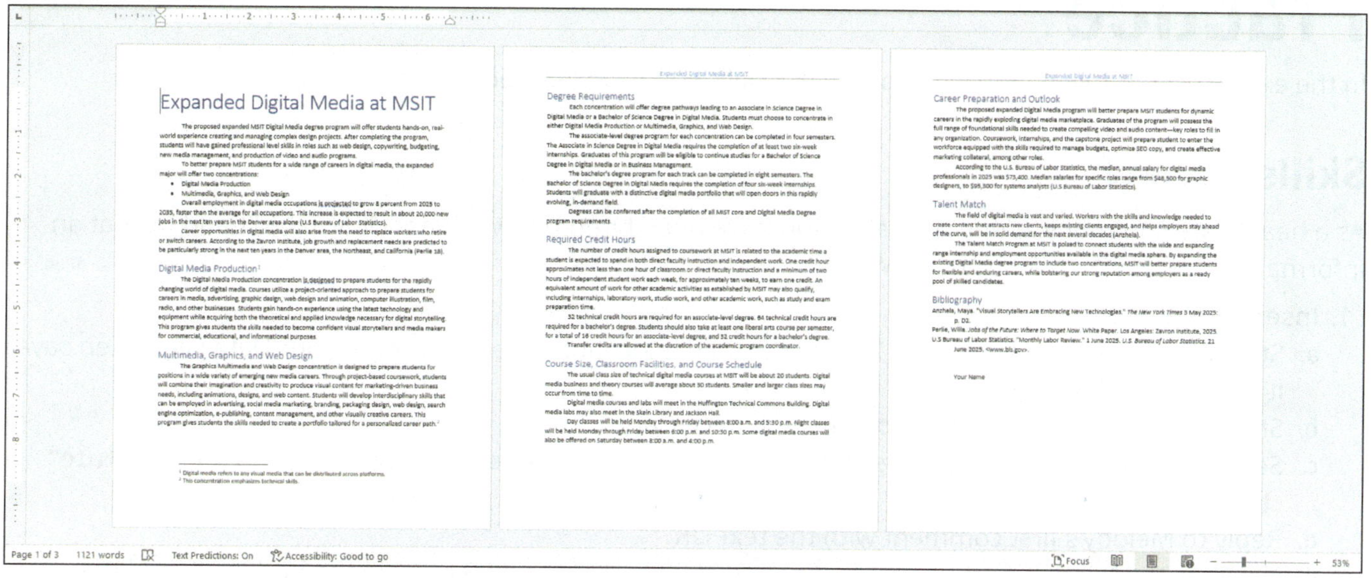

Figure 2-29: Results after inspecting document

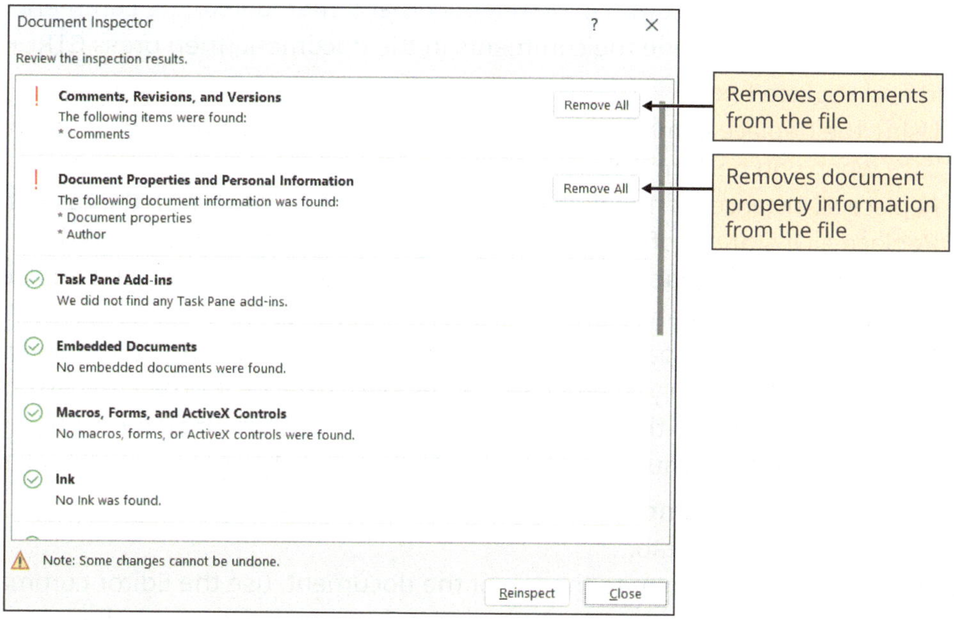

Table 2-3: Options on the Info screen

option	use to
Protect Document	Set a document to open as read-only so that users must opt into editing; encrypt a document so that a password is required to open it; restrict what kinds of changes can be made to a document and by whom; add a digital signature to a document to restrict access to editing, copying, and printing, and to verify its integrity; and mark a document as final so that it is read-only and cannot be edited
Check for Issues	Detect and remove unwanted information from a document, including document properties and comments; check for content that people with disabilities might find difficult to read; and check the document for features that are not supported by previous versions of Word
Version History	View and restore a previous version of a file stored on OneDrive
Manage Document	Browse and recover draft versions of unsaved files

Practice

In the exercises that follow, you will practice the skills you have learned in this module.

Skills Review

As a healthcare communications specialist, you have been hired by a wellness clinic to edit and format an informational report for clients, using Word.

1. **Insert comments.**
   a. Start Word, open the file IL_WD_2-2.docx from the location where you store your Data Files, then save it as **IL_WD_2_Lifestyle**.
   b. Show all the comments in the document, if necessary.
   c. Select Center in the title, then insert a new comment with the text **I will change this to "Institute" throughout.**
   d. Reply to Melody's first comment with the text **OK.**
   e. Navigate to Melody's next comment. Change 2022 to **2025** and 83 to **80** in the body text, and then mark the comment thread resolved.
   f. Navigate to the previous comment and edit your "OK." comment to add the sentence **I will add a footnote.**
   g. Navigate to the final comment in the document, then delete the comment thread.
   h. Save your changes, hide the comments in the document, then press CTRL+HOME.
2. **Find and replace text.**
   a. Using the Replace command, replace all instances of "Center" with **Institute**, taking care to match the case when you perform the search.
   b. Replace all instances of "medical" with **clinical**, taking care to match the case when you perform the replace.
   c. Replace all instances of "rehab" with **rehabilitation**, taking care to replace whole words only when you perform the replace. (Hint: Deselect Match case if it is selected.) Replace each instance of "rehab" individually rather than replacing all instances at once.
   d. Open the Navigation pane, then view all instances of "institute" in the document to make sure no errors occurred when you replaced Center with Institute. Correct any errors.
   e. Click the Pages link in the Navigation pane, click the thumbnail for each page to scroll through the document, click the thumbnail for page 1, close the Navigation pane, then save your changes.
3. **Check spelling and grammar and proofread and revise text.**
   a. Switch to the Review tab.
   b. Move the insertion point to the top of the document, use the Editor command to search for and correct spelling and grammar errors in the document, then close the Editor pane. (Hint: Ignore any suggested Refinements.)
   c. Use the Thesaurus to replace "enhance" in the first body paragraph with a different suitable word, then close the Thesaurus pane.
   d. Check the word count of the document.
   e. Proofread your document, correct any errors, then save your changes.
4. **Change line spacing and indents.**
   a. Change the line spacing of the entire document to 1.5.
   b. Change the line spacing of the first body paragraph to 1.15.
   c. Indent the first line of the first body paragraph .3". (Hint: Use the Paragraph dialog box.)
   d. Remove the paragraph space under the first body paragraph, then save your changes.
5. **Apply styles to text.**
   a. Apply the Title style to the title "North Coast Wellness Institute".
   b. Apply the Subtitle style to the subtitle "Lifestyle is Medicine".

c. Apply the Heading 1 style to each red heading in the document: "Jumpstart Health Living at North Coast Wellness Center" and "Clinical Services".
d. Apply the Heading 2 style to each blue heading in the document: "Lifestyle Medicine and Wellness", "Developing a Wellness Routine", "Staying Motivated", "Working with Our Medical Staff", "Rehabilitation", "Preventative Care", "Chronic Disease Management", and "Community Education".
e. With the insertion point in the first body paragraph, update the Normal style to match the first body paragraph.
f. Modify the Title style to be based on no style.
g. Modify the Subtitle, Heading 1, and Heading 2 styles to be based on no style.
h. Change the theme of the document to Gallery. (Hint: Use the Design tab.)
i. Select the title, change the font size to 36, then change the font color to Red, Accent 1, Darker 25%.
j. Select the subtitle, change the font size to 14, then add 24 points of space after the paragraph.
k. Select the heading "Jumpstart...", add 6 points of space after the paragraph, then update the Heading 1 style to match the selection
l. Select the heading "Lifestyle Medicine...", add 6 points of space before the paragraph, and 3 points of space after the paragraph, then update the Heading 2 style to match the selection.
m. Scroll to the bottom of page 1, click the first item in the bulleted list, add 6 points of space before the paragraph, then save your changes.

6. **Insert page numbers and page breaks.**
   a. Scroll to the bottom of page 2, then insert a manual page break before the heading "Clinical Services".
   b. Insert page numbers in the document at the bottom of the page.
   c. Close the Footer area, then scroll through the document to view the page number on each page.
   d. Turn on formatting marks, delete the manual page break at the bottom of page 2, then save your changes to the document.

7. **Add headers and footers.**
   a. Double-click the Footer area, then use the Go to Header button to move the insertion point to the Header area.
   b. Click the Header button, scroll down the gallery of built-in header designs, then select the Filigree header.
   c. Click the Document title content control in the header, then type **North Coast Wellness Institute**.
   d. Replace the text in the Author content control with your name, press END to move the insertion point out of the content control, then press SPACEBAR. (Note: If your name does not appear in the header, right-click the Author content control, click Remove Content Control, then type your name in the header.)
   e. Close headers and footers, then scroll to view the header and footer on each page.
   f. Open headers and footers, select the text in the Header area, including the paragraph mark after your name, change the alignment of the selected text to left, then remove the first line indent. (Hint: You can drag the indent marker on the ruler or use the Paragraph dialog box to remove the first line indent.)
   g. Remove the header and footer from the first page of the document, close headers and footers, then save your changes.

8. **Add footnotes and endnotes.**
   a. Press CTRL+HOME, scroll down, place the insertion point at the end of the first body paragraph, insert a footnote, then type **Healthcare resources include personnel, facilities, materials, and anything else that is used to provide medical care.**
   b. Place the insertion point at the end of the first paragraph under the Developing a Wellness Routine heading, insert a footnote, then type **Most wellness activities require only 30 minutes a day.**
   c. Place the insertion point at the end of the second paragraph under the Developing a Wellness Routine heading, insert a footnote, then type **Always consult a physician before beginning a new fitness program.**
   d. Change the number format of the footnotes to *, †, ‡ or another option, then save your changes.

Skills Review (Continued)

9. Insert citations.

a. Place the insertion point at the end of the first paragraph under the Lifestyle Medicine and Wellness heading (after "poor lifestyle" but before the period), then be sure the style for citations and bibliography is set to MLA Seventh Edition.

b. Insert a citation, add a new source, enter the source information shown in the Create Source dialog box in **Figure 2-30**, then click OK.

Figure 2-30

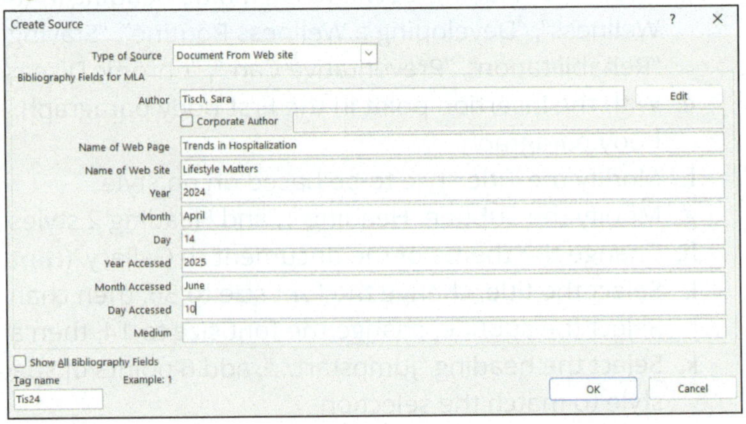

c. Place the insertion point at the end of the second paragraph under the Developing a Wellness Routine heading, insert a citation, then select Chao, Brian from the list of sources.

d. Edit the citation to include the page number **24**.

e. Scroll to page 2, place the insertion point at the end of the "Schedule your wellness activity" paragraph in the bulleted list, but before the ending period, insert a citation for Hagen, then save your changes.

10. Create a bibliography.

a. Press CTRL+END, then use the Bibliography command to insert a Works Cited list.

b. Open the Source Manager dialog box.

c. Delete the Mindfulness Institute source from the Current list.

d. Select the source Tisch, Sara: ... in the Current List, click Edit, show all Bibliography fields, add the URL **www.lifestylematters.org** to the source, click OK, click Yes, then click Close.

e. Update the bibliography field.

f. With the bibliography field selected, click the Bibliographies button above the Bibliography field, then select References. Pages 1 and 3 of the formatted document are shown in **Figure 2-31**.

g. Save your changes to the document, then submit it to your instructor without closing the document.

11. Inspect a document.

a. Save a copy of the document as **IL_WD_2_Lifestyle_Inspected** to the drive and folder where you store your Data Files.

b. Open the Navigation pane, click the Headings link, click the headings listed in the Navigation pane to scroll through the document, then close the Navigation pane.

c. Use the Go To command to move the insertion point to the top of page 1.

d. Use the Find and Replace dialog box to find all em dashes in the document, but do not replace the em dashes. (**Hint**: Scroll through the document using the Find Next button.)

e. Use the Find and Replace dialog box to find text formatted with the Heading 2 style, but do not replace the text.

f. Select a word in the document, look it up using the Search button on the References tab, then close the Search pane.

g. Show the comments in the document, then, using the Review tab, delete all the comments in the document.

h. Use the Check for Issues command to run the Document Inspector.

i. Remove all document property and personal information data from the document, then save your changes.

j. Submit a copy of the document to your instructor, close the document, then exit Word.

Figure 2-31

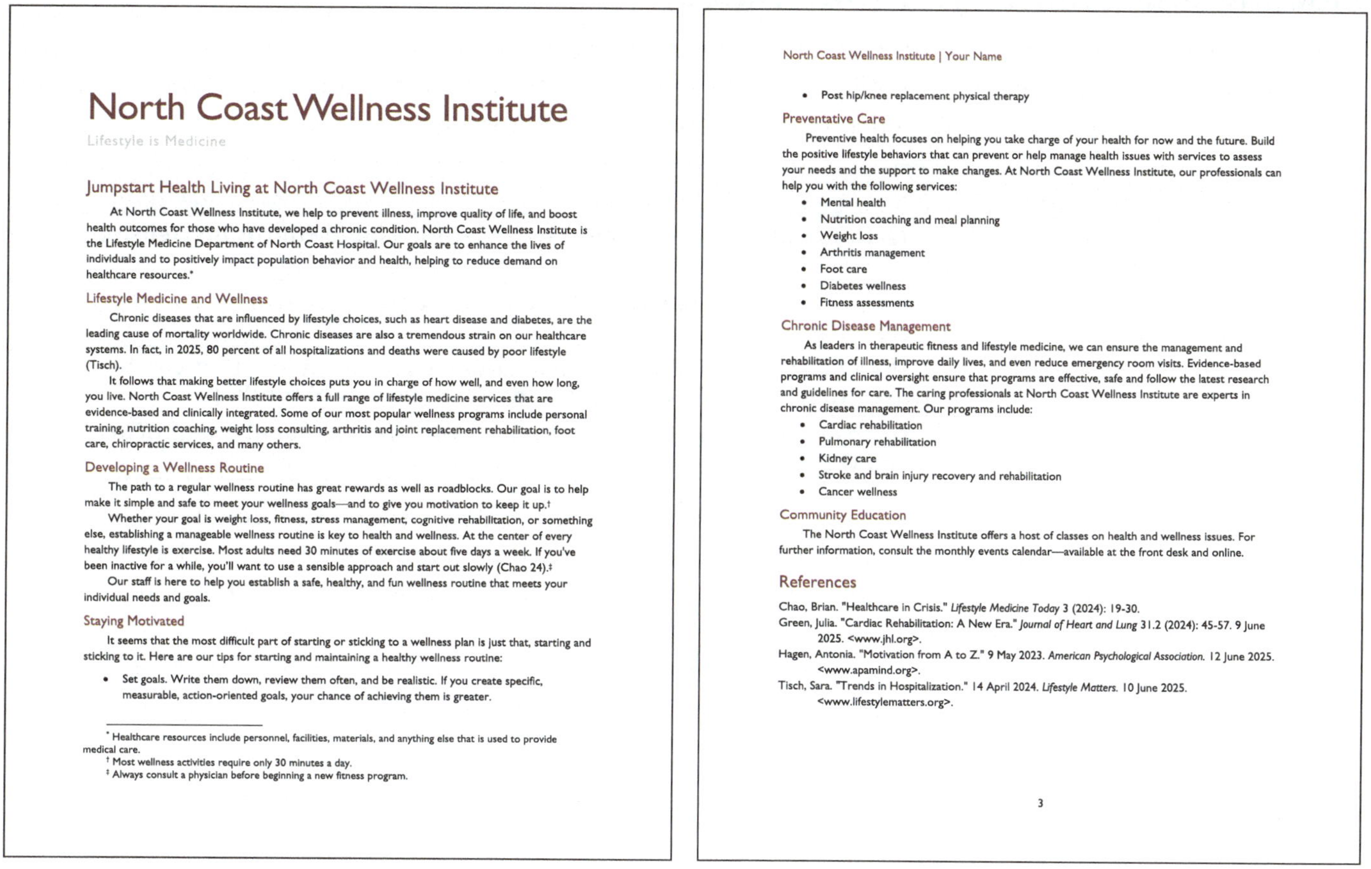
North Coast Wellness Institute

Lifestyle is Medicine

Jumpstart Health Living at North Coast Wellness Institute

At North Coast Wellness Institute, we help to prevent illness, improve quality of life, and boost health outcomes for those who have developed a chronic condition. North Coast Wellness Institute is the Lifestyle Medicine Department of North Coast Hospital. Our goals are to enhance the lives of individuals and to positively impact population behavior and health, helping to reduce demand on healthcare resources.*

Lifestyle Medicine and Wellness

Chronic diseases that are influenced by lifestyle choices, such as heart disease and diabetes, are the leading cause of mortality worldwide. Chronic diseases are also a tremendous strain on our healthcare systems. In fact, in 2025, 80 percent of all hospitalizations and deaths were caused by poor lifestyle (Tisch).

It follows that making better lifestyle choices puts you in charge of how well, and even how long, you live. North Coast Wellness Institute offers a full range of lifestyle medicine services that are evidence-based and clinically integrated. Some of our most popular wellness programs include personal training, nutrition coaching, weight loss consulting, arthritis and joint replacement rehabilitation, foot care, chiropractic services, and many others.

Developing a Wellness Routine

The path to a regular wellness routine has great rewards as well as roadblocks. Our goal is to help make it simple and safe to meet your wellness goals—and to give you motivation to keep it up.†

Whether your goal is weight loss, fitness, stress management, cognitive rehabilitation, or something else, establishing a manageable wellness routine is key to health and wellness. At the center of every healthy lifestyle is exercise. Most adults need 30 minutes of exercise about five days a week. If you've been inactive for a while, you'll want to use a sensible approach and start out slowly (Chao 24).‡

Our staff is here to help you establish a safe, healthy, and fun wellness routine that meets your individual needs and goals.

Staying Motivated

It seems that the most difficult part of starting or sticking to a wellness plan is just that, starting and sticking to it. Here are our tips for starting and maintaining a healthy wellness routine:

- Set goals. Write them down, review them often, and be realistic. If you create specific, measurable, action-oriented goals, your chance of achieving them is greater.

* Healthcare resources include personnel, facilities, materials, and anything else that is used to provide medical care.
† Most wellness activities require only 30 minutes a day.
‡ Always consult a physician before beginning a new fitness program.

North Coast Wellness Institute | Your Name

- Post hip/knee replacement physical therapy

Preventative Care

Preventive health focuses on helping you take charge of your health for now and the future. Build the positive lifestyle behaviors that can prevent or help manage health issues with services to assess your needs and the support to make changes. At North Coast Wellness Institute, our professionals can help you with the following services:

- Mental health
- Nutrition coaching and meal planning
- Weight loss
- Arthritis management
- Foot care
- Diabetes wellness
- Fitness assessments

Chronic Disease Management

As leaders in therapeutic fitness and lifestyle medicine, we can ensure the management and rehabilitation of illness, improve daily lives, and even reduce emergency room visits. Evidence-based programs and clinical oversight ensure that programs are effective, safe and follow the latest research and guidelines for care. The caring professionals at North Coast Wellness Institute are experts in chronic disease management. Our programs include:

- Cardiac rehabilitation
- Pulmonary rehabilitation
- Kidney care
- Stroke and brain injury recovery and rehabilitation
- Cancer wellness

Community Education

The North Coast Wellness Institute offers a host of classes on health and wellness issues. For further information, consult the monthly events calendar—available at the front desk and online.

References

Chao, Brian. "Healthcare in Crisis." *Lifestyle Medicine Today* 3 (2024): 19-30.
Green, Julia. "Cardiac Rehabilitation: A New Era." *Journal of Heart and Lung* 31.2 (2024): 45-57. 9 June 2025. <www.jhl.org>.
Hagen, Antonia. "Motivation from A to Z." 9 May 2023. *American Psychological Association.* 12 June 2025. <www.apamind.org>.
Tisch, Sara. "Trends in Hospitalization." 14 April 2024. *Lifestyle Matters.* 10 June 2025. <www.lifestylematters.org>.

3

Independent Challenge 1

The Center for Global Education at Coastal City College publishes a variety of newsletters and information reports related to work and study abroad opportunities for students. Your colleague has drafted the spring newsletter and forwarded the file to you. The file includes comments with instructions for finalizing the document. You need to add citations and footnotes and format the newsletter for distribution to patients.

a. Start Word, open the file IL_WD_2-3.docx from the drive and folder where you store your Data Files, save it as **IL_WD_2_SpringNewsletter**, then read the document to get a feel for its contents.

b. Show the comments in the document, scroll through the comments, reply to or resolve each comment, add a comment, then delete all comments from the document.

c. Format the newsletter using styles. Apply the Title style to the purple text, the Heading 1 style to the blue text, the Heading 2 style to the green text, and the Heading 3 style to the dark orange text. (You will format the masthead after formatting the body of the document.)

d. Apply a theme to the document. Choose a theme that suits the purpose and audience of the document. You can change the theme colors or style set if you wish.

e. Change the font size of the title so that the title fits on one line, if necessary.

f. Modify the Heading 1, Heading 2, and Heading 3 styles so that the font, font size, font color, and paragraph spacing of the headings gives the newsletter an attractive and cohesive appearance.

g. Using styles, format the first three lines of the document as a masthead for the newsletter. The masthead for this document should not compete with the title of the document for attention. After applying styles, apply other formats, such as font size, font color, text effects, paragraph alignment, and borders to customize the look of the masthead.

h. Add a header to the document using the Filigree header style. Type **Center for Global Education** in the Document title content control, then type your name in the Author content control. (Hint: If the Author content control shows different text, replace that text with your name.)

i. Add a page number to the bottom of each page using the page number style of your choice.

Independent Challenge 1 (Continued)

j. Remove headers and footers from the first page of the document.

k. Use the Find command or the Navigation pane to find the text specified in the table below, then add a footnote at each location, using the footnote text specified in the table.

Find text	Footnote text
best experiences of their lives	**Testimonials are posted on the Center for Global Education website.**
Australia (Perth, Wollongong)	**Perth is available fall semester only. Wollongong is available spring semester only.**
General Funding	**The CCC Financial Aid website includes a search engine that can be used to identify scholarships and other sources of funding.**
Laws and cultural attitudes in the host country	**For more information on local laws, visit the U.S. Department of State and U.S. Embassy webpages.**

l. Change the Citations and Bibliography style to MLA Seventh Edition. Use the Find command or the Navigation pane to find the text specified in the table below, then add a citation at each location, using the source specified in the table. Some citations include a page number. Remember to insert the citation before the period at the end of a sentence.

Find text	Citation source	Citation page number
study or work in another country	World Travel Institute	18
outcomes	World Health Organization	
public health concerns	Centers for Disease Control and Prevention	
Source:	Elliot, Margaret	132

m. Press CTRL+END, then add a bibliography to the newsletter.

n. Check the document for spelling and grammar errors, then use the thesaurus to replace a word with a synonym.

o. View the document in Multiple pages view, then make any formatting adjustments necessary so that the document flows smoothly between pages and is easy to read. **Figure 2-32** depicts a sample first page of the newsletter.

p. Save the document, submit a copy to your instructor, close the document, then exit Word.

Figure 2-32

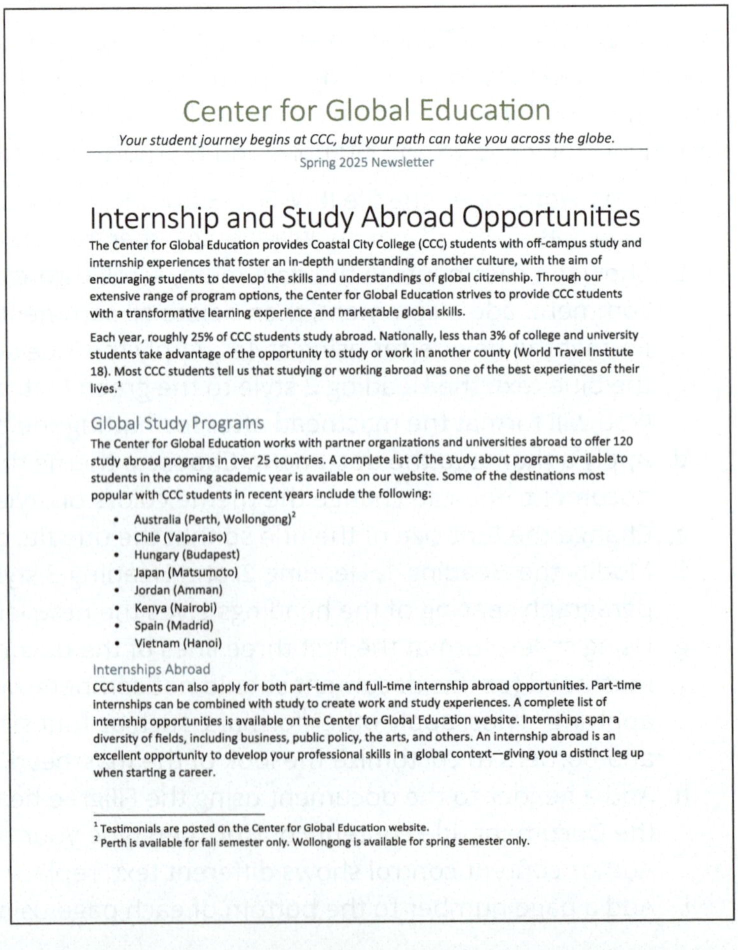

Center for Global Education

Your student journey begins at CCC, but your path can take you across the globe.

Spring 2025 Newsletter

Internship and Study Abroad Opportunities

The Center for Global Education provides Coastal City College (CCC) students with off-campus study and internship experiences that foster an in-depth understanding of another culture, with the aim of encouraging students to develop the skills and understandings of global citizenship. Through our extensive range of program options, the Center for Global Education strives to provide CCC students with a transformative learning experience and marketable global skills.

Each year, roughly 25% of CCC students study abroad. Nationally, less than 3% of college and university students take advantage of the opportunity to study or work in another county (World Travel Institute 18). Most CCC students tell us that studying or working abroad was one of the best experiences of their lives.[1]

Global Study Programs

The Center for Global Education works with partner organizations and universities abroad to offer 120 study abroad programs in over 25 countries. A complete list of the study about programs available to students in the coming academic year is available on our website. Some of the destinations most popular with CCC students in recent years include the following:

- Australia (Perth, Wollongong)[2]
- Chile (Valparaiso)
- Hungary (Budapest)
- Japan (Matsumoto)
- Jordan (Amman)
- Kenya (Nairobi)
- Spain (Madrid)
- Vietnam (Hanoi)

Internships Abroad

CCC students can also apply for both part-time and full-time internship abroad opportunities. Part-time internships can be combined with study to create work and study experiences. A complete list of internship opportunities is available on the Center for Global Education website. Internships span a diversity of fields, including business, public policy, the arts, and others. An internship abroad is an excellent opportunity to develop your professional skills in a global context—giving you a distinct leg up when starting a career.

[1] Testimonials are posted on the Center for Global Education website.
[2] Perth is available for fall semester only. Wollongong is available for spring semester only.

Independent Challenge 2

As an administrative assistant at a research institute, you frequently format the research papers written by the researchers and policymakers of your department. The format recommended by the *MLA Handbook for Writers of Research Papers*, a style guide that includes information on preparing, writing, and formatting research papers, is the standard format used by many schools, colleges, and universities. In this independent challenge, you will research the MLA guidelines for formatting a research paper and use the guidelines you find to format the pages of a research report.

a. Use your favorite search engine to search the web for information on the MLA guidelines for formatting a research report. Use the keywords **MLA Style** and **research paper format** to conduct your search.

b. Look for information on the proper formatting for the following aspects of a research paper: paper size, margins, title page or first page of the report, line spacing, paragraph indentation, and page numbers. Also, find information on proper formatting for citations and a works cited page. Print the information you find.

c. Start Word, open the file IL_WD_2-4.docx from the drive and folder where you store your Data Files, then save it as **IL_WD_2_ResearchReport**. Using the information you learned, format this document as a research report.

d. Correct spelling and grammar errors in the document.

e. Adjust the margins, set the line spacing, and add page numbers to the document in the format recommended by the MLA. Use **The Affordable Housing Crisis: Challenges and Solutions** as the title for your sample report, use your name as the author name, and use the name of the course you are enrolled in currently as well as the instructor's name for that course. Make sure to format the title page exactly as the MLA style dictates.

Figure 2-33

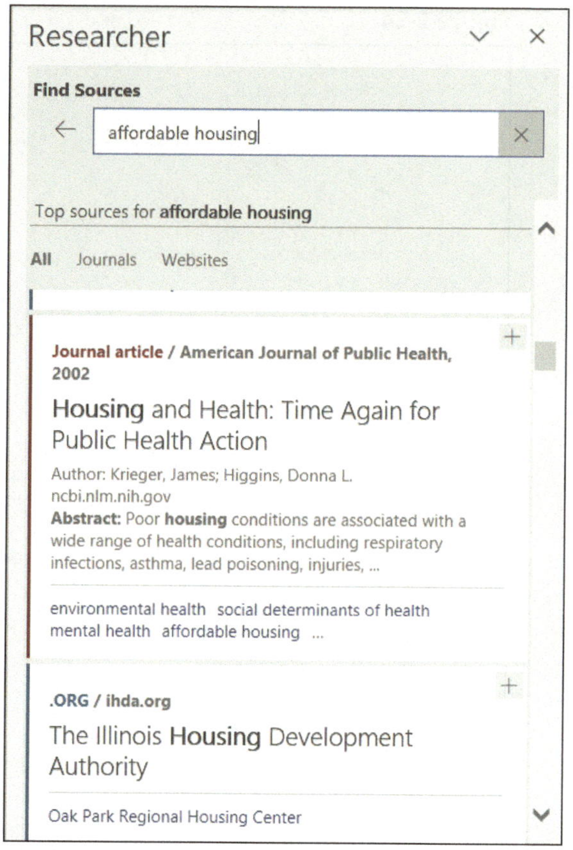

f. Format the remaining text as the body of the research report. Indent the first line of each paragraph rather than use quadruple spacing between paragraphs.

g. Create five sources and insert five citations in the document—including at least one journal article and one website. If possible, use the Researcher tool to add sources and citations. **Figure 2-33** depicts the Researcher pane with sample sources. You can also make up sources. (**Note**: For this practice document, you are allowed to make up sources. Never make up sources for real research papers.)

h. Add two citation placeholders to the document.

i. Create a works cited page, following MLA style. If necessary, edit the format of the citations and works cited page to conform to MLA format.

j. Save the document, submit a copy to your instructor, close the document, then exit Word.

Visual Workshop

Use a blank document to create the Works Cited page shown in **Figure 2-34**, then save the document as **IL_WD_2_GreenEnergyWorksCited**. Use 12-point Times New Roman for the text, double-space the lines in the document, and apply a hanging indent to the paragraphs in the list. Format "Works Cited" with the Heading 1 style and center the heading at the top of the document. Add your name and a page number to the header, then format the header text in 12-point Times New Roman. Correct spelling and grammar errors, remove the document property information from the file, then submit a copy to your instructor.

Figure 2-34

Your Name 1

Works Cited

Aran, Shea C. *Renewable Energy: Principles and Practices.* Sun Publishers, 2025.

Harris, Simon. "Renewable Power for Everyday Living." *Good Energy: Green from the Ground Up,* 18 Aug. 2024, www.goodenergy.com/article/renewable. Accessed 16 July 2025.

Hikari, Akira. "Solar Energy." *The Homeowner's Guide to Renewable Energy,* edited by Nuka Payne, Earth Press, 2025, pp. 209-17.

Roshni, Sushila. "Can Green Energy Replace Fossil Fuels?" *Green Energy Today,* www.greenenergytoday.org/replace-fossil-fuels.html. Accessed 14 July 2025.

Formatting Text and Graphics

Case

You have been asked to finalize an event planning report for move-in week at MSIT that will be distributed to other departments. After formatting the headings in the report, you use tabs and create tables to organize the other information so that it is easy to understand. Finally, you illustrate the report with images, shapes, and SmartArt to help convey the friendly and welcoming tone of move-in week.

Module Objectives

After completing this module, you will be able to:

- Use the Format Painter
- Set and modify tabs
- Add borders and shading
- Insert a table
- Insert and delete rows and columns
- Apply a table style
- Insert online pictures
- Size and scale a graphic
- Draw and format shapes
- Adjust and rotate shapes
- Arrange graphic objects
- Create SmartArt graphics
- Add alt text to objects

Files You Will Need

IL_WD_3-1.docx
IL_WD_3-2.docx
IL_WD_3-3.docx
IL_WD_3-4.docx
IL_WD_3-5.docx

Use the Format Painter

Case You enhance the appearance of the title and headings in the report by applying different font styles and text effects. You also insert the date and a copyright symbol in the document to mark the planning stage and indicate the report content is proprietary.

Objectives
- Apply formatting
- Clear formatting
- Insert the date
- Insert special characters

You can dramatically change the appearance of text by applying different font styles, font effects, and character-spacing effects. When you are satisfied with the formatting of specific text, you can quickly apply the same formats to other text in the document using the Format Painter. The **Format Painter** is a powerful Word feature that allows you to copy all the format settings applied to selected text to other text that you want to format the same way.

Steps

1. **sam** Start **Word**, open the file **IL_WD_3-1.docx** from the location where you store your Data Files, then save it as **IL_WD_3_PlanningReport**

Quick Tip To change the WordArt style currently applied to text, select the text, click the Text Effects and Typography button, then select a different WordArt style from the gallery.

2. Select the title **Welcoming New Students to the MSIT Campus**, click the **Text Effects and Typography button** in the Font group on the Home tab, click the **Fill: Blue; Accent color 1; Shadow style** (the second WordArt style in the first row), click the **Font Size arrow**, click **24**, click the **Font Color arrow**, then click **Orange, Accent 2, Darker 25%**
   The title is formatted in a 24-point WordArt style, orange.

3. Select the heading **What Does the Move-in Team Do?** to display the Mini toolbar, click the **Font Size arrow**, click **14**, click the **Bold button**, click the **Font Color arrow**, click the **Blue, Accent 1, Darker 25%** color in the theme colors, then deselect the text
   The heading is formatted in 14-point bold, dark blue.

Trouble Move the pointer over the document text to see the paintbrush pointer.

4. Select **What Does the Move-in Team Do?**, then click the **Format Painter button** in the Clipboard group on the Home tab
   The pointer changes to the paintbrush pointer, a paintbrush icon.

Quick Tip You can also click in the left margin to select the heading text.

5. Scroll down, drag the paintbrush pointer to select the heading **Move-in Week Planning and Budgeting**, then deselect the text
   The heading is formatted in 14-point bold, and dark blue, as shown in **Figure 3-1**.

6. Select **Move-in Week Planning and Budgeting** again, then double-click the **Format Painter button**
   Double-clicking the Format Painter button allows the Format Painter to remain active until you turn it off. By keeping the Format Painter active, you can apply formatting to multiple items.

Quick Tip You can also press ESC to turn off the Format Painter.

7. Scroll down, select the headings **Recruiting Move-in Team Volunteers** and **Administrative Team for Move-in Week**, then click the **Format Painter button** to turn off the Format Painter
   The headings are formatted in 14-point bold, and dark blue.

Quick Tip To insert the date as a field that is updated automatically, select the Update automatically check box.

8. Press **CTRL+END**, type **Prepared by**, press **SPACEBAR** and type your name followed by a comma, press **SPACEBAR**, click the **Insert tab**, then click the **Date and Time button** in the Text group
   The Date and Time dialog box opens with available formats for inserting the date and time.

Trouble If you do not see the copyright symbol, click More Symbols, select the code in the Character code box, type 00A9, click Insert, then click Close.

9. Select the **third format** in the list, click **OK** to insert the current date at the insertion point, press **ENTER**, then click the **Symbol button** in the Symbols group
   A gallery of commonly used symbols opens similar to the one in **Figure 3-2**. You may see a different selection of symbols depending on which symbols you insert most frequently. You can insert a symbol from this gallery or click More Symbols to open a larger gallery of symbols.

10. Click the **copyright symbol ©** in the gallery, press **SPACEBAR**, type **Mountain Springs Institute of Technology**, click the **Home tab**, press **CTRL+HOME**, then save your changes
    The copyright symbol is inserted before Mountain Springs Institute of Technology.

Figure 3-1: Formats copied and applied using the Format Painter

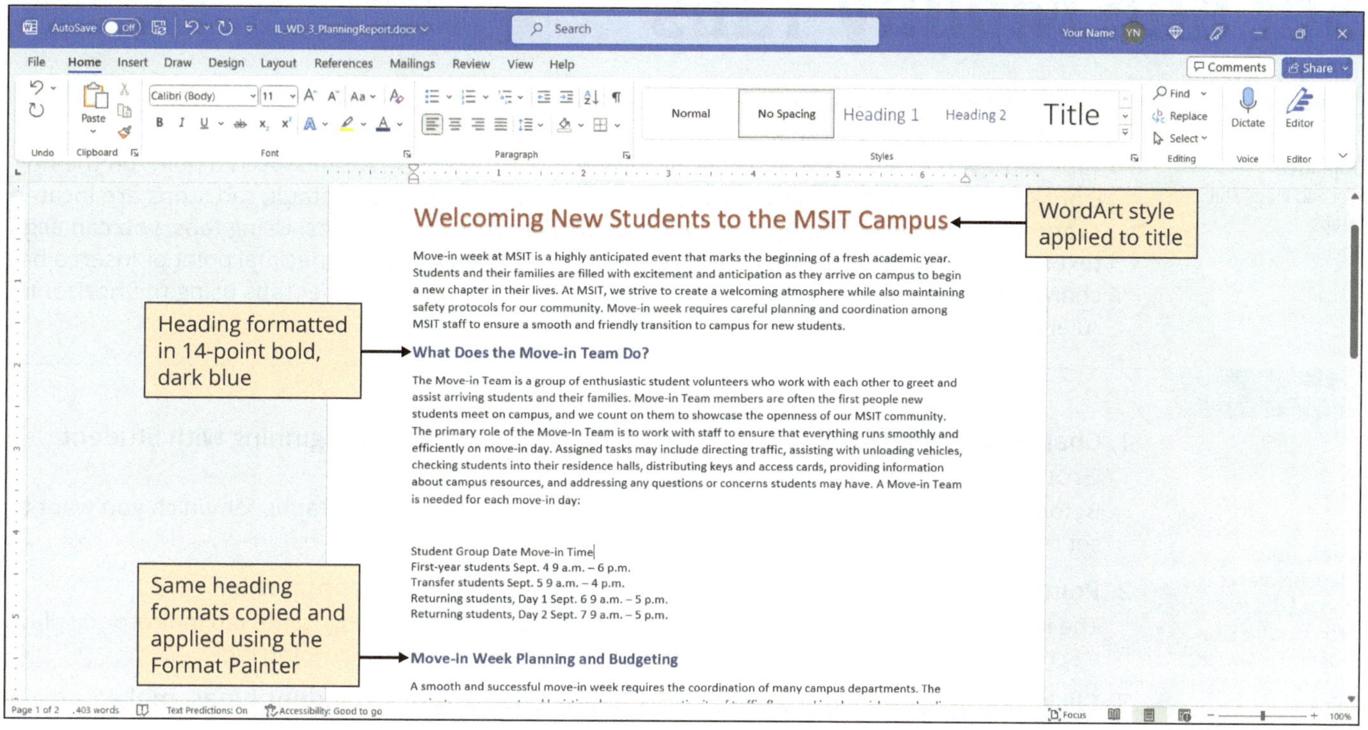

Figure 3-2: Symbol gallery

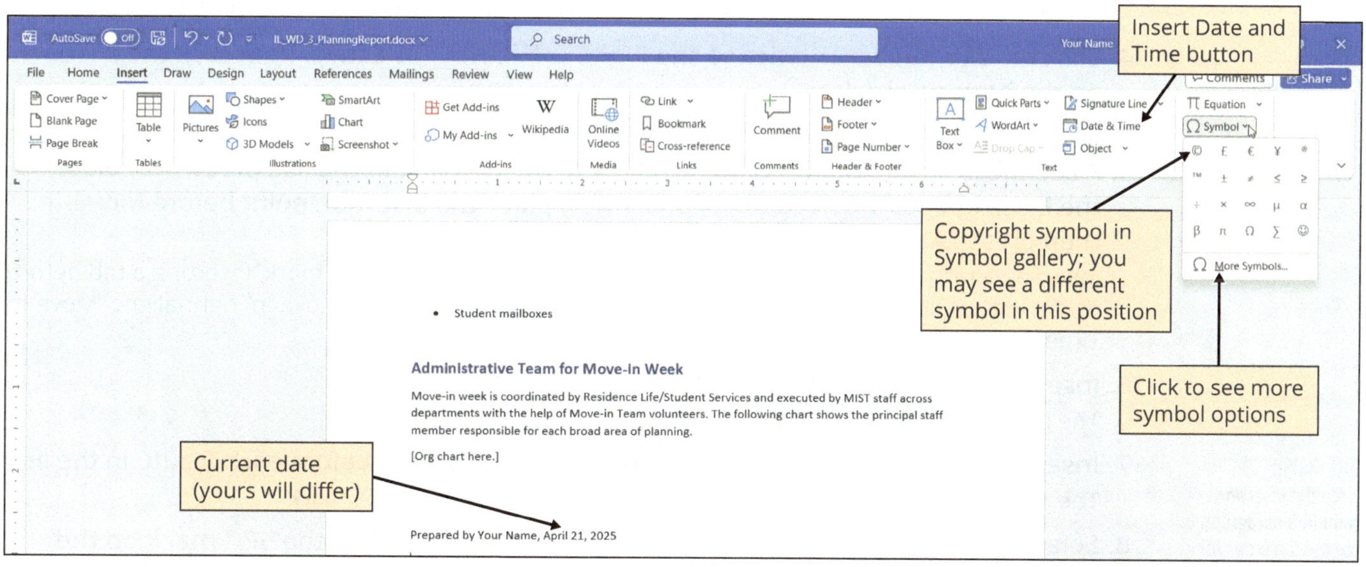

Clearing formatting from text

If you are unhappy with the way text is formatted, you can use the Clear All Formatting command to return the text to the default format settings. The default format includes font and paragraph formatting: text is formatted in 11-point Calibri, and paragraphs are left-aligned with 1.08 points of space between lines, 8 points of space after paragraphs, and no indents. To clear formatting from text and return it to the default format, select the text you want to clear, and then click the Clear All Formatting button in the Font group on the Home tab. If you prefer to return the text to the default font and remove all paragraph formatting, making the text 11-point Calibri, left-aligned, single-spaced, with no paragraph spacing or indents, select the text and then click the No Spacing button in the Styles group on the Home tab.

Set and Modify Tabs

Case You use tabs to format the move-in date and time information so that it is easy to read.

Objective
- Set and modify tab stops

Tabs allow you to align text at a specific location in a document. A **tab stop** is a point on the horizontal ruler that indicates the location at which to align text. By default, tab stops are located every 1⁄2" from the left margin, but you can also set custom tab stops. Using tabs, you can align text to the left, right, or center of a tab stop, or you can align text at a decimal point or insert a bar character. **Table 3-1** describes the different types of tab stops. You set tabs using the horizontal ruler or the Tabs dialog box.

Steps

1. **Change the zoom level to 140, then select the five-line list beginning with Student Group Date Move-in Time**
   Before you set tab stops for existing text, you must select the paragraphs for which you want to set tabs.

Quick Tip If the rulers are not displayed, click the Ruler check box in the Show group on the View tab.

2. **Point to the tab indicator at the far-left end of the horizontal ruler**
   The icon in the tab indicator indicates the active type of tab; pointing to the tab indicator displays a ScreenTip naming the active tab type. By default, left tab is the active tab type.

Quick Tip To remove a tab stop, drag it off the ruler.

3. **Click the tab indicator to see each of the available tab and indent types, make Left Tab the active tab type, click the 1" mark on the horizontal ruler, then click the 3¼" mark on the horizontal ruler**
   Clicking the horizontal ruler near the bottom inserts a tab stop of the active type for the selected paragraph or paragraphs. A left tab stop is inserted at the 1" mark and the 3¼" mark.

Trouble If you click more than twice, keep clicking until the Right Tab icon again appears.

4. **Click the tab indicator twice so the Right Tab icon is active, then click the 5" mark on the horizontal ruler**
   A right tab stop is inserted at the 5" mark on the horizontal ruler, as shown in **Figure 3-3**.

5. **Place the insertion point before Student in the first line in the list, press TAB, place the insertion point before Date, press TAB, place the insertion point before Move-in, then press TAB**
   Inserting a tab before "Student" left-aligns "Student Group" at the 1" mark, inserting a tab before "Date" left-aligns "Date" at the 3¼" mark, and inserting a tab before "Move-in" right-aligns "Move-in Time" at the 5" mark.

6. **Insert a tab at the beginning of each remaining line in the list**
   The paragraphs left-align at the 1" mark.

Quick Tip Place the insertion point in a paragraph to see the tab stops for that paragraph on the horizontal ruler.

7. **Insert a tab before each Sept. in the list, then insert a tab before each 9 a.m. in the list**
   The dates left-align at the 3¼" mark. The times right-align at the 5" mark.

8. **Select the five lines of tabbed text, drag the right tab stop to the 5½" mark on the horizontal ruler, then deselect the text**
   Dragging the tab stop moves it to a new location. The times right-align at the 5½" mark.

Quick Tip Double-click a tab stop on the ruler to open the Tabs dialog box.

9. **Select the last four lines of tabbed text, click the Launcher in the Paragraph group, then click Tabs at the bottom of the Paragraph dialog box**
   The Tabs dialog box opens, as shown in **Figure 3-4**. You can use the Tabs dialog box to set tab stops, change the position or alignment of existing tab stops, clear tab stops, and apply tab leaders to tabs. **Tab leaders** are lines that appear in front of tabbed text.

Quick Tip In the Tabs dialog box, click Set after changing the settings for each tab stop.

10. **Click 3.25" in the Tab stop position list box, click the 2 option button in the Leader section, click Set, click 5.5" in the Tab stop position list box, click the 2 option button in the Leader section, click Set, click OK, deselect the text, then save your changes**
    A dotted tab leader is added before each 3.25" and 5.5" tab stop in the last four lines of tabbed text, as shown in **Figure 3-5**.

Figure 3-3: Left and right tab stops on the horizontal ruler

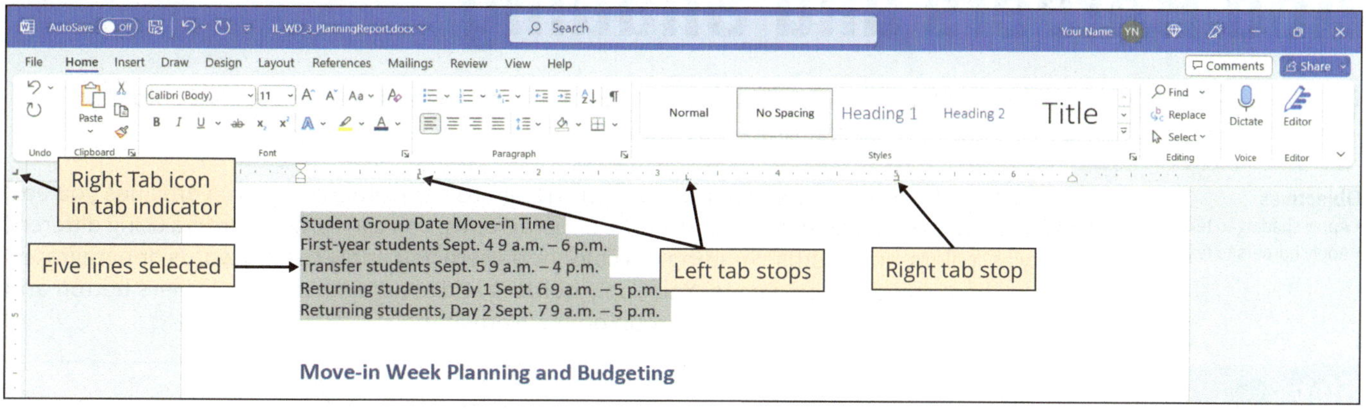

Figure 3-4: Tabs dialog box

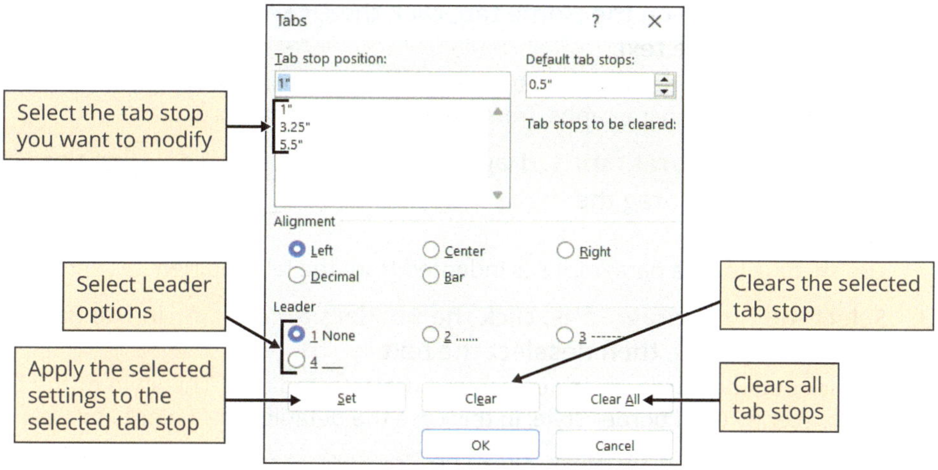

Figure 3-5: Tab leaders

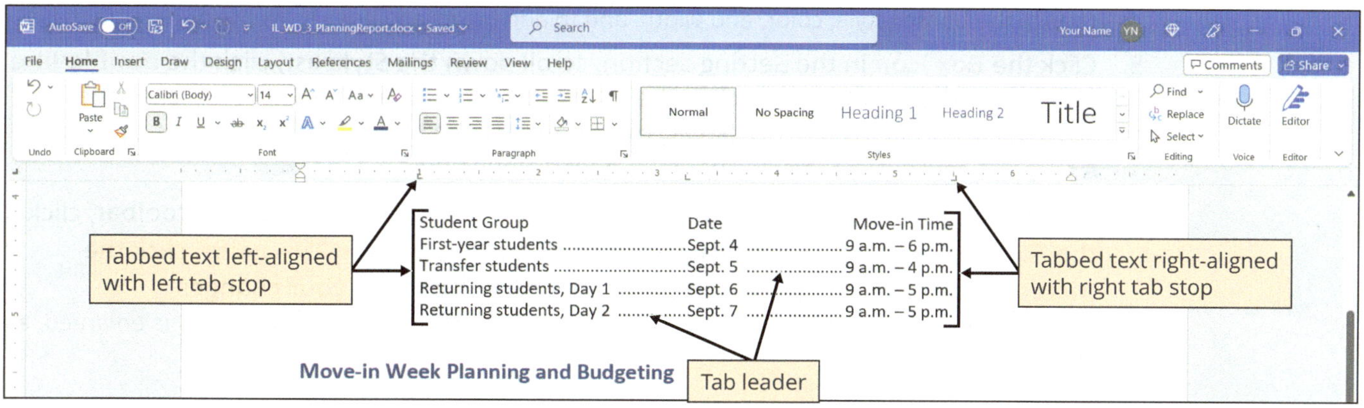

Table 3-1: Types of tabs

tab	use to
Left tab	Set the start position of text so that text runs to the right of the tab stop as you type
Center tab	Set the center align position of text so that text stays centered on the tab stop as you type
Right tab	Set the right or end position of text so that text moves to the left of the tab stop as you type
Decimal tab	Set the position of the decimal point so that numbers align around the decimal point as you type
Bar tab	Insert a vertical bar at the tab position

Add Borders and Shading

Case You enhance the tabbed text for move-in dates and times by adding shading to it. You also apply a border around the tabbed text to set it off from the rest of the document.

Objectives
- Apply shading to text
- Apply borders to text

Borders and shading can add color and artistic design to a document. **Borders** are lines you add above, below, to either side, or around words or paragraphs. You can format borders using different line styles, colors, and widths. **Shading** is a color or pattern you apply behind words or paragraphs to make them stand out on a page. You apply borders and shading using the Borders button and the Shading button in the Paragraph group on the Home tab.

Steps

1. **Select the five paragraphs of tabbed text, click the Shading arrow in the Paragraph group on the Home tab, click the Orange, Accent 2, Lighter 60% color, then deselect the text**
   Light orange shading is applied to the five paragraphs. Notice that the shading is applied to the entire width of the paragraphs, from the left to the right margin.
2. **Select the five paragraphs, drag the Left Indent marker to the ¾" mark on the horizontal ruler, drag the Right Indent marker to the 5¾" mark, then deselect the text**
   The shading for the paragraphs is indented from the left and right, as shown in **Figure 3-6**.
3. **Select the five paragraphs, click the Borders arrow in the Paragraph group, click Outside Borders, then deselect the text**
   A black outside border is added around the selected text. The style of the border added is the most recently used border style, in this case the default, a thin black line.
4. **Select the five paragraphs, click the Borders arrow, click No Border, click the Borders arrow, then click Borders and Shading**
   The Borders and Shading dialog box opens, as shown in **Figure 3-7**. You use the Borders tab to change the border style, color, and width, and to add boxes and lines to words or paragraphs.
5. **Click the Box icon in the Setting section, scroll down the Style list, click the double-line style, click the Color arrow, click the Blue, Accent 1, Darker 25% color, click the Width arrow, click 1½ pt, click OK, then deselect the text**
   A 1½-point dark blue double-line border is added around the tabbed text.
6. **Select the first line of tabbed text, click the Bold button on the Mini toolbar, click the Font Color arrow, click the Blue, Accent 1, Darker 25% color, click the Increase Font Size button, deselect the text, then save your changes**
   The Student Group, Date, and Move-in Time text changes to bold dark blue and is enlarged, as shown in **Figure 3-8**.

Underlining text

Another way to call attention to text and enhance the appearance of a document is to apply an underline style to words you want to highlight. The Underline arrow in the Font group displays straight, dotted, wavy, dashed, and mixed underline styles, along with a gallery of colors to choose from. To apply an underline to text, select it, click the Underline arrow, and then select an underline style from the list. For a wider variety of underline styles, click More Underlines in the list, and then select an underline style in the Font dialog box. You can change the color of an underline at any time by selecting the underlined text, clicking the Underline arrow, pointing to Underline Color, and then choosing from the options in the color gallery. If you want to remove an underline from text, select the underlined text, and then click the Underline button.

Figure 3-6: Shading applied to the tabbed text

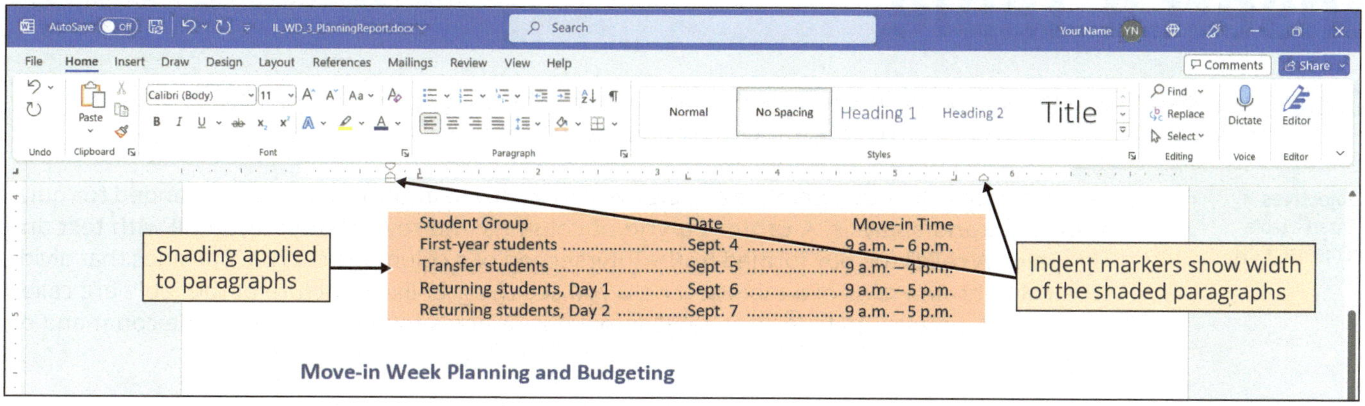

Figure 3-7: Borders tab in Borders and Shading dialog box

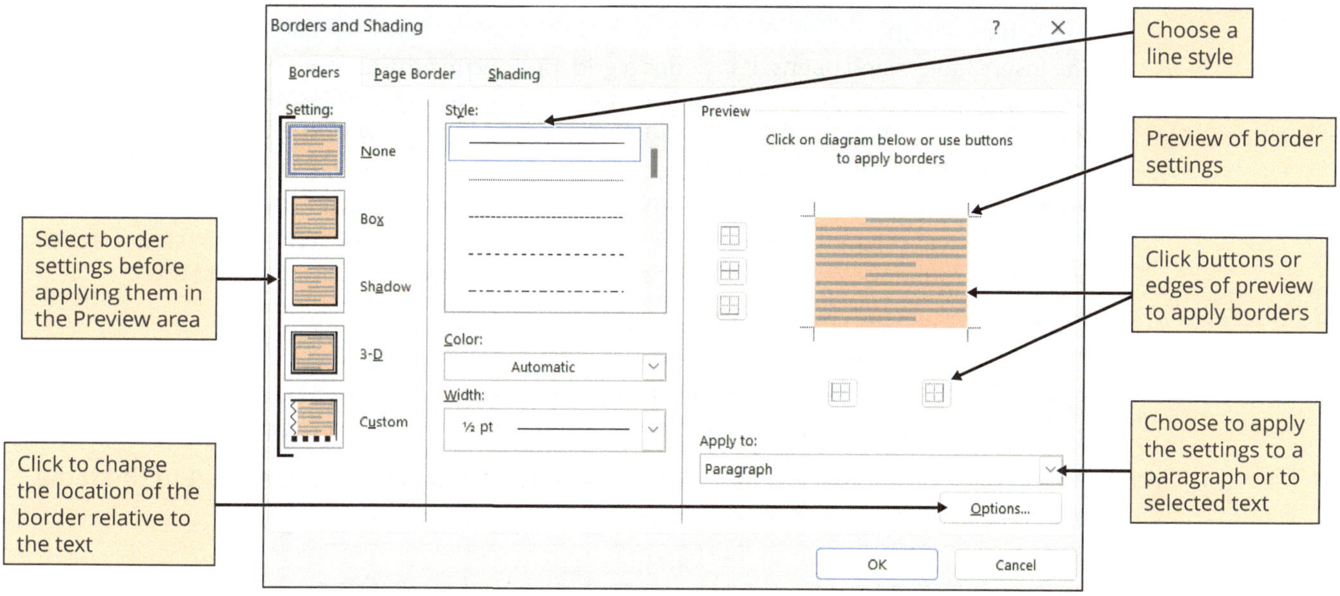

Figure 3-8: Borders and shading applied to the document

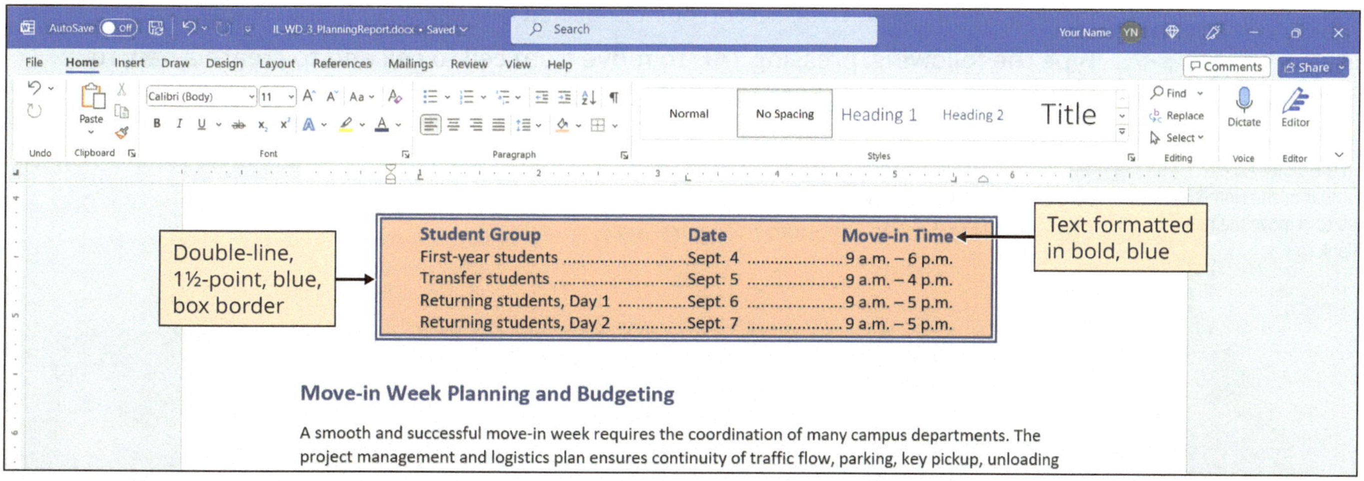

Insert a Table

Case You need to add the budget for move-in week to the report. The budget data will be easiest to read if it is organized as a table, so you insert a blank table and add the data to it.

Objectives
- Insert a table
- Enter table data

Adding a table to a document is a useful way to illustrate information that is intended for quick reference and analysis. A **table** is a grid of columns and rows that you can fill with text and graphics. A **cell** is the box formed by the intersection of a column and a row. The lines that divide the columns and rows of a table and help you see the grid-like structure of the table are called **borders**. A simple way to insert a table into a document is to use the Insert Table command on the Insert tab.

Steps

1. **Scroll down, place the insertion point in the blank paragraph above the Recruiting Move-in Team Volunteers heading, click the Insert tab, then click the Table button in the Tables group**
   The Insert Table menu opens. It includes a grid for selecting the number of columns and rows you want the table to contain, as well as commands for inserting a table. **Table 3-2** describes these commands. As you move the pointer across the grid, a preview of the table with the specified number of columns and rows appears in the document at the location of the insertion point.
2. **Point to the second box in the fourth row to select 2x4 Table, then click**
   A table with two columns and four rows is inserted in the document, as shown in **Figure 3-9**. Black borders surround the table cells. The insertion point is in the first cell in the first row.
3. **Type Expense, then press TAB**
   Pressing TAB moves the insertion point to the next cell in the row.
4. **Type Department, press TAB, then type Traffic and parking**
   Pressing TAB at the end of a row moves the insertion point to the first cell in the next row.
5. **Press TAB, type Transportation, press TAB, then type the following text in the table, pressing TAB to move from cell to cell**

Signage	Printing Services
Move-in staffing and information	Residence Life/Student Services

6. **Press TAB**
   Pressing TAB at the end of the last cell of a table creates a new row at the bottom of the table, as shown in **Figure 3-10**. The insertion point is located in the first cell in the new row.
7. **Type the following, pressing TAB to move from cell to cell and to create a new row**

Technology	IT
Tents and moving equipment	Facilities

8. **Save your changes**
   The completed table is shown in **Figure 3-11**.

Trouble
If you pressed TAB after the last row, click the Undo button on the Quick Access toolbar or the Home tab to remove the new blank row.

Figure 3-9: Blank table

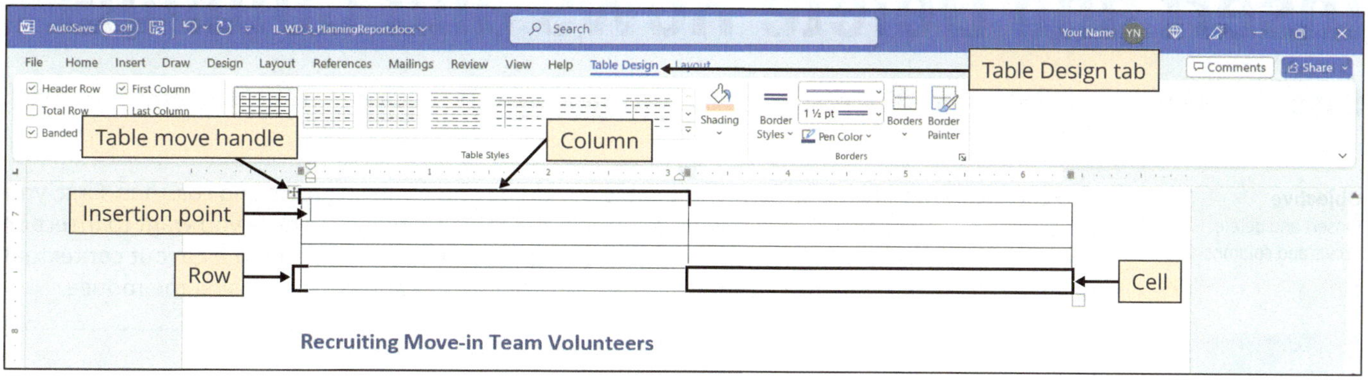

Figure 3-10: New row in table

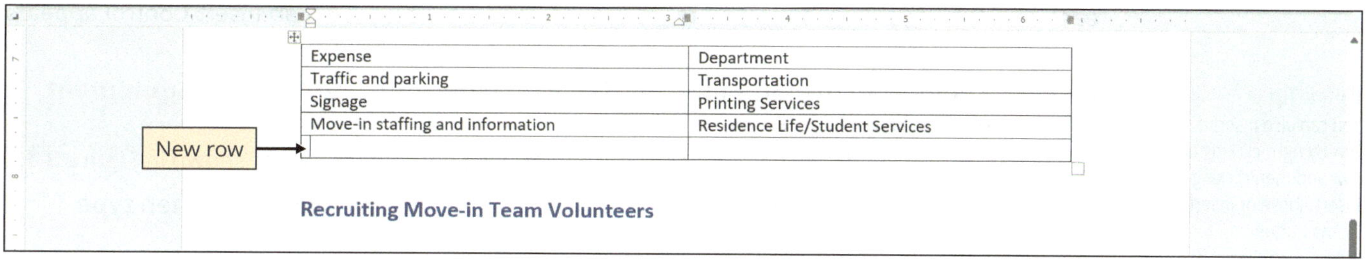

Figure 3-11: Text in the table

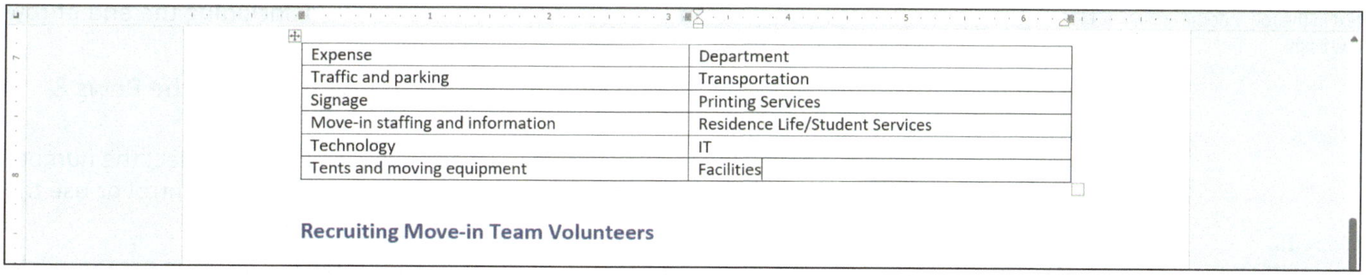

Table 3-2: Table menu commands

command	use to
Insert Table	Create a table with any number of columns and rows and select an AutoFit behavior
Draw Table	Create a complex table by drawing the table columns and rows
Convert Text to Table	Convert text that is separated by tabs, commas, or another separator character into a table
Excel Spreadsheet	Insert a blank Excel worksheet into the document as an embedded object
Quick Tables	Insert a preformatted table template and replace the placeholder data with your own data

Insert and Delete Rows and Columns

Case You add new rows and columns to the table to accommodate more expense data. You also delete the rows that prove to be unnecessary.

Objective
- Insert and delete rows and columns

You can easily modify the structure of a table by adding and removing rows and columns. First, you must click or select an existing row or column in the table to indicate where you want to insert or delete. You can select any element of a table using the Select command on the Layout contextual tab, but it is often more direct to select, add, and delete rows and columns using the mouse.

Steps

1. **Click the Home tab, click the Show/Hide ¶ button [¶] in the Paragraph group to display formatting marks, then move the pointer up and down the left edge of the table**
   An end of cell mark appears at the end of each cell, and an end of row mark appears at the end of each row. When you move the pointer to the left of two existing rows, an Insert Control appears outside the table.

> **Quick Tip**
> You can also insert a row by right-clicking a row and then clicking Insert Above or Insert Below button.

2. **Move the pointer to the left of the border above the Tents and moving equipment row, then click the Insert Control**
   A new row is inserted directly above the Tents and moving equipment row, as shown in **Figure 3-12**.
3. **Click the first cell of the new row, type Water and first aid, press TAB, then type Environmental Health and Safety**

> **Quick Tip**
> If the end of row mark is not selected, you have selected only the text in the row, not the row itself.

4. **Place the pointer in the margin to the left of the Signage row until the pointer changes to ↗, click to select the row, press and hold the mouse button, drag down to select the Move-in staffing and information row, then release the mouse button**
   The Signage and Move-in staffing and information rows are selected, including the end of row marks.
5. **Click the Layout contextual tab, then click the Insert Below button in the Rows & Columns group**
   Two new rows are added below the selected rows. To insert multiple rows, you select the number of rows you want to insert before inserting the rows, and then click an Insert Control or use the buttons on the Ribbon.

> **Quick Tip**
> If you select a row and press DELETE, you delete only the contents of the row, not the row itself.

6. **Click the Technology row, click the Delete button in the Rows & Columns group, click Delete Rows, select the two blank rows, click the Delete button on the Mini toolbar, then click Delete Rows**
   The Technology row and the two blank rows are deleted.

> **Quick Tip**
> To select a cell, place the pointer near the left border of the cell, then click.

7. **Place the pointer over the top border of the Department column until the pointer changes to ⬇, then click to select the entire column**
8. **Click the Insert Right button in the Rows & Columns group, then type Code**
   A new column is inserted to the right of the Department column, as shown in **Figure 3-13**.
9. **Place the pointer over the border between the Department and Code columns at the top of the table, click the Insert Control, then type Budget in the first cell of the new column**
   A new column for Budget is added between the Department and Code columns.

> **Quick Tip**
> You can use the arrow keys or press TAB to move the insertion point from cell to cell.

10. **Press DOWN ARROW to move the insertion point to the next cell in the Budget column, click the Home tab, click [¶] to turn off the display of formatting marks, enter the text shown in Figure 3-14 in each cell in the Budget and Code columns, then save your changes**
    Compare your table to **Figure 3-14**.

Figure 3-12: Inserted row

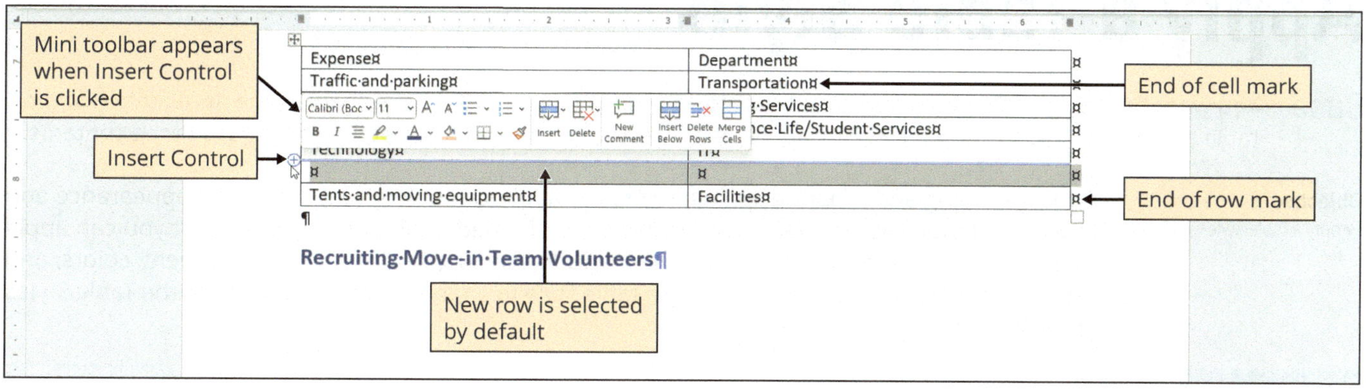

Figure 3-13: Inserted column

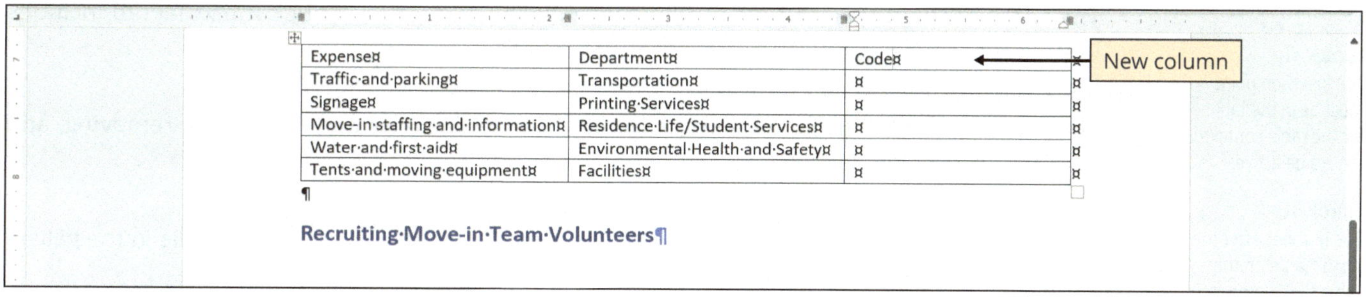

Figure 3-14: Text in Budget and Code columns

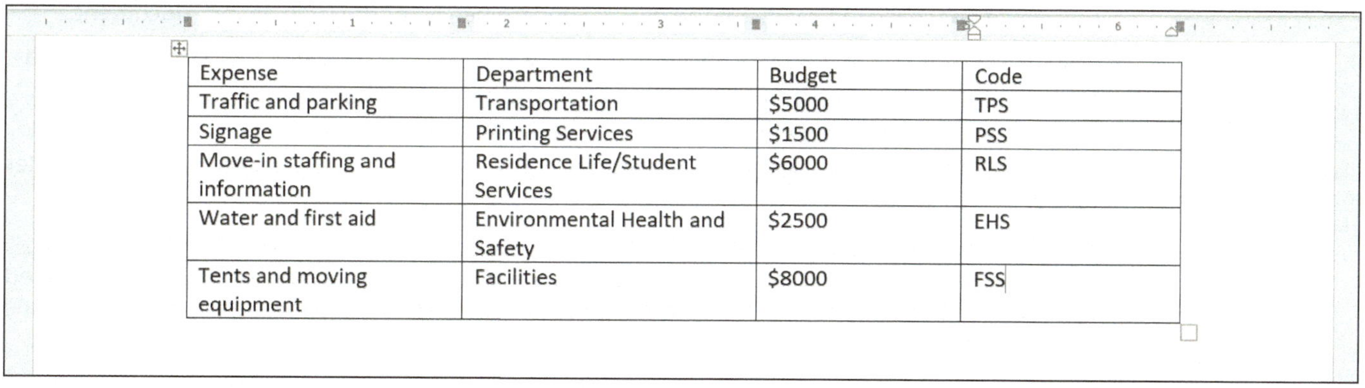

Expense	Department	Budget	Code
Traffic and parking	Transportation	$5000	TPS
Signage	Printing Services	$1500	PSS
Move-in staffing and information	Residence Life/Student Services	$6000	RLS
Water and first aid	Environmental Health and Safety	$2500	EHS
Tents and moving equipment	Facilities	$8000	FSS

Apply a Table Style

Case You want the budget information to stand out, so you apply a table style that enhances the appearance of the table and makes it easier to read. Before applying a style, you adjust the width of the columns to fit the contents.

Objective
- Apply a table style

Adding shading and other design elements to a table can help give it a polished appearance and make the data easier to read. Word includes predefined, built-in table styles that you can apply to a table to format it quickly. Table styles include borders, shading, fonts, alignment, colors, and other formatting effects. You can apply a table style to a table using the buttons in the Table Styles group on the Table Design tab.

Steps

Quick Tip The insertion point must be in the table for the table contextual tabs to be active.

Quick Tip The number after the word "Table" in the Table style name is the row identifier in the gallery of table styles.

Quick Tip Click Clear in the gallery of table styles to remove all borders, shading, and other style elements from a table.

Quick Tip You can also use the Select button in the Table group on the Layout contextual tab to select a table, row, column, or cell.

1. **Click the Layout contextual tab, click the AutoFit button in the Cell Size group, then click AutoFit Contents**
   The width of the table columns is adjusted to fit the text. The Layout contextual tab includes buttons for modifying the structure and size of a table.
2. **Click the Table Design tab**
   The Table Design tab includes buttons for applying table styles and for adding, removing, and customizing borders and shading in a table.
3. **Click the More button in the Table Styles group**
   The gallery of table styles opens, as shown in **Figure 3-15**. You point to a table style in the gallery to preview the style applied to the table.
4. **Move the pointer over the styles in the gallery, then click the Grid Table 5 Dark - Accent 1 style**
   The Grid Table 5 Dark - Accent 1 style is applied to the table, as shown in **Figure 3-16**. This style makes the data easier to read, but the dark colors are heavy for the tone of your document.
5. **Click the scroll arrows in the Table Styles group to scroll the gallery of styles, point to several styles to see each style applied to the table, click the More button in the Table Styles group, then click the Grid Table 3 - Accent 3 style**
   The Grid Table 3 - Accent 3 style is applied to the table. This style makes the table data easier to read.
6. **In the Table Style Options group, click the Banded Rows check box to clear it**
   The shading is removed from alternating rows in the table. When the banded columns or banded rows setting is active, the odd columns or rows are formatted differently from the even columns or rows to make the table data easier to read.
7. **Select the first column of the table, click the Font Color arrow on the Mini toolbar, click Orange, Accent 2, Darker 50%, select the first row of the table, click , then click Blue, Accent 1, Darker 25%**
   The text in the first column is dark orange and the text in the header row is blue.
8. **Select the Budget and Code columns, then click the Center button on the Mini toolbar**
   The text in the Budget and Code columns is center-aligned. You can also use the buttons in the Alignment group on the Layout contextual tab to change the alignment of text in cells.
9. **Click the table move handle, click the Home tab, click the Center button in the Paragraph group on the Ribbon, then deselect the table**
   Clicking the table move handle selects the entire table. Clicking the Center button with the entire table selected centered the table between the margins, as shown in **Figure 3-17**.
10. **Press CTRL+HOME, then save your changes**

Figure 3-15: Gallery of table styles

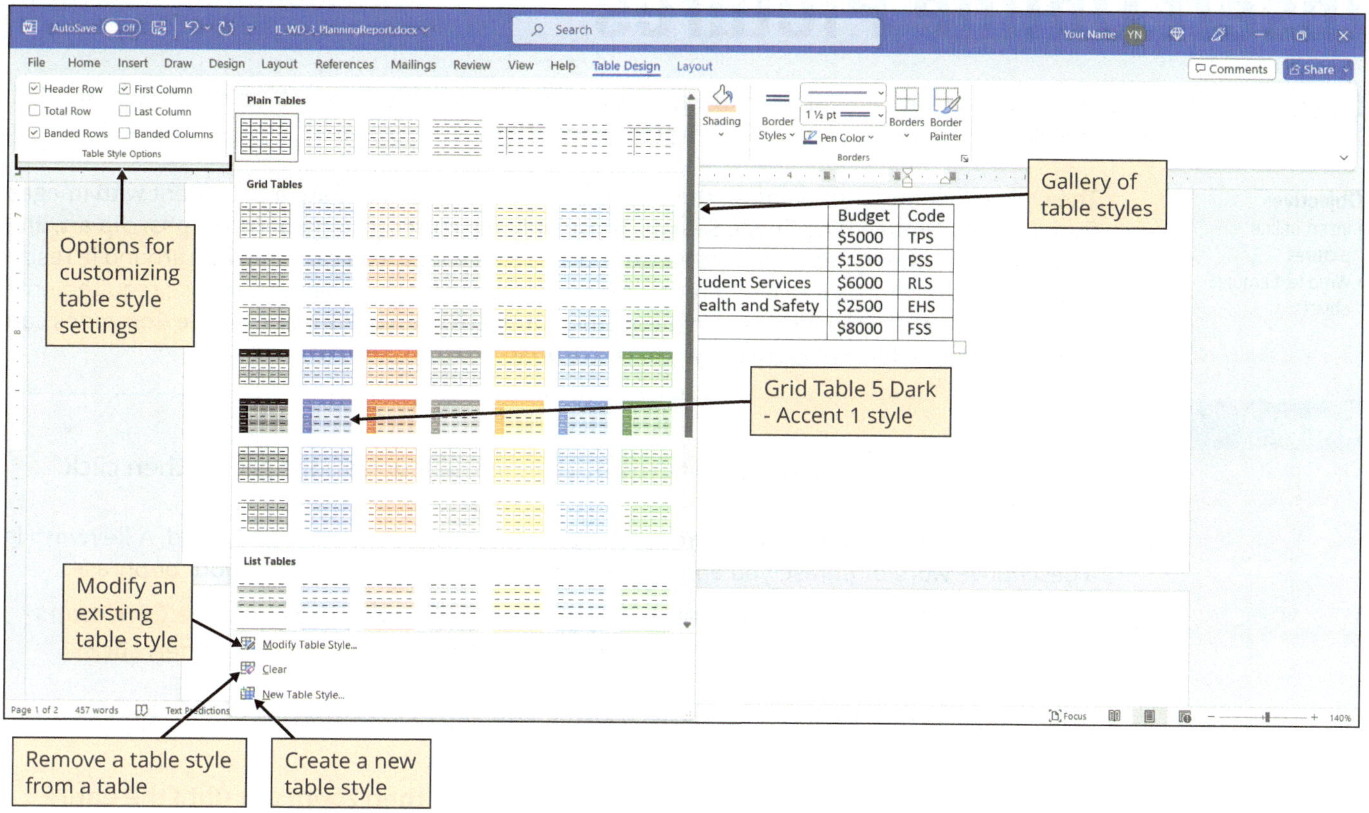

Figure 3-16: Grid Table 5 Dark - Accent 1 style applied to table

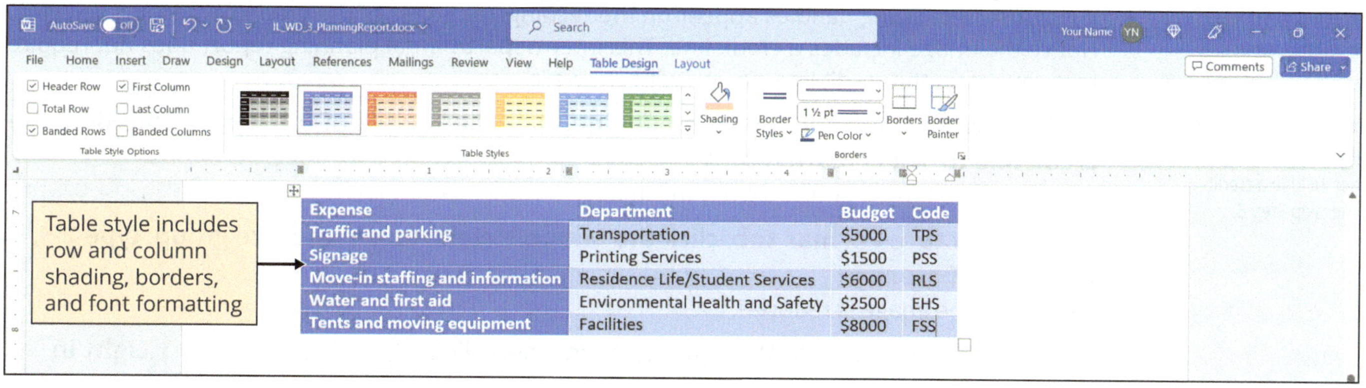

Figure 3-17: Completed table

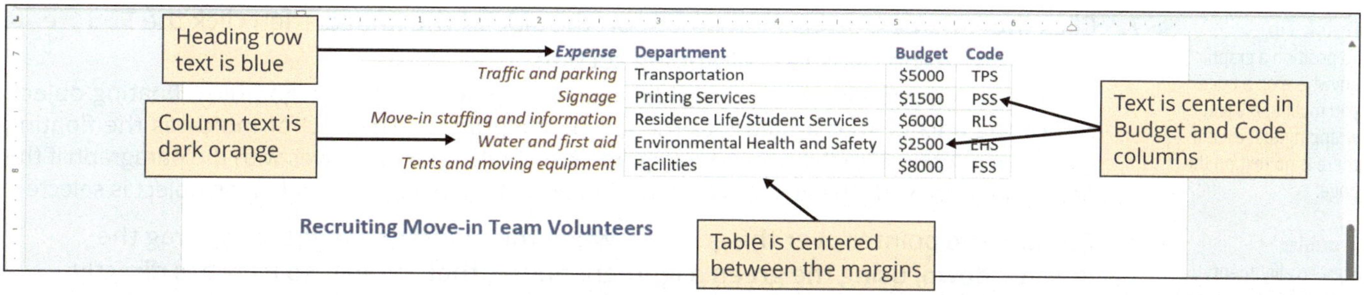

Insert Online Pictures

Case You illustrate the document with an online image that expresses the upbeat mood of move-in day. Note: To complete this lesson, your computer must be connected to the Internet.

Objectives
- Insert online pictures
- Wrap text around objects

The Online Pictures command on the Insert tab allows you to illustrate a document with images found online through Bing Image Search. These online pictures include photographs, clip art, line drawings, and other types of images. Once you insert an image, you can wrap text around it, resize it, enhance it, and move it to a different location. Always carefully review any license requirements for an image before you include it in a document. Images licensed under Creative Commons can be used by the public but carry copyright restrictions.

Steps

1. **Click the Insert tab, click the Pictures button in the Illustrations group, then click Online Pictures**
   The Online Pictures window opens. You can search for images related to a keyword. A **keyword** is a descriptive word or phrase you enter to obtain an image described by the word or phrase.
2. **Type college students in the search box, press ENTER, click the Creative Commons only check box if it is not already selected, click the Filter button, then click Clipart**
   Clip art images that have the keywords "college students" associated with them appear in the Online Pictures window, as shown in **Figure 3-18**.

Trouble
Select a different image that has similar rectangular dimensions if the image shown in **Figure 3-18** is not available to you.

3. **Click the image called out in Figure 3-18, click Insert, then zoom out until the entire image is visible on your screen**
   The image is inserted as an inline graphic at the location of the insertion point, as shown in **Figure 3-19**. Until you apply text wrapping to an inline graphic, it is part of the line of text in which it was inserted. Sizing handles appear on the rectangular edges of the graphic when it is selected. Notice the image includes a credit line. This inter-departmental planning report does not require that you retain the credit line, so you will remove it.

Trouble
If your graphic does not include a credit line, skip Step 5.

4. **Click the word Unknown in the credit line, click the border of the box surrounding the credit line to select it, then press DELETE**
   The credit line box is removed from the image.
5. **Click the Picture Format tab, click the Shape Height box in the Size group, type 2.5, then press Enter**
   The size of the image is reduced.
6. **Click the Color button in the Adjust group, then click Blue, Accent color 1 Light in the Recolor section**
   The color of the image changes from multi-colored to shades of blue. To move a graphic independently of the line of text in which it was inserted, you must make it a floating graphic.

Quick Tip
To position a graphic anywhere on a page, you must apply text wrapping to it even if there is no text on the page.

7. **Click the Layout Options button on the side of the image, then click the Square button in the With Text Wrapping section**
   The text wraps around the square sides of the graphic, making the graphic a floating object. Notice the anchor that appears to the left of the graphic. The anchor indicates the floating graphic is **anchored** to the nearest paragraph so that the graphic moves with the paragraph if the paragraph is moved. The anchor is a nonprinting symbol that appears when an object is selected.

Trouble
If green alignment guides do not appear, click the Align Objects button in the Arrange group, then click Use Alignment Guides.

8. **Position the pointer over the graphic, when the pointer changes to ✥, drag the graphic down, using the green alignment guides that appear, so its top is directly under the document title and its left aligns with the left margin, as shown in Figure 3-20, then release the mouse button**
   The graphic is positioned below the title on the left side of the page.
9. **Deselect the graphic, then save your changes**

Figure 3-18: Online Pictures window

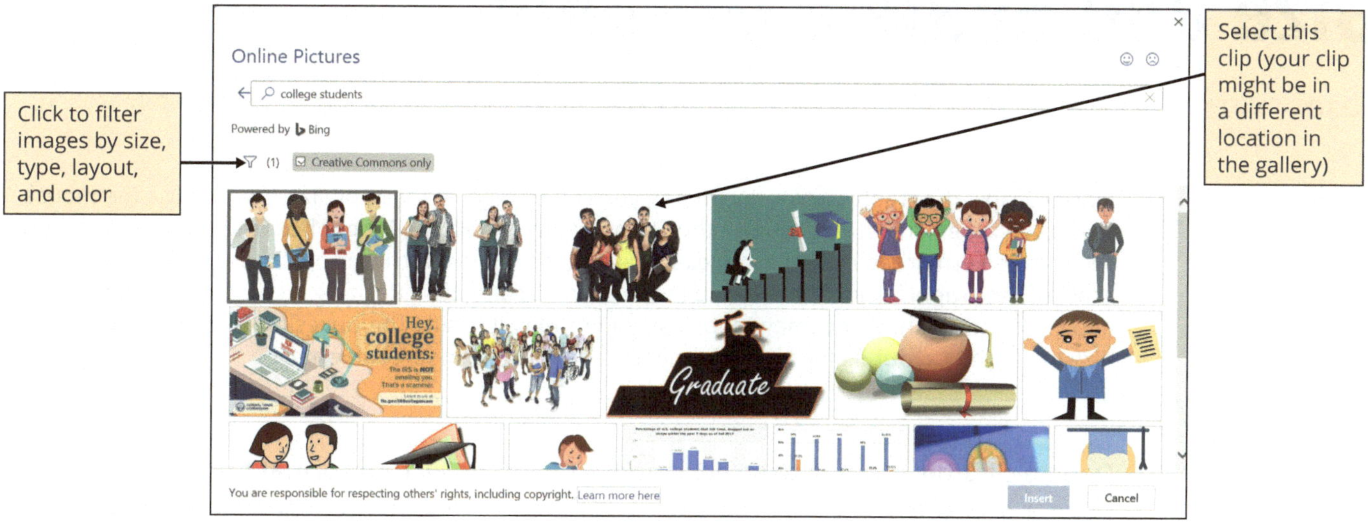

Figure 3-19: Inline graphic

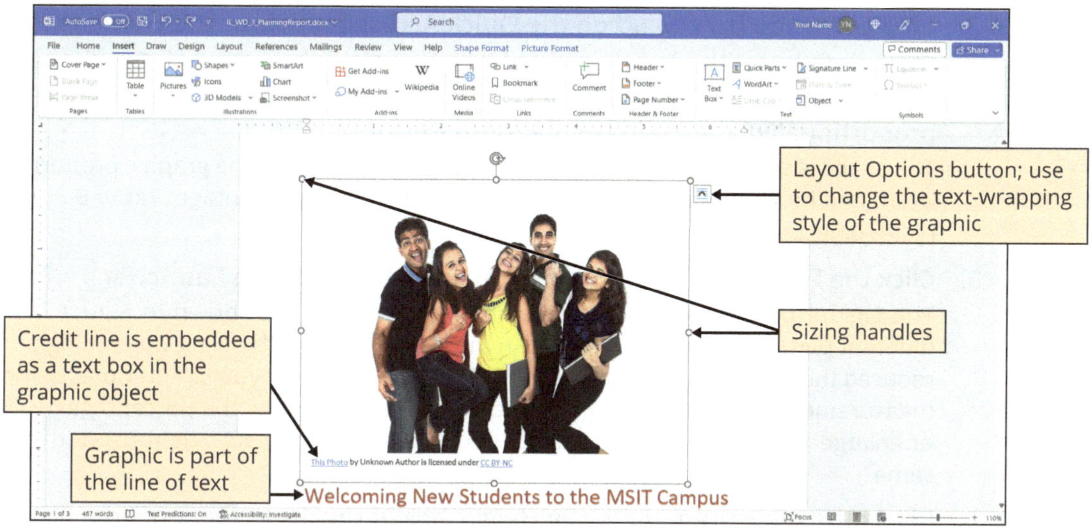

Figure 3-20: Graphic being moved to a new location

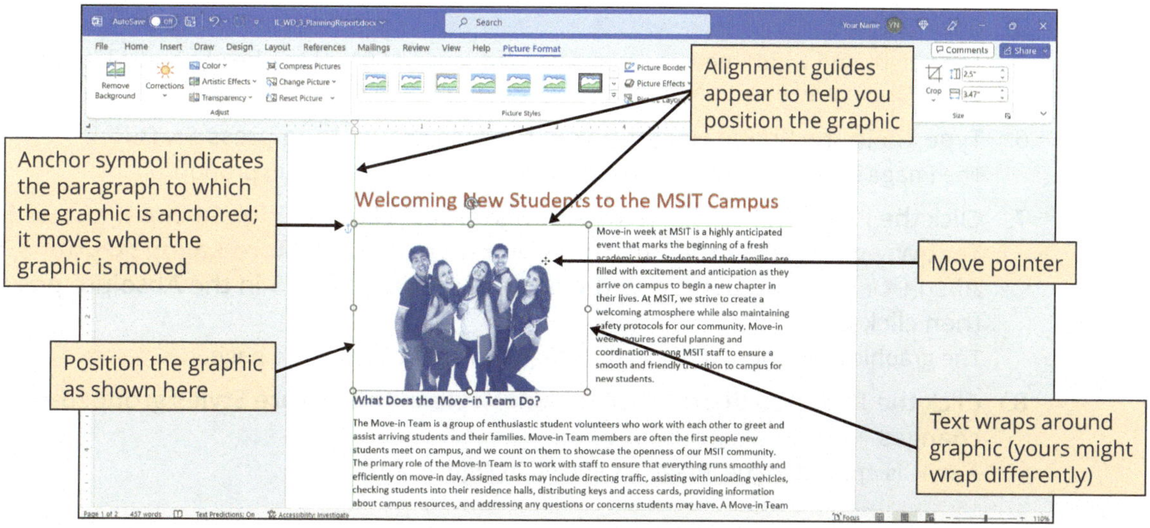

Size and Scale a Graphic

Case You reduce the size of the graphic and position it precisely on the page so that the text wraps smoothly around the graphic.

Objectives
- Resize a graphic
- Scale a graphic
- Position a graphic

Once you insert a graphic into a document, you can change its shape or size. You can use the mouse to drag a sizing handle, you can use the Shape Width and Shape Height boxes in the Size group on the Picture Format tab to specify an exact height and width for the graphic, or you can change the scale of the graphic using the Size tab in the Layout dialog box. Resizing a graphic with the mouse allows you to see how the image looks as you modify it. Using the boxes in the Size group or the Size tab in the Layout dialog box allows you to set precise measurements.

Steps

1. **Double-click the graphic to select it and activate the Picture Format tab, place the pointer over the middle-right sizing handle, when the pointer changes to ⇔, drag to the left until the graphic is about 2" wide**
   Refer to the ruler as you drag. When you release the mouse button, the image is taller than it is wide. Dragging a side, top, or bottom sizing handle changes only the width or height of a graphic.

Quick Tip
As you drag the corner handle, refer to the measurements in the Size group on the Ribbon to best approximate the size of the image.

2. **Click the Undo button on the Quick Access toolbar or the Home tab, place the pointer over the lower-right sizing handle, when the pointer changes to ⤡, drag up and to the left until the graphic is about 2.5" wide (the height will adjust proportionally), then release the mouse button**
   The image is smaller. Dragging a corner sizing handle resizes the graphic proportionally so that its width and height are reduced or enlarged by the same percentage. **Table 3-3** describes ways to resize objects using the mouse.

3. **Click the Picture Format tab if necessary, then click the Launcher in the Size group**
   The Layout dialog box opens with the Size tab active, as shown in **Figure 3-21**. Note that a different percentage may be entered in the Height and Width boxes, depending on how much you reduced the size of the graphic in Step 2. The Size tab allows you to enter precise height and width measurements for a graphic or to scale a graphic by entering the percentage you want to reduce or enlarge it by. When a graphic is sized to **scale** (or scaled), its height-to-width ratio remains the same.

Quick Tip
Deselect the Lock aspect ratio check box if you want to change a graphic's proportions.

4. **Select the measurement in the Height box in the Scale section, type 50, then click the Width box in the Scale section**
   The scale of the width changes to 50% and the Absolute measurements in the Height and Width sections decrease proportionally.

5. **Click OK**
   The height and width measurements are reduced to 50% of the height and width measurements in the Original size section of the dialog box.

6. **Type 1.5 in the Shape Height box in the Size group, then press ENTER**
   The image is enlarged to be 1.5" high, with the width changed in proportion.

7. **Click the Position button in the Arrange group, click Position in Top Right with Square Text Wrapping, click the Position button again, click More Layout Options, click the Absolute position button in the Vertical section, type .6 in the Absolute position box, then click OK**
   The graphic is positioned below the title on the right side of the page.

8. **Click the Dropped Shadow Rectangle style in the Picture Styles group, then save your changes**
   A style is applied to the image, as shown in **Figure 3-22**.

Figure 3-21: Size tab in the Layout dialog box

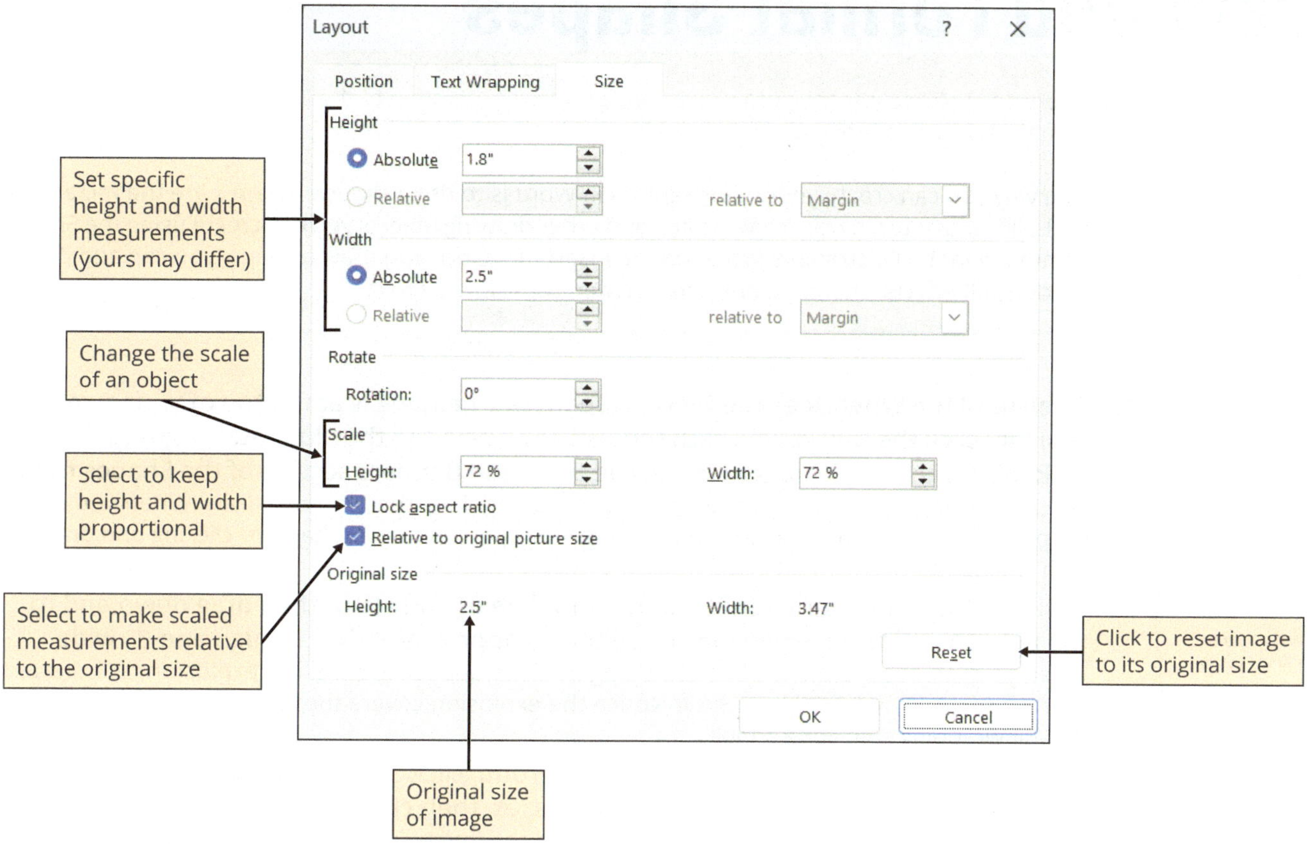

Figure 3-22: Style applied to resized image

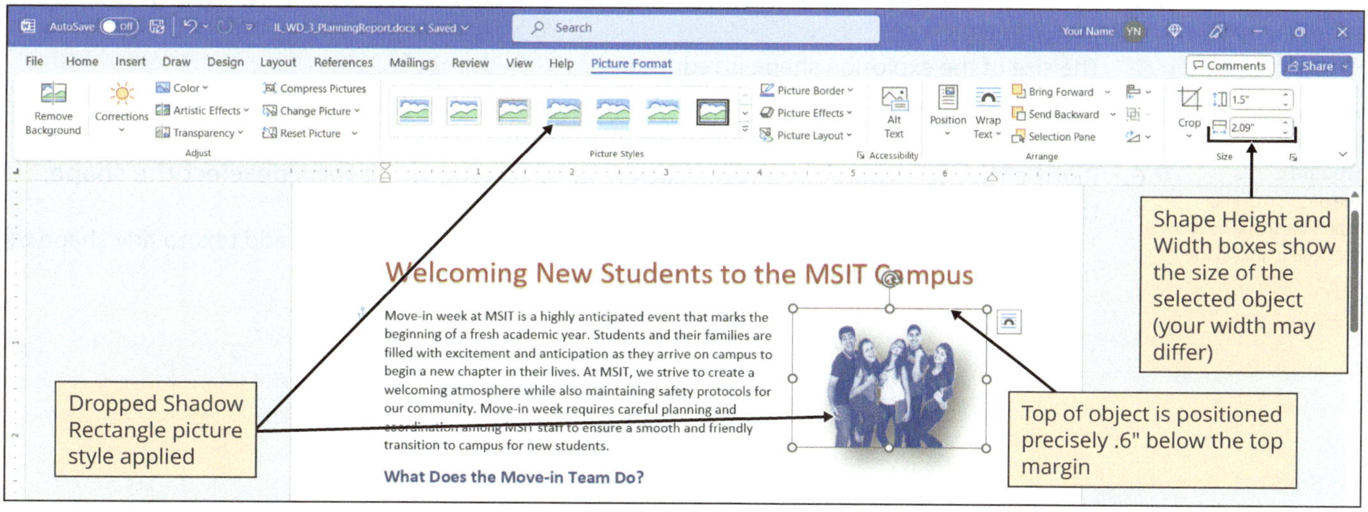

Table 3-3: Methods for resizing an object using the mouse

do this	to
Drag a corner sizing handle	Resize a clip art or bitmap graphic and maintain its proportions
Press SHIFT and drag a corner sizing handle	Resize any graphic object and maintain its proportions
Press CTRL and drag a side, top, or bottom sizing handle	Resize any graphic object vertically or horizontally while keeping the center position fixed
Press CTRL and drag a corner sizing handle	Resize any graphic object diagonally while keeping the center position fixed
Press SHIFT+CTRL and drag a corner sizing handle	Resize any graphic object while keeping the center position fixed and maintaining its proportions

Draw and Format Shapes

Case You add visual interest to the document by drawing a shape that calls attention to the Move-in Team information, and then you format, resize, arrange, and add text to it.

Objectives
- Insert a shape
- Apply styles to objects

One way you can create your own graphics in Word is to draw shapes. **Shapes** are the rectangles, ovals, lines, callouts, block arrows, stars, and other drawing objects you can create using the Shapes command in the Illustrations group on the Insert tab. Once you draw a shape, you can add colors, borders, fill effects, shadows, and three-dimensional effects to it.

Steps

1. **Scroll until the What Does the Move-in Team Do? heading is at the top of your screen, zoom in, click the Insert tab, click the Shapes button in the Illustrations group, then click the Explosion: 8 points icon in the Stars and Banners section of the Shapes menu**
   The Shapes menu contains categories of shapes and lines that you can draw. When you click a shape in the Shapes menu, the pointer changes to +. You draw a shape by clicking and dragging with this pointer.

2. **Position the + pointer over The in the first line of body text, then drag down and to the right to create an explosion shape that is approximately 1.5" high and 2" wide**
   When you release the mouse button, sizing handles appear around the explosion to indicate it is selected, as shown in **Figure 3-23**. Notice the explosion covers the text. In Front of Text is the default wrapping style for a shape.

3. **Click the More button in the Shape Styles group, click Subtle Effect - Blue Accent 1, click the Shape Effects button, point to Preset, then click Preset 1**
   The color of the shape changes to light blue and the image is formatted with a preset style that includes a shadow, bevel, and white contour.

4. **Type 1 in the Height box in the Size group, press TAB, type 1.5 in the Width box, then press ENTER**
   The size of the explosion shape is reduced.

5. **Click the Wrap Text button in the Arrange group, then click Tight**
   The text wraps to the jagged shape of the image.

6. **Right-click the explosion shape, click Add Text, type Have fun!, deselect the shape, then save your document**
   Text is added to the explosion shape, as shown in **Figure 3-24**. You can add text to any shape by right-clicking it and then clicking Add Text or Edit Text.

Quick Tip
To draw a perfect square or circle, click the Rectangle or Oval shape on the menu, then press SHIFT while you drag with the pointer.

Quick Tip
You can also use the Layout Options button to change the text wrapping style applied to an object.

Trouble
The position of your explosion shape does not need to match the figure exactly.

Figure 3-23: Shape in document

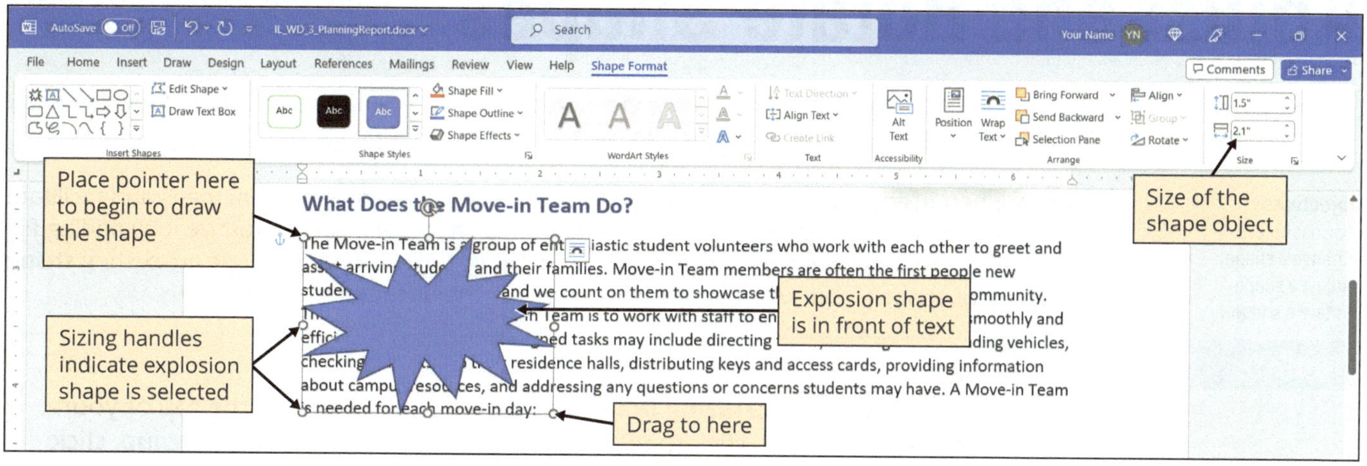

Figure 3-24: Text added to shape

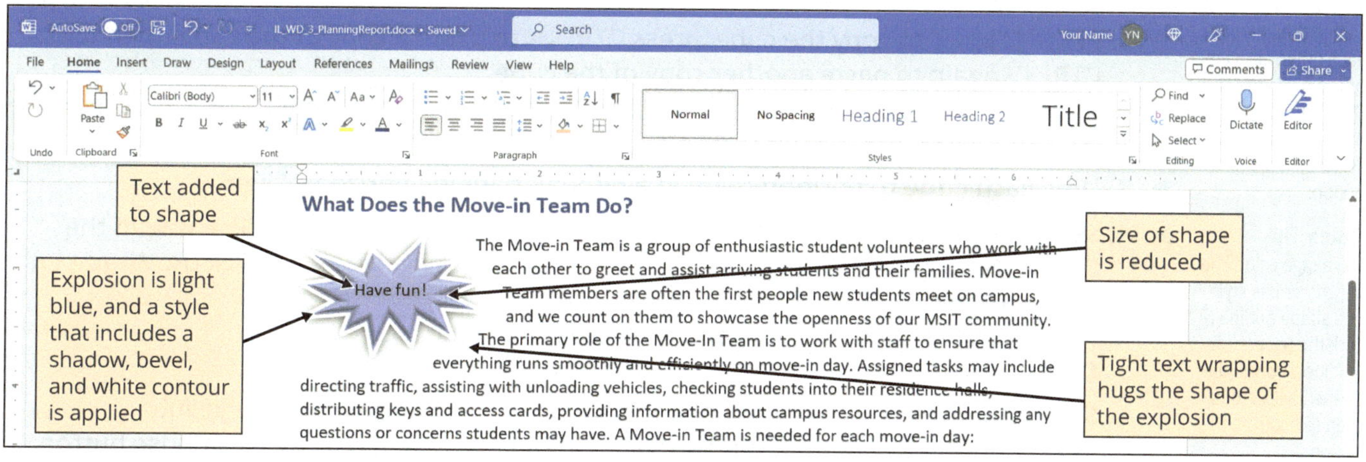

Correcting pictures, changing colors, and applying artistic effects

The Corrections command in the Adjust group on the Picture Format tab allows you to adjust a picture's relative lightness **(brightness)**, alter the difference between its darkest and lightest areas **(contrast)**, and change the sharpness of an image. To make these adjustments, select the image and then click the Corrections button to open a gallery of preset percentages applied to the selected picture. Point to an option in the gallery to preview it in the document; click an option in the gallery to apply it. You can also fine-tune brightness, contrast, or sharpness by clicking Picture Corrections Options in the Corrections gallery, and then using the sliders in the Picture Corrections section of the Format Picture pane to adjust the percentage.

The Color command in the Adjust group is used to change the vividness and intensity of color in an image **(color saturation)**, and to change the "temperature" of a photo by bringing out the cooler blue tones or the warmer orange tones **(color tone)**. The Color command is also used to recolor a picture to give it a stylized effect, such as sepia tone, grayscale, or duotone (using theme colors). To make changes to the colors in a picture, select it, click the Color button, and then select one of the color modes or variations in the gallery that opens, or click Picture Color Options to fine-tune color settings using the Format Picture pane.

The Artistic Effects command in the Adjust group allows you to make a photo look like a drawing, a painting, a photocopy, a sketch, or some other artistic medium. To experiment with applying an artistic effect, select a photo, click the Artistic Effects button, and then point to each effect to preview it applied to the photo.

After you adjust a picture, you can undo any changes by clicking the Reset Picture arrow in the Adjust group. This command discards all formatting changes made to a picture, including size, cropping, borders, and effects.

Adjust and Rotate Shapes

Case You decide to illustrate page 2 of the document with shapes that suggest moving boxes. You start by drawing cube shapes, and then you format, adjust, and resize each cube shape to be unique.

Objectives
- Format objects
- Change a shape
- Adjust a shape
- Rotate a shape

Shapes, when used appropriately, can be used as visual cues to help present ideas and facilitate the message of a document. Once you have inserted a shape, you can customize it by adding fill, adjusting its interior proportions, resizing it, and rotating it. You can also change an existing shape to a different shape to see which shape works best for the document.

Steps

1. **Scroll until the heading Recruiting Move-in Team Volunteers is at the top of your screen, click the Insert tab, click the Shapes button in the Illustrations group, click the Cube icon in the Basic Shapes section of the Shapes menu, then click a blank area of page 2**

   A 1.33" cube shape is inserted in the document.

Quick Tip
To align shapes with each other, select two or more shapes, click the Align button in the Arrange group, then select an alignment option.

2. **Press CTRL+C to copy the cube, press CTRL+V to paste a copy of the cube, then press CTRL+V again to paste another copy of the cube**

   Two cubes are pasted for a total of three overlapping cubes. These pasted objects have the same text wrapping style as the source object—In Front of Text.

3. **Drag each cube to position them in a non-overlapping horizontal line**

Quick Tip
To change color, line weight, or line style of a shape outline, click the Shape Outline arrow in the Shape Styles group, then select from the options.

4. **Select the first cube, click the Shape Format tab, click the Shape Fill arrow in the Shape Styles group, click Orange, Accent 2, select the third cube, click the Shape Fill arrow, then click Blue, Accent 1, Lighter 40%**

   The first cube is orange, the second cube is blue, and the third cube is light blue, as shown in **Figure 3-25**.

5. **Select the orange cube (the first cube), position the pointer over the yellow adjustment handle, drag the handle up about 1/8", then release the mouse button**

   Dragging an adjustment handle changes the internal proportions of a shape. The orange cube becomes taller and shallower.

6. **Select the light blue cube (the third cube), drag the yellow adjustment handle down about 1/2", then release the mouse button**

   The light blue cube becomes shorter and deeper.

7. **Select the orange cube, position the pointer over the top right sizing handle, drag down and left until the cube is approximately .8" high and .9" wide, select the light blue cube, position the pointer over the top right sizing handle, then drag down and right until the cube is approximately 1" high and 2" wide**

   The cubes are resized to be unique from each other. The measurements don't have to be exact.

Quick Tip
To rotate a graphic object 90 degrees, click the Rotate Objects button in the Arrange group, then click Rotate Right or Rotate Left. To flip a graphic object, click the Rotate Objects button, then click Flip Vertical or Flip Horizontal.

8. **Select the orange cube, press CTRL+C, press CTRL+V, drag the copied cube to a blank area, click the Edit Shape button in the Insert Shapes group, point to Change Shape, then click the Star: 5 points icon in the Stars and Banners section**

   The rectangle changes to a star. Notice that changing the object shape does not change the format settings applied to the object.

9. **Drag the yellow adjustment handle in the star down about 1/8"**

   The star becomes narrower.

10. **Drag the rotate handle on the star right about 1/4", then save your changes**

    The star is rotated right, as shown in **Figure 3-26**.

Figure 3-25: Cubes with fill color applied

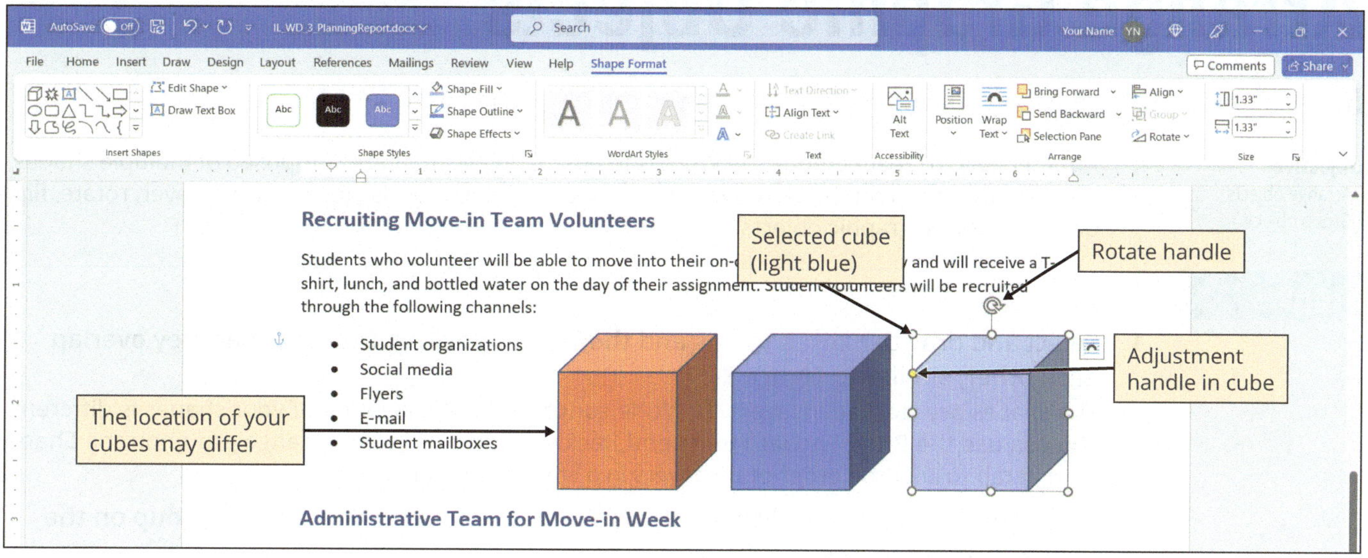

Figure 3-26: Cube shapes adjusted and resized, and star shape adjusted and rotated

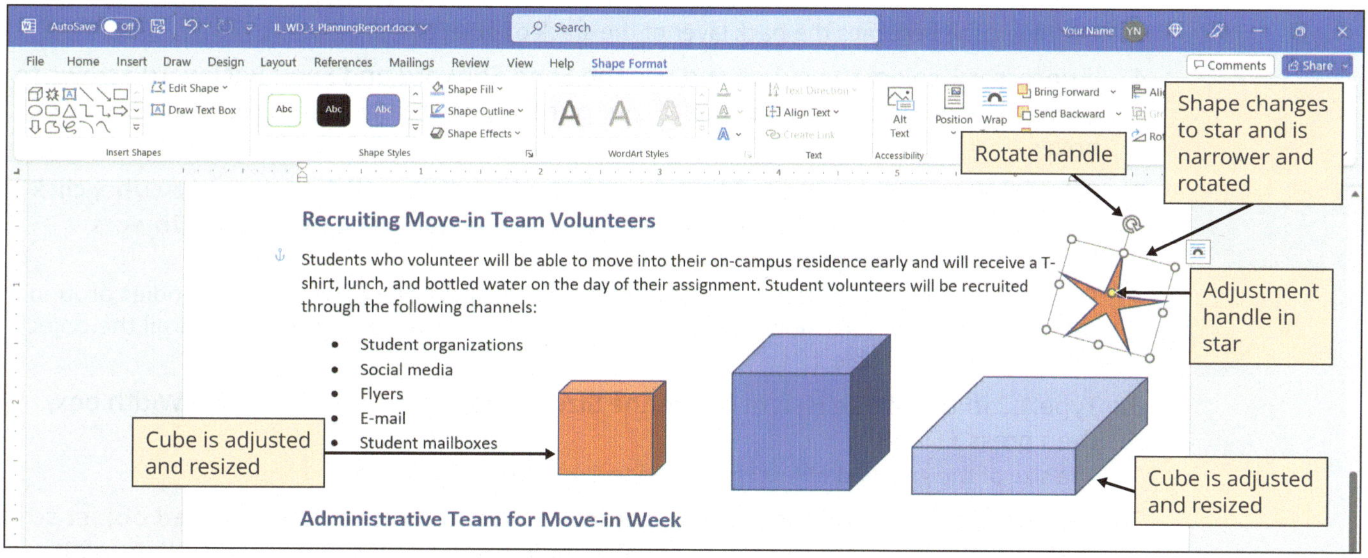

Enhancing graphic objects with styles and effects

Another way to make a document fun and visually appealing for the reader is to apply a style or an effect to a graphic object. To apply a style, select the object and then choose from the style options in the Styles group on the active Format tab for that type of object. Styles include a preset mixture of effects, such as shading, borders, shadows, and other settings. The Effects command in the Styles group on the active Format tab gives you the power to apply a customized variety of effects to an object, including a shadow, bevel, glow, reflection, soft edge, or 3-D rotation. To apply an effect, select the object, click the Effects command for that type of object, point to the type of effect you want to apply, and then select from the options in the gallery that opens. To further customize an effect, click the Options command for that type of effect at the bottom of the gallery to open the Format Shape pane. The best way to learn about styles and effects is to experiment by applying them to an object and seeing what works.

Arrange Graphic Objects

Case You group the four shapes into a single object that you can resize and position easily.

Objectives
- Arrange objects
- Group objects

Another way to create graphics in Word is to create objects that are composed of multiple shapes. The Arrange group on the Shape Format tab includes commands you can use to layer, rotate, flip, align, and group graphic objects.

Steps

1. **Select and drag the three cubes and the star to position them so that they overlap each other, similar to Figure 3-27**
   The shapes are stacked in layers. Don't be concerned if the layering of your shapes is different. You can use the Bring Forward and Send Backward arrows in the Arrange group on the Shape Format tab to shift the order of the layers in a stack of graphic objects.
2. **Select the orange cube, click the Bring Forward arrow in the Arrange group on the Shape Format tab, then click Bring to Front**
   The orange cube becomes the front layer of the stack of objects.
3. **Select the blue cube, click the Send Backward arrow in the Arrange group, then click Send to Back**
   The blue cube becomes the back layer of the stack of objects.
4. **If necessary, select the cubes and use the Send Forward and Send Backward arrows to change the order of the layers until the four shapes are layered to resemble a stack of boxes**
5. **Select the star, press and hold CTRL, click the blue cube, click the orange cube, click the light blue cube so that all four shapes are selected, click the Group Objects button in the Arrange group, then click Group**
   The four cube objects and the star object become a single object with sizing handles around a surrounding border, as shown in Figure 3-28. Any formatting applied will affect all the objects within the grouped object.
6. **Type 1.2 in the Shape Height box in the Size group, type 1.6 in the Shape Width box, then press ENTER**
   The size of the grouped object is reduced to 1.2" high and 1.6" wide.
7. **Use the pointer and the green alignment guides to position the grouped object so that its top aligns with the top of the first bullet point and the right side aligns with the right margin, as shown in Figure 3-29, then release the mouse button**
   The grouped object is positioned below the first body paragraph on the right side of the page.
8. **Save your changes**

Figure 3-27: Cubes layered in document

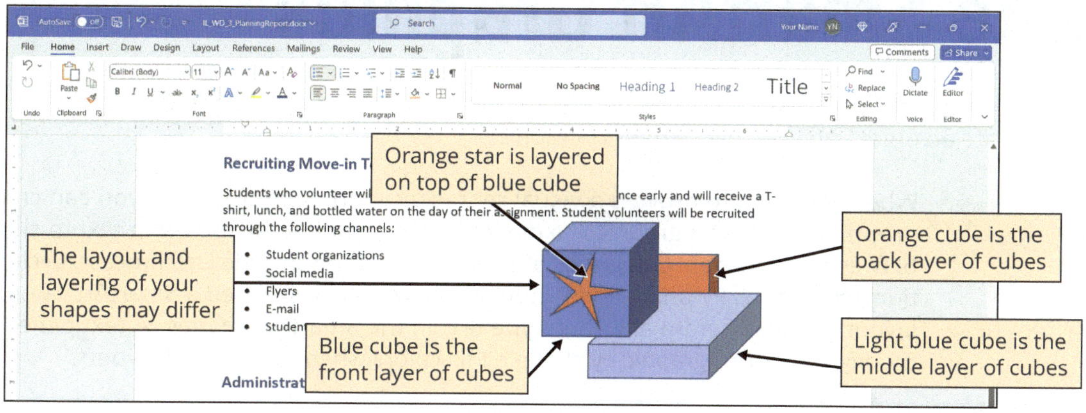

Figure 3-28: Grouped object

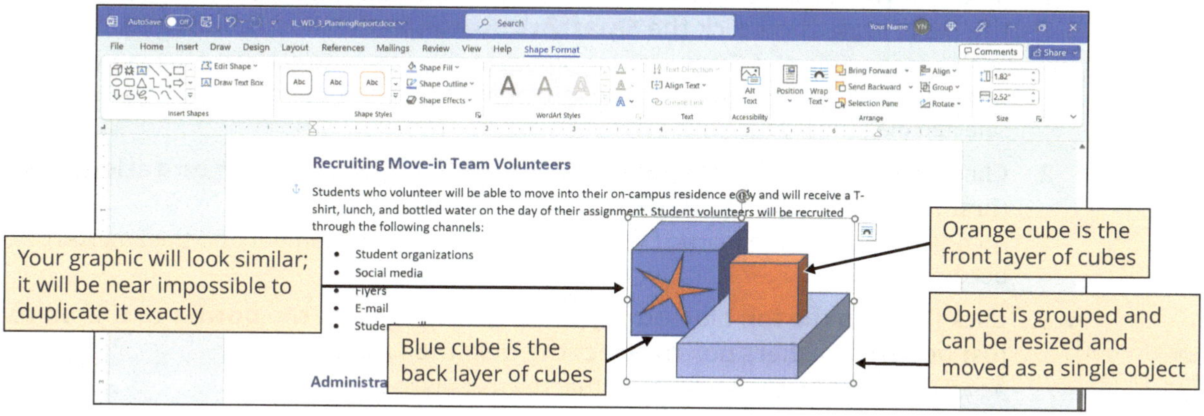

Figure 3-29: Positioning the grouped object

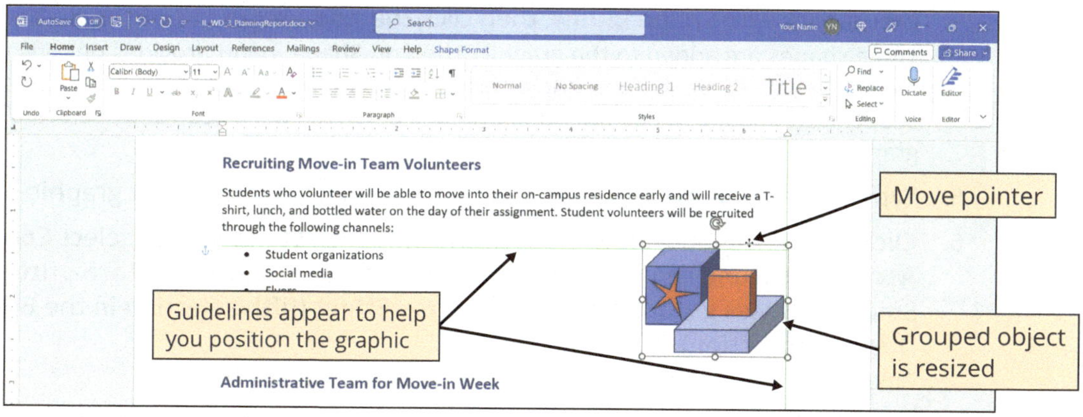

Creating an illustration in a drawing canvas

A **drawing canvas** is a workspace for creating your own graphics. It provides a frame-like boundary between an illustration and the rest of the document so that the illustration can be sized, formatted, and positioned like a single graphic object. If you are creating an illustration that includes multiple shapes, such as a flow chart, it is helpful to create the illustration in a drawing canvas. To draw shapes or lines in a drawing canvas, click the Shapes button in the Illustrations group on the Insert tab, click New Drawing Canvas to open a drawing canvas in the document, and then create and format your illustration in the drawing canvas. When you are finished, right-click the border of the drawing canvas and then click Fit to resize the drawing canvas to fit the illustration. You can then resize the illustration by dragging a border of the drawing canvas. Once you have resized a drawing canvas, you can wrap text around it and position it. By default, a drawing canvas has no border or background so that it is transparent in a document, but you can add fill and borders to it if you wish.

Create SmartArt Graphics

Case To help recipients of the planning document better understand the management structure for move-in week, you create an organizational chart SmartArt graphic.

Objectives
- Insert SmartArt
- Customize SmartArt

When you want to provide a visual representation of information, you can create a **SmartArt graphic**. A SmartArt graphic is a diagram that combines shapes with text to show relationships between information. Categories of SmartArt diagrams include List, Process, Cycle, Hierarchy, Relationship, Matrix, Pyramid, and Picture. Once you have selected a SmartArt category, you select a layout for the diagram and then type text in the SmartArt shapes or text pane. You can further modify a SmartArt graphic by changing fill colors, shape styles, and layouts.

Steps

1. **Scroll down, select [Org chart here.] under the Administrative Team... heading, click the Insert tab, then click the SmartArt button in the Illustrations group**
   The Choose a SmartArt Graphic dialog box opens. You use it to select the category of diagram you want to create and the layout and design for the diagram. The right pane shows a preview of the selected diagram layout.
2. **Click Hierarchy in the left pane, select the Name and Title Organization Chart style (first row, third column) in the middle pane, then click OK**
   An organization chart SmartArt object is inserted in the document and the SmartArt Design tab becomes active.
3. **Click [Text] in the top blue box, type Rachel Tong, click the border of the white box just beneath Rachel's box to select the box, then type Director**
   As you type, the font size adjusts so that the text fits in each text box.

   Quick Tip
   You can type directly in the shapes, or you can use the text pane to enter the text.
4. **Click the blue box below and to the left to select it, press DELETE, click the right-most blue box in the bottom row to select it, click the Add Shape arrow in the Create Graphic group, click Add Shape Below, then click the Add Shape button again two times**
   Three shapes are added to the graphic. The Add Shape menu provides options for adding more shapes below, above, before, and after to your SmartArt graphic. You can also add an Assistant shape. New shapes will be added depending on which box is currently selected in the SmartArt graphic.
5. **Type the text shown in Figure 3-30 in each box of the SmartArt graphic**
6. **Click the Change Colors button in the SmartArt Styles group, select Colored Fill - Accent 2 (second selection in the Accent 2 section), click the More button in the SmartArt Styles group, then click Intense Effect (fifth selection in the Best Match for Document section)**
   Color and a SmartArt style are applied to the organizational chart.
7. **Click the Olga McMahon box to select it, click the Format tab, click the Shape Fill arrow in the Shape Styles section, then click Blue, Accent 1**
   The orange box changes to blue. You can also format each element of a SmartArt graphic individually.
8. **Click outside the object to deselect it, save your changes, click the View tab, then click Multiple Pages in the Zoom group**
   The completed document layout is shown in **Figure 3-31**.

Figure 3-30: Organizational chart

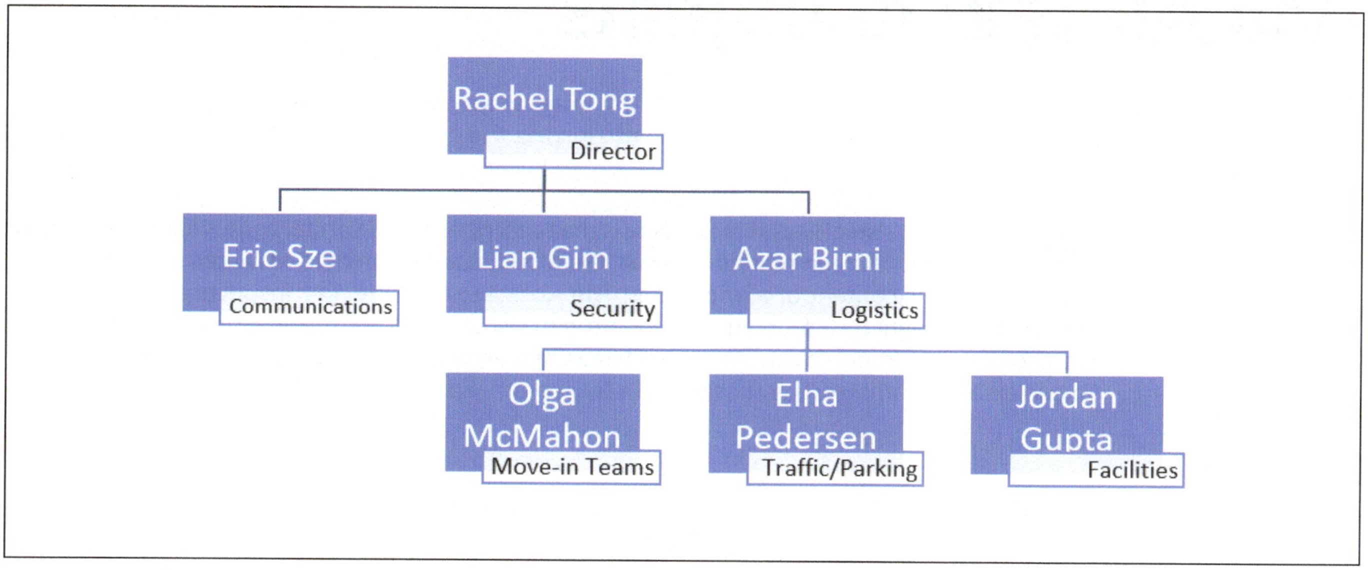

Figure 3-31: Completed document layout

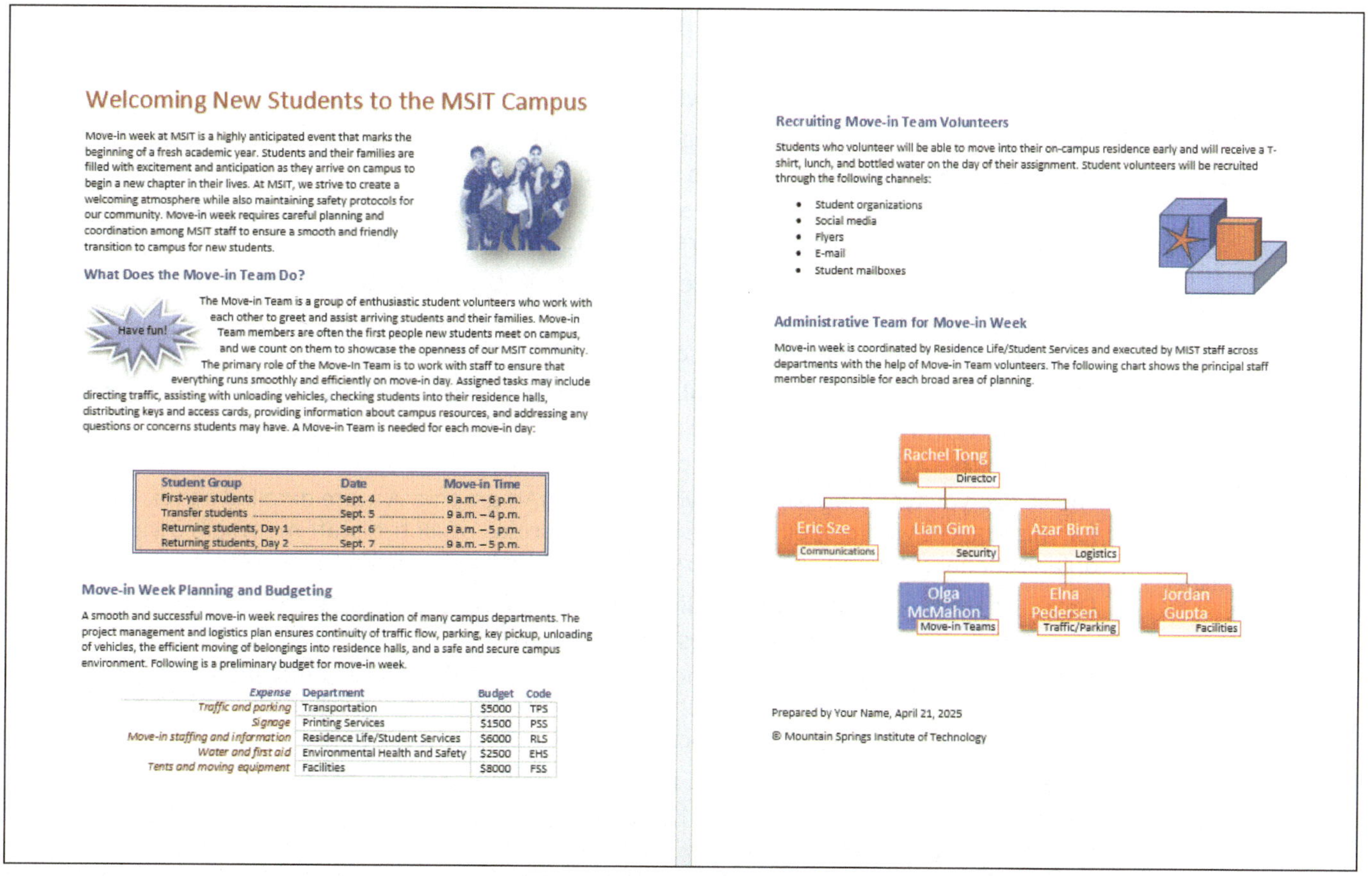

Welcoming New Students to the MSIT Campus

Move-in week at MSIT is a highly anticipated event that marks the beginning of a fresh academic year. Students and their families are filled with excitement and anticipation as they arrive on campus to begin a new chapter in their lives. At MSIT, we strive to create a welcoming atmosphere while also maintaining safety protocols for our community. Move-in week requires careful planning and coordination among MSIT staff to ensure a smooth and friendly transition to campus for new students.

What Does the Move-in Team Do?

Have fun!

The Move-in Team is a group of enthusiastic student volunteers who work with each other to greet and assist arriving students and their families. Move-in Team members are often the first people new students meet on campus, and we count on them to showcase the openness of our MSIT community. The primary role of the Move-In Team is to work with staff to ensure that everything runs smoothly and efficiently on move-in day. Assigned tasks may include directing traffic, assisting with unloading vehicles, checking students into their residence halls, distributing keys and access cards, providing information about campus resources, and addressing any questions or concerns students may have. A Move-in Team is needed for each move-in day:

Student Group	Date	Move-in Time
First-year students	Sept. 4	9 a.m. – 6 p.m.
Transfer students	Sept. 5	9 a.m. – 4 p.m.
Returning students, Day 1	Sept. 6	9 a.m. – 5 p.m.
Returning students, Day 2	Sept. 7	9 a.m. – 5 p.m.

Move-in Week Planning and Budgeting

A smooth and successful move-in week requires the coordination of many campus departments. The project management and logistics plan ensures continuity of traffic flow, parking, key pickup, unloading of vehicles, the efficient moving of belongings into residence halls, and a safe and secure campus environment. Following is a preliminary budget for move-in week.

Expense	Department	Budget	Code
Traffic and parking	Transportation	$5000	TPS
Signage	Printing Services	$1500	PSS
Move-in staffing and information	Residence Life/Student Services	$6000	RLS
Water and first aid	Environmental Health and Safety	$2500	EHS
Tents and moving equipment	Facilities	$8000	FSS

Recruiting Move-in Team Volunteers

Students who volunteer will be able to move into their on-campus residence early and will receive a T-shirt, lunch, and bottled water on the day of their assignment. Student volunteers will be recruited through the following channels:

- Student organizations
- Social media
- Flyers
- E-mail
- Student mailboxes

Administrative Team for Move-in Week

Move-in week is coordinated by Residence Life/Student Services and executed by MIST staff across departments with the help of Move-in Team volunteers. The following chart shows the principal staff member responsible for each broad area of planning.

Rachel Tong
Director
Eric Sze
Communications
Lian Gim
Security
Azar Birni
Logistics
Olga McMahon
Move-in Teams
Elna Pedersen
Traffic/Parking
Jordan Gupta
Facilities

Prepared by Your Name, April 21, 2025

© Mountain Springs Institute of Technology

Add Alt Text to Objects

Case Before distributing the document, you add alt text to several images to make them accessible to people who use screen readers. Finally, you run the Accessibility Checker to inspect the document for other accessibility issues and resolve any accessibility errors.

Objectives
- Add alt text to images
- Check documents for accessibility

Alternative text, also called **alt text**, is text that describes the essential content and meaning of an image or object. Screen readers read alt text aloud, enabling people who are visually impaired to access the full content of a document. The **Accessibility Checker** inspects a document for elements that might be a problem for readers with visual impairment, and it recommends actions for resolving each issue. To run the Accessibility Checker, you use the Check Accessibility command. To add alt text to an object, you use the Alt Text command.

Steps

Quick Tip
You can also add or edit alt text by right-clicking an object, clicking Edit Alt Text, and then typing the alt text in the Alt Text pane.

Quick Tip
To hear the document read aloud by a screen reader, click the View tab, click the Immersive Reader command in the Immersive group, then click Read Aloud.

1. **Click the clip art graphic on page 1 to select it, click the Picture Format tab, then click the Alt Text button in the Accessibility group**
   The Alt Text pane opens, as shown in **Figure 3-32**. You use this pane to type alternative text for the selected object. The pane includes an option for generating automatic alt text. You can experiment with this option or write your own alt text.
2. **Click the text box in the Alt Text pane, then type Five happy college students posing for a photo and laughing.**
   The alt text you typed is associated with the selected image.
3. **Click the explosion shape on page 1 to select it, then click the Mark as decorative check box in the Alt Text pane to select it**
   The explosion shape is marked as decorative. Objects that are decorative in a document are for visual interest only and do not require alt text for screen readers.
4. **Click the grouped object on page 2 to select it, then click the Mark as decorative check box in the Alt Text pane**
   The grouped object is marked as decorative.
5. **Click the SmartArt graphic to select it, click the text box in the Alt Text pane, then type An organizational chart showing the administrative structure for move-in week, with Rachel Tong as director.**
   The alt text you typed is associated with the SmartArt graphic. A more detailed alt-text description for this graphic would spell out the names and roles of all the staff members included in the organizational chart and would describe the relationships between those roles.
6. **Deselect the SmartArt graphic, click the Review tab, then click the Check Accessibility button in the Accessibility group**
   The Accessibility pane opens. It shows the results of the accessibility inspection and offers suggestions for how to resolve each issue. The Accessibility Checker identifies one potential accessibility issue in the planning document.
7. **Click Image or object not inline in the Accessibility pane, then click Picture 1**
   Picture 1, the clip art graphic on page 1, is identified by the Accessibility Checker as a floating object—i.e., not part of a line of text ("inline"). The clip art graphic is selected in the document, as shown in **Figure 3-33**. Two actions for fixing the accessibility issue are recommended by the Accessibility Checker: convert the floating object to an inline object or mark it as decorative. Since the image is not essential to the meaning and purpose of the planning document, you mark the clip art graphic as decorative.
8. **Click Mark as decorative**
   The clip art graphic is marked as decorative, removing the alt text associated with it. The Accessibility pane now indicates the document is free of accessibility issues.
9. **Close the Accessibility pane, close the Alt Text pane, deselect the clip art graphic, then save your changes**
10. **sam Submit the document to your instructor, close the file, then exit Word**

Figure 3-32: Alt Text pane

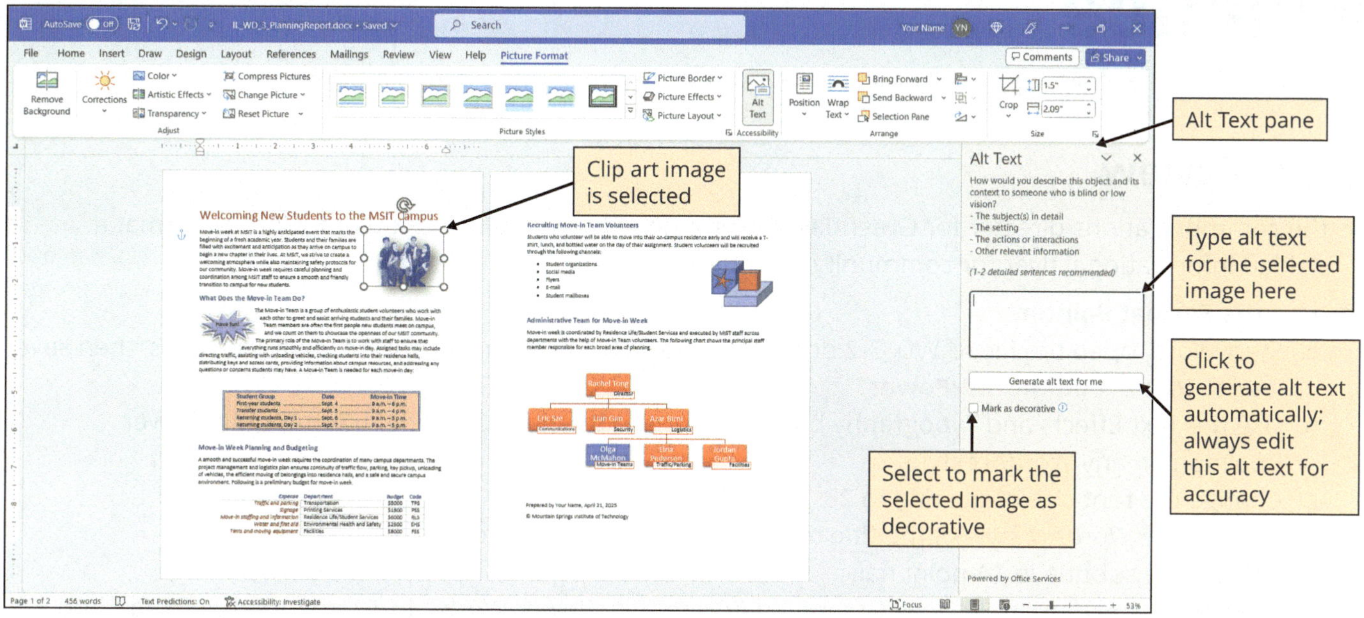

Figure 3-33: Accessibility pane

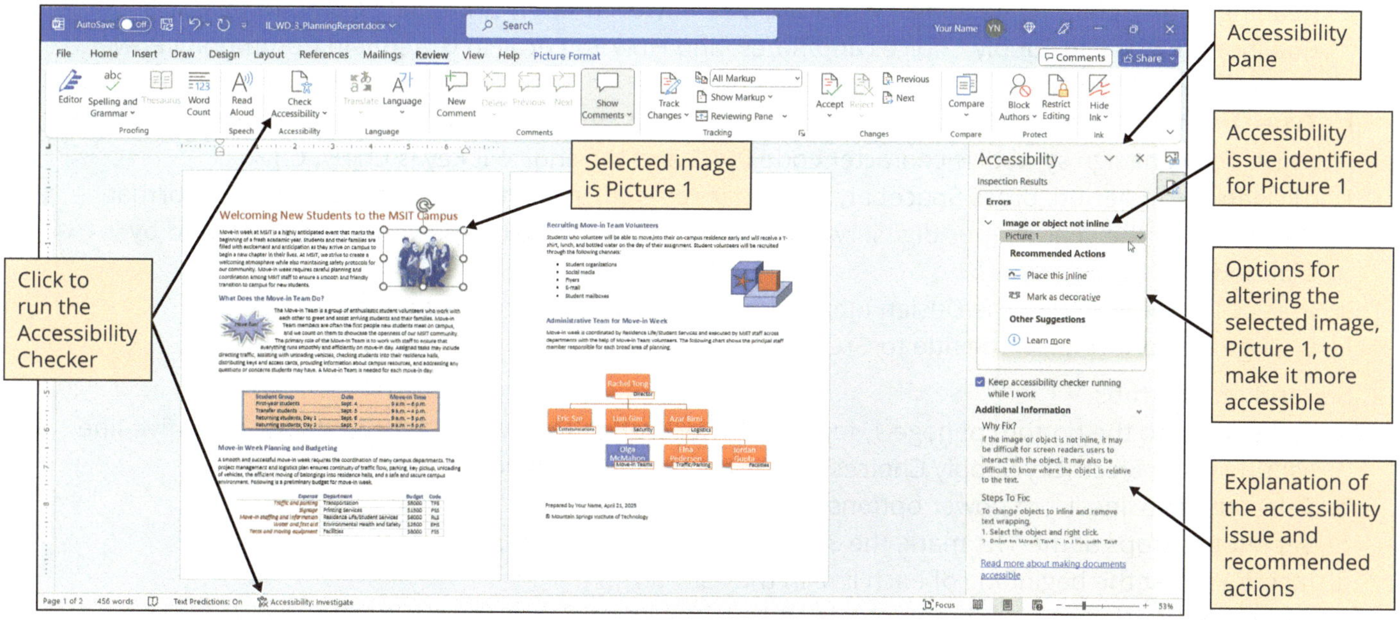

Practice

In the exercises that follow, you will practice the skills you have learned in this module.

Skills Review

As the communications director for Greenfield Community Power Coalition, you use Word to format a two-sided informational flyer for community members.

1. **Use the Format Painter.**
   a. Start Word, open the file IL_WD_3-2.docx from the location where you store your Data Files, then save it as **IL_WD_3_CommunityPower**.
   b. Use the Text Effects and Typography button to format the title "Greenfield Community Power Coalition" in any WordArt style.
   c. Change the font size of the title to 28.
   d. Change the WordArt style of the title to the third style in the third row.
   e. Format the subtitle in 14-point italic.
   f. Format the heading "How Does Greenfield Community Power Work?" in 14-point italic with a Blue, Accent 1, Darker 25% font color.
   g. Use the Format Painter to copy the format of the How Does Greenfield Community Power Work? heading to the following headings: Why Purchase Power through Greenfield Community Power Coalition?, Electricity Supply Choices and Rates, and How To Enroll in Greenfield Community Power.
   h. Press CTRL+END to go to the end of the document,
   i. Type **Our rates start at 15.5 per kilowatt-hour (kWh).**, then insert a cent sign symbol (¢) after 15.5. (**Hint**: The cent sign symbol is character code 00A2 and the shortcut key is Ctrl+/, C.)
   j. Click after the period, press Spacebar, type **Last revised**, insert the current date using a format that includes the year as four digits, type a comma, type **by**, then type your name followed by a period.
   k. Press CTRL+HOME, click the Design tab, then change the theme colors to Green.
   l. Change the font color of the title to Green, Accent 1, Darker 25%, then save your changes.

2. **Set and modify tabs.**
   a. Scroll down to the bottom of page 1, format "Power Option Renewable," the first line in the five-line list under the Electricity Supply Choices and Rates heading, in bold.
   b. Select the five-line list of power options.
   c. Set left tab stops at the 1½" mark, the 3¾" mark, and the 5" mark.
   d. Insert a tab at the beginning of each line in the list.
   e. In the first line, insert a tab before Renewable. In the second line, insert a tab before 22. In the remaining lines, insert a tab before 33, 50, and 100.
   f. Select the five lines of tabbed text, then drag the second tab stop to the 4" mark on the horizontal ruler.
   g. Drag the third tab stop at the 5" mark off the ruler to remove it.
   h. Select the five lines of tabbed text, open the Tabs dialog box, then change the alignment of the 4" tab stop to Center.
   i. Select the last four lines of tabbed text, open the Tabs dialog box, then apply a dotted line tab leader to the 4" tab stop.
   j. Save your changes to the document.

3. **Add borders and shading.**
   a. Select "Power Option," then apply an underline.
   b. Use the Underline arrow in the Font group to change the color of the underline to Green, Accent 1.
   c. Use the Format Painter to copy the underline formatting from "Power Option" to "Renewable."
   d. Click the heading Electricity Supply Choices and Rates, add 6 points of space after the paragraph, then open the Borders and Shading dialog box.
   e. Use the Borders tab to apply a ½-point width, Turquoise, Accent 6 colored border below the heading.
   f. Use the Format Painter to apply the same paragraph and border settings to the other headings in the report: How Does..., Why Purchase..., and How To Enroll...
   g. Scroll to the end of the document, click in the Our rates... paragraph, then center the paragraph.
   h. Apply Turquoise, Accent 6, Lighter 80% shading to the paragraph.
   i. Add a ½-point, Turquoise, Accent 6 box border around the paragraph.
   j. Save your changes.

4. **Insert a table.**
   a. Turn on formatting marks, click in the middle blank paragraph above the How To Enroll in Greenfield Community Power heading, then insert a table that contains three columns and three rows.
   b. Type the text shown below in the table, pressing TAB to add rows as necessary.

22%	Green Basic	$94/month
33%	Green Plus	$97/month
50%	Green Enhanced	$101/month
65%	Green Clean	$108/month
100%	Green Complete	$116/month
22%	PowerHub	$122/month

   c. Save your changes.

5. **Insert and delete rows and columns.**
   a. Insert a row above the top row, type **Renewable Content** in the first cell, type **Power Options** in the second cell, then type **Estimated Cost** in the third cell.
   b. Delete the 65% row.
   c. Insert a column to the left of the Estimated Cost column, then type **Rate/kWh** in the first cell.
   d. Type the following prices in the empty cells in the new column, starting at the top of the table: **15.5¢**, **16.2¢**, **16.9¢**, **19.3¢**, **20.3¢**. (Hint: Insert the cent sign symbol.)
   e. Save your changes.

6. **Apply a table style.**
   a. Select the table, then use the AutoFit command to fit the table to the contents.
   b. Click the Table Design tab, preview table styles applied to the table, and then apply an appropriate style.
   c. Apply the Grid Table 6 Colorful - Accent 1 style to the table, add the Header Row, Total Row, and First Column table style options, remove the Banded Rows, Banded Columns, and Last Column table style options, if necessary, then change the font color of the header row to Turquoise, Accent 6, Darker, 25%.
   d. Change the font color of the last row to black, remove the bold formatting from the last row, then apply bold to the 22% cell in the last row.
   e. Center the text in the Renewable Content and Rate/kWh columns.
   f. Center the table between the margins, then save your changes.

Skills Review (Continued)

7. **Insert online pictures.** (Note: To complete these steps, your computer must be connected to the Internet.)
   a. Press CTRL+HOME, then open the Online Pictures window.
   b. Search using Bing Image Search to find images related to the keyword **energy**. Click the Filter link in the Online Pictures window, select Clipart on the Filter menu to filter the search results, then verify the Creative Commons only check box is selected.
   c. Insert the renewable energy clip art image shown in **Figure 3-34**. (Note: Select a different image if this one is not available to you. It is best to select an image that is similar in shape to the image shown in **Figure 3-34**.)
   d. Scroll down. If the image includes a credit line, click the text in the credit line, select the box that surrounds the credit line, then delete the credit line box.
   e. Use the Shape Width box in the Size group on the Picture Format tab to change the width of the image to 3".
   f. Use the Position command to position the image in the top right with square text wrapping.
   g. Change the color of the image to Lime, Accent color 2 Dark.
   h. Use the Artistic Effects button to apply the Glow Edges artistic effect to the image (fifth row, third column).
   i. Use the Reset Picture arrow to reset the picture (but not the size), then save your changes.

Figure 3-34

8. **Size and scale a graphic.**
   a. Resize the image proportionally so that it is about **1"** high and **1.5"** wide.
   b. Drag the image so its top is aligned with the first line of body text and its left side is aligned with the left margin.
   c. Resize the image so that it is precisely **1.5"** high and **2.25"** wide. Deselect the Lock aspect ratio check box, if necessary.
   d. Position the image so its Horizontal absolute position is 0" to the right of the margin and its Vertical absolute position is 1" below the margin.
   e. Add ¾-point Turquoise, Accent 6 picture border around the image, then save your changes.

9. **Draw and format shapes.**
   a. Scroll until the Why Purchase Power... heading is at the top of your screen.
   b. Click the Shapes button, click the Cloud shape, then click in the numbered list below the Why Purchase... heading.
   c. Resize the shape to be **.8"** high and **.8"** wide.
   d. Fill the shape with Turquoise, Accent 6, then apply the Preset 3 shape effect.
   e. Change the shape of the object to Sun.
   f. Apply square text wrapping, then position the shape in the bottom left corner of the page.

10. **Adjust and rotate shapes.**
    a. Draw a teardrop shape in a blank space on the page, then resize it to **1"** high and **1"** wide.
    b. Select the sun shape, then use the Format Painter to copy the format of the sun shape to the teardrop shape.

c. Rotate the teardrop shape left about 45 degrees so that the yellow adjustment handle is at the top of the shape, then drag the yellow adjustment handle up about ¼".
d. Draw a lightning bolt shape near the teardrop shape, then resize it to be about **1"** high and **.4"** wide.
e. Fill the shape with Lime, Accent 3, then apply the Preset 3 shape effect.
f. Draw a sun shape near the teardrop shape, resize it to be about **.8"** high and **.8"** wide, then drag the adjustment handle right slightly.
g. Fill the sun shape with Orange from the Standard Colors section, apply the Preset 3 shape effect, then save your changes.

11. Arrange graphic objects.

a. Position the lightning bolt shape on top of the teardrop shape.
b. Position the orange sun so that it overlaps the teardrop slightly, then use the Send Backward arrow to send the orange sun to the back.
c. Select the teardrop shape, press and hold CTRL, select the lightning bolt shape, select the orange sun shape, then group the shapes into a single object.
d. Resize the grouped object to be **1"** high and **1"** wide, then apply square text wrapping to the object.
e. Position the grouped object so it aligns with the right margin and the first line of body text under the Why Purchase... heading. (**Hint**: Make sure the object is under the border.)
f. Select the turquoise sun shape, copy it, then paste a copy.
g. Drag the pasted copy of the sun shape to a blank area of the page, adjust the sun shape, reduce the size of the sun shape, then rotate the sun shape.
h. Position the rotated sun shape in the blank space to the right of the tabbed text.
i. Change the fill color of the two turquoise suns to orange, then save your changes.

12. Create SmartArt graphics.

a. Scroll to the end of the document, click in the middle blank paragraph above the Our rates... shaded paragraph, then click the SmartArt button.
b. Select Process in the list of SmartArt types, select the Accent Process style, then click OK.
c. Change the colors of the SmartArt object to the Colorful - Accent Colors style.
d. Enter text in the SmartArt object so that the process diagram appears as shown in **Figure 3-35**.
e. Resize the SmartArt object to be **3.2"** high, then save your changes.
f. Adjust the size or position of objects as needed so that your document resembles the document shown in the figure. View your document in two-page view and compare it to the document shown in **Figure 3-36**.

Figure 3-35

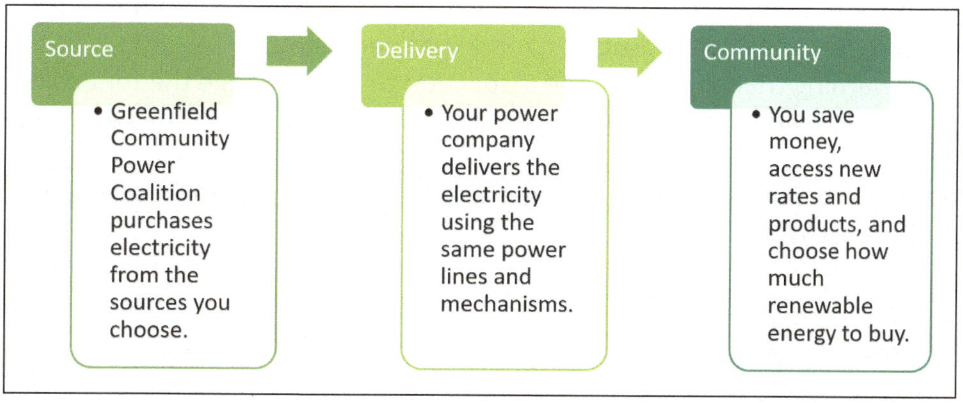

Skills Review (Continued)

Figure 3-36

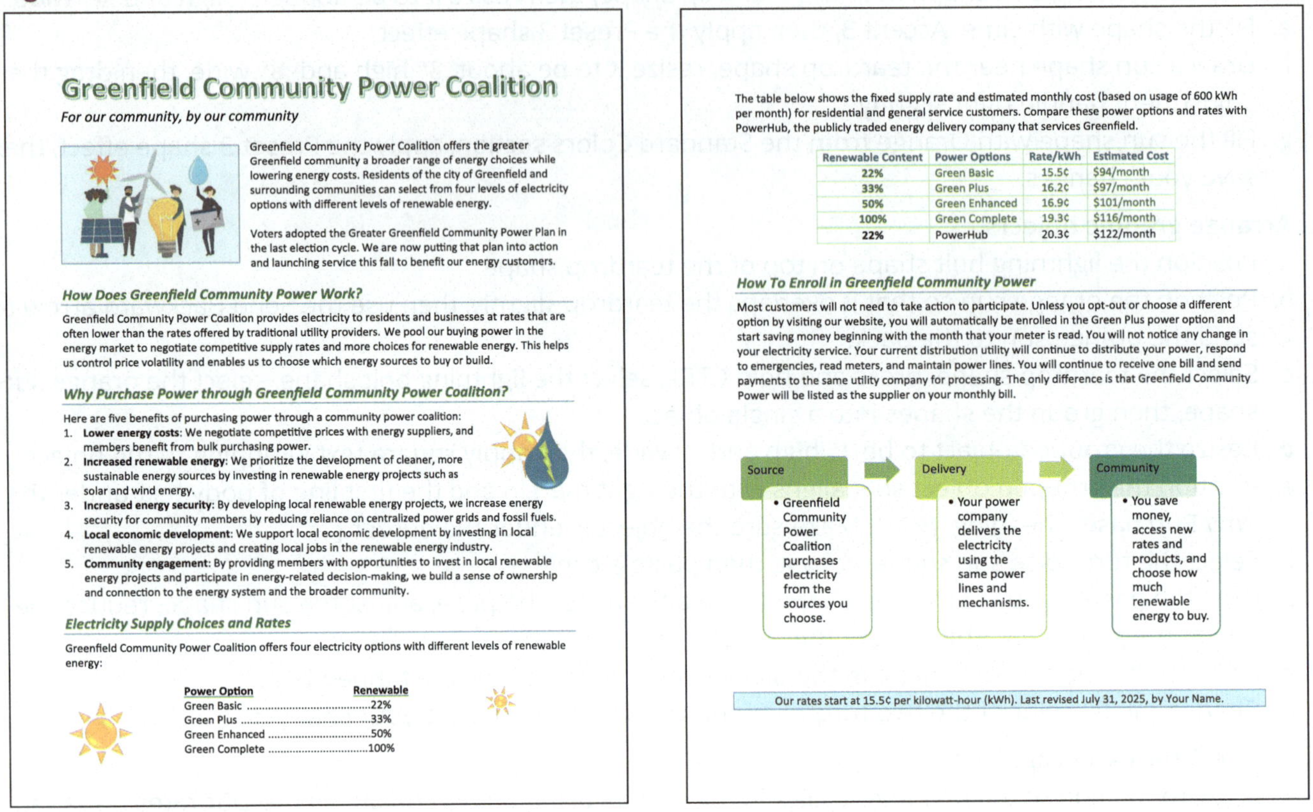

Greenfield Community Power Coalition

For our community, by our community

Greenfield Community Power Coalition offers the greater Greenfield community a broader range of energy choices while lowering energy costs. Residents of the city of Greenfield and surrounding communities can select from four levels of electricity options with different levels of renewable energy.

Voters adopted the Greater Greenfield Community Power Plan in the last election cycle. We are now putting that plan into action and launching service this fall to benefit our energy customers.

How Does Greenfield Community Power Work?

Greenfield Community Power Coalition provides electricity to residents and businesses at rates that are often lower than the rates offered by traditional utility providers. We pool our buying power in the energy market to negotiate competitive supply rates and more choices for renewable energy. This helps us control price volatility and enables us to choose which energy sources to buy or build.

Why Purchase Power through Greenfield Community Power Coalition?

Here are five benefits of purchasing power through a community power coalition:

1. **Lower energy costs**: We negotiate competitive prices with energy suppliers, and members benefit from bulk purchasing power.
2. **Increased renewable energy**: We prioritize the development of cleaner, more sustainable energy sources by investing in renewable energy projects such as solar and wind energy.
3. **Increased energy security**: By developing local renewable energy projects, we increase energy security for community members by reducing reliance on centralized power grids and fossil fuels.
4. **Local economic development**: We support local economic development by investing in local renewable energy projects and creating local jobs in the renewable energy industry.
5. **Community engagement**: By providing members with opportunities to invest in local renewable energy projects and participate in energy-related decision-making, we build a sense of ownership and connection to the energy system and the broader community.

Electricity Supply Choices and Rates

Greenfield Community Power Coalition offers four electricity options with different levels of renewable energy:

Power Option	Renewable
Green Basic	22%
Green Plus	33%
Green Enhanced	50%
Green Complete	100%

The table below shows the fixed supply rate and estimated monthly cost (based on usage of 600 kWh per month) for residential and general service customers. Compare these power options and rates with PowerHub, the publicly traded energy delivery company that services Greenfield.

Renewable Content	Power Options	Rate/kWh	Estimated Cost
22%	Green Basic	15.5¢	$94/month
33%	Green Plus	16.2¢	$97/month
50%	Green Enhanced	16.9¢	$101/month
100%	Green Complete	19.3¢	$116/month
22%	PowerHub	20.3¢	$122/month

How To Enroll in Greenfield Community Power

Most customers will not need to take action to participate. Unless you opt-out or choose a different option by visiting our website, you will automatically be enrolled in the Green Plus power option and start saving money beginning with the month that your meter is read. You will not notice any change in your electricity service. Your current distribution utility will continue to distribute your power, respond to emergencies, read meters, and maintain power lines. You will continue to receive one bill and send payments to the same utility company for processing. The only difference is that Greenfield Community Power will be listed as the supplier on your monthly bill.

Our rates start at 15.5¢ per kilowatt-hour (kWh). Last revised July 31, 2025, by Your Name.

13. Add alt text to objects.
    a. Select the clip art graphic on page 1, use the Alt Text command to open the Alt Text pane, then type the following alt text: **A group of people holding solar panels, wind turbines, lightbulbs, and water, representing renewable energy sources.**
    b. Select the grouped object on page 1, mark it as decorative in the Alt Text pane, then select and mark the two sun shapes as decorative.
    c. Click the SmartArt graphic, then type the following alt text In the Alt Text pane: **A chart detailing the electricity source, delivery process, and community benefits for Greenfield Community Power customers.**
    d. Use the Check Accessibility command on the Review tab to run the Accessibility Checker.
    e. Resolve each error that appears in the inspection results. Since the clip art object is not essential to the meaning and purpose of the document, mark it as decorative.
    f. Consider each warning that appears in the inspection results. Change the font color of the white text in the SmartArt graphic to black, then verify that no accessibility issues are flagged in the document.
    g. Close the Accessibility pane, save your changes to the document, submit it to your instructor, close the file, and then exit Word.

Independent Challenge 1

The senior center where you work publishes a variety of helpful tips and information sheets related to health and safety issues for older adults. Your colleague has assembled a tip sheet on fall prevention and has asked you to format it so it highlights the important information. Design and formatting elements will make the document attractive to readers.

a. Start Word, open the file IL_WD_3-3.docx from the drive and folder where you store your Data Files, save it as **IL_WD_3_FallPrevention**, then read the document to get a basic understanding of its contents.
b. Select the entire document, then change the font to 10-point Arial.
c. Change all four document margins to Narrow 0.5".
d. Change the font size of the first line, "Healthy Aging", to 14, and apply italic.
e. Change the font size of the second line, the title "Fall Prevention...", to 20.
f. Change the font size of the heading "Discuss your medications with your healthcare provider" to 14, then add a single bottom border with the Blue, Accent 1 color, and a width of 1/2 pt.
g. Use the Format Painter to copy the format of the "Discuss your medications..." heading to the following headings in the tip sheet: Stay active and keep moving, Wear appropriate footwear, Improve lighting and remove home hazards, and Use assistive devices.
h. Insert an online picture that is a photograph. Select a photograph that is appropriate to the content. (Hint: Use the Filter link in the Online Pictures window to filter for photographs.)
i. Remove the credit line box from the image, if necessary.
j. Resize the image proportionally so that it is approximately 2.5" wide, wrap text around the image, then position the photograph above the "Discuss your medications..." heading. **Figure 3-37** shows a sample layout.
k. Change the theme colors to a theme color set that works with the photograph you selected. (Hint: Use the Theme Colors button on the Design tab.)
l. Enhance the photograph with corrections, colors, artistic effects, borders, or styles.
m. Using heart shapes, create an image similar to the one shown in the completed document in **Figure 3-37**. Apply a fill color to the larger heart and a different fill color to the smaller heart.
n. Use the adjustment handle to alter the shape of the hearts if necessary. Group the two heart shapes into a single object, then position the grouped object in the top-right corner of the page.
o. Apply font colors to the document that work with the photograph you selected, then adjust the color and style of the borders as necessary.
p. Add your name to the footer, then examine the document carefully for formatting errors and make any necessary adjustments. Adjust the size and placement of the photograph if necessary, so that all the text fits on a single page.
q. Check the document for accessibility, mark each image as decorative, and make any other necessary adjustments.
r. Save the tip sheet, submit it to your instructor, then close the file and exit Word.

Figure 3-37

Healthy Aging

Fall Prevention: Simple Tips to Prevent Falls

Fall prevention is an important topic for seniors to consider. As we age, physical changes and health conditions, including the medications prescribed to treat those conditions, make falls more likely. If you are an older adult, fall prevention is essential to maintaining your independence, mobility, and overall health. In fact, falls are a leading cause of injury, hospitalization, and extended periods of rehabilitation for older adults. By implementing fall protection strategies, you can reduce your risk of injury from falls, maintain your quality of life, and reduce your healthcare costs. Prevent falls with these simple fall prevention measures.

Discuss your medications with your healthcare provider

Make a list of your prescription and non-prescription medications to review with your healthcare provider for side effects and interactions. Medications that make you tired or affect your thinking could put you at greater risk for a fall. Also discuss any dizziness, joint pain, numbness in your feet, or shortness of breath you experience. Your healthcare provider can evaluate your muscle strength, balance, and gait, and make recommendations for fall prevention strategies.

Stay active and keep moving

Independent Challenge 2

The healthcare communications agency where you work has been contracted by City Health Clinic to redesign an info sheet on their supportive care services for expectant and new parents. The client would like the info sheet to include graphics, tables, and other elements that make the document visually interesting. The info sheet must also be accessible to people who are visually impaired and using a screen reader. You design the document to highlight the important information and add alt text so that readers of all abilities can access the content of the graphic images.

a. Start Word, open the file IL_WD_3-4.docx from the drive and folder where you store your Data Files, then save it as **IL_WD_3_SupportiveCare**.
b. Read the document to get a basic understanding of the contents, use CTRL+A to select all the text in the document, then clear all formatting from the text.
c. Determine the font and font sizes you will use for the body text, title, subtitle, and headings.
d. Select all the text again, change the style to No Spacing, then apply the font you intend to use for the body text to all the text in the report.
e. Format the title and subtitle using a font, font size, and font color of your choice.
f. Format the heading Mission and Goals using a font, font size, and font color of your choice, then, use the Format Painter to copy the formatting of the Mission and Goals heading to the Workshops and Support Groups and Advocacy Initiatives headings.
g. Format the subheading Emotional support using a font, font size, and font color of your choice, then use the Format Painter to copy the formatting of the Emotional support heading to the following headings: Education, Advocacy, Building community, Prenatal classes, Infant care classes, Breastfeeding support groups, Postpartum support groups, Prenatal yoga classes, Access to quality healthcare, Maternal and infant health, and Policy reform
h. Scroll down. Above the Advocacy Initiatives heading, insert a table with three columns and six rows, then enter the following text.

Class/Workshop	Day	Time
Prenatal	Tues., Thurs.	7–9 p.m.
Infant care	Mon., Wed.	6–7 p.m.
Breastfeeding	Mon., Wed., Fri.	10–11 a.m.
Postpartum	Tues., Thurs	10–11 a.m.
Yoga	Mon., Wed., Fri.	7–8 p.m.

i. Autofit the table to the content, apply an appropriate table style to the table, adjust the formatting, then center the table between the margins.
j. Scroll to the top of the document. Using shapes, create a graphic to illustrate the document. The graphic should be composed of two or more shapes. For example, you might draw an abstract design or something else you think will represent the content.
k. Format the shapes with fills, outlines, and effects. Use the adjustment and rotate handles to alter the shapes as necessary.
l. Position the shapes so that they overlap, use the Bring Forward and Send Backward buttons to adjust the layers, then group the shapes into a single object.
m. Resize the grouped object, wrap text around it, and position it in the document.

n. Create a SmartArt graphic similar to **Figure 3-38**. Use the Alternating Hexagons SmartArt style (List group), then format the SmartArt graphic using colors, styles, and effects.
o. Resize the SmartArt graphic and position it in the document.
p. Use the Multiple Pages button to view both pages of the document, then adjust the size and position of the graphics.
q. Select the shapes graphic you created in steps j–m, use the Alt Text button to open the Alt Text pane, then mark the shapes graphic as decorative.
r. Select the SmartArt graphic, then type a description of the SmartArt graphic in the Alt Text pane.
s. Use the Check Accessibility button on the Review tab to check the document for accessibility issues, and make any necessary adjustments.
t. Add your name to the footer, save your changes to the document, submit it to your instructor, close the file, and then exit Word.

Figure 3-38

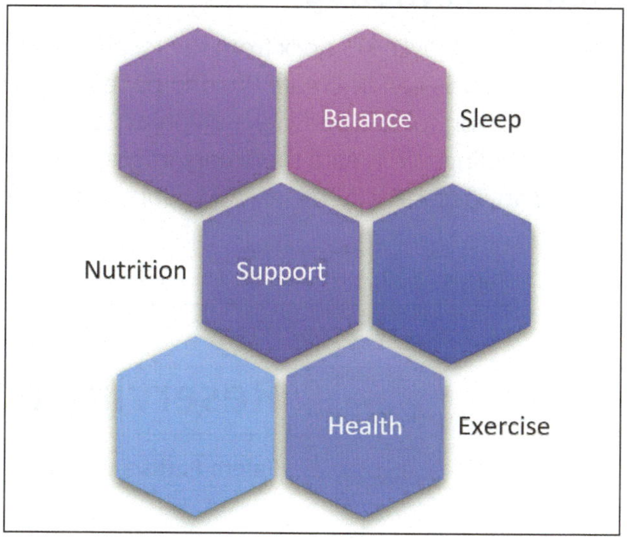

Visual Workshop

Open the file IL_WD_3-5.docx from the location where you store your Data Files, then save the document as **IL_WD_3_ReserveFAQ**. Create the one-page flyer shown in **Figure 3-39**. Change all four margins to .75". Use 12-point Calibri for the body text, 28-point Calibri for the title, 14-point Calibri for the subtitle, and 14-point Calibri for the headings. To create the SmartArt graphic object, use the Accent Process style from the Process group. Resolve any accessibility issues. Add your name to the footer, then submit a copy of the flyer to your instructor.

Figure 3-39

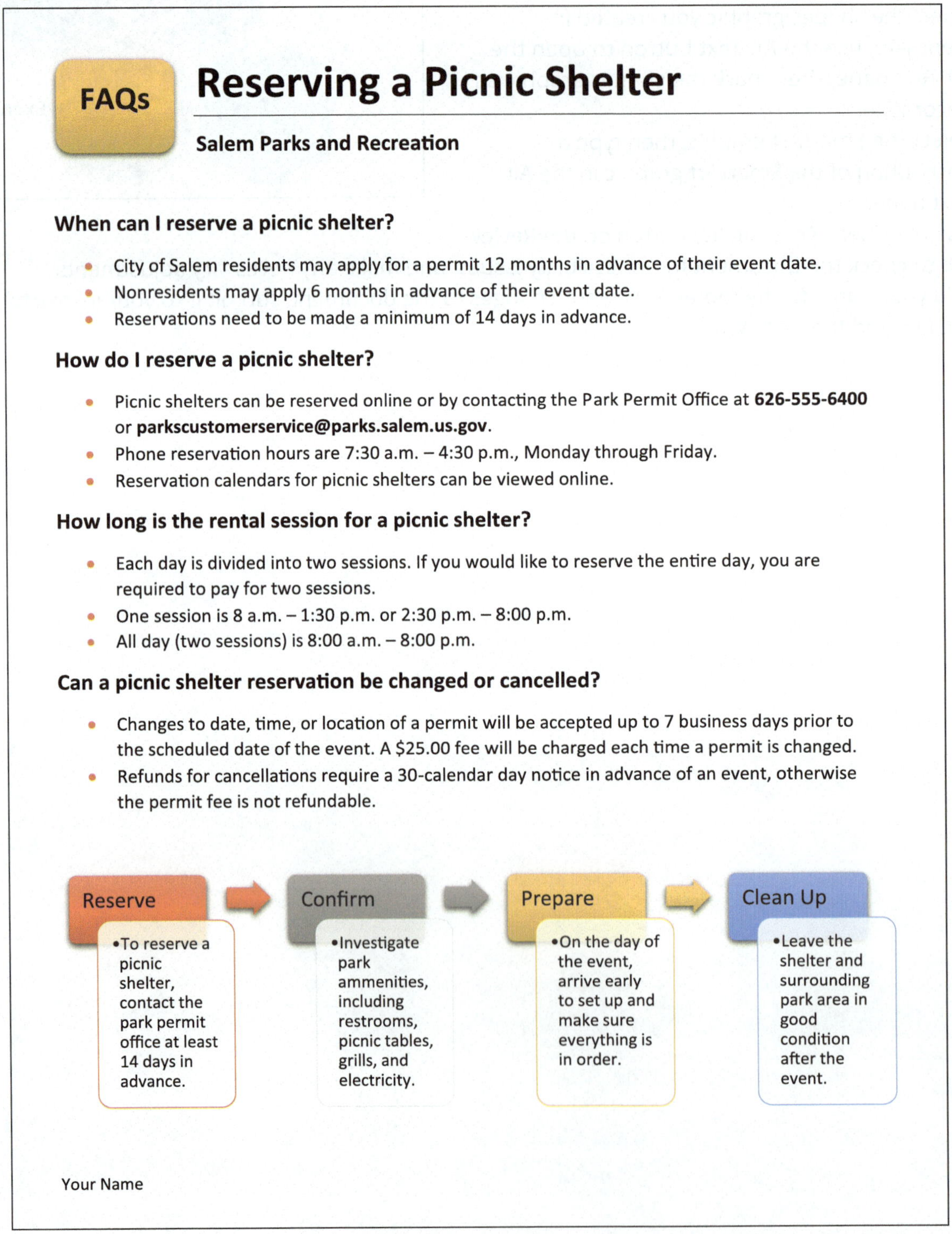

FAQs

Reserving a Picnic Shelter

Salem Parks and Recreation

When can I reserve a picnic shelter?

- City of Salem residents may apply for a permit 12 months in advance of their event date.
- Nonresidents may apply 6 months in advance of their event date.
- Reservations need to be made a minimum of 14 days in advance.

How do I reserve a picnic shelter?

- Picnic shelters can be reserved online or by contacting the Park Permit Office at **626-555-6400** or **parkscustomerservice@parks.salem.us.gov**.
- Phone reservation hours are 7:30 a.m. – 4:30 p.m., Monday through Friday.
- Reservation calendars for picnic shelters can be viewed online.

How long is the rental session for a picnic shelter?

- Each day is divided into two sessions. If you would like to reserve the entire day, you are required to pay for two sessions.
- One session is 8 a.m. – 1:30 p.m. or 2:30 p.m. – 8:00 p.m.
- All day (two sessions) is 8:00 a.m. – 8:00 p.m.

Can a picnic shelter reservation be changed or cancelled?

- Changes to date, time, or location of a permit will be accepted up to 7 business days prior to the scheduled date of the event. A $25.00 fee will be charged each time a permit is changed.
- Refunds for cancellations require a 30-calendar day notice in advance of an event, otherwise the permit fee is not refundable.

Your Name

Formatting Tables and Documents

Case

You are preparing a prospectus for an advertising campaign for MSIT Bookstore, the campus bookstore. The goal of the ad campaign is to increase awareness of MSIT Bookstore among the student population and drive more foot traffic to the store. You format the budget information in the prospectus as a table, so that it is easier to read and analyze, and then you add headers, footers, and a cover page to the prospectus to guide readers and give the prospectus a more formal appearance.

Module Objectives

After completing this module, you will be able to:

- Modify character spacing
- Increase and decrease indents
- Divide a document into sections
- Format headers and footers
- Modify a table
- Modify rows and columns
- Sort table data
- Split and merge cells
- Perform calculations in tables
- Modify table style options
- Customize a table format
- Insert a cover page

Files You Will Need

IL_WD_4-1.docx
IL_WD_4-2.docx
IL_WD_4-3.docx

Modify Character Spacing

Case You stylize the appearance of the headings in the prospectus by formatting the headings in small caps, making the characters narrower, and adjusting the character spacing.

Objective
- Modify character spacing

A powerful way to change the appearance of text is to modify character spacing. **Character spacing** is formatting that changes the scale (or width) of characters, expands or condenses the amount of space between characters, raises or lowers characters relative to the line of text, and adjusts the kerning of characters. **Kerning** is the space between standard combinations of letters. You use the Advanced tab in the Font dialog box to modify character spacing.

Steps

1. **sam Start Word, open the file IL_WD_4-1.docx from the location where you store your Data Files, save it as IL_WD_4_BookstoreProspectus, then drag the Zoom slider to 120.**

2. **Select the heading Executive Summary, click the Font Size arrow [11] on the Mini toolbar, then click 48**
   The font size of the heading is enlarged to 48.

3. **Click the Launcher in the Font group on the Home tab to open the Font dialog box, click the Small caps check box in the Effects area on the Font tab, then click OK**
   The lowercase characters change to small capital characters. You can use the options on the Font tab to apply other font effects, as well, including Subscript, Superscript, and Strikethrough.

4. **Click the Launcher in the Font group, then click the Advanced tab in the Font dialog box**
   The Advanced tab in the Font dialog box is shown in **Figure 4-1**. You use the options on the Advanced tab to change the scale and spacing of characters or to raise or lower the characters.

5. **Click the Scale arrow, click 80%, click the Spacing arrow, click Expanded, then click OK**
   Decreasing the scale of the characters makes them narrower and gives the text a tall, thin appearance. Expanding the spacing increases the amount of white space between characters.

6. **Click the Font Size arrow [11] in the Font group, click 24, double-click the Format Painter button in the Clipboard group, then move the pointer over the document text to show the Format Painter pointer**
   The font size of the heading changes to 24. The Format Painter is turned on and the pointer changes to the Format Painter pointer.

7. **Scroll down, select the headings Advertising Campaign Development Timeline and Budget and Costing, click the Format Painter button to turn off the Format Painter, press CTRL+HOME, then save your changes**
   The headings are formatted the same; they are 24-point, small caps, character scale of 80%, with character spacing expanded by 1 point, as shown in **Figure 4-2**.

Figure 4-1: Advanced tab in Font dialog box

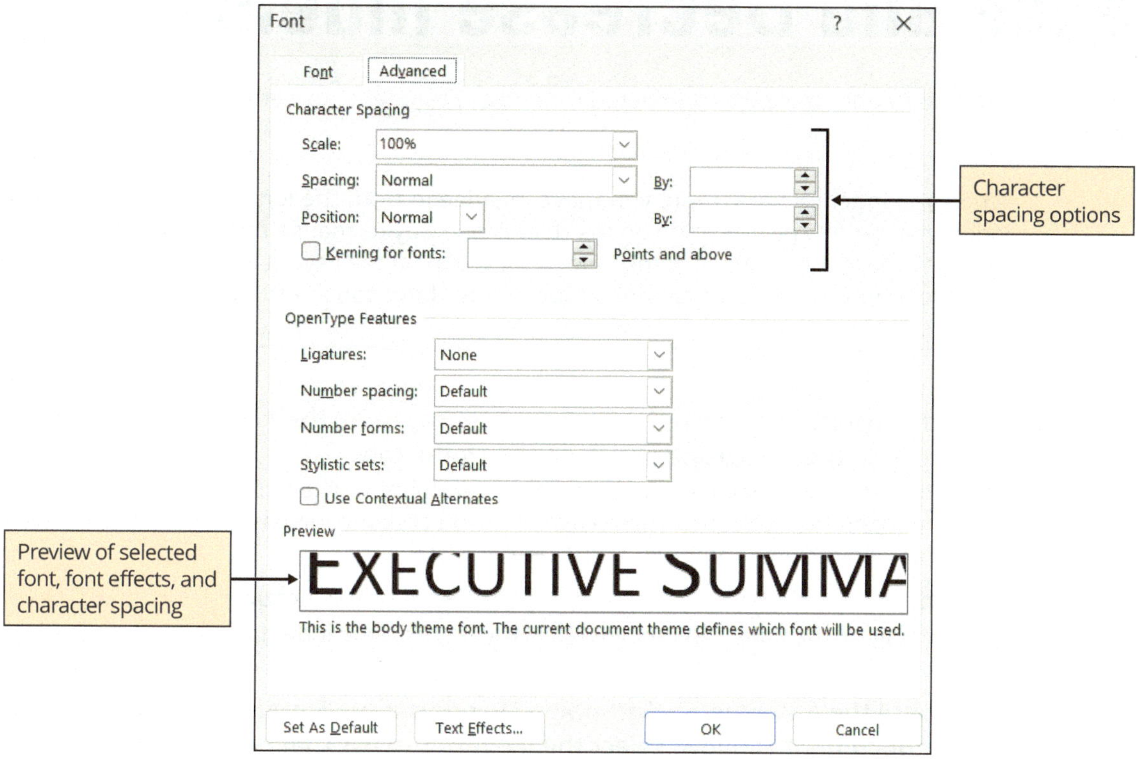

Figure 4-2: Font and character spacing effects applied to text

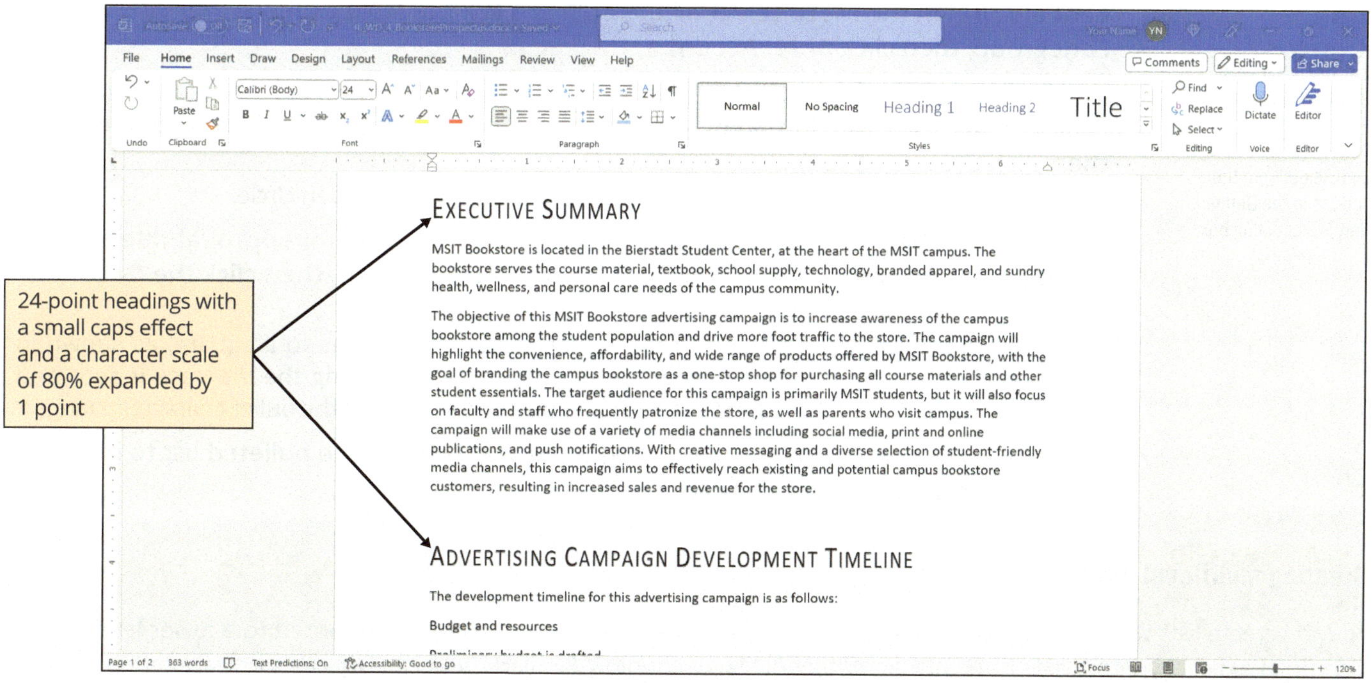

Increase and Decrease Indents

Case You format the development timeline as a bulleted list and apply indents to better organize the information for readers.

Objectives
- Increase and decrease indents
- Change bullet characters

When you indent a paragraph, you move its edge in from the left or right margin. Dragging an indent marker to a new location on the ruler is one way to change the indentation of a paragraph, changing the indent settings in the Paragraph group on the Layout tab is a second way, and using the indent buttons in the Paragraph group on the Home tab is a third.

Steps

Quick Tip
To create a right indent, drag the right indent marker on the horizontal ruler to the left.

Quick Tip
To create mirror indents, select the Mirror indents check box on the Indents and Spacing tab in the Paragraph dialog box.

Quick Tip
To use a symbol or a picture for a bullet character, click the Bullets arrow, click Define New Bullet, and then select from the options in the Define New Bullet dialog box.

1. **Place the insertion point in the first body paragraph, then click the Increase Indent button in the Paragraph group on the Home tab**
   The entire paragraph is indented ½" from the left margin. The left indent marker also moves to the ½" mark on the horizontal ruler. Each time you click the Increase Indent button, the left edge of a paragraph moves another ½" to the right.
2. **Click the Decrease Indent button in the Paragraph group**
   The left edge of the paragraph moves ½" to the left, and the indent marker moves back to the left margin.
3. **Scroll until the Advertising Campaign Development Timeline heading is at the top of your document window, select the eleven-line list that begins with Budget and resources, click the Bullets arrow in the Paragraph group, then click the black round bullet**
   The 11 paragraphs are formatted as a bulleted list using the black round bullet symbol, as shown in **Figure 4-3**.
4. **Click a bullet in the list to select all the bullets, click the Font Color arrow in the Font group, then click Blue, Accent 1, Darker 25%**
   The bullet characters all change to blue.
5. **Click to place the insertion point in Preliminary budget is drafted in the bulleted list, then click the Increase Indent button**
   The list item is indented ½" and the bullet character changes to an open circle.
6. **Click to place the insertion point in Bookstore marketing team approval due in the bulleted list, click the Increase Indent button three times, then click the Decrease Indent button once**
   The list item is indented further and the bullet character changes to a square, as shown in **Figure 4-4**. You promote and demote items in a bulleted list using the Increase Indent and Decrease Indent buttons. Each time you promote or demote an item, the bullet character changes.
7. **Click the Increase Indent button to indent the items in the bulleted list to match Figure 4-5, then save your changes**

Creating multilevel lists

You can create lists with hierarchical structures by applying a multilevel list style to a list. To create a multilevel list, also called an outline, begin by applying a multilevel list style using the Multilevel List arrow in the Paragraph group on the Home tab, then type your outline, pressing ENTER after each item. To demote items to a lower level of importance in the outline, place the insertion point in the item, then click the Increase Indent button in the Paragraph group on the Home tab. Each time you indent a paragraph, the item is demoted to a lower level in the outline. Similarly, you can use the Decrease Indent button to promote an item to a higher level in the outline. You can also create a hierarchical structure in any bulleted or numbered list by using the Increase Indent button and the Decrease Indent button to demote and promote items in the list. To change the multilevel list style applied to a list, select the list, click the Multilevel List arrow, and then select a new style.

Figure 4-3: Bulleted list

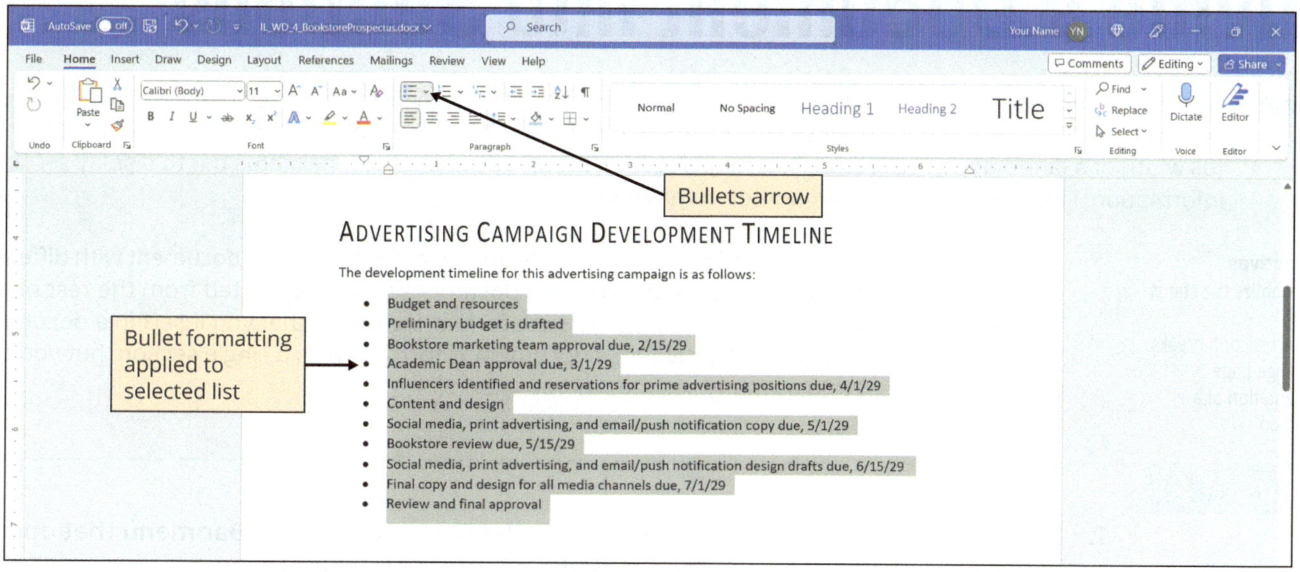

Figure 4-4: Demoted items in list

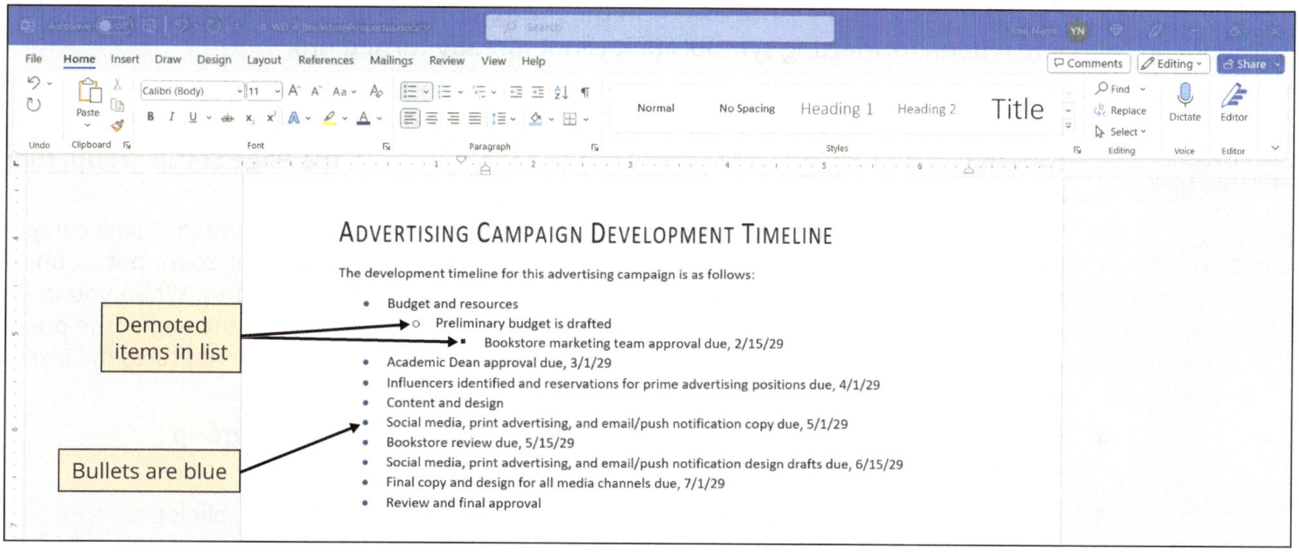

Figure 4-5: Multilevel list

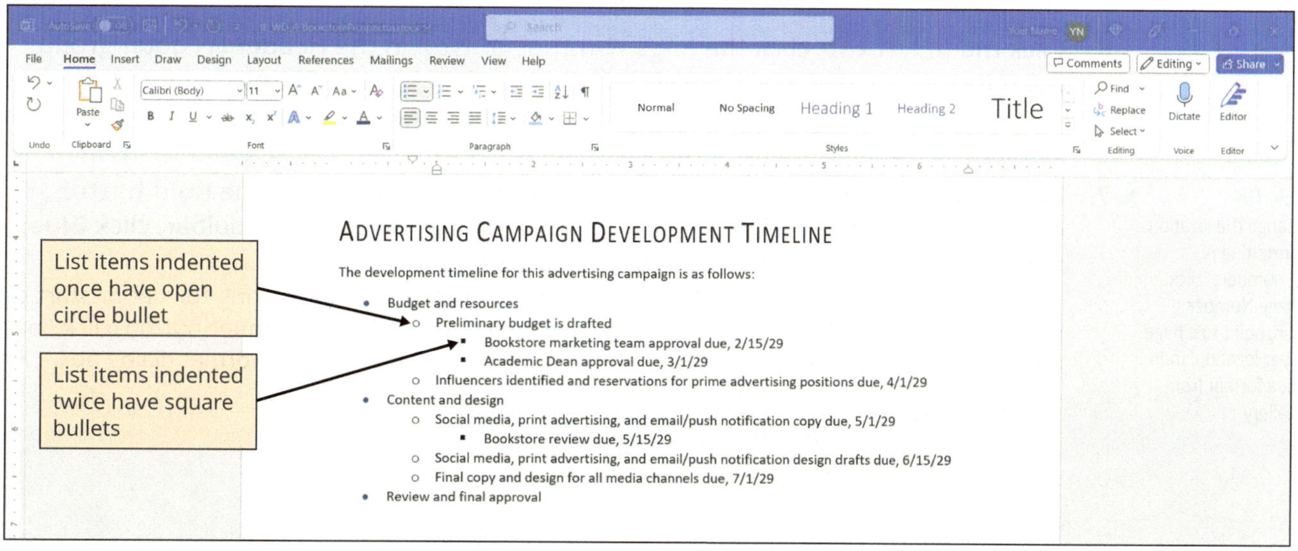

Divide a Document into Sections

Case You insert a next page section break above the Budget and Costing table to divide the document into two sections. You then apply landscape page orientation to the section that contains the table, so that the table can span the full width of a landscape page. Before inserting a section break, you customize the status bar to display section information. Finally, you add a page number in the footer.

Objectives
- Customize the status bar
- Insert section breaks
- Change page orientation of a section

Dividing a document into sections allows you to format each section of the document with different page layout settings. A **section** is a portion of a document that is separated from the rest of the document by section breaks. **Section breaks** are formatting marks that you insert in a document to show the end of a section. By default, a document is formatted as a single section, but you can divide a document into as many sections as you like.

Steps

Quick Tip
Use the Customize Status Bar menu to turn on and off the display of information in the status bar.

Quick Tip
To delete a break, click to the left of the break with the selection pointer to select it, then press DELETE.

Quick Tip
To change the location or formatting of page numbers, click the Page Number button, point to a page number location, then select a format from the gallery.

1. **Right-click the status bar, click Section on the Customize Status Bar menu that opens (if it is not already checked), then click the document to close the menu**
   The status bar indicates the insertion point is located in Section 1 of the document.

2. **Click the Show/Hide ¶ button ¶ in the Paragraph group to show paragraph marks and hidden formatting symbols (if it is not already turned on)**
   Turning on formatting marks allows you to display the section breaks you insert in a document.

3. **Place the insertion point in the blank paragraph above the Budget and Costing heading, click the Layout tab, click the Breaks button in the Page Setup group, then click Next Page in the Section Breaks section**
   Word inserts a next page section break, shown as a dotted double line, above the blank paragraph above the heading, as shown in **Figure 4-6**. You might need to scroll or zoom out to observe both the section break and the insertion point in your document window. When you insert a section break at the beginning of a paragraph, Word inserts the break at the end of the previous paragraph. The document now has two sections. Notice that the status bar indicates the insertion point is in Section 2.

4. **Click the View tab, click the Multiple Pages button in the Zoom group**
   Both pages of the document appear in the document window.

5. **Verify that the insertion point is in Section 2, click the Layout tab, click the Orientation button in the Page Setup group, then click Landscape**
   The page orientation of Section 2 changes to landscape, as shown in **Figure 4-7**. The page orientation of Section 1 does not change.

6. **Click the Insert tab, click the Page Number button in the Header & Footer group, point to Bottom of Page, then click Plain Number 3 in the Simple section**
   A page number field containing the number 2 is right-aligned in the Footer area at the bottom of pages 1 and 2 of the document. The document text is dimmed.

7. **Zoom in, select the page number at the bottom of page 2, click the Bold button B on the Mini toolbar, click the Font Color arrow A on the Mini toolbar, click Blue, Accent 1, Darker 25% then save your changes**
   The page number is bold and blue. If you want to change the numbering format or start page numbering with a different number, you can simply click the Page Number button, click Format Page Numbers, and then choose from the options in the Page Number Format dialog box.

Figure 4-6: Next Page section break

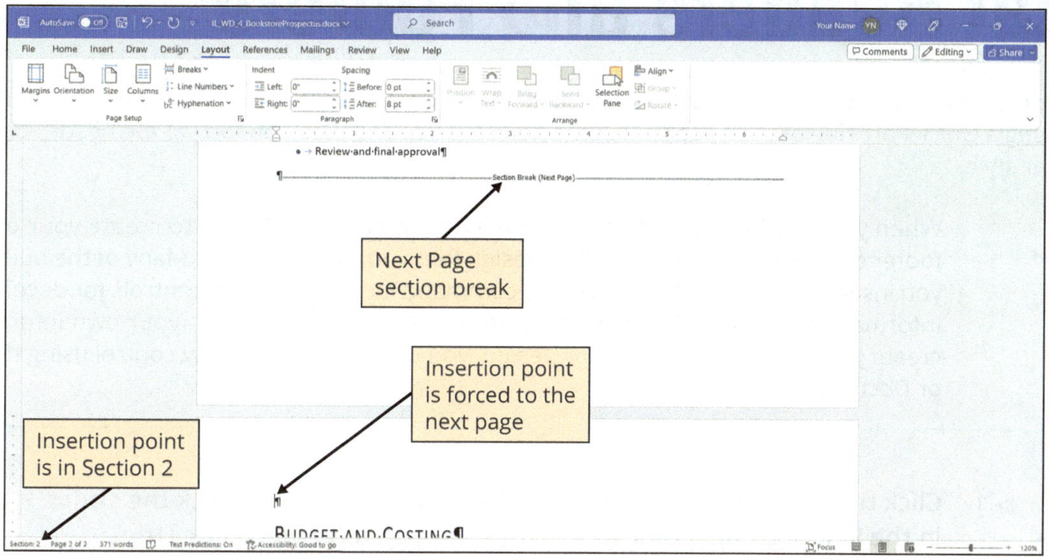

Figure 4-7: Section 2 with landscape page orientation

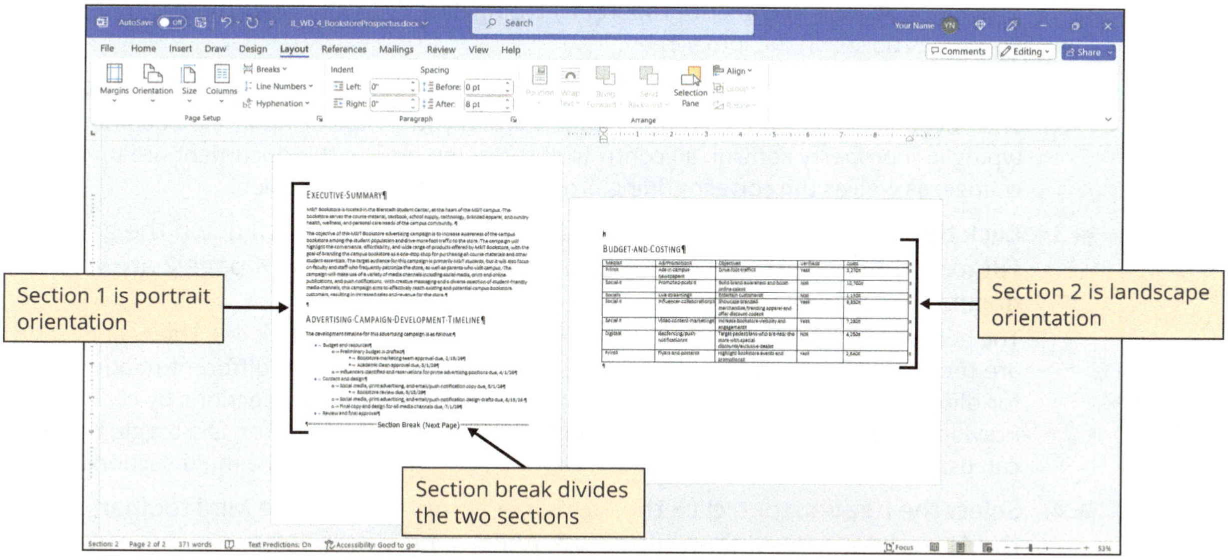

Using sections to vary the layout of a document

Dividing a document into sections allows you to vary the layout of a document. In addition to applying different page orientation settings to sections, you can apply different margins, paper size, columns, vertical alignment, header and footer, page numbering, footnotes, endnotes, and other page layout settings. For example, if you are formatting a report that includes a large chart, you might want to change the page margins for the chart only. To do this, you would insert a section break before and after the chart to create a section that contains only the chart, and then you would change the margin settings for that section only. If the chart does not fill the page from top to bottom, you could also change the vertical alignment of the chart so that it is centered vertically on the page. To do this, use the Vertical alignment arrow on the Layout tab of the Page Setup dialog box.

To check or change the page layout settings for an individual section, place the insertion point in the section, then open the Page Setup dialog box. Select any options you want to change, click the Apply to arrow, click This section, then click OK. When you select This section, the settings are applied to the current section only. When you select This point forward, the settings are applied to the current section and all sections that follow it. If you select Whole document, the settings are applied to all the sections in the document. Use the Apply to arrow in the Columns dialog box or the Footnote and Endnote dialog box to change those settings for a section.

Format Headers and Footers

Case You want the prospectus to include a header that identifies the title of the document. You create the header by inserting a Quick Part Title property control in the header area, and then you format the header using a built-in header style.

Objectives
- Format headers and footers
- Insert property controls

When you add headers and footers to a document, you choose to create your own header or footer design or start with a built-in design that you can customize. Many of the built-in styles that you insert using the Header or Footer command include property controls for document property information such as title, date, or author that you customize with your own information. If you create your own header or footer design, you can insert a property control using the Quick Parts or Document Info commands.

Steps

Trouble
If the Header & Footer contextual tab is not showing, click the Header & Footer tab.

1. **Click the Go to Header button in the Navigation group, click the Quick Parts button in the Insert group, point to Document Property, then click Title**
   A property control for the Title property is added to the header. A **property control** is a content control that contains document property information, such as title, company, or author. You can assign or update a document property by typing directly in a property control or by typing in the Properties boxes on the Info screen.

2. **Type MSIT Bookstore Advertising Campaign Prospectus in the Title property control**
   The document title is added to the header. When you assign or update a document property by typing in a property control, all controls of the same type in the document are updated with the change, as well as the corresponding property field on the Info screen.

Trouble
If your name is not entered in the Author property control, right-click the Author control, click Remove Content Control, select the text that remains, then type your name.

3. **Click the Header button in the Header & Footer group, scroll down the gallery, click Filigree, then scroll until the bottom of page 1 and the top of page 2 are visible in the document window**
   The header design changes to the Filigree design, as shown in **Figure 4-8**. The headers and footers are the same in Section 1 and Section 2. If you wanted to create different headers and footers for different sections, you would need to break the link between sections by clicking the Link to Previous button in the Navigation group. The Link to Previous button is a toggle button that you can use to link and unlink headers and footers between sections in a multi-section document.

Quick Tip
To remove a header, click in the Header or Footer area, click the Header button in the Header & Footer group, then click Remove Header. To remove a footer, click the Footer button, then click Remove Footer.

4. **Select the header text, click the Font Size arrow [11] on the Mini toolbar, click 12, click the Font color arrow, then click Blue, Accent 1, Darker 50%**
   The font color of the header text changes to dark blue. You can customize the format of a header or footer after applying a built-in header or footer style to it.

5. **Click the Close Header and Footer button in the Close group**
   The header and footer areas close and are dimmed. The body of the document is now active.

6. **Click the Home tab, click the Show/Hide ¶ button [¶], then save your changes**

Figure 4-8: Filigree header

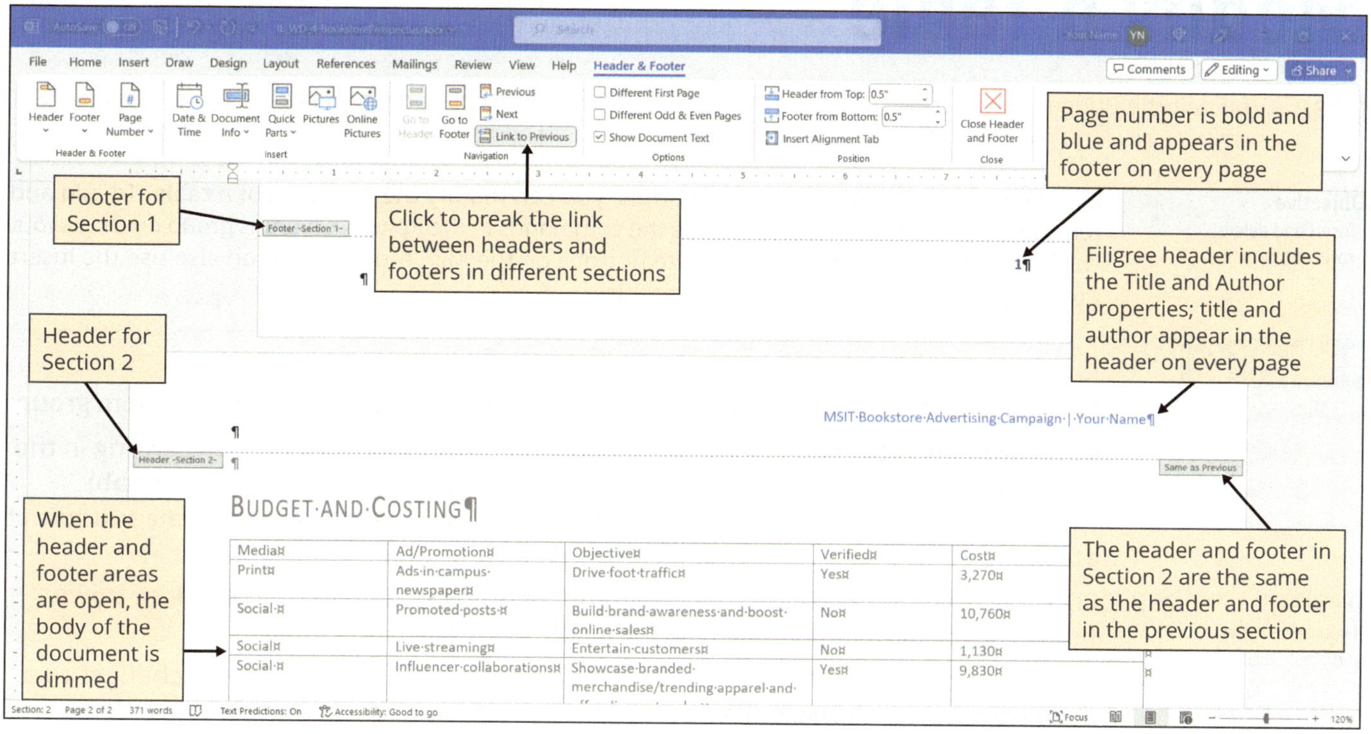

Adding a custom header or footer to the gallery

When you design a header that you want to use again in other documents, you can add it to the Header gallery by saving it as a building block. Building blocks are reusable pieces of formatted content or document parts, including headers and footers, page numbers, and text boxes, that are stored in galleries. **Building blocks** include predesigned content that comes with Word, as well as content that you create and save for future use. For example, you might create a custom header that contains your company name and logo and is formatted using the fonts, borders, and colors you use in all company documents.

To add a custom header to the Header gallery, select all the text in the header, including the last paragraph mark, click the Header button, and then click Save Selection to Header Gallery. In the Create New Building Block dialog box that opens, type a unique name for the header in the Name box, click the Gallery arrow and select the appropriate gallery, verify that the Category is General, and then type a brief description of the new header design in the Description box. This description appears in a ScreenTip when you point to the custom header in the gallery. When you are finished, click OK. The new header appears in the Header gallery under the General category.

To remove a custom header from the Header gallery, click the Header button in the Header & Footer group, scroll to the new header, right-click it in the Header gallery, click Organize and Delete, make sure the appropriate building block is selected in the Building Blocks Organizer that opens, click Delete, click Yes, and then click Close. You can follow the same process to add or remove a custom footer to the Footer gallery.

Modify a Table

Case You edit the Budget and Costing table to update it with the most recent budget and costing information. You remove a row and column of data that are no longer needed and add a row to the table for a new budget item.

Objective
- Insert and delete rows and columns

By adding and deleting rows and columns, you can modify the structure of a table. To add and remove rows and columns, you can use the commands in the Rows & Columns group on the Layout contextual tab, or the Insert and Delete buttons on the Mini toolbar. You can also use the Insert Controls to add rows and columns to a table.

Steps

1. **Click page 2, if necessary, click the View tab, then click Page Width in the Zoom group**
2. **Scroll until the table is at the top of the document window, click Live streaming in the table, then click the Layout contextual tab (to the right of the Table Design tab)**
   The buttons on the Layout tab (the contextual tab for tables) can be used to alter the structure of a table.
3. **Click the Delete button in the Rows and Columns group, then click Delete Rows**
   The Live streaming row is deleted from the table.
4. **Place the pointer over the Verified column top border until the pointer changes to a downward arrow ⬇, then click**
   The entire Verified column is selected, as shown in **Figure 4-9**.
5. **Click the Delete button on the Mini toolbar, then click Delete Columns**
   The Verified column is deleted from the table.
6. **Place the right-pointing arrow pointer at the left edge of the table over the border between the Promoted posts and Influencer collaborations rows to display the Insert Control, then click the Insert Control**
   A new row is added between the Promoted posts and Influencer collaborations rows.
7. **Click in the first cell in the new row, type Digital, press TAB, type Email newsletters, press TAB, type Share special offers and coupons, press TAB, type 1,250, then save your changes**
   Text is added to the new row, as shown in **Figure 4-10**.

Quick Tip
If you select a row and press DELETE, you delete only the contents of the row, not the row in the table.

Quick Tip
To select a cell, place the pointer near the left border of the cell, then click.

Copying and moving rows and columns

You can copy and move rows and columns within a table in the same manner you copy and move text. Select the row or column you want to move, then use the Copy or Cut button to place the selection on the Clipboard. Place the insertion point in the location where you want to insert the row or column, then click the Paste button to paste the selection. Rows are inserted above the row containing the insertion point; columns are inserted to the left of the column containing the insertion point. You can also copy or move columns and rows by selecting them and using the pointer to drag them to a new location in the table. To copy or move an entire table, select the entire table and then use the Cut, Copy, and Paste commands.

Figure 4-9: Column is selected

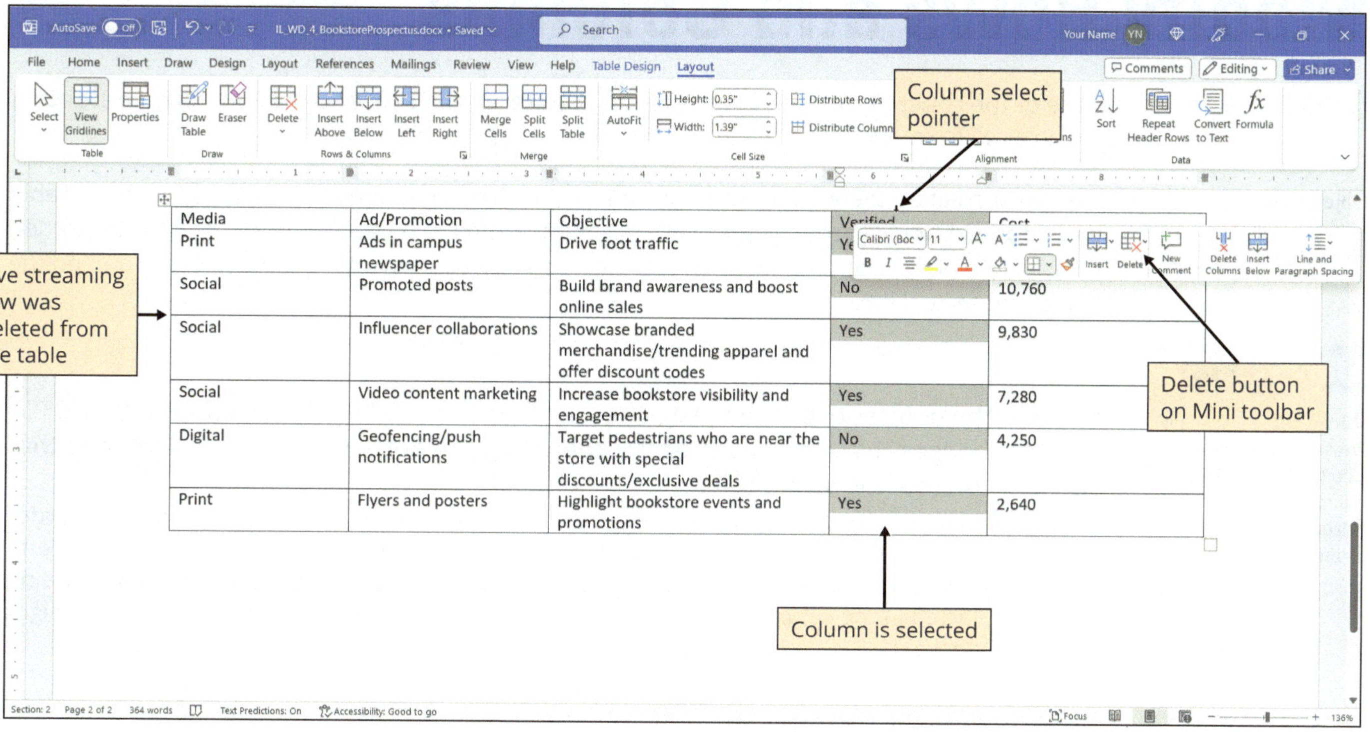

Figure 4-10: New row in table

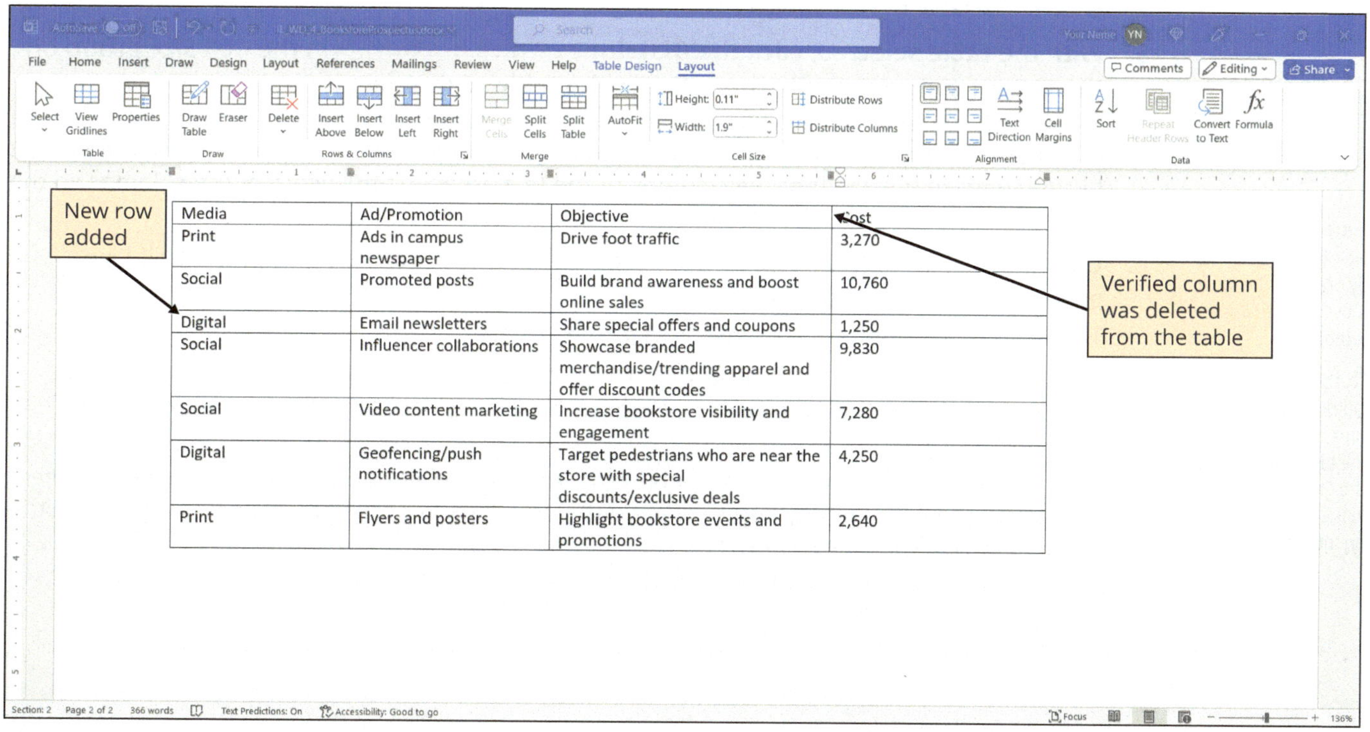

Modify Rows and Columns

Case You adjust the size of the columns and rows in the table to better fit the text, and then you center the text vertically in each table cell to create the appearance of more white space in the table.

Objectives
- Resize columns
- Format table cells

Once you create a table, you can easily adjust the size of columns and rows to make the table easier to read. You can change the width of columns and the height of rows by dragging a border, by using the AutoFit command, or by setting precise measurements in the Cell Size group on the Layout contextual tab.

Steps

Quick Tip
Press ALT as you drag a border to display the column width or row height measurements on the ruler.

1. **Position the pointer over the border between Media and Ad/Promotion until the pointer changes to a resize pointer, then drag the border left to approximately the ¾" mark on the horizontal ruler**
   The dotted line that appears as you drag represents the border. Dragging the column border changes the width of the first and second columns: the first column is narrower and the second column is wider. When dragging a border to change the width of an entire column, make sure no cells are selected in the column. You can also drag a row border up or down to change the height of the row above it.

2. **Position the pointer over the Ad/Promotion column right border until the pointer changes to a resize pointer, then double-click**
   Double-clicking a column border automatically resizes the column to fit the text.

3. **Double-click the Objective column right border with the resize pointer, then double-click the Cost column right border with the resize pointer**
   The widths of the Objective and Cost columns are adjusted.

4. **Move the pointer over the table, then click the table move handle that appears outside the upper-left corner of the table**
   Clicking the table move handle selects the entire table.

5. **With the table selected, click the Distribute Rows button in the Cell Size group on the Layout contextual tab, then click in the table to deselect it**
   All the rows in the table become the same height, as shown in **Figure 4-11**. You can also use the Distribute Columns button to make all the columns the same width, or you can use the AutoFit button to make the width of the columns fit the text, to adjust the width of the columns so the table is justified between the margins, or to set fixed column widths.

Quick Tip
Quickly move a table by dragging the table move handle to a new location.

6. **Click in the Objective column, click the Table Column Width box in the Cell Size group, type 5.3, then press ENTER**
   The width of the Objective column changes to 5.3".

Quick Tip
Quickly center a table on a page by selecting the table and clicking the Center button in the Paragraph group on the Home tab.

7. **Click the Select button in the Table group, click Select Table, click the Align Center Left button in the Alignment group, click to deselect the table, then save your changes**
   The text is centered vertically in each table cell, as shown in **Figure 4-12**. You can use the alignment buttons in the Alignment group to change the vertical and horizontal alignment of the text in selected cells or the entire table.

Figure 4-11: Resized columns and rows

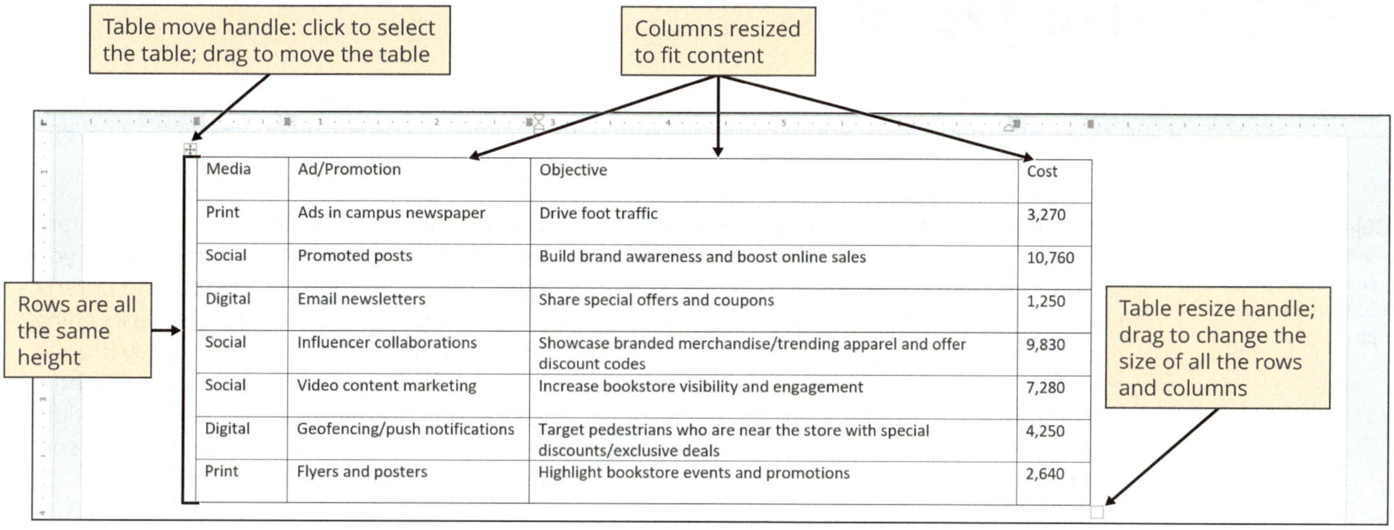

Figure 4-12: Text centered vertically in cells

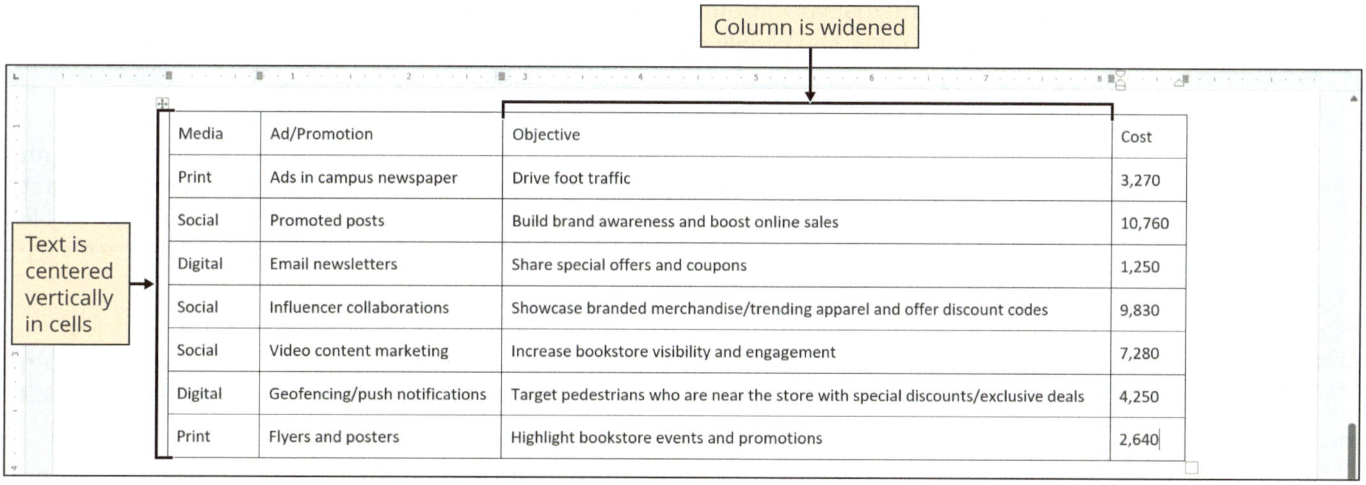

Setting advanced table properties

When you want to wrap text around a table, indent a table, or set other advanced table properties, you click the Properties command in the Table group on the Layout tab to open the Table Properties dialog box, shown in **Figure 4-13**. Using the Table tab in this dialog box, you can set a precise width for the table, change the horizontal alignment of the table between the margins, indent the table, and set text wrapping options for the table. You can also click Options on the Table tab to open the Table Options dialog box, which you use to customize the table's default cell margins and the spacing between table cells. Alternatively, click Borders and Shading on the Table tab to open the Borders and Shading dialog box, which you can use to create a custom format for the table.

The Row, Column, and Cell tabs in the Table Properties dialog box allow you to set an exact height for rows, specify an exact width for columns, and indicate an exact size for individual cells. The Alt Text tab is used to add alternative text for a table, such as a description of its content, so that the table can be understood by a person using a screen reader.

Figure 4-13: Table Properties dialog box

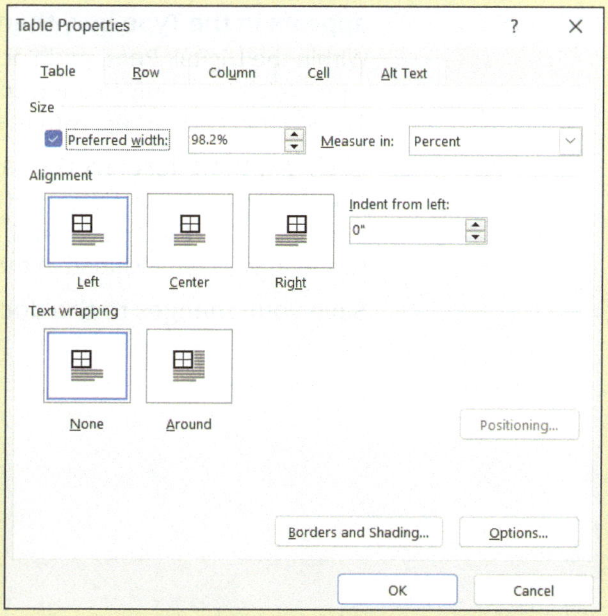

Sort Table Data

Case You sort the table so that all ads and promotions of the same media type are listed together. You also add secondary sort criteria so that the ads and promotions within each media type are listed in descending order by cost.

Objectives
- Sort table data by one or more criteria
- Sort lists and paragraphs

Tables are often easier to interpret and analyze when the data is **sorted**, which means the rows are organized in alphabetical or sequential order based on the data in one or more columns. When you sort a table, Word arranges all the table data according to the criteria you set. You set sort criteria by specifying the column (or columns) you want to sort by and indicating the sort order—ascending or descending—you want to use. **Ascending order** lists data alphabetically or sequentially (from A to Z, 0 to 9, or earliest to latest). **Descending order** lists data in reverse alphabetical or sequential order (from Z to A, 9 to 0, or latest to earliest). You can sort using the data in one column or multiple columns. When you sort by multiple columns, you must select primary, secondary, and tertiary sort criteria. You use the Sort command in the Data group on the Layout tab to sort a table.

Steps

1. **Click to place the insertion point anywhere in the table**
   To sort an entire table, you simply need to place the insertion point anywhere in the table. If you want to sort specific rows only, then you must select the rows you want to sort.

2. **Click the Sort button in the Data group on the Layout tab**
   The Sort dialog box opens, as shown in **Figure 4-14**. You use this dialog box to specify the column or columns you want to sort by, the type of information you are sorting (text, numbers, or dates), and the sort order (ascending or descending). Column 1 is selected by default in the Sort by list box. Since you want to sort your table first by the information in the first column—the media type (Print, Digital, or Social)—you don't change the Sort by criteria.

Quick Tip
To repeat the header row on every page of a table that spans multiple pages, click the Repeat Header Rows button in the Data group on the Layout tab.

3. **Click the Header row option button in the My list has section to select it**
   The table includes a **header row**, which is the first row of a table that contains the column headings. You must select the Header row option button first when you do not want the header row included in the sort.

4. **Click the Descending option button in the Sort by section**
   The information in the Media column will be sorted in descending—or reverse alphabetical—order, so that the "Social" promotion types will be listed first, followed by the "Print" promotion types, and then the "Digital" promotion types.

5. **Click the Then by arrow in the first Then by section, click Cost, verify that Number appears in the Type box, then click the Descending option button**
   Within the Digital, Print, and Social groups, the rows will be sorted by the cost of the promotion type, which is the information contained in the Cost column. The rows will appear in descending order within each group, with the most expensive promotion type listed first.

6. **Click OK, then deselect the table**
   The rows in the table are sorted first by the information in the Media column and second by the information in the Cost column, as shown in **Figure 4-15**. The first row of the table, which is the header row, is not included in the sort.

7. **Save your changes to the document**

Figure 4-14: Sort dialog box

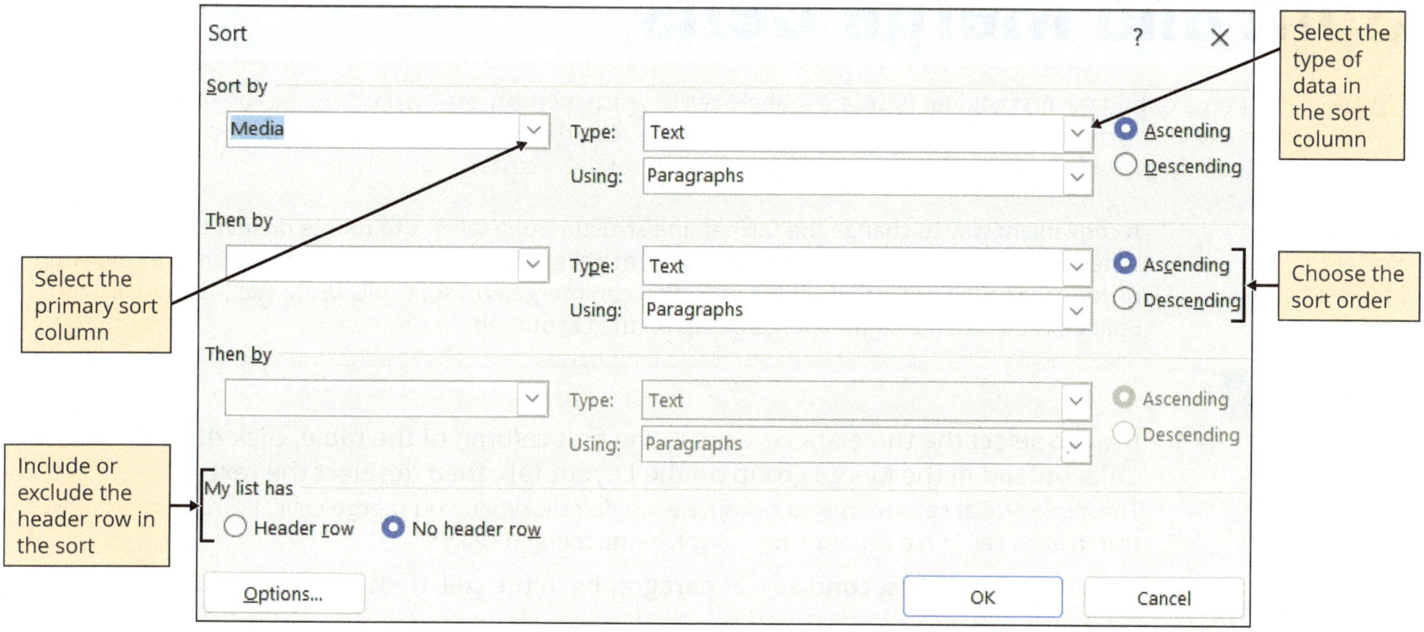

Figure 4-15: Sorted table

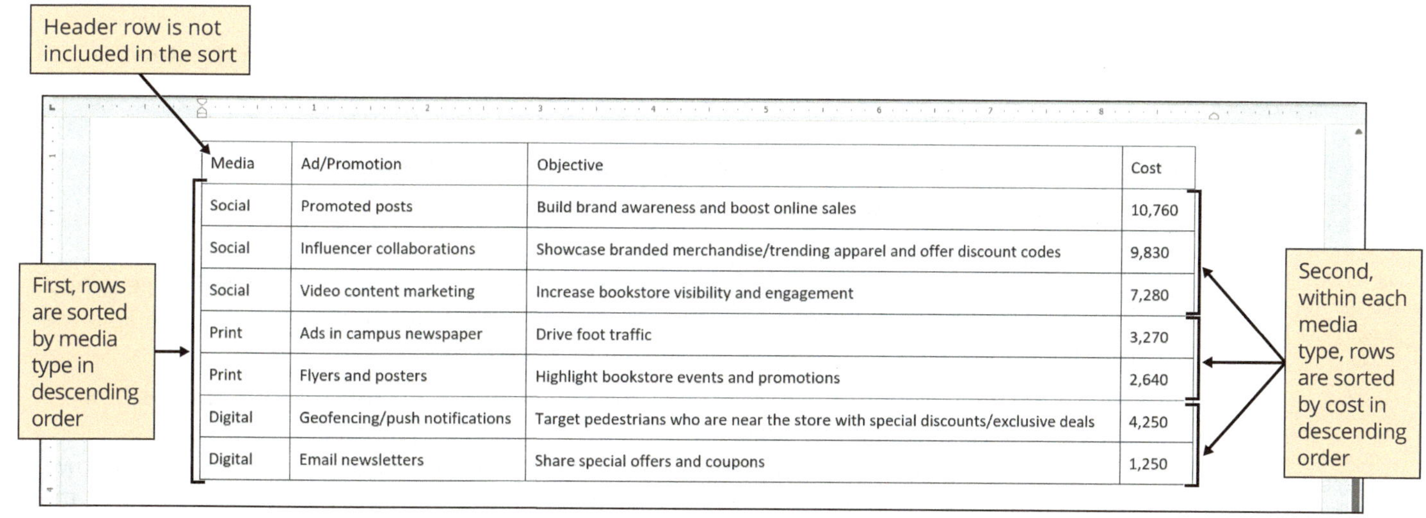

Media	Ad/Promotion	Objective	Cost
Social	Promoted posts	Build brand awareness and boost online sales	10,760
Social	Influencer collaborations	Showcase branded merchandise/trending apparel and offer discount codes	9,830
Social	Video content marketing	Increase bookstore visibility and engagement	7,280
Print	Ads in campus newspaper	Drive foot traffic	3,270
Print	Flyers and posters	Highlight bookstore events and promotions	2,640
Digital	Geofencing/push notifications	Target pedestrians who are near the store with special discounts/exclusive deals	4,250
Digital	Email newsletters	Share special offers and coupons	1,250

Sorting lists and paragraphs

In addition to sorting table data, you can use the Sort command to alphabetize text or sort numerical data. When you want to sort data that is not formatted as a table, such as lists and paragraphs, you use the Sort command in the Paragraph group on the Home tab. To sort lists and paragraphs, select the items you want included in the sort, then click the Sort button. In the Sort Text dialog box, use the Sort by arrow to select the sort by criteria (such as paragraphs or fields), use the Type arrow to select the type of data (text, numbers, or dates), and then click the Ascending or Descending option button to choose a sort order.

When sorting text information in a document, the term "fields" refers to text or numbers that are separated by a character, such as a tab or a comma. For example, you might want to sort a list of names alphabetically. If the names you want to sort are listed in "Last name, First name" order, then last name and first name are each considered a field. You can choose to sort the list in alphabetical order by last name or by first name. Use the Options button in the Sort Text dialog box to specify the character that separates the fields in your lists or paragraphs, along with other sort options.

Split and Merge Cells

Case You merge cells in the first column to create a single cell for each media type—Social, Print, and Digital. You also add a new blank row to the bottom of the table and split the cells in the row to create three new blank rows with a different structure. These rows will eventually be used to total the costs.

Objectives
- Split cells
- Merge cells

A convenient way to change the format and structure of a table is to merge or split the table cells. When you **merge** cells, you combine adjacent cells into a single cell. When you **split** a cell, you divide an existing cell into multiple cells. You can merge and split cells using the Merge Cells and Split Cells commands in the Merge group on the Layout tab.

Steps

1. **Drag to select the three Social cells in the first column of the table, click the Merge Cells button in the Merge group on the Layout tab, then deselect the text**
   The three Social cells merge to become a single cell. When you merge cells, Word converts the text in each cell into a separate paragraph in the merged cell.

Trouble
If you click below the table to deselect it, the active tab changes to the Home tab. If necessary, click in the table, then click the Layout tab to continue with the steps in this lesson.

2. **Select the first and second Social paragraphs in the cell, then press DELETE**
3. **Drag to select the two Print cells in the first column, click the Merge Cells button, type Print, drag to select the two Digital cells, click the Merge Cells button, then type Digital**
   The three Social cells merge to become one cell, the two Print cells merge to become one cell, and the two Digital cells merge to become one cell.
4. **Click the Email newsletters cell, then click the Insert Below button in the Rows & Columns group**
   A row is added to the bottom of the table.
5. **Drag to select the first three cells in the new last row of the table, click the Merge Cells button, then deselect the cell**
   The three cells in the row merge to become a single cell.
6. **Click the first cell in the last row, then click the Split Cells button in the Merge group**
   The Split Cells dialog box opens, as shown in **Figure 4-16**. You use this dialog box to split the selected cell or cells into a specific number of columns and rows.

Quick Tip
To split a table in two, click the row you want to be the first row in the second table, then click the Split Table button in the Merge group.

7. **Type 1 in the Number of columns box, press TAB, type 3 in the Number of rows box, click OK, then deselect the cells**
   The single cell is divided into three rows of equal height. When you split a cell into multiple rows, the width of the original column does not change. When you split a cell into multiple columns, the height of the original row does not change.

Quick Tip
If the cell you split contains text, all the text appears in the upper-left cell.

8. **Click the last cell in the Cost column, click the Split Cells button, type 1 in the Number of columns box, press TAB, type 3 in the Number of rows box, click OK, then save your changes**
   The cell is split into three rows, as shown in **Figure 4-17**. The last three rows now have only two columns.

Changing cell margins

By default, table cells have .08" left and right cell margins with no spacing between the cells, but you can adjust these settings for a table using the Cell Margins button in the Alignment group on the Layout tab. First, place the insertion point in the table, and then click the Cell Margins button to open the Table Options dialog box. Enter new settings for the top, bottom, left, and right cell margins in the boxes in the Default cell margins section of the dialog box, or select the Allow spacing between cells check box and then enter a setting in the Cell spacing section to increase the spacing between table cells. You can also deselect the Automatically resize to fit contents check box in the Options section of the dialog box to turn off the setting that causes table cells to widen to fit the text as you type. Any settings you change in the Table Options dialog box are applied to the entire table.

Figure 4-16: Split Cells dialog box

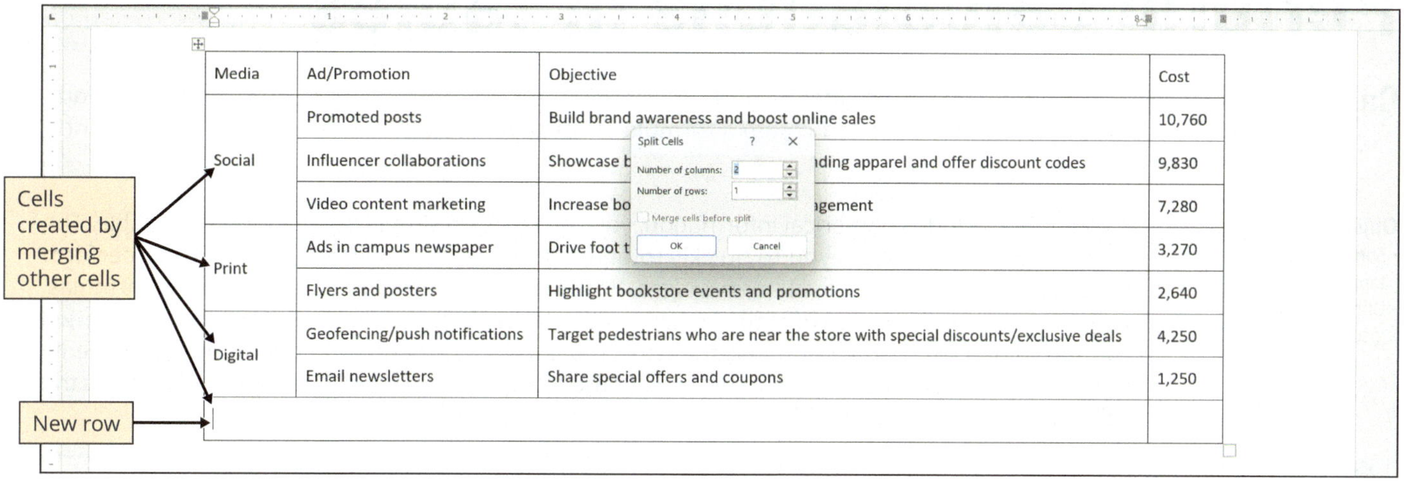

Figure 4-17: Cells split into three rows

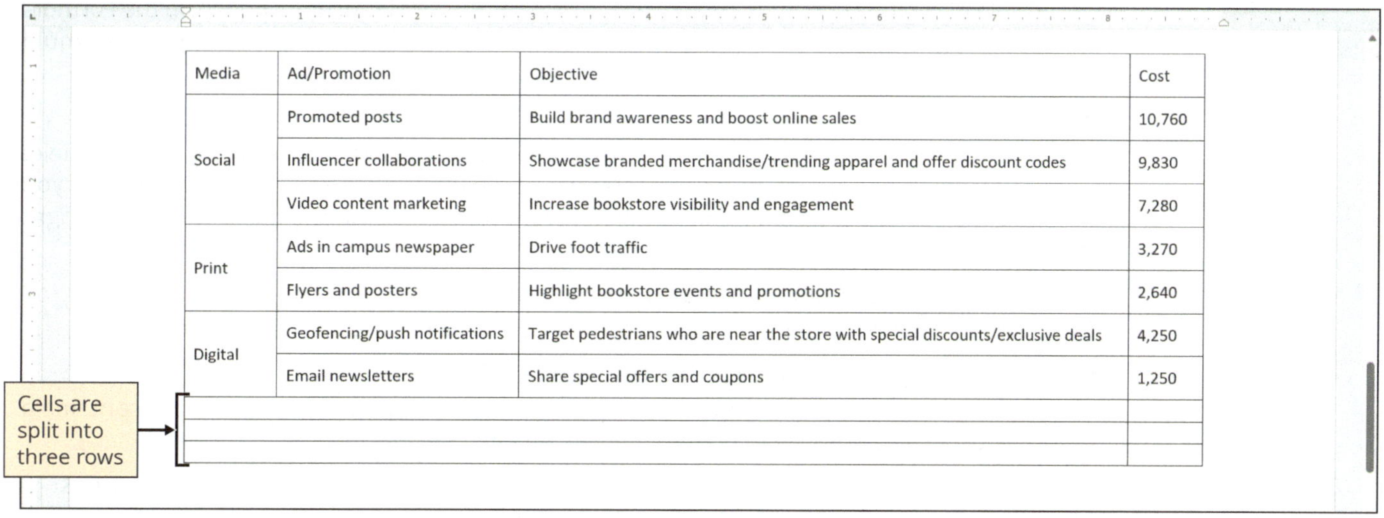

Media	Ad/Promotion	Objective	Cost
Social	Promoted posts	Build brand awareness and boost online sales	10,760
	Influencer collaborations	Showcase branded merchandise/trending apparel and offer discount codes	9,830
	Video content marketing	Increase bookstore visibility and engagement	7,280
Print	Ads in campus newspaper	Drive foot traffic	3,270
	Flyers and posters	Highlight bookstore events and promotions	2,640
Digital	Geofencing/push notifications	Target pedestrians who are near the store with special discounts/exclusive deals	4,250
	Email newsletters	Share special offers and coupons	1,250

Using tables to lay out a page

Tables are often used to display information for quick reference and analysis, but you can also use tables to structure the layout of a page. You can insert any kind of information in the cell of a table—including graphics, bulleted lists, charts, and other tables (called **nested tables**). For example, you might use a table to lay out a résumé, a newsletter, or a webpage. When you use a table to lay out a page, you generally remove the table borders to hide the table structure from the reader. After you remove borders, it can be helpful to display the table gridlines on the screen while you work. **Gridlines** are dotted lines that show the boundaries of cells but do not print. If your document will be viewed online—for example, if you are planning to email your résumé to potential employers—you should turn off the display of gridlines before you distribute the document so that it appears the same online as it is displayed when printed. To turn gridlines off or on, click the View Gridlines button in the Table group on the Layout tab.

Perform Calculations in Tables

Case You use the Formula command to calculate the total cost of the bookstore advertising campaign. You also add information about the budgeted cost and create a formula to calculate the difference between the total and budgeted costs.

Objectives
- Sum numbers in a table
- Update a field
- Insert a formula

If your table includes numerical information, you can perform simple calculations in the table. The Formula command allows you to quickly total the numbers in a column or row, and to perform other simple calculations, such as averages. When you calculate data in a table using formulas, you use cell references to refer to the cells in the table. Each cell has a unique **cell reference** composed of a letter and a number; the letter represents its column and the number represents its row. For example, the cell in the third row of the fourth column is cell D3. **Figure 4-18** shows the cell references in a simple table.

Steps

Quick Tip
You must type a zero in any blank cell in a row or column before using the SUM function.

1. **Click the first blank cell in column 1, type Total Cost, press TAB, then click the Formula button in the Data group on the Layout tab**
   The Formula dialog box opens, as shown in **Figure 4-19**. The SUM function appears in the Formula box followed by the reference for the cells to include in the calculation, (ABOVE). The formula =SUM(ABOVE) indicates that Word will sum the numbers in the cells above the active cell.

2. **Click OK**
   Word totals the numbers in the cells above the active cell and inserts the resulting sum as a field. You can use the SUM function to quickly total the numbers in a column or a row. If the cell you select is at the bottom of a column of numbers, Word totals the column. If the cell is at the right end of a row of numbers, Word totals the row.

3. **Select 1,250 in the cell above the total, then type 1,675**
   If you change a number that is part of a calculation, you must recalculate the field result.

4. **Press DOWN ARROW, right-click the cell, then click Update Field**
   The resulting sum in the cell is updated. When the insertion point is in a cell that contains a formula, you can also press F9 to update the field result.

5. **Press TAB, type Budgeted in the cell below Total Cost, press TAB, type 40,000, press TAB, type Difference in the cell below Budgeted, then press TAB**
   The insertion point is in the last cell of the table.

6. **Click the Formula button**
   The Formula dialog box opens. Word proposes to sum the numbers above the active cell, but you want to insert a formula that calculates the difference between the total and budgeted costs. You can type simple custom formulas using a plus sign (+) for addition, a minus sign (–) for subtraction, an asterisk (*) for multiplication, and a slash (/) for division.

Quick Tip
Cell references are determined by the number of columns in each row, not by the number of columns in the table. Rows 9 and 10 have only two columns: A and B.

7. **Select =SUM(ABOVE) in the Formula box, then type =B9–B10**
   You must type an equal sign (=) to indicate that the text following the equal sign (=) is a formula. You want to subtract the budgeted cost in the second column of row 10 from the total cost in the second column of row 9; therefore, you type a formula to subtract the value in cell B10 from the value in cell B9.

8. **Click OK, then save your changes**
   The difference appears in the cell, as shown in **Figure 4-20**.

Figure 4-18: Cell references in a table

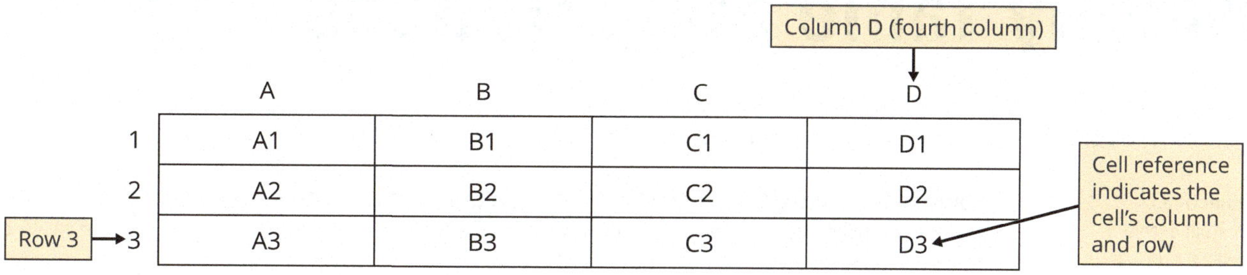

Figure 4-19: Formula dialog box

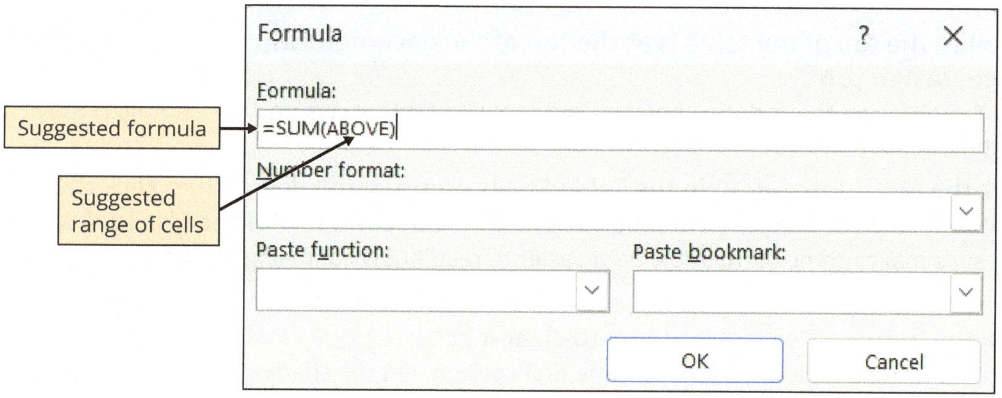

Figure 4-20: Difference calculated in table

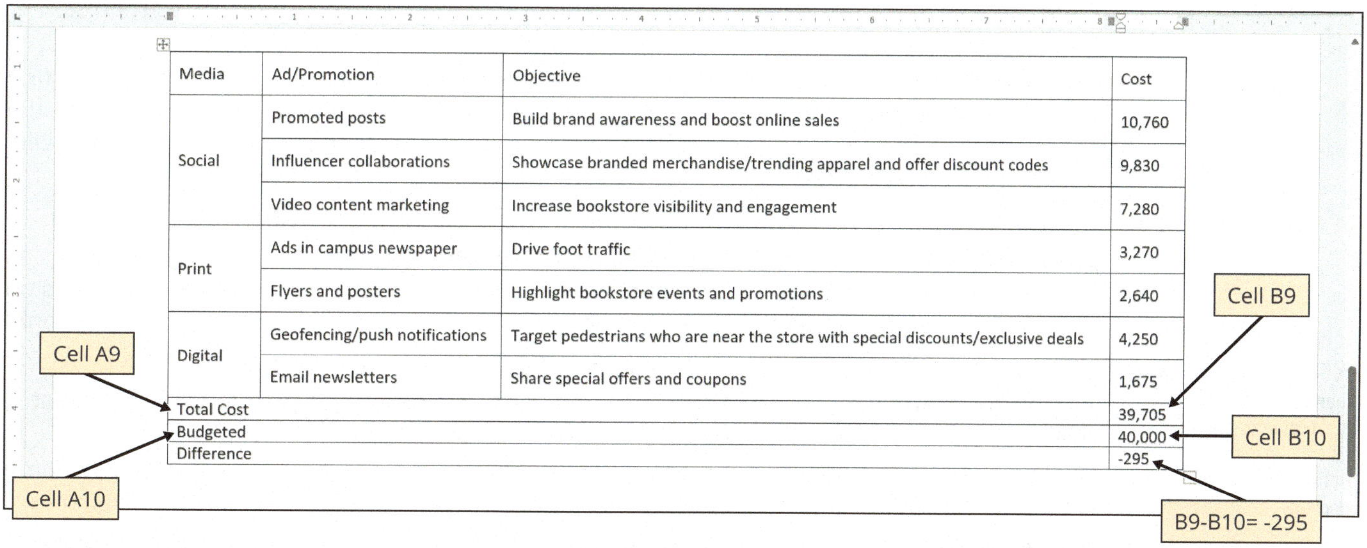

Media	Ad/Promotion	Objective	Cost
Social	Promoted posts	Build brand awareness and boost online sales	10,760
	Influencer collaborations	Showcase branded merchandise/trending apparel and offer discount codes	9,830
	Video content marketing	Increase bookstore visibility and engagement	7,280
Print	Ads in campus newspaper	Drive foot traffic	3,270
	Flyers and posters	Highlight bookstore events and promotions	2,640
Digital	Geofencing/push notifications	Target pedestrians who are near the store with special discounts/exclusive deals	4,250
	Email newsletters	Share special offers and coupons	1,675
Total Cost			39,705
Budgeted			40,000
Difference			-295

Working with formulas

In addition to the SUM function, Word includes formulas for averaging, counting, and rounding data, to name a few. To use a Word formula, delete any text in the Formula box, type =, click the Paste function arrow in the Formula dialog box, select a function, and then insert the cell references of the cells you want to include in the calculation in parentheses after the name of the function. When entering formulas, you must separate cell references by a comma. For example, if you want to average the values in cells A1, B3, and C4, enter the formula =AVERAGE(A1,B3,C4). You must separate cell ranges by a colon. For example, to total the values in cells A1 through A9, enter the formula =SUM(A1:A9). To display the result of a calculation in a particular number format, such as a decimal percentage (0.00%), click the Number format arrow in the Formula dialog box and select a number format. Word inserts the result of a calculation as a field in the selected cell.

Modify Table Style Options

Case You want the table information to stand out, so you apply a table style to the table, adjust the table style options, and then change the alignment of text in the table cells.

Objectives
- Format a table
- Align text in table cells

Applying a table style is a fast way to format a table using borders, shading, fonts, alignment, colors, and other formatting effects. Once you apply a table style, you can use the table style options to customize the format of the table, and the alignment buttons to adjust the position of text within the table.

Steps

1. **Scroll so the top of the table is at the top of the document window, then click the Table Design tab**

   The Table Design tab includes buttons for applying table styles and for adding, removing, and customizing borders and shading in a table.

> **Quick Tip**
> Click Clear in the gallery of table styles to remove all borders, shading, and other style elements from the table.

2. **Click the More button in the Table Styles group, scroll down, then click the List Table 2 – Accent 1 style (the second style in the second row of the List Tables section)**

   This style makes some of the table data easier to read but is confusing, as shown in **Figure 4-21**.

3. **In the Table Style Options group, click the First Column check box to clear it, then click the Banded Rows check box to clear it**

   The bold formatting is removed from the first column and the shading is removed from the table rows. When the banded columns or banded rows setting is active, the odd columns or rows are formatted differently from the even columns or rows.

4. **Click the Banded Columns check box to clear it, then click the First Column check box to select it**

   The shading is removed from the table columns and the bold formatting is restored to the first column, making the organization of the table data easier to understand. You can also use the check boxes in the Table Style Options group to change the Header row, Total row, and Last Column formatting in a table.

5. **Click the Layout contextual tab, then click the View Gridlines button in the Table group to display table gridlines if they are not already displayed**

   The View Gridlines button is a toggle button. You use it to turn the display of table gridlines on and off. Gridlines display on the screen but do not print. You want the gridlines to be turned on.

> **Trouble**
> When you select the Media column, the first column in the last three rows is also selected.

6. **Click the table move handle, click the Align Center Left button in the Alignment group, select the Media column, click the Align Center button, select the Cost column, then click the Align Center Right button**

   First, the data in the table is left-aligned and centered vertically, then the data in the Media column is centered, and finally, the data in the Cost column is right-aligned.

7. **Select the last three rows of the table, click the Bold button B on the Mini toolbar twice, then click the Align Center Right button in the Alignment group on the Layout tab on the Ribbon**

   The text in the last three rows is right-aligned and bold is applied.

> **Quick Tip**
> You can also use the alignment buttons in the Paragraph group on the Home tab to change the alignment of text in a table.

8. **Select the first row of the table, click the Center button on the Mini toolbar, click the Font Size arrow 11 on the Mini toolbar, click 12, deselect the row, then save your changes**

   The text in the header row is centered and enlarged, as shown in **Figure 4-22**.

Figure 4-21: List Table 2 - Accent 1 style applied to table

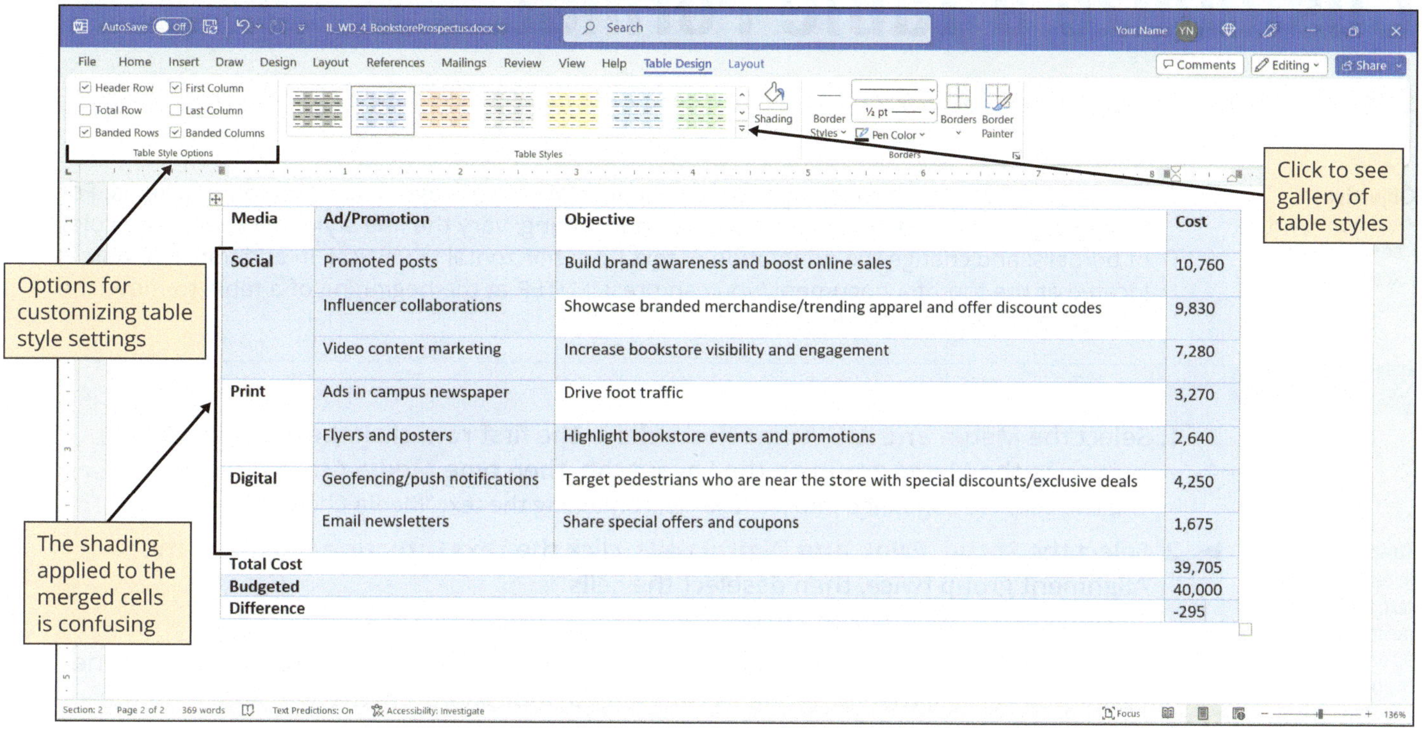

Figure 4-22: Table format modified with table style options

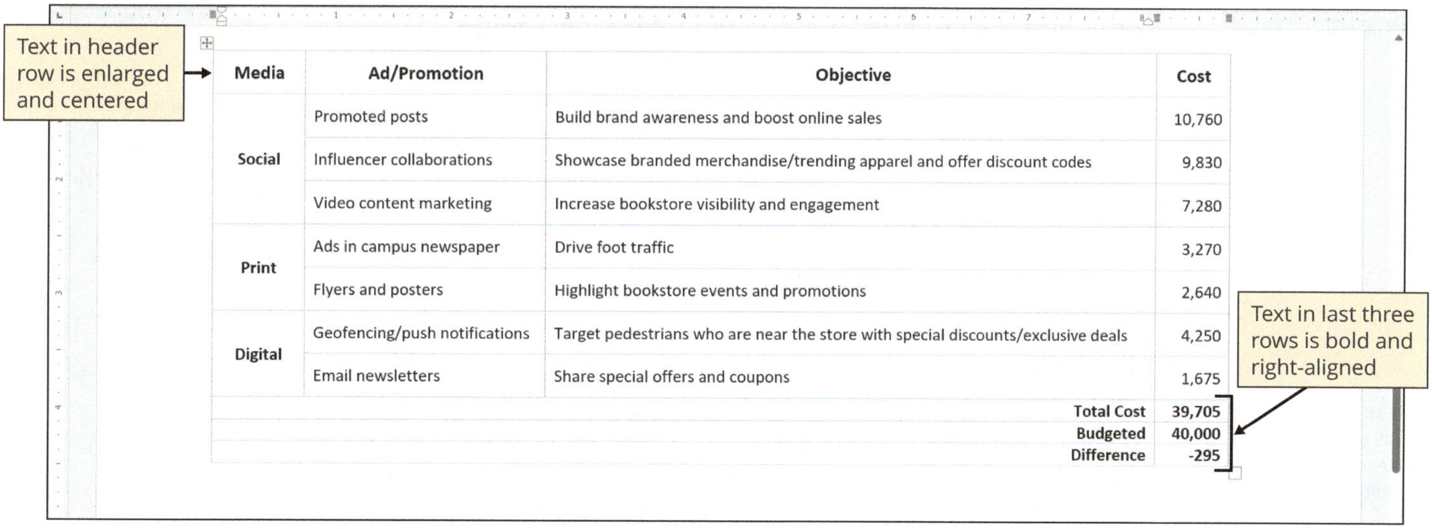

Customize a Table Format

Case You adjust the text direction, shading, and borders in the table to make it colorful and easier to understand at a glance.

Objectives
- Add shading and borders to a table
- Rotate text

You can also use the formatting tools available in Word to create your own table designs. For example, you can add or remove borders and shading; vary the line style, thickness, and color of borders; and change the orientation of text from horizontal to vertical. In addition, if a table is located at the top of a document, you can press ENTER at the beginning of a table to move the table down one line in the document.

Steps

1. **Select the Media and Ad/Promotion cells in the first row, click the Merge Cells button in the Merge group on the Layout tab, then type Media Channel**
   The two cells are combined into a single cell containing the text "Media Channel".

Quick Tip In cells with vertical text, the I-beam pointer is rotated 90 degrees, and the buttons in the Alignment group change to vertical alignment.

2. **Select the Social, Print, and Digital cells, click the Text Direction button in the Alignment group twice, then deselect the cells**
   The text in each cell is rotated 270 degrees.
3. **Position the pointer over the Social cell right border until the pointer changes to the resize pointer +||+, then drag the border left to approximately the 1/3" mark on the horizontal ruler**
   The width of the column containing the vertical text narrows.

Trouble The Colors button is located on the Design tab, not the Table Design tab.

4. **Click the Design tab, click the Colors button, scroll down the Colors list, then click Aspect**
   The color palette for the document changes to Aspect.
5. **Click Social to place the insertion point in the Social cell, click the Table Design tab, then click the Shading arrow in the Table Styles group**
   The gallery of shading colors for the Aspect theme color palette opens.
6. **Click Red, Accent 2, Lighter 40% in the gallery as shown in Figure 4-23, click the Print cell, click the Shading arrow, click Orange, Accent 1, Lighter 40%, click the Digital cell, click the Shading arrow, then click Dark Green, Accent 4, Lighter 40%**
   Colored shading is applied to each cell.
7. **Select the header row, click the Shading arrow on the Mini toolbar, click Dark Purple, Accent 5, Darker 25%, click the Font color arrow on the Mini toolbar, then click White, Background 1**
   Shading is applied to the header row and the font color changes to white for better contrast.

Quick Tip You use the Borders menu to both add and remove borders.

8. **Click the Borders arrow in the Borders group, click View Gridlines to turn off the display of gridlines, select the last three rows of the table, click the Borders arrow, click No Border on the Borders menu, then click in the table to deselect the rows**
   The top, bottom, left, and right borders are removed from each cell in the selected rows.

Quick Tip To change the color, line weight, line style, or border style of an existing border, adjust the active settings in the Borders group, click the Border Painter button, then click the border with the Border Painter pointer.

9. **Select the Total Cost row, click the Borders arrow, then click Top Border**
   The active border color is black. A black top border is added to the Total Cost row. You can use the buttons in the Borders group to change the active color, line weight, line style, and border style settings before adding a border to a table.
10. **Click the Pen Color button in the Borders group, click Orange, Accent 1, click the Border Painter button to turn off the Border painter, select the Total Cost row, if necessary, click the Borders arrow, click Top Border, click the 40,000 cell, click the Borders arrow, click Bottom Border, then save your changes**
    The active border color changes to orange, the color of the top border of the Total Cost row changes to orange, and an orange bottom border is added to the 40,000 cell. The completed table is shown in **Figure 4-24**.

Figure 4-23: Gallery of shading colors from the Aspect theme color palette

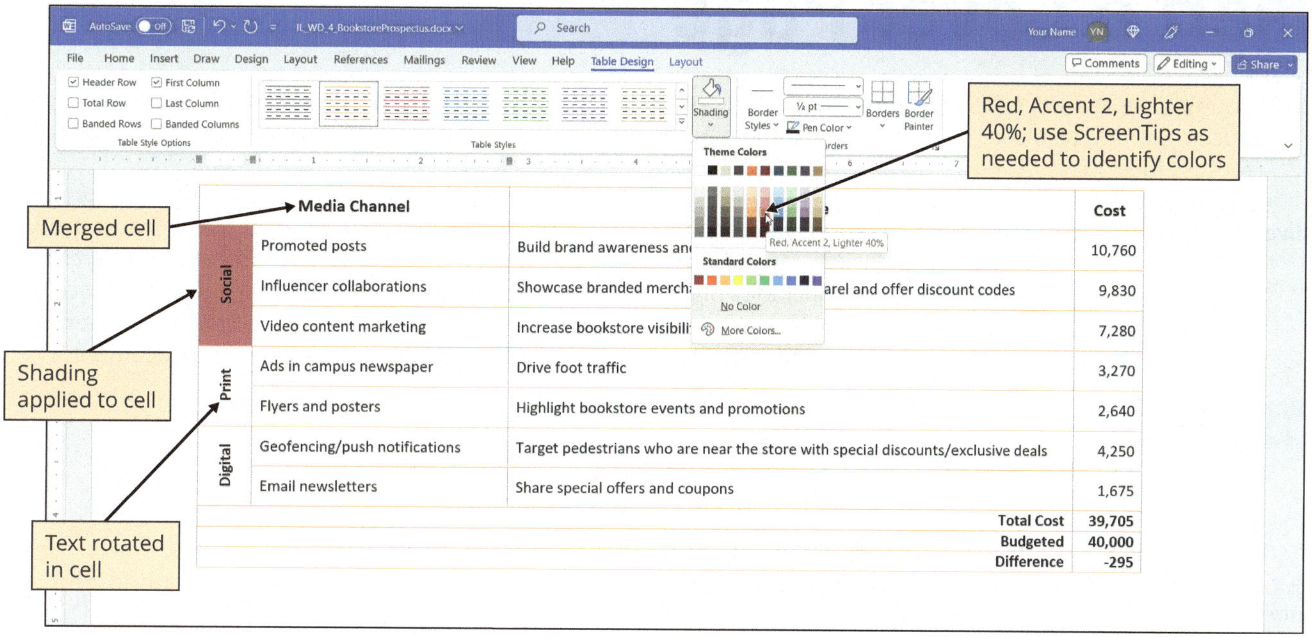

Figure 4-24: Completed table

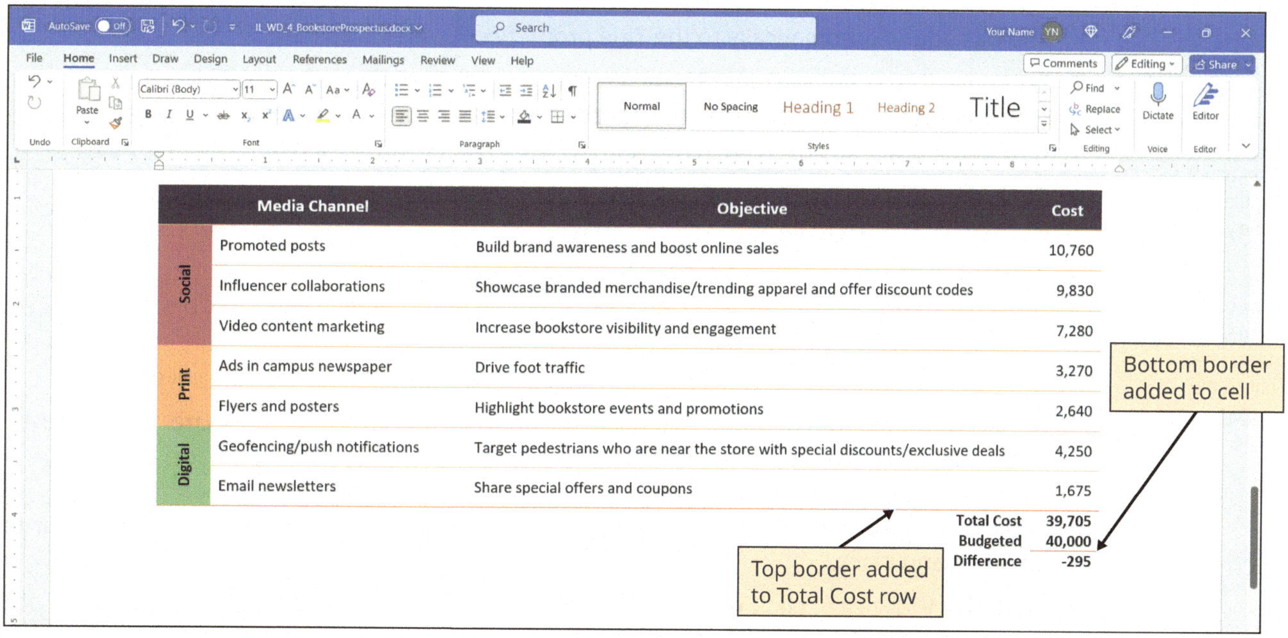

Drawing a table

The Word Draw Table feature allows you to draw table cells exactly where you want them. To draw a table, click the Table button on the Insert tab, and then click Draw Table. If a table is already started, you can click the Draw Table button in the Draw group on the Layout tab to turn on the Draw pointer, and then click and drag to draw a cell. Using the same method, you can draw borders within the cell to create columns and rows or draw additional cells attached to the first cell. Click the Draw Table button or press [ESC] to turn off the draw feature. The borders you draw are added using the active line style, line weight, and pen color settings found in the Borders group on the Table Design tab.

If you want to remove a border from a table, click the Eraser button in the Draw group to activate the Eraser pointer, and then click the border you want to remove. Click the Eraser button or press [ESC] to turn off the erase feature. You can use the Draw pointer and the Eraser pointer to change the structure of any table, not just the tables you draw from scratch.

Insert a Cover Page

Case You finalize the advertising campaign prospectus by inserting a cover page that mirrors the design of the document. You also add a "Confidential" watermark to indicate the document is confidential until it is approved for distribution.

Objectives
- Insert and customize a cover page
- Add a watermark

To quickly finalize a report, you can insert one of the many predesigned cover pages that come with Word. Cover page designs range from plain and straightforward to colorful and attention-grabbing. Each cover page design includes placeholder text and property controls that you can replace with your own information. You can also customize a document by adding a watermark. A **watermark** is a WordArt or other graphic object that appears lightly shaded behind text in a document.

Steps

1. **Click the View tab, then click the Multiple Pages button**
   Both pages of the document appear in the document window.
2. **Click the Insert tab, then click the Cover Page arrow in the Pages group**
   The gallery of cover pages opens. Each page design includes placeholder text and property controls. The page designs are shown using the active color palette, which is Aspect.
3. **Scroll down the gallery, then click Ion (Dark)**
   The Ion Dark cover page is added at the beginning of the document. Notice that the document title was added automatically to the Title property control.
4. **Zoom in on the cover page, then scroll down to view the title, subtitle, author, company name, and company address controls at the bottom of the page**
   Your name is already entered in the Author property control, as shown in **Figure 4-25**.
5. **Click the Document Subtitle property control, then type Mountain Springs Institute of Technology**
6. **Right-click the Company Name property control, click Remove Content Control, right-click the Company address property control, click Remove Content Control, then press [Backspace] three times**
   The Company Name and Company address controls are removed from the cover page.
7. **Scroll to the top of the page, click the Year property control, click the Year arrow, click Today, select the year, click the Increase Font Size button on the Mini toolbar three times, click the Font Color arrow, then click Black, Text 1**
   The current year replaces the placeholder text in the Year property control, and the year text is enlarged and black.
8. **Click the View tab, click the Multiple Pages button, click to place the insertion point in the middle of page 2, click the Design tab, then click the Watermark button in the Page Background group**
   A gallery of watermarks opens. You can apply one of the preformatted watermarks or create a custom watermark.
9. **Click Confidential 1, then save your changes**
   The word "Confidential" appears lightly shaded behind the text on each page of the document, but not on the cover page. The completed document is shown in **Figure 4-26**.
10. **sam Submit the document to your instructor, close the file, then exit Word**

Quick Tip
To remove a cover page, click the Cover Page arrow, then click Remove Current Cover Page.

Trouble
If your name is not entered in the Author property control, right-click the Author control, click Remove Content Control, select the text that remains, then type your name.

Trouble
If you are unable to remove the property control, deselect the control, then try step 6 again.

Quick Tip
To remove a watermark, click the Watermark button, then click Remove Watermark.

Figure 4-25: Ion Dark cover page

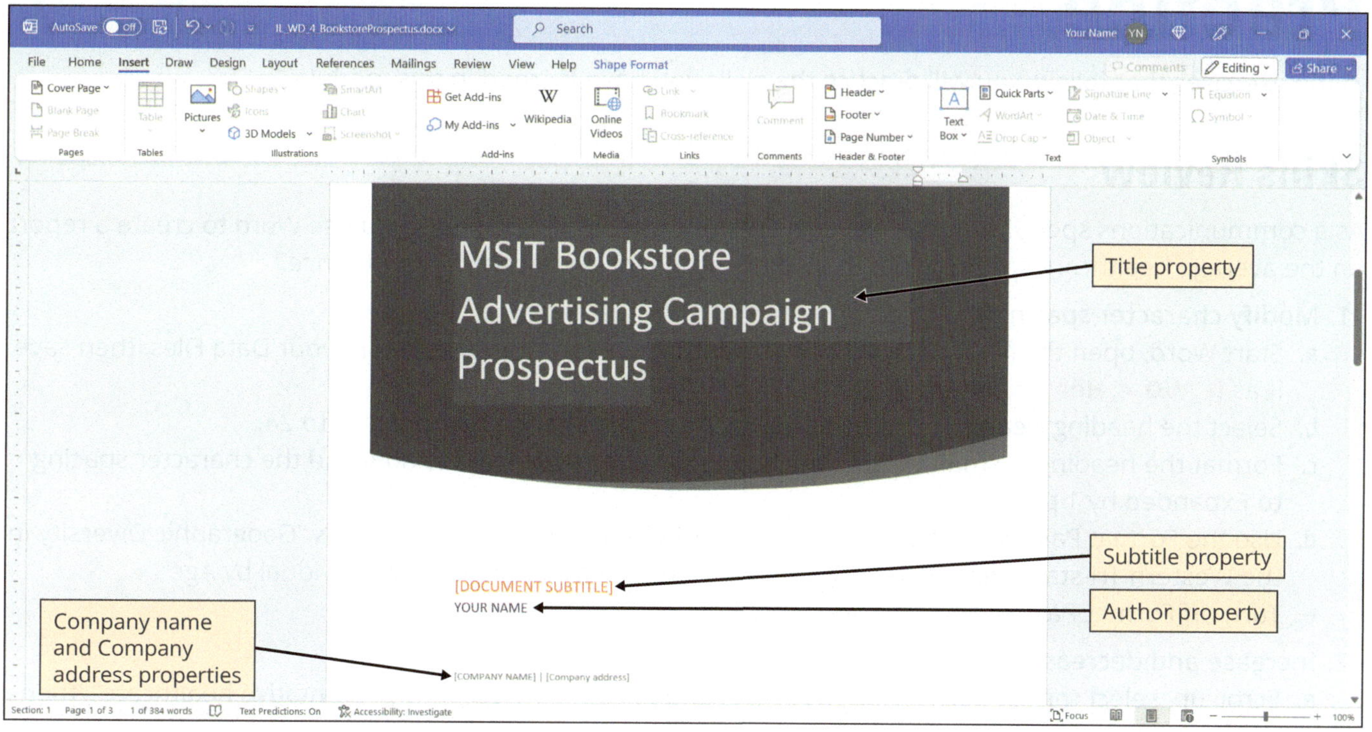

Figure 4-26: Completed document

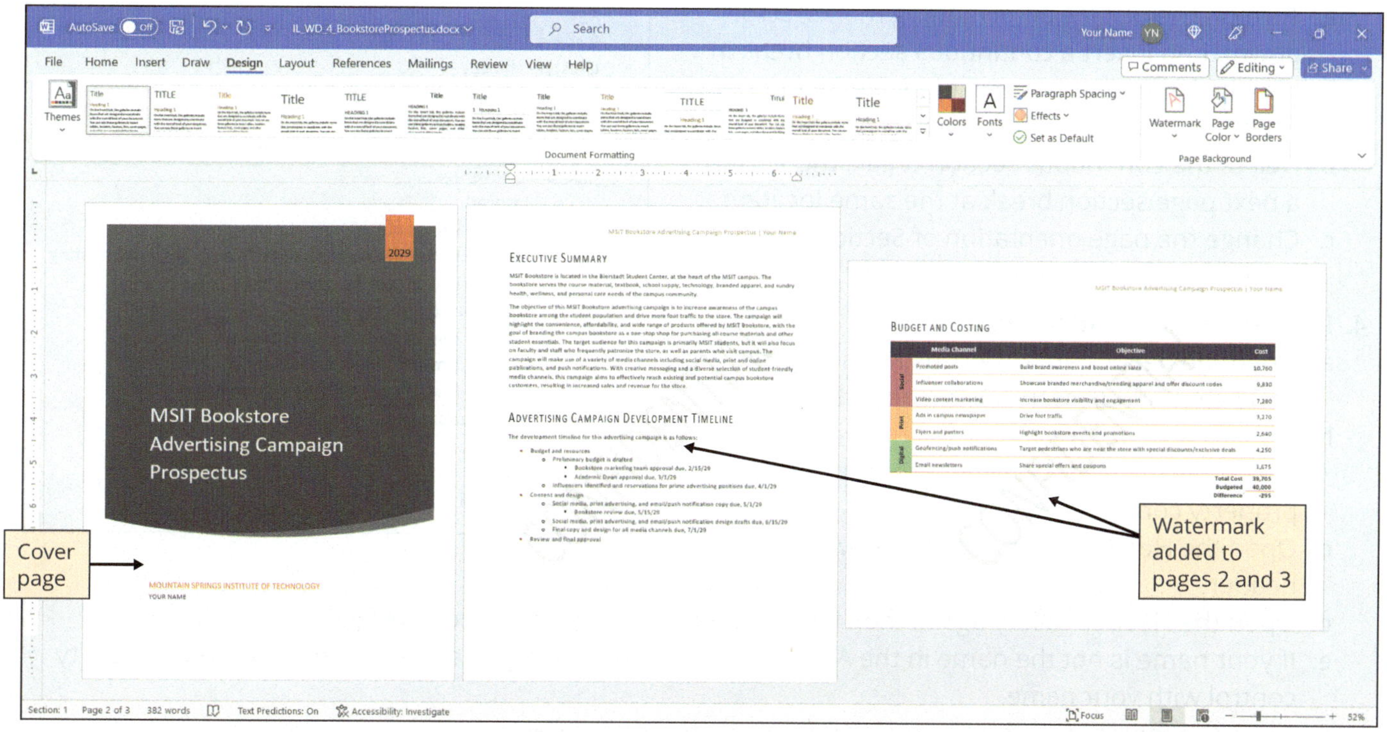

Practice

In the exercises that follow, you will practice the skills you have learned in this module.

Skills Review

As a communications specialist at the Western Tri-state Nursing Association, you use Word to create a report on the average healthcare spending per individual by age for an upcoming conference.

1. **Modify character spacing.**
   a. Start Word, open the file IL_WD_4-2.docx from the location where you store your Data Files, then save it as **IL_WD_4_HealthSpending**.
   b. Select the heading Health Spending Varies by Age, then change the font size to 24.
   c. Format the heading in small caps, then change the character scale to 80% and the character spacing to Expanded by 1 point.
   d. Use the Format Painter to copy the formatting of the heading to the headings "Geographic Diversity in the Western Tri-state Region" and "Average Annual Health Spending Per Individual by Age".
   e. Turn off Format Painter and save your changes.
2. **Increase and decrease indents.**
   a. Scroll up, select the list that begins with "Age" and ends with "Access to preventative healthcare", then apply square bullets to the list.
   b. Change the font color of the bullet characters to Blue, Accent 1.
   c. Using the Increase and Decrease Indent buttons, create the multilevel list shown in **Figure 4-27**, then save your changes.
3. **Divide a document into sections.**
   a. Turn on the display of formatting marks, scroll down, then insert a continuous section break in the blank paragraph above the Average Annual Health Spending Per Individual by Age heading.
   b. Delete the continuous section break, then insert a next page section break at the same location.
   c. Change the page orientation of Section 2 to landscape, then save your changes.
4. **Format headers and footers.**
   a. Open the header area, then, using the Quick Parts command, insert a Title property control.
   b. Type **Health Spending Per Individual by Age in the Western Tri-state Region** in the Title property control.
   c. Open the Header gallery, then remove the header.
   d. Open the Header gallery again, then insert a header using the Filigree design.
   e. If your name is not the name in the Author property control, replace the text in the Author property control with your name.
   f. Go to the footer area, then insert a footer using the Whisp design.
   g. Close the footer area, turn off the display of formatting marks, then save your changes.

Figure 4-27

- Age
- Income
- Lifestyle choices
  - Eating habits and nutrition
  - Exercise habits
  - Smoking and alcohol consumption
- Insurance coverage
  - Insured
    - Lower out-of-pocket expenses
    - Better access to specialists and diagnostic testing
    - Lower cost for prescription drugs
  - Not insured or under-insured
    - Higher up-front costs for healthcare
    - Limited range of providers
    - Higher cost for prescription drugs
- Geographic location
  - Urban
  - Rural
- Access to preventative healthcare

5. **Modify a table.**
   a. Scroll to page 2 to display the table in your document window.
   b. Insert a table row above the Jasper row, then type the following text in the new row:

Seneca	**5**	**1,491**	**2,321**	**3,675**	**7,476**	**15,534**	**23,734**

   c. Delete the Greene row, then delete the Zone column.
   d. Insert a column to the right of the 71+ column, type **Pop. (M)** in the header row, then enter the following numbers in each cell in the column: **4.7**, **6.2**, **1.6**, **2.3**, **2.1**, **3.8**.
   e. Move the Pop. (M) column to the right of the County column, then save your changes.
6. **Modify rows and columns.**
   a. Select the table, then change the font size of the table to 12.
   b. Drag the border between the first and second columns right to resize the first column to be about 1.25" wide.
   c. Double-click the border between the second and third columns to resize the Pop. (M) column.
   d. Double-click the right border of the age range columns (0-5, 5-17, 18-30, 31-54, 55-70, and 71+) to resize the columns.
   e. Select the six age range columns, then distribute the columns evenly.
   f. Select the table, set the row height to exactly .4", then save your changes.
7. **Sort table data.**
   Perform three separate sorts, making sure to select that your list has a header row, as follows:
   a. Sort the table data in descending order by the information in the 0-5 column, then click OK.
   b. Sort the table data in descending order by population, then click OK.
   c. Sort the table data by county in alphabetical order, click OK, then save your changes.
8. **Split and merge cells.**
   a. Insert a row above the header row, then merge the first cell in the new row with the County cell.
   b. Merge the second cell in the new row with the Pop. (M) cell.
   c. Merge the six remaining blank cells in the first row into a single cell, then type **Average Yearly Individual Expenditure by Age Group** in the merged cell.
   d. Select the second column (from Pop. (M) to 4.7), open the Split Cells dialog box, clear the Merge cells before split check box, then split the cells into two columns.
   e. Type **PD Rank** as the heading for the new column, then enter the following text in the remaining cells in the column: **4**, **6**, **3**, **5**, **1**, and **2**.
   f. Add a new row to the bottom of the table.
   g. Merge the first three cells in the new row, then type **Average Spending (Dollars)** in the merged cell.
   h. AutoFit the content of the table to fit the window, then save your changes.
9. **Perform calculations in tables.**
   a. Place the insertion point in the last cell in the 0-5 column.
   b. Open the Formula dialog box, delete the text in the Formula box, type **=average(above)**, click the Number format arrow, click #,##0, then click OK.
   c. Repeat Step b to insert the average premium in the last cell in each remaining age range column (5-17, 18-30, 31-54, 55-70, 71+). (Hint: You can also copy and paste the formula from one column to another. Copy the result, paste it into a different column, select the entire copied number, and then press [F9] to update the result for the current column.)
   d. Change the value of the 5-17 premium for Seneca County from 2,321 to **1,880**.
   e. Recalculate the average premium for 5-17. (Hint: Right-click the cell and select Update Field, or use F9.)
   f. Save your changes.

Skills Review (Continued)

10. Modify table style options.

a. Click the Design tab, then change the theme colors to Green.
b. Click the Table Design tab, then apply the Grid Table 4– Accent 1 style to the table.
c. Remove the table style from the First Column and Banded Rows.
d. Add the Total Row, Last Column, and Banded Columns styles.
e. Add the First Column and Banded Rows styles.
f. Remove all table style options except the Header Row option.
g. Use the Clear command in the Table Styles gallery to clear all formatting from the table.
h. Apply the Grid Table 1 Light – Accent 1 style (first row in the Grid section) to the table. Add the Header Row style and remove the First Column style.
i. Apply bold to the age range column headings (0-5, 5-17, 18-30, 31-54, 55-70, 71+), and the bottom row of the table.
j. Center the table title, Average Annual Health Spending Per Individual by Age, then save your changes.

11. Customize a table format.

a. Use the Align Center button in the Alignment group on the Layout tab for the table to center the text in every cell vertically and horizontally.
b. Center right-align the numbers in columns 4–9, but not the column headings.
c. Center left-align the county names in column 1, but not the column heading.
d. Center right-align the text in the bottom row. Make sure the text in the header row is still centered.
e. Select all the cells in the header row, including the 0-5, 5-17, 18-30, 31-54, 55-70, 71+ column headings, apply Green, Accent 1, Darker 25% shading, then change the font color to White, Background 1.
f. Apply Green, Accent 1, Lighter 80% shading to the Butte, Hillsborough, and Seneca rows.
g. Change the font color of the bottom row to Green, Accent 1, Darker 25%.
h. Add a ½-point white bottom border to the Average Yearly Individual Expenditure by Age Group cell in the header row, then save your changes. (**Hint**: Click in the cell, then, using the buttons in the Borders group on the Table Design tab, verify that the weight is ½ pt, change the pen color to white, click the Border Painter button to turn off the Border Painter, if necessary, then use the Borders button to apply the bottom border.)

12. Insert a cover page.

a. Change the view to multiple pages, then insert the Filigree cover page.
b. Remove the Filigree cover page, then insert the Ion (Light) cover page.
c. Zoom in on the cover page, and verify that the name in the Author property control is your name. If not, remove the property control, select the text that remains, then replace it with your name.
d. Type **Western Tri-State Nursing Association** in the Document subtitle property control.
e. Select today's date in the Year property control.
f. Select the year, then change the font size to 18.
g. Zoom out to display all pages of the document, click page 2, then insert the Confidential 1 watermark.
h. Remove the watermark, insert the Do Not Copy 1 watermark, then save your changes.
i. Compare your document to **Figure 4-28**, then make any necessary adjustments.
j. Save your changes, submit a copy to your instructor, close the file, then exit Word.

Figure 4-28

2029

Health Spending Per Individual by Age in the Western Tri-state Region

WESTERN TRI-STATE NURSING ASSOCIATION

YOUR NAME

Health Spending Varies by Age

The healthcare spending of an individual can vary significantly by age, influenced by various factors such as income, lifestyle, geographic location, and healthcare needs. This report explores health spending patterns by age in the Western Tri-state region, with the goal of helping policymakers and medical professionals make informed decisions regarding healthcare coverage and patient care.

Factors that influence healthcare spending by individuals include the following:

- Age
- Income
- Lifestyle choices
  - Eating habits and nutrition
  - Exercise habits
  - Smoking and alcohol consumption
- Insurance coverage
  - Insured
    - Lower out-of-pocket expenses
    - Better access to specialists and diagnostic testing
    - Lower cost for prescription drugs
  - Not insured or under-insured
    - Higher up-front costs for healthcare
    - Limited range of providers
    - Higher cost for prescription drugs
- Geographic location
  - Urban
  - Rural
- Access to preventative healthcare

Geographic Diversity in the Western Tri-state Region

The Western Tri-state region is comprised of major population centers, sprawling suburbs, small cities and towns, rural communities, and thousands of acres of national forest. A significant proportion of the region's residents are retirees. The cost of living, availability of healthcare facilities, and prevalence of certain health conditions vary across the region, impacting individual healthcare spending. Healthcare costs and spending can differ significantly between urban and rural areas.

Average Annual Health Spending Per Individual by Age

County	Pop. (M)	PD Rank	Average Yearly Individual Expenditure by Age Group					
			0-5	5-17	18-30	31-54	55-70	71+
Beaver	1.6	4	1,987	1,182	2,272	7.783	16,387	26,028
Butte	2.1	6	3,214	1,835	3,764	8,387	16,351	26,265
Columbia	3.8	3	2,155	1,922	2,988	7,823	18,597	25,183
Hillsborough	2.3	5	2,973	2,415	2,897	9,997	14,865	24,117
Jasper	6.2	1	2,856	1,968	3,545	6,045	15,739	27,163
Seneca	4.7	2	1,491	1,880	3,675	7,476	15,534	23,734
Average Spending (Dollars)			**2,446**	**1,867**	**3,190**	**6,623**	**16,246**	**25,415**

Key:
Pop. (M)=Population in Millions
PD=Population Density

Note: Spending refers to total annual spending per individual, regardless of who is paying (insurance or the individual).

Source: Healthcare Research Association

Independent Challenge 1

You work in the corporate office at Elite Body Works Fitness and Training, an operator of fitness centers in seven locations. In preparation for a meeting of the board of directors, you create a summary report that shows quarterly new clients by location for fiscal year 2029. You format the information as a table and prepare the document for presentation to the board.

a. Start Word, then save a new blank document as **IL_WD_4_NewClients2029** to the location where you store your Data Files.
b. Type the table heading **New Fitness Clients, Fiscal Year 2029** at the top of the document, then press ENTER.
c. Insert a table with five columns and four rows, then enter the data shown in **Figure 4-29** into the table, adding rows as necessary. (*Note*: *Do not format the text or the table at this time.*)

Figure 4-29

Location	Q1	Q2	Q3	Q4
Providence, RI	575	725	1378	989
Buffalo, NY	297	467	956	821
Columbus, OH	476	812	1366	1151
Birmingham, AL	256	697	878	373
Richmond, VA	278	511	752	498
St. Petersburgh, FL	412	675	834	732
Charlotte, NC	567	634	988	876

d. Resize the columns to fit the text.
e. Sort the table rows in alphabetical order by Location.
f. Add a new row to the bottom of the table, type **Total** in the first cell, then enter a formula in each remaining cell in the new row to calculate the sum of the cells above it.
g. Add a new column to the right side of the table, type **Total** in the first cell, then enter a formula in each remaining cell in the new column to calculate the sum of the cells to the left of it. (Hint: Make sure the formula you insert in each cell sums the cells to the left, not the cells above. In the last cell in the last column, you can sum the cells to the left or the cells above; either way, the total should be the same.)
h. Apply a table style to the table. Select a style that enhances the information contained in the table, and adjust the Table Style Options to suit the content.
i. Right-align the numerical data in the table, then adjust the alignment of the text in the header row and first column to suit the design of the table.
j. Enhance the table with fonts, font colors, shading, and borders to make the table attractive and easy to read at a glance.
k. Increase the font size of the table heading to 24 points, change the character scale to 80%, then expand the character spacing by 1 point.
l. AutoFit the table to fit the window, then adjust the row height so the table is easy to read.
m. Add a header to the document that includes the title property. Type **Elite Body Works Fitness and Training** in the Title property control.
n. Add the Austin cover page to the document. Type **Quarterly Report, Fiscal Year 2029** for the subtitle, add your name as the author, and then remove the Abstract content control.
o. Save your changes, submit the file to your instructor, close the file, then exit Word.

Independent Challenge 2

A well-written and well-formatted résumé gives you an advantage when it comes to getting a job interview. In a winning résumé, the content and format support your career goals and effectively present your background and qualifications. One simple way to create a résumé is to lay out the page using tabs, indents, bullets, borders, and paragraph alignment. In this exercise, you research guidelines for writing and formatting résumés. You then create your own résumé using indents, borders, and other formatting features. (*Note*: Keep in mind that certain formatting can be confusing for screen readers and applicant tracking systems (ATS), so it's best to avoid tables, headers and footers, text boxes, images, and other graphic elements when creating a résumé that will be scanned by an ATS. Many résumé templates found on the internet use tables to lay out a page.)

a. Use your favorite search engine to search the web for information on writing and formatting résumés. Use the keywords **resume advice**.
b. Find helpful advice on writing and formatting résumés from at least two websites.
c. Think about the information you want to include in your résumé. The header should include your name and contact information. The body should include information on your education, work experience, and skills. You may want to add additional information.
d. Sketch a layout for your résumé. Include in your sketch the borders, indents, bullets, and other formatting features you will use. **Figure 4-30** shows a sample layout for a résumé, but you can create your own unique design.
e. Start Word, open a new blank document, then save it as **IL_WD_4_NewResume** to the location where you store your Data Files.
f. Set appropriate margins, then type your résumé. Take care to use a professional tone and keep your language to the point.
g. Format your résumé with fonts, character spacing, indents, tabs, borders, bullets, and other formatting features. Adjust the spacing between sections by modifying line and paragraph spacing.
h. When you are satisfied with the content and format of your résumé, check it for spelling and grammar errors.
i. Save your changes, preview your résumé, submit a copy to your instructor, close the file, then exit Word.

Figure 4-30

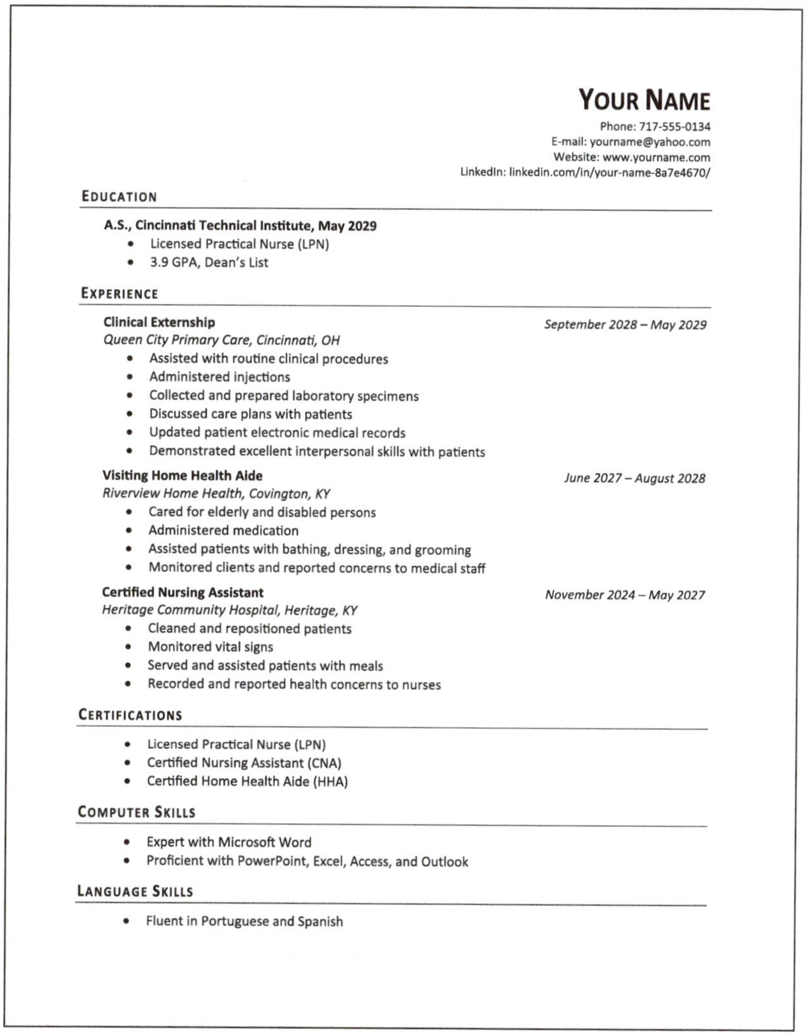

YOUR NAME
Phone: 717-555-0134
E-mail: yourname@yahoo.com
Website: www.yourname.com
LinkedIn: linkedin.com/in/your-name-8a7e4670/

EDUCATION

A.S., Cincinnati Technical Institute, May 2029
- Licensed Practical Nurse (LPN)
- 3.9 GPA, Dean's List

EXPERIENCE

Clinical Externship *September 2028 – May 2029*
Queen City Primary Care, Cincinnati, OH
- Assisted with routine clinical procedures
- Administered injections
- Collected and prepared laboratory specimens
- Discussed care plans with patients
- Updated patient electronic medical records
- Demonstrated excellent interpersonal skills with patients

Visiting Home Health Aide *June 2027 – August 2028*
Riverview Home Health, Covington, KY
- Cared for elderly and disabled persons
- Administered medication
- Assisted patients with bathing, dressing, and grooming
- Monitored clients and reported concerns to medical staff

Certified Nursing Assistant *November 2024 – May 2027*
Heritage Community Hospital, Heritage, KY
- Cleaned and repositioned patients
- Monitored vital signs
- Served and assisted patients with meals
- Recorded and reported health concerns to nurses

CERTIFICATIONS
- Licensed Practical Nurse (LPN)
- Certified Nursing Assistant (CNA)
- Certified Home Health Aide (HHA)

COMPUTER SKILLS
- Expert with Microsoft Word
- Proficient with PowerPoint, Excel, Access, and Outlook

LANGUAGE SKILLS
- Fluent in Portuguese and Spanish

Visual Workshop

Open the file IL_WD_4-3.docx from the location where you store your Data Files, save it as **IL_WD_4_2029ProjectedRevenue**, then format the document as shown in **Figure 4-31**. The headings are formatted with an 80% character scale and character spacing expanded by 0.1 point. The Plain Table 3 table style is applied to the table. The theme colors are Red Violet. Add a total row and total column to the table. Use a formula to insert the totals in the Total column and Total row. Sort the table rows by Total in descending order. Type your name in the header, save the document, then submit a copy to your instructor.

Figure 4-31

Your Name

Zenna Group Health Insurance

Projected Revenue in Billions, Fiscal Year 2029

	Q1	Q2	Q3	Q4	TOTAL
PACIFIC	$28.48	$28.94	$30.39	$30.66	$118.47
MID ATLANTIC	$25.26	$25.83	$25.97	$26.15	$103.21
SOUTH ATLANTIC	$22.65	$22.98	$23.34	$23.24	$92.21
NEW ENGLAND	$19.21	$20.42	$20.73	$19.82	$80.18
EAST SOUTH CENTRAL	$18.44	$18.96	$18.82	$19.27	$75.49
EAST NORTH CENTRAL	$17.59	$18.32	$17.84	$18.66	$72.41
WEST SOUTH CENTRAL	$17.84	$18.16	$17.98	$18.39	$72.37
MOUNTAIN	$16.54	$17.26	$16.92	$17.41	$68.13
WEST NORTH CENTRAL	$15.67	$15.81	$16.18	$15.93	$63.59
TOTAL	$181.68	$186.68	$188.17	$189.53	$746.06

Working with Styles, Themes, and Building Blocks

Case

You are preparing a Frequently Asked Questions (FAQ) sheet for the MSIT Libraries. You create a customized style and theme for the FAQ document and then simplify the process of designing the document layout by using predesigned building blocks. You save the reusable customized theme and content you created so that you can easily use them again in other MSIT Libraries documents.

Module Objectives

After completing this module, you will be able to:

- Add hyperlinks
- Modify document margins
- Create paragraph styles
- Format with themes
- Customize a theme
- Insert Quick Parts
- Create building blocks
- Insert building blocks
- Use a document template
- Create and Edit PDF files in Word

Files You Will Need

IL_WD_5-1.docx
IL_WD_5-2.docx
IL_WD_5-3.docx
IL_WD_5-4.docx
IL_WD_5-5.docx
IL_WD_5-6.docx

Add Hyperlinks

Case MSIT students will receive the FAQ document by email or view it on the MSIT website. To make it easier for students to contact a librarian or access additional library information, you add several hyperlinks to the document.

Objectives
- Insert a hyperlink
- Share documents

A **hyperlink** is text or a graphic that, when clicked, "jumps" the viewer to a different location or program. When a document is viewed on screen, hyperlinks allow readers to link (or jump) to a webpage, an email address, a file, or a specific location in a document. When you create a hyperlink in a document, you select the text or graphic you want to use as a hyperlink, and then you specify the location you want to jump to when the hyperlink is clicked. You create a hyperlink using the Link button in the Links group on the Insert tab. Text that is formatted as a hyperlink appears as colored, underlined text.

Steps

1. **sam Start Word, open the file IL_WD_5-1.docx from the location where you store your Data Files, save it as IL_WD_5_StudentFAQ, then drag the Zoom slider to 120**
   The document includes FAQ (Frequently Asked Questions), the MIST Libraries logo, and a preformatted sidebar. A **sidebar** is a text box that is positioned adjacent to the body of a document and contains auxiliary information.

Quick Tip By default, Word automatically creates a hyperlink to an email address or URL when you type an email address or a URL in a document.

2. **Select send us an email at the end of the first body paragraph, click the Insert tab, then click the Link button in the Links group**
   The Insert Hyperlink dialog box opens, as shown in **Figure 5-1**. You use this dialog box to specify the location you want to jump to when the hyperlink—in this case, "send us an email"—is clicked.
3. **Click E-mail Address in the Link to section**
   The Insert Hyperlink dialog box changes so you can create a hyperlink to an email address.
4. **Type your email address in the E-mail address box, type Help Desk Inquiry in the Subject box, then click OK**
   As you type, Word automatically adds mailto: in front of your email address. After you close the dialog box, the hyperlink text—send us an email—is formatted in blue and underlined. Before distributing a document, it's important to test any hyperlinks you added.

Trouble If an email message does not open, close any window that opens and continue with Step 7.

5. **Press and hold CTRL, then click the send us an email hyperlink**
   An email message addressed to you with the subject "Help Desk Inquiry" opens in the default email program.
6. **Close the email message window, clicking No if you are prompted to save**
   The hyperlink text changed color, indicating the hyperlink has been followed.

Quick Tip To remove a hyperlink, right-click it, then click Remove Hyperlink. Removing a hyperlink removes the link, but the text remains.

7. **Scroll down, select Find and reserve a group study room at the end of the second paragraph, click the Link button, click Existing File or Web Page in the Link to section of the Insert Hyperlink dialog box, type www.example.org in the Address box, then click OK**
   As you type the web address, Word automatically adds "http://" in front of "www." The text "Find and reserve a group study room." is formatted as a hyperlink to the web page www. example.org. When clicked, the hyperlink will open the webpage in the default browser window. If you point to a hyperlink in Word, the link to the location appears in a ScreenTip. You can edit ScreenTip text to make it more descriptive.

Quick Tip You can also edit the hyperlink destination or the hyperlink text.

8. **Right-click reserve in the Find and reserve a group study room hyperlink, click Edit Hyperlink, click ScreenTip in the Edit Hyperlink dialog box, type Search for and reserve a group study room at any MSIT Library. in the ScreenTip text box, click OK, click OK, save your changes, then point to the Find and reserve a group study room hyperlink in the document**
   The ScreenTip you created appears above the Find and reserve a group study room hyperlink, as shown in **Figure 5-2**.

Figure 5-1: Insert Hyperlink dialog box

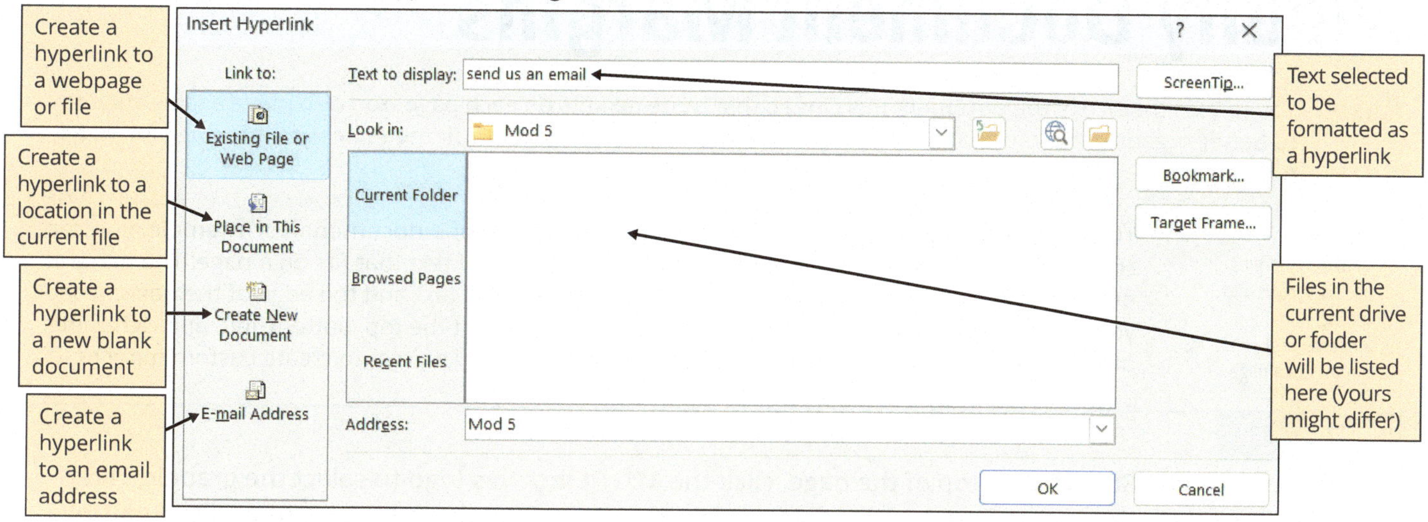

Figure 5-2: Hyperlinks in the document

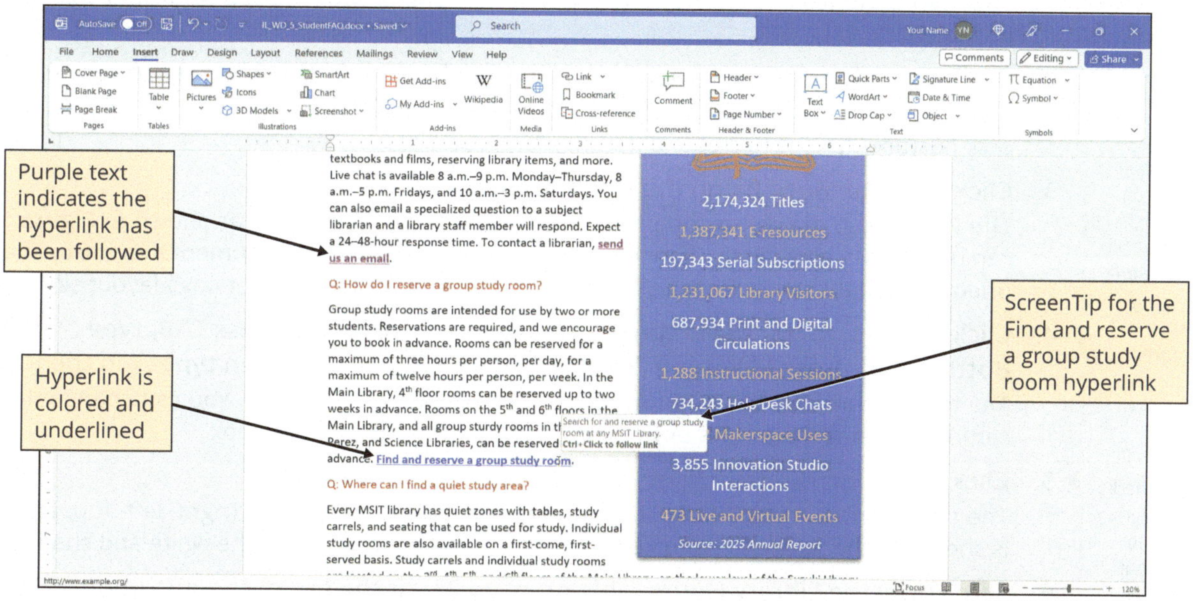

Sharing documents from Word and checking compatibility

Word includes several options for distributing and sharing documents over the Internet directly from within Word, including saving a document to OneDrive for others to view and edit, emailing a document, presenting a document online so others can view it in a web browser, sending an Adobe PDF to others for review, and posting a document to a blog. To share a document, open the file in Word, click the File tab, click Share, then click one of the Share options. You can also use the Share button on the title bar to save a document to an online location.

When you email a document from within Word, the document is sent as an attachment to an email message using your default email program. You can choose to attach the document as a Word file, a .pdf file, or an .xps file, or to send it as an Internet fax. When you click an option, a message window opens that includes the filename of the current file as the message subject and the file as an attachment. Type the email address(es) of the recipient(s) in the To and Cc boxes, type any message you want in the message window, then click Send. The default email program sends a copy of the document to each recipient. Note that faxing a document directly from Word requires registration with a third-party Internet fax service.

Before you share a document with others, it's a good idea to check it for compatibility with previous versions of Word. Click the File tab, click Info, click Check for Issues, click Check Compatibility, select the versions you want to check for in the Microsoft Word Compatibility Checker dialog box, then click OK.

Modify Document Margins

Case You reduce the size of the document margins so that more text fits on each page. You also move a table column to better organize the information, and resize the table columns to better fit the table within the new margins on the page.

Objectives
- Set custom margins
- Move table rows and columns
- Change vertical alignment of a page

The Page Setup options enable you to change the layout of a document. For example, you can change the margins in a document to control the amount of text that fits on a page. The margins of a document are the blank areas between the edge of the text and the edge of the page. When you create a document in Word, the default margins are 1" at the top, bottom, left, and right sides of the page, but you can increase or decrease the size of any margin to create custom margins.

Steps

1. **Scroll to the top of the page, click the MSIT Libraries logo to select the graphic, click the Shape Format tab, click the Position button in the Arrange group, click Position in Top Right with Square Text Wrapping, then deselect the logo graphic**
   The logo graphic is now a floating graphic that aligns with the top and right margins of the document.
2. **Click the Layout tab, then click the Margins button in the Page Setup group**
   The Margins menu opens. You can select predefined margin settings from this menu, or you can click Custom Margins to create different margin settings.
3. **Click Custom Margins on the Margins menu**
   The Page Setup dialog box opens with the Margins tab displayed, as shown in **Figure 5-3**. You can use the Margins tab to change the top, bottom, left, or right document margin, to change the orientation of the pages from portrait to landscape, and to alter other page layout settings.
4. **Click the Top down arrow three times until 0.7" appears, press TAB, type .7 in the Bottom box, press TAB, type .7 in the Left box, press TAB, then type .7 in the Right box**
   The top, bottom, left, and right margins of the report will all be .7". You can change the margin settings by using the arrows or by typing a value in the appropriate box.
5. **Click OK**
   The document margins change to .7". The location of each margin (right, left, top, and bottom) is shown on the horizontal and vertical rulers at the intersection of the white and shaded areas.
6. **Scroll until the Library Hours table on page 2 is at the top of the document window, then click the Home tab**
7. **Place the pointer over the top of the fifth column (the Main Library column) in the table, click to select the Main Library column, click the Cut button in the Clipboard group, click in the Suzuki Library cell, then click the Paste button in the Clipboard group**
   The Main Library column moves to become the second column in the table.
8. **Click in the table, click the Layout contextual tab for tables, click the AutoFit button in the Cell Size group, click AutoFit Window, click the View tab, click the Multiple Pages button in the Zoom group, then save your changes**
   The table is resized to fit the new margin settings, as shown in **Figure 5-4**.

Quick Tip
The minimum allowable margin settings depend on your printer and the size of the paper you are using. Word displays a warning message if you set margins that are too narrow for your printer.

Trouble
Click the Ruler check box in the Show group on the View tab to display the rulers if they are not already displayed.

Quick Tip
To copy or move a table row, select the row, click the Copy or Cut button in the Clipboard group, place the insertion point in the location you want to insert the row, then click the Paste button. Use the Paste Options button to determine the formatting of a pasted column or row.

Figure 5-3: Margins tab in Page Setup dialog box

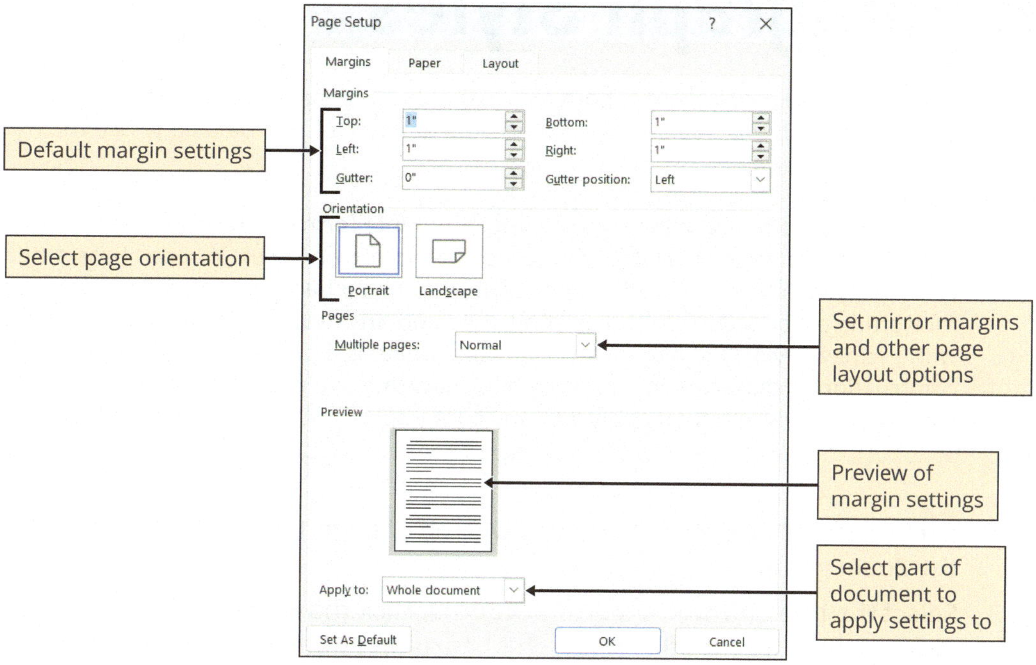

Figure 5-4: Document with smaller margins

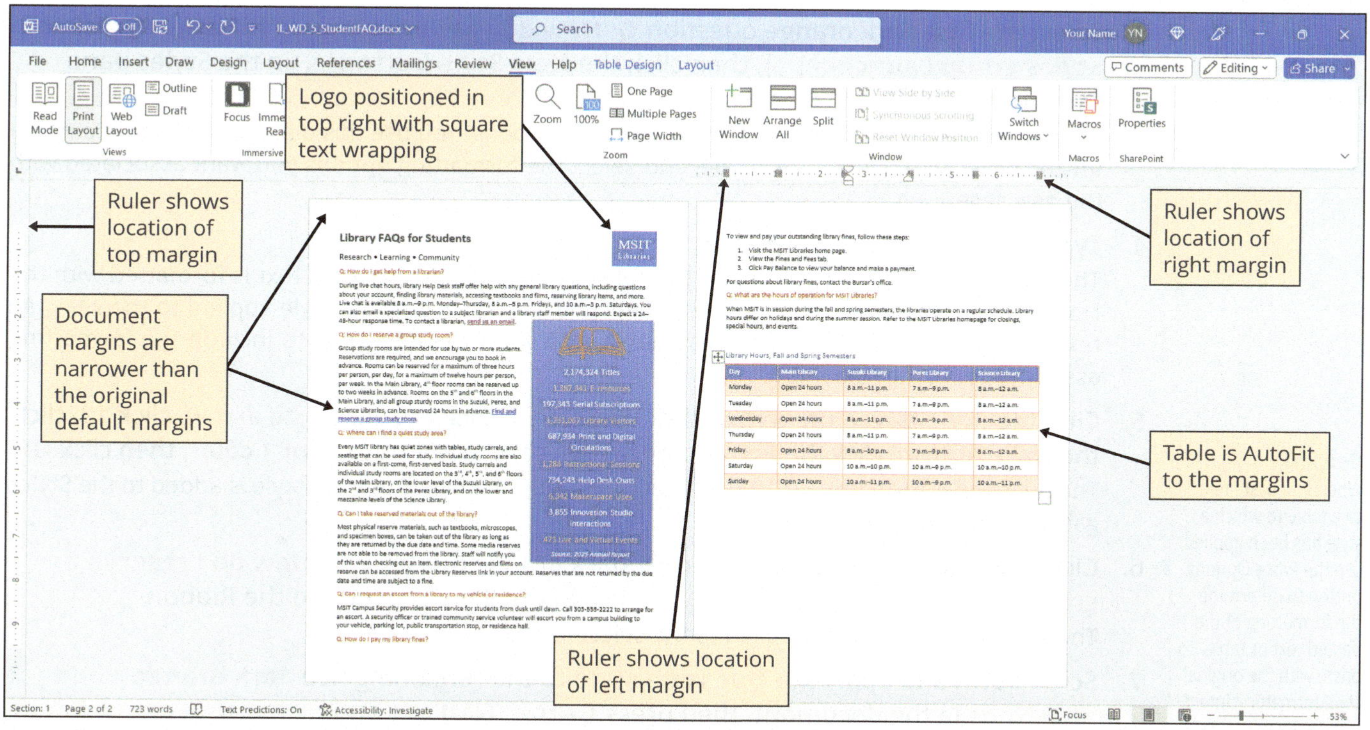

Changing vertical alignment

By default, text is aligned vertically at the top margin of a document, but you can change the vertical alignment of text to align with the bottom margin, to be centered between the top and bottom margins, or to be justified. To change the vertical alignment of text, click the Layout tab in the Page Setup dialog box, click the Vertical alignment arrow, then click the alignment option you want. Using the Apply to arrow on the Layout tab, you can choose to apply the vertical alignment settings to the whole document, to the current section, or to the current section and all sections that follow it. When you are finished, click OK.

Create Paragraph Styles

Case You apply two built-in styles to the title and subtitle text in the document and then create a new paragraph style called Question and apply it to the FAQ questions in the document. You will be able to use the new Question style in other library FAQ documents.

Objectives
- Create styles
- Resolve style conflicts
- Create web pages

Applying a style to text allows you to apply multiple format settings to text in one easy step. In addition to using built-in styles, you can create your own styles. You can base a new style on an existing style, or you can base it on no style. When you base a style on an existing style, both the formatting associated with the existing style and any new formatting you apply are associated with the new style. One type of style you can create is a paragraph style. A **paragraph style** is a combination of character and paragraph formats that you name and store as a set. You can create a paragraph style and then apply it to any paragraph.

Steps

1. **Click Library FAQs for Students at the top of page 1, then click the 100% button in the Zoom group**

2. **Select the title Library FAQs for Students, click the Home tab, click Title in the Styles group, select the subtitle Research • Learning • Community, then click Subtitle in the Styles group**
   The built-in Title and Subtitle styles are applied to the selected text.

   > **Trouble**
   > Don't be concerned if the logo graphic is also selected. The graphic is anchored to the Library FAQs for Students paragraph.

3. **Select the first dark orange question Q: How do I get help from a librarian?, click the Styles group Launcher, then click the New Style button in the Styles pane that opens**
   The Create New Style from Formatting dialog box opens. You use this dialog box to enter a name for the new style, select a style type, and select the formatting options you want associated with the new style.

4. **Type Question in the Name box**
   The Question style is based on the Normal style because the selected text is formatted with the Normal style. When you create a new style, you can base it on the style applied to the selected text, to another style, or to no preset style. You want the new style to include the formatting associated with the Heading 1 style.

5. **Click the Style based on arrow, click Heading 1, click the Font Size arrow, click 12, click the Italic button, click the Font Color arrow, click the Blue, Accent 1 color, then click OK**
   The question is formatted in 12-point italic blue, and the new Question style is added to the Styles gallery, as shown in **Figure 5-5**.

6. **Close the Styles pane, select the next dark orange question Q: How do I reserve a group study room?, then click Question in the Styles gallery on the Ribbon**
   The new Question style is applied to the selected text.

   > **Quick Tip**
   > When you paste text or a table to which a style has been applied, use the Paste Options button to determine the formatting of the pasted text or table. To paste with the original style formatting intact, use the Keep Source Formatting option.

7. **Scroll down and apply the Question style to the remaining five dark orange questions in the document, then press CTRL+HOME**
   The new Question style is applied to every FAQ question in the document.

8. **Click the first blue question, then press SHIFT+F1**
   The Reveal Formatting pane opens, as shown in **Figure 5-6**. This pane lists exactly which styles and formats are applied to the character, paragraphs, and section of the selected text.

   > **Quick Tip**
   > Another way to open the Reveal Formatting pane is to click the Launcher in the Styles group, click the Style Inspector button in the Styles pane, then click the Reveal Formatting button.

9. **Click several other paragraphs, notice the format settings in the Reveal Formatting pane for each paragraph, close the Reveal Formatting pane, close all other panes if necessary, then save your changes**

Figure 5-5: New style in Styles gallery

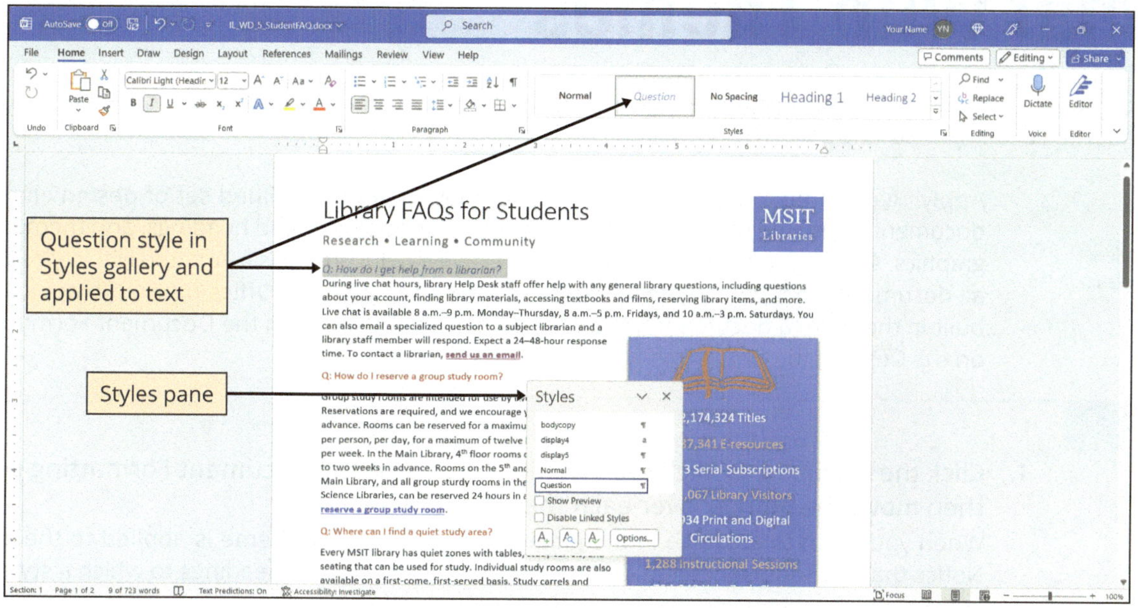

Figure 5-6: Reveal Formatting pane

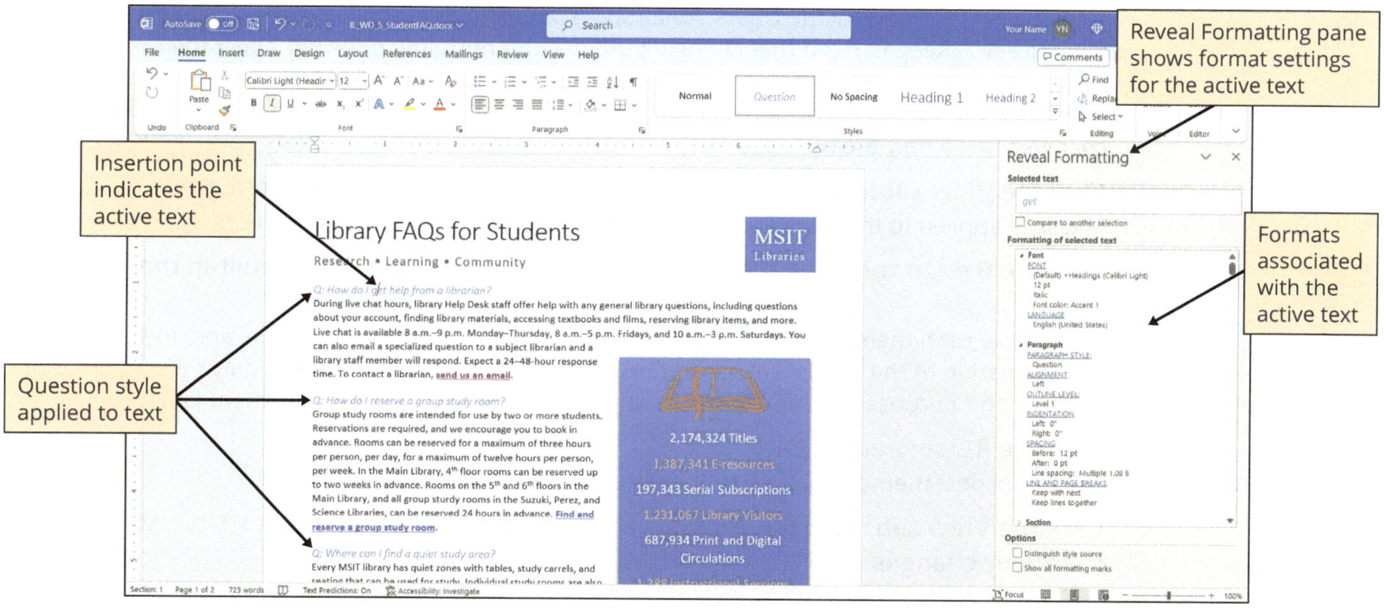

Saving a document as a webpage

Creating a webpage and posting it on the Internet or an intranet is a powerful way to share information with other people. You can design a webpage from scratch in Word, or you can use the Save As command to save an existing document in HTML format so it can be viewed with a browser. When you save an existing document as a webpage, Word converts the content and formatting of the Word file to HTML and displays the webpage in Web Layout view, which shows the webpage as it will appear in a browser. Any formatting that is not supported by web browsers is either converted to similar supported formatting or removed from the webpage.

To save a document as a webpage, open the Save As dialog box, and then select a Web Page format in the Save as type list. You have the option of saving the document in Single File Web Page (.mht or .mhtml) format, or in Web Page or Web Page, Filtered (.htm or .html) format. In a single file webpage, all the elements of the webpage, including the text and graphics, are saved together in a single MIME encapsulated aggregate HTML (MHTML) file, making it simple to publish your webpage or send it via email. By contrast, if you choose to save a webpage as an .htm file, Word automatically creates a supporting folder in the same location as the .htm file. This folder has the same name as the .htm file plus the suffix files, and it houses the supporting files associated with the webpage, such as graphics.

Format with Themes

Case You apply a theme that suits the purpose of the FAQ sheet—to quickly answer common questions—and aligns with the scholarly aesthetic of MSIT Libraries.

Objectives
- Apply a theme
- Change the style set
- Change the default theme

Applying a theme to a document is a quick way to apply a unified set of design elements to a document, including theme colors, theme fonts for body text and headings, and theme effects for graphics. Applying a theme is particularly effective if a document is formatted with styles. By default, all documents that you create in Word are formatted with the Office theme. To apply a different built-in theme to a document, you use the Themes command in the Document Formatting group on the Design tab.

Steps

1. **Click the Design tab, click the Themes button in the Document Formatting group, then move the pointer over each theme in the gallery**
   When you point to a theme in the gallery, a preview of the theme is applied to the document. Notice that the font colors and the fonts for the body text and headings to which a style has been applied change when you preview each theme.

Trouble
If the Facet theme is not available, select any other theme.

2. **Click the Facet theme**
   A complete set of new theme colors, fonts, styles, and effects is applied to the document, as shown in **Figure 5-7**. Keep in mind that changing the document theme does not affect the formatting of text to which font formatting has been applied. Only document content that uses theme colors, text that is formatted with a style (including default body text), and table styles and graphic effects change when a new theme is applied.

3. **Click the View tab, then click the Multiple Pages button in the Zoom group**
   The style applied to the table at the bottom of the last page reflects the Facet theme.

Quick Tip
To restore the document to the default theme for the template on which the document is based, click the Themes button, then click Reset to Theme from Template.

4. **Click the Design tab, click the Themes button, then point to each built-in theme in the gallery**
   Notice how each theme affects the formatting of the text, sidebar, and table, and, in some cases, the pagination of the document. It's important to choose a theme that not only mirrors the tone, content, and purpose of your document but also meets your goal for document length.

5. **Click the Retrospect theme**
   The Retrospect theme is applied to the document as shown in **Figure 5-8**.

6. **Click the View tab, click the 100% button in the Zoom group, press CTRL+HOME, then save your changes**

Changing the style set

Applying a different style set is another quick way to change the appearance of an entire document. Style sets include font and paragraph settings for headings and body text so that when you apply a new style set to a document, all the body text and all the headings that have been formatted with a style change to the format settings for the active style set. You apply styles to a document using the styles available in the Styles group on the Home tab. You apply a style set using the style sets available in the Document Formatting group on the Design tab.

You can also save a group of font and paragraph settings as a new style set. To do this, click the More button in the Document Formatting group, then click Save as a New Style Set. If you want to return a document to its original style set, click the More button, then click Reset to the Default Style Set.

Figure 5-7: Facet theme applied to document

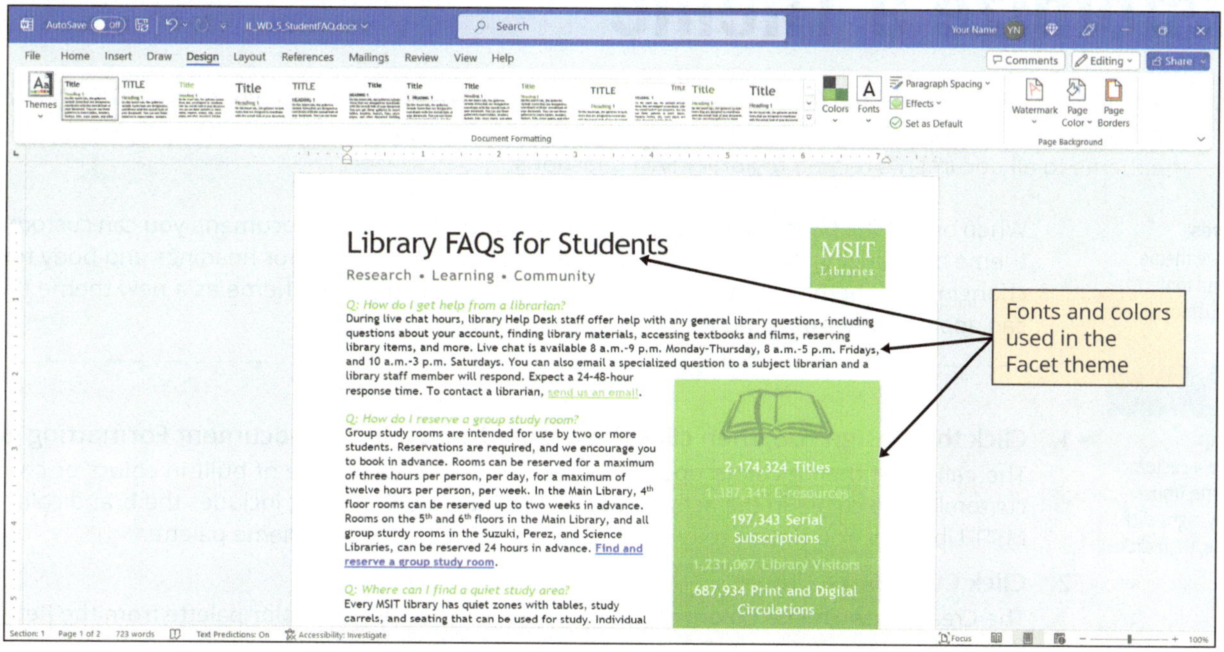

Figure 5-8: Retrospect theme applied to document

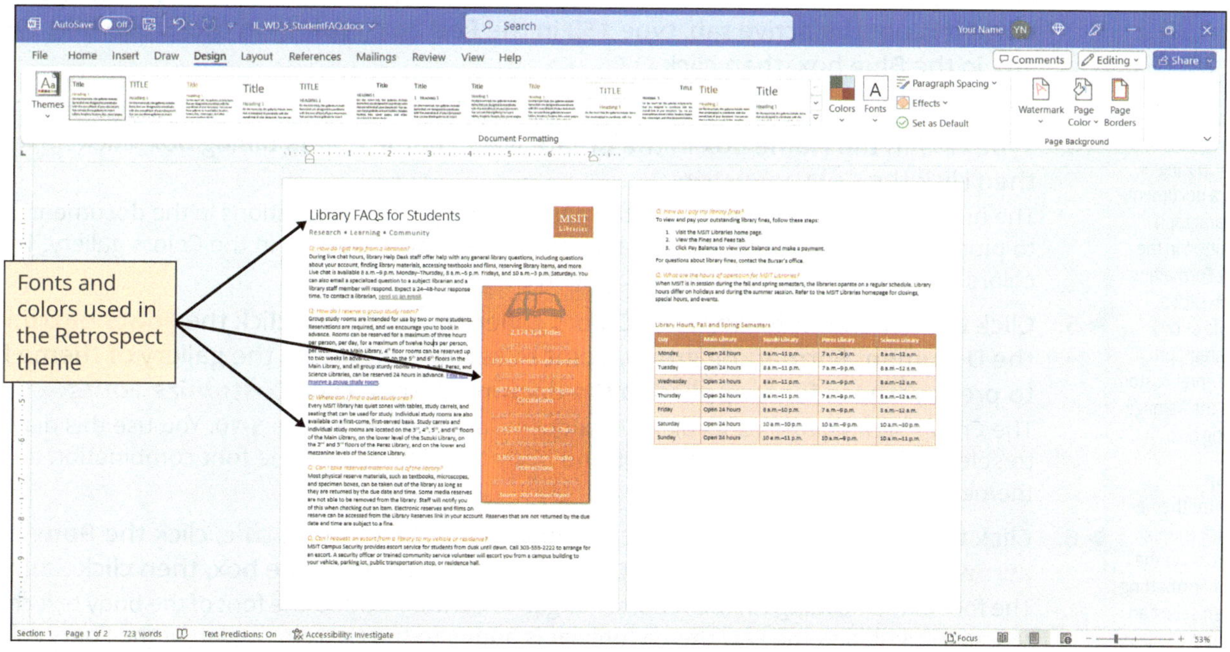

Changing the default theme

By default, all new documents created in Word are formatted with the Office theme, but you can change your settings to use a different theme as the default. To change the default theme to a different built-in theme, press CTRL+N to open a new blank document, click the Themes button in the Document Formatting group on the Design tab, and then click the theme you want to use as the default. If you want to customize the theme before saving it as the new default, use the Colors, Fonts, and Effects buttons in the Document Formatting group to customize the settings for theme colors, fonts, and effects. Alternatively, click the More button in the Document Formatting group then select a new style set to use in the new default theme. When you are satisfied with the settings for the new default theme, click the Set as Default button in the Document Formatting group. The Themes gallery will be updated to reflect your changes.

Customize a Theme

Case You tweak the theme colors and fonts to create a new theme that uses the brand color of the MSIT Libraries—a particular color that is used in the library logo. You then save the settings as a new theme so that you can apply the theme to all documents related to library FAQ questions.

Objectives
- Customize theme colors and fonts
- Save a custom theme

When one of the built-in Word themes is not quite right for your document, you can customize the theme by changing the theme colors, selecting new theme fonts for headings and body text, and changing the theme effects. You can then save the customized theme as a new theme that you can apply to other documents.

Steps

Quick Tip
To remove a custom color palette from the gallery, right-click the palette, then click Delete.

1. **Click the Design tab, then click the Colors button in the Document Formatting group**
   The gallery of theme colors opens. You can select a new palette of built-in colors or choose to customize the colors in the active palette. You want a palette that includes the brand color of the MSIT Libraries. You decide to tweak the colors in the Retrospect theme palette.

2. **Click Customize Colors**
   The Create New Theme Colors dialog box opens and shows the color palette from the Retrospect theme, as shown in **Figure 5-9**. You use this dialog box to change the colors in the active palette and to save the set of colors you create with a new name.

3. **Click the Accent 1 arrow, click More Colors, click the Custom tab in the Colors dialog box if it is not the active tab, type 153 in the Red box, type 51 in the Green box, type 102 in the Blue box, then click OK**
   The Accent 1 color changes from dark orange to plum.

Quick Tip
To change the line and paragraph spacing applied to a document, click the Paragraph Spacing button in the Document Formatting group, then click a Built-In style or click Custom Paragraph Spacing to enter custom settings in the Manage Styles dialog box.

4. **Type FAQ in the Name box in the Create New Theme Colors dialog box, click Save, then click the Colors button**
   The new color scheme is saved with the name FAQ, the orange questions in the document change to plum, and the FAQ color scheme appears in the Custom section in the Colors gallery. The FAQ colors can now be applied to any document.

5. **Click the document to close the Colors gallery if necessary, click the Fonts button in the Document Formatting group, point to several options in the gallery of theme fonts to preview those fonts applied to the document, then click Customize Fonts**
   The Create New Theme Fonts dialog box opens, as shown in **Figure 5-10**. You use this dialog box to select different fonts for headings and body text and to save the font combination as a new theme font set.

Quick Tip
To customize theme effects, click the Effects button in the Document Formatting group, then select an effect from the gallery.

6. **Click the Heading font arrow, scroll down, click Century Gothic, click the Body font arrow, scroll down, click Calibri Light, type FAQ in the Name box, then click Save**
   The font of the headings in the report changes to Century Gothic, the font of the body text changes to Calibri Light, and the FAQ theme font set is added to the Custom section of the Fonts gallery.

Quick Tip
To remove a custom theme from the gallery, right-click the theme, then click Delete.

7. **Click the Themes button, click Save Current Theme, type FAQ in the File name box in the Save Current Theme dialog box, then click Save**
   The FAQ theme colors and FAQ theme fonts are saved together as a new theme called FAQ in the default location for document themes.

8. **Save your changes, then click the Themes button**
   The new theme appears in the Custom section of the Themes gallery, as shown in **Figure 5-11**.

Figure 5-9: Create New Theme Colors dialog box

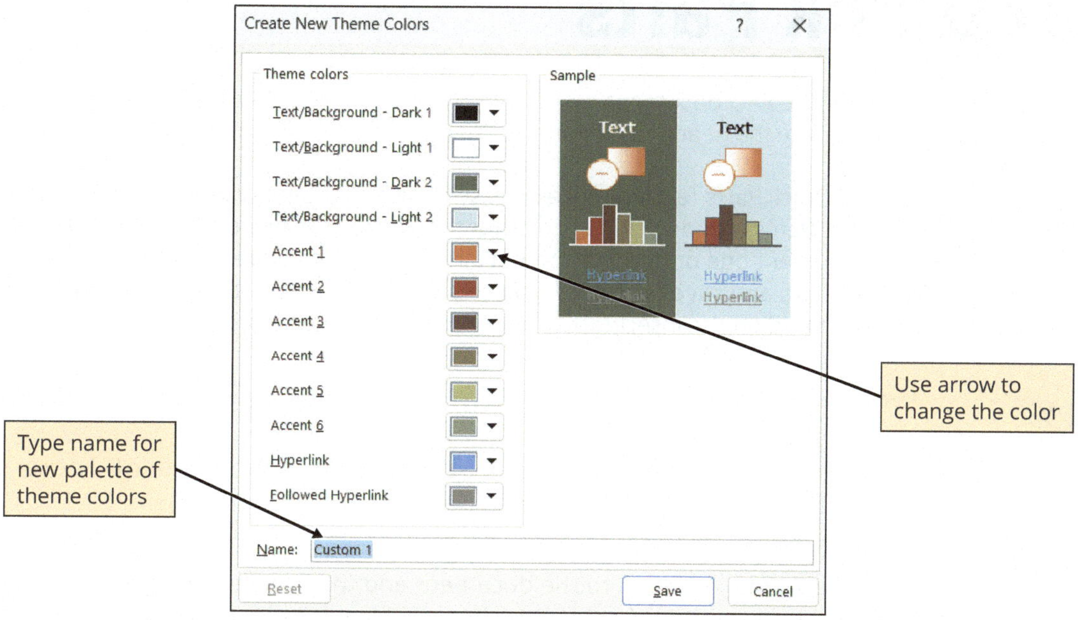

Figure 5-10: Create New Theme Fonts dialog box

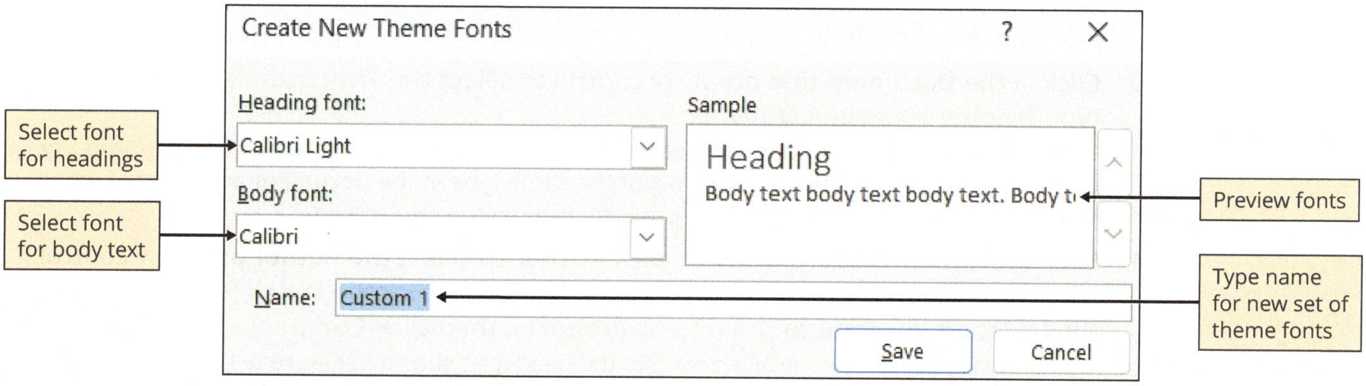

Figure 5-11: Custom theme in the Themes gallery

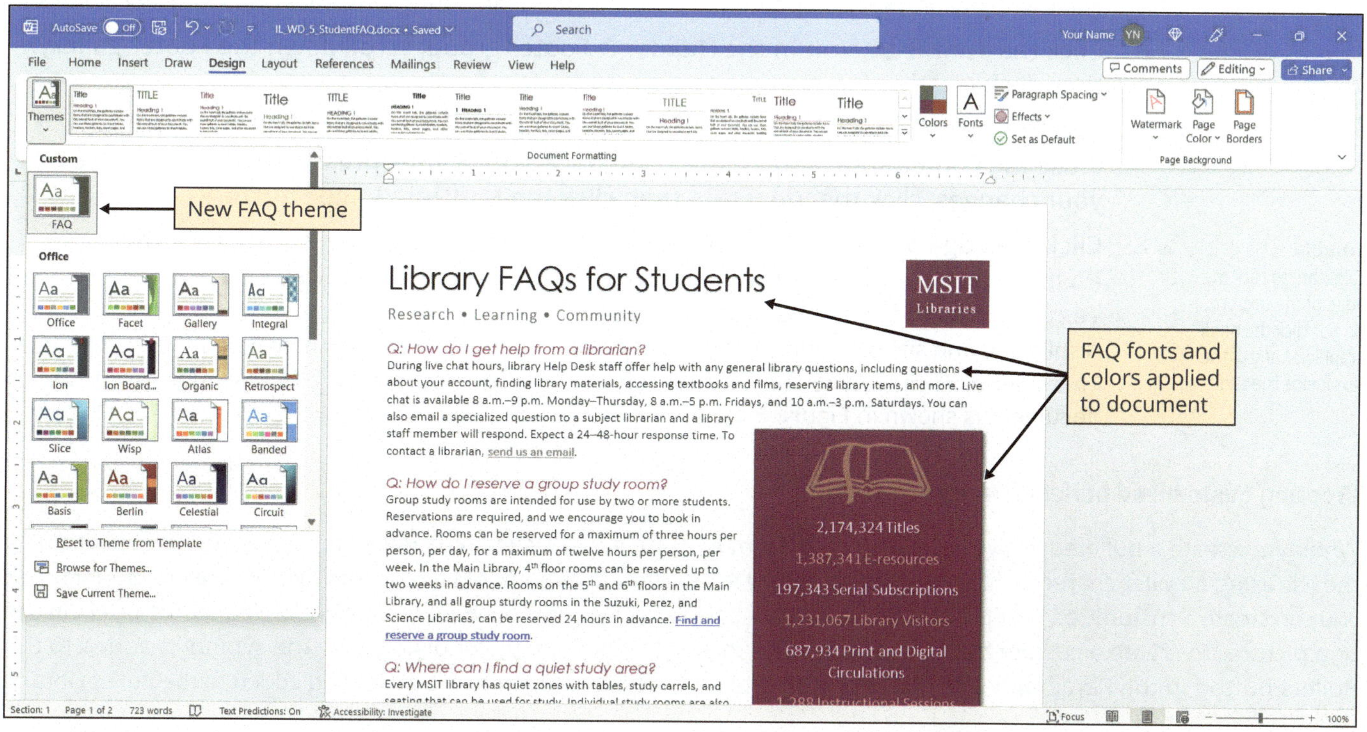

Insert Quick Parts

Case You finalize the design of the FAQ document by adding a header building block and a footer building block to the document. You customize the header by adding a document property to it using the Quick Parts command.

Objectives
- Insert headers and footers
- Update a document property
- Insert and delete a property control

The Word Quick Parts feature makes it easy to insert reusable pieces of content into a document. Quick Parts items include fields, such as for the date or a page number; document properties, such as the document title or author; and building blocks, which are customized content that you can create, format, and save for future use. You insert a Quick Part into a document using the Quick Parts command on the Insert tab or on the Header & Footer tab.

Steps

Quick Tip
When you update a document property on the Info screen, the property controls in the document are updated with the new information.

Trouble
Zoom in and out on the document as necessary.

Quick Tip
Your Author property control might contain your name or other customized text.

Trouble
Take care to click the edge of the text box; do not click the book graphic or any of the text inside the text box.

1. **Click the Insert tab, then click the Header button in the Header & Footer group**
   The Header gallery opens and displays the list of predesigned headers.

2. **Scroll down the Header gallery, then click Filigree**
   The Filigree header is added to the document and the Header area opens. The Filigree header includes property controls for the Document Title and Author. A **property control** is a content control that contains document property information, such as title, company, or author. You can assign or update a document property by typing directly in a property control or by typing in the Properties boxes on the Info screen.

3. **Click in the Document title property control to select the Title property control, then type Frequently Asked Questions**
   The document title is added to the header. When you assign or update a document property by typing in a property control, all controls of the same type in the document are updated with the change, as well as the corresponding property field on the Info screen.

4. **Click the Author property control, click Author to select the Author property control, press DELETE to delete the Author property control, click the Quick Parts button in the Insert group, point to Document Property, then click Company**
   The Company property control is added to the header as shown in **Figure 5-12**.

5. **Type Mountain Springs Institute of Technology Libraries**
   The Company property is updated to become Mountain Springs Institute of Technology Libraries.

6. **Click the Footer button in the Header & Footer group, scroll down the Footer gallery, then click Austin**
   The Austin footer includes a page number field and a page border, as shown in **Figure 5-13**.

7. **Close the Footer area, press CTRL+END, type your name, press CTRL+HOME, save your changes, click the View tab, then click the Multiple Pages button**

8. **Click the edge of the sidebar to select it, click the Shape Format tab, click the Position button in the Arrange group, click Position in Bottom Left with Square Text Wrapping, then save your changes**
   A solid line and sizing handles surround the box so you know the box is selected.
   The sidebar is moved to the bottom left corner. The completed Library FAQs for Students document is shown in **Figure 5-14**.

Creating customized bullet characters

When you create a bulleted list, you can choose to format the list using a bullet character from the Bullet Library, or you can create a customized bullet character using a symbol or a picture. To create a custom bullet character, click the Bullets button in the Paragraph group on the Home tab, then click Define New Bullet. In the Define New Bullet dialog box, click Symbol to open the Symbol gallery, double-click the symbol you want to use as a bullet, then click OK in the Define New Bullet dialog box. The symbol is added to the active paragraph as a bullet and added to the Bullet Library.

Figure 5-12: Document Title property control in Filigree header

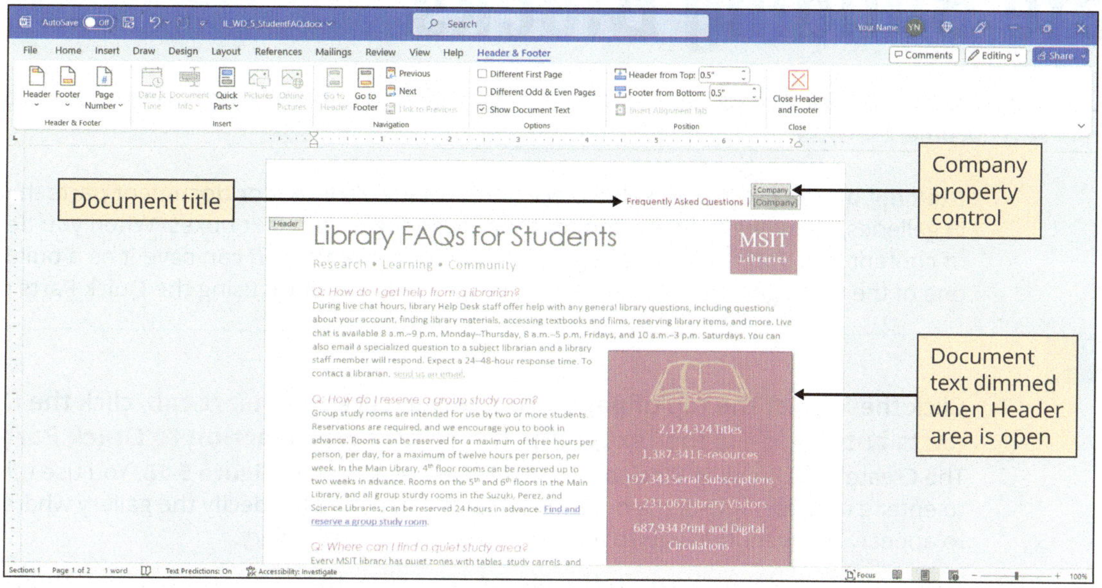

Figure 5-13: Company property control in Austin footer

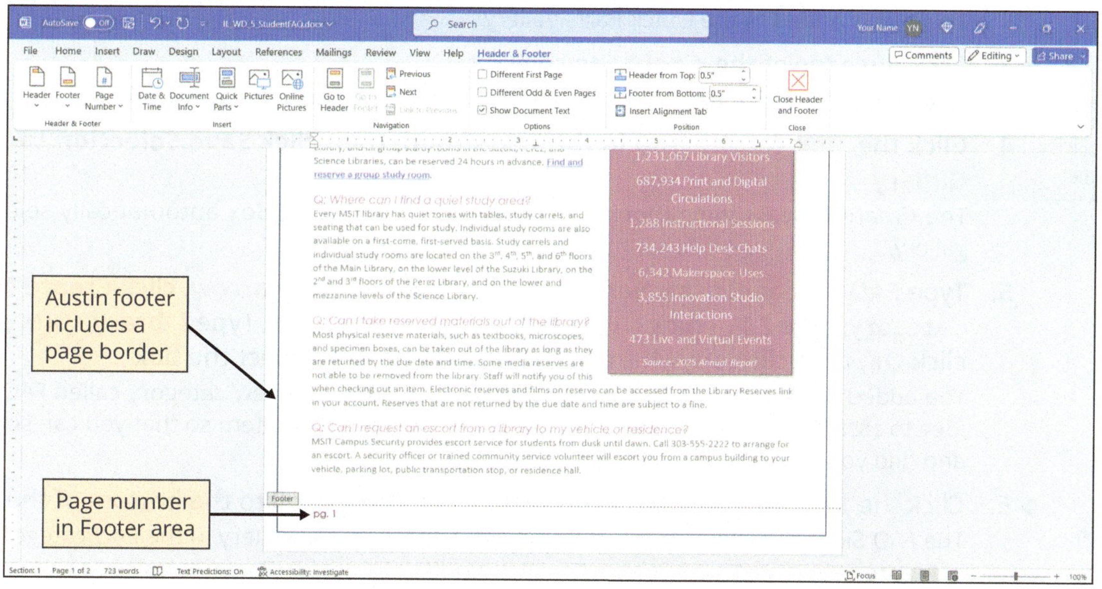

Figure 5-14: Completed Library FAQs for Students document

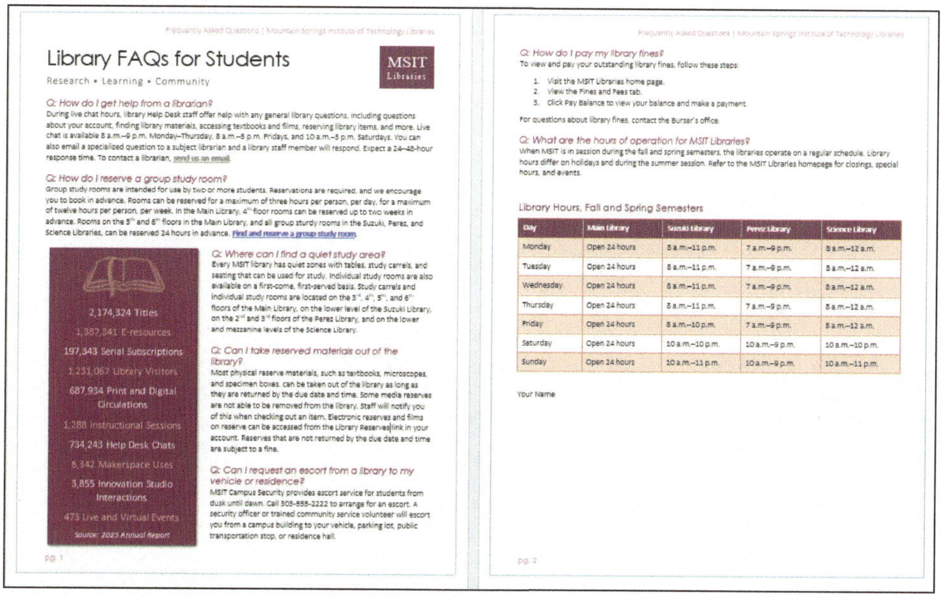

Create Building Blocks

Case You save the MSIT Libraries logo and the sidebar as building blocks so that you can easily include them in other library FAQ documents.

Objective
- Save a custom building block

Building blocks are the reusable pieces of formatted content or document parts that are stored in galleries, including headers and footers, cover pages, and text boxes. When you design a piece of content that you want to use again in other documents, you can save it as a building block in one of the Word galleries. You save an item as a building block using the Quick Parts command.

Steps

1. **Click the logo at the top of page 1 to select it, click the Insert tab, click the Quick Parts button in the Text group, then click Save Selection to Quick Part Gallery**
   The Create New Building Block dialog box opens, as shown in **Figure 5-15**. You use this dialog box to enter a unique name and a description for the item and to specify the gallery where you want it to appear. You want the logo to appear in the Quick Parts gallery.
2. **Type MSIT Libraries Logo in the Name box, click the Description box, type MSIT Libraries logo in top-right corner of page, then click OK**
   The logo is added to the Quick Parts gallery.
3. **Click the edge of the sidebar to select it**
   A solid line and sizing handles surround the box so you know the box is selected.
4. **Click the Text Box button in the Text group, then click Save Selection to Text Box Gallery**
   The Create New Building Block dialog box opens with Text Box automatically selected as the gallery.
5. **Type FAQ Sidebar in the Name box, click the Category arrow, click Create New Category, type FAQ, click OK, click the Description box, type Library stats sidebar, click OK, then click anywhere in the document to deselect the box**
   You added the sidebar to the Text Box gallery and created a new category called FAQ. It's a good idea to assign a descriptive category name to a building block item so that you can sort, organize, and find your building blocks easily.
6. **Click the Text Box button in the Text group, then scroll to the bottom of the gallery**
   The FAQ Sidebar building block is displayed in the Text Box gallery in the FAQ category, as shown in **Figure 5-16**.
7. **Click the document to close the gallery, then save your changes**

Trouble
Take care to click the edge of the text box; do not click the book graphic or any of the text inside the text box.

Quick Tip
To store paragraph formatting with a building block, make sure to also select the final paragraph mark.

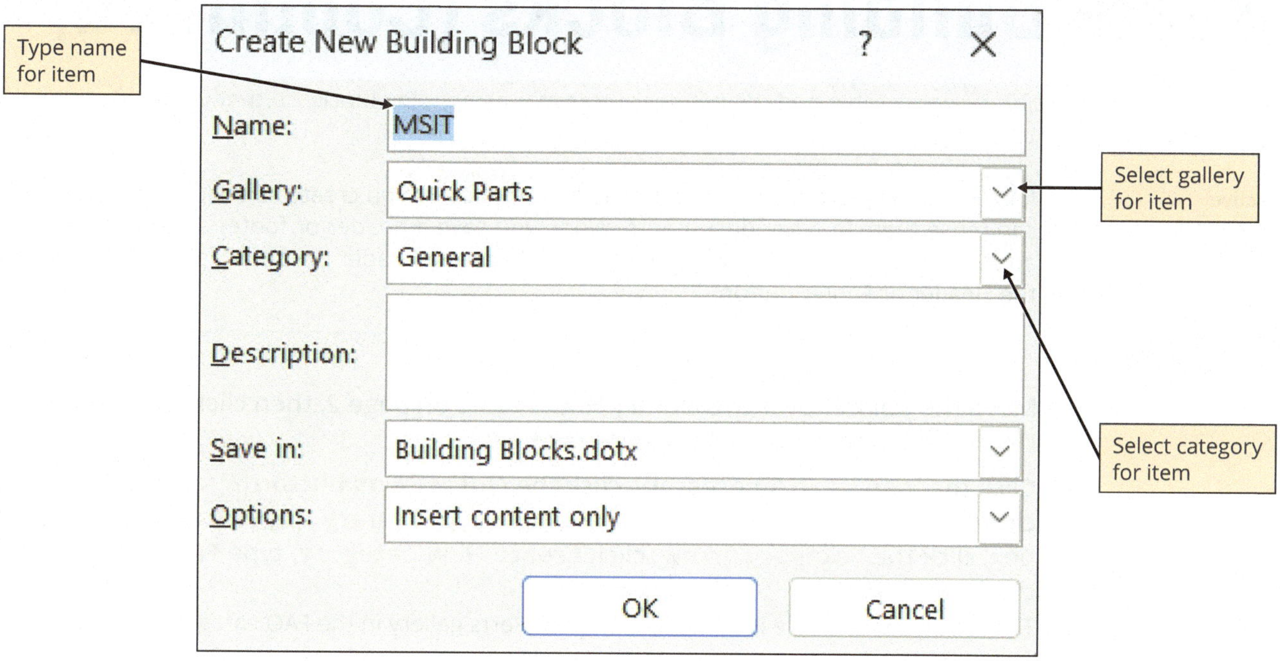

Figure 5-15: Create New Building Block dialog box

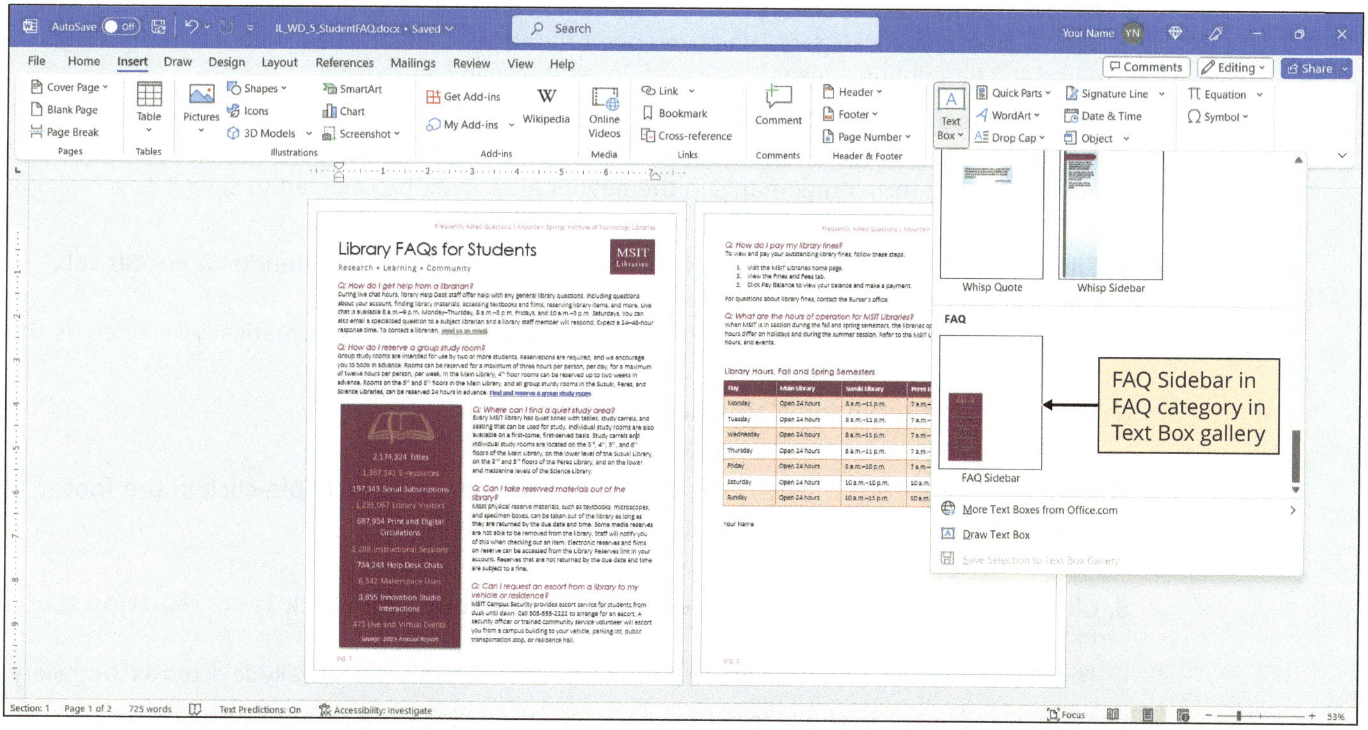

Figure 5-16: New building block in Text Box gallery

Inserting icons in a document

Word includes hundreds of icon images that you can insert into documents to visually communicate using symbols. To insert an icon in a document, click the Icons button in the Illustrations group on the Insert tab, scroll the gallery of icons in the Insert Icon dialog box, select an icon, then click Insert. The icon is inserted as a graphic object at the location of the insertion point. Like any graphic object, you can use the options on the Graphics Format tab to size, position, and format the icon graphic.

Create Building Blocks (Continued)

Case You save the Library Hours table and the header and footer as building blocks so that you can easily include them in other Library FAQ documents.

Objective
- Save a custom building block

It is useful to save the customized headers and footers you create as building blocks so that you can reuse them in other documents. When you save a header or footer as a building block, it is added to the Header or Footer gallery. You can save a header or footer as a building block using the Header or Footer button.

Steps

1. Move the pointer over the Library Hours table on page 2, then click the **table move handle** to select the Library Hours table
2. Click the **Insert tab** if necessary, click the **Quick Parts button** in the Text group, click **Save Selection to Quick Part Gallery**, type **Library Hours Table** in the Name box, click the **Category arrow**, click **Create New Category**, type **FAQ**, click **OK**, then click **OK**
   The Library Hours table is saved in the Quick Parts gallery in the FAQ category.
3. Click the **Quick Parts button** in the Text group to verify that the item was added to the gallery, then point to (but do not click) the **MSIT Libraries Logo** item in the gallery
   The gallery includes the Library Hours Table item in the FAQ category and the MSIT Libraries Logo item in the General category. When you point to the MSIT Libraries Logo item in the gallery, the name and description appear in a ScreenTip, as shown in **Figure 5-17**.
4. Click the document to close the gallery, double-click the **header** to open it, then triple-click in the header to select all the text and formatting in the header
   All the text and formatting marks in the header area must be selected to save it as a building block.
5. Click the **Header button** in the Header & Footer group on the Header & Footer tab, then click **Save Selection to Header Gallery**
   The Create New Building Block dialog box opens with Headers automatically selected as the gallery.
6. Type **FAQ Header** in the Name box, then click **OK**
   The header is added to the Header gallery under the General category.
7. Click the **Go to Footer button** in the Navigation group, then triple-click in the footer area to select the page number and the page border
   When the page border is selected, the whole page is shaded.
8. Click the **Footer button** in the Header & Footer group, then click **Save Selection to Footer Gallery**
   The Create New Building Block dialog box opens with Footers automatically selected as the gallery.
9. Type **FAQ Footer** in the Name box, click **OK**, then close the Header and Footer
   The footer is added to the Footer gallery under the General category. You now will be able to insert the building blocks you created into a different FAQ document.
10. sam Save the document, submit it, then close the document without exiting Word

Figure 5-17: Items in Quick Parts gallery

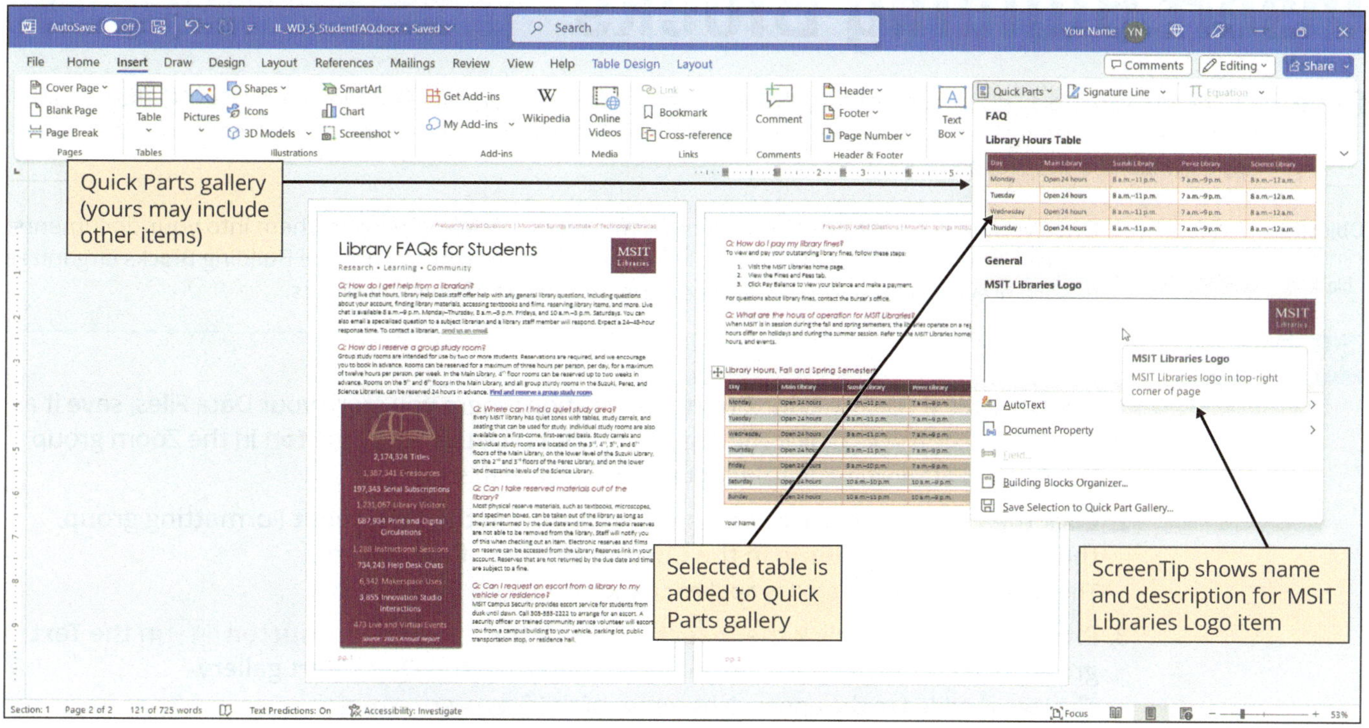

Renaming a building block and editing other properties

You can edit the properties of a building block at any time, including changing its name, gallery location, category, and description. To modify building block properties, simply right-click the item in a gallery, then click Edit Properties. In the Modify Building Block dialog box that opens, edit the item's name or description, or assign it to a new gallery or category. When you are finished, click OK, then click Yes in the warning box that opens. You can also modify the properties of a building block by selecting the item in the Building Blocks Organizer, then clicking Edit Properties.

Insert Building Blocks

Case You need to create a FAQ document for MSIT Faculty. You open the Faculty FAQ file, apply the FAQ theme, and then insert the building blocks you created so that all the FAQ documents have common content and a consistent appearance and aesthetic.

Objective
- Insert a building block

Once you have created customized building blocks, it is easy to insert them into your documents. You can insert a building block directly from a gallery, or you can use the Building Blocks Organizer to sort, preview, insert, delete, and edit the properties of building blocks.

Steps

1. **Open the file IL_WD_5-2.docx from the location where you store your Data Files, save it as IL_WD_5_FacultyFAQ, click the View tab, then click the 100% button in the Zoom group**
   The Faculty FAQ document includes text formatted with styles.
2. **Click the Design tab, click the Themes button in the Document Formatting group, then click the FAQ theme in the Custom section of the gallery**
   The FAQ theme you created is applied to the document.
3. **Press CTRL+HOME, click the Insert tab, click the Quick Parts button in the Text group, then click the MSIT Libraries Logo item in the Quick Part gallery**
   The logo is added to the upper-right corner of the first page.
4. **Press CTRL+END, click the Quick Parts button, then click the Library Hours item in the Quick Part gallery**
   The Library Hours table is added to the end of the document.
5. **Scroll up, click anywhere on page 1, click the Header button in the Header & Footer group, scroll down the Header gallery, click FAQ Header in the General section, click the Footer button, scroll down the Footer gallery, click FAQ Footer in the General section, then click the Close Header and Footer button**
   The custom header and footer you created are added to pages 1 and 2. The property information that appears in the header and footer—in this case, the document title and the company name—are the property information for the current document.
6. **Click the Q: How do I place physical items on reserve? paragraph, click the Insert tab, click the Quick Parts button in the Text group, then click Building Blocks Organizer**
   The Building Blocks Organizer opens, as shown in **Figure 5-18**. The Building Blocks Organizer includes a complete list of the built-in and customized building blocks from every gallery. You use the Building Blocks Organizer to sort, preview, insert, delete, and edit the properties of building blocks.
7. **Click the Category column heading in the list of building blocks**
   The building blocks are sorted and grouped by category.
8. **Scroll down the list to locate the items in the FAQ category, click the FAQ Sidebar item to select it, then click Insert**
   The FAQ Sidebar is inserted on page 1. The sidebar is anchored to the Q: How do I place physical items on reserve? paragraph, which is the current position of the insertion point.
9. **With the sidebar selected, click the Shape Format tab, if necessary, click the Position button in the Arrange group, click Position in Middle Right with Square Text Wrapping, click the View tab, then click the Multiple Pages button**
   The sidebar is moved to the middle right side of the page
10. **Click the logo to select it, click the Position button in the Arrange group, click Position in Top Left with Square Text Wrapping, press CTRL+END, press ENTER, then type your name**
    The logo is moved to the top left corner of the page, and your name is added to the end of the document. The completed Faculty FAQ document is shown in **Figure 5-19**.
11. **Save your changes, submit the document, then close the file without exiting Word**

Quick Tip
To edit the content of a building block, insert the item in a document, edit the item, then save the selection to the same Quick Parts gallery using the same name.

Quick Tip
To delete a building block, select it in the Building Blocks Organizer, then click Delete.

Trouble
If you are working on your personal computer and you want to save the building blocks you created, click Save to save the Building Blocks.dotx file.

Figure 5-18: Building Blocks Organizer

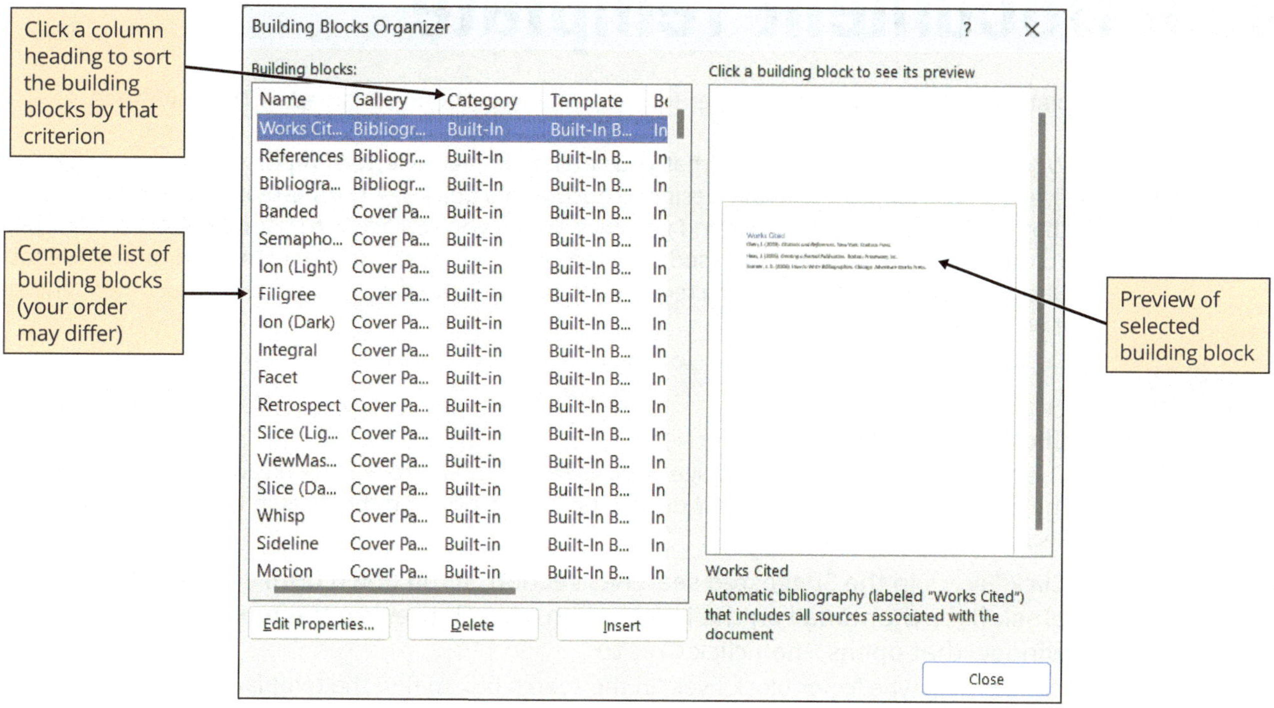

Figure 5-19: Completed Faculty FAQ document

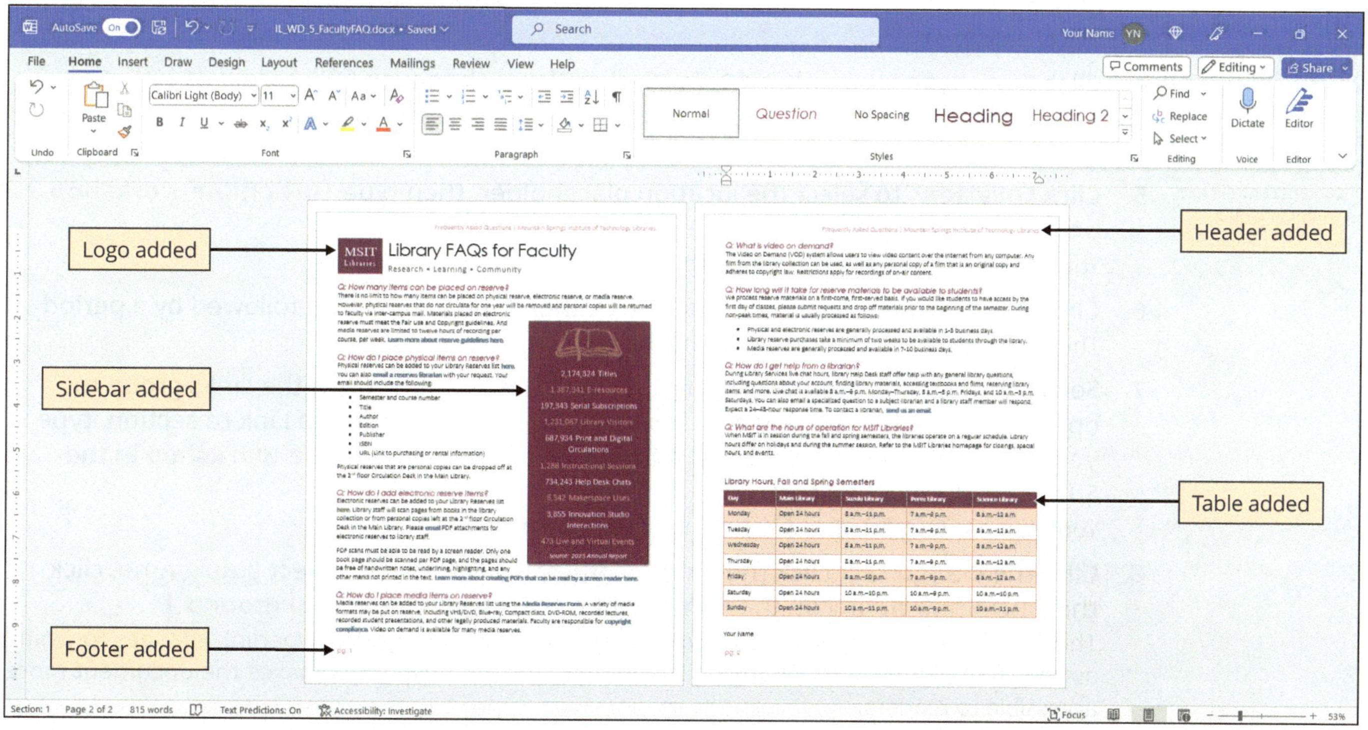

Use a Document Template

Case You use a template to create a promotional flyer for an online workshop sponsored by MSIT Libraries.

Objective
- Customize a template

Word includes many templates that you can use to create letters, reports, brochures, calendars, flyers, and other professionally designed documents quickly. A **template** is a formatted document that contains placeholder text and graphics, which you replace with your own text and graphics. To create a document that is based on a template, you use the New command on the File tab in Backstage view, and then select a template to use. You can then customize the document and save it with a new filename.

Steps

Quick Tip
You must have an active Internet connection to search for templates.

Trouble
Templates change over time. If this template is not available, select another flyer template or just read the steps to understand how to work with templates.

Quick Tip
Some templates might include document property information or content controls for information such as a date.

1. **Click File, then click New**
   The New screen opens in Backstage view, as shown in **Figure 5-20**. You can select a template from the gallery shown in this window or use the search box and the links in the Suggested searches section to find templates.
2. **Click Flyers in the Suggested searches section, scroll down until you find the Color block flyer thumbnail on the New screen, click it, preview the template in the preview window that opens, then click Create**
   You can also type "color block flyer" in the search box to find the template. The Color block flyer template opens as a new document in the document window. It contains placeholder text, which you can replace with your own information.
3. **Click Event Name or Heading Here in the document to select the placeholder text, then type Can I Quote That? A Fair Use Workshop**
   Clicking placeholder text selects the entire placeholder. The text you typed replaces the placeholder text.
4. **Click Date, type November 12, 2029, click Time, then type 10:30 a.m. – 11:45 a.m.**
   As you type the month, AutoComplete suggests text to insert. The workshop date and time are added to the flyer.
5. **Click Locations to select the location placeholder, then type This online workshop provides copyright and fair use strategies for students.**
   You can replace placeholder text with any text that suits your purpose.
6. **Click Website, type To register, contact, then type your name followed by a period**
   The text you type replaces the placeholder text.
7. **Select your name, click the Insert tab, click the Link button in the Links group to open the Insert Hyperlink dialog box, click Email address in the Link to section, type your email address in the Email address text box, type Fair Use Workshop in the Subject text box, then click OK**
   Your name is formatted as a hyperlink to your email address.
8. **Click the Design tab, click the Themes button, click Savon, select your name, click the Font Color arrow on the Mini toolbar, then click White Background 1**
   The Savon theme is applied to the document and the color of the hyperlink changes to white, as shown in **Figure 5-21**. Changing the font color of the hyperlink makes the document more accessible to readers.
9. **Save the document as IL_WD_5_FairUseFlyer to the location where you store your Data Files**

Figure 5-20: New screen in Backstage view

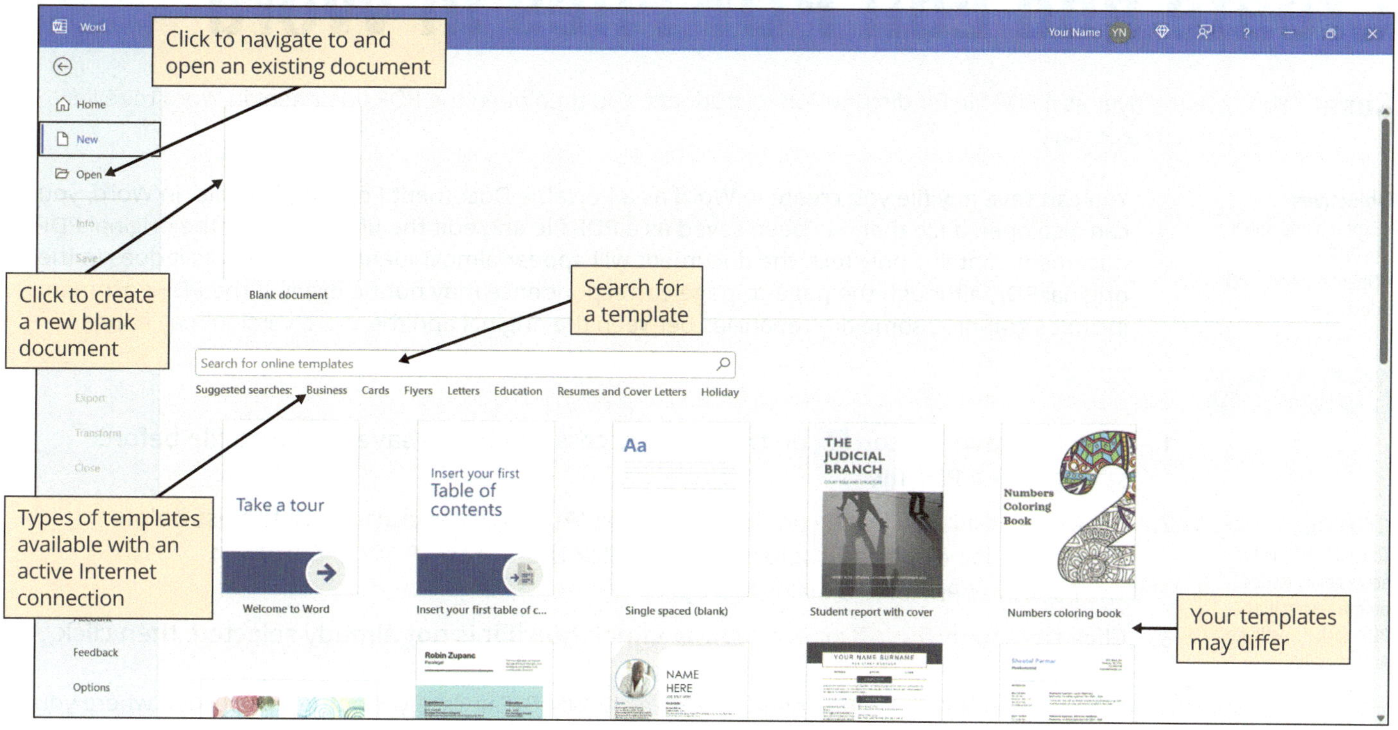

Figure 5-21: Document created using the Color block flyer template

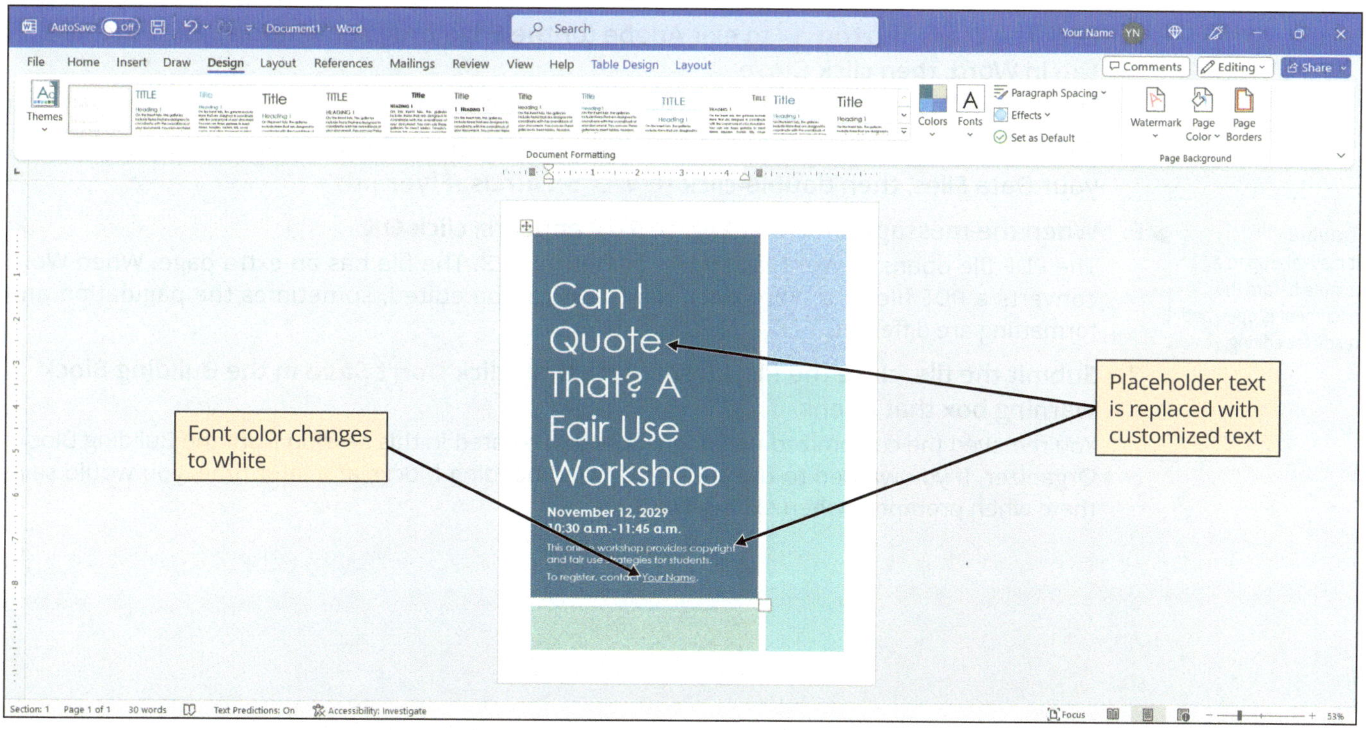

Create and Edit PDF Files in Word

Case You save the flyer as a PDF file for distribution to students. You then open the PDF document in Word to review and edit it if necessary.

Objectives
- Export a document to PDF
- Open and edit a PDF document

You can save any file you create in Word as a Portable Document Format (PDF) file. In Word, you can also open a file that has been saved as a PDF file and edit the file in Word. If the original PDF document contains only text, the document will appear almost identical in Word as it does in the original PDF, although the page-to-page correspondence may not be exact. If the PDF document includes graphics, some discrepancies between the original and the Word version may appear.

Steps

Quick Tip
To check the file for accessibility issues before saving it as a PDF, click Investigate Accessibility.

Trouble
It may take up to a minute before the document is open and ready for editing.

1. **Click the Save button on the Quick Access toolbar to save the Word file before saving it as a PDF file**
2. **Click the File tab, click Export, click Create PDF/XPS Document in the list below Export if it is not already selected, then click the Create PDF/XPS button**
   The Publish as PDF or XPS dialog box opens.
3. **Click the Open file after publishing check box if it is not already selected, then click Publish**
   In a few moments, the document is saved as IL_WD_5_FairUseFlyer.pdf to the location where you store your Data Files, and it opens in an Adobe Acrobat window or an Edge browser window if Acrobat is not installed. Another way to save a file as a PDF is to click the File tab, click Save As, navigate to the location where you want to save the file, click the Save as type arrow in the Save As dialog box, click PDF as the Save as type, then click Save. The file will be saved as a PDF document.
4. **Click the Close button to exit Adobe (or the Edge browser window), click the File tab in Word, then click Close**
   The PDF file closes in Adobe and the Word file closes in Word.
5. **Click the File tab, click Open, click Browse, navigate to the location where you store your Data Files, then double-click IL_WD_5_FairUseFlyer.pdf**
6. **When the message shown in Figure 5-22 appears, click OK**
   The PDF file opens in Word, as shown in Figure 5-23. The file has an extra page. When Word converts a PDF file to a Word document that can be edited, sometimes the pagination and formatting are different.
7. **Submit the file, close the file, close Word, then click Don't Save in the Building Block warning box that opens**
   You removed the customized building blocks you created in this session from the Building Blocks Organizer. If you wanted to use the customized building blocks at a later time, you would save them when prompted when exiting Word.

Figure 5-22: Message box that can appear when opening a PDF file in Word

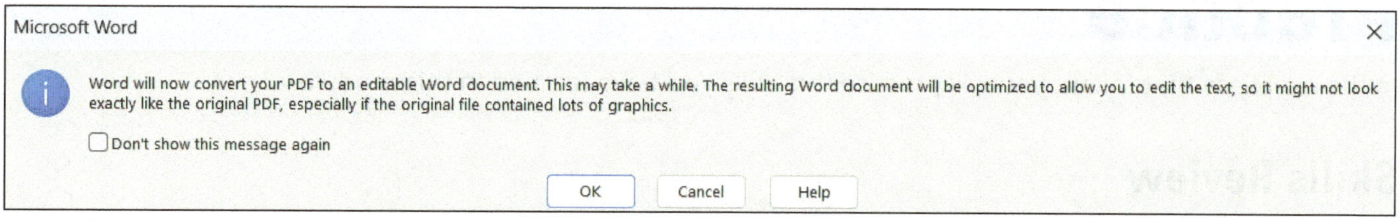

Figure 5-23: PDF file open in Word

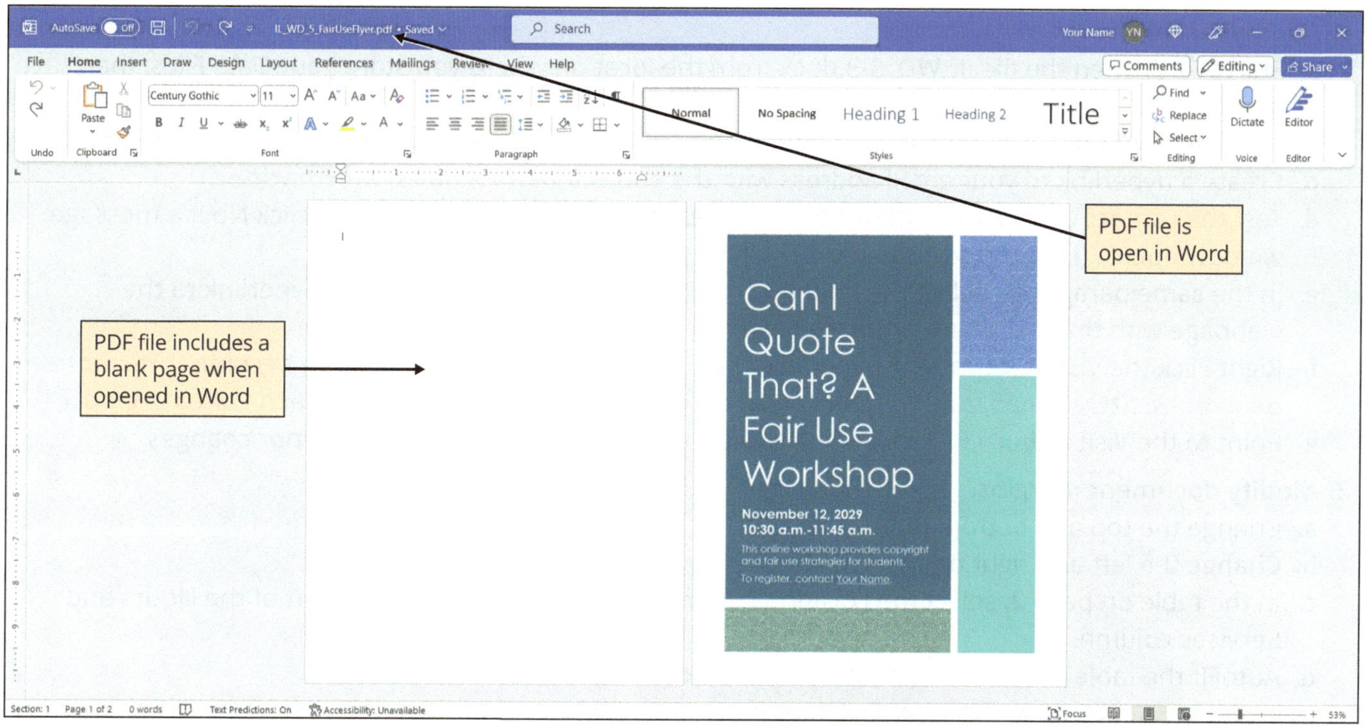

Opening non-native files directly in Word

By default, Microsoft Word saves files in one of its proprietary formats. The saved file is called a native Word file because it is saved in a file format that is native to Word, such as .docx for Word documents and .dotx for Word templates. A Word file may not be recognized by other software programs.

Sometimes you may need to open a file in Word that is a non-native file—that is, a file created with a different software program. Depending on the program used to create the original file, you may not be able to open the non-native file in Word. For example, you will get an error message if you attempt to open an Excel or PowerPoint file in Word.

When you are working with a different program and you want to work with that file in Word, you can save the file as a PDF file, as a txt, or as an rtf file. You can open and work on any of these three non-native file formats in Word. For example, you can save an Excel file as a PDF file, then open and work on the file in Word.

Practice

In the exercises that follow, you will practice the skills you have learned in this module.

Skills Review

As the newly hired executive assistant at Visit Auburn, an economic development and tourism authority, you use Word to format two flyers that share some content. You also create a business card for yourself in your new role.

1. **Add hyperlinks.**
   a. Start Word, open the file IL_WD_5-3.docx from the location where you store your Data Files, then save it as **IL_WD_5_MissionVision**.
   b. Select the bold text "Contact us" in the fourth paragraph, then open the Insert Hyperlink dialog box.
   c. Create a hyperlink to your email address with the subject **Visit Auburn Information**.
   d. Test the contact us hyperlink, then close the message window that opens and click No if a message window opens. (**Hint**: Press and hold CTRL then click the hyperlink.)
   e. In the same paragraph, select the bold text "Visit Auburn Blog," then create a hyperlink to the webpage with the URL **www.example.org**.
   f. Right-click the Visit Auburn Blog hyperlink, then edit the hyperlink ScreenTip to become **Information on events, attractions, and happenings in Fairview County and the Northern Lakes region**.
   g. Point to the Visit Auburn Blog hyperlink to view the new ScreenTip, then save your changes.
2. **Modify document margins.**
   a. Change the top and bottom margins to **.75"**.
   b. Change the left and right margins to **.6"**.
   c. In the table on page 2, select the Location column, cut it, then paste it to the left of the Hours and Services column.
   d. AutoFit the table to the contents, then save your changes.
3. **Create paragraph styles.**
   a. Scroll to page 1, apply the Title style to the "Visit Auburn: Mission and Vision" heading, then change the font color to Gold, Accent 4, Darker 25%.
   b. Apply the Subtitle style to the "Welcome to the heart of the Northern Lakes region, where business and leisure are celebrated" heading, then click the Increase Font Size button three times.
   c. Apply the Heading 1 style and Gold, Accent 4, Darker 25% font color to the red headings: "Core Values and Goals," "How We Work," and "Visitor Information Centers."
   d. Select the purple heading "Business Partnerships," click the Launcher in the Styles group, then click the New Style button in the Styles pane to open the Create New Style from Formatting dialog box.
   e. Create a new style called **Visit Auburn** that is based on the Heading 2 style, is italic, and has a Blue, Accent 1, Darker 25% font color.
   f. Apply the Visit Auburn style to each purple heading: "Community Partnerships," "Support for Infrastructure," and "Market Research and Analysis."
   g. Open the Reveal Formatting pane, examine the format settings applied to several paragraphs, close all open panes, then save your changes.

4. **Format with themes.**
   a. Change the view to Multiple Pages, then change the Style Set to Basic (Simple). (**Hint**: Use the Style Sets gallery in the Document Formatting group on the Design tab.)
   b. Open the Themes gallery, apply the Wisp theme (or any other theme), then zoom in to view each page.
   c. Apply the Organic theme, scroll to examine how it applied to both pages, zoom out to 50%, then save your changes.

5. **Customize a theme.**
   a. Click the Theme Colors button, then change the theme colors to Paper.
   b. Click the Theme Colors button again, click Customize Colors, click the Accent 4 arrow, click More Colors, click the Custom tab if it is not the active tab, type **175** in the Red box, type **75** in the Green box, type **108** in the Blue box, then click OK. The Accent 4 color is now a darker shade of plum.
   c. Name the palette of new theme colors **Visit Auburn**, then save it.
   d. Change the theme fonts to Century Gothic, then change the paragraph spacing to Open. (**Hint**: Use the Theme Fonts and Paragraph Spacing buttons in the Document Formatting group on the Design tab.)
   e. Save the current theme with the name **Visit Auburn**, then save your changes.

6. **Insert Quick Parts.**
   a. Change the view to 100%, then insert the Retrospect header from the Header gallery.
   b. Click the Document Title property control, if necessary, then type **Visit Auburn**.
   c. Press TAB, remove the Date control, insert a Category property control, then type **Mission and Vision**.
   d. Click the table move handle to select the table in the header, then change the font color to Black, Text 1.
   e. Go to the footer, insert the Retrospect footer from the Footer gallery, then click the Footer from Bottom down arrow in the Position group on the Header & Footer tab twice.
   f. Type your name in the Author property control, select the table in the footer, change the font color to Black, Text 1, close headers and footers, then save your changes.

7. **Create Building Blocks.**
   a. Change the view to Multiple Pages, click the edge of the chart object on page 1 to select it, click the Insert tab, then use the Quick Parts button to save the selection as a Quick Part. (*Note*: Sizing handles and a solid border appear around the chart object when it is selected.)
   b. Name the building block **Pie Chart**, assign it to the Quick Parts gallery, create a new category called **Visit Auburn**, then click OK twice.
   c. Zoom in on page 2, turn on the display of paragraph and other formatting marks, select the block of text and table beginning with the heading Visitor Information Centers through the end of the Visit Auburn hyperlink, including the paragraph mark after the hyperlink, save the selected block of text and table as a Quick Part, name the building block **Visitor Information Centers**, assign it to the Quick Parts gallery, assign it to the Visit Auburn category, then click OK.
   d. Open the Header area, click the Table move handle to select the entire header, then save the header to the Header Gallery, using the name **Visit Auburn header**, creating a **Visit Auburn category**, then clicking OK twice.
   e. Move to the Footer area, click the Table move handle to select the entire footer, then save the footer to the Footer Gallery, using the name **Visit Auburn footer**, creating a **Visit Auburn category**, then clicking OK twice.
   f. Close the Header and Footer areas, save your changes, submit the document, then close the file without exiting Word. The completed document is shown in **Figure 5-24**.

Skills Review (Continued)

Figure 5-24

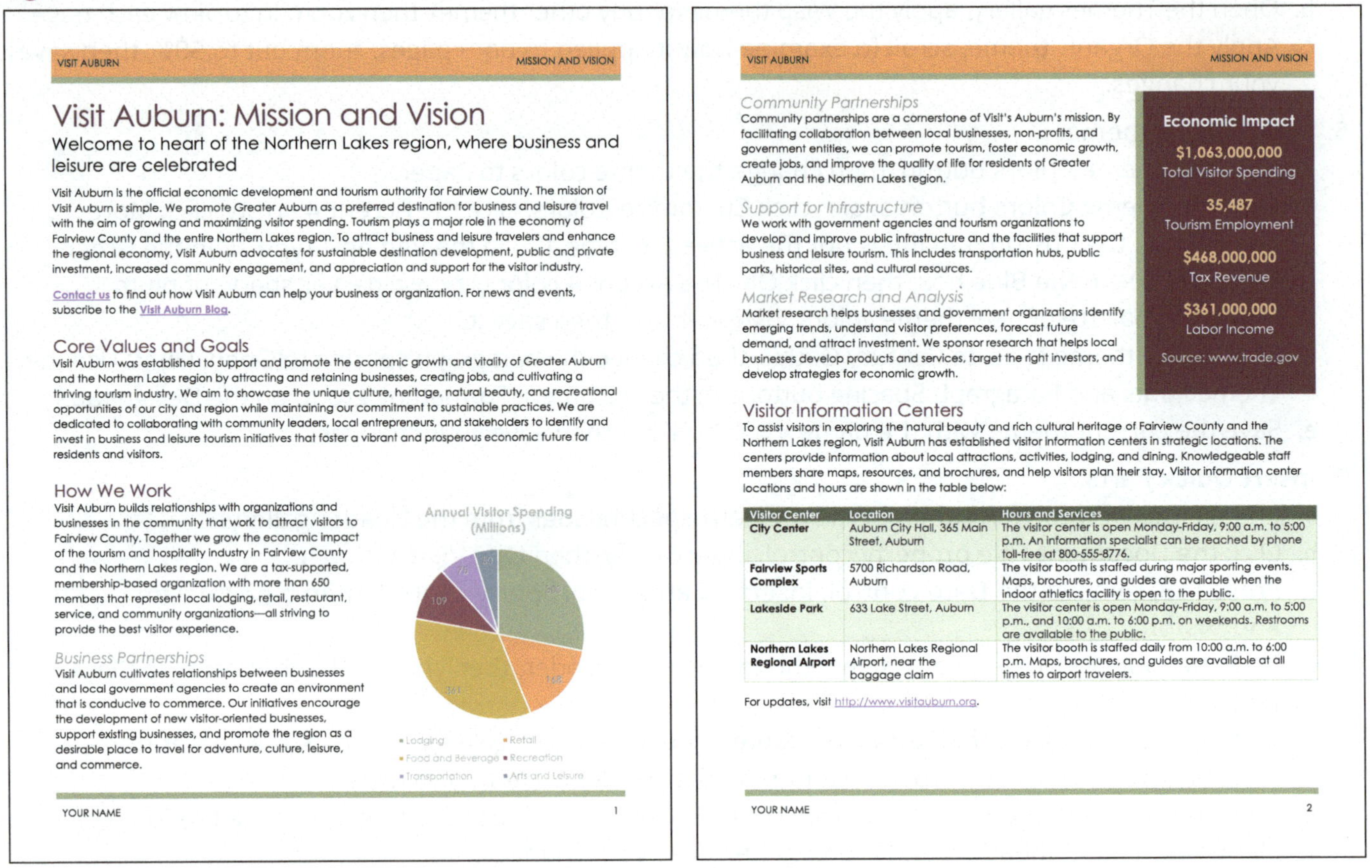

VISIT AUBURN MISSION AND VISION

Visit Auburn: Mission and Vision

Welcome to heart of the Northern Lakes region, where business and leisure are celebrated

Visit Auburn is the official economic development and tourism authority for Fairview County. The mission of Visit Auburn is simple. We promote Greater Auburn as a preferred destination for business and leisure travel with the aim of growing and maximizing visitor spending. Tourism plays a major role in the economy of Fairview County and the entire Northern Lakes region. To attract business and leisure travelers and enhance the regional economy, Visit Auburn advocates for sustainable destination development, public and private investment, increased community engagement, and appreciation and support for the visitor industry.

Contact us to find out how Visit Auburn can help your business or organization. For news and events, subscribe to the Visit Auburn Blog.

Core Values and Goals

Visit Auburn was established to support and promote the economic growth and vitality of Greater Auburn and the Northern Lakes region by attracting and retaining businesses, creating jobs, and cultivating a thriving tourism industry. We aim to showcase the unique culture, heritage, natural beauty, and recreational opportunities of our city and region while maintaining our commitment to sustainable practices. We are dedicated to collaborating with community leaders, local entrepreneurs, and stakeholders to identify and invest in business and leisure tourism initiatives that foster a vibrant and prosperous economic future for residents and visitors.

How We Work

Visit Auburn builds relationships with organizations and businesses in the community that work to attract visitors to Fairview County. Together we grow the economic impact of the tourism and hospitality industry in Fairview County and the Northern Lakes region. We are a tax-supported, membership-based organization with more than 650 members that represent local lodging, retail, restaurant, service, and community organizations—all striving to provide the best visitor experience.

Business Partnerships

Visit Auburn cultivates relationships between businesses and local government agencies to create an environment that is conducive to commerce. Our initiatives encourage the development of new visitor-oriented businesses, support existing businesses, and promote the region as a desirable place to travel for adventure, culture, leisure, and commerce.

Annual Visitor Spending (Millions)

Lodging, Retail, Food and Beverage, Recreation, Transportation, Arts and Leisure

YOUR NAME 1

VISIT AUBURN MISSION AND VISION

Community Partnerships

Community partnerships are a cornerstone of Visit's Auburn's mission. By facilitating collaboration between local businesses, non-profits, and government entities, we can promote tourism, foster economic growth, create jobs, and improve the quality of life for residents of Greater Auburn and the Northern Lakes region.

Support for Infrastructure

We work with government agencies and tourism organizations to develop and improve public infrastructure and the facilities that support business and leisure tourism. This includes transportation hubs, public parks, historical sites, and cultural resources.

Market Research and Analysis

Market research helps businesses and government organizations identify emerging trends, understand visitor preferences, forecast future demand, and attract investment. We sponsor research that helps local businesses develop products and services, target the right investors, and develop strategies for economic growth.

Economic Impact

$1,063,000,000 Total Visitor Spending

35,487 Tourism Employment

$468,000,000 Tax Revenue

$361,000,000 Labor Income

Source: www.trade.gov

Visitor Information Centers

To assist visitors in exploring the natural beauty and rich cultural heritage of Fairview County and the Northern Lakes region, Visit Auburn has established visitor information centers in strategic locations. The centers provide information about local attractions, activities, lodging, and dining. Knowledgeable staff members share maps, resources, and brochures, and help visitors plan their stay. Visitor information center locations and hours are shown in the table below:

Visitor Center	Location	Hours and Services
City Center	Auburn City Hall, 365 Main Street, Auburn	The visitor center is open Monday-Friday, 9:00 a.m. to 5:00 p.m. An information specialist can be reached by phone toll-free at 800-555-8776.
Fairview Sports Complex	5700 Richardson Road, Auburn	The visitor booth is staffed during major sporting events. Maps, brochures, and guides are available when the indoor athletics facility is open to the public.
Lakeside Park	633 Lake Street, Auburn	The visitor center is open Monday-Friday, 9:00 a.m. to 5:00 p.m., and 10:00 a.m. to 6:00 p.m. on weekends. Restrooms are available to the public.
Northern Lakes Regional Airport	Northern Lakes Regional Airport, near the baggage claim	The visitor booth is staffed daily from 10:00 a.m. to 6:00 p.m. Maps, brochures, and guides are available at all times to airport travelers.

For updates, visit http://www.visitauburn.org.

YOUR NAME 2

8. **Insert Building Blocks.**
   a. Open the file IL_WD_5-4.docx from the location where you store your Data Files, save it as **IL_WD_5_KeyInitiatives**, then apply the Visit Auburn theme.
   b. Insert the Visit Auburn header from the Visit Auburn category in the Header gallery.
   c. Insert the Visit Auburn footer from the Visit Auburn category in the Footer gallery and replace the information in the Author control with your name if necessary.
   d. Click the Taste Auburn heading on page 2, open the Quick Parts gallery, then insert the Pie Chart from the Visit Auburn category. Select the pie chart object, then position it in the top right corner with square text wrapping. (**Hint**: Take care to select only the chart object and not any elements inside the chart object.)
   e. Press CTRL END to position the insertion point at the end of the document, then open the Building Blocks Organizer.
   f. Click the Category heading to sort the items by category, scroll to locate the items in the Visit Auburn category, click the Visitor Information Centers item, then click Insert.
   g. Adjust the placement of the items, if necessary, then apply Purple, Accent 4, Darker 25% font color to the title "Visit Auburn: Key Initiatives" and the headings "Sustainable Fairview County," "Recommend Auburn," "Welcome Neighbors Tourism Campaign," and "Taste Auburn."
   h. Save your changes, then submit the document. The completed document is shown in **Figure 5-25**.
   i. Close the file without exiting Word.

Figure 5-25

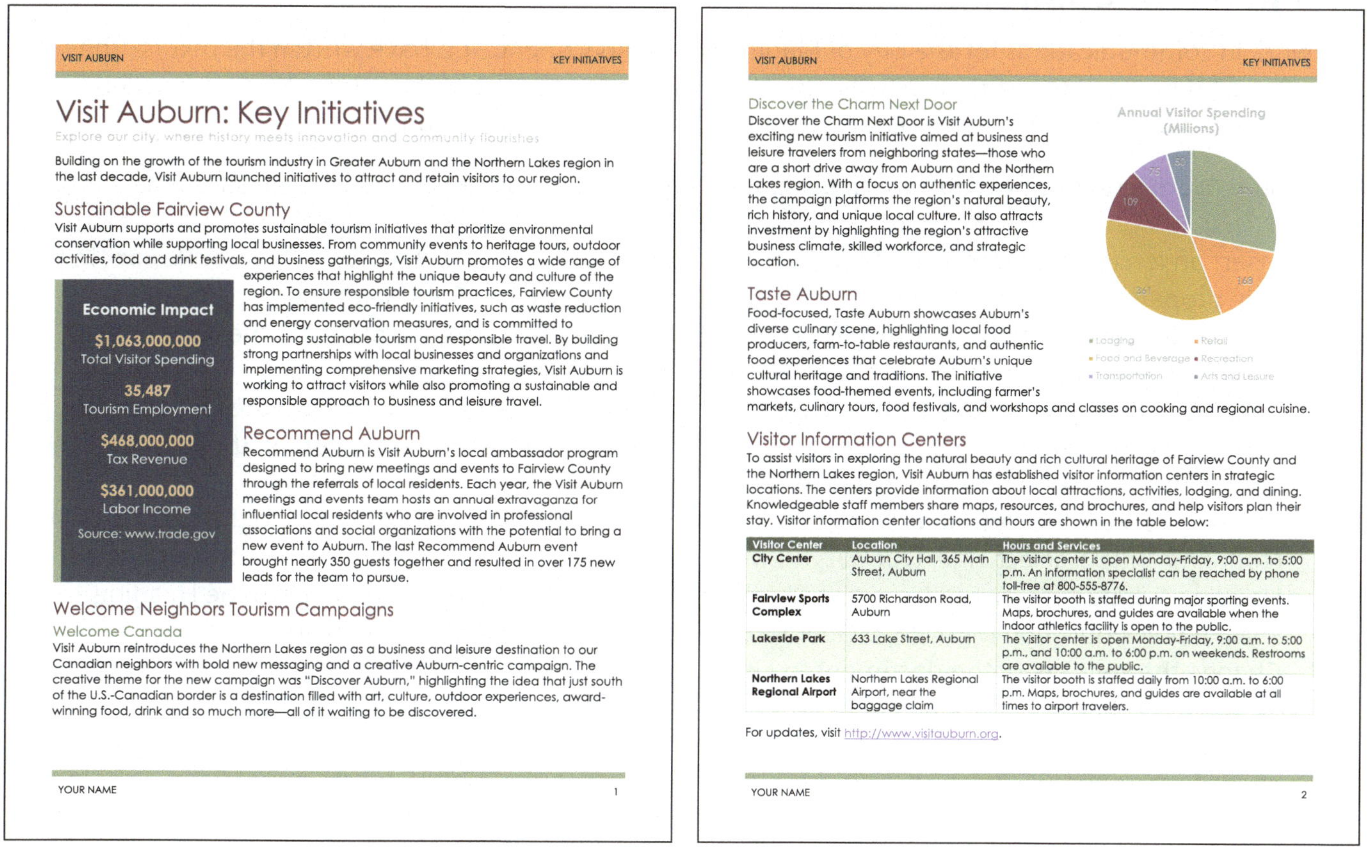

VISIT AUBURN KEY INITIATIVES

Visit Auburn: Key Initiatives

Explore our city, where history meets innovation and community flourishes

Building on the growth of the tourism industry in Greater Auburn and the Northern Lakes region in the last decade, Visit Auburn launched initiatives to attract and retain visitors to our region.

Sustainable Fairview County

Visit Auburn supports and promotes sustainable tourism initiatives that prioritize environmental conservation while supporting local businesses. From community events to heritage tours, outdoor activities, food and drink festivals, and business gatherings, Visit Auburn promotes a wide range of experiences that highlight the unique beauty and culture of the region. To ensure responsible tourism practices, Fairview County has implemented eco-friendly initiatives, such as waste reduction and energy conservation measures, and is committed to promoting sustainable tourism and responsible travel. By building strong partnerships with local businesses and organizations and implementing comprehensive marketing strategies, Visit Auburn is working to attract visitors while also promoting a sustainable and responsible approach to business and leisure travel.

Economic Impact

$1,063,000,000
Total Visitor Spending

35,487
Tourism Employment

$468,000,000
Tax Revenue

$361,000,000
Labor Income

Source: www.trade.gov

Recommend Auburn

Recommend Auburn is Visit Auburn's local ambassador program designed to bring new meetings and events to Fairview County through the referrals of local residents. Each year, the Visit Auburn meetings and events team hosts an annual extravaganza for influential local residents who are involved in professional associations and social organizations with the potential to bring a new event to Auburn. The last Recommend Auburn event brought nearly 350 guests together and resulted in over 175 new leads for the team to pursue.

Welcome Neighbors Tourism Campaigns

Welcome Canada

Visit Auburn reintroduces the Northern Lakes region as a business and leisure destination to our Canadian neighbors with bold new messaging and a creative Auburn-centric campaign. The creative theme for the new campaign was "Discover Auburn," highlighting the idea that just south of the U.S.-Canadian border is a destination filled with art, culture, outdoor experiences, award-winning food, drink and so much more—all of it waiting to be discovered.

YOUR NAME 1

VISIT AUBURN KEY INITIATIVES

Discover the Charm Next Door

Discover the Charm Next Door is Visit Auburn's exciting new tourism initiative aimed at business and leisure travelers from neighboring states—those who are a short drive away from Auburn and the Northern Lakes region. With a focus on authentic experiences, the campaign platforms the region's natural beauty, rich history, and unique local culture. It also attracts investment by highlighting the region's attractive business climate, skilled workforce, and strategic location.

Taste Auburn

Food-focused, Taste Auburn showcases Auburn's diverse culinary scene, highlighting local food producers, farm-to-table restaurants, and authentic food experiences that celebrate Auburn's unique cultural heritage and traditions. The initiative showcases food-themed events, including farmer's markets, culinary tours, food festivals, and workshops and classes on cooking and regional cuisine.

Visitor Information Centers

To assist visitors in exploring the natural beauty and rich cultural heritage of Fairview County and the Northern Lakes region, Visit Auburn has established visitor information centers in strategic locations. The centers provide information about local attractions, activities, lodging, and dining. Knowledgeable staff members share maps, resources, and brochures, and help visitors plan their stay. Visitor information center locations and hours are shown in the table below:

Visitor Center	Location	Hours and Services
City Center	Auburn City Hall, 365 Main Street, Auburn	The visitor center is open Monday-Friday, 9:00 a.m. to 5:00 p.m. An information specialist can be reached by phone toll-free at 800-555-8776.
Fairview Sports Complex	5700 Richardson Road, Auburn	The visitor booth is staffed during major sporting events. Maps, brochures, and guides are available when the indoor athletics facility is open to the public.
Lakeside Park	633 Lake Street, Auburn	The visitor center is open Monday-Friday, 9:00 a.m. to 5:00 p.m., and 10:00 a.m. to 6:00 p.m. on weekends. Restrooms are available to the public.
Northern Lakes Regional Airport	Northern Lakes Regional Airport, near the baggage claim	The visitor booth is staffed daily from 10:00 a.m. to 6:00 p.m. Maps, brochures, and guides are available at all times to airport travelers.

For updates, visit http://www.visitauburn.org.

YOUR NAME 2

9. **Use a document template.**
   a. Click the File tab, click New, then scroll through the gallery of templates.
   b. Create a new document using the Modern Business Cards template. (**Hint**: Use the Search box to find the template, if necessary.)
   c. In the upper-left business card, click the Your Name placeholder, then type your name.
   d. Click the Street Address, City, ST ZIP Code placeholder, type **Visit Auburn**, then press ENTER.
   e. Click the Telephone placeholder, type **315-555-8484**, click the Email placeholder, type **ext. 109**, click the Twitter handle placeholder, type your email address, click the Web address placeholder, then type **www.visitauburn.com**.
   f. Click the Design tab, then change the theme colors to Median.
   g. Save the document with the filename **IL_WD_5_BusinessCard** to the location where you store your Data Files.

10. **Create and edit PDF files in Word.**
    a. Click the File tab, click Export, click the Create PDF/XPS button, then click Publish.
    b. View the business cards in Adobe or your browser, then click to exit Adobe or your browser.
    c. Submit the Word file, click the File tab in Word, then click Close.
    d. Click the File tab, click Open, navigate to the location where you store your Data Files, then open **IL_WD_5_BusinessCard.pdf**.
    e. Submit the PDF file, close the file, do not save changes to the Building Blocks.dotx file if prompted, then exit Word.

Independent Challenge 1

You work in communications for the City of Madison Fire Department. You have written the text for the semi-annual report on department activities, and now you need to format the report. You'll use styles, themes, and Quick Parts to give the report a cohesive and polished appearance.

a. Start Word, create a new document using the Report design (blank) template, then save it as **IL_WD_5_MadisonFireSAR**.
b. Insert an Ion (Light) cover page. Type **City of Madison Fire Department Semi-Annual Report** in the Title property control, then type **Overview and Highlights** in the Subtitle property control.
c. Type your name in the Author property control, then use the Date control to add the current date.
d. Scroll to the next page (contains "Title"), select all the body text on the page under the Heading 1 heading (starting with "To get started..."), insert the text file IL_WD_5-5.docx from the location where you store your Data Files. (**Hint**: Click the Object button arrow in the Text group on the Insert tab, click Text from File, then locate and insert the text file.)
e. Scroll up to view the format and content of the report. Press CTRL+HOME, scroll to the second page (contains "Title"), select Title, type **City of Madison Fire Department Semi-Annual Report**, select Heading 1, type **A Message from the Chief**, then format the following headings in the Heading 1 style: Public Education Highlights, Operations Highlights, and Training Highlights.
f. Change the style set of the document to Lines (Simple), then reduce the font size of the title at the top of the second page of the document (not on the cover page) to 28 points.
g. Notice how different styles change the appearance of a document by applying the following heading styles to the School Education Program subheading under the Public Education Highlights heading: the Heading 1 style, the Heading 2 style, then the Heading 3 style. (**Hint**: Open the Styles pane, click Options, then click All Styles in the Select styles to show box.)
h. Apply the Heading 3 style to the following subheadings: Neighborhoods Program and Social Media Outreach.
i. Insert a Next Page section break after the end of the last paragraph above the chart (ends with "...City of Madison"), switch to multiple pages view, select the chart object on the last page, open the Page Setup dialog box from the Layout tab, then change the vertical alignment of the page containing the chart to Center.
j. Using the Cover Page command, remove the current cover page, then use the Cover Page command again to insert a different cover page for the report from the Built-in category. Update or remove the content and property controls as necessary. (**Hint**: Scroll as needed to display the Built-in options.)
k. Starting on the first page of the report (contains the text of the report), add a footer to the report that includes a page number and your name. You can customize a built-in footer or create your own. Navigate to the footer on the last page of the report (contains the chart), click the Different First Page check box in the Options group on the Header & Footer ribbon to deselect it, click Page Number in the Header & Footer group, click Format Page Numbers, then click the Continue from previous section option button. Close the footer and verify that the three pages of the report text (not including the cover page) are numbered 1, 2, and 3 similar to the sample report shown in **Figure 5-26**.
l. Experiment with different themes, theme colors, theme fonts, theme effects, and paragraph spacing, then use these tools to customize the appearance of the report.
m. Adjust the elements of the report as necessary to make sure the document is accessible, each page has a cohesive and polished appearance, and the text fits comfortably on four pages. Figure 5-26 shows a sample finished report using the Retrospect theme, the Semaphore built-in cover page, and the Integral built-in footer.
n. Save your changes to the document, submit the document to your instructor, close the document, then exit Word.

Figure 5-26

AUGUST 1, 2029

CITY OF MADISON FIRE DEPARTMENT
SEMI-ANNUAL REPORT
OVERVIEW AND HIGHLIGHTS

YOUR NAME

City of Madison Fire Department Semi-Annual Report

A Message from the Chief

It is our honor to serve the City of Madison and provide the highest level of fire protection and emergency medical services to our community.

Over the past six months, our firefighters and medical response teams have worked tirelessly to ensure the safety and wellbeing of our citizens, often at great personal risk. We have responded to structural fires, hazardous material spills, motor vehicle accidents, natural disasters, and emergency medical incidents, among others. In addition, we have been actively involved in community education and outreach programs to provide the citizens of Madison with the knowledge and resources required to prevent and prepare for emergency situations.

This report highlights the achievements and accomplishments of our department during the past six months. It provides an overview of the initiatives we have undertaken to educate the public, improve our services and operations, and train our firefighters, EMS teams, support staff, and volunteers. We are dedicated to transparency, accountability, and continuous improvement.

Our hope is that this report provides valuable insights into the exceptional work our firefighters and emergency medical responders do on a daily basis. We extend our sincere appreciation to the citizens of Madison for their support and commitment to public safety, which allows us to provide vital services to all members of our community.

Public Education Highlights

We continued to engage with the Madison community through public education and outreach programs. Our programs are aimed at enhancing public safety awareness of fire prevention and emergency response protocols.

School Education Program

Our department provided age-appropriate fire safety education for over 13,000 students in eighteen Madison elementary schools. Children learned how to recognize fire hazards at home, and how to practice safe escape routes in case of a fire.

Neighborhoods Program

To encourage citizens to take an active role in fire prevention and safety, we launched a Neighborhoods Program in partnership with Madison's neighborhood associations.

As part of this program, seven Madison fire stations held open houses where community members were able visit the station, touch and experience emergency vehicles and equipment, and meet emergency responders in person. The program also offered free home inspections, free smoke detectors, and neighborhood-specific fire prevention education activities.

YOUR NAME 1

Social Media Outreach

Our department produced fire safety videos that showed simple and practical tips for preventing fires and staying safe in an emergency. These videos were shared on our social media accounts and across other media channels.

We also used our social media accounts to share stories, photos, and videos about real emergency incidents that occurred in Madison, to respond to questions and concerns from community members, and to build trust and rapport with citizens.

Operations Highlights

The Madison Fire Department continued to see an increase in the demand for emergency services, with over 4,600 response call incidents in the past six months. These included medical emergencies, rescue operations, hazardous materials incidents, and fire-related emergencies.

We maintained our progress on improving response time to emergency calls as part of our commitment to ensuring the safety and well-being of citizens. On average, we were able to respond to emergency calls in 6.5 minutes, an improvement over the previous six months.

In addition, we continued to focus on recruiting and retaining exceptional firefighters and medical first responders. Through our outreach programs, we recruited a diverse pool of applicants. Six firefighters and ten emergency medical responders were hired in the past six months, and our retention rate was 87%.

Training Highlights

Our training and professional development efforts were targeted at training our firefighters on new techniques and technologies and at keeping our emergency medical responders up to date with best practices in the field.

Firefighters received training on hazardous materials response, including identification, containment, and decontamination protocols for various hazardous materials. Firefighters also received training on high angle, confined space, trench, vehicle, water, and structural collapse emergency rescues.

Emergency medical responders received training on cardiopulmonary resuscitation (CPR), automated external defibrillators (AED), and basic life support.

Our training programs improved the overall quality and effectiveness of the emergency response services we provided to the City of Madison.

YOUR NAME 2

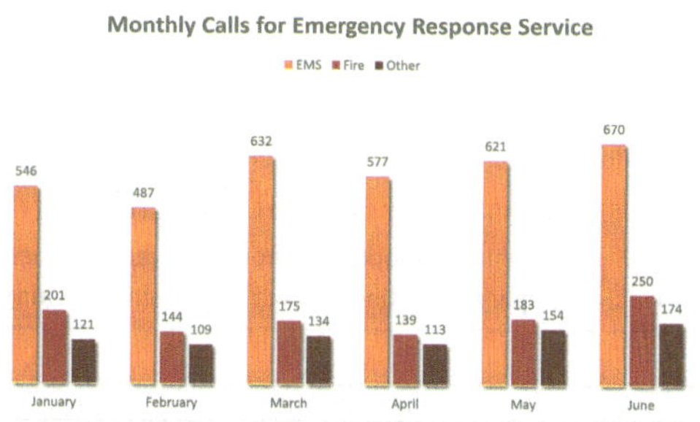

YOUR NAME 3

Independent Challenge 2

The Human Resources (HR) department at the company where you work publishes a blog each month on different HR topics. The blog is published on the company intranet and distributed electronically to employees. It's your job to format the blog posts and prepare them for electronic distribution. In this exercise you design a layout for a blog post, add hyperlinks to it, then save the document as a PDF file and as a webpage.

a. Start Word, open the file IL_WD_5-6.docx from the location where you store your Data Files, then save it as **IL_WD_5_HRBlog** to the location where you store your Data Files.
b. In the third line of the document, replace YOUR NAME with your name.
c. Replace each instance of bold green text in the document with a hyperlink to the appropriate website for each source, shown in the table below. Include a ScreenTip in each hyperlink.

Source	Website URL	ScreenTip
OSHA	www.osha.gov	Occupational Health and Safety Administration
Department of Labor	www.dol.gov	Resources from the U.S. Department of Labor
NIMH	www.nimh.nih.gov	National Institute of Mental Health (NIMH)

d. Test each link to make sure it works, then make any necessary adjustments.
e. Apply styles to the document. Format the first three lines of text using styles of your choice, then apply a heading style to each blue heading in the document.
f. Apply a style set to the document.
g. Apply a theme to the document. Customize the theme fonts, theme colors, and paragraph spacing to achieve the appearance you want. **Figure 5-27** shows a sample layout.

Figure 5-27

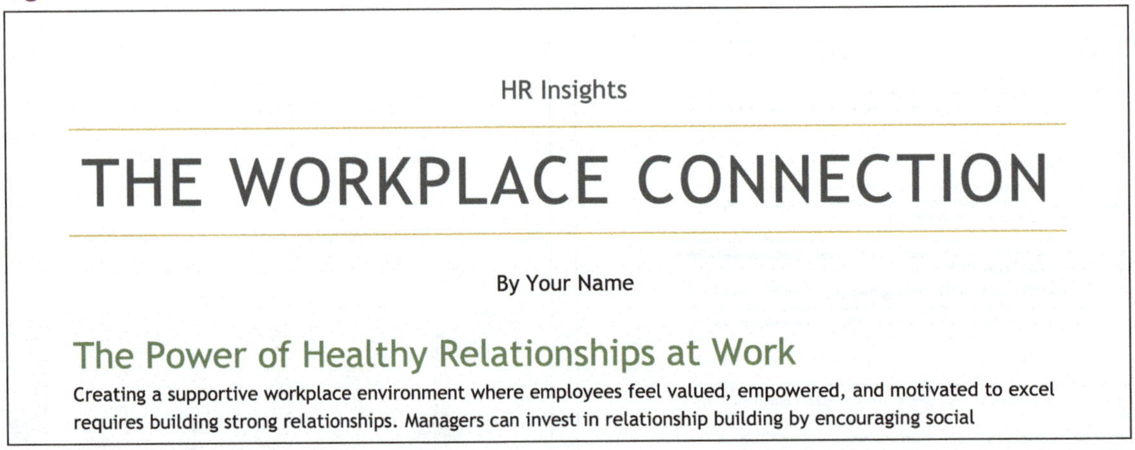

h. Create a new bullet character using a symbol and apply the new symbol bullet to the four bulleted lists in the document.
i. Adjust the margins, alignment, colors, and other formatting so the blog post is readable and the layout is attractive, then save your changes and submit the file.
j. Check the document for compatibility with earlier versions of Word.
k. Save the document as a PDF file, submit the PDF file, then close Adobe or your browser.
l. Save document as a Single File Web Page, view the webpage in Word, submit the webpage file, then save your changes.
m. Close all open files, then exit Word.

Visual Workshop

Create the invoice shown in **Figure 5-28**. Start with the Invoice (Simple modern) template, apply the Office theme, and change the theme fonts to Trebuchet MS. In the upper-right corner of the page, replace the logo placeholder with an icon. (**Hint**: Right-click the logo placeholder, point to Change Picture, click From Icons, then search for "computer" and select the icon shown in the figure.) Enlarge the icon to be approximately .8" wide and center it horizontally in the table cell. In the invoice header and the body of the invoice, replace the placeholder text with the text shown in Figure 5-28. In the table, delete the Quantity and Unit Price columns, autofit the table to fit the window, and then adjust the width of the table columns to resemble Figure 5-28. In the footer area, replace the placeholder text with the text shown in Figure 5-28 and remove any hyperlinks. Save the document as **IL_WD_5_Invoice7689**.

Figure 5-28

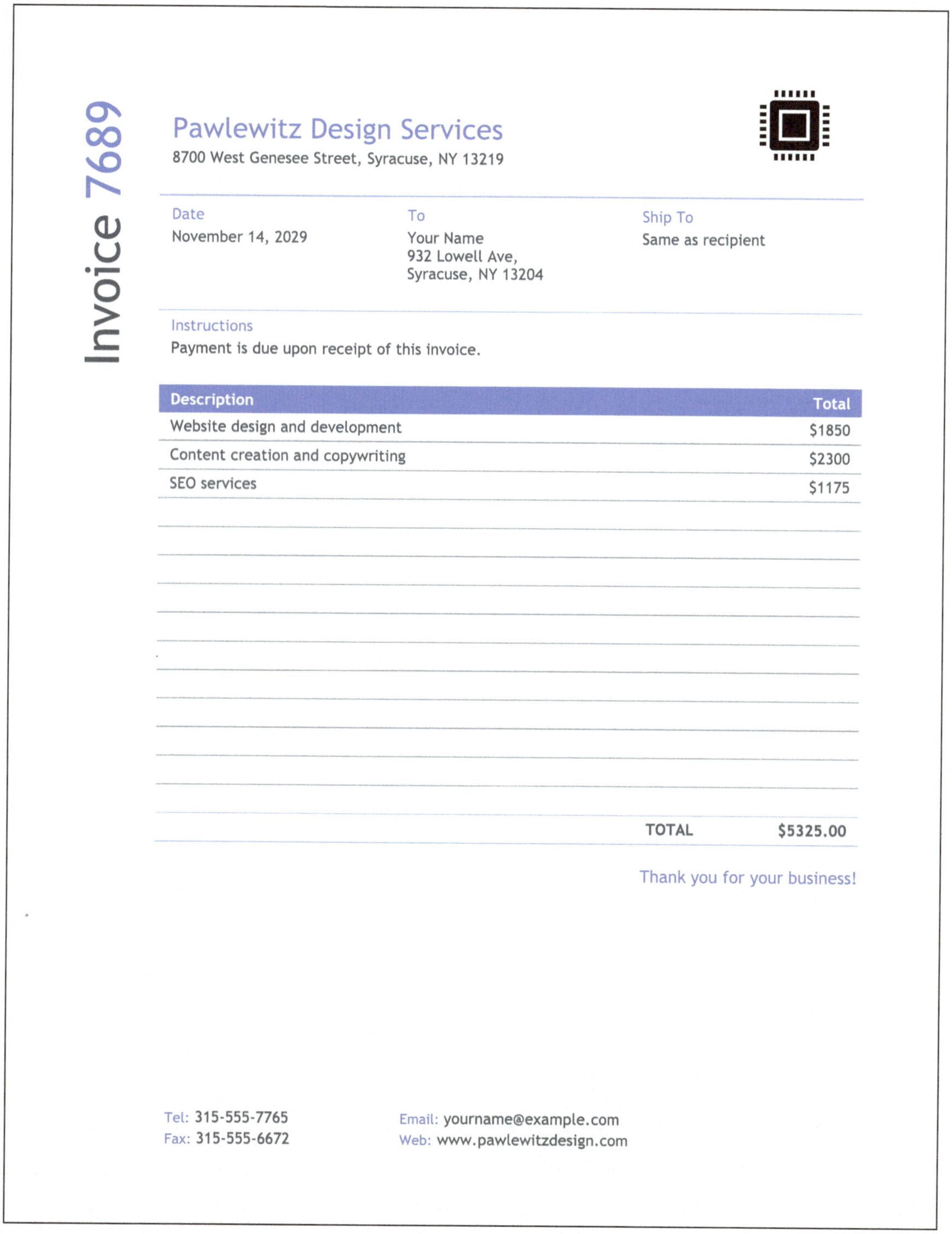

Invoice 7689

Pawlewitz Design Services
8700 West Genesee Street, Syracuse, NY 13219

Date	To	Ship To
November 14, 2029	Your Name 932 Lowell Ave, Syracuse, NY 13204	Same as recipient

Instructions
Payment is due upon receipt of this invoice.

Description	Total
Website design and development	$1850
Content creation and copywriting	$2300
SEO services	$1175
TOTAL	$5325.00

Thank you for your business!

Tel: 315-555-7765
Fax: 315-555-6672
Email: yourname@example.com
Web: www.pawlewitzdesign.com

Merging Word Documents

Case

You need to send a letter to people who recently registered for the MSIT Alumni Leadership Conference, hosted by the alumni affairs and development office at MSIT. The letter confirms participants' enrollment in a specific conference workshop and acknowledges receipt of a nonrefundable deposit. You also need to send an information packet to all the people attending the upcoming conference. You use a mail merge to create a personalized form letter for people who recently registered for the conference and mailing labels for the information packet.

Module Objectives

After completing this module, you will be able to:

- Explain mail merge
- Create a main document
- Design a data source
- Enter and edit records
- Add merge fields
- Use merge rules
- Merge data
- Create labels
- Sort and filter records

Files You Will Need

IL_WD_6-1.docx
Support_WD_6_LabelsData.accdb
IL_WD_6-2.docx
IL_WD_6-3.docx
IL_WD_6-4.docx
Support_WD_6_ParticipantData.accdb

Explain Mail Merge

Case You decide to use the Mail Merge pane to create your form letters and the commands on the Mailings tab to create your mailing labels. Before beginning, you explore the steps involved in performing a mail merge.

Objectives
- Identify the elements of a mail merge
- State the benefits of performing a mail merge

When you perform a **mail merge**, you merge a standard Word document with a file that contains customized information for many individuals or items. The standard document is called the **main document**. The file with the unique data for individual people or items is called the **data source**. Merging the main document with a data source results in a **merged document** that contains customized versions of the main document, as shown in **Figure 6-1**. The Mail Merge pane steps you through the process of setting up and performing a mail merge. You can also perform a mail merge using the commands on the Mailings tab.

Details

- **Create the main document**
  The main document contains the text—often called **boilerplate text**—that appears in every version of the merged document. The main document also includes the merge fields, which indicate where the customized information is inserted when you perform the merge. You insert the merge fields in the main document after you have created or selected the data source. You can create a main document using one of the following: a new blank document, the current document, a template, or an existing document.

- **Create a data source or select an existing data source**
  The data source is a file that contains the unique information for each individual or item, such as a person's name. It provides the information that varies in every version of the merged document. A data source is composed of data fields and data records. A **data field** is a category of information, such as last name, first name, street address, city, or postal code. A **data record** is a complete set of related information for an individual or an item, such as one person's name and address. Think of a data source file as a table: the header row contains the names of the data fields (the **field names**), and each row in the table is an individual data record. You can create a new data source or you can use an existing data source, such as a data source created in Word, an Outlook contact list, an Access database, or an Excel worksheet.

- **Identify the fields to include in the data source and enter the records**
  When you create a new data source, you must first identify the fields to include, such as first name, last name, and street address if you are creating a data source that will include addresses. It is also important to think of and include all the fields you will need (not just the obvious ones) before you begin to enter data. For example, if you are creating a data source that includes names and addresses, you might need to include fields for a person's middle name, title, apartment number, department name, or country, even if some records in the data source will not include that information. Once you have identified the fields and set up your data source, you are ready to enter the data for each record.

- **Add merge fields to the main document**
  A **merge field** is a placeholder that you insert in the main document to indicate where the data from each record should be inserted when you perform the merge. For example, you insert a ZIP Code merge field in the location where you want to insert a ZIP Code. The merge fields in a main document must correspond with the field names in the associated data source. Merge fields must be inserted, not typed, in the main document. The Mail Merge pane and the Mailings tab provide access to the dialog boxes you use to insert merge fields.

- **Merge the data from the data source into the main document**
  Once you have established your data source and inserted the merge fields in the main document, you are ready to perform the merge. You can merge to a new file, which contains a customized version of the main document for each record in the data source, or you can merge directly to a printer or an email message.

Figure 6-1: Mail Merge Process

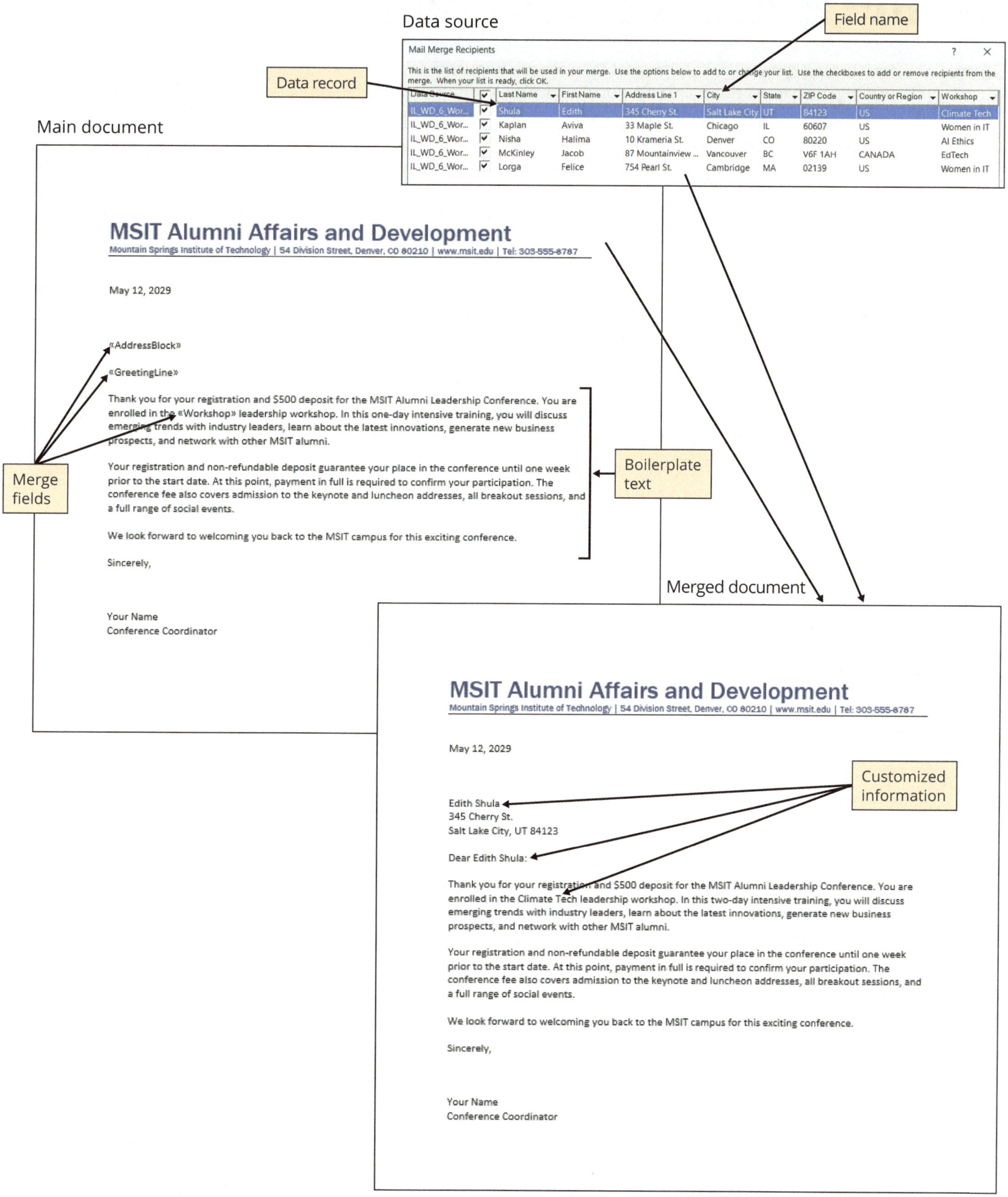

Create a Main Document

Case You have already drafted boilerplate text for a form letter confirming conference registration. You decide to use this existing form letter for your main document. You start the mail merge process by opening the Mail Merge pane and saving the existing letter as a main document.

Objectives
- Start a mail merge
- Create a letter main document

The first step in performing a mail merge is to set up the main document—the file that contains the boilerplate text. You can create a main document from scratch, save an existing document as a main document, or use a mail merge template to create a main document. The Mail Merge pane walks you through the process of selecting the type of main document you want to create.

Steps

Trouble
If the Mailings tab is not available on the Ribbon, right-click the Ribbon, click Customize the Ribbon, select the Mailings check box in the Main tabs list box to enable it, and then click OK.

Quick Tip
If you choose "Use the current document" and the current document is blank, you can create a main document from scratch. Either type the boilerplate text at this step or wait until the Mail Merge pane prompts you to do so.

1. **sam Start Word, open a blank document, click the Mailings tab, click the Start Mail Merge button in the Start Mail Merge group, then click Step-by-Step Mail Merge Wizard**
   The Mail Merge pane opens, as shown in **Figure 6-2**, and displays information for the first step in the mail merge process: Select document type, which is the type of merge document to create. Options for documents include Letters, E-mail messages, Envelopes, Labels, and Directory.
2. **Make sure the Letters option button is selected, then click Next: Starting document to continue with the next step**
   The Mail Merge pane displays the options for the second step: Select starting document, which is the main document. You can use the current document, start with a mail merge template, or use an existing file.
3. **Select the Start from existing document option button, make sure (More files...) is selected in the Start from existing box, then click Open**
   The Open dialog box opens.
4. **Navigate to the location where you store your Data Files, select the file IL_WD_6-1.docx, then click Open**
   Notice the filename in the title bar is Document1. When you create a main document that is based on an existing document, Word gives the main document a default temporary filename.
5. **Click the Save button on the Quick Access toolbar, then save the main document as IL_WD_6_ConferenceLetterMain to the location where you store your files**
   It's a good idea to include "main" in the filename so that you can easily recognize the file as a main document.
6. **Replace Current Date at the beginning of the document with the current date, scroll to and select Irene Vanja in the signature line at the end of the letter, type your name, press CTRL+HOME, then save your changes**
   The edited main document is shown in **Figure 6-3**. You will continue with the next step, selecting recipients, in the next lesson.

Figure 6-2: Step 1 of 6 Mail Merge pane

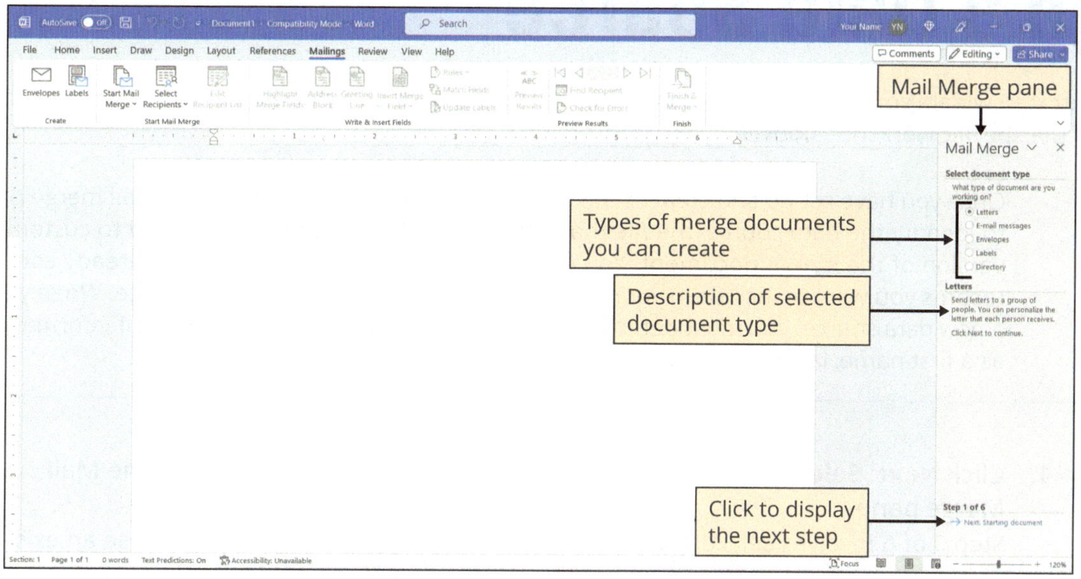

Figure 6-3: Main document with Step 2 of 6 Mail Merge pane

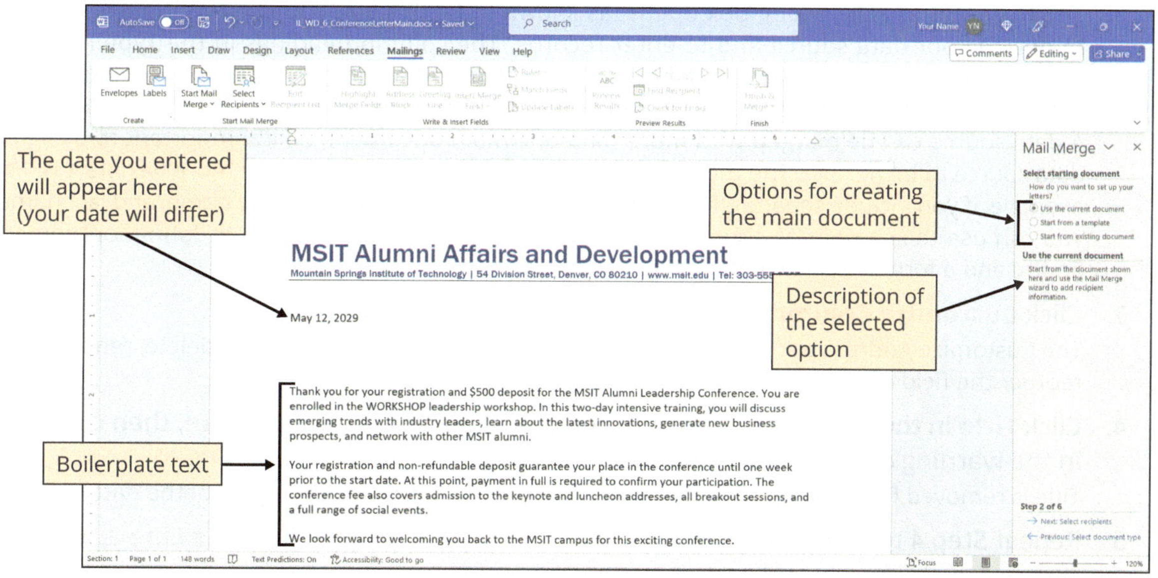

Using a mail merge template

If you are creating letters or faxes, you can use a mail merge template to start your main document. Each template includes placeholder text, which you can replace, and merge fields, which you can match to the field names in your data source. To create a main document that is based on a mail merge template, click the File tab, click New, type "mail merge" in the Search for online templates box, click the Start searching button, select one of the mail merge templates to use as your main document, and then click Create. You can then use the Mail Merge pane or the Ribbon to begin a mail merge using the current document. In the Step 2 of 6 Mail Merge pane, click the Use the current document option button, and then click Next. Once you have created the main document, you can customize the main document with your own information: edit the placeholder text; change the document format; or add, remove, or modify the merge fields.

Before performing the merge, make sure to match the names of the merge fields used in the template with the field names used in your data source. To match the field names, click the Match Fields button in the Write & Insert Fields group on the Mailings tab, and then use the arrows in the Match Fields dialog box to select the field name in your data source that corresponds to each address field component in the main document.

Design a Data Source

Case You create a new data source that includes fields for the conference participant's name and address, and the name of the specific workshop booked by the participant.

Objectives
- Create a data source
- Add and remove fields in a data source

Once you have set up and created the main document, the next step in the mail merge process is to identify the data source, the file that contains the information that is used to customize each version of the merge document. You can use an existing data source that already contains the records you want to include in your merge, or you can create a new data source. When you create a new data source, you must determine the fields to include—the categories of information, such as a first name, last name, city, or postal code—and then add the records.

Steps

Quick Tip
Data sources created and saved as an Access database use the .accdb file extension; data sources created and saved in Word as part of the Mail Merge process use the .mdb file extension.

1. **Click Next: Select recipients to display Step 3 of 6 at the bottom of the Mail Merge pane**
   Step 3 of 6 involves selecting a data source to use for the merge. You can use an existing data source from Access, use a list of contacts created in Microsoft Outlook, or create a new data source.

2. **Select the Type a new list option button, then click Create**
   The New Address List dialog box opens, as shown in **Figure 6-4**. You use this dialog box both to design your data source and to enter records. The column headings in the Type recipient information... section of the dialog box are fields that are commonly used in form letters, but you can customize your data source by adding and removing columns (fields) from this table. A data source can be merged with more than one main document, so it's important to design a data source to be flexible. The more fields you include in a data source, the more flexible it is. For example, if you include separate fields for a person's title, first name, middle name, and last name, you can use the same data source to create an envelope addressed to "Mr. John Montgomery Smith" and a form letter with the greeting "Dear John".

3. **Click Customize Columns**
   The Customize Address List dialog box opens. You use this dialog box to add, delete, rename, and reorder the fields in the data source.

4. **Click Title in the list of field names to select it, if necessary, click Delete, then click Yes in the warning dialog box that opens**
   Title is removed from the list of field names. The Title field is no longer a part of the data source.

5. **Repeat Step 4 to delete the following fields: Company Name, Address Line 2, Home Phone, Work Phone, and E-mail Address**
   The fields are removed from the data source.

6. **Click Add, type Workshop in the Add Field dialog box, then click OK**
   A field called "Workshop", which you will use to indicate the workshop booked by the participant, is added to the data source.

7. **Make sure Workshop is selected in the list of field names, then click Move Up until Workshop is at the top of the list**
   The field name "Workshop" is moved to the top of the list, as shown in **Figure 6-5**. Although the order of field names does not matter in a data source, it's convenient to arrange the field names logically to make it easier to enter and edit records.

8. **Click OK**
   The New Address List dialog box shows the customized list of fields, with the Workshop field first in the list. The next step is to enter each record you want to include in the data source. You add records to the data source in the next lesson.

Figure 6-4: New Address List dialog box

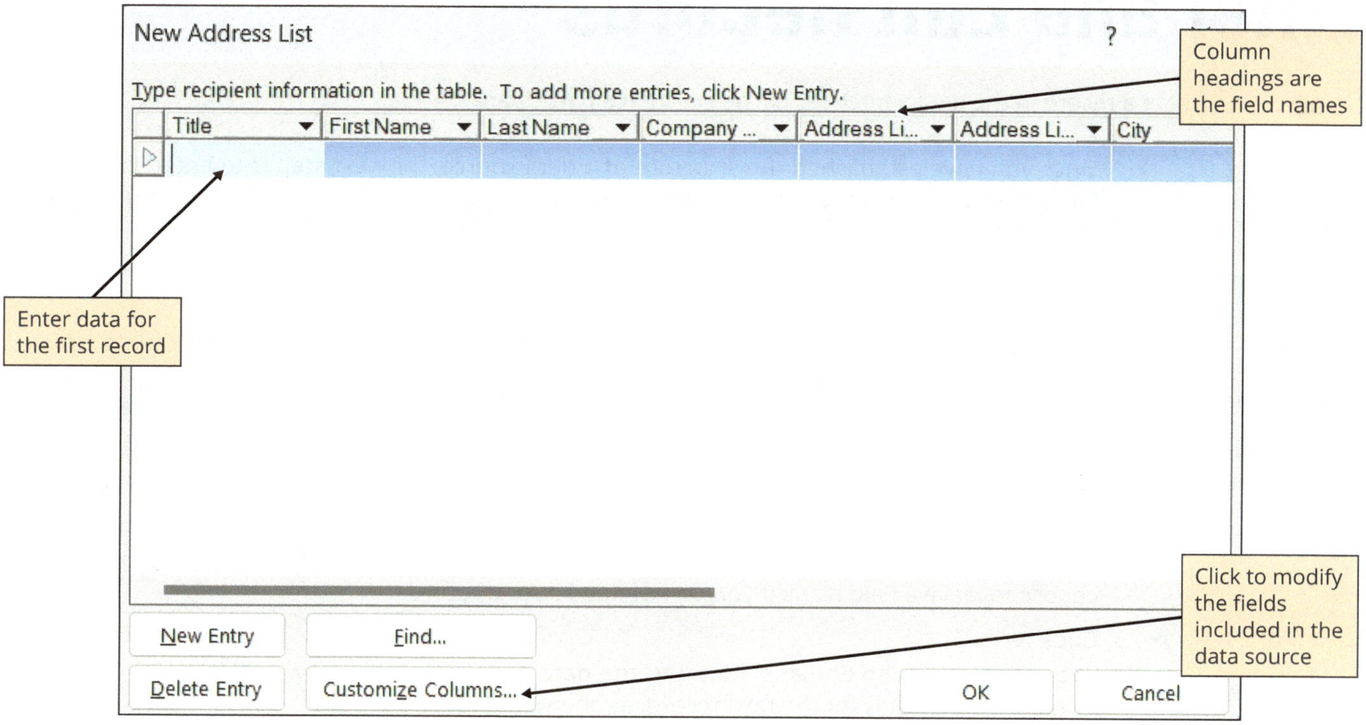

Figure 6-5: Customize Address List dialog box

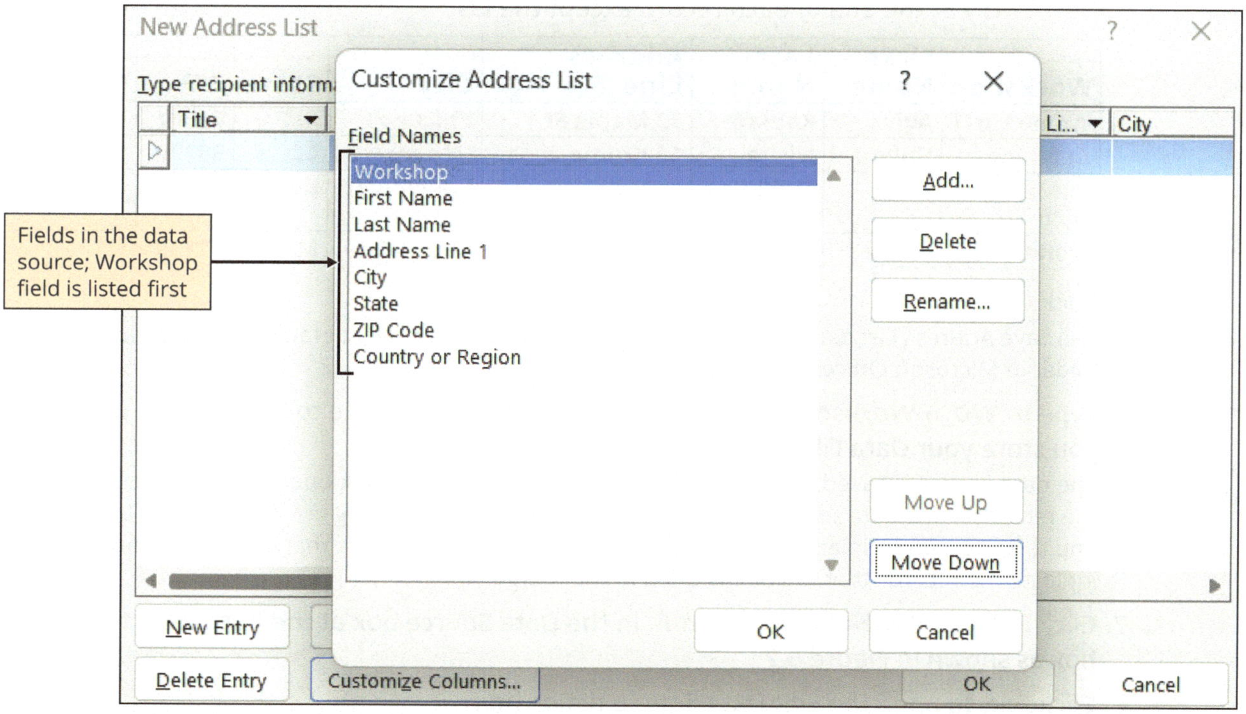

Merging with an Outlook data source

If you maintain lists of contacts in Microsoft Outlook, you can use one of your Outlook contact lists as a data source for a merge. To merge with an Outlook data source, click the Select from Outlook contacts option button in the Step 3 of 6 Mail Merge pane, then click Choose Contacts Folder to open the Choose Profile dialog box. In this dialog box, use the Profile Name arrow to select the profile you want to use, then click OK to open the Select Contacts dialog box. In this dialog box, select the contact list you want to use as the data source, and then click OK. All the contacts included in the selected folder appear in the Mail Merge Recipients dialog box. Here, you can refine the list of recipients to include in the merge by sorting and filtering the records. When you are satisfied, click OK in the Mail Merge Recipients dialog box.

Enter and Edit Records

Case You create a record in the data source for each conference participant.

Objectives
- Add a record
- Edit a recipient list

Once you have established the structure of a data source, the next step is to enter the records. Each record includes the complete set of information for each individual or item you include in the data source.

Steps

Quick Tip
Be careful not to add spaces or extra punctuation after an entry in a field, or these will appear when the data is merged.

1. **Verify the insertion point is in the Workshop box in the New Address List dialog box, type Climate Tech, then press TAB**
   "Climate Tech" appears in the Workshop field, and the insertion point moves to the next column, the First Name field.

2. **Type Edith, press TAB, type Shula, press TAB, type 345 Cherry St., press TAB, type Salt Lake City, press TAB, type UT, press TAB, type 84123, press TAB, then type US**
   Data is entered in all the fields for the first record. You used each field for this record, but you can choose to leave a field blank if you do not need it for a record.

Quick Tip
You can also press TAB at the end of the last field to start a new record.

3. **Click New Entry**
   The record for Edith Shula is added to the data source, and the New Address List dialog box displays empty fields for the next record, as shown in **Figure 6-6**.

4. **Enter the following four records, pressing TAB to move from field to field, and clicking New Entry at the end of each record except the last:**

Workshop	First Name	Last Name	Address Line 1	City	State	ZIP	Country
Women in IT	Aviva	Kaplan	33 Maple St.	Chicago	IL	60607	US
AI Ethics	Halima	Nisha	10 Krameria St.	Denver	CO	80220	US
Climate Tech	Jacob	McKinley	87 Mountainview Dr.	Vancouver	BC	V6F 1AH	CANADA
Women in IT	Felice	Lorga	754 Pearl St.	Cambridge	MA	02139	US

5. **Click OK**
   The Save Address List dialog box opens. Data sources are saved by default in the My Data Sources folder in Microsoft Office Address Lists (*.mdb) format.

Trouble
If a check mark appears in the blank record under Felice Lorga, click the check mark to eliminate the record from the merge.

6. **Type IL_WD_6_WorkshopData in the File name box, navigate to the location where you store your Data Files, then click Save**
   The data source is saved, and the Mail Merge Recipients dialog box opens. The dialog box shows the records in the data source in table format. You can use the dialog box to sort and filter records, and to select the recipients to include in the mail merge. The check marks in the second column indicate the records that will be included in the merge.

7. **Click IL_WD_6_WorkshopData.mdb in the Data Source box at the bottom of the dialog box as shown in Figure 6-7**

8. **Click Edit to open the Edit Data Source dialog box**
   You use this dialog box to edit a recipient list, including adding and removing fields, editing field names, adding and removing records, and editing existing records.

9. **Click Climate Tech in the Workshop field of the Jacob McKinley record to select it, then type EdTech, as shown in Figure 6-8**

Quick Tip
If you want to add new records or modify existing records, click Edit recipient list in the Mail Merge pane.

10. **Click OK in the Edit Data Source dialog box, click Yes, then click OK in the Mail Merge Recipients dialog box**
    The file type and filename of the data source attached to the main document now appear under Use an existing list heading in the Mail Merge pane.

Figure 6-6: Record in New Address List dialog box

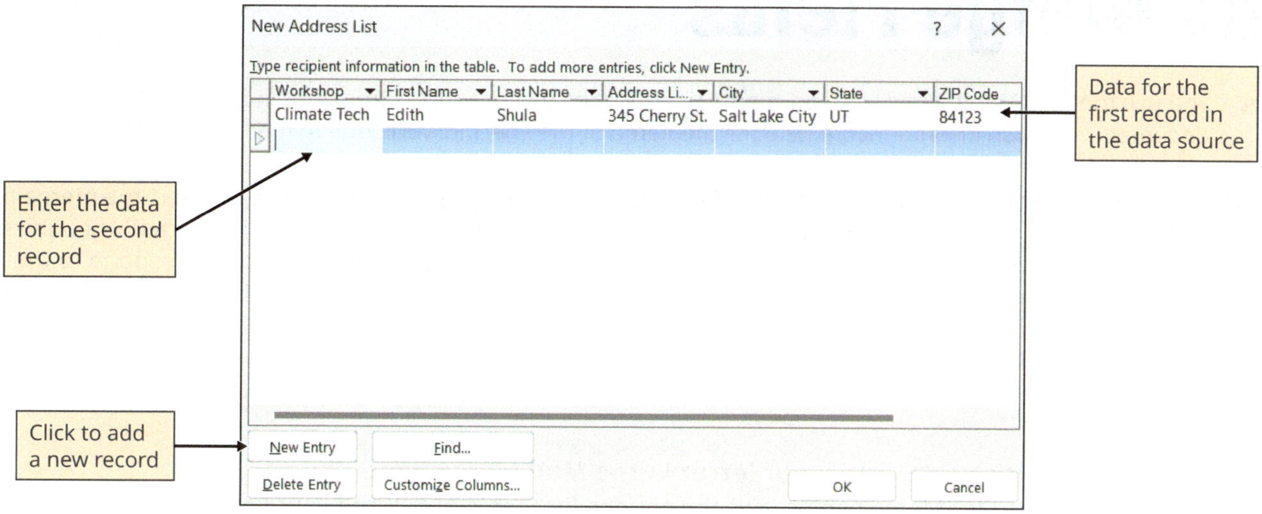

Figure 6-7: Data Source selected in the Mail Merge Recipients dialog box

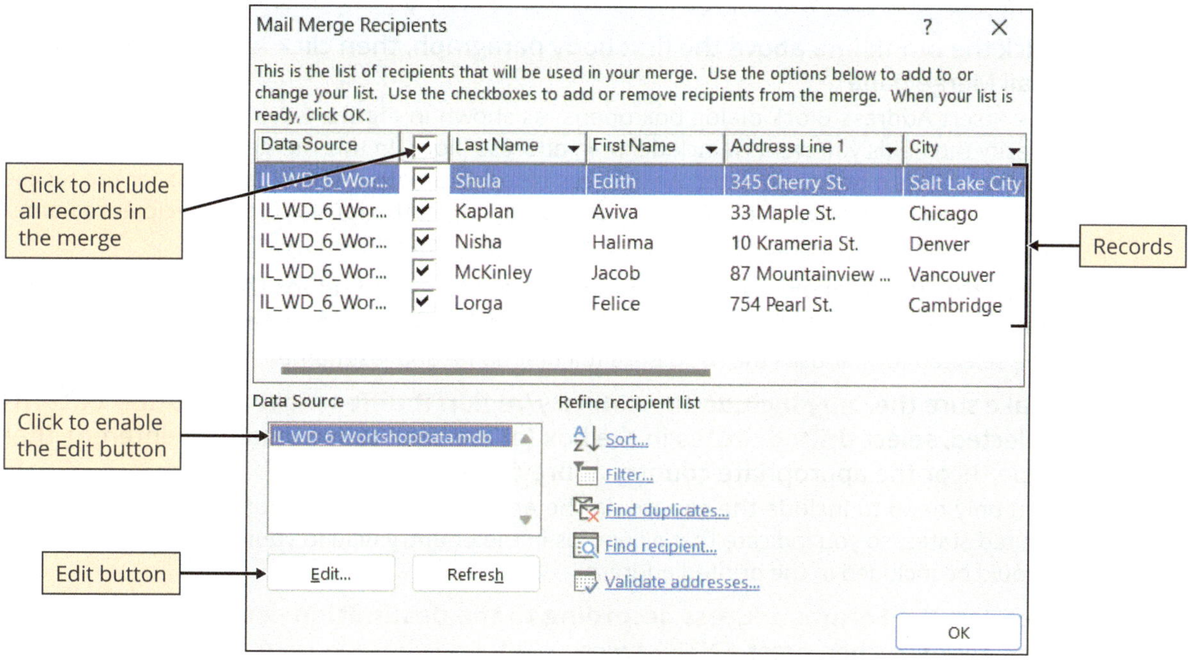

Figure 6-8: Edit Data Source dialog box

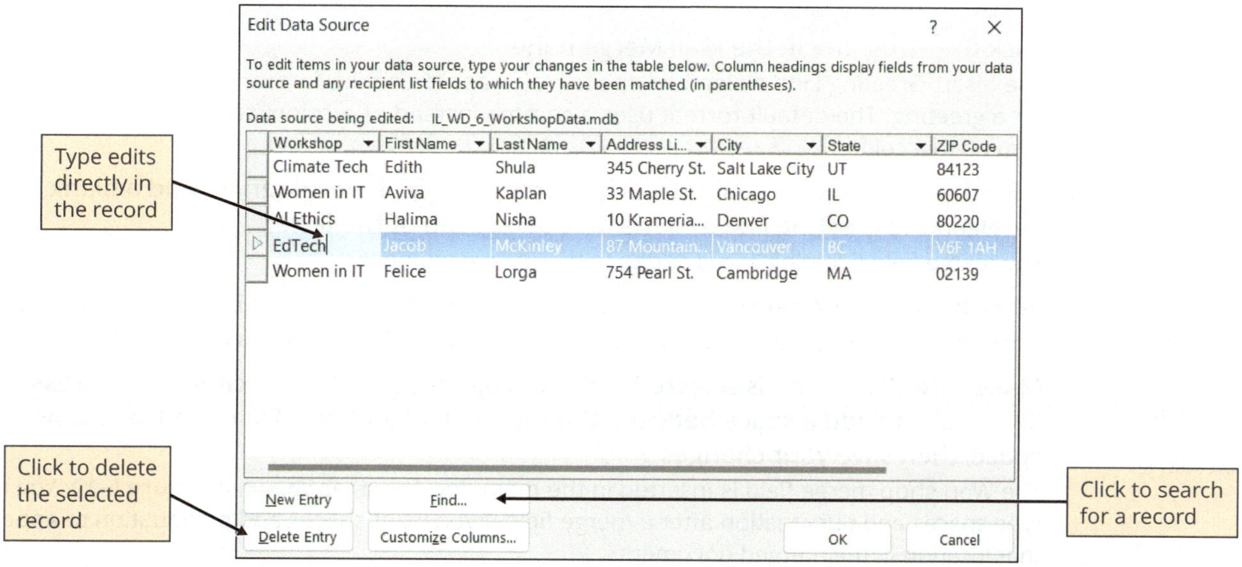

Add Merge Fields

Case You use the Mail Merge pane to insert merge fields for the inside address and greeting of the letter in the main document. You also insert a merge field for the name of the specific workshop in the body of the letter.

Objectives
- Insert merge fields
- Customize an address block and greeting field

After you have created and identified the data source, the next step is to insert the merge fields in the main document. Merge fields serve as placeholders for text that is inserted when the main document and the data source are merged. The names of merge fields correspond to the field names in the data source. You can insert merge fields using the Mail Merge pane or the Address Block, Greeting Line, and Insert Merge Field buttons in the Write & Insert Fields group on the mailings tab. You cannot type merge fields into the main document.

Steps

Quick Tip
You can also click the Address Block button in the Write & Insert Fields group on the Mailings tab to insert an address block.

1. **Click Next: Write your letter in the Mail Merge pane**
   The Mail Merge pane shows the options for Step 4 of 6: Write your letter. During this step, you write or edit the boilerplate text and insert the merge fields in the main document. Since your form letter is already written, you are ready to add the merge fields to it.
2. **Click the blank line above the first body paragraph, then click Address block in the Mail Merge pane**
   The Insert Address Block dialog box opens, as shown in **Figure 6-9**. You use this dialog box to specify the fields you want to include in an address block. In this merge, the address block is the inside address of the form letter. An address block automatically includes fields for the recipient's name, street, city, state, and ZIP code, but you can select the format for the recipient's name and indicate whether to include a company name or country in the address.
3. **Scroll the list of formats for a recipient's name to get a feel for the kinds of formats you can use, then click Joshua Randall Jr. if it is not already selected**
   The selected format uses the recipient's full first name and last name.
4. **Make sure the Only include the country/region if different than: option button is selected, select United States in the box (or another country name if entered), then type US or the appropriate country abbreviation**
   You only need to include the country in the address block if the country is different from the United States, so you indicate that all entries in the Country field in your data source, except "US", should be included in the printed address.

Quick Tip
You cannot simply type chevrons around a field name. You must insert merge fields using the Mail Merge pane or the buttons in the Write & Insert Fields group on the Mailings tab.

5. **Deselect the Format address according to the destination country/region check box, click OK, then press ENTER twice**
   The merge field AddressBlock is added to the main document. Chevrons (<< and >>) surround a merge field to distinguish it from the boilerplate text.
6. **Click Greeting line in the Mail Merge pane**
   The Insert Greeting Line dialog box opens. You want to use the format "Dear Joshua Randall Jr.:" for a greeting. The default format uses a comma instead of a colon, so you have to change the comma to a colon.
7. **Click the , arrow, click :, click OK, then press ENTER, if necessary to add a blank line between the greeting line and the first paragraph of the letter**
   The merge field GreetingLine is added to the main document.

Quick Tip
You can also click the Insert Merge Field button or arrow in the Write & Insert Fields group on the Mailings tab to insert a merge field.

8. **In the body of the letter select WORKSHOP, then click More items in the Mail Merge pane**
   The Insert Merge Field dialog box opens and displays the list of field names included in the data source.
9. **Make sure Workshop is selected in the dialog box, click Insert, click Close, press SPACEBAR to add a space between the merge field and "workshop" if there is no space, then save your changes**
   The Workshop merge field is inserted in the main document, as shown in **Figure 6-10**. You must type spaces and punctuation after a merge field if you want spaces and punctuation to appear in that location in the merged documents.

Figure 6-9: Insert Address Block dialog box

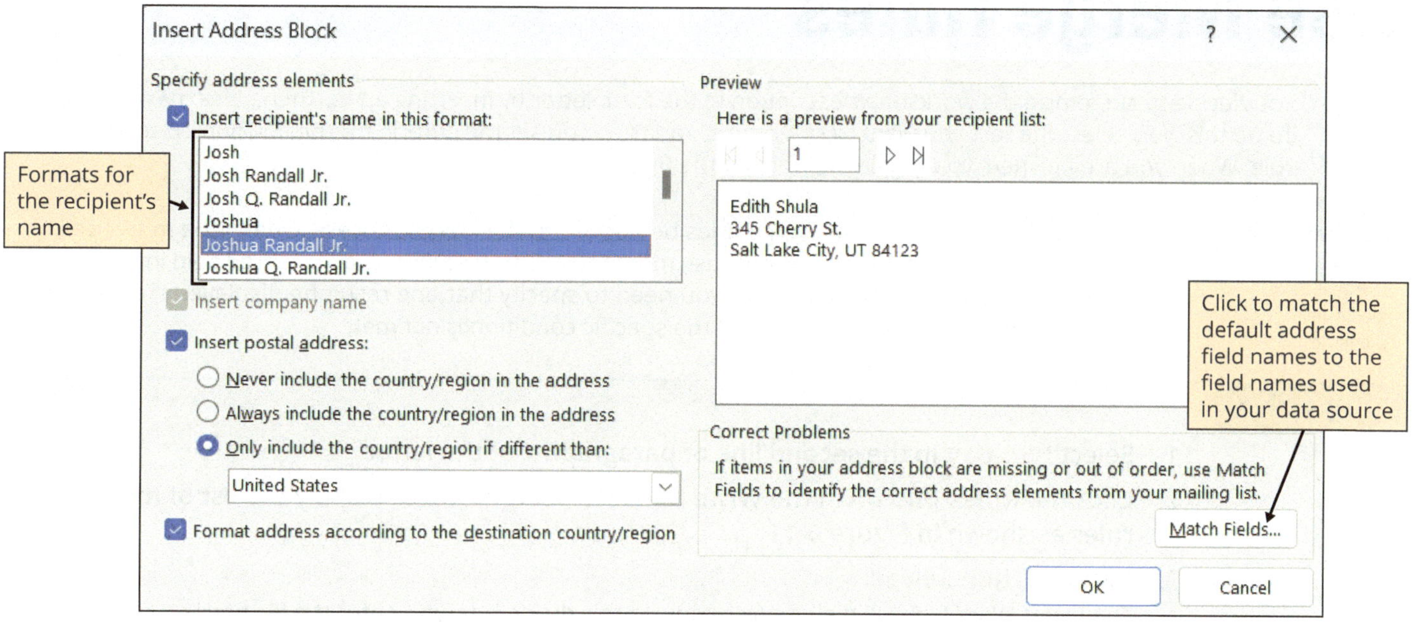

Figure 6-10: Merge fields in the main document

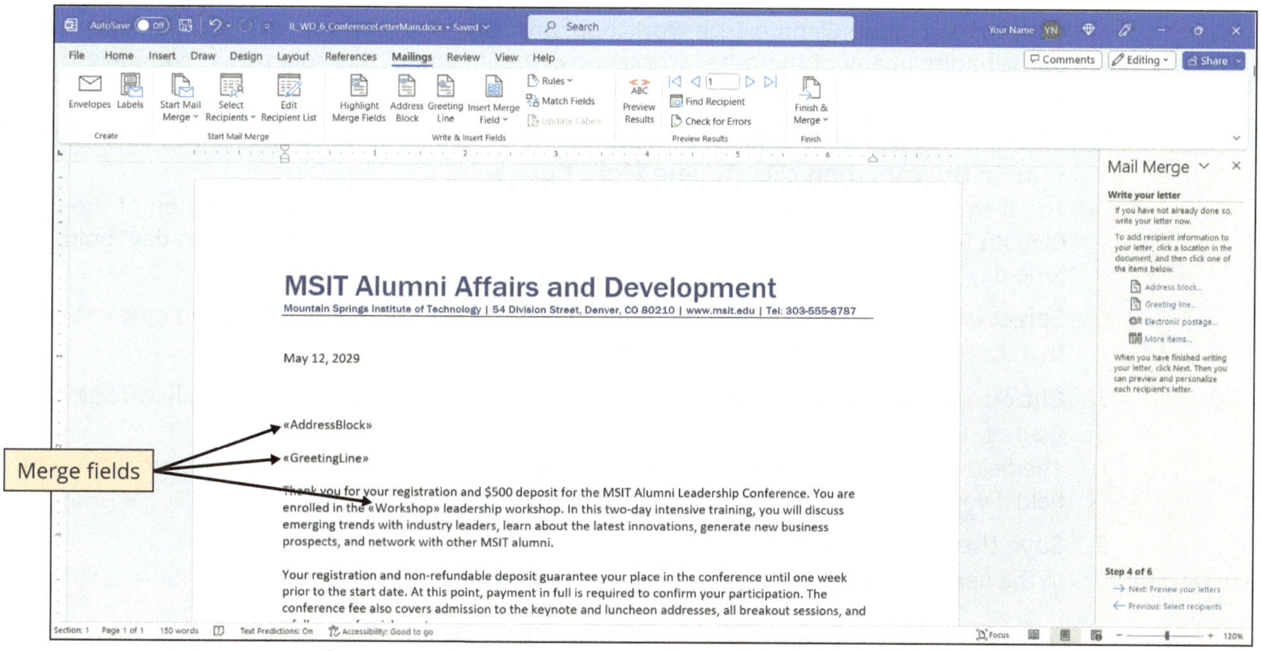

Matching fields

The merge fields you insert in a main document must correspond with the field names in the associated data source. If you are using the Address Block merge field, you must make sure that the default address field names correspond to the field names used in your data source. If the default address field names do not match the field names in your data source, click Match Fields in the Insert Address Block dialog box, then use the arrows in the Match Fields dialog box to select the field name in the data source that corresponds to each default address field name. You can also click the Match Fields button in the Write & Insert Fields group on the Mailings tab to open the Match Fields dialog box.

Use Merge Rules

Case You decide to customize the workshop description in the form letter by inserting an If...Then...Else merge field. To do this, you select the text you want to customize, and then you set the criteria for the If...Then...Else merge rule. When you are finished, you toggle and format the field code.

Objectives
- Specify a merge rule
- Use an IF field
- Modify field properties

You can specify that certain merge rules be applied to the merge process. One of the most useful of these merge rules is the If...Then...Else merge rule. This rule inserts an IF merge field into a main document. You use an IF field when you need to specify that one result be displayed if a specific condition is met and another result if the specific condition is *not* met.

Steps

1. **Select two-day in the second line of paragraph 1 of the letter**
2. **Click the Rules button in the Write & Insert Fields group to display the list of merge rules as shown in Figure 6-11**
3. **Click If...Then...Else...**
   The Insert Word Field: IF dialog box opens. In this dialog box, you enter the IF criteria.
4. **Enter criteria for the If...Then...Else rule as shown in Figure 6-12, click OK, then press SPACEBAR to add a space between "two-day" and "intensive", if necessary**
   You specify that "two-day" will appear as the workshop duration in every letter to people participating in the Climate Tech workshop, and "one-day" will appear in every letter to people participating in any of the other workshops. The If...Then...Else rule turns "two-day" into an IF Merge field that you can view using the Toggle feature.
5. **Select two-day (it turns gray, indicating it is a field and not regular text), click the right mouse button, then click Toggle Field Codes**
   The IF merge field is displayed as shown in **Figure 6-13**. You want the duration of the two-day Climate Tech workshop to stand out, so you modify the field code to make "two-day" bold, leaving "one-day" as regular text.
6. **Select two-day in the merge field (it becomes a darker gray), click the right mouse button, click Font, select Bold in the Font style box, then click OK**
7. **Click one-day in the merge field, click the right mouse button, then click Toggle Field Codes**
   The field properties of the merge field "two-day" are now modified. You only know it is a merge field if you click on it to view the gray shading.
8. **Save the document**
   In the next lesson, you will preview and then complete the merge.

Figure 6-11: List of merge rules

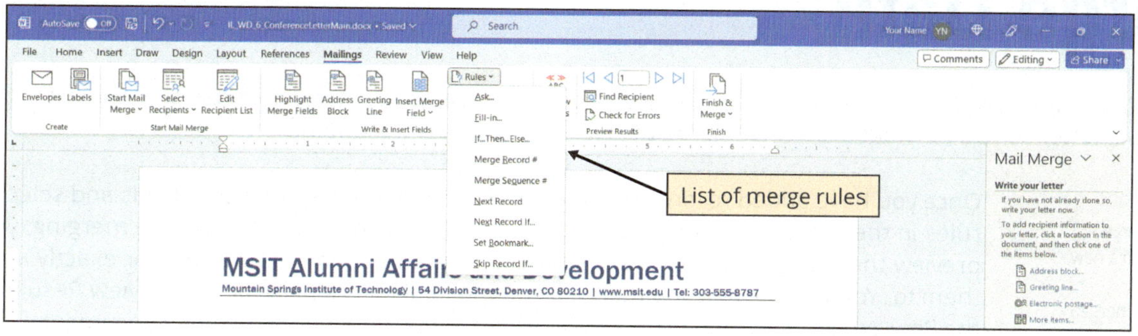

Figure 6-12: Insert Word Field: IF dialog box

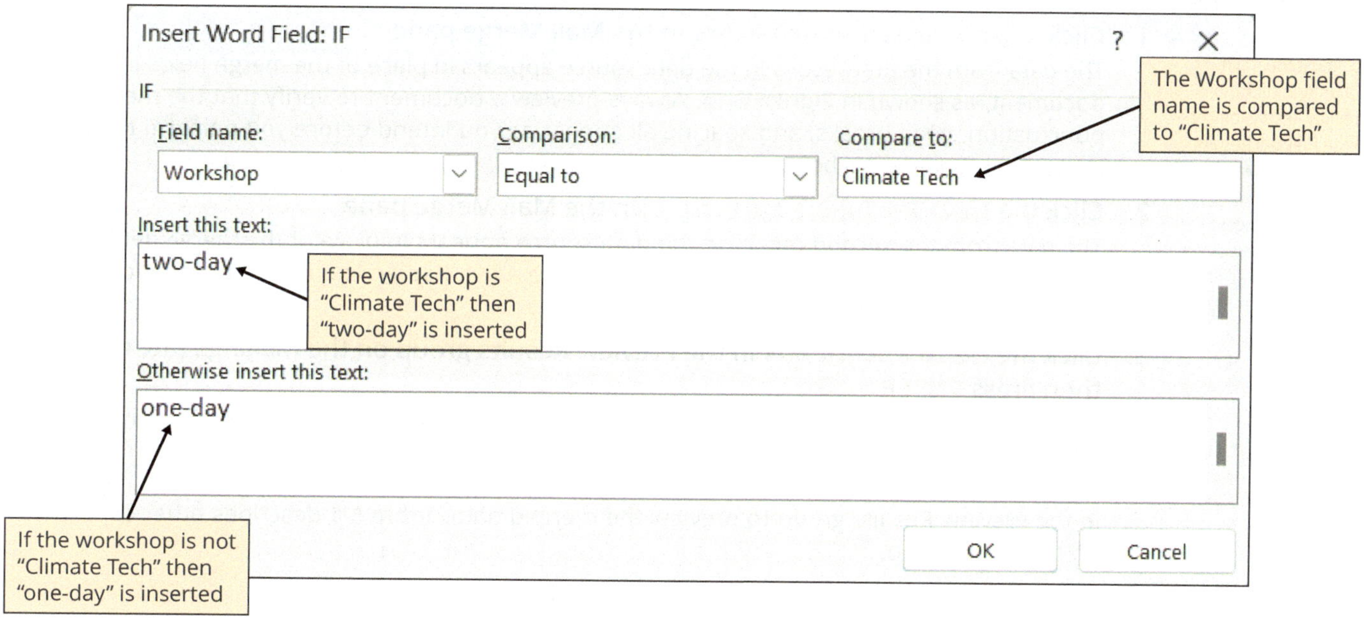

Figure 6-13: Toggled IF merge field

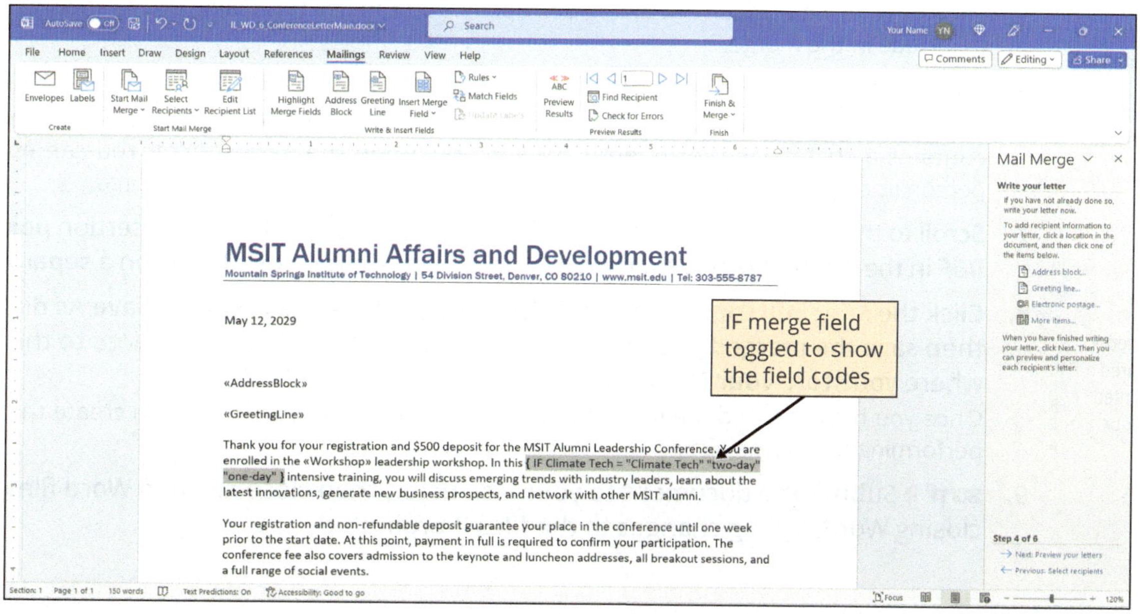

Merge Data

Case Before merging the form letter with the data source, you preview the merge to make sure the data appears in the letter as you intended. You then merge the two files to a new document.

Objectives
- Preview a merge
- Merge data to a new document
- Customize a merged document

Once you have added records to your data source and inserted merge fields and selected merge rules in the main document, you are ready to perform the merge. Before merging, you should preview the merged data to make sure the printed documents will appear exactly as you want them to. You can preview the merge using the Mail Merge pane or the Preview Results button in the Preview Results group on the Mailings tab. When you merge the main document with the data source, you must choose between merging to a new file or directly to a printer.

Steps

Quick Tip
To adjust the main document, click the Preview Results button in the Preview Results group on the Mailings tab, then make any necessary changes. Click the Preview Results button again to preview the merged data.

1. **Click Next: Preview your letters in the Mail Merge pane**
   The data from the first record in the data source appears in place of the merge fields in the main document, as shown in **Figure 6-14**. Always preview a document to verify that the merge fields, punctuation, page breaks, and spacing all appear as you intend before you perform the merge. Notice that "two-day" is bold.

2. **Click the Next Recipient button [>>] in the Mail Merge pane**
   The data from the second record in the data source appears in place of the merge fields. Notice that "two-day" has changed to "one-day" because Aviva Kaplan is enrolled in the Women in IT workshop. Also, notice that "one-day" is not bold.

3. **Click the Go to Record box in the Preview Results group on the Mailings tab, type 4, then press ENTER**
   The data for the fourth record appears in the document window. The non-US country name, in this case, CANADA, is included in the address block, just as you specified. You can also use the **First Record** [|◁], **Previous Record** [◁], **Next Record** [▷], and **Last Record** [▷|] buttons in the Preview Results group to preview the merged data. **Table 6-1** describes other commands on the Mailings tab.

4. **Click Next: Complete the merge in the Mail Merge pane**
   The options for Step 6 of 6 appear in the Mail Merge pane. Merging to a new file creates a document with one letter for each record in the data source. This allows you to edit the individual letters.

Quick Tip
If your data source contains many records, you can merge directly to a printer to avoid creating a large file.

5. **Click Edit individual letters to merge the data to a new document**
   The Merge to New Document dialog box opens. You can use this dialog box to specify the records to include in the merge.

6. **Make sure the All option button is selected, then click OK**
   The main document and the data source are merged to a new document called Letters1, which contains a customized form letter for each record in the data source. You can now further personalize the letters without affecting the main document or the data source.

7. **Scroll to the fourth letter (addressed to Jacob McKinley), place the insertion point before V6F in the address block, then press ENTER to place the postal code on a separate line**

Quick Tip
Print only one letter if you are required to submit a printed document to your instructor.

8. **Click the Save button [💾] on the Quick Access toolbar to open the Save As dialog box, then save the merged document as IL_WD_6_ConferenceLetterMerge to the location where you store your Data Files**
   Once you have created the main document and the data source, you can create the letters by performing the merge again.

9. **sam Submit the document to your instructor, then close all open Word files without closing Word, saving changes to the files if prompted**

Figure 6-14: Preview of merged data

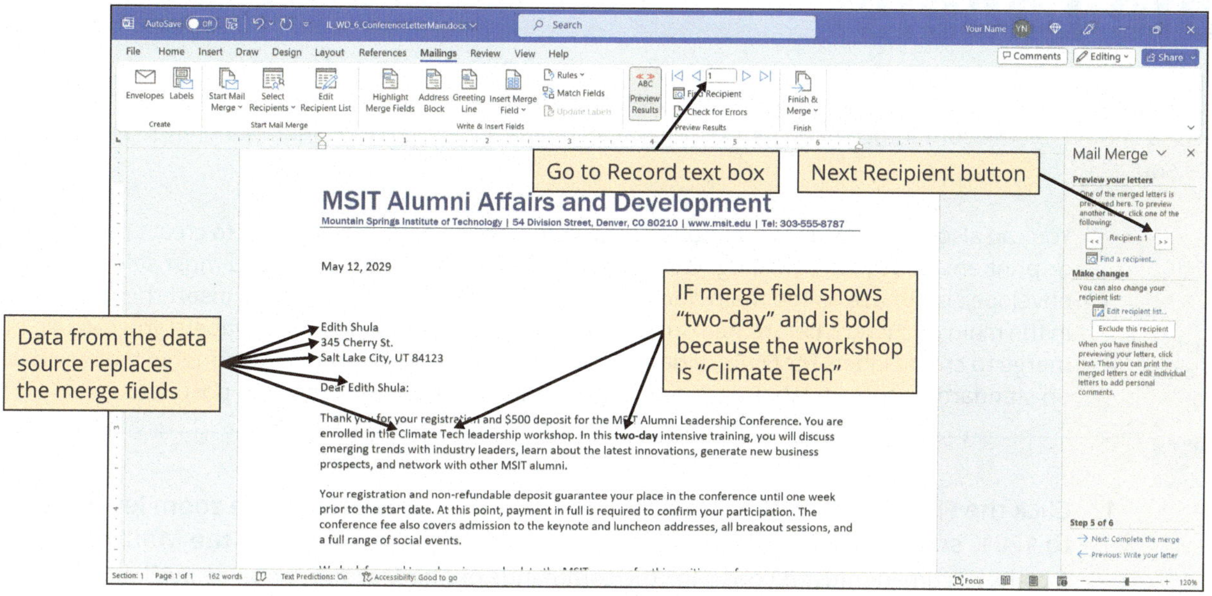

Table 6-1: Commands on the Mailings tab

command	use to
Envelopes	Create and print an individual envelope
Labels	Create and print an individual label
Start Mail Merge	Select the type of mail merge document to create and start the mail merge process
Select Recipients	Attach an existing data source to a main document or create a new data source
Edit Recipient List	Edit, sort, and filter the associated data source
Highlight Merge Fields	Highlight the merge fields in the main document
Address Block	Insert an Address Block merge field in the main document
Greeting Line	Insert a Greeting Line merge field in the main document
Insert Merge Field	Insert a merge field from the data source in the main document
Rules	Set rules to control how Word merges the data in the data source with the main document
Match Fields	Match the names of address or greeting fields used in a main document with the field names used in the data source
Update Labels	Update all the labels in a label main document to match the content and formatting of the first label
Preview Results	Switch between viewing the main document with merge fields or with merged data
Find Recipient	Search for a specific record in the merged document
Check for Errors	Check for and report errors in the merge
Finish & Merge	Specify whether to merge to a new document or directly to a printer or to email, then complete the merge

Opening Merge Files

The Word file you have designated as "Main" in the filename is linked to the data source that you attached to it. When you open the Word file, a message appears advising you that "Opening this document will run the following SQL command:". When you click Yes, the data from the data source attached to the merge file will be placed in the document. If you wish to run the merge again, you need to click Yes when this message is displayed.

Create Labels

Case You decide to use the commands on the Mailings tab to create mailing labels for the information packet you need to send to all the conference participants. You create a new label main document and attach an existing data source.

Objectives
- Create a label main document
- Merge with an existing data source
- Update mailing labels

You can also use the Mail Merge pane or the commands on the Mailings tab to create mailing labels or print envelopes for a mailing. When you create labels or envelopes, you must select a label or envelope size to use as the main document, select a data source, and then insert the merge fields in the main document before performing the merge. In addition to mailing labels, you can use mail merge to create labels for DVDs, videos, and other items, and to create documents that are based on standard or custom label sizes, such as business cards, name tags, and postcards.

Steps

1. **Click the File tab, click New, click Blank document, make sure the zoom level is set to 120% so that the label text will appear on the screen, then click the Mailings tab**
   A blank document must be open for the commands on the Mailings tab to be available.

Quick Tip
To create an envelope mail merge, click Envelopes to open the Envelope Options dialog box, and then select from the options.

2. **Click the Start Mail Merge button in the Start Mail Merge group, click Labels, click the Label vendors arrow in the Label Options dialog box, then click Microsoft if Microsoft is not already displayed**
   The Label Options dialog box opens, as shown in **Figure 6-15**. You use this dialog box to select a label size for your labels and to specify the type of printer you plan to use. The name Microsoft appears in the Label vendors box. You can use the Label vendors arrow to select other brand name label vendors, such as Avery, Staples, or Office Depot. Many standard-sized labels for mailings, business cards, postcards, and other types of labels are listed in the Product number box. The type, height, width, and page size for the selected product are displayed in the Label information section.

Quick Tip
If your labels do not match FIGURE 6-16, click the Undo button on the Quick Access toolbar, then repeat Step 3, making sure to click the second instance of 30 Per Page.

3. **Click the second instance of 30 Per Page in the Product number list, click OK, click the Layout contextual tab (to the right of the Table Design tab), click the View Gridlines button in the Table group to turn on the display of gridlines if they are not displayed, then click the Mailings tab**
   A table with gridlines appears in the main document, as shown in **Figure 6-16**. Each table cell is the size of a label for the label product you selected.

4. **Save the label main document with the filename IL_WD_6_ConferenceLabelsMain to the location where you store your Data Files**
   Next, you need to select a data source for the labels. You open a data source in Microsoft Access and resave it with a new name, then attach it to the main document.

Trouble
Click Enable Content if it appears in a yellow bar in the Access window.

5. **Open File Explorer, navigate to the location where you store your Data Files, then double-click Support_WD_6_LabelsData.accdb**
   The data source opens in Access, which is a database program often used to create recipient lists for mail merges.

Quick Tip
To create or change the return address for an envelope mail merge, click the File tab, click Options, click Advanced in the left pane of the Word Options dialog box, then scroll down the right pane and enter the return address in the Mailing address box in the General section.

6. **Click the File tab, click Save As, click the Save As button, navigate to the location where you store your Data Files, change the name of the file to IL_WD_6_LabelsDataSource, click Save, then click the ✕ in the top right corner of the Access window to exit Access**

7. **Return to the labels document in Word, click the Mailings tab, click the Select Recipients button in the Start Mail Merge group, then click Use an Existing List**
   The Select Data Source dialog box opens.

8. **Navigate to the location where you store your Data Files, open the file IL_WD_6_LabelsDataSource.accdb, then save your changes**
   The data source file is attached to the label main document, and <<Next Record>> appears in every cell in the table except the first cell, which is blank. In the next lesson, you sort and filter the records before performing the mail merge.

Figure 6-15: Label Options dialog box

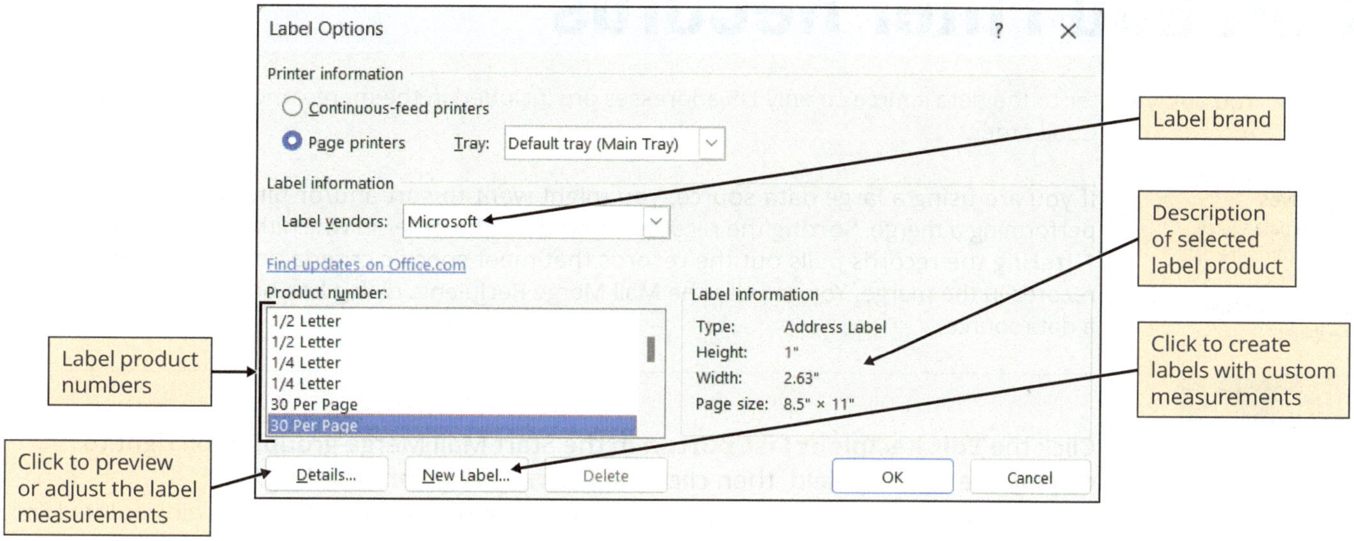

Figure 6-16: Label main document

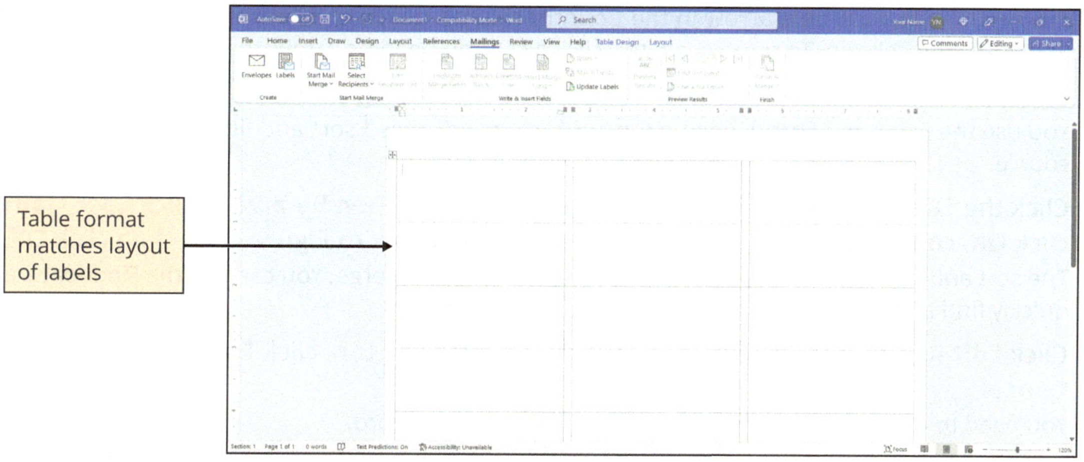

Printing individual envelopes and labels

The Mail Merge feature enables you to easily print envelopes and labels for mass mailings, but you can also quickly format and print individual envelopes and labels using the Envelopes or Labels commands in the Create group on the Mailings tab. Simply click the Envelopes button or Labels button to open the Envelopes and Labels dialog box. On the Envelopes tab, shown in **Figure 6-17**, type the recipient's address in the Delivery address box and the return address in the Return address box. Click Options to open the Envelope Options dialog box, which you use to select the envelope size, change the font and font size of the delivery and return addresses, and change the printing options. When you are ready to print the envelope, click Print in the Envelopes and Labels dialog box. The procedure for printing an individual label is similar to printing an individual envelope: enter the label text in the Address box on the Labels tab, click Options to select a label product number, click OK, and then click Print. Be sure to have envelopes loaded into your printer.

Figure 6-17: Envelopes and Labels dialog box

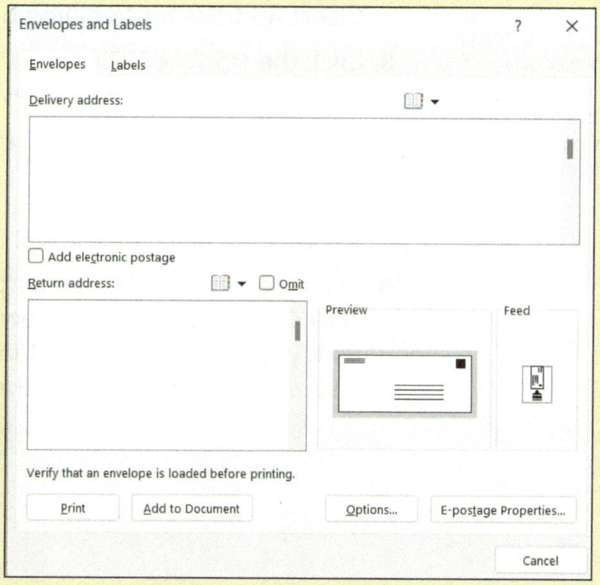

Sort and Filter Records

Case You apply a filter to the data source so only US addresses are included in the merge and then you sort those records in ZIP Code order.

Objectives
- Filter a data source
- Sort records in a data source
- Find a mail merge recipient

If you are using a large data source, you might want to sort and/or filter the records before performing a merge. **Sorting** the records determines the order in which the records are merged. **Filtering** the records pulls out the records that meet specific criteria and includes only those records in the merge. You can use the Mail Merge Recipients dialog box both to sort and to filter a data source.

Steps

1. **Click the Edit Recipient List button in the Start Mail Merge group, scroll right to display the Country field, then click the Country column heading**
   The records are sorted in ascending alphabetical order by country, with Canadian records listed first.
2. **Click the Country column heading arrow, then click US on the menu that opens**
   A filter is applied to the data source so only the records with "US" in the Country field will be merged. The grayish-blue arrow in the Country column heading indicates that a filter has been applied to the column. To remove a filter, click a column heading arrow, then click (All).
3. **Click Sort in the Refine recipient list section of the dialog box**
   You use the Filter and Sort dialog box to apply more advanced sort and filter options to the data source.
4. **Click the Sort by arrow, click ZIP Code, click the first Then by arrow, click Last Name, click OK, compare the Mail Merge Recipients dialog box to Figure 6-18, then click OK**
   The sort and filter criteria you set are saved for the current merge. You can use the Find feature to quickly find and then edit a mail merge recipient's record.
5. **Click Edit Recipient List, click Find recipient, type Graton, click Find Next, then click Cancel**
   You need to open the data source to make a change to a record.
6. **Double-click the filename in the Data Source box, click Find, type Graton, click Find Next, click Cancel, verify that Graton is selected, type San Leandro, click OK, click Yes, then click OK**
   With your recipients list filtered, sorted, and edited, you are ready to complete the merge.
7. **Click the Address Block button in the Write & Insert Fields group, then click OK in the Insert Address Block dialog box to add the Address Block merge field to the first label**
8. **Click the Update Labels button in the Write & Insert Fields group to copy the merge field from the first label to every label in the main document**
9. **Click the Preview Results button in the Preview Results group**
   A preview of the merged label data appears in the main document, as shown in **Figure 6-19**. Only US addresses are included, and the labels are organized in ZIP Code order, with recipients with the same ZIP Code listed in alphabetical order by Last Name.
10. **Click the Finish & Merge button in the Finish group, click Edit Individual Documents, click OK in the Merge to New Document dialog box, replace Anastasia Lieberstein with your name in the first label, save the document as IL_WD_6_ConferenceLabels_USZipMerge, submit the labels, then save and close all open files and exit Word**

Quick Tip
Use the options on the Filter Records tab to apply more than one filter to the data source.

Quick Tip
Sorting and filtering a data source does not alter the records in a data source; it simply reorganizes the records for the current merge only.

Quick Tip
To change the font or paragraph formatting of merged data, format the merge fields, including the chevrons, before performing a merge.

Figure 6-18: US records sorted in zip code order

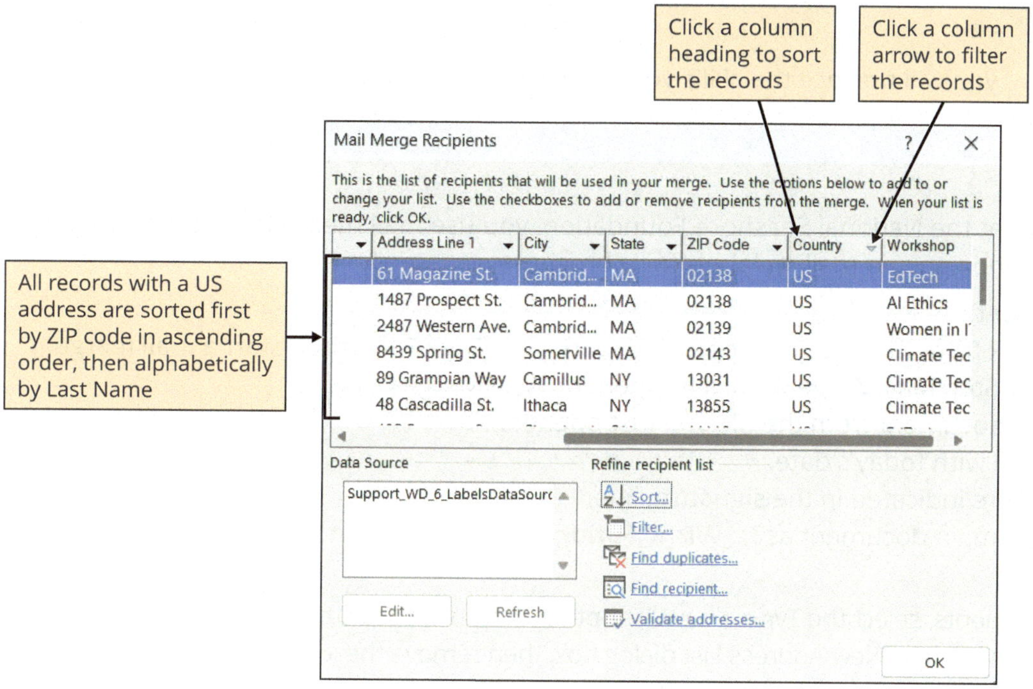

Figure 6-19: Merged labels

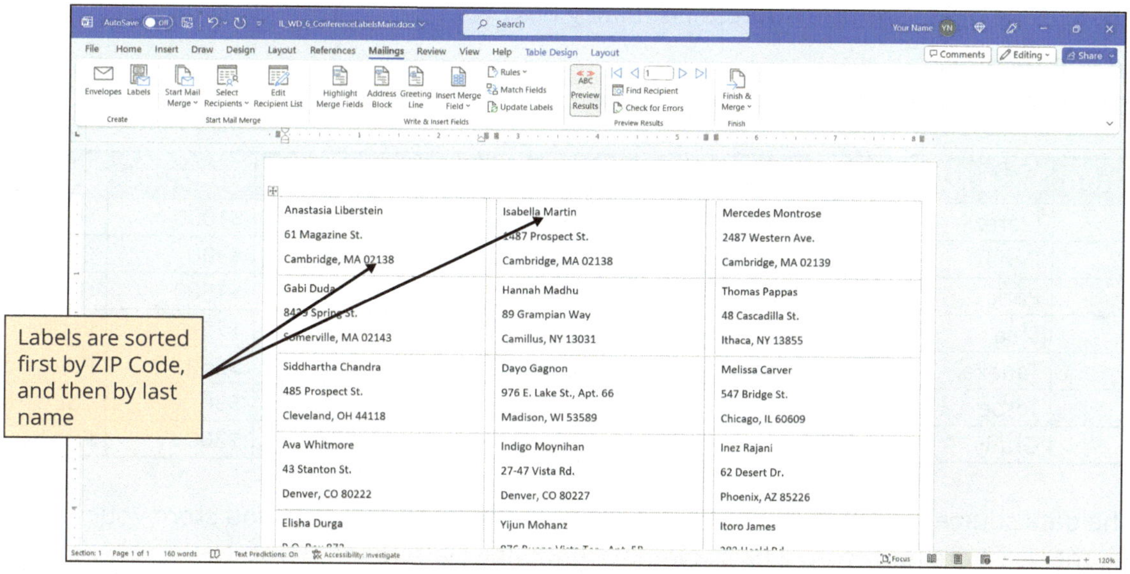

Inserting individual merge fields

You must include proper punctuation, spacing, and blank lines between the merge fields in a main document if you want punctuation, spaces, and blank lines to appear between the data in the merge documents. For example, to create an address line with a city, state, and ZIP Code, you insert the City merge field, type a comma and a space, insert the State merge field, type a space, and then insert the ZIP Code merge field: <<City>>, <<State>> <<ZIP Code>>.

You can insert an individual merge field by clicking the Insert Merge Field arrow in the Write & Insert Fields group and then selecting the field name from the menu that opens. Alternatively, you can click the Insert Merge Field button to open the Insert Merge Field dialog box, which you can use to insert several merge fields at once by clicking a field name in the dialog box, clicking Insert, clicking another field name, clicking Insert, and so on. When you have finished inserting the merge fields, click Close to close the dialog box. You can then add spaces, punctuation, and lines between the merge fields you inserted in the main document.

Practice

In the exercises that follow, you will practice the skills you have learned in this module.

Skills Review

As fundraising coordinator at the National Seashore Foundation, you use mail merge to create thank you letters for a fundraising campaign and mailing labels for a brochure.

1. **Create a main document.**
   a. Open IL_WD_6-2.docx from the location where you store your Data Files, then start a mail merge by using the Step-by-Step Mail Merge Wizard to open the Mail Merge pane.
   b. Create a letter main document from the file you just opened.
   c. Replace Current Date with today's date.
   d. Type your name where indicated in the signature line.
   e. Save the mail merge main document as **IL_WD_6_FundraisingLetterMain**.
2. **Design a data source.**
   a. Click Next: Select recipients, select the Type a new list option button in Step 3 of 6... pane, then click Create.
   b. Click Customize Columns in the New Address List dialog box, then remove these fields from the data source: Title, Company Name, Address Line 2, Country or Region, Home Phone, Work Phone, and E-mail Address.
   c. Add an **Amount** field and a **Seashore** field to the data source. Be sure these fields follow the ZIP Code field.
   d. Click OK to close the Customize Address List dialog box.
3. **Enter and edit records.**
   a. Add the records shown below to the data source.

First Name	Last Name	Address Line 1	City	State	ZIP Code	Amount	Seashore
Pablo	Juarez	32-56 Beacon St.	Brooklyn	NY	20201	$1000	Fire Island
Sylvia	Pena	776 Ocean Rd.	Eureka	CA	95503	$300	Cape Hatteras
Amanda	Park	998 Main St.	Jackson	MS	38203	$1500	Gulf Islands
Gaby	Shia	3345 Gulf Rd.	Houston	TX	77036	$75	Padre Island
Mari	Tanaka	173 Maria St.	Santa Rosa	CA	95401	$250	Point Reyes
Richard	Tesse	323 Piedmont Rd.	Charlotte	NC	28205	$50	Cape Hatteras
Victoria	Grady	45-23 30th Ave.	Astoria	NY	11102	$200	Fire Island

   b. Save the data source as **IL_WD_6_FundraisingData** to the location where you store your Data Files.
   c. Change the seashore for record 2 (Sylvia Pena) from Cape Hatteras to **Point Reyes**.
   d. Click OK as needed to close all dialog boxes.
4. **Add merge fields.**
   a. Click Next: Write your letter, then in the blank line above the first body paragraph, insert an Address block merge field, then click OK.
   b. Press ENTER twice, insert a Greeting Line merge field using the default greeting line format, then press ENTER.
   c. In the first body paragraph, replace AMOUNT with the Amount merge field.
   d. In the second body paragraph, replace SEASHORE with the Seashore merge field. (*Note*: Make sure to insert a space before or after each merge field as needed.)
   e. Save your changes to the main document.
5. **Use merge rules.**
   a. Select National Seashore at the end of paragraph 2, then select the If...Then...Else merge rule.
   b. Select Seashore as the field name, then enter criteria for the rule so that when "Point Reyes" is the record in the Seashore field, "National Seashore and Tomales Bay State Park" is displayed, and if not, then "National Seashore" is displayed.

c. Toggle the field codes and verify the code is { IF { MERGEFIELD Seashore } = "Point Reyes" "National Seashore and Tomales Bay State Park" "National Seashore" }. (**Hint**: Toggle "Fire Island" to display {MERGEFIELD Seashore}.)

d. Select the entire field code, then change the font of the field code to Times New Roman.

6. **Merge data.**

   a. Click Next: Preview your letters to preview the merged data, then use the Next Record button to scroll through each letter, examining it carefully for errors. Check that the merge rule worked.

   b. Click the Preview Results button on the Mailings tab, make any necessary adjustments to the main document, save your changes, then click the Preview Results button to return to the preview of the document.

   c. Click Next: Complete the merge, click Edit individual letters, then merge all the records to a new file.

   d. Save the merged document as **IL_WD_6_FundraisingLetterMerge** to the location where you store your Data Files. The first letter is shown in **Figure 6-20**. Submit the file or a copy of the last letter per your instructor's directions, then save and close all open files but not Word.

Figure 6-20

National Seashore Foundation
8749 North Carolina Avenue NW, Washington, DC 20004, www.seashorefoundation.org

Current Date

Pablo Juarez
32-56 Beacon St.
Brooklyn, NY 20201

Dear Pablo Juarez,

We are delighted to receive your generous contribution of $1000 to the National Seashore Foundation.

Our national seashores not only provide outstanding recreational opportunities but play a vital role in educating visitors about the ecological significance of coastal landscapes. Your donation is crucial to helping us protect the pristine beauty, fragile ecosystems, diverse habitats, and cultural heritage of Fire Island National Seashore.

Sincerely,

Your Name
Executive Director

7. **Create labels.**

   a. Open a new blank document, click the Start Mail Merge button in the Start Mail Merge group on the Mailings tab, then create a Labels main document.

   b. In the Label Options dialog box, select Avery US Letter, select 5160 Address Labels, then click OK.

   c. Click the Select Recipients button, then open the IL_WD_6_FundraisingData.mdb file you created.

   d. Save the label main document as **IL_WD_6_FundraisingLabelsMain** to the location where you store your Data Files.

8. **Sort and filter records.**

   a. Click the Edit Recipient List button, filter the records so that only the records with Fire Island in the Seashore field are included in the merge, sort the records in City order, then click OK as needed to return to the labels document.

   b. Insert an Address Block merge field using the default settings, update the labels, then click the Preview Results button.

   c. Open the Recipient List, find the record for Amanda Park, then change the Seashore to Fire Island.

   d. Verify that Amanda's record appears, examine the merged data for errors, then correct any mistakes.

   e. Click the Finish & Merge button, then click the Edit Individual Documents to merge all the records to an individual document, as shown in **Figure 6-21**.

Figure 6-21

Victoria Grady 45-23 30th Ave. Astoria, NY 11102	Pablo Juarez 32-56 Beacon St. Brooklyn, NY 20201	Amanda Park 998 Main St. Jackson, MS 38203

Skills Review (Continued)

f. Save the merged file as **IL_WD_6_FundraisingLabelsFireIslandOnlyMerge** to the location where you store your Data Files.

g. In the first label, change Victoria Grady to your name, submit the document to your instructor, save and close all open Word files, then exit Word.

Independent Challenge 1

As a care coordinator at Merrimack Family Health, you handle patient correspondence regarding health and wellness screenings. You need to send a letter and informational brochure to patients who are overdue for a mammogram or skin check, reminding them to make an appointment. You'll use Mail Merge to create the letter and a sheet of labels.

a. Start Word, open IL_WD_6-3.docx from the location where you store your Data Files, save the document as **IL_WD_6_ScreeningLetter**, add the current date, replace Your Name with your name in the signature block, then save and close the file.

b. Start a new blank document in Word, then using either the commands on the Mailings tab or the Mail Merge pane (the wizard), create a letter main document using the document you just saved. Save the main document as **IL_WD_6_ScreeningLetterMain**.

c. Create a new recipient list using the data shown below. Remove any field names that are not included.

First Name	Last Name	Address Line 1	City	State	ZIP Code	Screening	Doctor
Kate	Joss	77 Mountain Rd.	Greenfield	NH	03047	skin check	Hines
Ming	Putu	997 Stoddard Rd.	Hillsboro	NH	03244	mammogram	Hines
Beatrice	Cary	82 Tilton St.	Manchester	NH	03104	mammogram	Xuan
Agnes	Dezi	437 Hudson Rd.	Manchester	NH	03103	skin check	Hines
Sung	Nkruma	88 River Rd.	Sunapee	NH	03782	mammogram	Xuan

d. Name the data source **IL_WD_6_ScreeningData**.

e. Sort the data source by Last Name, then edit the data by changing the address for Ms. Agnes Dezi to **4125 Warner St**.

f. Insert an Address Block and a Greeting Line merge field in the main document.

g. Customize the Greeting Line merge field by selecting Joshua as the greeting line format. When the merge is run, "Dear" will be followed by the first name of the recipient.

h. Replace "DOCTOR" and "SCREENING" with the appropriate merge fields.

i. Replace "MEDICAL CONDITION" with an If...Then...Else merge rule. Select Screening as the field name, then enter the criteria for the rule so that when "mammogram" is the record in the Screening field, "breast cancer" is displayed, and if not, then "skin cancer" is displayed.

j. Replace "TIME" with an If...Then...Else merge rule. Select Screening as the field name, then enter the criteria for the rule so that when "mammogram" is the record in the Screening field, "one year" is displayed, and if not, then "eighteen months" is displayed.

k. Toggle the field codes to verify the accuracy and make any necessary adjustments.

l. Preview the merged letters, make any spacing adjustments required, then examine the letters for errors and correct any mistakes. The second letter is shown in **Figure 6-22**.

m. Merge all the records to a new document, save it as **IL_WD_6_ScreeningLetterMerge**, then close the document.

n. Save and close **IL_WD_6_ScreeningLetterMain**.

o. Open a new blank document, then using the Mail Merge pane (the wizard) or the commands on the Mailings tab, select Labels as the main document, and select the label type **Microsoft** and the second instance of 30 Per Page.

p. Select recipients from the IL_WD_6_ScreeningData.mdb file you just created.

Figure 6-22

Merrimack Family Health
5557 Old Mill Road, Suite 459
Manchester, NH 03104
603-555-9348
merrimackfamilyhealth.org

Current Date

Agnes Dezi
4125 Warner St.
Manchester, NH 03103

Dear Agnes,

Your healthcare provider, Dr. Hines, recommends an annual screening for skin cancer. Our records indicate it has been over eighteen months since your last skin check. Please call our office to schedule an appointment.

Regular health screenings are essential to maintaining wellness and diagnosing potential health issues at an early stage. As always, our goal is to provide you with the best possible healthcare.

Please have your insurance information handy when you call to schedule an appointment.

Sincerely,

Your Name
Care Coordinator

q. Save the label main document as **IL_WD_6_ScreeningLabelsMain** to the location where you store your Data Files.

r. Insert an Address Block merge field using the default settings, update the labels, then preview the results.

s. Filter the records so that only the records with mammogram in the Screening field are included in the merge, then sort the records in ZIP Code order.

t. Examine the merged data for errors, then correct any mistakes. The three labels should appear as shown in **Figure 6-23**.

u. Merge all the records to an individual document, save the merged file as **IL_WD_6_ScreeningLabelsMammogramOnlyMerge** to the location where you store your Data Files.

v. Change the name on the first label to your name.

w. Submit the files or a copy of the label sheet and the first merge letter per your instructor's directions, close all open Word files, save changes, and then exit Word.

Figure 6-23

Beatrice Cary 82 Tilton St. Manchester, NH 03104	Ming Putu 997 Stoddard Rd. Hillsboro, NH 03244	Sung Nkruma 88 River Rd. Sunapee, NH 03782

Independent Challenge 2

As program coordinator for the Atlanta World Teacher Exchange Initiative, you are responsible for communicating with participants. You want to send a letter to all Georgia participants enrolled in the Japan and Costa Rica Exchange Teaching programs to inform them of an in-person orientation session to be held in Atlanta, and to offer a discount on their account balance if paid in full by a certain date. You'll use Mail Merge to create the letter and create an envelope for one letter.

a. Start Word, open a blank document, then using either the commands on the Mailings tab or the Mail Merge pane (the wizard), create a letter main document using the file IL_WD_6-4.docx from the location where you store your Data Files.
b. Replace Current Date with the current date and Your Name with your name in the signature block, then save the main document as **IL_WD_6_TeacherLetterMain**.
c. Use the file **Support_WD_6_ParticipantData.accdb** from the location where you store your Data Files as the data source.
d. Sort the data source by Last Name, then filter the data so that only records with GA as the state are included in the merge.
e. Insert an Address Block and a Greeting Line merge field in the main document (separate with a blank line).
f. Replace "AMOUNT" with the Amount merge field, and then remove the space between "$" and the merge field.
g. Replace "PROGRAM" with the Program merge field.
h. Replace "CITY" with an If...Then...Else merge rule. Select Program as the field name, then enter the criteria for the rule so that when "Japan" is the record in the Program field, "Tokyo" is displayed, and if not, then "San Jose" is displayed.
i. Toggle the field code to verify the IF field is correct.
j. In the third body paragraph, replace "DATE" with an If...Then...Else merge rule. Select Program as the field name, then enter the criteria for the rule so that when "Japan" is the record in the Program field, "February 15" is displayed, and if not, then "February 20" is displayed.
k. Toggle the field code to verify the IF field is correct.
l. Toggle off the field code, select "February 15" then apply Bold formatting.
m. In the second body paragraph, select 5% discount, then use the If...Then...Else merge rule to change 5% discount to **3% discount** if the Amount field is greater than or equal to "1000." (**Hint**: You need to modify the Comparison operator to select Greater Than or Equal To.)
n. Toggle the field code to verify the IF field is correct.
o. Toggle off the field code, select "5% discount," then apply Bold formatting.
p. Preview results, then scroll through the letters to verify that the merge rules worked.
q. Merge all the records to a new document, then save it as **IL_WD_6_TeacherLetterMerge**.
r. Select the recipient address in the first merge letter, then click the Envelopes button in the Create group on the Mailings tab to open the Envelopes and Labels dialog box. (*Note*: You will create one envelope and include it as part of the merge document. If you were doing a mail merge, you would create a separate envelope merge.)
s. On the Envelopes tab in the Envelopes and Labels dialog box, verify that the Omit check box is not selected, then in the Return address box, type your name, press ENTER, type **Atlanta World Teacher Exchange Initiative**, press ENTER, type **5050 Peachtree Street**, press ENTER, then type **Atlanta, GA 31429**.

t. Click Options to open the Envelope Options dialog box, click the Envelope Options tab if it is not the active tab, then make sure the Envelope size is set to Size 10.

u. Click the Printing Options tab, select the appropriate Feed method for your printer, then click OK.

v. Click Add to Document, then click No if a message box opens asking if you want to save the new return address as the default return address. The dialog box closes without printing the envelope and the envelope is added as the first page of the merge document as shown in **Figure 6-24**.

w. Submit the file or a copy of the envelope and the first merge letter per your instructor's directions, close all open Word files, save changes, and then exit Word.

Figure 6-24

Your Name
Atlanta World Teacher Exchange Initiative
5050 Peachtree Street
Atlanta, GA 31429

Varghese Abia
Montgomery School
24 LeClair Blvd.
Fifty Lakes, GA 31429

Visual Workshop

Using mail merge, create the data source shown in **Figure 6-25** for the postcard main document shown in **Figure 6-26**. Use Avery US Letter 3263 Postcard labels for the main document. Save the data source as **IL_WD_6_ClientData**, save the merge document as **IL_WD_6_BirthdayPromotionCardMerge**, and save the main document as **IL_WD_6_BirthdayPromotionCardMain**, all to the location where you store your Data Files. Notice that the postcard label main document is formatted as a table. To lay out the postcard, insert a nested table with two columns and one row in the upper-left postcard; add the text and merge field to the nested table; and then remove the outside borders on the nested table. The font for the postcard text is Century Gothic. The font for the address block is Calibri. Submit a copy of the postcards to your instructor.

Figure 6-25

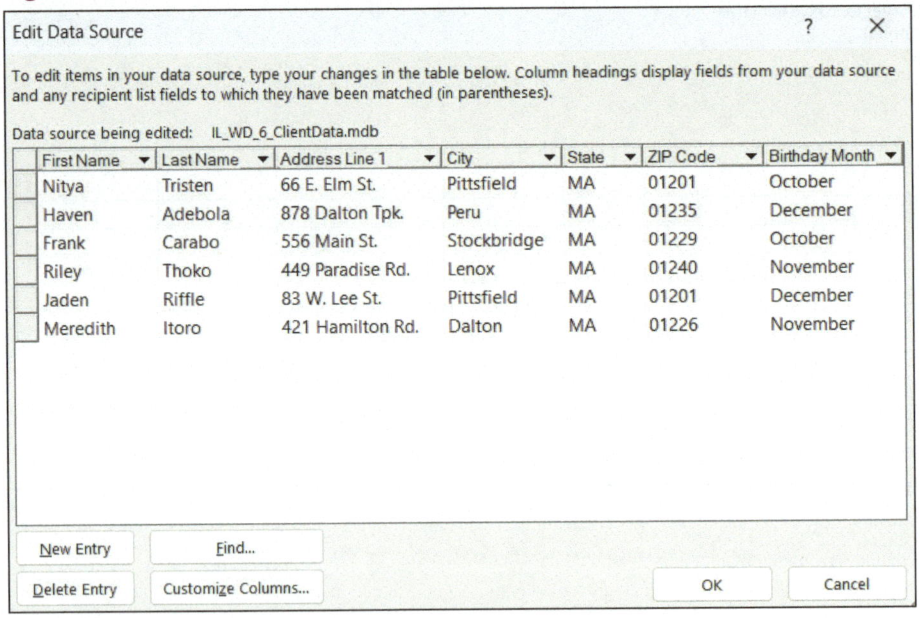

Figure 6-26

Illustrating Documents with Graphics

Case

You have been asked to edit and finalize a two-page information sheet that will be distributed to students interested in attending the Mountain Springs Institute of Technology (MSIT) in Denver, Colorado. The document includes reasons why students should choose MSIT, information about job opportunities, and a checklist detailing how to apply to MSIT.

Module Objectives

After completing this module, you will be able to:

- Use the Office Clipboard
- Insert sections and columns
- Insert SmartArt graphics
- Modify SmartArt graphics
- Crop and rotate a picture
- Position a graphic
- Insert shapes
- Use Drawing tools
- Insert WordArt
- Insert a text box
- Insert a Word file

Files You Will Need

IL_WD_7-1.docx
Support_WD_7_Business.jpg
Support_WD_7_Engineering.jpg
Support_WD_7_OtherDesign.docx
Support_WD_7_Programs.docx
Support_WD_7_Services.docx
IL_WD_7-2.docx
Support_WD_7_Financing.jpg
Support_WD_7_Goals.docx
Support_WD_7_Growth_NewDesign.docx
Support_WD_7_Process.docx
Support_WD_7_RiskChart.jpg
IL_WD_7-3.docx
Support_WD_7_Class.jpg
Support_WD_7_PatientEducation.docx
Support_WD_7_Teddy.jpg
IL_WD_7-4.docx
Support_WD_7_GreenTech.docx
Support_WD_7_Draft.docx
IL_WD_7-5.docx

Use the Office Clipboard

Case You use the Clipboard to store address text and a picture you need to move within the information sheet. You want the address text to appear in the document footer on both pages of the information sheet and the picture to appear at the top of the document in the document heading.

Objectives
- Copy and cut items to the Clipboard
- Paste items from the Clipboard

You can use the Office Clipboard to collect text and graphics from files created in any Office program and then insert them into your Word documents. The Office Clipboard (the Clipboard) holds up to 24 items at a time. To display the Clipboard, you simply click the launcher in the Clipboard group on the Home tab. You add items to the Clipboard using the Cut and Copy commands. The last item you collect is always added at the top of the Clipboard.

Steps

Quick Tip
You can set the Clipboard pane to open automatically when you cut or copy two items consecutively by clicking Options on the Clipboard pane and then selecting Show Office Clipboard Automatically.

Quick Tip
If you add a 25th item to the Clipboard, the first item you collected is deleted.

Quick Tip
To delete an individual item from the Clipboard, click the arrow next to the item, then click Delete.

1. **sam Start Word, open IL_WD_7-1.docx from the location where you store your Data Files, save it as IL_WD_7_InformationSheet, then click the Launcher in the Clipboard group on the Home tab**
   The Office Clipboard opens in the Clipboard pane. In this pane, each object and text selection you copied or cut in a current Office session is listed. The Clipboard pane will be empty if you have not copied or pasted anything recently.
2. **If items appear in the Clipboard pane, click Clear All, then select the two lines of text at the top of the document from Prepared by Your Name at Mountain Springs . . . to the phone number**
   With the text selected, you can choose to either copy it or cut it. You want to move this text to the document footer, so you need to cut it.
3. **Click the Cut button in the Clipboard group**
   The text is removed from the document and placed in the Clipboard as shown in **Figure 7-1**. The icon next to the item indicates it is cut or copied from a Word document. You can continue to cut or copy additional items to the Clipboard, including objects such as charts and pictures.
4. **Click the picture of the person and the mountains, then click the Cut button in the Clipboard group**
   The picture is displayed at the top of the Clipboard pane because it is the most recent item collected. As new items are collected, the existing items move down the Clipboard. Clicking an item on the Clipboard pastes the item in the document at the location of the insertion point. Items remain on the Clipboard until you delete them or close all open Office programs.
5. **Press CTRL+HOME to move to the top of the document, press ENTER two times, press Up Arrow two times to move to the first line in the document, then click the picture in the Clipboard**
   The picture is inserted at the top of your document.
6. **Click the Insert tab, click the Footer button in the Header & Footer group, click the Blank style, click Prepared by ... in the Clipboard, then press BACKSPACE and DELETE as needed to remove any extra blank lines**
7. **Press CTRL+E to center the text as shown in Figure 7-2, replace Your Name with your name, click the Close Header and Footer button in the Close group, then click the Close button on the Clipboard pane**
   The text is pasted into the footer and will appear on both pages of the information sheet.

Figure 7-1: Text copied to the Clipboard

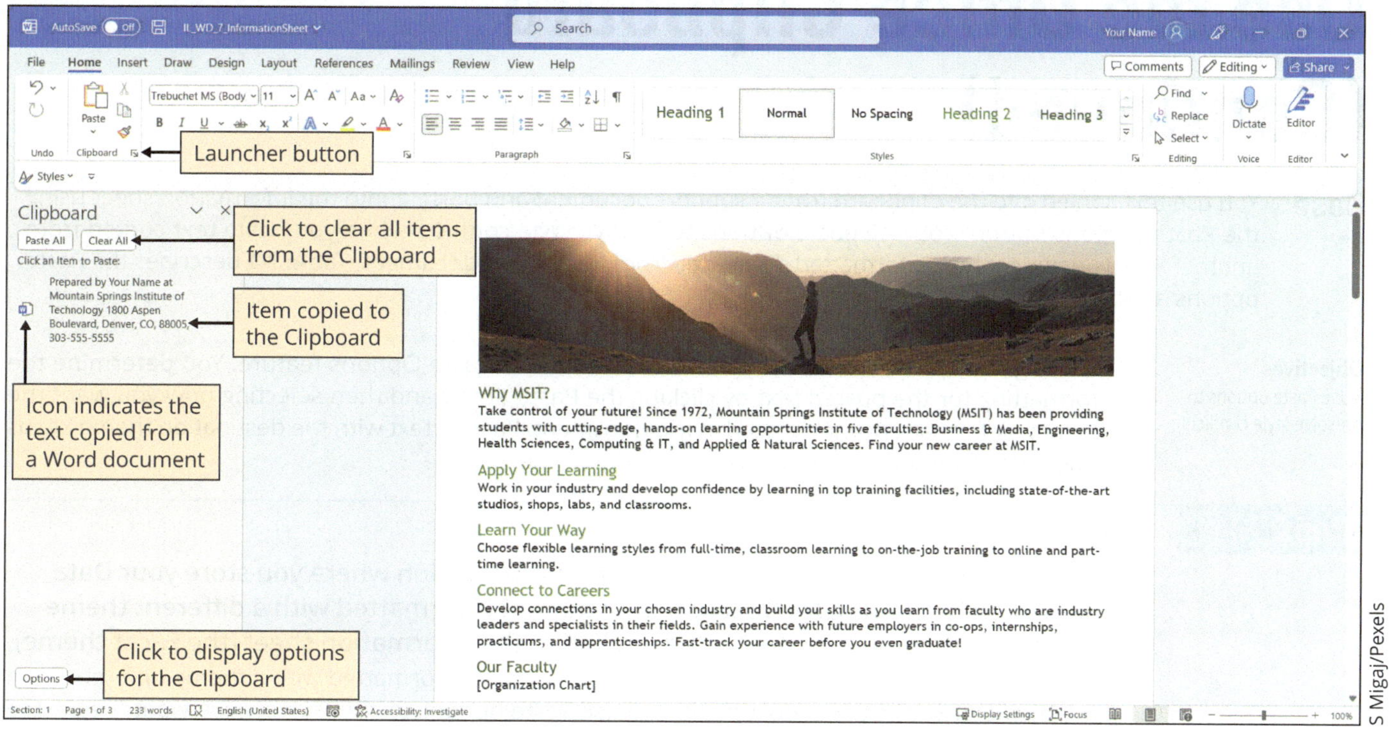

Figure 7-2: Footer text copied and formatted

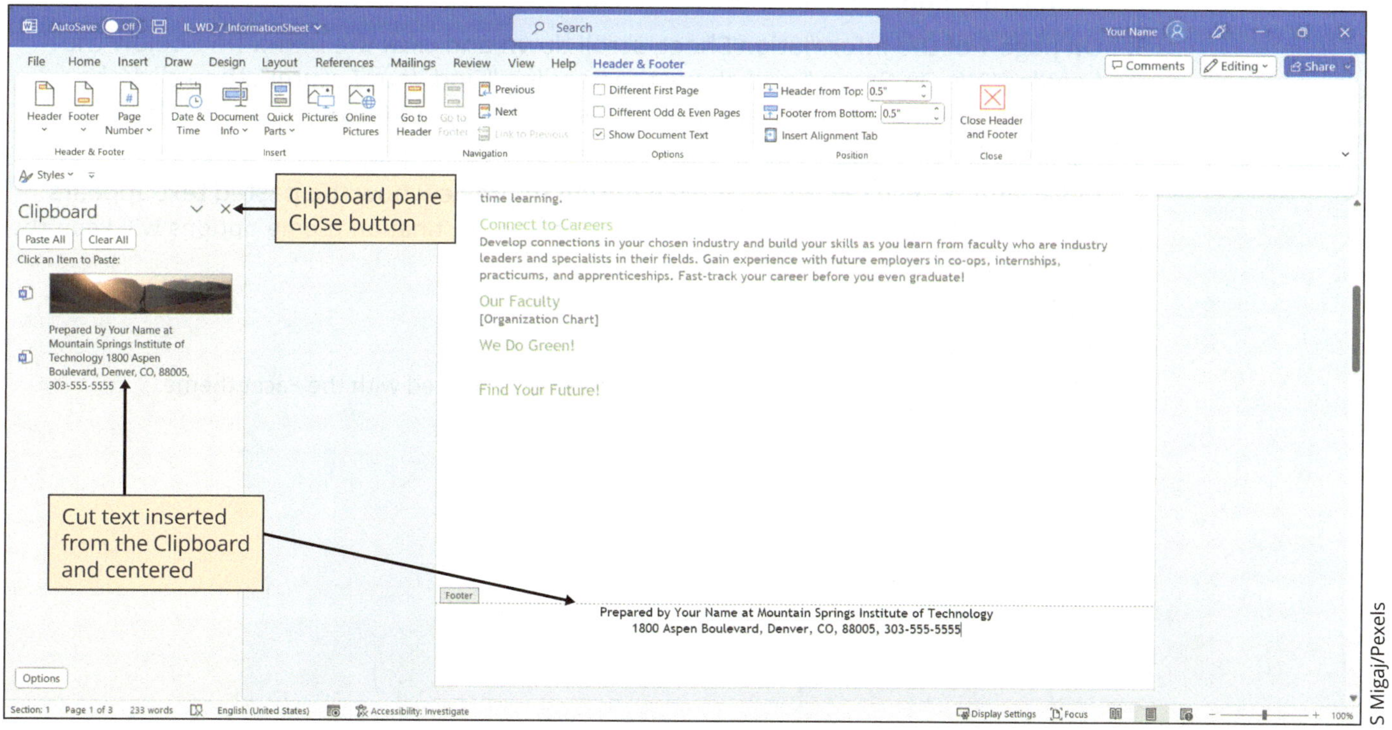

Use the Office Clipboard (Continued)

Case You use text copied into the Clipboard from a support document and paste it into the Information sheet using the Paste Options button. You use paste options to resolve style conflicts when you paste text copied from another Word document that is formatted differently from the current document. **Table 7-1** describes the Paste options available.

Objectives
- Use Paste options to resolve style conflicts

Pasting text in a document can be controlled by the Paste Options feature. You determine the formatting for the pasted text by clicking the Paste arrow and then selecting how you want the text to be formatted when placed in the document. Pasting text with the destination theme keeps document formatting consistent.

Steps

1. **Open Support_WD_7_Programs.docx from the location where you store your Data Files, then notice that the text in this document is formatted with a different theme (the Berlin theme) from the theme applied to the information sheet (the Facet theme)**
   When you copy text from another Word document that is formatted with a theme different from the theme of your current document, you use Paste options to choose how you want the pasted text formatted.
2. **Press CTRL+A to select all the text in the document, click the Copy button in the Clipboard group, then close the document**
3. **On page 1 of the Information Sheet, scroll down and click the blank line below the heading "We Do Green!" and above the heading "Find Your Future!", then click the Paste arrow in the Clipboard group to display the list of Paste options as shown in Figure 7-3**
4. **Move your mouse pointer over each option to preview how the pasted text appears**
   As you'll notice by exploring the Paste options, the Destination theme options will keep the document formatting consistent throughout.
5. **Click the Use Destination Theme (H) button**
6. **Save the document**
   The text is copied into the current document and is formatted with the Facet theme.

Figure 7-3: Paste options

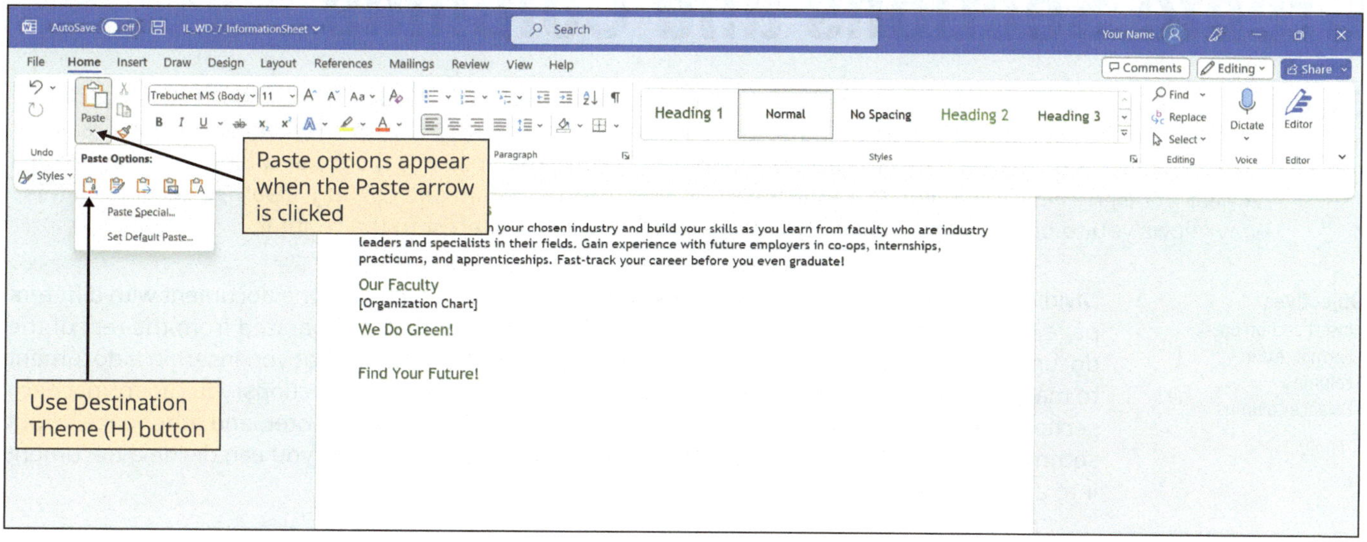

Table 7-1: Paste options

paste option	description
Use Destination Theme	The formatting applied to text copied from a source file is changed to match the formatting applied to text in the destination file.
Keep Source Formatting	The formatting applied to the copied text in the source file is retained, even if the formatting is different from the formatting applied to text in the destination file.
Merge Formatting	The copied text takes on the style characteristics of the paragraph where it is pasted.
Picture	The copied text is pasted as a picture that you can resize and move like any graphic object.
Keep Text Only	Only the text, with no formatting, is pasted into the destination file.

Create Sections and Columns

Case You display paragraph marks and then insert a section break to divide the document into two sections because you want to format the text in the second section in two columns. You then insert a Next Page section break to create a third section, format text in Section 3 in three columns, then balance the three columns so they are all similar in height. Finally, you create a fourth section that is formatted in one column. Inserting sections in this way allows you to present text in a variety of ways, thereby adding interest to the content.

Objectives
- Insert section breaks
- Format text in columns
- Balance columns

Dividing a document into sections allows you to format each section of the document with different page layout settings. A **section** is a portion of a document that is separated from the rest of the document by section breaks. **Section breaks** are formatting marks that you insert in a document to mark the end of a section. Once you have divided a document into sections, you can format each section with different column, margin, page orientation, header and footer, and other page layout settings. By default, a document is formatted as a single section, but you can divide a document into as many sections as you like.

Steps

Quick Tip
Turning on formatting marks allows you to observe the section breaks that you insert in a document.

Trouble
If Section 2 does not appear in the status bar in the lower-left corner of your screen, right-click the status bar, click **Section** to add a check mark next to it, then click outside the menu.

Quick Tip
When you delete a section break, you delete the section formatting of the text before the break. That text becomes part of the following section and assumes the formatting of that section.

1. **Click the Show/Hide ¶ button ¶ in the Paragraph group to turn on formatting marks, if necessary**
2. **Click to the left of the heading "Why MSIT?" near the top of the document, click the Layout tab, then click the Breaks button in the Page Setup group**
   The Breaks menu opens. You use this menu to insert different types of section breaks. Refer to **Table 7-2**.
3. **Click Continuous**
   Word inserts a continuous section break, shown as a dotted double line below the picture and above the "Why MSIT?" heading. Refer to **Figure 7-4**. When you insert a section break at the beginning of a paragraph, Word inserts the break at the end of the previous paragraph. The section break stores the formatting information for the previous section. The status bar indicates that the insertion point is in Section 2.
4. **Click the Columns button in the Page Setup group, then click More Columns**
5. **Click Right in the Presets section, click the Spacing down arrow twice until 0.3" appears, compare the dialog box to Figure 7-5, then click OK**
   Section 2 is formatted in two unequal columns with .3" of spacing between columns.
6. **Click the View tab, click Multiple Pages in the Zoom group to display both pages of the information sheet, click to the left of "We Do Green!" in column 1, click the Layout tab, click Breaks, then click Next Page**
   "We Do Green!" and its accompanying text move to the top of page 2 and Section 3 appears on the status bar.
7. **Click the Columns button, click More Columns, click Three, change the spacing between columns to .2", then click OK**
   All the text and pictures on the page are formatted in three narrow columns.
8. **Go to 100% view, click to the left of the paragraph mark following the text "business services." at the end of the description of the Business & Media programs at the bottom of the first column on page 2, click Breaks in the Page Setup group on the Layout tab, then click Continuous**
   You inserted a Continuous section break to balance the columns only in the "We Do Green!" section so each column is approximately the same height. Text in the balanced columns flows automatically from the bottom of one column to the top of the next column.
9. **Verify that the insertion point appears to the left of the paragraph mark below the "We Do Green!" paragraph, click the Columns button in the Page Setup group, click One, then save the document**
   You create another section (Section 4) because you want the remaining information in the document to extend the full width of the page.

Figure 7-4: Continuous section break

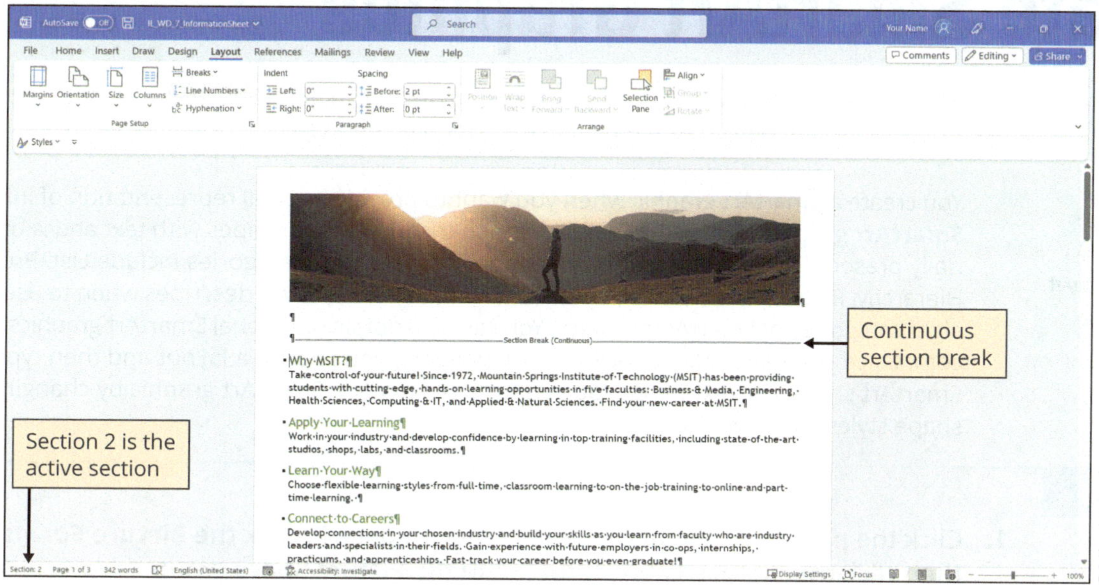

S Migaj/Pexels

Figure 7-5: Columns dialog box

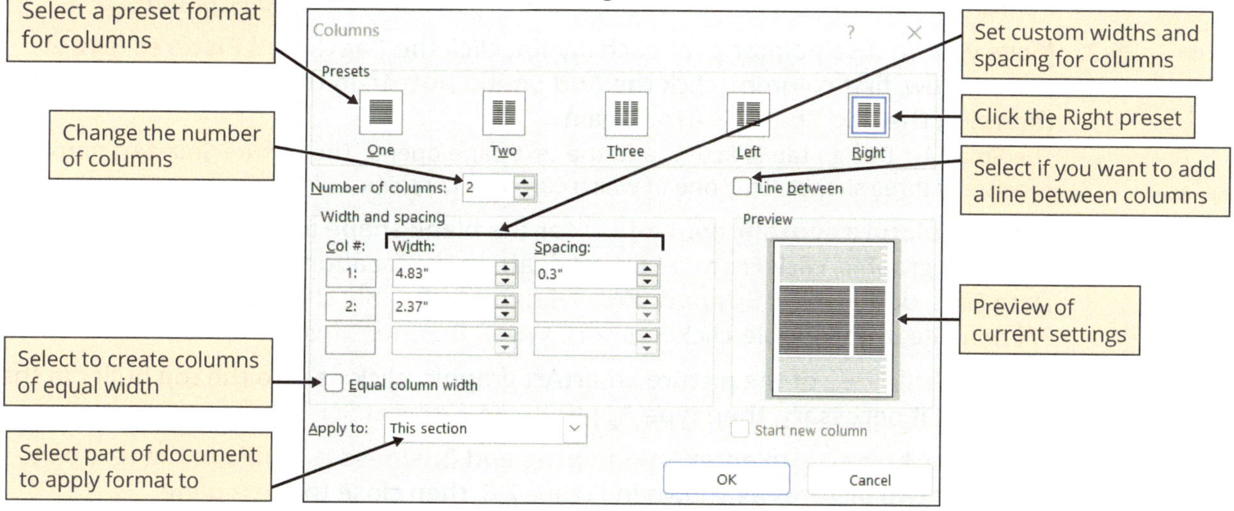

Table 7-2: Types of section breaks

section	function
Next page	Begins a new section and moves the text following the break to the top of the next page
Continuous	Begins a new section on the same page
Even page	Begins a new section and moves the text following the break to the top of the next even-numbered page
Odd page	Begins a new section and moves the text following the break to the top of the next odd-numbered page

Changing page layout settings for a section

Dividing a document into sections allows you to vary the layout of a document. In addition to applying different column settings to sections, you can apply different margins, page orientations, paper sizes, text alignment, headers and footers, page numbering, footnotes, endnotes, and other page layout settings. To check or change the page layout settings for an individual section, place the insertion point in the section, then open the Page Setup dialog box. Select any options you want to change, click the Apply to arrow, click This section, then click OK. When you select This section in the Apply to box, the settings are applied to the current section only. When you select This point forward, the settings are applied to the current section and all sections that follow it. If you select Whole document in the Apply to box, the settings are applied to all the sections in the document.

Create SmartArt Graphics

Case You create a picture SmartArt graphic on page 2 of the information sheet because you want to illustrate with pictures three of the MSIT programs that are focused on green technology.

Objectives
- Insert a picture SmartArt Graphic
- Change the SmartArt layout

You create a SmartArt graphic when you want to provide a visual representation of information. A **SmartArt graphic** is a customizable diagram that combines shapes with text and is used to pictorially present lists, processes, and relationships. SmartArt categories include List, Process, Cycle, Hierarchy, Relationship, Matrix, Pyramid, and Picture. **Table 7-3** describes when to use each of the eight categories of SmartArt graphics. You can also obtain additional SmartArt graphics from Office.com. Once you have selected a SmartArt category, you choose a layout and then type text in the SmartArt shapes or text pane. You can further modify a SmartArt graphic by changing fill colors, shape styles, and layouts.

Steps

Quick Tip
To insert a new SmartArt graphic, click the Insert tab, then click the SmartArt button in the Illustrations group and select a layout.

Trouble
If the text pane does not open, click the **Expand button** on the left side of the SmartArt graphic to open it.

Quick Tip
You can also click the Text Pane button in the Create Graphic group on the SmartArt Design tab to open and close the text pane.

1. **Click the picture of the phone and plants on page 2, click the Picture Format tab, then click the Picture Layout button in the Picture Styles group**
   A selection of picture SmartArt layouts is displayed. You can create a picture SmartArt graphic from any picture inserted in a document, and then you can add additional pictures.
2. **Move your mouse pointer over each layout, click the Captioned Pictures layout (second row, first column), click the Add Shape button in the Create Graphic group, then click the Add Shape button again**
   The SmartArt Design tab is active, and the text pane opens. The picture SmartArt graphic now consists of three shapes, only one of which currently contains a picture.
3. **Click the picture content control for the blank shape in the middle of the SmartArt graphic, click From a File, navigate to the location where you store your Data Files, double-click Support_WD_7_Engineering.jpg, click in the last shape, click From a File, then double-click Support_WD_7_Business.jpg**
4. **Click a blank area of the picture SmartArt graphic, click next to the top bullet in the text pane if necessary, then type Applied and Natural Sciences**
5. **Use Down Arrow to enter Engineering and Business & Media in the text pane for the other two pictures as shown in Figure 7-6, then close the text pane**
6. **Click the More button in the Layouts group on the SmartArt Design tab, then click the Bending Picture Caption layout (second row, second column)**
   You can experiment with how you want the SmartArt graphic to appear by selecting different picture layouts. You set a precise height and width for the SmartArt graphic.
7. **Click the Format tab, click the Size button to display the Height and Width boxes if necessary, select the measurement in the Height box, type 3.4, press TAB to select the measurement in the Width box, type 5.7, then press ENTER**
   You can also format the appearance of each shape in a SmartArt graphic.
8. **Click away from the picture SmartArt graphic to deselect it, click the phone picture, press and hold SHIFT, then click the other two pictures so all three pictures in the picture SmartArt graphic are selected**
9. **Click the Format tab, click the Shape Effects button in the Shape Styles group, point to Bevel, click Round (first column, first row in the Bevel section), click away from the picture SmartArt graphic to deselect it, then save the document**
   The picture SmartArt graphic appears as shown in **Figure 7-7**.

Figure 7-6: Data for the picture

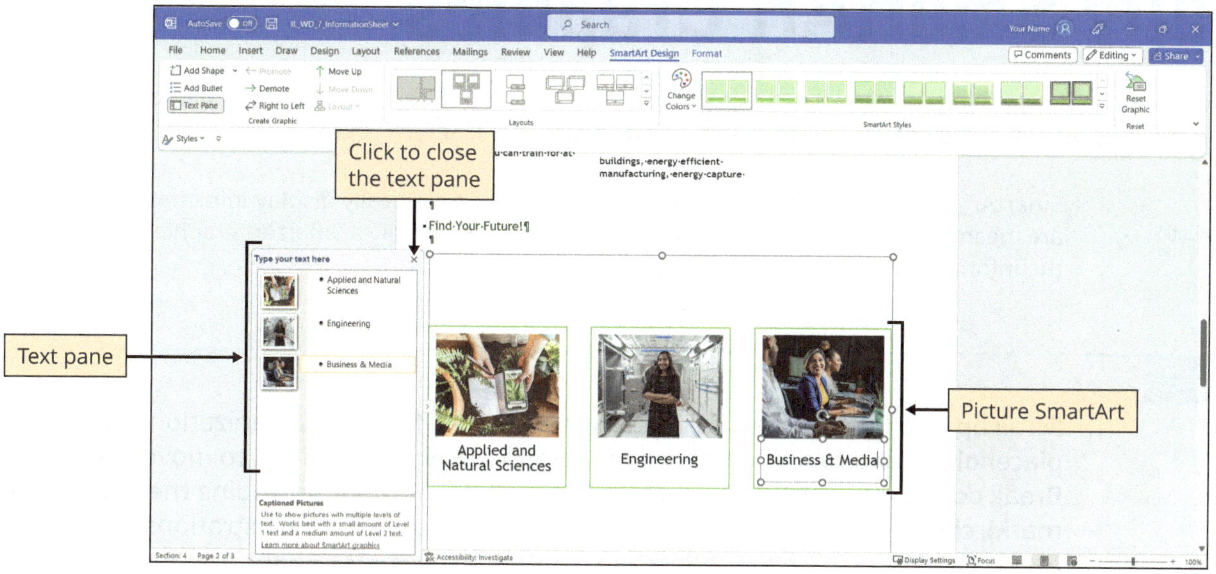

Antoni Shkraba/Pexels; ThisIsEngineering/Pexels; Jopwell/Pexels

Figure 7-7: Sized and formatted picture SmartArt graphic

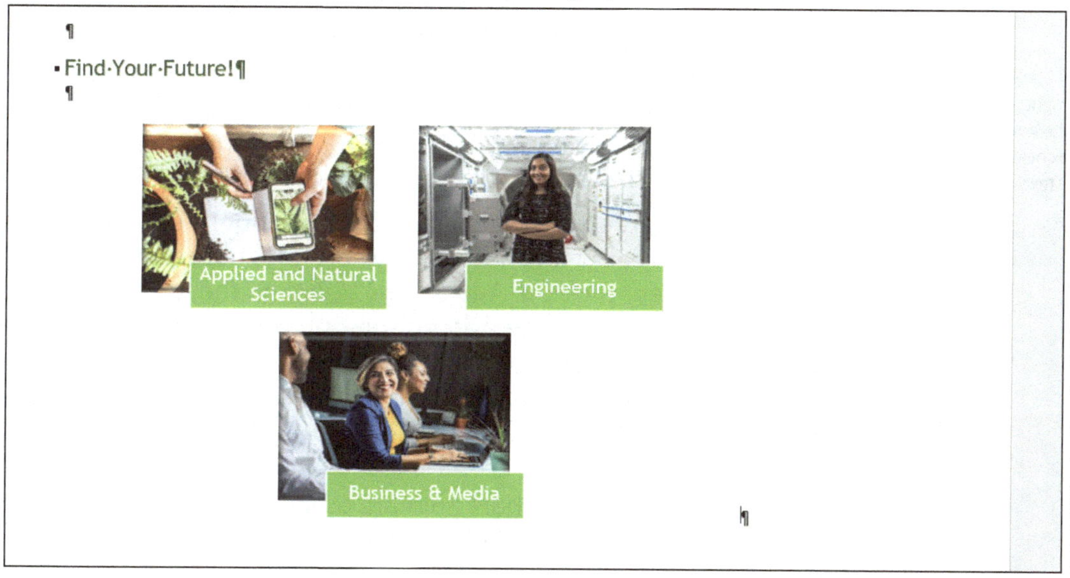

Antoni Shkraba/Pexels; ThisIsEngineering/Pexels; Jopwell/Pexels

Table 7-3: Eight categories of SmartArt graphics

category	when to use
List	To show nonsequential information
Process	To show steps in a process or timeline
Cycle	To show a continual process
Hierarchy	To show an organization chart or decision tree
Relationship	To illustrate connections between the shapes in the graphic
Matrix	To show how parts relate to a whole
Pyramid	To show proportional relationships with the largest component on the bottom
Picture	To use pictures to convey or emphasize visual content

Inserting a picture into a SmartArt shape

You can fill any shape in a SmartArt graphic with a picture, even if the shape does not include a Picture content control. Click the shape, click the Format tab, click the Shape Fill arrow, click Picture, click From a File, navigate to the location of the picture, then click Insert. The picture is inserted into the shape.

Modify SmartArt Graphics

Case You insert an organization chart that lists the top executives at MSIT on page 1 of the information sheet, and then modify it by adding, removing, and resizing individual shapes in the SmartArt graphic, and applying 3D effects.

Objectives
- Build an organization chart
- Modify SmartArt shapes

SmartArt graphics provide you with many options to graphically display information in ways that are meaningful to readers. Sometimes you may need to modify a SmartArt graphic to better convey the information.

Steps

1. **Scroll up to page 1 of the information sheet, click after the [Organization Chart] placeholder, and to the left of the paragraph mark, press ENTER to move the Section Break down, select the [Organization Chart] placeholder (including the paragraph mark), click the Insert tab, click the SmartArt button in the Illustrations group, click Hierarchy in the left pane, select the Name and Title Organization Chart style (first row, third column), then click OK**
   An organization chart from the Hierarchy category is inserted into the document. You use charts in the Hierarchy category to illustrate the chain of command within a company or organization.

Trouble
Click at the far-right edge of the white box to select the box below Jared and enter text.

2. **Close the Text pane if it is open, increase the zoom to 250%, scroll to view the whole graphic, click in the top box, type Jared Irvin, click in the box below Jared, then type President**
   By default, an assistant box is attached to the top box in the Organization chart. Space is limited on the page, so you remove the assistant box and add two subordinates to one of the Level 2 boxes.

3. **Click the edge of the green box below and to the left of Jared's box, press DELETE, click the SmartArt Design tab if it is not already selected, note that the far-left box in the bottom row is selected, click the Add Shape arrow in the Create Graphic group, click Add Shape Below, then click the Add Shape button (not the arrow) to add another shape to the right of the shape you just inserted**
   The Add Shape menu provides options (such as below, after, and above) for adding more shapes to your SmartArt graphic. The new shapes are added based on the currently selected box and the menu selection.

4. **Enter text so the organization chart appears as shown in Figure 7-8**
   After entering text in a SmartArt graphic, you sometimes need to modify the size so the text doesn't wrap.

5. **Click a blank area of the SmartArt graphic, click the Format tab, then change the height of the graphic to 2" and the width to 4.5"**
   You can also rearrange the shapes in a SmartArt graphic.

6. **Click the Sara Wong box, click the SmartArt Design tab, then click the Move Down button in the Create Graphic group**
   The Move Down command moves the box to the right and on the same level as the other two boxes. The two subordinate boxes attached to Sara's box are also moved. Table 7-4 explains the different ways in which you can move shapes in a SmartArt graphic.

Quick Tip
Choose from a wide variety of effects to format a SmartArt graphic.

7. **Click a blank area of the SmartArt graphic, click the Change Colors button in the SmartArt Styles group, select Colored Fill – Accent 2 (second selection in the Accent 2 section), click the More button in the SmartArt Styles group, then click Cartoon (third selection in the 3D section)**

8. **Click the Inez Ramirez box, press and hold SHIFT, click the remaining four subordinate boxes: Sara Wong, Gary Lawson, Kris Olsen, and Olive Metz, release SHIFT, click the Format tab, type 1 in the Width box, then press ENTER**

9. **Return to 100% view, click away from the chart, then save the document**
   The width of all the subordinate boxes in the Organization chart is changed to 1" as shown in Figure 7-9.

Figure 7-8: Text for the organization chart

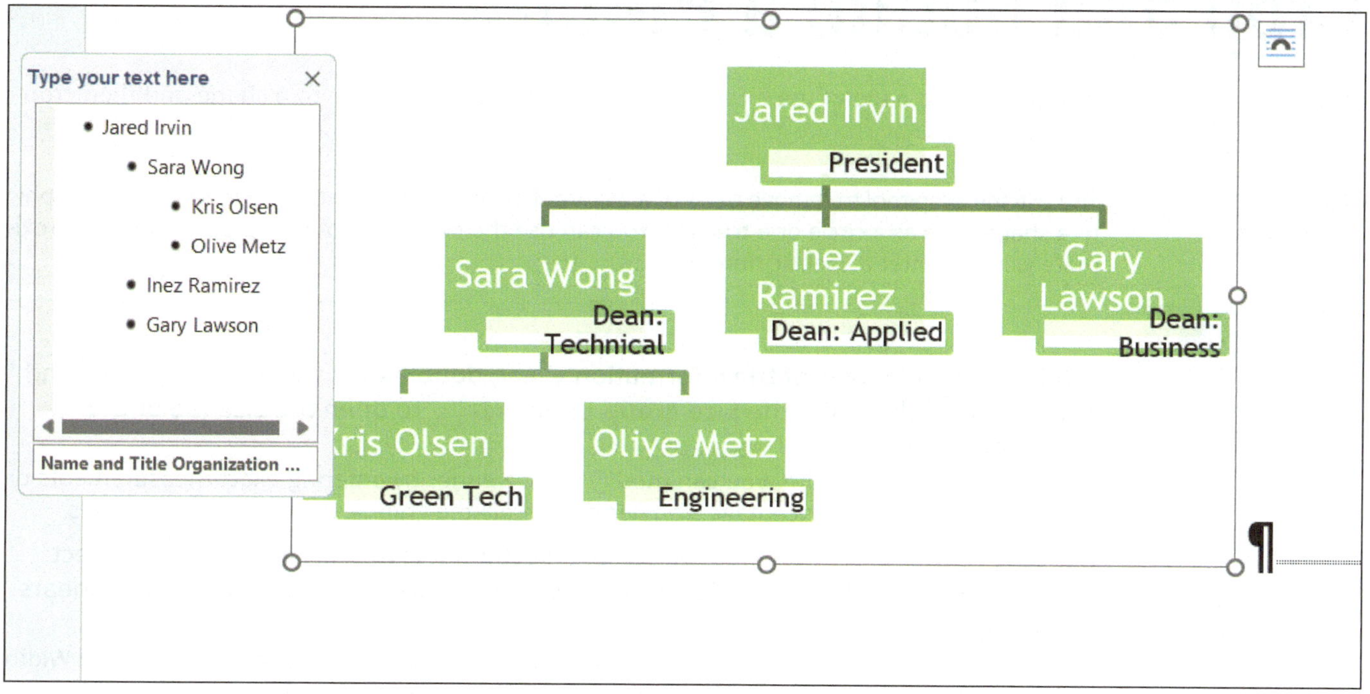

Figure 7-9: Completed organization chart

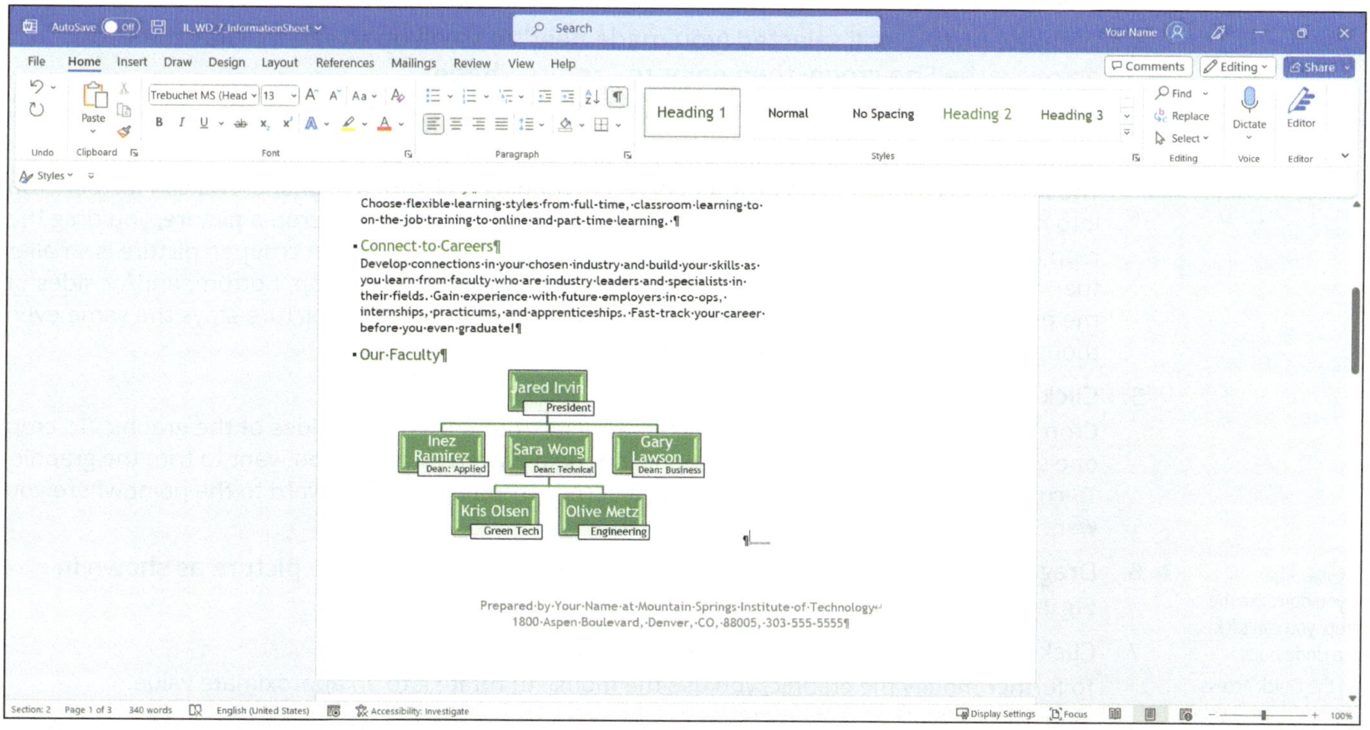

Table 7-4: Options for moving shapes in a SmartArt graphic

option	click to move
Promote	a subordinate box up one level
Demote	a subordinate box down one level
Right to Left	a box to the far left or right of the current row of boxes
Move Up	a box to the left of the adjacent box on the current row
Move Down	a box to the right of the adjacent box on the current row

Crop and Rotate a Picture

Case To add interest to the second page of the information sheet, you crop a picture to a shape and then crop additional portions of it, and finally rotate it.

Objectives
- Crop a picture
- Rotate a picture

You use the Crop tool to remove parts of a picture that you do not want. You can also crop a graphic to a shape such as a circle or a triangle. You can use the mouse to rotate a graphic to an approximate value or enter a specific number.

Steps

1. **Scroll to the third page of the information sheet, double-click the picture of the hand holding a leaf, then click the Size group Launcher to open the Size tab of the Layout dialog box**
Before cropping the picture, you can modify its size either by entering exact measurements or scaling the graphic to a percentage. You decide to scale the graphic to maintain proportions.

Trouble
Make sure you enter 40 in the Scale section toward the bottom of the Size dialog box.

2. **Click the Lock aspect ratio check box to select it if it is not already selected, select 100% in the Height box in the Scale section, type 40, press TAB, verify that 40 appears in the Width box, then click OK**
The scale of the width changes to 40% and the Absolute measurements in the Height and Width sections increase proportionally. When the Lock aspect ratio check box is selected, you need to enter only a height or width measurement. Word calculates the other measurement so that the resized graphic is proportional.

3. **With the picture still selected (you made need to scroll up to see it), click the Crop arrow in the Size group, then point to Crop to Shape**
A selection of shapes is displayed as shown in **Figure 7-10**. You can crop any picture to any shape.

4. **Click the Oval shape (first selection in the first row of Basic Shapes)**
The picture is cropped to an oval shape. After cropping a picture to a shape, you can further crop it to remove portions of the picture that you do not want. When you crop a picture, you drag the crop handle associated with the part of the picture you want to crop. A cropped picture is smaller than the original picture because you take away content from the top, bottom, and/or sides of the picture. However, when you resize a picture, the content of the picture stays the same even though the picture is made smaller or larger.

5. **Click the Crop button to reveal the crop marks**
Cropping handles (solid black lines) appear on all four corners and sides of the graphic. To crop one side of a graphic, drag a side cropping handle inward to where you want to trim the graphic. To crop two adjacent sides at once, drag a corner cropping handle inward to the point where you want the corner of the cropped image to be.

Quick Tip
If you don't like the crop, you can click the Undo button on the Quick Access Toolbar to undo your last crop action.

6. **Drag the right-side crop mark to set the size and shape of the picture as shown in Figure 7-11**

7. **Click the Crop button again to turn off the crop feature**
To further modify the graphic, you use the mouse to rotate it to an approximate value.

8. **Click the Rotate handle at the top of the picture, then drag the mouse to rotate the picture so it appears similar to Figure 7-12**

9. **Click away to deselect the picture, then save the document**

Figure 7-10: Shapes for cropping a picture to

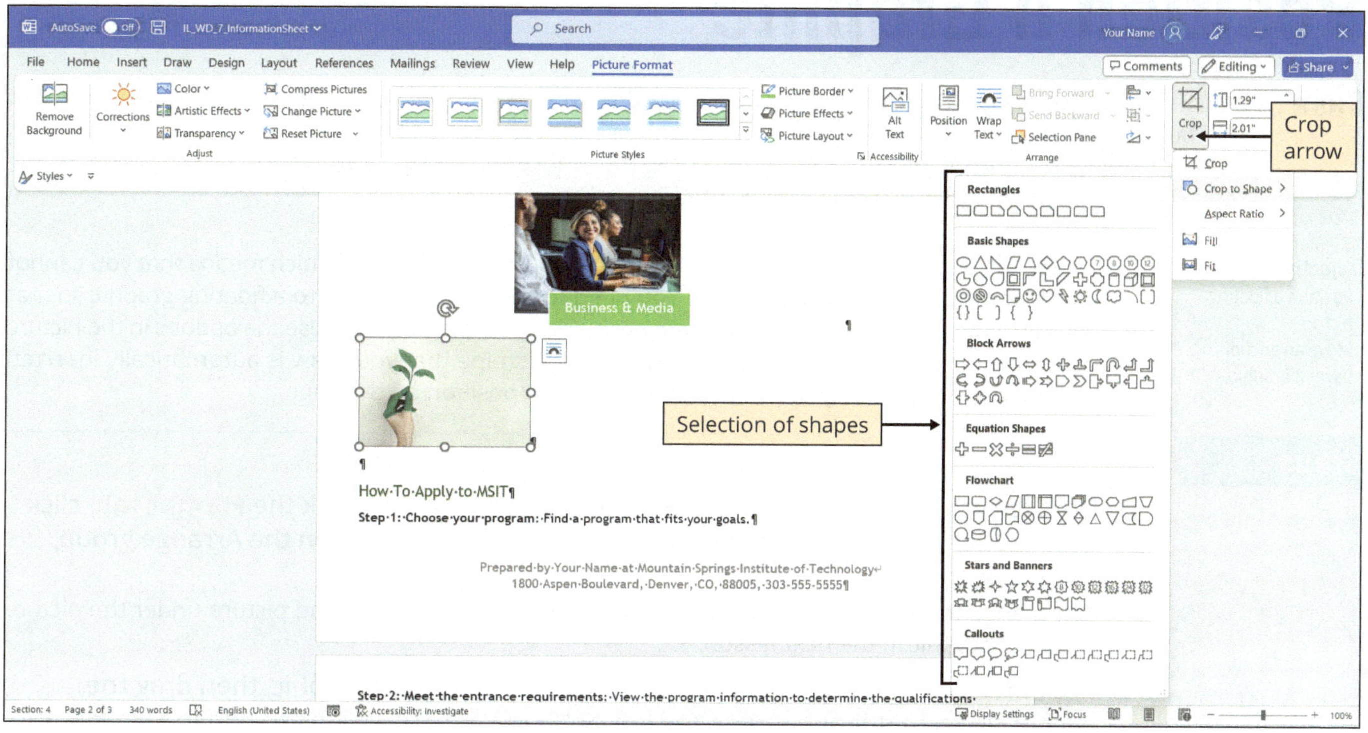

Jopwell/Pexels; Alena Koval/Pexels

Figure 7-11: Cropping a picture

Alena Koval/Pexels

Figure 7-12: Rotating a picture

Alena Koval/Pexels

Position a Graphic

Case To further enhance the graphics on page 2, you make both the picture SmartArt graphic and the picture of the hand holding the leaf into floating graphics so you can position the picture of the hand at a precise location on the page in relation to the picture SmartArt graphic. You then move the anchor attached to the picture SmartArt graphic so that it moves with the heading "Find Your Future!"

Objectives
- Position a floating picture
- Move an anchor
- Layer a graphic

By default, a picture inserted into a document is in line with the text, which means that you cannot use your mouse to move the picture. You need to convert the picture to a floating graphic so that you can either move it to an approximate position in your document or use the options in the Picture dialog box to set a precise location on the page. A shape that you draw is automatically inserted as a floating shape that you can use your mouse to position on the page.

Steps

1. **Double-click a white area of the picture SmartArt graphic, click the Format tab, click the Arrange button if necessary, click the Wrap Text button in the Arrange group, then click Through**

   You change the wrap setting to Through so that you can layer the hand picture under the picture SmartArt graphic in the next lesson.

2. **Click the anchor ⚓ at the top left of the picture SmartArt graphic, then drag the anchor up so that it appears to the left of "Find Your Future!" as shown in Figure 7-13**

3. **Deselect the picture SmartArt graphic, click the first paragraph mark below "Find Your Future!", then press ENTER**

   Notice how the picture SmartArt graphic does not move. Because you moved the anchor up to attach the graphic to the paragraph above, the graphic only moves when you also move its attached paragraph. An anchor is attached to any graphic object such as a picture, SmartArt, or shape that you insert in Word. You can attach the graphic to any paragraph by moving its anchor.

4. **Click the cropped picture of the hand holding the leaf, click the Layout Options button at the top-right corner of the picture, click the Through button in the With Text Wrapping section, click the Fix position on page option button, then click See more**

   On the Position tab in the Layout dialog box, you set a precise position for the picture.

5. **Select the contents of the Absolute position box in the Horizontal section, type 1.3, click the to the right of arrow, then click Left Margin**

6. **Select the contents of the Absolute position box in the Vertical section, type 5.4, click the below arrow, click Top Margin, compare the Layout dialog box to Figure 7-14, then click OK**

   The position of the picture is now set 1.3" to the right of the left margin and 5.4" from the top margin. The picture slightly overlaps the picture SmartArt graphic and the "How to Apply to MSIT" heading, and text wraps around the SmartArt graphic. When you make changes to text wrapping options for graphics and pictures, you often need to readjust the position of surrounding text.

7. **As shown in Figures 7-15A and 7-15B, click the anchor attached to the leaf picture and drag it up to the paragraph mark below the "Find Your Future!" heading**

8. **Click the paragraph mark below "Find Your Future!", then press ENTER eight times to move the "How to Apply to MSIT" heading and text down**

9. **Click a white area of the picture SmartArt graphic, click the Format tab, click the Bring Forward arrow in the Arrange group, then click Bring to Front**

   In addition to bringing an object to the front, you can use Send It Back to send it behind other objects. You use the Bring Forward and Send Back layering options when you have more than two objects to layer in relation to each other.

10. **Click away from the SmartArt graphic, then save the document**

Figure 7-13: Anchor repositioned

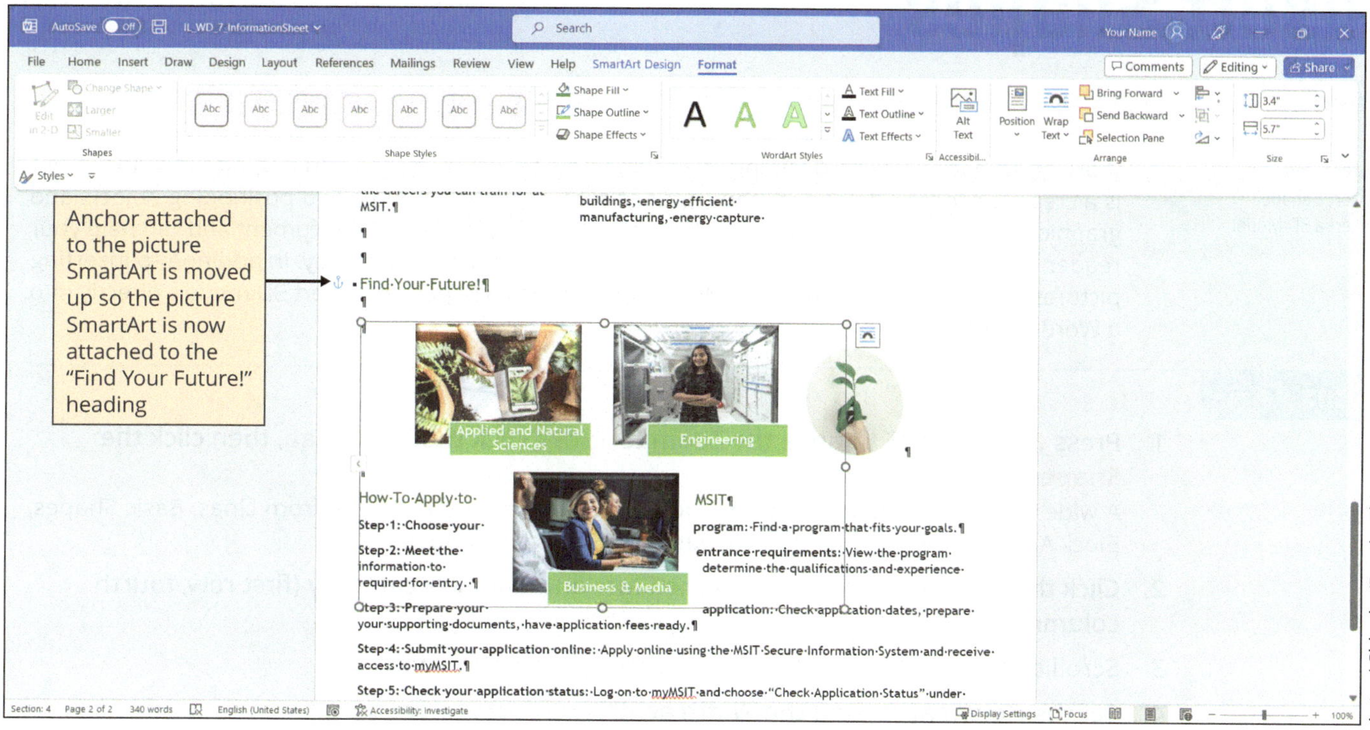

Antoni Shkraba/Pexels; ThisIsEngineering/Pexels; Jopwell/Pexels; Alena Koval/Pexels

Figure 7-14: Layout dialog box

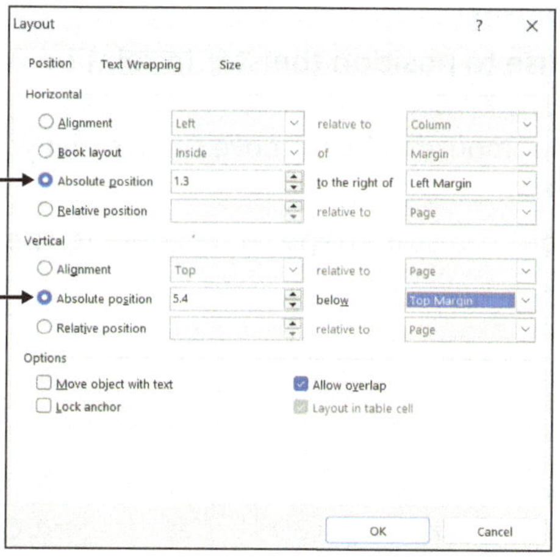

Figure 7-15A & 15B: Repositioning the anchor attached to the leaf picture

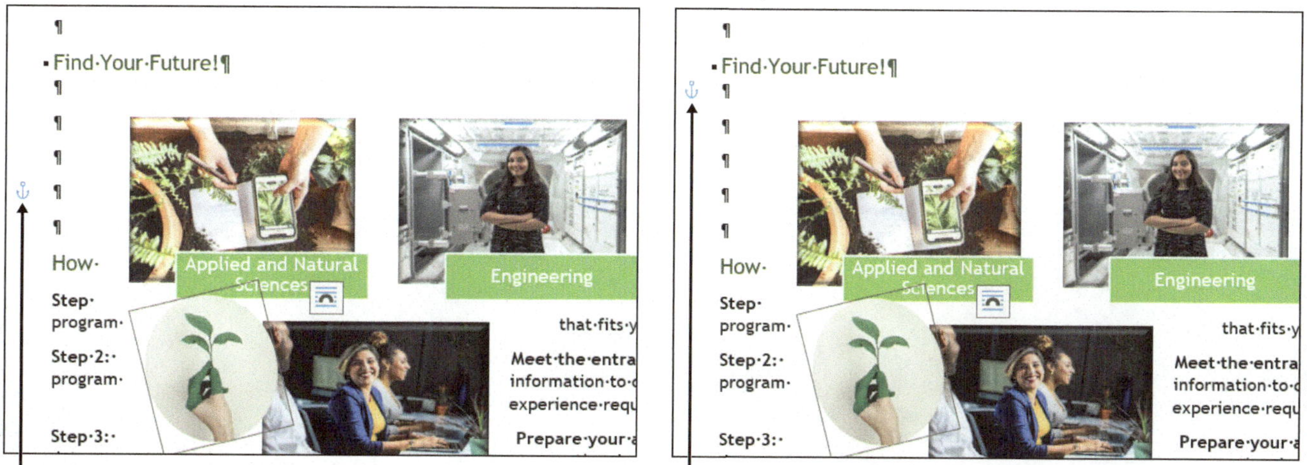

Antoni Shkraba/Pexels; ThisIsEngineering/Pexels; Jopwell/Pexels; Alena Koval/Pexels

Antoni Shkraba/Pexels; ThisIsEngineering/Pexels; Jopwell/Pexels; Alena Koval/Pexels

Insert Shapes

Case You draw a star shape on page 1 to draw attention to the president of MSIT in the organization chart.

Objectives
- Insert a shape
- Insert a 3D Model

Working with layouts and deciding where and how to insert images and graphics in a document is a creative process. You have many options for wrapping, layering, and positioning objects and graphics in a document relative to each other. Graphics enhance any document and can help your reader understand the concepts and ideas that you are trying to convey. In addition to inserting pictures and SmartArt graphics into Word, you can draw shapes and insert 3D models directly into a Word document.

Steps

1. **Press CTRL+HOME, change the Zoom to 150%, click the Insert tab, then click the Shapes button**
   A wide range of shapes in six categories is available. You can choose from Lines, Basic Shapes, Block Arrows, Flowchart shapes, Callouts, and Stars and Banners.
2. **Click the Star: 5 Points shape in the Stars and Banners category (first row, fourth column)**
3. **Scroll down and draw a star next to the organization chart**
4. **Set the Height at .4" and the Width at .4"**
5. **Click the Shape Fill arrow in the Shape Styles group, then click the Gold, Accent 3 color box (top row)**
6. **Use your mouse to position the star in relation to the organization chart SmartArt as shown in Figure 7-16**
   You can use your mouse to freely move shapes that you draw in Word without needing to modify wrapping options.
7. **Click away from the star shape to deselect it, then save the document**

Quick Tip
You can also use the arrow keys to position the star by moving it in small increments.

Inserting and Editing 3D Models

You can use 3D models to creatively enhance your documents. You create a 3D model by either inserting a 3D model file or selecting a 3D model from the stock 3D models provided online. To insert a 3D model, click the Insert tab, then click the 3D Models arrow to show two options: This Device and Stock 3D Models. To select a stock 3D model, click Stock 3D Models, click the model category you require, click the model you wish to use, then click Insert.

Figure 7-17 shows the 3D model of a car from the Vehicles category. Once you have inserted a 3D model, you use the options on the 3D Model tab to add additional models, return the model to its original settings, change the 3D model view, add Alt text, arrange the position of the 3D model with relation to other objects on the page, and modify the size of the 3D model. **Figure 7-18** shows how the 3D model of the car has been rotated.

Figure 7-16: Star shape filled and positioned

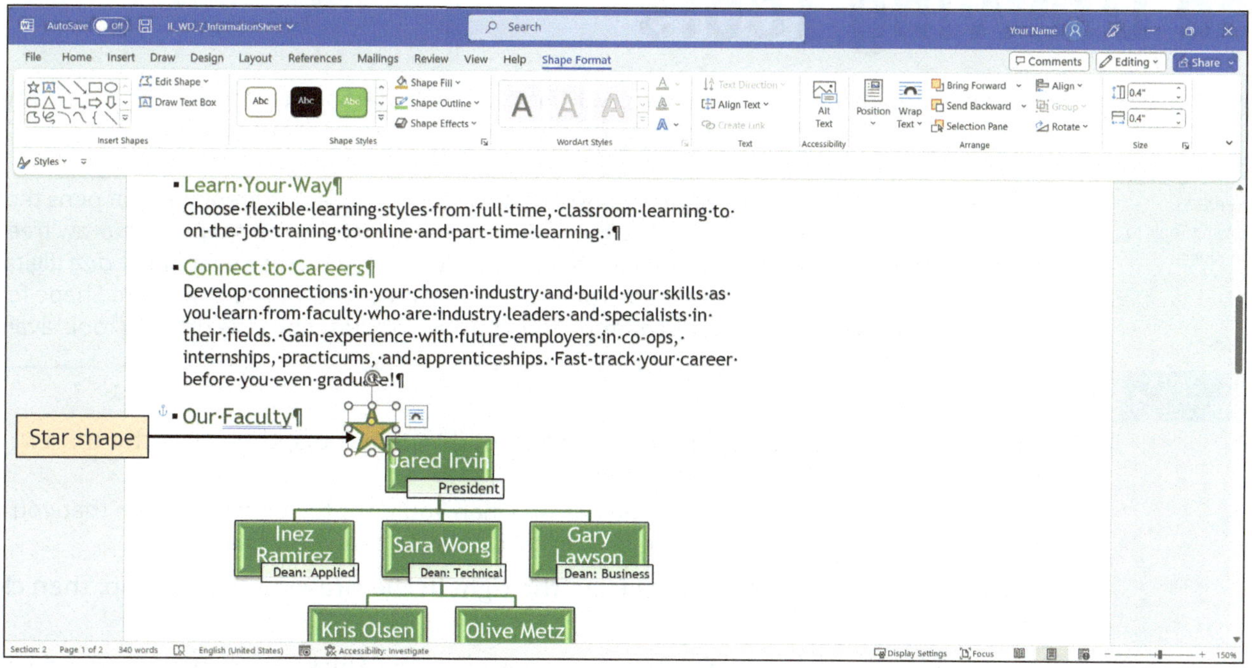

Figure 7-17: 3D Model inserted

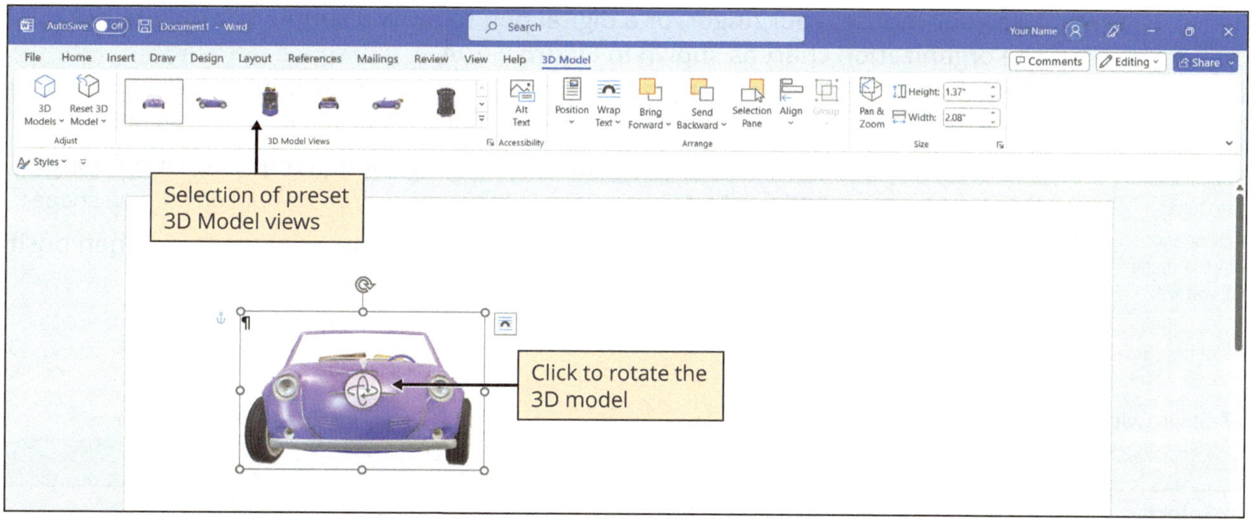

Figure 7-18: Rotating the 3D model

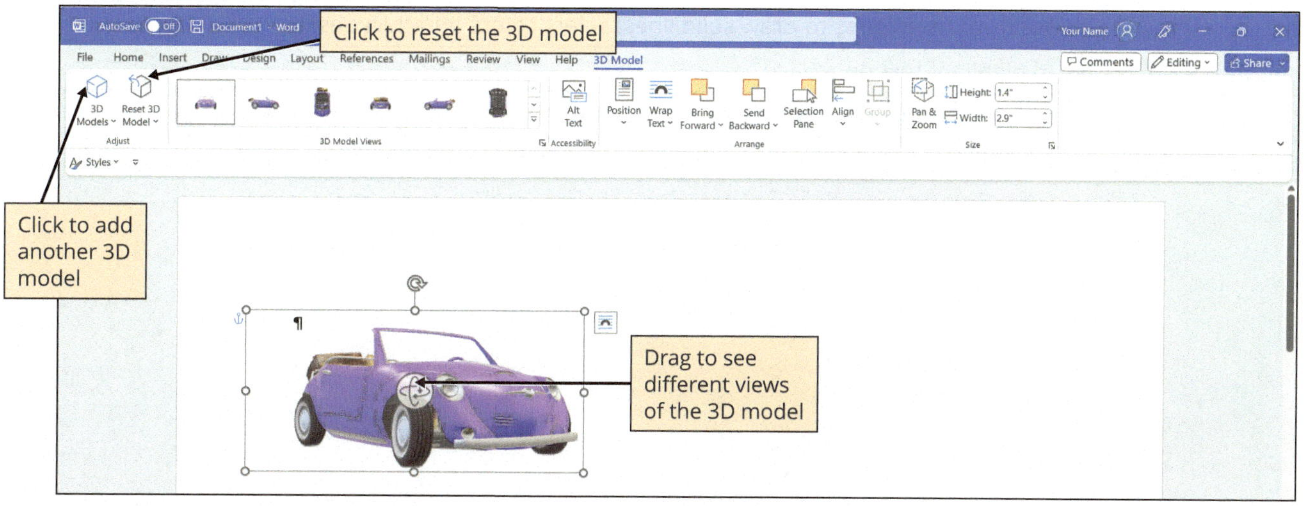

Use Drawing Tools

Case You use drawing tools to draw a triangle representing MSIT below the WordArt object at the top of the document. Once you've drawn an object, you can resize and position it the same way you do a drawn shape.

Objectives
- Use Drawing Tools to draw an object

On the Draw tab, you can access a variety of drawing tools such as different types of pens that you can use to draw shapes and lines. The term **ink** is used to describe the shapes you draw freehand using the drawing tools. If you have a touch-enabled device, you can use your finger or a digital pen to draw an object. You can draw shapes and lines freehand or you can use the Ink to Shape feature to convert a drawn shape into a geometric shape. **Table 7-5** describes the drawing tools available.

Steps

1. **Click the Draw tab to display the selection of drawing tools, then click the Ink to Shape button in the Convert group**
   You must first select the Ink to Shape button when you want to convert a shape that you draw freehand with a mouse, your finger, or a digital pen into a geometric shape.
2. **Click the pen tool that is fourth from the right in the Drawing Tools group, then click the down arrow**
3. **As shown in Figure 7-19, click the 2mm option in the Thickness section (second from the right), then click the Green color option (third column in the third row)**
4. **Use your mouse, your finger, or a digital pen to draw a simple triangle to the right of the organization chart as shown in Figure 7-20A**
   As soon as you remove your finger or pen or release the mouse button, the shape is converted into a triangle as shown in **Figure 7-20B** because you selected the Ink to Shape option.
5. **Click the Select Objects button in the Drawing Tools group to turn off the pen**
   You can now move and position the drawing in the same way you would any drawn shape.
6. **Refer to Figure 7-21: change the Height and Width of the triangle to .6", then position it over the picture at the top of the information sheet**
7. **Save the document**

Trouble
You may need to practice a few times to draw a freehand triangle that is similar to **Figure 7-20**. Click the Undo button on the Quick Access Toolbar and try drawing the shape again until you are satisfied.

Table 7-5: Drawing tools

tool	description
Lasso Select	Select several inked shapes at once.
Eraser	Erase ink that has been drawn on the page.
Pens	Choose from three pens to draw solid lines; select colors and thicknesses.
Highlighter	Use to highlight text on a page.
Track Changes	Use to select text using natural gestures (for example, your finger or a digital pen)

Figure 7-19: Selecting pen options

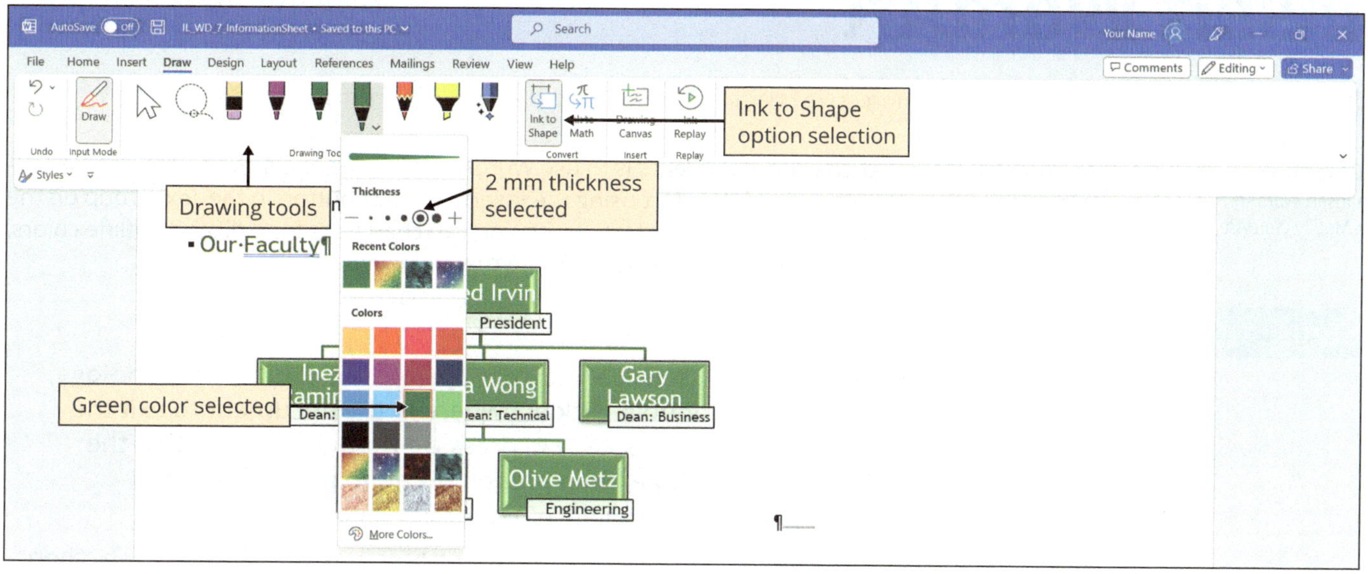

Figure 7-20A & 20B: Freeform shape changed to geometric shape with Ink to Shape selected

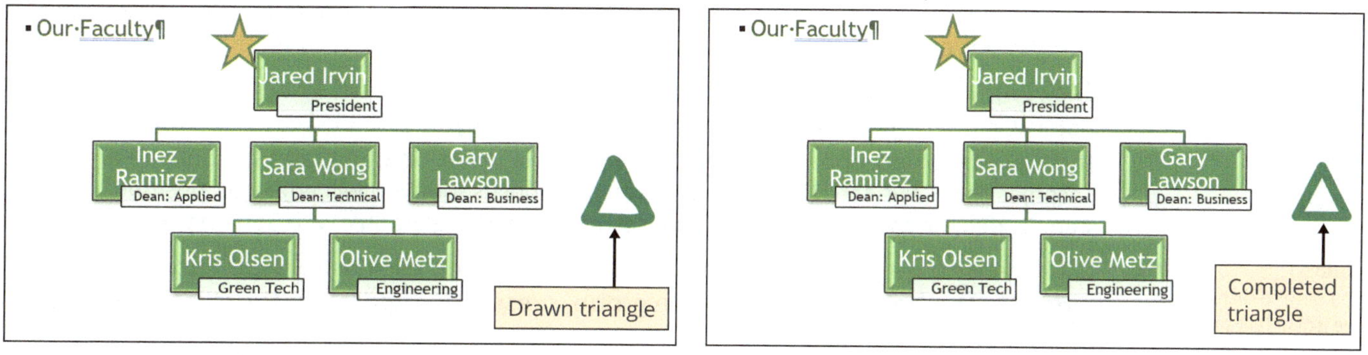

Figure 7-21: Triangle sized and positioned

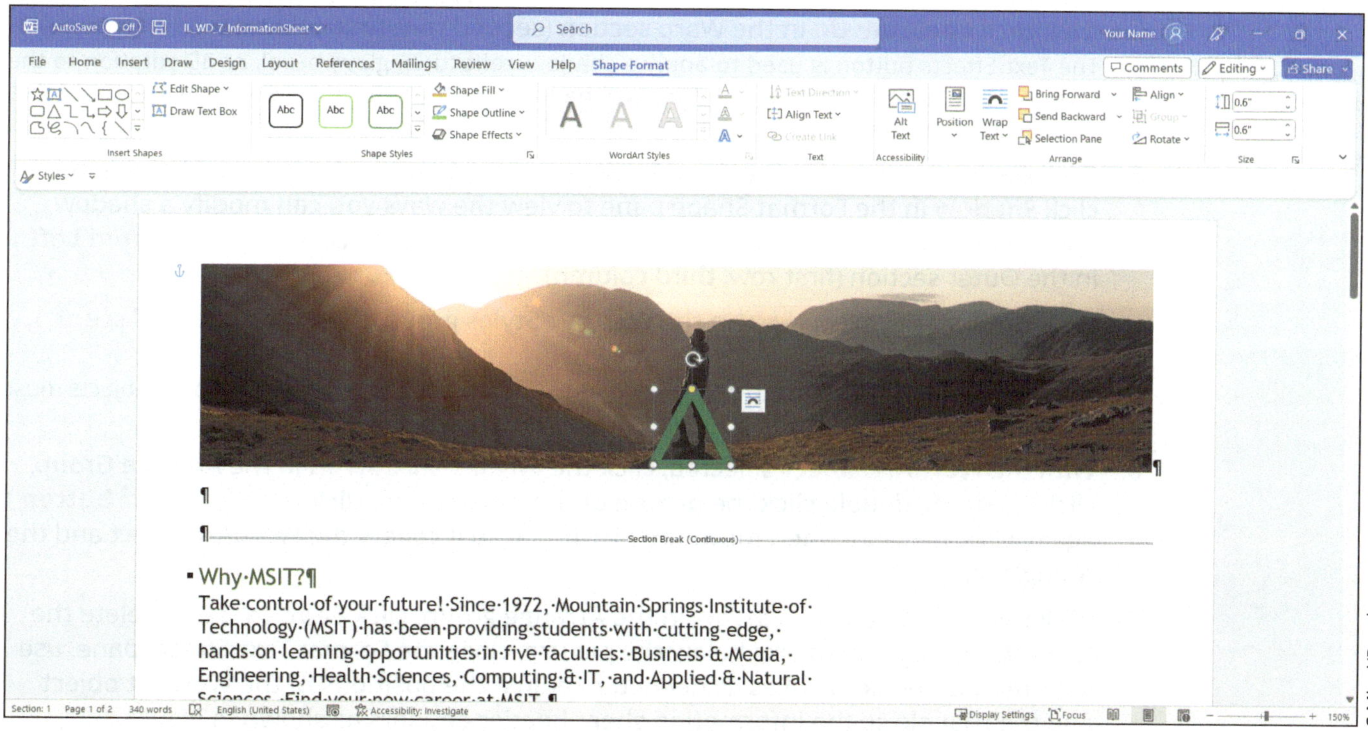

S Migaj/Pexels

Insert WordArt

Case You use WordArt to create an impressive heading from existing text for the information sheet.

Objectives
- Insert WordArt
- Modify WordArt

Another way to enhance your documents is to use WordArt. **WordArt** is a drawing object that contains decorative text. You create WordArt using the Insert WordArt button in the Text group on the Insert tab. Once you have created a WordArt object, you can change its font, fill and outline colors, borders, shadows, shape, and other effects to create the impact you desire.

Steps

1. **Double-click in the Footer area, select Mountain Springs Institute of Technology, press CTRL+C to copy the text, double-click anywhere in the document to exit the footer area, press CTRL+HOME, press ENTER, press Up Arrow [↑] to position the insertion point at the top of the page, then press CTRL+V to paste the text**
   You want to convert "Mountain Springs Institute of Technology" into a WordArt object.
2. **Select the text Mountain Springs Institute of Technology, click the Insert tab, then click the Insert WordArt button in the Text group**
   The WordArt gallery opens as shown in **Figure 7-22** with styles you can choose for your WordArt. You can convert existing text to a WordArt object or you can click the Insert tab and click the Insert WordArt button in the text group to insert a WordArt object that you type.
3. **Click Fill: White; Outline: Dark Green, Accent color 2; Hard Shadow: Dark Green, Accent color 2 (the fourth style in the bottom row)**
   The WordArt object appears at the location of the insertion point, and the Shape Format tab becomes the active tab. The triangle shape also moves, but you will adjust its position in a later step. By default, the WordArt object is inserted as a floating graphic with Square text wrapping.

Quick Tip
You can also change the font or font size of WordArt text using the Mini toolbar.

4. **Click the Home tab, change the font size to 24 point, click the Shape Format tab, type .7 in the Height box in the Size group, press TAB, type 7.5 in the Width box, then press ENTER**
   The WordArt object spans the page between the left and right margins.

Quick Tip
Use the Text Effects and Typography button in the Font group on the Home tab to apply text effects to regular text.

5. **Click the Text Effects button in the WordArt Styles group, point to Transform, then click Chevron: Up in the Warp section (second row, first column)**
   The Text Effects button is used to apply a shadow, reflection, glow, bevel, or 3D rotation to the text. It is also used to change the shape of the text. The Transform gallery shows the available shapes for WordArt text.
6. **Click the Launcher in the WordArt Styles group to open the Format Shape pane, click Shadow in the Format Shape pane to view the ways you can modify a shadow applied to a WordArt object, click the Presets button, then click Offset: Bottom Left in the Outer section (first row, third column)**
7. **Click the Text Fill arrow in the WordArt Styles group, then click Green, Accent 1, Lighter 80%**
   You want the WordArt object to appear on top of the picture. The wrapping for both objects must be changed to Through.
8. **With the WordArt object selected, click the Wrap Text button in the Arrange Group, click Through, double-click the picture of the mountains, click the Wrap Text button again, click Through, then move the picture up so it covers the WordArt object and the triangle shape**
9. **Click the Send Backward arrow in the Arrange group, click Send to Back, delete the two extra paragraph marks below the picture, close the Format Text Effects pane, use your mouse and keystrokes as needed to adjust the positions of the WordArt object and the triangle so the information sheet header appears as shown in Figure 7-23, then save the document**

Figure 7-22: WordArt gallery

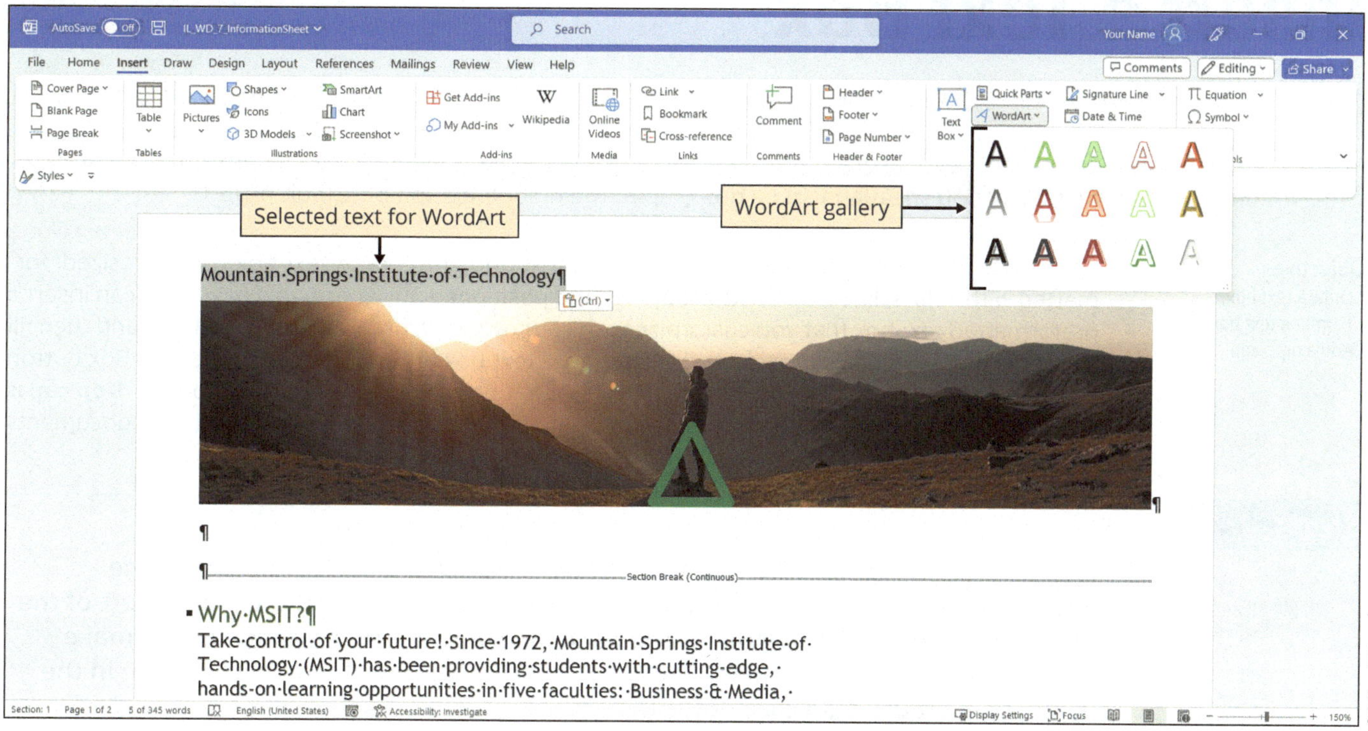

S Migaj/Pexels

Figure 7-23: Completed header

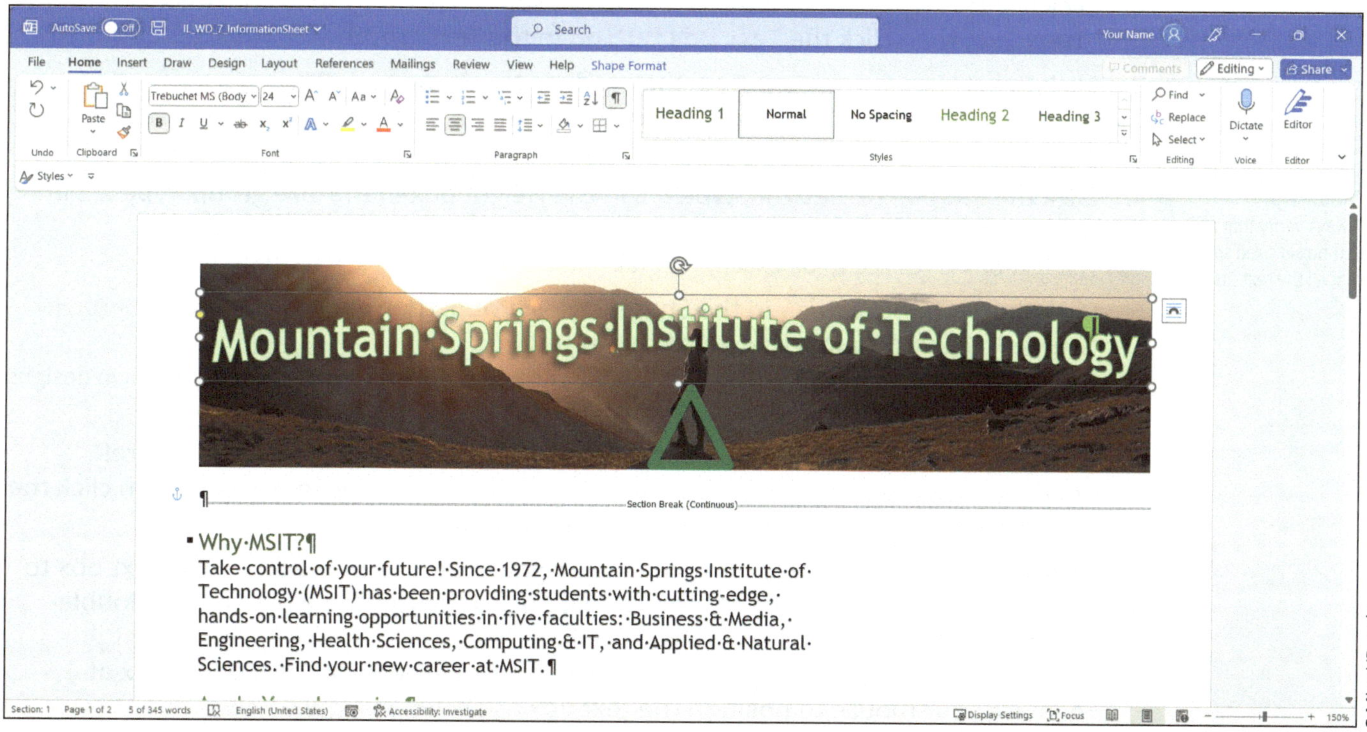

S Migaj/Pexels

Insert a Text Box

Case To further add interest to the information sheet, you decide to present some of the text in boxes and add a drop cap. First, you draw a text box in column 2 on page 1 of the information sheet, resize and position the text box on the page, and then fill it with text and format it with a text box style. You then insert a preformatted text box on page 2 of the information sheet and add a drop cap to the first paragraph of text on page 1.

Objectives
- Draw a text box
- Format a text box
- Add a drop cap

A **text box** is a container that you can fill with text and graphics. A text box can be resized; formatted with colors, lines, and text wrapping; and positioned anywhere on a page. You can insert a preformatted text box that you customize with your own text, draw an empty text box and then fill it with text, or select existing text and then draw a text box around it. You use the Text Box button in the Text group, or the Shapes button in the Illustrations group to create a text box. A **drop cap** is a large initial capital letter that is often used to set off the first paragraph of an article in documents such as information sheets, newsletters, and books.

Steps

1. **Press CTRL+END, select the text from "How to Apply to MSIT" to the end of the document, press CTRL+X to cut the text, scroll up to page 1 and click to the left of the paragraph mark at the bottom of the page following the organization chart (make sure you don't select the chart), click the Layout tab, click the Breaks button in the Page Setup group, then click Column**

   The insertion point is positioned at the top of column 2 on page 1 where you want to draw the text box.

2. **Click the Home tab, click the Paste button, select the text you just pasted, click the Insert tab, then click the Text Box button in the Text group**

3. **Click Draw Horizontal Text Box, then reduce the Zoom to 100%**

   The selected text is formatted as a text box in column 2 on page 1 as shown in **Figure 7-24**. When you draw a text box around existing text or graphics, the text box becomes a floating object.

Quick Tip
Always verify that a text box is sized so that all the text fits.

4. **Click the Shape Format tab, type 6.2 in the Height box in the Size group, type 2.2 in the Width box, then press ENTER**

   The text box is resized to be exactly 6.2" tall and 2.2" wide.

5. **Click the More button in the Shape Styles group, then click Subtle Effect – Dark Green, Accent 2 (fourth row, third column)**

   A style that includes green shading is applied to the text box. You can also create your own designs using the Shape Fill and Shape Outline buttons in the Shape Styles group.

6. **Go to page 2 of the information sheet, click to the left of the "Find Your Future!" heading, click the Insert tab, click the Text Box button in the Text group, then click the Austin Quote preformatted style (middle selection in the first row)**

7. **Drag the left-middle sizing handle to the right to reduce the width of the text box to approximately 2", move the text box down and to the right to a blank area, double-click in the text box, type Contact Kris Olsen for information about current job opportunities in the green technology sector., set the width of the text box at 2.5", then use your mouse to position the text box as shown in Figure 7-25**

8. **Click away from the text box, press CTRL+HOME, click in the paragraph below the "Why MSIT?" heading in Column 1, click the Insert tab, click the Drop Cap button in the Text group, then click Dropped**

   A drop cap is added to the paragraph. You can modify the size and font of the drop cap.

9. **With the drop cap still selected, click the Drop Cap button, click Drop Cap Options, click the Lines to drop down arrow to show 2, click OK, deselect the drop cap, then save the document**

Figure 7-24: Text enclosed in a text box

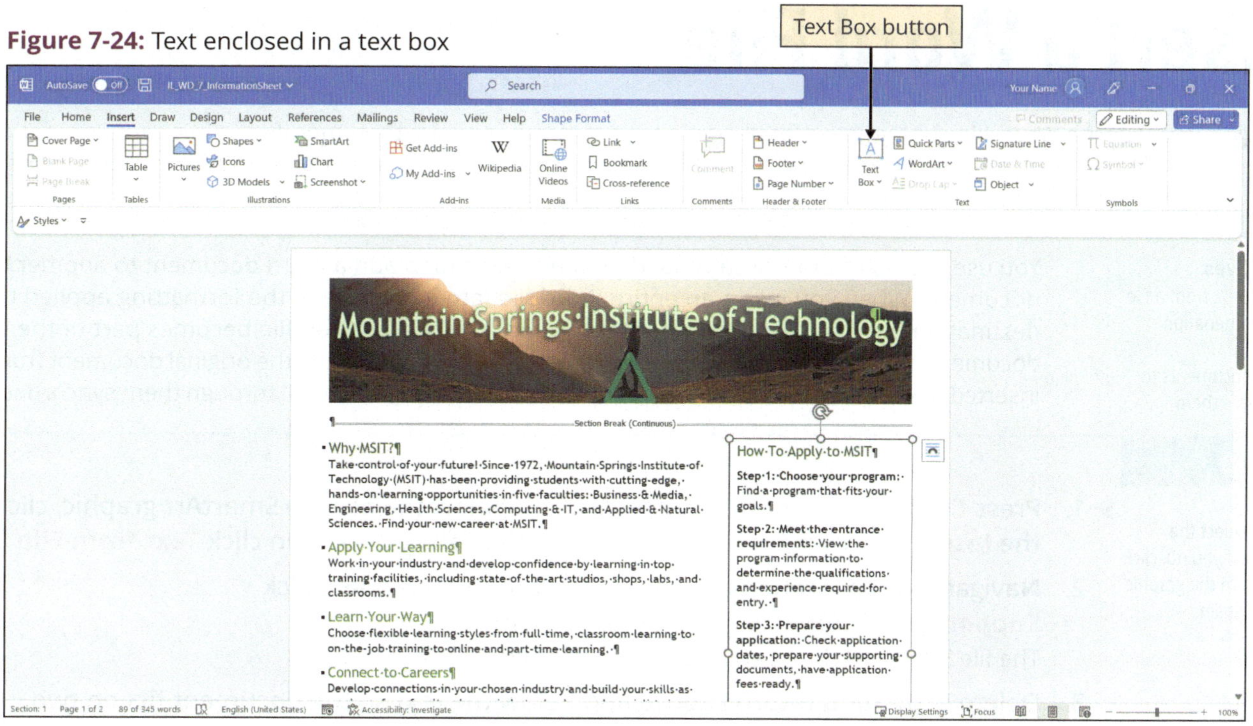

S Migaj/Pexels

Figure 7-25: Text box sized and positioned

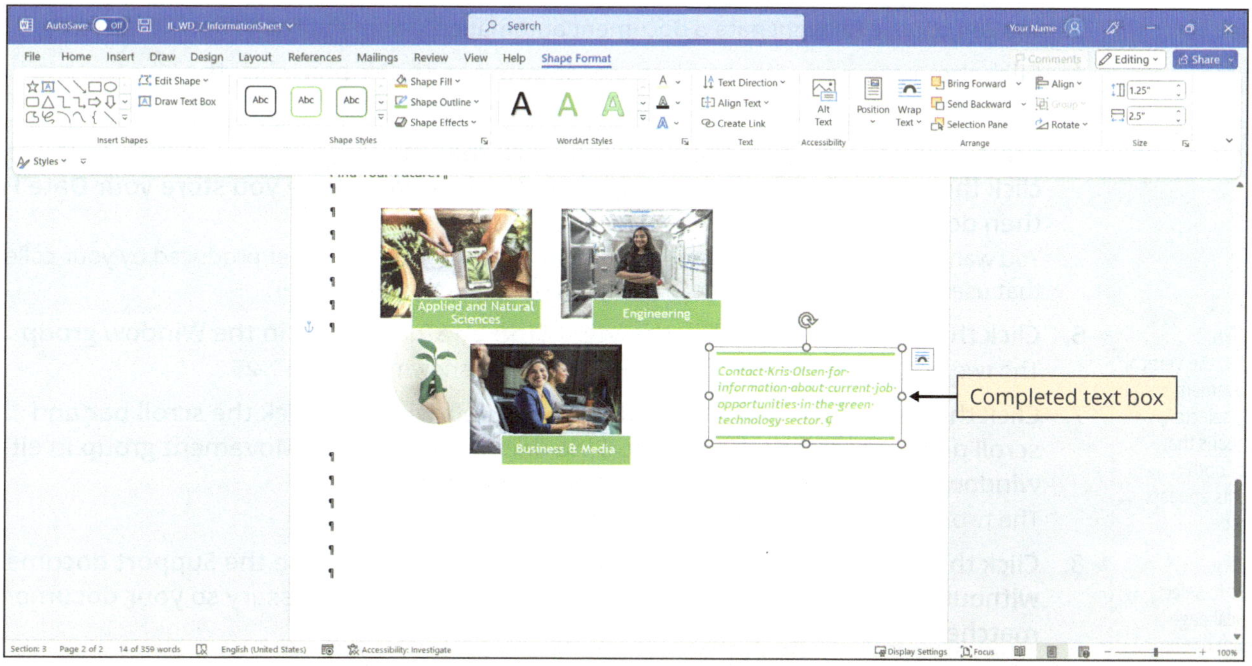

Antoni Shkraba/Pexels; ThisIsEngineering/Pexels; Jopwell/Pexels; Alena Koval/Pexels

Linking text boxes

If you are working on a longer document, you might want text to begin in a text box on one page and then continue in a text box on another page. By creating a **link** between two or more text boxes, you can force text to flow automatically from one text box to another, allowing you to size and format the text boxes any way you wish. To link two or more text boxes, you must first create the original text box, fill it with text, and then create a second, empty text box. Then, to create the link, select the first text box, click the Create Link button in the Text group on the Shape Format tab to activate the pointer, and then click the second text box with the pointer. Any overflow text from the first text box flows seamlessly into the second text box. As you resize the first text box, the flow of text adjusts automatically between the two linked text boxes. If you want to break a link between two linked text boxes so that all the text is contained in the original text box, select the original text box, and then click the Break Link button in the Text group.

Insert a Word File

Case You insert a Word file containing information about campus services, then modify the hyphenation options. Finally, you view the completed information sheet side by side with an information sheet created by a colleague to compare them.

Objectives
- Insert text from a file
- Set hyphenation options
- View documents to compare them

You use the Text from File command on the Insert tab to add a Word document to another Word document. When you insert an entire Word file into a document, the formatting applied to the destination file is applied to the content you insert. The inserted file becomes part of the Word document, similar to an embedded object, and you cannot return to the original document from the inserted file. You can also view two documents side by side and scroll through them synchronously.

Steps

Trouble
Do not select the graphic. If you do, click away from the graphic and try again.

1. **Press CTRL+END, click a paragraph mark below the picture SmartArt graphic, click the Insert tab, click the Object arrow in the Text group, then click Text from File**
2. **Navigate to the location where you store your Data Files, click Support_WD_7_Services.docx, then click Insert**
   The file Support_WD_7_Services.docx is inserted.
3. **Delete extra hard returns above and below the text so the document fits on two pages, if necessary, click the Layout tab, click the Hyphenation arrow in the Page Setup group, then click Hyphenation Options**
   You can choose to hyphenate a document automatically or manually.
4. **Click the Automatically hyphenate document check box, click the Hyphenate words in CAPS check box to deselect it, then click OK**
5. **Press CTRL+HOME, click the View tab, click the One Page button in the Zoom group, click the File tab, click Open, navigate to the location where you store your Data Files, then double-click Support_WD_7_OtherDesign.docx**
   You want to compare this finished document to an information sheet produced by your colleague that uses the Retrospect theme and a different picture in the banner.

Quick Tip
By default, the Vertical page movement option is selected, which means that page 1 of both documents appears side by side.

6. **Click the View tab, then click the View Side by Side button in the Window group**
   The two information sheets appear side by side as shown in **Figure 7-26**.
7. **Click the Other Design information sheet (left window), click the scroll bar and scroll down, then click the Side to Side button in the Page Movement group in either window to display the two pages of each document**
   The two pages of the support document are displayed.

Quick Tip
You need to select the Vertical page movement option to continue working normally in Word.

8. **Click the Vertical button in the Page Movement group, close the Support document without saving it, then make any spacing adjustments necessary so your document matches Figure 7-27**
9. **sam Save your changes, submit a copy to your instructor, then close the file and exit Word**

Configuring line numbers

To add line numbers to selected text, click the Line Numbers button in the Page Setup group on the Layout tab. You can then choose to number lines continuously, restart numbering on each new page or section, or suppress for the current paragraph. You can also choose to display the numbers at intervals. Word counts the number of lines in a document. This is helpful if you want to refer to a specific line in a document such as in a legal contract.

Figure 7-26: Two documents viewed side by side

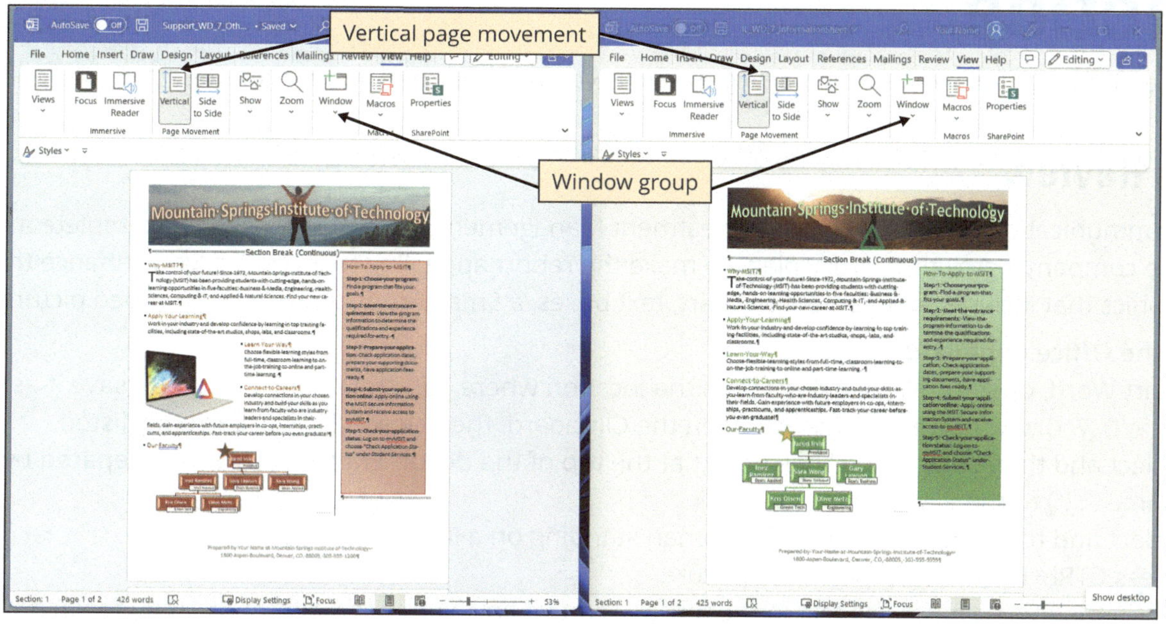

Min An/Pexels; S Migaj/Pexels

Figure 7-27: Completed information sheet

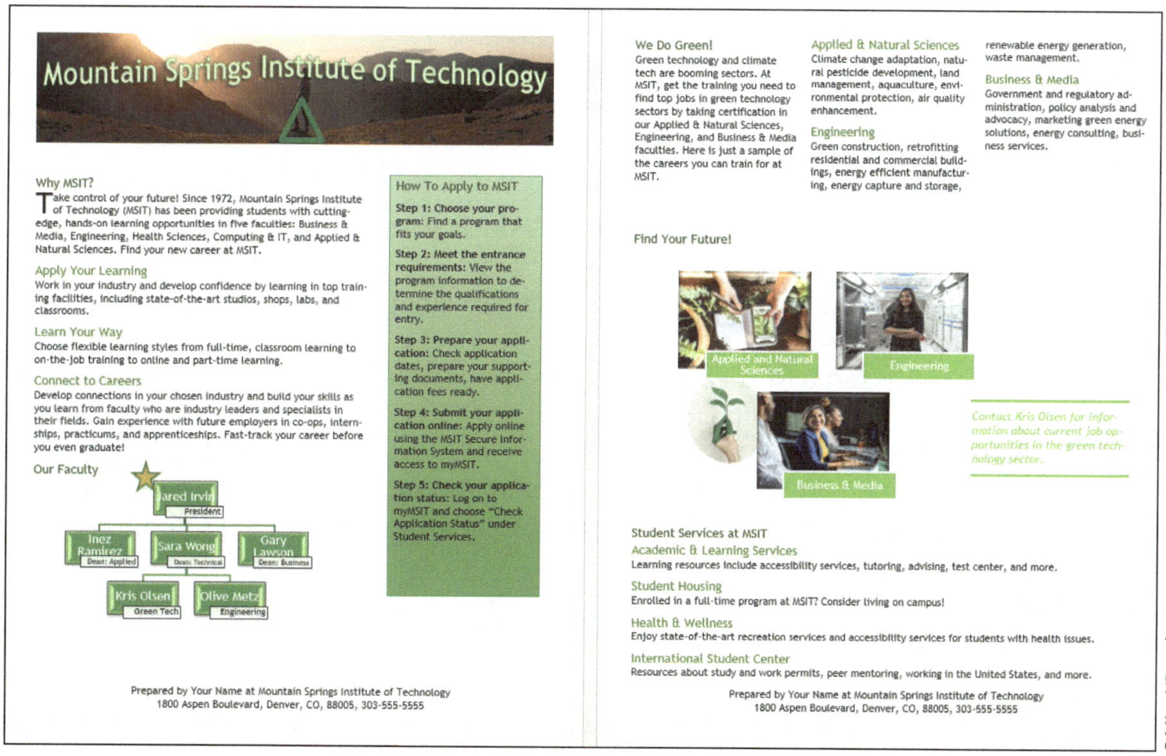
Mountain Springs Institute of Technology

Why MSIT?
Take control of your future! Since 1972, Mountain Springs Institute of Technology (MSIT) has been providing students with cutting-edge, hands-on learning opportunities in five faculties: Business & Media, Engineering, Health Sciences, Computing & IT, and Applied & Natural Sciences. Find your new career at MSIT.

Apply Your Learning
Work in your industry and develop confidence by learning in top training facilities, including state-of-the-art studios, shops, labs, and classrooms.

Learn Your Way
Choose flexible learning styles from full-time, classroom learning to on-the-job training to online and part-time learning.

Connect to Careers
Develop connections in your chosen industry and build your skills as you learn from faculty who are industry leaders and specialists in their fields. Gain experience with future employers in co-ops, internships, practicums, and apprenticeships. Fast-track your career before you even graduate!

Our Faculty
Jared Irvin — President
Inez Ramirez — Dean: Applied
Sara Wong — Dean: Technical
Gary Lawson — Dean: Business
Kris Olsen — Green Tech
Olive Metz — Engineering

How To Apply to MSIT
Step 1: Choose your program: Find a program that fits your goals.
Step 2: Meet the entrance requirements: View the program information to determine the qualifications and experience required for entry.
Step 3: Prepare your application: Check application dates, prepare your supporting documents, have application fees ready.
Step 4: Submit your application online: Apply online using the MSIT Secure Information System and receive access to myMSIT.
Step 5: Check your application status: Log on to myMSIT and choose "Check Application Status" under Student Services.

Prepared by Your Name at Mountain Springs Institute of Technology
1800 Aspen Boulevard, Denver, CO, 88005, 303-555-5555

We Do Green!
Green technology and climate tech are booming sectors. At MSIT, get the training you need to find top jobs in green technology sectors by taking certification in our Applied & Natural Sciences, Engineering, and Business & Media faculties. Here is just a sample of the careers you can train for at MSIT.

Applied & Natural Sciences
Climate change adaptation, natural pesticide development, land management, aquaculture, environmental protection, air quality enhancement.

Engineering
Green construction, retrofitting residential and commercial buildings, energy efficient manufacturing, energy capture and storage, renewable energy generation, waste management.

Business & Media
Government and regulatory administration, policy analysis and advocacy, marketing green energy solutions, energy consulting, business services.

Find Your Future!
Applied and Natural Sciences
Engineering
Business & Media

Contact Kris Olsen for information about current job opportunities in the green technology sector.

Student Services at MSIT
Academic & Learning Services
Learning resources include accessibility services, tutoring, advising, test center, and more.
Student Housing
Enrolled in a full-time program at MSIT? Consider living on campus!
Health & Wellness
Enjoy state-of-the-art recreation services and accessibility services for students with health issues.
International Student Center
Resources about study and work permits, peer mentoring, working in the United States, and more.

Prepared by Your Name at Mountain Springs Institute of Technology
1800 Aspen Boulevard, Denver, CO, 88005, 303-555-5555

S Migaj/Pexels; Antoni Shkraba/Pexels; ThisIsEngineering/Pexels; Jopwell/Pexels; Alena Koval/Pexels

Inserting online videos and online pictures in a document

You can also illustrate your documents with graphics and media that you have found on the web and have permission to use. The Online Video command in the Media group on the Insert tab allows you to insert videos found on the web into your Word documents and play them. Click the Online Video button, type the URL or embed code in the Insert Video dialog box, then click Insert. Use the Pictures button in the Illustrations group to insert images from the web. Click Online Pictures on the Pictures button menu to open the Online Pictures window, type a keyword or phrase in the search box for the image you want to find, then press ENTER. Select an image from the search results, click Insert to add it to the document, then format the item as you would any other graphic object. Videos inserted in a document include a play button that you can click to view the video right in Word.

Practice

In the exercises that follow, you will practice the skills you have learned in this module.

Skills Review

As the communications assistant at Trent Investment Management, you've been asked to complete a report about the company's growth strategy plan. To make the report appealing to investors, you enhance the report with graphics that include an organization chart, text boxes, a SmartArt diagram and a cropped picture.

1. **Use the Office Clipboard.**
   a. Start Word, open IL_WD_7-2.docx from the location where you store your Data Files, save it as **IL_WD_7_GrowthStrategyReport**, open the Clipboard, then clear all items currently listed.
   b. Select and then cut the two lines of text at the top of the document (starting with "Prepared by Your Name . . .") to the Clipboard.
   c. Select and then cut the picture of a woman standing on a line graph to the Clipboard.
   d. Press CTRL+HOME, then paste the picture.
   e. Open the footer, paste the text in the footer, remove any extra lines, center the text, replace "Your Name" with your name, then exit the footer.
   f. Open Support_WD_7_Goals.docx from the location where you store your Data Files, select and copy all the text, then close the document.
   g. Click the blank line below the "Organization Chart" placeholder, paste the text using the Use Destination Theme paste option, close the Clipboard, then save the document.
2. **Create sections and columns.**
   a. Turn on formatting marks, if necessary.
   b. Place the insertion point to the left of the heading "Growth Strategy Team", then insert a continuous section break.
   c. In Section 2, turn on columns with the following settings: Right preset, spacing between set at .4", and the Line between option selected.
   d. In Multiple Pages view, insert a Next Page section break to the left of "Growth Strategy Questions".
   e. In Section 3, turn on columns with the following settings: Three, spacing between at .2", and the Line between option deselected.
   f. Insert a Continuous section break to the left of the paragraph mark following the text "with the proposed growth strategies?" towards the bottom of column 1 to balance the columns containing the Growth Strategy Questions text.
   g. Click the paragraph mark above the "Growth Strategy Resources" heading on page 2, turn on one column (Section 4), then save the document.
3. **Create SmartArt graphics.**
   a. Click the picture of the people applauding on page 2, then create a picture SmartArt graphic using the Bending Picture Blocks layout.
   b. Add two shapes to the picture SmartArt.
   c. Insert **Support_WD_7_Financing.jpg** in the first blank shape, then insert **Support_WD_7_RiskChart .jpg** in the second blank shape.
   d. Expand the text pane, if necessary, label the three boxes as follows: **Employee Support, Financial Resources**, and **Risk Analysis**, then close the text pane. (Hint: Press the down arrow, *not* ENTER, to move to the next bullet. If you press ENTER, click the Undo button.)
   e. Change the layout to Picture Frame (second row, third column).
   f. Set the height of the picture SmartArt graphic to 3.2" and the width to 5.7".
   g. Use SHIFT to select the three pictures in the picture SmartArt graphic, apply the Slant bevel shape effect (first row, fourth column), then save the document.

4. **Modify SmartArt graphics.**
   a. On page 1 of the Growth Strategy Report, select the "Organization Chart" placeholder and the paragraph mark following it, then insert a Hierarchy SmartArt graphic using the Name and Title Organization Chart style.
   b. Click a white area of the chart, then set the height of the organization chart at 2.4" and the width at 4.7".

Figure 7-28

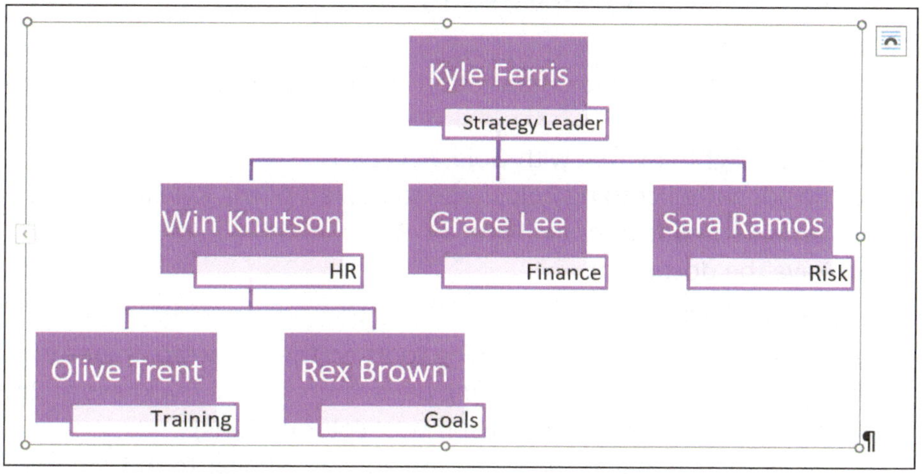

   c. Add and remove shapes and text so the organization chart appears as shown in **Figure 7-28**.
   d. Use the Move Down command to move the box for Win Knutson so it and its subordinate boxes appear in the middle of row 2.
   e. Change the colors of the chart to Colorful Range– Accent Colors 2 to 3 (second selection in the Colorful range).
   f. Apply the Inset SmartArt style from the 3D section.
   g. Select all five of the subordinate boxes, set the width at 1.1", then save the document.

5. **Crop and rotate a picture.**
   a. Scroll to the end of the report, double-click the picture of the laptop and vase, then scale the picture to 75%. (Hint: Remember to verify that the Lock aspect ratio check box is selected so the picture is resized proportionally.)
   b. Crop the picture to the Teardrop shape (second row, third selection from the left in the Basic Shapes category).
   c. Refer to **Figure 7-29**. Further crop the picture and use the mouse to slightly rotate it to the left.
   d. Deselect the picture, then save the document.

Figure 7-29

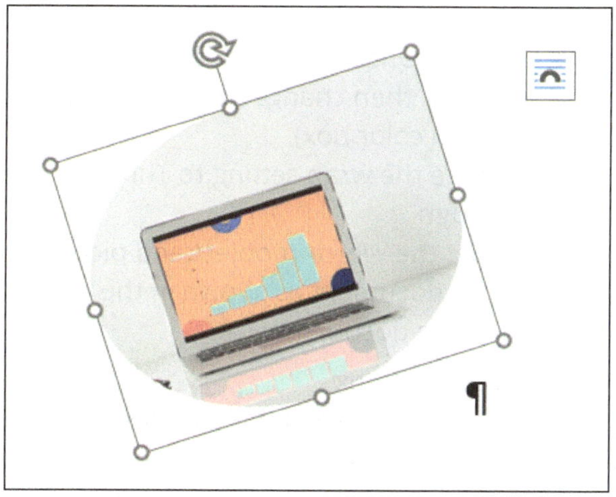

Mikael Blomkvist/Pexels

6. **Position a graphic.**
   a. On page 2, change the wrapping of the SmartArt graphic to Through. Don't worry that text will wrap around it.
   b. Drag the anchor for the picture SmartArt up so it appears to the left of the "Growth Strategy Resources" heading.
   c. Scroll down and click the teardrop-shaped picture, cut the picture, then paste it at the paragraph mark above the "Growth Strategy Resources" heading.
   d. Adjust the size of the teardop shape to 1.04" in Height and 1.3" in Width, change the wrapping of the teardrop shape to Through, then on the Position tab in the Layout dialog box, set the position of the picture at 4.3" to the right of the Left Margin and 5.5" below the Page.
   e. Find the anchor for the teardrop shape (above and to the left of the shape), then drag the anchor up so it appears on the line below the "Growth Strategy Resources" heading.
   f. Click the picture SmartArt graphic, then change the layering to Bring to Front so that the graphic slightly overlaps the teardrop picture.
   g. Click the paragraph mark above "Growth Considerations", press ENTER until the "Growth Considerations" paragraph is moved below the picture SmartArt graphic, then save the document.

Skills Review (Continued)

7. **Insert Shapes**
   a. Scroll up to view the organization chart, then draw a Lightning Bolt shape that is approximately 1" in height.
   b. Fill the lightning bolt with Gold, Accent 5.
   c. Position the lightning bolt shape to the left of the Kyle Ferris box and slightly overlap it. Refer to the completed document in **Figure 7-30**.
   d. Save the document

8. **Use Drawing Tools**
   a. Display the selection of drawing tools on the Draw tab, then turn on the Ink to Shape function.
   b. Select one of the three drawing pens, then set the thickness at 2mm and the color at Galaxy (second selection in the second to last row of color options).
   c. Draw a circle that when converted appears similar to the circle in **Figure 7-30**.
   d. Turn off the pen, size and position the circle as shown in **Figure 7-30**, then save the document.

9. **Create WordArt.**
   a. Press CTRL+HOME to move to the top of the document, press ENTER, press CTRL+HOME, then type **Growth Strategy Report**.
   b. Convert the text "Growth Strategy Report" to a WordArt object using the Fill: White; Outline: Purple, Accent color 1; Glow, Purple, Accent color 1 (second row, fourth column).
   c. Set the height of the WordArt object at .6" and the width at 6.7".
   d. Transform the WordArt object with the Chevron: Up effect (first column, second row in the Warp section).
   e. Add the Offset: Left shadow effect to the WordArt object (second row, third column in the Outer section), then change the fill color of the WordArt object to Light Gray, Background 2 (first row, third column color box).
   f. Change the wrap setting to Through, then change the wrap setting of the wide picture below to Through.
   g. Adjust the WordArt object and picture so the WordArt object appears in front of the picture at the top of the document as shown in the completed document in **Figure 7-30**.
   h. Save the document.

10. **Create a text box.**
   a. Scroll to and select the text from "Growth Considerations" to the end of the document, then cut it.
   b. Scroll up to page 1, click to the left of the Section Break at the top of column 2 on page 1, then paste the copied text in the new column.
   c. Select the text again, then insert it into a text box using the Draw Text Box option.
   d. Set the height of the text box to 6.3" and the width to 2.2".
   e. Apply the Subtle Effect – Purple, Accent 1 shape style to the text box.
   f. Remove the two paragraph marks above "Growth Strategy Resources", then insert a text box using the Austin Quote preformatted text box.
   g. Size and position the text box, then type **Contact Olive Trent for information about upcoming employee training sessions.** as shown in the completed report in **Figure 7-30**.
   h. On page 1 of the report, insert a drop cap that is dropped two lines in the paragraph under the "Growth Strategy Team" heading.
   i. Save the document.

Figure 7-30

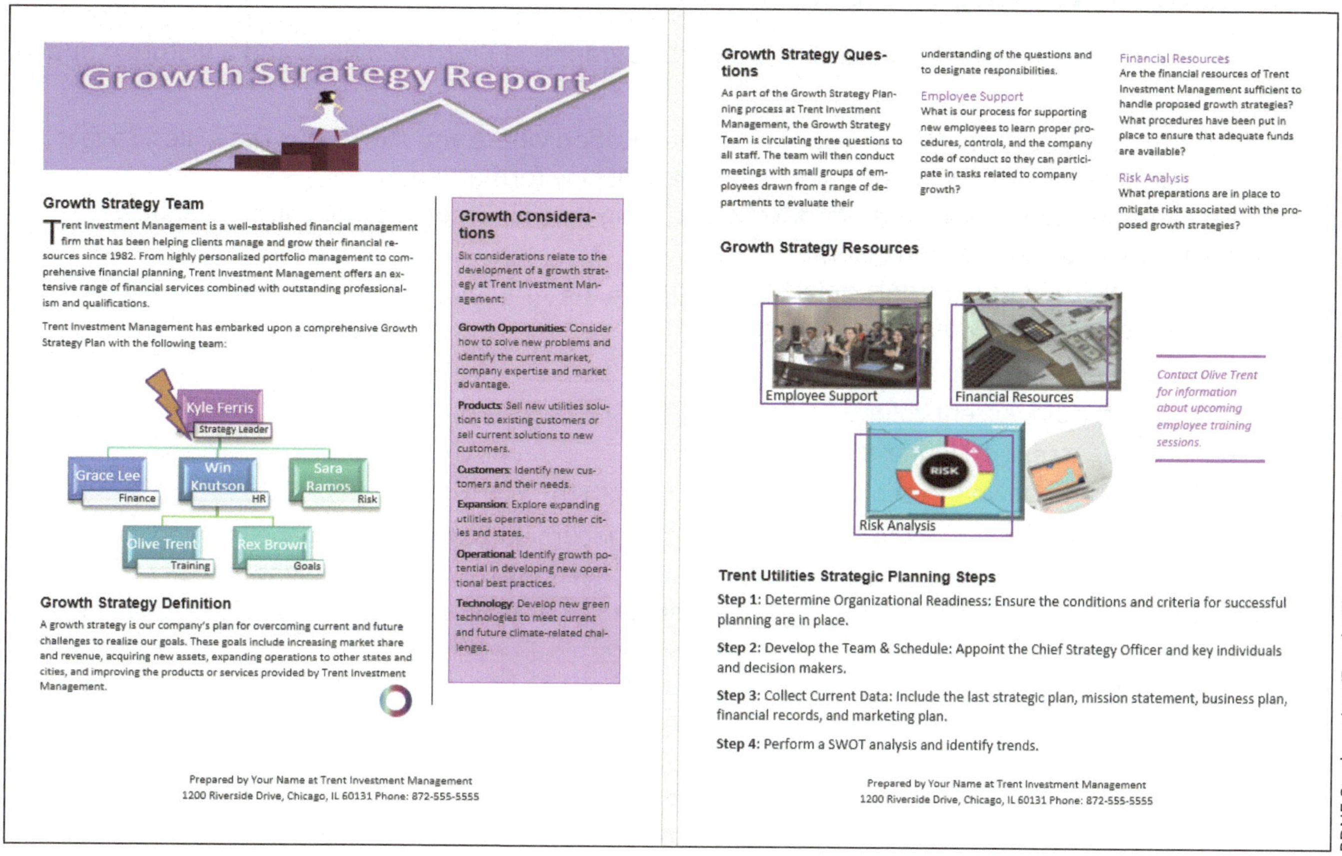
Growth Strategy Report

Growth Strategy Team

Trent Investment Management is a well-established financial management firm that has been helping clients manage and grow their financial resources since 1982. From highly personalized portfolio management to comprehensive financial planning, Trent Investment Management offers an extensive range of financial services combined with outstanding professionalism and qualifications.

Trent Investment Management has embarked upon a comprehensive Growth Strategy Plan with the following team:

Growth Strategy Definition

A growth strategy is our company's plan for overcoming current and future challenges to realize our goals. These goals include increasing market share and revenue, acquiring new assets, expanding operations to other states and cities, and improving the products or services provided by Trent Investment Management.

Growth Considerations

Six considerations relate to the development of a growth strategy at Trent Investment Management:

Growth Opportunities: Consider how to solve new problems and identify the current market, company expertise and market advantage.

Products: Sell new utilities solutions to existing customers or sell current solutions to new customers.

Customers: Identify new customers and their needs.

Expansion: Explore expanding utilities operations to other cities and states.

Operational: Identify growth potential in developing new operational best practices.

Technology: Develop new green technologies to meet current and future climate-related challenges.

Prepared by Your Name at Trent Investment Management
1200 Riverside Drive, Chicago, IL 60131 Phone: 872-555-5555

Growth Strategy Questions

As part of the Growth Strategy Planning process at Trent Investment Management, the Growth Strategy Team is circulating three questions to all staff. The team will then conduct meetings with small groups of employees drawn from a range of departments to evaluate their understanding of the questions and to designate responsibilities.

Employee Support
What is our process for supporting new employees to learn proper procedures, controls, and the company code of conduct so they can participate in tasks related to company growth?

Financial Resources
Are the financial resources of Trent Investment Management sufficient to handle proposed growth strategies? What procedures have been put in place to ensure that adequate funds are available?

Risk Analysis
What preparations are in place to mitigate risks associated with the proposed growth strategies?

Growth Strategy Resources

Contact Olive Trent for information about upcoming employee training sessions.

Trent Utilities Strategic Planning Steps

Step 1: Determine Organizational Readiness: Ensure the conditions and criteria for successful planning are in place.

Step 2: Develop the Team & Schedule: Appoint the Chief Strategy Officer and key individuals and decision makers.

Step 3: Collect Current Data: Include the last strategic plan, mission statement, business plan, financial records, and marketing plan.

Step 4: Perform a SWOT analysis and identify trends.

Prepared by Your Name at Trent Investment Management
1200 Riverside Drive, Chicago, IL 60131 Phone: 872-555-5555

Monstera/Pexels

RDNE Stock project/Pexels; Tima Miroshnichenko/Pexels; Monstera/Pexels; Mikael Blomkvist/Pexels

11. **Insert a Word file.**
    a. Click to the left of a paragraph mark below the picture SmartArt graphic on page 2 to position the insertion point, then insert the Word file **Support_WD_7_Process.docx** from the location where you store your Data Files.
    b. Add or remove any extra hard returns so that the document fits on two pages.
    c. Change the hyphenation options so that the text in the document is automatically hyphenated and words in CAPS are *not* hyphenated.
    d. Press CTRL+HOME, then view the document in One Page view.
    e. Open **Support_WD_7_Growth_NewDesign.docx** from the location where you store your Data Files.
    f. View the two documents side by side, then change the page movement to Side to Side.
    g. Return the page movement to Vertical, close the Support document, then make any spacing adjustments necessary so that the two pages of the Growth Strategy Report appear as shown in **Figure 7-30**.
    h. Save the document, submit a copy to your instructor, then close the file and exit Word.

Independent Challenge 1

At Pinetree Medical Clinic in Bangor, ME, you've been asked to take over the writing and formatting of the clinic's quarterly newsletter. The two pages of the newsletter are printed on both sides of one page and distributed to staff. In addition, patients and staff can download a PDF of the newsletter from the clinic's website. You open a draft of the Summer newsletter and format it in sections with columns, and then add

Independent Challenge 1 (Continued)

graphic objects, including text boxes, a drawing, a SmartArt graphic, a WordArt object, and a picture cropped to a shape.

a. Start Word, open the file IL_WD_7-3.docx from the location where you store your Data Files, save it as **IL_WD_7_PinetreeClinicSummerNewsletter**, then display formatting marks.
b. Create "Summer Newsletter" as a WordArt object using the Fill: Green, Accent color 1; Shadow WordArt style (first row, second column).
c. Increase the width of the WordArt object to 5", change the wrapping to Through, then modify the WordArt object using the following settings:
   - Shadow: Offset: Bottom in the Outer section
   - Glow: 5 point; Gold, Accent color 3
   - Text Fill: Gold, Accent 3, Lighter 80%
   - Transform: Wave: Down (first column in the fifth row in the Warp section)
d. Crop the picture of the forest scene at the top of the document to the Wave shape (second row, second shape from the right in the Stars and Banners section), then set the height of the cropped picture at 1.8" and the width at 6.5". (Hint: deselect the Lock aspect ratio check box in the Size dialog box so the shape is not resized proportionally.)
e. Change the text wrapping of the cropped shape to Through, then use layering and your mouse to position the WordArt object in front of the cropped shape at the top of the page as shown in the completed newsletter in **Figure 7-31**.
f. Open the Clipboard, clear the contents, select the text from the "Giving Back" heading to the end of the paragraph under "Pinetree Kids", then cut it to the Clipboard.
g. Cut the picture of the women running to the Clipboard.
h. Paste the cut text at the second paragraph mark below the "Summer Newsletter" heading and picture, then paste the picture following the text you just pasted.
i. Insert a Next Page Section break to the left of the "Clinic News" heading so it appears in Section 2 at the top of a new page.
j. Scroll up, then insert a Continuous section break on the left of the "Giving Back" heading below the "Summer Newsletter" header and picture.
k. Turn on columns with the following settings: Two and .3 spacing between.
l. Balance the two columns by inserting a Continuous section break after "$3,000." at the end of the "Pinetree Kids" paragraph.
m. Click the picture of the women running and turn on One column, then make the picture into a picture SmartArt graphic using the Bending Picture Blocks layout and add two shapes.
n. Fill the first new shape with the picture file **Support_WD_7_Class.jpg** and the second new shape with the picture file **Support_WD_7_Teddy.jpg**.
o. Change the layout of the picture SmartArt graphic to Captioned Pictures, then change the height of the picture SmartArt graphic to 2.2" and the width to 6.5" so that it extends in one line of boxes across the bottom of page 1 as shown in the completed newsletter in **Figure 7-31**. Enter the required captions.
p. On page 2 of the document, make the text "Congratulations" and the paragraph that follows it into a text box formatted with the Subtle Effect - Gold, Accent 3 shape style.
q. Anchor the text box to the paragraph above it ("New Emergency Room Procedures") by dragging the anchor currently attached to the text box up so it appears to the left of the paragraph above.
r. On a blank line below the text box, then insert the Word file **Support_WD_7_PatientEducation.docx**.
s. With the Ink to Shape option activated, use one of the drawing pens with 2mm thickness and the Green color to draw a triangle and then position it to the right of the text so it appears similar to **Figure 7-31**.
t. View the newsletter in Multiple Pages view, then compare it to **Figure 7-31** and make any spacing adjustments.
u. Save your changes, submit a copy to your instructor, close the document, then exit Word.

Figure 7-31

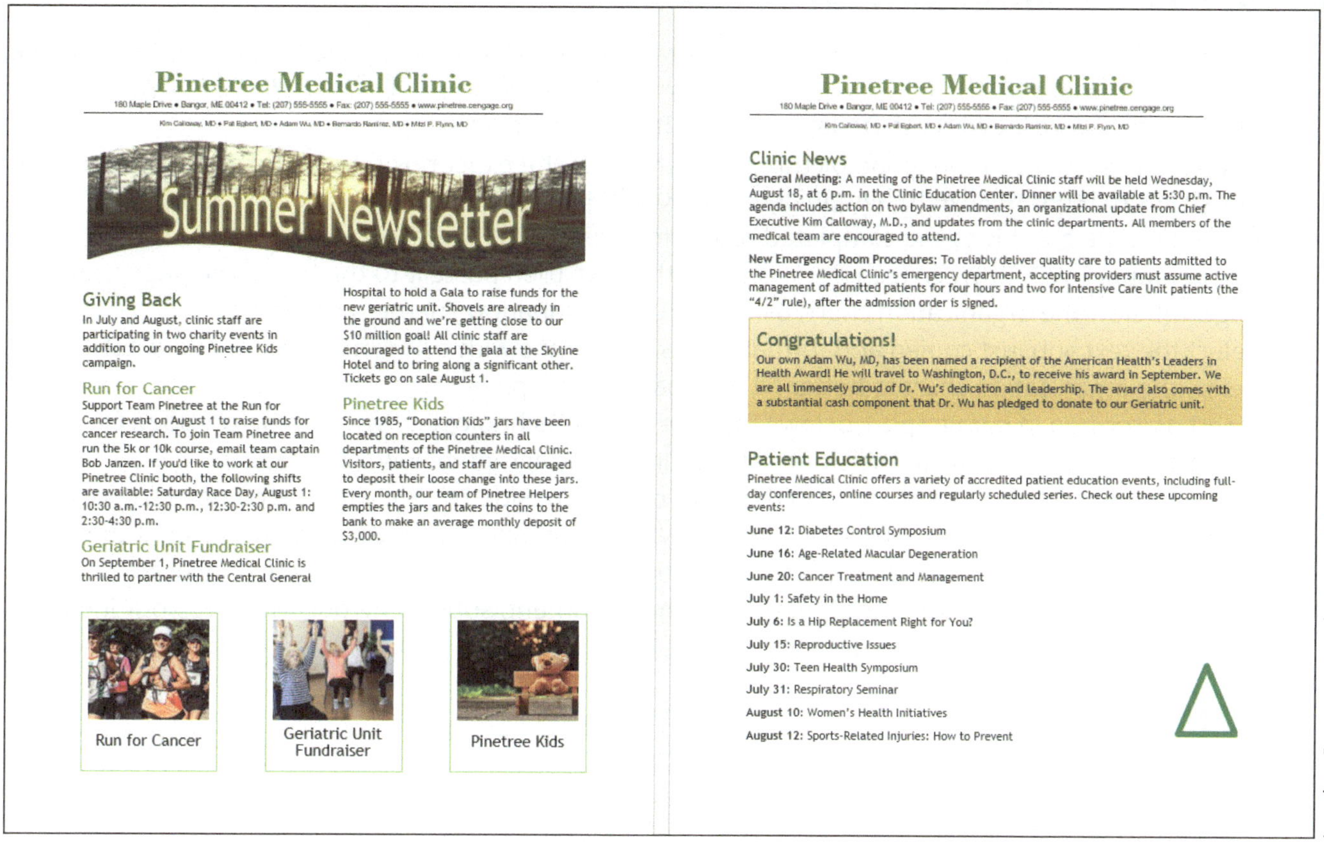
Pinetree Medical Clinic
180 Maple Drive • Bangor, ME 00412 • Tel: (207) 555-5555 • Fax: (207) 555-5555 • www.pinetree.cengage.org
Kim Calloway, MD • Pat Egbert, MD • Adam Wu, MD • Bernardo Ramirez, MD • Mitzi P. Flynn, MD

Summer Newsletter

Giving Back
In July and August, clinic staff are participating in two charity events in addition to our ongoing Pinetree Kids campaign.

Run for Cancer
Support Team Pinetree at the Run for Cancer event on August 1 to raise funds for cancer research. To join Team Pinetree and run the 5k or 10k course, email team captain Bob Janzen. If you'd like to work at our Pinetree Clinic booth, the following shifts are available: Saturday Race Day, August 1: 10:30 a.m.-12:30 p.m., 12:30-2:30 p.m. and 2:30-4:30 p.m.

Geriatric Unit Fundraiser
On September 1, Pinetree Medical Clinic is thrilled to partner with the Central General Hospital to hold a Gala to raise funds for the new geriatric unit. Shovels are already in the ground and we're getting close to our $10 million goal! All clinic staff are encouraged to attend the gala at the Skyline Hotel and to bring along a significant other. Tickets go on sale August 1.

Pinetree Kids
Since 1985, "Donation Kids" jars have been located on reception counters in all departments of the Pinetree Medical Clinic. Visitors, patients, and staff are encouraged to deposit their loose change into these jars. Every month, our team of Pinetree Helpers empties the jars and takes the coins to the bank to make an average monthly deposit of $3,000.

Run for Cancer | Geriatric Unit Fundraiser | Pinetree Kids

Pinetree Medical Clinic
180 Maple Drive • Bangor, ME 00412 • Tel: (207) 555-5555 • Fax: (207) 555-5555 • www.pinetree.cengage.org
Kim Calloway, MD • Pat Egbert, MD • Adam Wu, MD • Bernardo Ramirez, MD • Mitzi P. Flynn, MD

Clinic News
General Meeting: A meeting of the Pinetree Medical Clinic staff will be held Wednesday, August 18, at 6 p.m. in the Clinic Education Center. Dinner will be available at 5:30 p.m. The agenda includes action on two bylaw amendments, an organizational update from Chief Executive Kim Calloway, M.D., and updates from the clinic departments. All members of the medical team are encouraged to attend.

New Emergency Room Procedures: To reliably deliver quality care to patients admitted to the Pinetree Medical Clinic's emergency department, accepting providers must assume active management of admitted patients for four hours and two for Intensive Care Unit patients (the "4/2" rule), after the admission order is signed.

Congratulations!
Our own Adam Wu, MD, has been named a recipient of the American Health's Leaders in Health Award! He will travel to Washington, D.C., to receive his award in September. We are all immensely proud of Dr. Wu's dedication and leadership. The award also comes with a substantial cash component that Dr. Wu has pledged to donate to our Geriatric unit.

Patient Education
Pinetree Medical Clinic offers a variety of accredited patient education events, including full-day conferences, online courses and regularly scheduled series. Check out these upcoming events:

June 12: Diabetes Control Symposium
June 16: Age-Related Macular Degeneration
June 20: Cancer Treatment and Management
July 1: Safety in the Home
July 6: Is a Hip Replacement Right for You?
July 15: Reproductive Issues
July 30: Teen Health Symposium
July 31: Respiratory Seminar
August 10: Women's Health Initiatives
August 12: Sports-Related Injuries: How to Prevent

Independent Challenge 2

You work for Watson Technology, a green technology solutions consulting firm based in Maryland. You've been asked to prepare an update for stakeholders that describes some of the company's latest green technology initiatives and includes information about the company. First, you create an organization chart to present the company personnel and then you create a graphic that includes the company's new slogan. Finally, you paste information from another document and format it as a text box that includes drop caps, and then view the document side by side with another update document.

a. Start Word, open the file IL_WD_7-4.docx from the drive and folder where you store your Data Files, then save it as **IL_WD_7_StakeholdersUpdate**.
b. Use the information contained in the table to create a SmartArt graphic organization chart that uses the Horizontal Hierarchy style in the Hierarchy category. (Hint: Press SHIFT+ENTER after you type a name so that you can enter the position).
c. Apply the Polished SmartArt style from the 3-D section of the SmartArt style, then apply the Colored Fill – Accent 4 color scheme.
d. Apply the Hard Edge Bevel style to all the boxes in the organization chart.
e. Set the height of the chart to 2.5".
f. When you have entered the names and positions for the organization chart, delete the table containing the text for the chart.
g. Under the "New Slogan" heading on page 2, create a graphic that includes the globe picture and a WordArt object as follows:
   - Crop the picture to an oval and then continue to crop to remove as much of the background as possible so the globe fills the space.
   - Change the text wrapping to Through.

Independent Challenge 2 (Continued)

- Type **Technology for the Future!** at the paragraph mark above the globe picture, then create a WordArt object from the text using the Fill: Green; Accent color 4; Soft Bevel WordArt style.
- Format the WordArt with the Deflate: Bottom Transform effect.
- Reduce the height of the globe picture to 2", then set the exact position of the globe picture on the page at Centered relative to Margin and 3" below Page.
- Compare the graphic to the completed report in **Figure 7-32**.

h. Open Support_WD_7_GreenTech.docx, copy all the text, then paste it to the left of the page break on page 1 (below the organization chart) using the Use Destination Theme paste option.

i. Select the text you just copied and format it in two columns with a line in between. Add a hard return below the organization chart to better fill the space on the page.

j. Insert a drop cap in paragraph 1 below "Top Five Green Technologies" and set the dropped to 2, then insert another drop cap with the same settings in the paragraph below "New Slogan".

k. Open Support_WD_7_Draft.docx, view the draft document side by side with the completed update, scroll the two documents, then close Support_WD_7_Draft and return the Page Movement to Vertical.

l. Set the hyphenation options so that the text in the document is automatically hyphenated.

m. Type your name in the document footer, save the document, submit the document to your instructor, then close the document and exit Word.

Figure 7-32

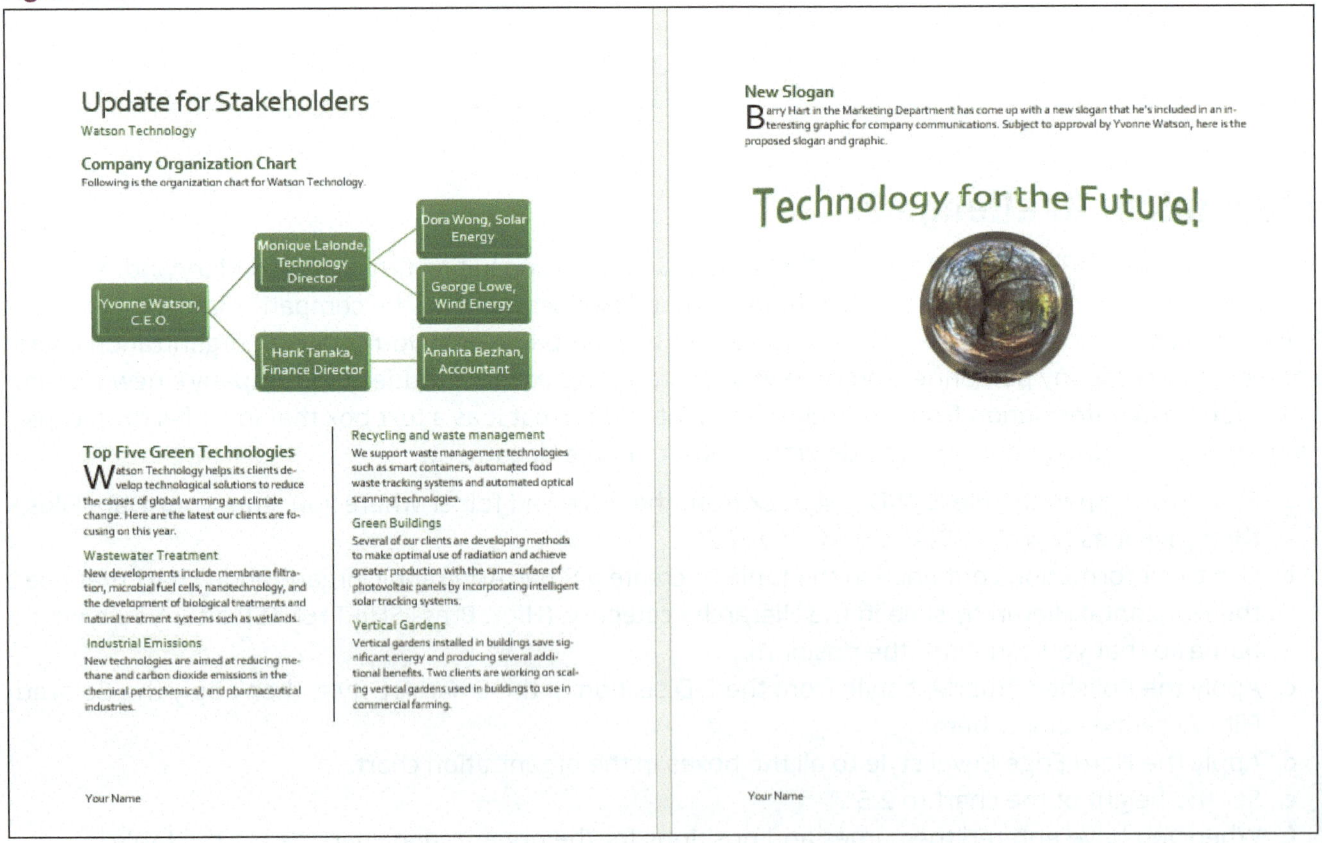

Pixabay/Pexels

Visual Workshop

Open IL_WD_7-5.docx from the drive and folder where you store your Data Files, then save the document as **IL_WD_7_ParkPlan**. Format the text and graphics in the document to match **Figure 7-33**. You will need to move text, create a WordArt object and a picture SmartArt graphic, format selected text in columns, and enclose some of the text in a text box. The WordArt object is formatted with the Fill: Dark Green, Accent color 3; Sharp Bevel and the width of the object increased to 6". To create the picture SmartArt graphic from the four pictures, create a graphic from the first picture (the view of the tent), add three shapes, then cut and paste each picture into a shape. Select the Bending Picture Caption layout, a height of 3.1" and a width of 6". Apply the Gradient Loop – Accent 3 color scheme and the Inset 3-D style. Apply the Subtle Effect, Dark Green, Accent 3 style to the text box. Format the sun shape with the Intense Effect – Orange, Accent 5 style and set the height and width at 1.4". Remember you can move the anchor icon attached to a graphic to help you move objects and text on the page. Add your name to the footer, save the document, submit a copy to your instructor, then close the document and exit Word.

Figure 7-33

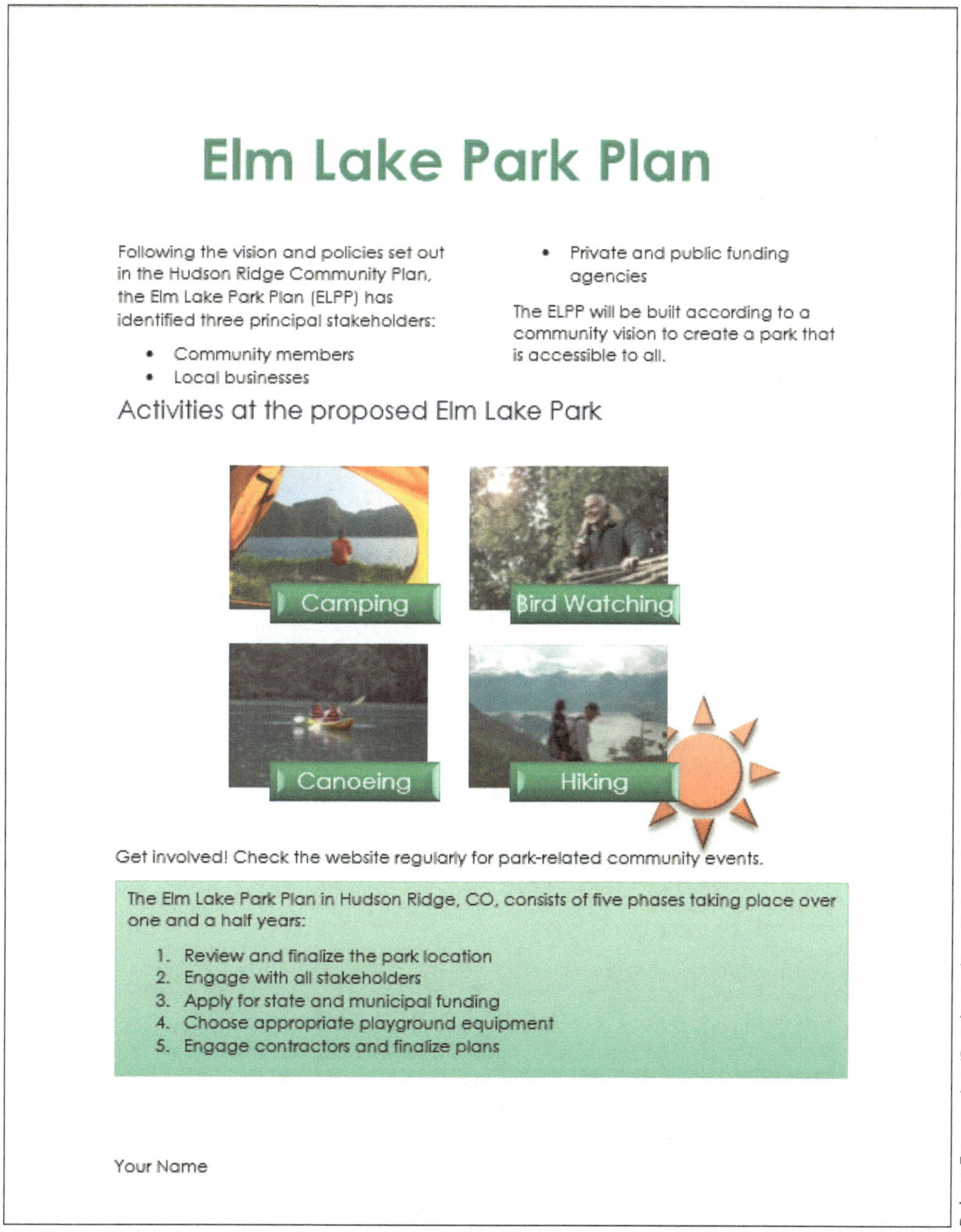

Elm Lake Park Plan

Following the vision and policies set out in the Hudson Ridge Community Plan, the Elm Lake Park Plan (ELPP) has identified three principal stakeholders:

- Community members
- Local businesses
- Private and public funding agencies

The ELPP will be built according to a community vision to create a park that is accessible to all.

Activities at the proposed Elm Lake Park

Camping

Bird Watching

Canoeing

Hiking

Get involved! Check the website regularly for park-related community events.

The Elm Lake Park Plan in Hudson Ridge, CO, consists of five phases taking place over one and a half years:

1. Review and finalize the park location
2. Engage with all stakeholders
3. Apply for state and municipal funding
4. Choose appropriate playground equipment
5. Engage contractors and finalize plans

Your Name

Robert Forever Ago/Pexels; Andrea Piacquadio/Pexels; Shivkumar Sd/Pexels; Josh Willink/Pexels

Integrating with Other Programs and Collaborating

Case

You work in the Office for International Students, which is part of Student Services at Mountain Springs Institute of Technology (MSIT) in Denver, Colorado. One of your colleagues, Marilyn Kendall, has drafted an analysis in a Word document of current international student enrolment. She has asked you to enhance the document with embedded objects from PowerPoint and Excel and charts that you create in Word. You then use collaboration tools in Word to edit questions for a survey aimed at international students who use MSIT student services.

Module Objectives

After completing this module, you will be able to:

- Embed and edit an Excel file
- Insert objects from other programs
- Link an Excel chart
- Link a PowerPoint slide
- Manage links
- Insert charts
- Format and edit charts
- Track changes
- Work with tracked changes
- Manage reviewers
- Compare documents

Files You Will Need

IL_WD_8-1.docx
Support_WD_8-1.xlsx
Support_WD_8-2.xlsx
Support_WD_8-3.pptx
IL_WD_8-2.docx
IL_WD_8-3.docx
IL_WD_8-4.docx
IL_WD_8-5.docx
Support_WD_8-4.xlsx
Support_WD_8-5.xlsx
Support_WD_8-6.pptx
IL_WD_8-6.docx
IL_WD_8-7.docx
IL_WD_8-8.docx
IL_WD_8-9.docx
Support_WD_8-7.xlsx
Support_WD_8-8.pptx
Support_WD_8-9.xlsx
IL_WD_8-10.docx
IL_WD_8-11.docx
Support_WD_8-10.pptx
Support_WD_8-11.xlsx

Embed and Edit an Excel File

Case The Word document contains placeholder text to designate where you need to insert objects. You embed an Excel worksheet listing the eight countries where most international students come from, and then edit the embedded worksheet in Word using Excel tools to provide updated information.

Objectives
- Embed an Excel file
- Edit an embedded Excel file

You embed an object, such as an Excel file, in Word when you want to be able to edit the file in Word. You edit the embedded object directly in Word using commands on the Ribbon associated with Excel, the source program. Because the objects are not connected or linked, the edits you make to an embedded object are not made to the object in the source file, and edits you make to the object in the source file are not made to the embedded object.

Steps

1. **sam Start Word, open the file IL_WD_8-1.docx from the location where you store your Data Files, save it as IL_WD_8_InternationalStudentsReport, then click the Show/Hide button ¶ in the Paragraph group to turn on paragraph marks if they are not displayed**

2. **Delete the placeholder text EXCEL WORKSHEET after the "Programs" paragraph on the first page but not the paragraph mark so a blank line still appears above the page break**

3. **Click the Insert tab, then click the Object button in the Text group**
   The Object dialog box opens. You use the Object dialog box to create a new object using the commands of a program other than Word or to insert an object already created in another program.

4. **Click the Create from File tab, click the Browse button, navigate to the drive and folder where you store your Data Files, click Support_WD_8-1.xlsx, then click Insert**
   The path to the file Support_WD_8-1.xlsx is displayed in the File name box. Because you want to create an embedded object, you leave the Link to file check box blank as shown in **Figure 8-1**.

> **Trouble**
> The Excel ribbon may not open in Word if you already have an Excel workbook open on your system. Close the Excel workbook before proceeding with these steps.

5. **Click OK, then double-click the embedded worksheet object**
   The embedded object opens in an Excel object window, and the Excel Ribbon opens in place of the Word Ribbon. The title bar at the top of the window contains the Word filename, indicating that you are still working within a Word file.

> **Quick Tip**
> Double-click the Excel object when you want to make changes to the data.

6. **Click cell B3, type 150, press ENTER, click cell B11, then click the Bold button B in the Font group on the Excel Ribbon**
   The total number of students entered in cell B11 increases from 628 to 718. Because you did not select the link option when you embedded the Excel file into the Word document, the changes you make to the embedded file are *not* made in the original Excel source file.

> **Trouble**
> If you are working on more than one screen, Excel may open on a different screen. Close the worksheet in Excel after completing Step 9.

7. **Click the Page Layout tab on the Excel Ribbon, click the Themes button in the Themes group, then select Banded**
   You formatted the embedded Excel file with the same theme (Banded) that has been applied to the Word document. The worksheet object appears in Word as shown in **Figure 8-2**.

8. **Click cell A1, then click to the right of the worksheet object to return to Word**
   The Excel Ribbon closes, and the Word Ribbon opens. In Word, the embedded object is part of the paragraph and can be formatted as such.

> **Quick Tip**
> Click the Excel object once to select the object and make changes to the object but not the data.

9. **Click the worksheet object to select it, click the Home tab, click the Center button in the Paragraph group, click anywhere in the Word document to deselect the worksheet object, then save the document**

Figure 8-1: Create from File tab in the Object dialog box

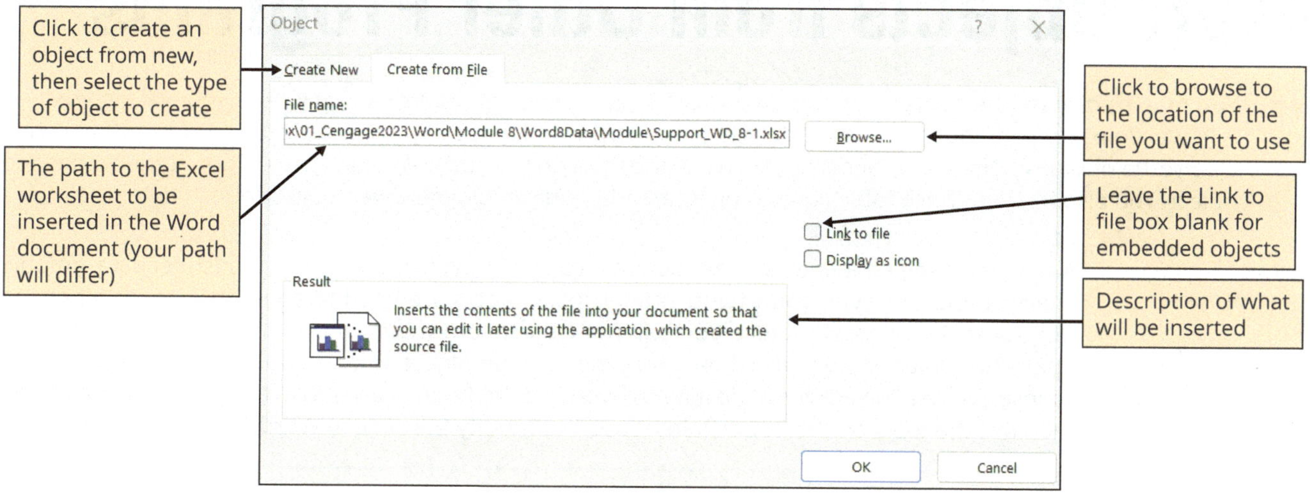

Figure 8-2: Excel worksheet embedded in Word document

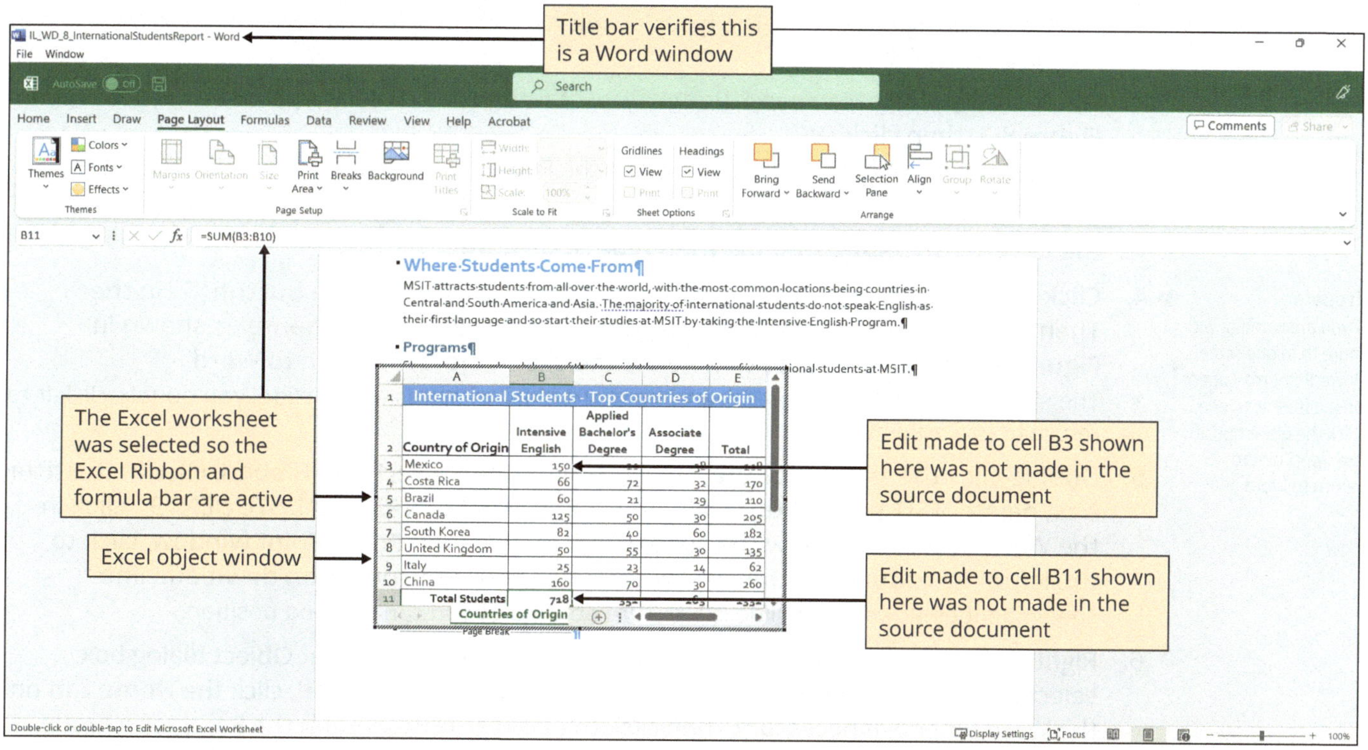

Understanding Object Linking and Embedding

The ability to share information with other programs is called **object linking and embedding (OLE)**. Two programs are involved in the OLE process. The **source program** is the program in which information is originally created, and the **destination program** is the program the information is copied to. An embedded object uses the features of another program such as Excel, but it is stored as part of the Word document.

Insert Objects from Other Programs

Case You plan to discuss the contents of the document at an upcoming staff meeting where you will also deliver a PowerPoint presentation with more details about support services for international students. You insert a PowerPoint slide on the report title page, then use the tools on the PowerPoint Ribbon to format the embedded object. You also insert a Quick Table containing a calendar indicating a new web page's launch date.

Objectives
- Insert a PowerPoint slide
- Insert a Quick Table

An **object** is self-contained information that can be in the form of text, spreadsheet data, graphics, charts, tables, or even sound and video clips. Objects are used to share information between programs. To insert an object, you use the Object command on the Insert tab. This command opens the Object dialog box where you can create an object or insert an existing file as an object. To insert a new PowerPoint slide in Word, you use the Create New tab in the Object dialog box and then use the tools on the PowerPoint Ribbon to modify the slide in Word.

Steps

1. **Press CTRL+HOME to move to the top of the document, click the Insert tab, then click the Object button in the Text group**
   The Object dialog box opens. The types of objects that you can create new in Word are listed in the Object type: list.
2. **Scroll down, select Microsoft PowerPoint Slide in the Object type: list as shown in Figure 8-3, then click OK**
   A blank PowerPoint slide appears along with the PowerPoint Ribbon.
3. **Click the Click to add title box, type Report on MSIT International Students, click the Click to add subtitle box, then type your name**
4. **Click the Design tab on the PowerPoint Ribbon, click the More button in the Themes group to open the Themes gallery, click the Banded theme as shown in Figure 8-4, then click in the text below the slide object to return to Word**
   The slide is inserted into Word as an object. To make changes to the slide, you double-click it to return to PowerPoint.

Trouble
If you are working with more than one screen, PowerPoint may open on a different screen. Click the Close button in PowerPoint to return to Word.

5. **Double-click the slide, click the Design tab on the PowerPoint Ribbon, click in the title box, delete MSIT so the title reads "REPORT ON INTERNATIONAL STUDENTS", click in the Word document below the slide object to close the PowerPoint window, click to the left of Introduction, then press ENTER to move Introduction down one line**
   The embedded PowerPoint slide is a picture object that you can size and position.
6. **Right-click the slide, click Picture, click the Size tab in the Format Object dialog box, select the contents of the Absolute Height box, type 2.7, click OK, click the Home tab on the Word Ribbon, if necessary, then click the Center button in the Paragraph group**
   Another object that you can insert into Word is a Quick Table. You use Quick Tables when you want to choose one of Word's built-in table forms.
7. **Press CTRL+END, scroll up slightly and delete CALENDAR but not the paragraph mark, click the Insert tab, click the Table button, point to Quick Tables to display the gallery of built-in tables, then click Calendar 2**
   A table already formatted as a calendar is inserted into the document. You can modify the formatting of the calendar to make it easier to enter data.
8. **Click the Table Select handle in the top-left corner of the table to select the entire table, drag the right edge of the table so it is even with the text at the right margin, click the Layout tab to the right of the Table Design tab, then click the Distribute Columns button in the Cell Size group**
9. **Click after 3 in the box for May 3, press ENTER, type LAUNCH!, remove the blank line after the table to match Figure 8-5 then save the document**
   The Calendar 2 Quick Table appears as shown in Figure 8-5.

Quick Tip
You can modify the text in the calendar to list the dates for a different month.

Figure 8-3: Create New tab in the Object dialog box

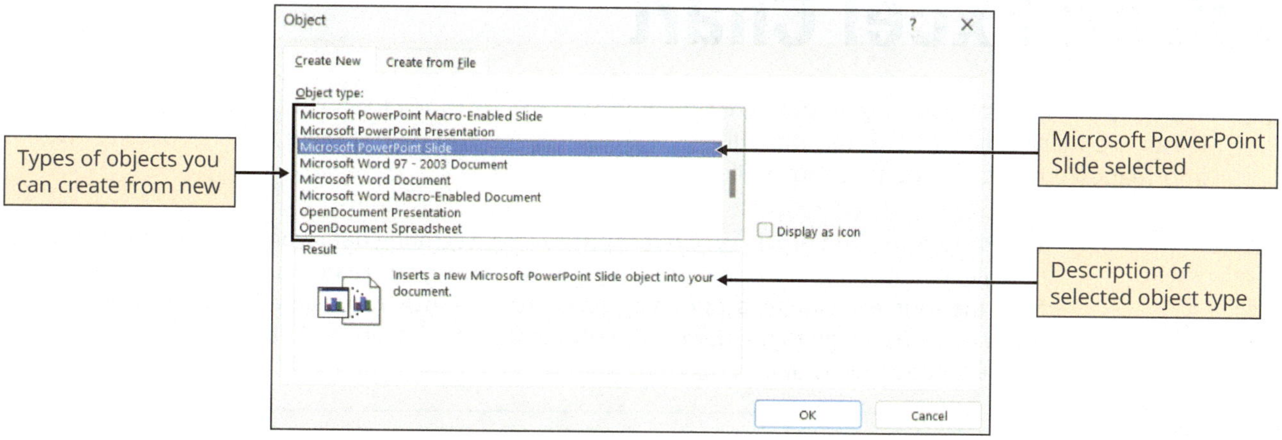

Figure 8-4: Banded theme selected

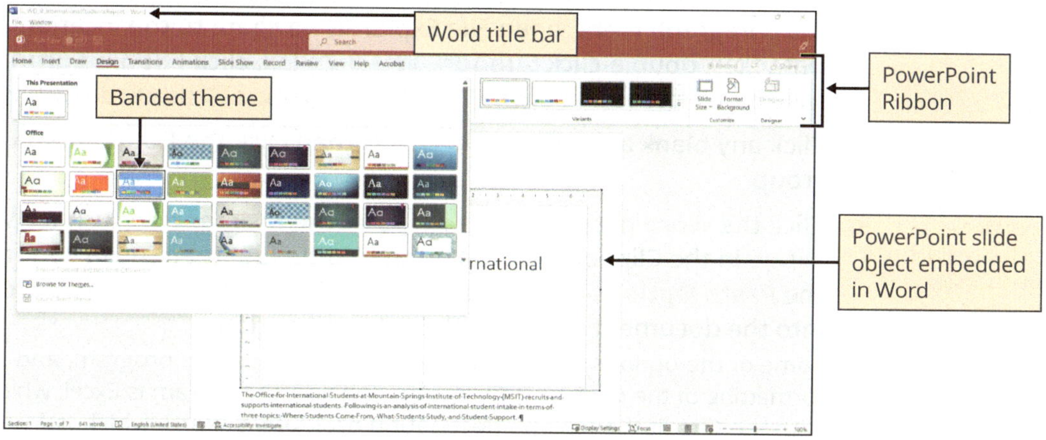

Figure 8-5: Calendar 2 Quick Table inserted and resized

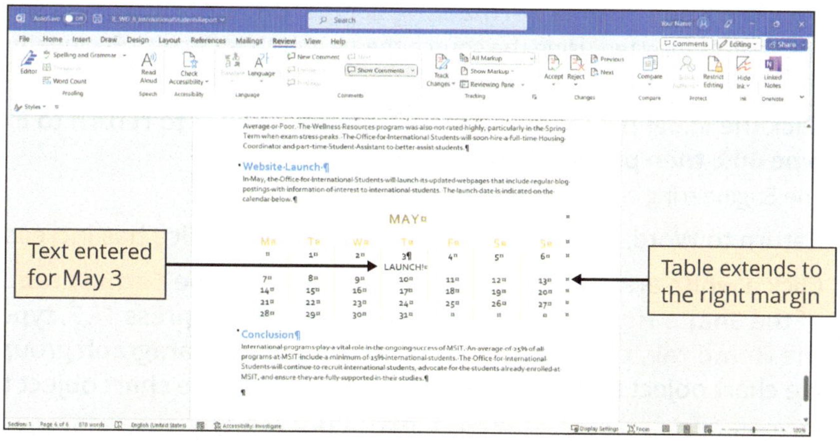

Publishing a blog directly from Word

A blog, which is short for weblog, is an informal journal that is created by an individual or a group and available to the public on the Internet. A blog usually conveys ideas, comments, and opinions and is written using a strong personal voice. The person who creates and maintains a blog, the blogger, typically updates the blog regularly. If you have or want to start a blog, you can configure Word to link to your blog site so that you can write, format, and publish blog entries directly from Word.

To blog directly from Word, you must first obtain a blog account with a blog service provider. Resources, such as the Word Help system and online forums, provide detailed information on obtaining and registering your personal blog account with Word. To create a new blog post, click the File tab, click New, then double-click Blog post (or search for an online template if one does not appear on your New screen) to open a predesigned blog post document that you can customize with your own text, formatting, and images. You can also publish an existing document as a blog post by opening the document, clicking the File tab, clicking Share, and then clicking Post to Blog. In either case, Word prompts you to log onto your personal blog account.

Link an Excel Chart

Case You copy a pie chart illustrating student enrolment in five areas of study from Excel (the source file) and paste it into the Word report (the destination file) as a linked object. You then update the linked object with new information entered in Excel (the source file).

Objectives
- Copy an Excel chart to Word
- Update a linked chart in Word

The Paste command provides several options for integrating data from a source file into a destination file. When you select one of the paste link options, you create a linked object. The data copied from the source file in one program is pasted as a link into the destination file in another program. If you make a change to the data in the source file, the data in the linked object that you copied to the destination file is updated.

Steps

1. **Press CTRL+HOME, scroll to page 2 and delete AREAS OF STUDY PIE CHART, but not the paragraph mark, open File Explorer, navigate to the location where you store your Data files, double-click Support_WD_8-2.xlsx, click Enable Editing if prompted, then save it in Excel as Support_WD_8_InternationalStudyAreas**

2. **Click any blank area of the pie chart, then click the Copy button in the Clipboard group**

Trouble
Be sure a solid border with sizing handles surrounds the pie chart and all its related components. If only one component is selected, click outside the chart area, then repeat Step 2.

3. **Click the Word program button on the taskbar to return to Word, click the Paste arrow in the Clipboard group on the Home tab, then move your mouse over each of the Paste Options to read each ScreenTip and preview how the chart will be pasted into the document based on the selected option**
   Some of the options retain the formatting of the source program, and some options adopt the formatting of the destination program. The source program is Excel, which is currently formatted with the Circuit theme. The destination program is Word, which is formatted with the Banded theme.

4. **Click the Keep Source Formatting & Link Data (F) button as shown in Figure 8-6**
   The chart is inserted using the source theme, which is Circuit. "Engineering" (the green slice) is the chosen area of study for 28% of the international students.

5. **Click the Excel program button on the taskbar to return to Excel, click cell B2, type 400, then press ENTER**
   The Engineering slice increases to 35%.

6. **Return to Word, then verify that the Engineering slice has increased to 35%**

Trouble
If the pie chart did not update, click the chart, click the Chart Design tab, and then click the Refresh Data button in the Data group.

7. **Click a white area inside the chart border, click the Format tab, select the contents of the Shape Height box in the Size group, type 4, press TAB, type 6, press ENTER, click the Home tab, click the Center button in the Paragraph group, click away from the pie chart object to deselect it, then compare the pie chart object to Figure 8-7**

Trouble
If the Shape Width box is dim and does not accept a value, click to the right of the chart and click the chart border again to be sure the entire chart object is selected.

8. **Click the Excel program button on the taskbar, save and close the workbook, then exit Excel**
   The IL_WD_8_InternationalStudentsReport.docx file in Word is again the active document.

9. **Save the document**

Figure 8-6: Selecting a link paste option

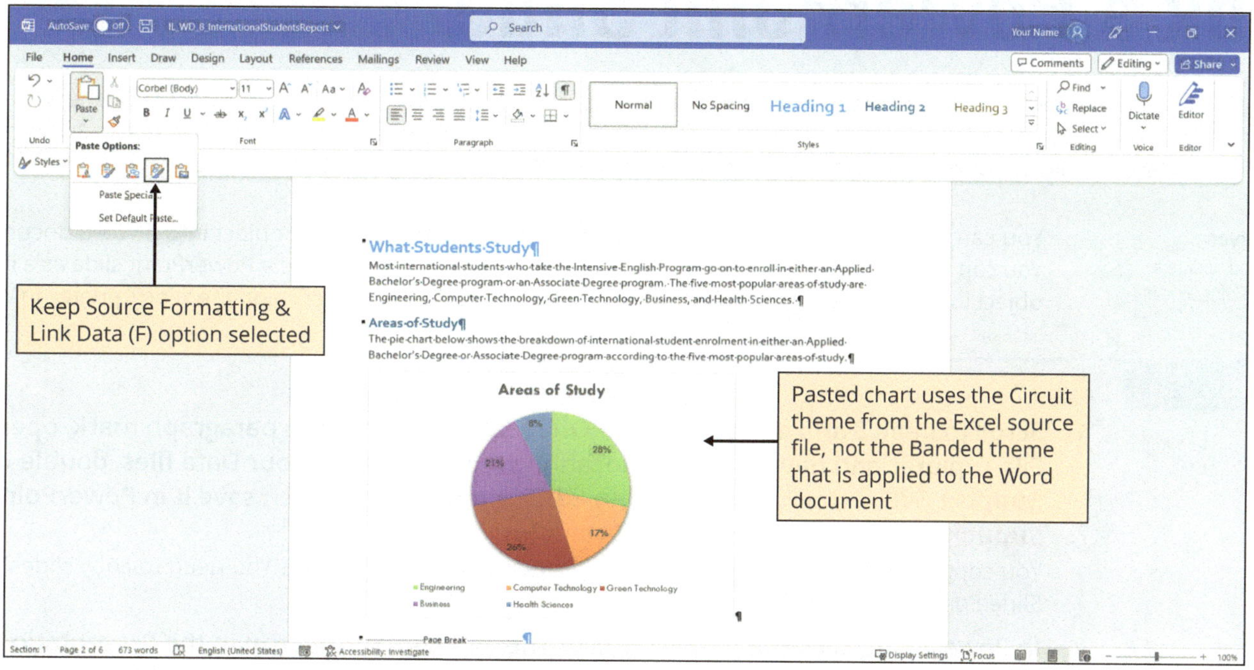

Figure 8-7: Linked pie chart updated in Word

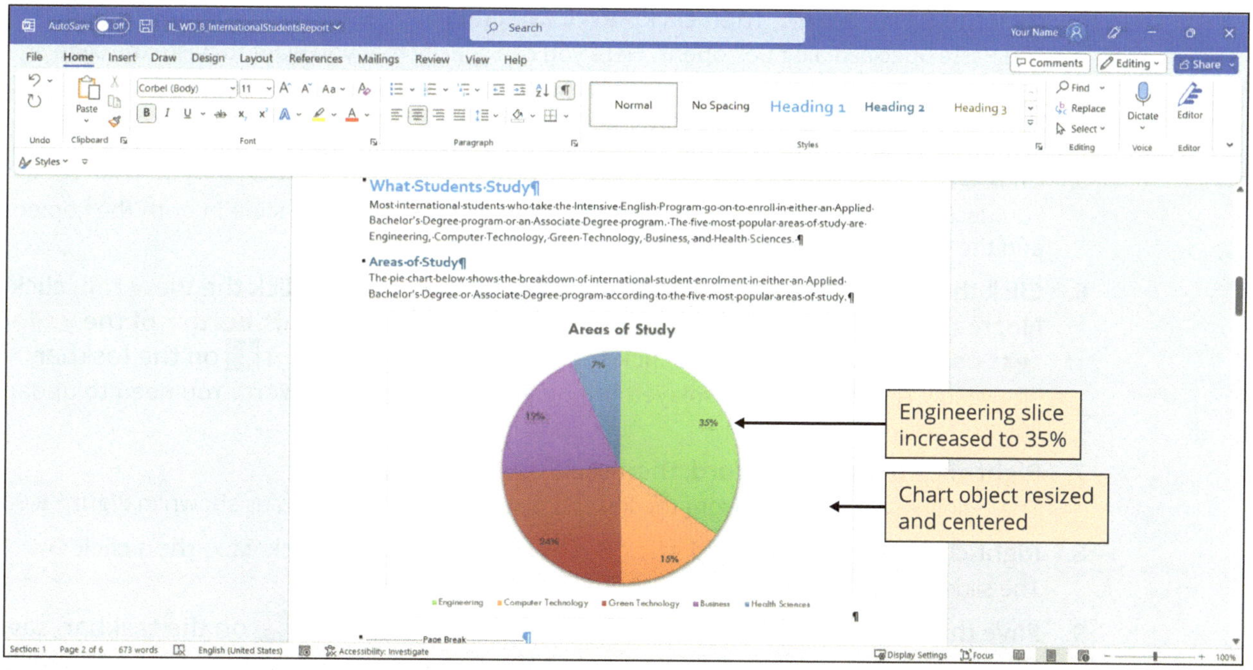

Using the Object dialog box to create a linked file

In addition to using the Paste options, you can create a linked object using the Object dialog box. You open the Object dialog box by clicking Object in the Text group on the Insert tab and then clicking the Create from File tab. You click the Browse button to navigate to and then select the file you want to link, click the Link to file check box to be sure that box is active (has a check mark), and then click OK. The file you select is inserted in the destination file as a linked object.

You create a linked object using one of the options available on the Paste menu when you want to copy only a portion of a file, such as selected cells or a chart in an Excel worksheet. You create a linked object using the Link to file check box in the Object dialog box when you want to insert the entire file, such as the entire worksheet in an Excel file.

Link a PowerPoint Slide

Case You open a PowerPoint presentation that contains a slide displaying the new image proposed for the opening page of the updated international student support website, copy the slide into Word and paste it as a link, then update the file in PowerPoint so that it also updates in Word.

Objectives
- Link and update a PowerPoint Slide in Word

You can use the Paste Special command to insert a slide as a linked object into a Word document. You can also use the Create New tab in the Object dialog box to create a PowerPoint slide as a linked object in Word. When you make changes to the linked slide in PowerPoint, the slide updates in Word.

Steps

1. **Scroll to page 3 and delete POWERPOINT SLIDE, but not the paragraph mark, open File Explorer and navigate to the location where you store your Data files, double-click Support_WD_8-3.pptx, click Enable Editing if prompted, then save it in PowerPoint as Support_WD_8_InternationalWebpageImage**

   You copy the slide from PowerPoint and paste it as a link into Word. You need to copy slides from Slide Sorter view in PowerPoint.

2. **In PowerPoint, click the View tab, click the Slide Sorter button in the Presentation Views group, click the Home tab, then click the Copy button in the Clipboard group**

3. **Click the Word Program button on the taskbar to return to the report in Word, click the Paste arrow, then click Paste Special**

   The Paste Special dialog box opens. Here you can specify that you want to paste the slide as a link.

4. **Click Microsoft PowerPoint Slide Object, then click the Paste link option button as shown in Figure 8-8**

5. **Click OK**

   You decide that you want to remove the yellow text box from the slide in both the copied slide and the original slide in PowerPoint.

6. **Click the PowerPoint program button on the taskbar, click the View tab, click the Normal button in the Presentation Views group, click the left border of the yellow text box, press DELETE, then click the Word program button on the taskbar**

   The yellow text box is still displayed on the PowerPoint slide in Word. You need to update the linked slide.

7. **Right-click the slide in Word, then click Update Link**

   The yellow box is removed from the linked PowerPoint slide in Word as shown in **Figure 8-9**.

8. **Right-click the slide in Word, click Borders and Shading, click Box, then click OK**

   The slide is enclosed in a border in Word.

9. **Save the document, click the PowerPoint program button on the taskbar, save the PowerPoint presentation, then click the Word program button on the taskbar**

   You are returned to the document in Word.

Figure 8-8: Paste Special dialog box

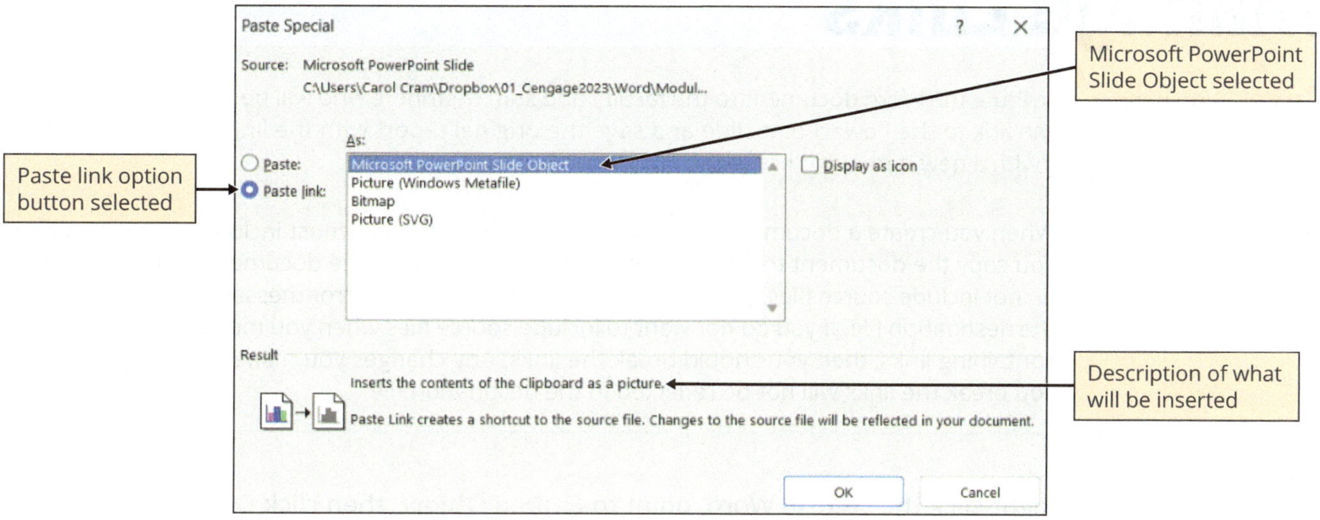

Figure 8-9: PowerPoint slide copied into Word as a link

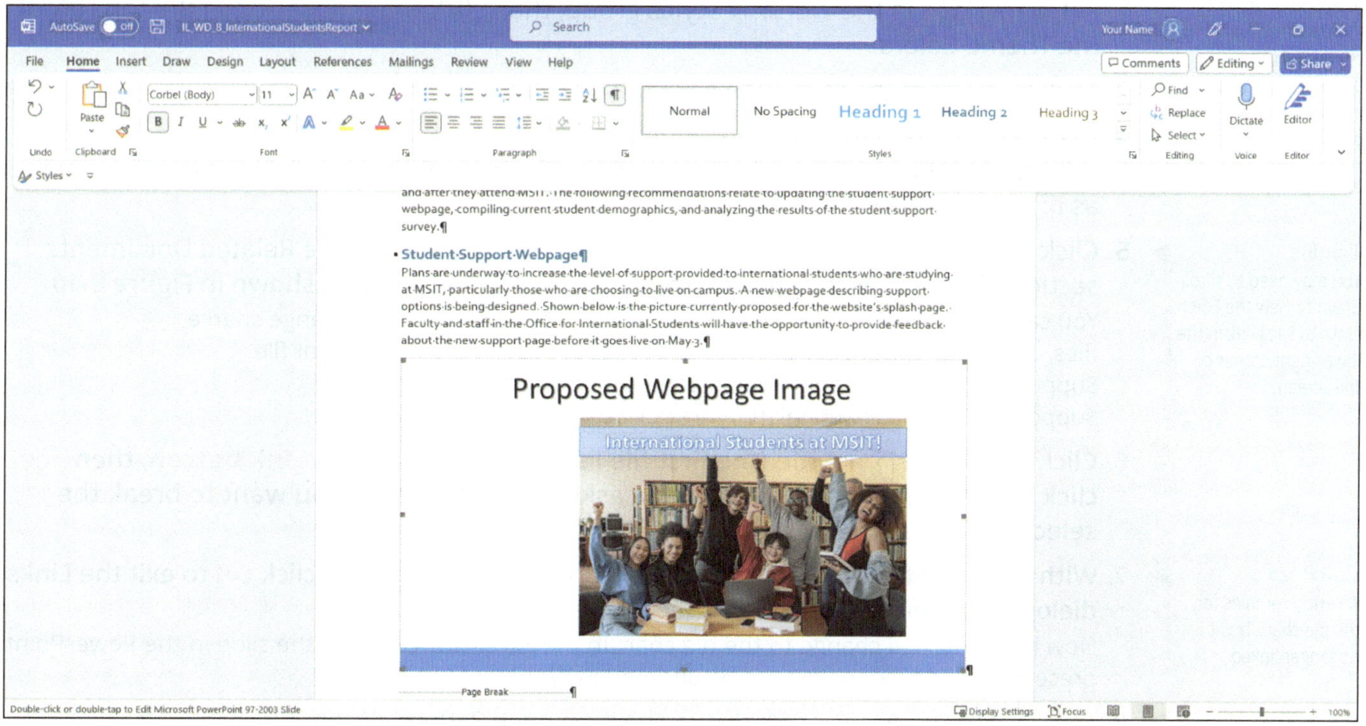

Yan Krukau/Pexels

Creating a PowerPoint presentation from a Word outline

When you create a PowerPoint presentation from a Word outline, the Word document is the source file and the PowerPoint document is the destination file. Headings formatted with heading styles in the Word source file are converted to PowerPoint headings in the PowerPoint destination file. For example, each line of text formatted with the Heading 1 style becomes its own slide. To create a PowerPoint presentation from a Word outline, create and then save the outline in Word, close the document, then launch PowerPoint. In PowerPoint, click the New Slide list arrow, click Slides from Outline, navigate to the location where you stored the Word document, then double-click the filename. The Word outline is converted to a PowerPoint presentation, which you can modify in the same way you modify any PowerPoint presentation. Any changes you make to the presentation in PowerPoint are *not* reflected in the original Word document.

Manage Links

Case You need to distribute the Word document to the faculty and staff members who will be attending the meeting. First, you edit the link to the PowerPoint slide and save the original report with the links intact, and then you save the report with a new name and break the links.

Objectives
- Edit a link to a file
- Break links

When you create a document that contains linked objects, you must include all source files when you copy the document to a new location or when you email the document to a colleague. If you do not include source files, you (or your colleague) will receive error messages when trying to open the destination file. If you do not want to include source files when you move or email a document containing links, then you should break the links. Any changes you make to the source files after you break the links will not be reflected in the destination file.

Steps

1. **Right-click the slide in Word, point to Linked Object, then click Open Link**
   You make additional changes to the slide in PowerPoint.
2. **Select the text Proposed Webpage Image, click the Shape Format tab, click the Text Fill arrow in the WordArt Styles group, then click Blue, Accent 2 in the top row of the Theme Colors**
3. **Click away from the text, then save the presentation**
4. **Return to Word, right-click the slide in Word, click Update Link, add your name where indicated in the document footer, save the document, then save the document again as IL_WD_8_InternationalStudentsReport_Meeting**
5. **Click the File tab, click Info, then click Edit Links to Files in the Related Documents section of the Properties pane to open the Links dialog box as shown in Figure 8-10**
   You can use the Links dialog box to update links, open source files, change source files, and break existing links. Two source files are listed: the PowerPoint file Support_WD_8_InternationalWebpageImage.pptx and the Excel file Support_WD_8_InternationalStudyAreas.xlsx.
6. **Click the PowerPoint file (the first file listed), click the Break Link button, then click Yes in response to the message asking if you are sure you want to break the selected link**
7. **With the Excel file selected click Break Link button, click Yes, click OK to exit the Links dialog box, then click to exit Backstage view**
   Now if you make a change to the pie chart in the Excel source file or the slide in the PowerPoint presentation, neither object will be updated in Word.
8. **Scroll up to the Areas of Study pie chart on page 2, then click the pie chart**
   The Word Ribbon is still active, and the chart contextual tabs are available. When you broke the link to the source file, Word converted the pie chart from a linked object to a chart object.
9. **Click the Chart Design tab, click the More button in the Chart Styles group, click Style 9, save the document, then compare it to Figure 8-11**
   The Style 9 chart style is applied to the chart and the theme is updated to match the theme of the document (Banded).
10. **Click the PowerPoint program button on the taskbar, then exit PowerPoint**

Quick Tip
After you break links, the Update Links command cannot be used to update information in the destination file.

Trouble
You may need to scroll down to view the Edit Links to Files link in the lower-right corner of the screen.

Quick Tip
An entry remains for the pie chart, but it is no longer linked.

Quick Tip
You can use commands on the Chart Design and Format tabs to modify the chart object, but you cannot change the content of the pie chart.

Figure 8-10: Links dialog box

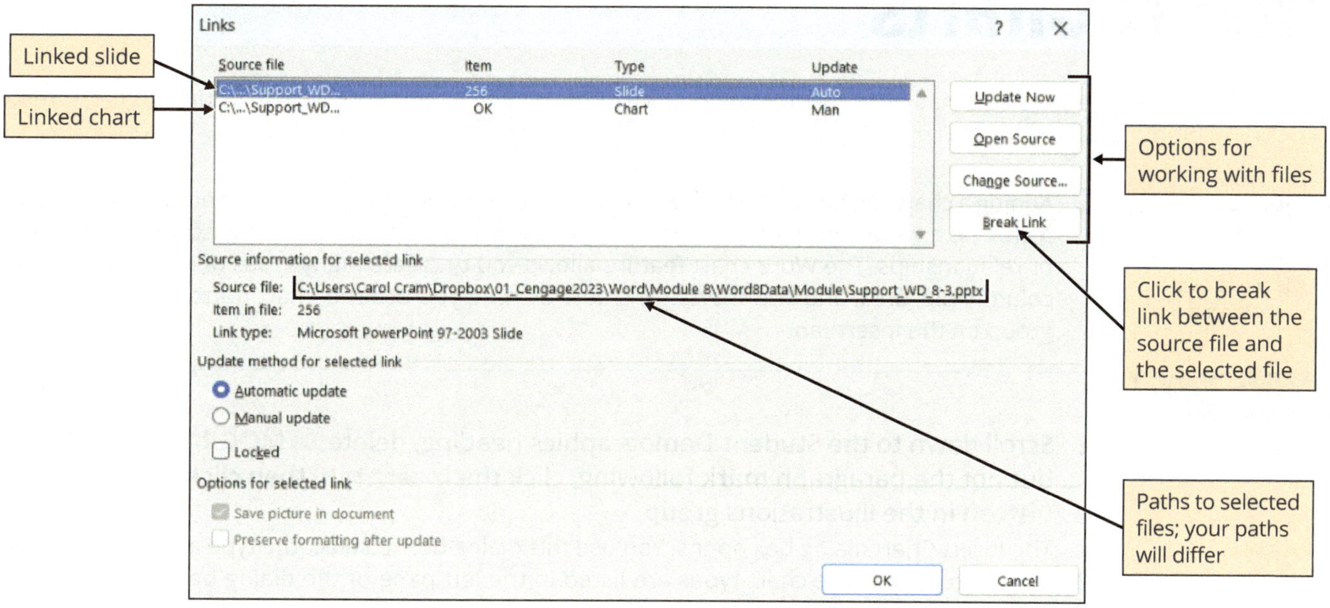

Figure 8-11: Formatted pie chart

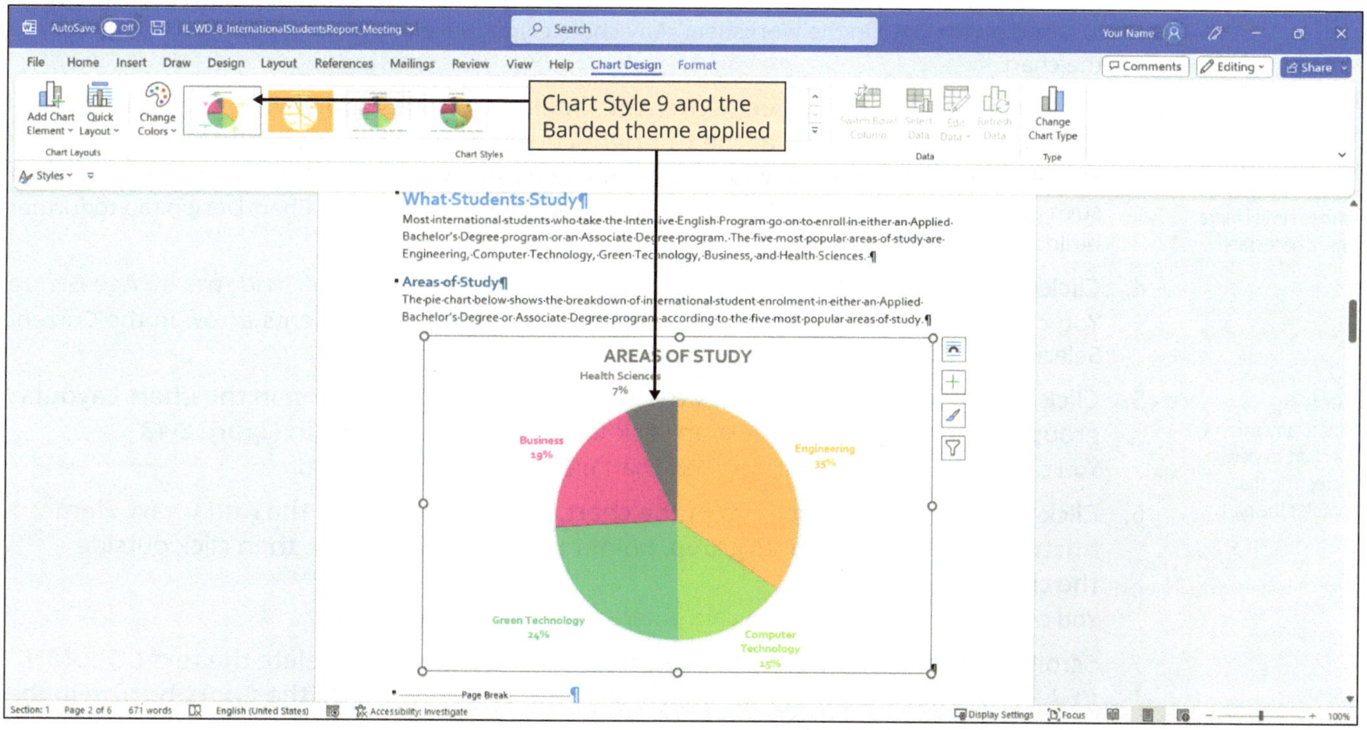

Insert Charts

Case You create a pie chart that illustrates the breakdown of international students by age group and then create a column chart from data contained in a table in the Word document.

Objectives
- Insert a pie chart
- Insert a column chart
- Add and remove chart elements

Adding a chart can be an effective way to illustrate a document that includes numerical information. A **chart** is a visual representation of numerical data and usually is used to illustrate trends, patterns, or relationships. The Word chart feature allows you to create many types of charts, including bar, column, pie, area, and line charts. To create a chart, you use the Chart button in the Illustrations group on the Insert tab.

Steps

1. **Scroll down to the Student Demographics heading, delete DEMOGRAPHIC PIE CHART but not the paragraph mark following, click the Insert tab, then click the Chart button in the Illustrations group**
   The Insert Chart dialog box opens. You use this dialog box to select the type and style of chart you intend to create. The chart types are listed in the left pane of the dialog box, and the styles for each chart type are listed in the right pane. You want to create a pie chart.
2. **Click Pie, then click OK**
   A worksheet opens in the Microsoft Word window, and a pie chart appears in the document. The worksheet and the chart contain placeholder data that you replace with your own data. The chart is based on the data in the worksheet. Any change you make to the data is made automatically to the chart.

Trouble
Drag the bottom or a corner of the worksheet object down to reveal more rows, if necessary.

3. **Click cell A1 in the worksheet, enter the labels and values shown in Figure 8-12, then click the Close button ☒ at the top-right corner of the Excel worksheet**
   The pie chart appears in the Word document. You can add additional elements to the pie chart such as a chart title and data labels. You work with the options on the Chart Design tab to further build the pie chart.
4. **Click the chart title Students to select it, then type International Students by Age Group**
   You can click any chart element to select it or use the Chart Elements arrow in the Current Selection group on the Format tab to select a chart element.

Quick Tip
Point to any part of a chart to view a ScreenTip that identifies the part.

5. **Click the Chart Design tab, click the Add Chart Element button in the Chart Layouts group, point to Data Labels, then click Outside End as shown in Figure 8-13**
   You can also remove and then reinsert chart elements such as a legend.
6. **Click the legend at the bottom of the chart, press DELETE, click the Add Chart Element button in the Chart Layouts group, point to Legend, click Right, then click outside the chart**
   You create a column chart from data entered in a table in the report.
7. **Scroll to "Student Support Survey Results" on the next page, delete the text COLUMN CHART, but not the paragraph mark, click the Insert tab, click the Chart button in the Illustrations group, then click OK**
   By default, a clustered column chart is inserted. You need to designate the data in the table as the data required for the column chart.
8. **Scroll up, click in the table, click the Table Select handle ⊞ to select all the text in the table, press CTRL+X to cut the table from the Word document, click cell A1 in the Excel worksheet, then press CTRL+V to paste the chart data into the Excel worksheet**
9. **Right-click a cell in column D, point to Delete, click Table Columns, close the Excel worksheet, click the chart title, type International Student Ages, compare the chart to Figure 8-14, then save the document**
   In the next lesson, you will further enhance both of the charts you created in this lesson.

Figure 8-12: Data for pie chart

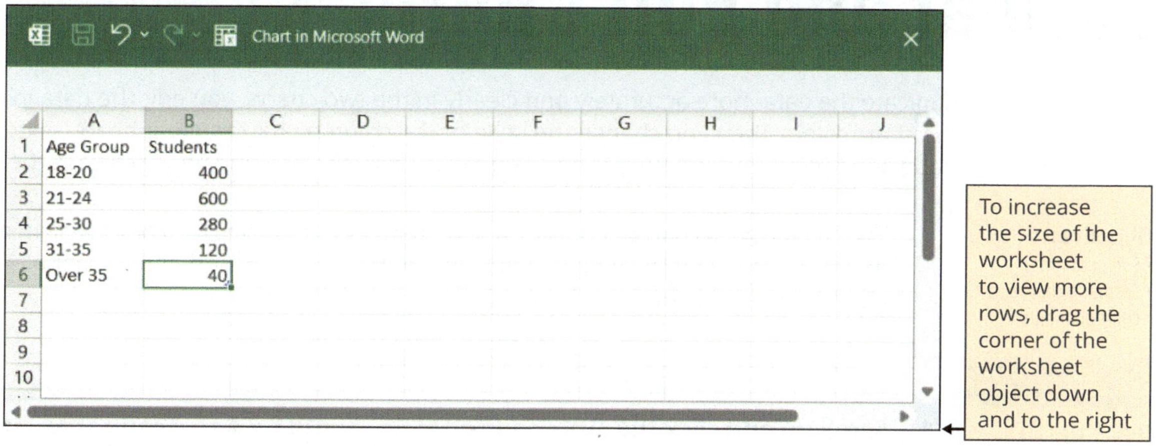

Figure 8-13: Adding data labels to a chart

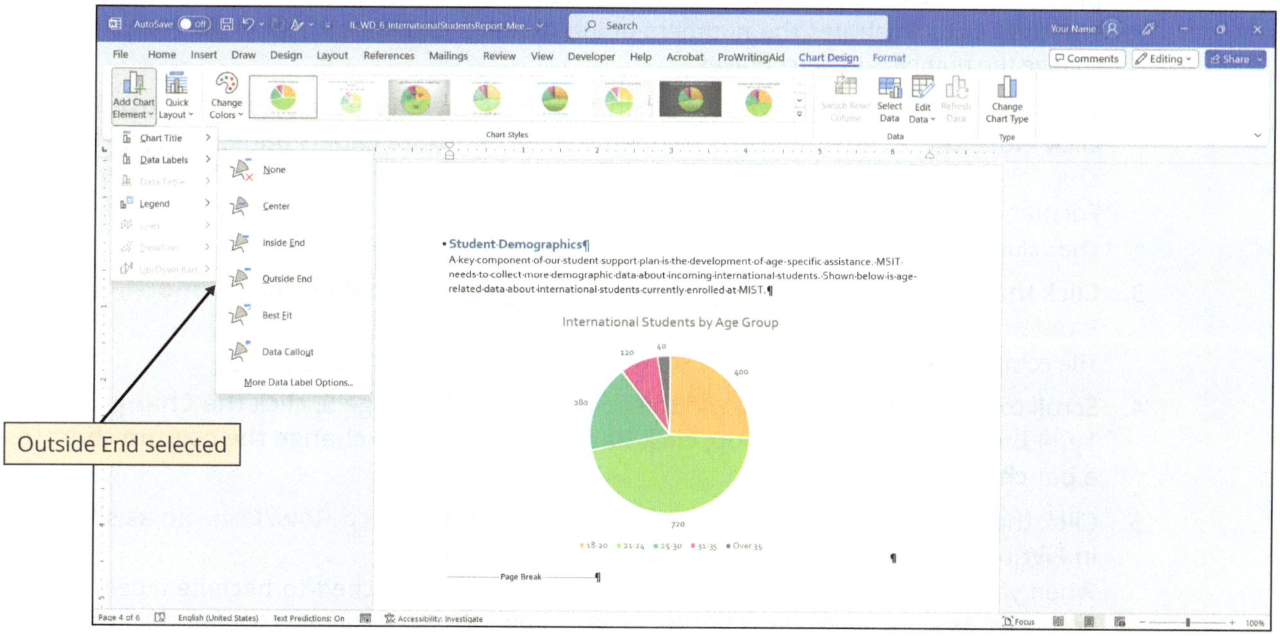

Figure 8-14: Column chart created in Word

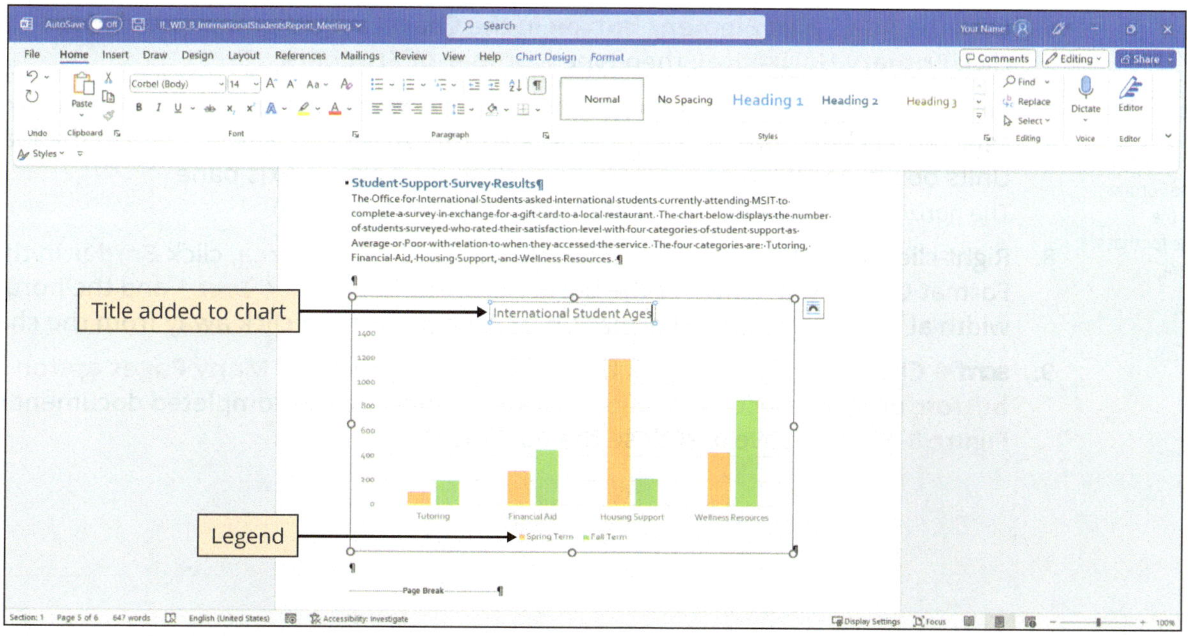

Format and Edit Charts

Case To communicate the data more accurately and clearly in the two charts, you edit the data in the pie chart and change the chart colors, then you change the style of the column chart to a bar chart, switch chart rows and columns, add and format an axis and axis title, change the chart colors, and finally enclose the chart in a border.

Objectives
- Edit chart data
- Format a chart and chart elements

You can format a chart by applying a new chart style, changing the colors assigned to chart elements, and even changing the type of chart. In addition, you can add and format a chart axis and add a chart border, then edit chart data.

Steps

Quick Tip
You can resize a chart in Word like any other graphic object.

1. Scroll up and click the **"International Students by Age Group" pie chart**, click the **Chart Design tab**, click the **Edit Data button** in the Data group, click cell **B3**, type **720**, press **ENTER**, then close the Excel worksheet
   The chart data illustrates the numbers of international students in each age group. You can change the numbers to percentages.
2. Click the **Add Chart Element button** in the Chart Layouts group, point to **Data Labels**, click **More Data Label Options** to open the Format Data Labels pane, click the **Value check box** to deselect it, click the **Percentage check box** to select it, then close the Format Data Labels pane
   The values are converted to percentages. You can change the colors of the chart.
3. Click the **Change Colors button** in the Chart Styles group, then click **Monochromatic Palette 1 (Gold gradient, dark to light)**
   The completed pie chart appears as shown in **Figure 8-15**.
4. Scroll to and click a blank area of the **column chart** on page 5, click the **Change Chart Type button** in the Type group, click **Bar**, then click **OK** to change the column chart to a bar chart
5. Click the **Select Data button** in the Data group, click **Switch Row/Column** as shown in **Figure 8-16**, then click **OK** and close the Excel window
   When you switch rows and columns, the series data is switched to become labels for the horizontal axis, and data on the horizontal axis is now the series data. In the bar chart, the chart displays "Fall Term" and "Spring Term", etc. on the vertical axis and the number of students on the horizontal axis.

Quick Tip
To format any chart element, select it, then click the Format Selection button in the Current Selection group on the Format tab to open the Format pane for that chart element.

6. Click the **Add Chart Element button** in the Chart Layouts group, point to **Axis Titles**, click **Primary Horizontal**, then type **Number of Students**
7. Right-click any **number** on the **horizontal axis**, verify all the numbers on the axis are selected, click **Format Axis** to open the Format Axis pane, select **200.0** in the Major Units box, type **100**, press **ENTER**, then close the Format Axis pane
   The horizontal axis now displays increments of 100 instead of 200.
8. Right-click a blank area in the **chart**, click **Format Chart Area**, click **Border** in the Format Chart Area pane, set the border color to **Dark Gray**, **Text 1** and the border width at **1.25 pt**, close the Format Chart Area pane, then click away from the chart
9. sam Click the **View tab**, click the **Zoom button**, click the **Many Pages option button**, drag to select **2 x 3 pages**, click **OK**, compare the completed document to **Figure 8-17**, then save and close the document

Figure 8-15: Edited pie chart

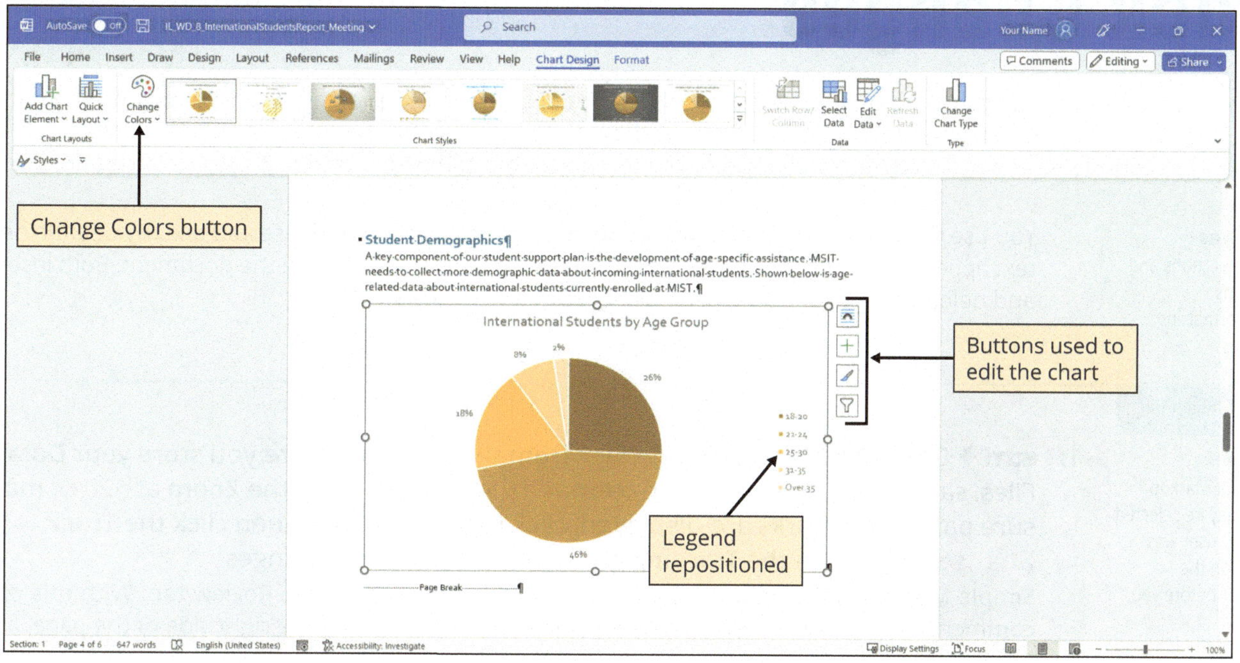

Figure 8-16: Select Data Source dialog box

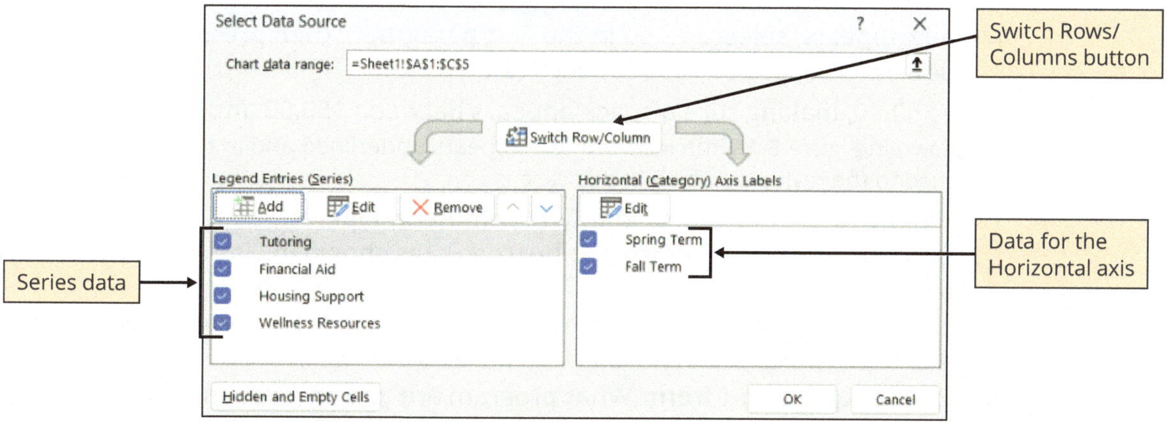

Figure 8-17: Completed report

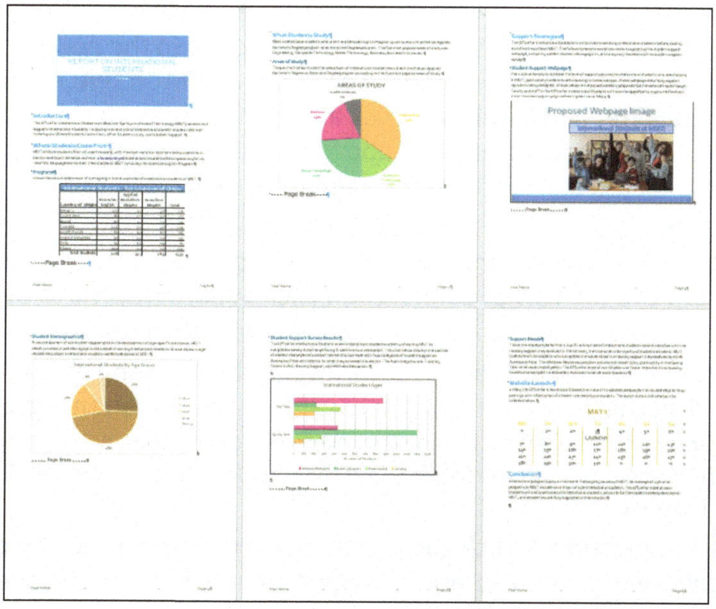

Yan Krukau/Pexels

Track Changes

Case You open questions for an online survey of international students attending MSIT. The document contains comments and changes made by Marilyn Kendall, the director of the Office for International Students. You review her comments and make additional changes to the text and some of the formatting. All these changes are tracked.

Objectives
- Track insertions and deletions
- Track formatting changes

You use the Track Changes command to indicate deleted text and inserted text. By default, deleted text appears as ~~strikethrough~~ and inserted text appears underlined in the document. Both insertions and deletions appear in the color assigned to the reviewer.

Steps

Trouble
A different markup option may be selected if another user was working on the computer before you.

1. **sam Open the file IL_WD_8-2.docx from the location where you store your Data Files, save it as IL_WD_8_InternationalStudentSurvey, set the Zoom at 120%, make sure paragraph marks are displayed, click the Review tab, then click the Track Changes button in the Tracking group to turn on Track Changes**
   Simple Markup is the default option in the Tracking group on the Review tab. With this option, comment icons and the comments they represent appear along the right side of the page, and no other tracked changes appear. When the Track Changes button is active, every change you make to the document will appear in colored text.
2. **Click Simple Markup in the Tracking group, click All Markup, or verify that All Markup already appears, select $30.00 in the first paragraph, then press DELETE**
   The deleted text appears as strikethrough text.
3. **Type $50.00, making sure a space appears between $50.00 and "gift card"**
   As shown in Figure 8-18, the inserted text appears underlined and in the same color as the color assigned to the reviewer, which in this case is you.
4. **Click in the Reply box below Marilyn's comment, type OK, click the Post Reply button, click the More thread actions button as shown in Figure 8-19, then click Resolve Thread**
   The comment is grayed out and the comment button to the right of the first paragraph now includes a check mark to indicate that the comment has been.
5. **Select all of question 1 from "What program are you enrolled in at MSIT" to "Associate Degree" including the paragraph mark, click the Home tab, then click the Cut button in the Clipboard group**
   The text you selected appears as deleted text, and the subsequent questions have been renumbered.

Quick Tip
You press BACKSPACE to remove a lettered line in a list and to leave a blank line.

6. **Click after More than 10 times in the last option in the new question 1, press ENTER, click the Paste button in the Clipboard group, press BACKSPACE and then DELETE to remove the extra letter and blank line, click after More than 10 times, press ENTER, then press BACKSPACE to add a blank line above question 2 and remove the extra lettered line**
   Both the cut text and the pasted text appear in a new color and are double-underlined.
7. **Select the document title, click the Increase Font Size button in the Font group two times to increase the font to 20 pt, click the Font Color arrow, select Blue, Text 2 in the top row of colors, then click in paragraph 1 to deselect the text**
   The formatting changes appear next to the newly formatted text.
8. **Click the Review tab, click All Markup in the Tracking group, click Simple Markup, then click the Show Comments button in the Comments group to deselect it**
   A bar appears in the left margin next to every line of text that includes a change, and a blank comment icon in the right margin next to any line that includes a comment. Notice that the resolved comment is not included.
9. **Scroll to Question 4, click the Comment icon to read the comment by Marilyn Kendall, select received and change it to accessed, then save the document**
   The new text is inserted.

Figure 8-18: Text inserted with Track Changes feature active

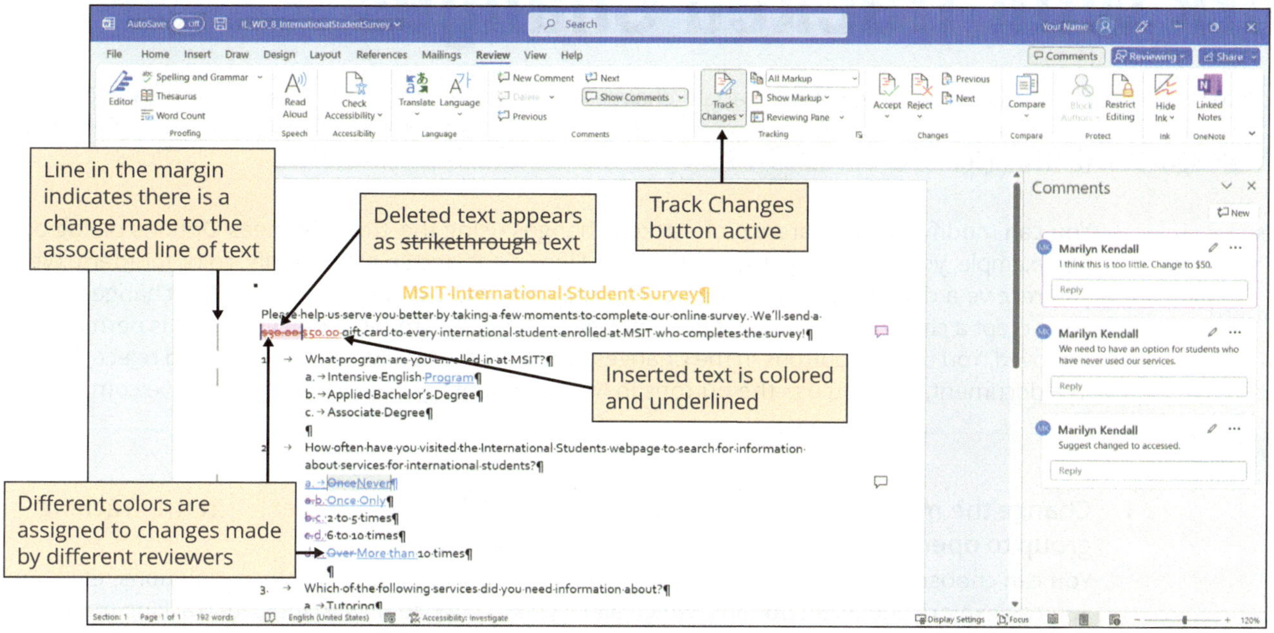

Figure 8-19: Resolving a Comment thread

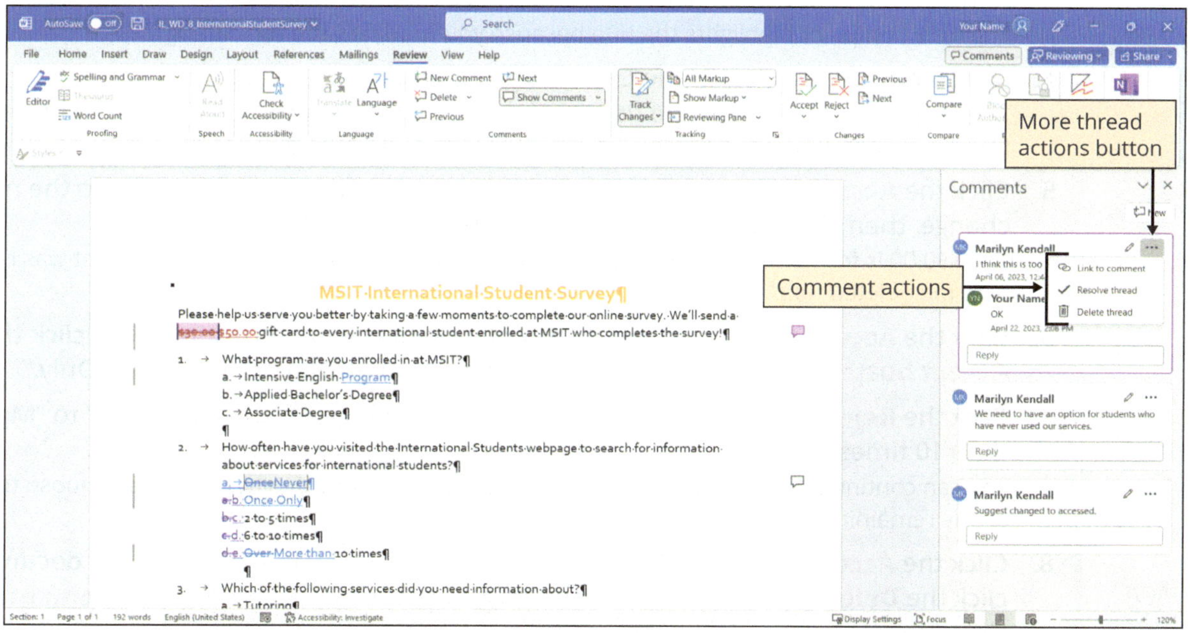

Using Paste and Paste All with tracked changes

If Track Changes is on when you are pasting items from the Clipboard, each item you paste is inserted in the document as a tracked change. If you cut an individual item and then paste it from the Clipboard into a new location, the item is inserted in a new color and with double underlining, which indicates that the item has been moved. If, however, you use the Paste All button on the Clipboard pane to paste all the items on the Clipboard at once, the items are pasted in the document as inserted text at the location of the insertion point. When you use the Paste All button, the items are pasted in the order in which you collected them, from the first item you collected (the item at the bottom of the Clipboard) to the most recent item you collected (the item at the top of the Clipboard).

Work with Tracked Changes

Case You decide to modify the appearance of the tracked changes in the document so they are easier to identify. You then accept or reject the tracked changes and remove all the comments so you have a clean copy for sending to colleagues for further input.

Objectives
- Change Track Changes options
- Accept and reject changes

You can modify the appearance of tracked changes using the Track Changes Options dialog box. For example, you can change the formatting of insertions and select a specific color for them. When you receive a document containing tracked changes, you can accept or reject the changes. When you accept a change, inserted text becomes part of the document and deleted text is permanently removed. You use the buttons in the Changes group on the Review tab to accept and reject changes in a document, and you use the buttons in the Comments group to find and remove comments.

Steps

1. **Change the markup back to All Markup, then click the Launcher in the Tracking group to open the Track Changes Options dialog box**
   You can choose which tracking methods to indicate (formatting, insertions, deletions, etc.), and you can explore advanced options, which allow you to choose how to indicate tracking methods.
2. **Click Advanced Options, click the Insertions arrow, click Double underline as shown in Figure 8-20, click OK, then click OK**
3. **Press CTRL+HOME, then click the Next Change button in the Changes group to move to the first tracked change in the document**
   The insertion point highlights the title because you modified the formatting.
4. **Click the Accept arrow in the Changes group, then click Accept and Move to Next**
   The formatting changes to the title are accepted, and the insertion point moves to the next tracked change, which is deleted text ($30.00) in the first paragraph.
5. **Click the Accept button to accept the deletion and automatically move to the next change, then click the Accept button again to accept $50.00**
   The $50.00 is formatted as black text to indicate it has been accepted. The comment was removed with the deleted text.
6. **Click the Accept button to accept the deletion of the first question, then click the Accept button twice more to accept the insertion of "Never" and "Once Only."**
7. **Click the Reject button two times to reject the change of "Over 10 times" to "More than 10 times"**
   You can continue to review and accept or reject changes individually, or you can choose to accept all the remaining changes in the document.
8. **Click the Accept arrow, click Accept All Changes, scroll to the end of the document, click the Delete arrow in the Comments group, then click Delete All Comments in Document**
   All the tracked changes in the document are accepted, including the question that was moved and renumbered, and the last comment removed.
9. **sam Scroll to the bottom of the document, click the Track Changes button in the Tracking group to turn off Track Changes, type your name where indicated in the footer, close the footer, view the document in One Page view, compare it to Figure 8-21, then save and close the document, but do not exit Word**

Quick Tip
You should always review all changes and comments before you use any of the Accept All Changes or Delete All Comments commands.

Figure 8-20: Advanced Track Changes dialog box

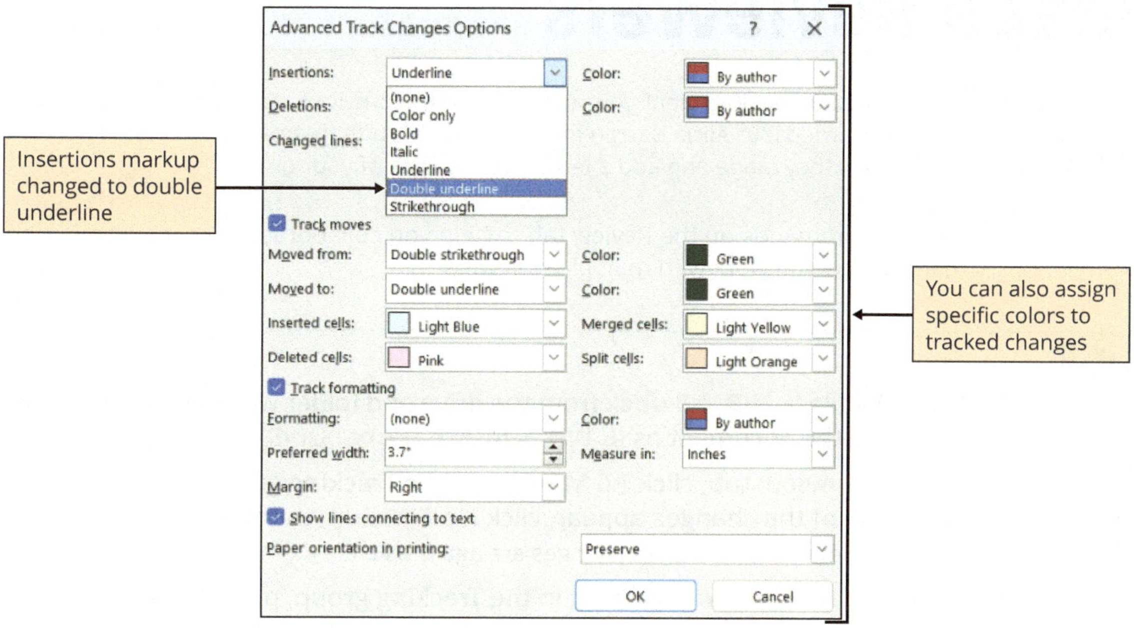

Figure 8-21: Completed document with tracked changes accepted and comments deleted

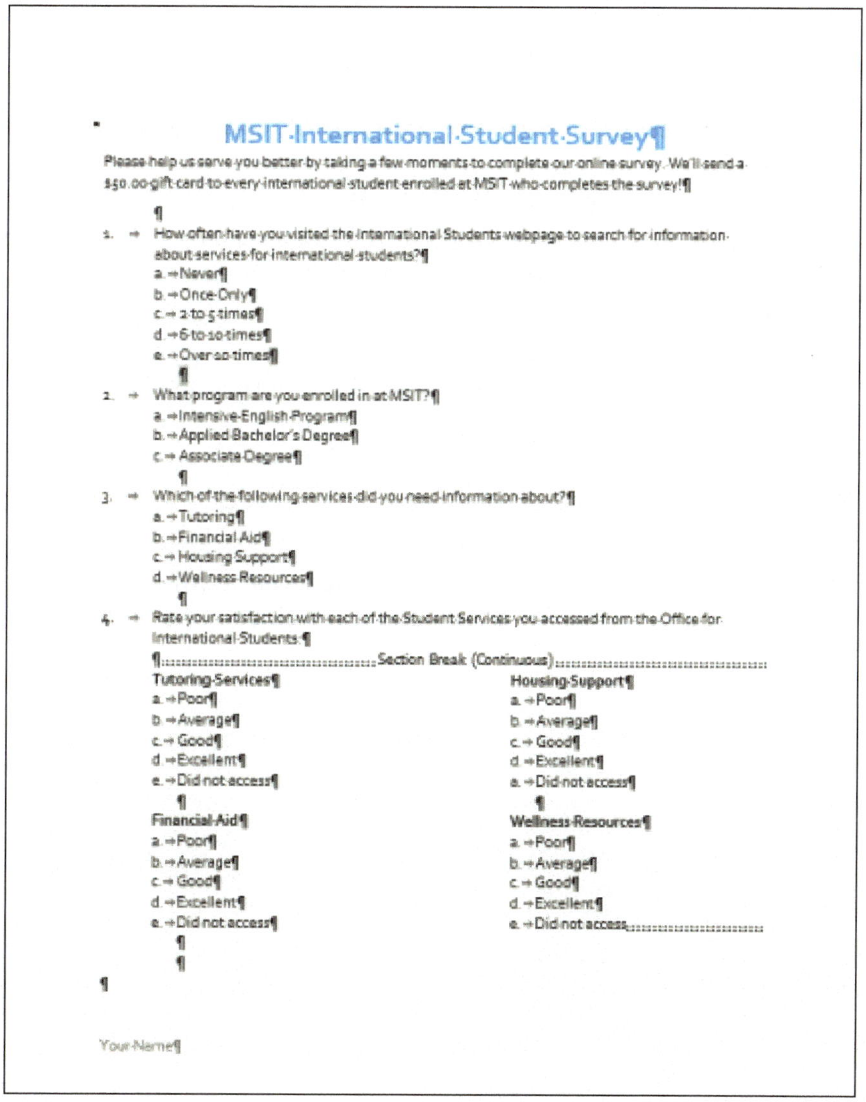
MSIT International Student Survey

Please help us serve you better by taking a few moments to complete our online survey. We'll send a $50.00 gift card to every international student enrolled at MSIT who completes the survey!

1. How often have you visited the International Students webpage to search for information about services for international students?
   a. Never
   b. Once Only
   c. 2 to 5 times
   d. 6 to 10 times
   e. Over 10 times
2. What program are you enrolled in at MSIT?
   a. Intensive English Program
   b. Applied Bachelor's Degree
   c. Associate Degree
3. Which of the following services did you need information about?
   a. Tutoring
   b. Financial Aid
   c. Housing Support
   d. Wellness Resources
4. Rate your satisfaction with each of the Student Services you accessed from the Office for International Students.

Section Break (Continuous)

Tutoring Services
a. Poor
b. Average
c. Good
d. Excellent
e. Did not access

Financial Aid
a. Poor
b. Average
c. Good
d. Excellent
e. Did not access

Housing Support
a. Poor
b. Average
c. Good
d. Excellent
a. Did not access

Wellness Resources
a. Poor
b. Average
c. Good
d. Excellent
e. Did not access

Your Name

Manage Reviewers

Case You emailed a copy of the Survey document you completed in the previous lesson to Ravi Singh, who edited the document and then forwarded it to Alicia Barton for her input. Alicia then emailed the edited document back to you. You view the changes they made and add a few more changes of your own.

Objectives
- View changes from multiple users

You use commands on the Review tab to help you collaborate with one or more people and to manage how you work with multiple reviewers.

Steps

Quick Tip
Additional changes in No Markup view will appear as tracked changes when you use All Markup view as long as the Track Changes button remains active.

Trouble
The option may be Show Only Comments and Formatting in Balloons.

Quick Tip
You can also change the username and initials by clicking the File tab, and then clicking Options to open the Word Options dialog box.

Quick Tip
Your name appears as one of the reviewers because you made a tracked change.

1. **Open the file IL_WD_8-3.docx from the drive and folder where you store your Data Files, then save the document as IL_WD_8_InternationalStudentSurvey_Colleagues**
2. **Click the Review tab, click All Markup in the Tracking group, click No Markup, note that none of the changes appear, click No Markup, then click All Markup**
   All the comments and tracked changes are again visible.
3. **Click the Show Markup button in the Tracking group, point to Balloons, click Show Revisions in Balloons, click Show Markup again, point to Balloons, then click Show Only Formatting in Balloons**
4. **Move your pointer over gift card in paragraph 1 to view the comment made by Ravi Singh in a box above the comment marker, as shown in Figure 8-22**
5. **Click the Show Markup button, then point to Specific People**
   A list of the people who commented on or made changes to the document appears, as shown in Figure 8-23.
6. **Click Alicia Barton to deselect it, click the Launcher in the Tracking group, click Change User Name to open the Word Options dialog box, select the contents of the User name box, type your name if necessary, press TAB, type your initials, click OK, then click OK**
7. **Press CTRL+HOME, click the Accept button to accept the deletion in the title, click the Accept button twice to accept the insertion of "assess", select gift card, then type e-coupon**
   The text "gift card" is marked as deleted, and the text "e-coupon" is marked as inserted.
8. **Click Show Markup, point to Specific People, click Alicia Barton to select it, click the Accept arrow, then click Accept All Changes and Stop Tracking**
9. **Delete all comments in the document, type your name where indicated in the document footer, save the document, then close the document but do not exit Word**

Figure 8-22: Manage reviewers

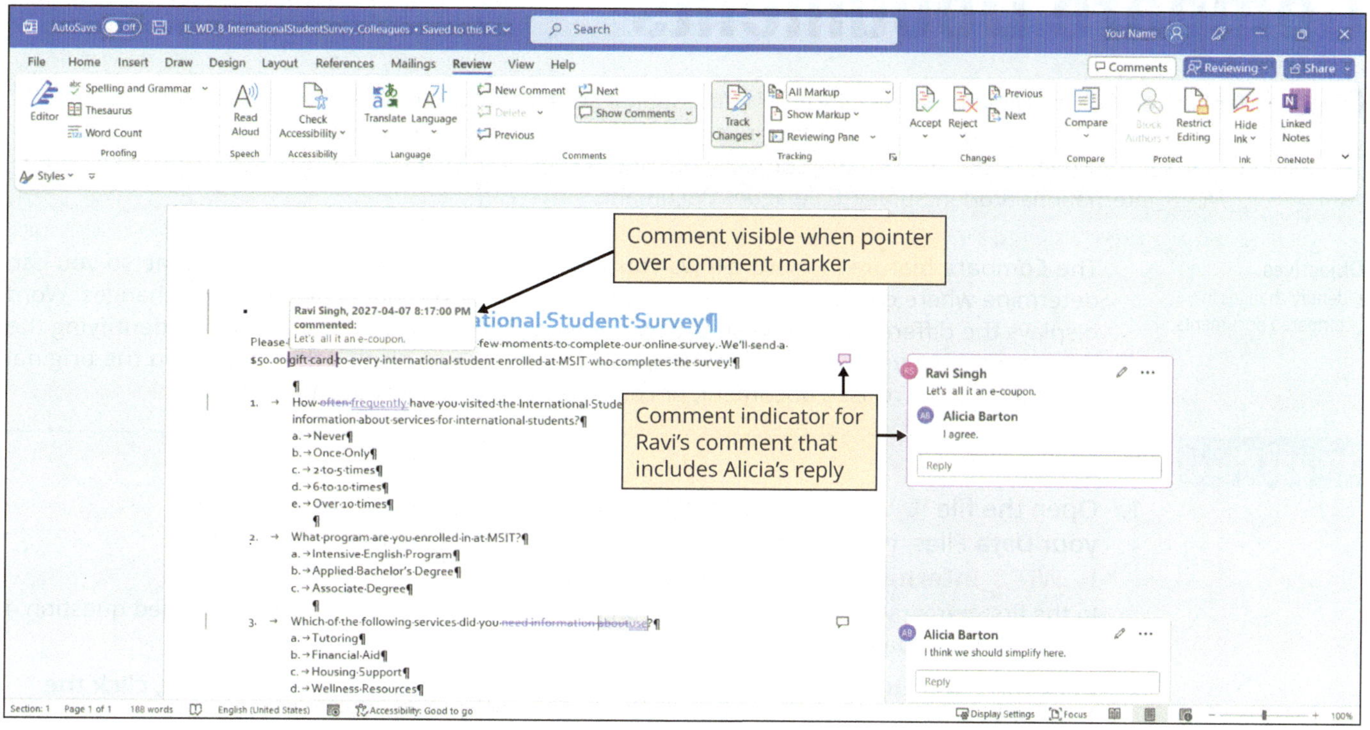

Figure 8-23: Indicating reviewers

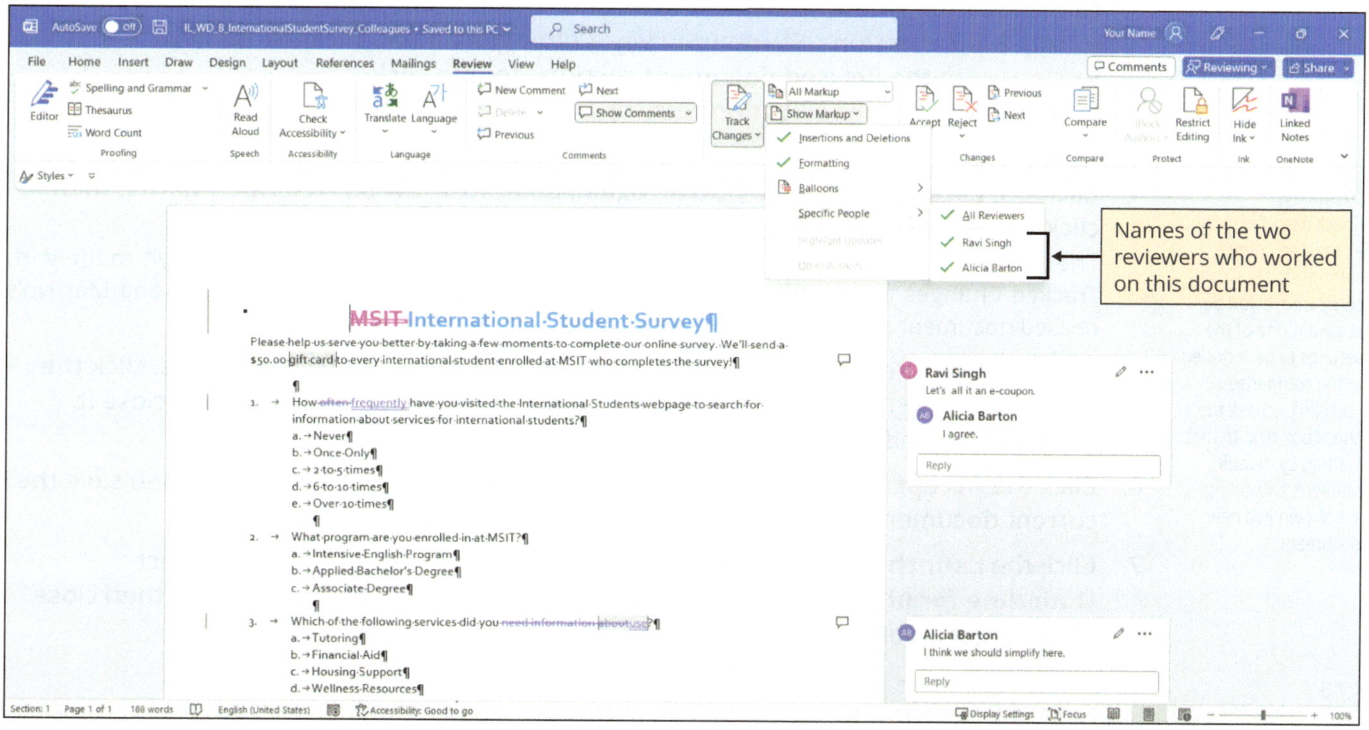

Compare Documents

Case Marilyn Kendall, the Director of the Office for International Students at MSIT, has reviewed the latest version of the Student Survey that you and your colleagues have edited. Marilyn made changes to the document but did not turn Track Changes on. You use the Compare feature to check the changes that Marilyn made against the IL_WD_8_InternationalStudentSurvey_Colleagues document.

Objectives
- Identify changes in compared documents

The Compare feature in Word allows you to compare two documents at one time so you can determine where changes have been made when a user has not activated Track Changes. Word displays the differences between the two documents as tracked changes. After identifying the documents that you want to compare, you can choose to display the changes in the original document, in the revised document, or combined into one new document.

Steps

1. **Open the file IL_WD_8-4.docx from the drive and folder where you store your Data Files, type your name in the footer, then save the document as IL_WD_8_InternationalStudentSurvey_Director**
   In the first paragraph, Marilyn changed "online survey" to "survey" and then changed question 4 so it begins "Evaluate each of the ..."

2. **Click the File tab, click Close, click the Review tab if it is not the active tab, click the Compare button in the Compare group, then click Compare**
   In the Compare Documents dialog box, you specify which two documents you want to compare.

3. **Click the Browse button in the Original document section, navigate to the location where you save the files for this module, double-click IL_WD_8_InternationalStudentSurvey_Colleagues.docx, click the Browse button in the Revised document section, double-click IL_WD_8_InternationalStudentSurvey_Director.docx, then click More**
   The edited and expanded Compare Documents dialog box is shown in **Figure 8-24**.

> **Quick Tip**
> Check marks identify all the document settings that will be compared. If you do not want one of the settings to be included in the comparison, you can uncheck the check box next to that setting. By default, Marilyn's two changes are shown in a new document.

4. **Click OK, click the Compare button again, point to Show Source Documents, then click Show Both**
   The screen splits into three. The document containing the two changes Marilyn made with Tracked Changes turned off appears in the larger pane. The original document and Marilyn's revised document appear in the two right panes as shown in **Figure 8-25**

5. **Review the information in the Revisions pane and in the split screen panes, click the Close button in the top-right corner of the Original document pane to close it, close the Revised document, then close the Revisions pane**

6. **Click the Accept arrow in the Changes group, click Accept All Changes, then save the current document as IL_WD_8_InternationalStudentSurvey_Final**

7. **Click the Launcher in the Tracking group, click Advanced Options, select Underline for insertions, click OK, click OK, submit all to your instructor, then close all open documents and exit Word**

Figure 8-24: Compare Documents dialog box

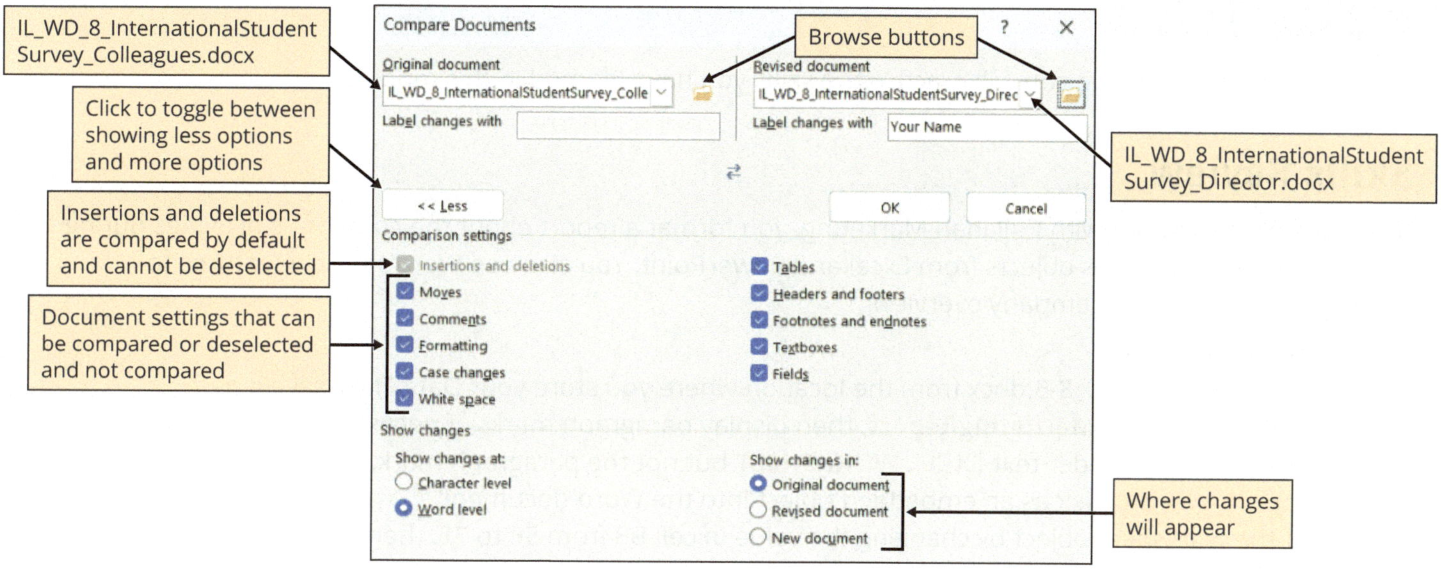

Figure 8-25: Comparing documents

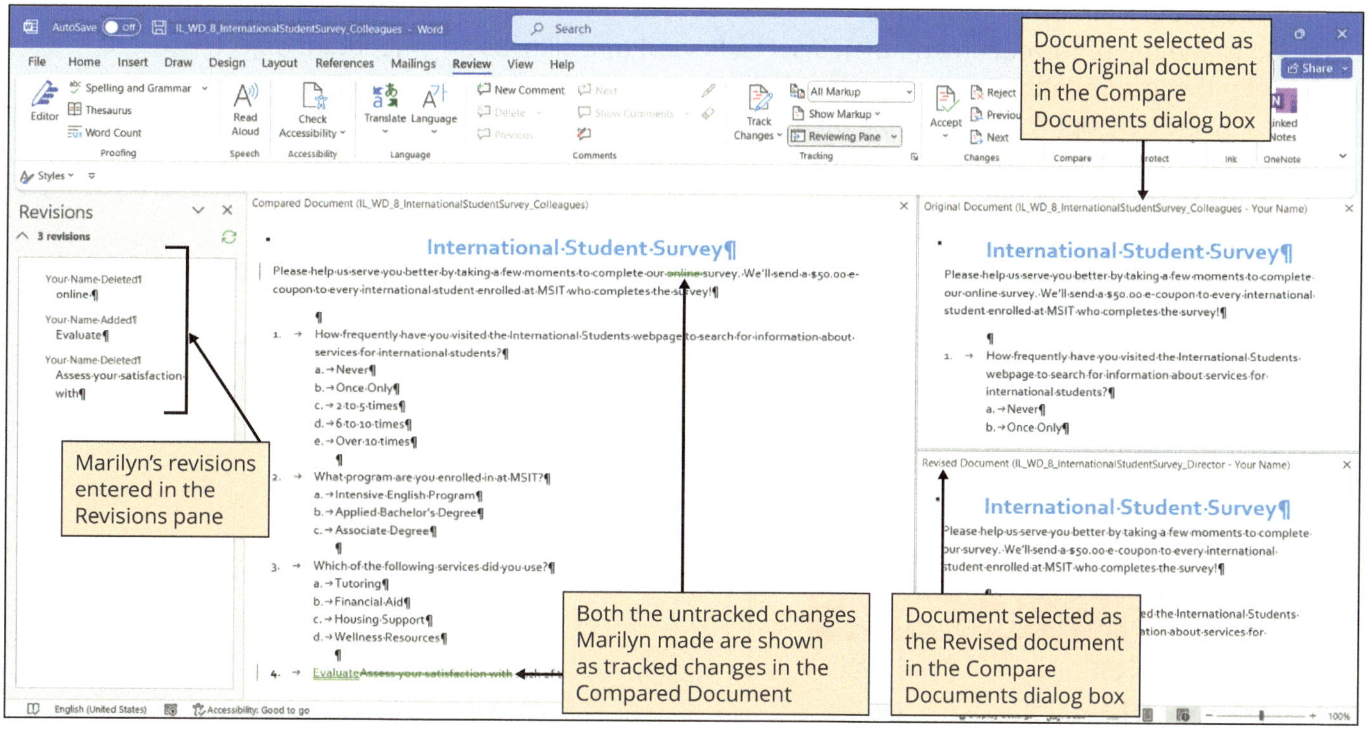

Practice

In the exercises that follow, you will practice the skills you have learned in this module.

Skills Review

As a marketing assistant with Callahan Marketing, you format a report about the company's activities during the past year that includes objects from Excel and PowerPoint. You also use Word's review features to develop a final copy of a company overview.

1. **Embed an Excel file.**
   a. Open the file IL_WD_8-5.docx from the location where you store your Data Files, save it as **IL_WD_8_CallahanMarketingReport**, then display paragraph marks, if necessary.
   b. Delete the placeholder text **EXCEL WORKSHEET** but not the paragraph mark, then insert the file **Support_WD_8-4.xlsx** as an embedded object into the Word document.
   c. Edit the worksheet object by changing the value in cell B3 from 56 to **75**, then enhance the value in cell B8 with bold.
   d. Apply the Quotable theme to the Excel workbook, then click cell A1 before returning to Word.
   e. In Word, center the worksheet object, save the document, then close the Excel workbook if necessary.
2. **Insert objects from other programs.**
   a. Go to the top of the document, then insert a PowerPoint slide as an embedded object.
   b. Enter the text **Callahan Marketing Year in Review** as the slide title, then enter your name as the subtitle.
   c. In PowerPoint, apply the Quotable theme to the slide object, then return to Word.
   d. Double-click the slide object, apply the red variant (far right), then click in the text below the slide object to return to Word.
   e. Set the absolute height of the slide object to **2.2"**, then center the slide object.
   f. Scroll to page 4, select and delete QUICK TABLE but not the paragraph mark below the "Client Evaluations" paragraph, then insert the Tabular List Quick Table.
   g. Select the last three rows in the table, click the right mouse button, click Delete Rows, then as shown in **Figure 8-26**, enter and format the data. (Hint: Right-align the data in column 2 and apply the Grid Table 4 – Accent 6 table style to the table to match the red formatting applied to other objects in the document).
   h. Save the document.

Figure 8-26

Rating	Responses
Five Star	1280
Four Star	1150
Three Star	378
Two Star	180
One Star	12

3. **Link an Excel chart.**
   a. Scroll up to page 2 and delete EXCEL PIE CHART, but not the paragraph mark, open Support_WD_8-5.xlsx from File Explorer, then save it in Excel as **Support_WD_8_ServiceRevenue**.
   b. Copy the pie chart, then paste it in Word using the Keep Source Formatting & Link Data (F) paste option.
   c. Note that the orange slice for Social Media Marketing accounts for 10% of the company revenue.

d. Return to Excel, change the value in cell B4 to **400,000**, then verify the value of the Social Media Marketing slice (12%).
e. Return to Word and verify that the orange slice is now 12%.
f. Switch to Excel, then save and close the workbook.
g. In Word, change the width of the pie chart to **5"**, then center the pie chart and save the document.

4. **Link a PowerPoint slide.**
   a. Scroll to and delete POWERPOINT SLIDE but not the paragraph mark, open **Support_WD_8-6.pptx** from File Explorer, then save it in PowerPoint as **Support_WD_8_Workshops**.
   b. Go to Slide Sorter view in PowerPoint, copy the slide, then paste it in Word as a linked PowerPoint Slide Object.
   c. Return to PowerPoint, view the slide in Normal view, then delete the red text box.
   d. Switch to Word and update the linked slide to reflect the change.
   e. Save the document, go to PowerPoint, then save the PowerPoint presentation.

5. **Manage document links.**
   a. In Word, right-click the linked slide, then edit the link.
   b. In PowerPoint, select the text "Digital Marketing Workshops", then change the fill color of the text to Red, Accent 6, Lighter 80%.
   c. Update the link in Word, then save the document.
   d. Save and close the PowerPoint presentation.
   e. Save the Word document again as **IL_WD_8_CallahanMarketingReport_Distribution**.
   f. Go to the Links dialog from the File tab, then break the link to the PowerPoint slide.
   g. Break the link to the Excel pie chart.
   h. Exit Backstage view, then save the document.

6. **Create charts.**
   a. Scroll to page 4, use CTRL+C to copy the Ratings Quick Table, then delete CUSTOMER PIE CHART but not the paragraph mark following.
   b. Insert a pie chart.
   c. Click cell A1 in the Worksheet window, then use CTRL+V to paste the table data into the Excel worksheet, then close the worksheet.
   d. Change the chart title to **Client Evaluations**.
   e. Add data labels at the Outside End position.
   f. Delete the legend, insert a legend to the right of the pie chart.
   g. Scroll up to page 3 and select COLUMN CHART, but not the paragraph mark, then insert a Clustered Column Chart (the default chart type).
   h. Select the table above the chart, use CTRL+X to cut the table, then use CTRL+V to paste the table into cell A1 of the Excel worksheet. Remove the extra row in the Excel table, then double-click the column header between each column to widen the columns to view the data.
   i. Close the Excel worksheet, enter **Annual Revenue by Location** as the chart title, then save the document.

7. **Format and edit charts.**
   a. Scroll down to the Client Evaluations pie chart, change the height to **3"** and the width to **3"**, then center the chart.
   b. Edit the chart data by changing 180 to **220** in cell B5.
   c. Format the data labels to display percentages instead of values.
   d. Apply the Style 12 chart style to the pie chart.
   e. Change 180 to **220** in the Quick Table so it matches the chart.
   f. Scroll up to the column chart.
   g. Change the chart type to Bar.
   h. Switch the rows and columns so the city names appear on the Vertical axis.
   i. Add an Axis Title to the Primary Horizontal Axis with the text **Revenue**.
   j. Format the Primary Horizontal Axis to indicate increments of $150,000 in the Major box.
   k. Format the chart area with a Dark Teal, Accent 1 border with a weight of 3 points.

Skills Review (Continued)

l. Reduce the height of the chart to **3"** and the width to **5.5"**, then center it.

m. View the report so that all four pages fit in the document window, compare the completed report to **Figure 8-27**, then save and close the document and exit Excel and PowerPoint if necessary.

Figure 8-27

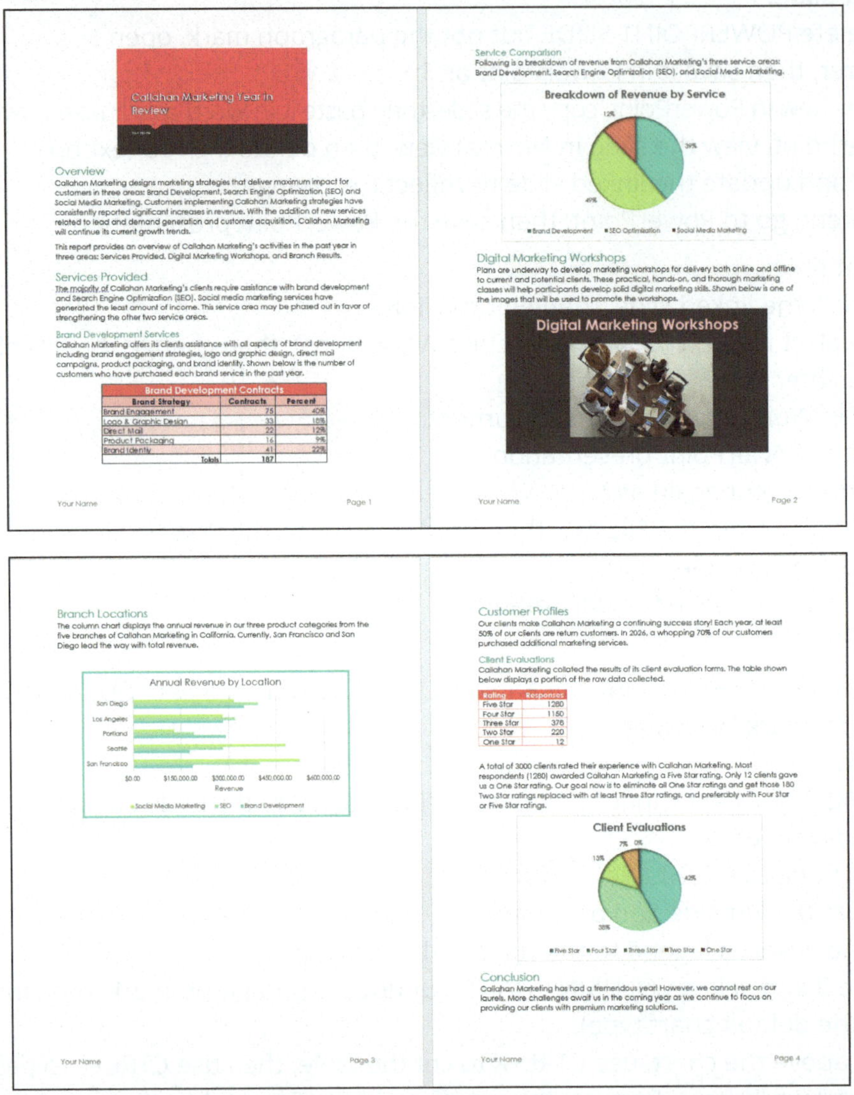

fauxels/Pexels

8. **Track changes.**
   a. Open the file IL_WD_8-6.docx from the location where you store your Data Files, save it as **IL_WD_8_CallahanMarketingOverview**, then turn on Track Changes from the Review tab if necessary.
   b. Select All Markup, if necessary, read the comment attached to "comprehensive" in the first paragraph, then reply to Wanda's comment with **I agree** and then resolve the thread.
   c. Scroll to the Company Background heading, cut the heading "Company Background" and the paragraph following, then paste them above the "Expansion Plans" heading.
   d. Select the document title at the top of the document, decrease the font size to 28 pt, then change the font color to Green, Accent 6.
   e. Scroll to the Expansion Plans paragraph, read the comment by Wanda Han, change "five" to "seven", then save the document.
9. **Work with tracked changes.**
   a. Open the Advanced Track Changes Options dialog box, display deletions as Double strikethrough, then click OK to exit all open dialog boxes.
   b. Go to the beginning of the document, then use the buttons in the Changes group to go to the first change.

c. Accept the change to the title formatting, then accept the changes in the first two body paragraphs.
d. Accept the change to seven, then reject the change from twenty to fifteen so the number is again twenty.
e. Accept all the remaining changes in the document, then delete all comments.
f. Save and close the document.

10. Manage reviewers.

a. Open the file IL_WD_8-7.docx from the drive and folder where you store your Data Files, then save the document as **IL_WD_8_CallahanMarketingOverview_Staff**.
b. Show All Markup, if necessary.
c. Display revisions in balloons, then show formatting in balloons.
d. Read the comment made by Danielle in the first paragraph, then read the comment made by Anita.
e. Display the list of people who worked on the document, then deselect Anita.
f. Change the username to your name, if necessary.
g. Go to the beginning of the document, accept the formatting of the title, accept the insertion in the title, accept the deletion of the subtitle, then go to "comprehensive" and change it to **customized**.
h. Display the list of people who worked on the document again, select Anita Ramos, then accept all changes and stop tracking.
i. Type your name where indicated in the document footer, save the document, then close the document but do not exit Word.

11. Compare documents.

a. Open the file IL_WD_8-8.docx from the drive and folder where you store your Data Files, type your name in the footer, then save the document as **IL_WD_8_CallahanMarketingOverview_Owner**.
b. Jeb Callahan, the owner of the company, made two changes to the document without turning on tracked changes. He changed "premier" to "leading" in the Company Overview paragraph and then changed "launched" to "incorporated" in the Company Background paragraph.
c. Close the document, then on the Review tab, click the Compare button and open the Compare Documents dialog box.
d. Open **IL_WD_8_CallahanMarketingOverview_Staff.docx** as the original document, then open **IL_WD_8_CallahanMarketingOverview_Owner.docx** as the revised document.
e. Close the Compare Documents dialog box, then display both the original and revised documents.
f. Review the information in the Revisions pane and in the split screen pane, note Jeb's two changes, close the Original document pane, close the Revised document pane, then close the Revisions pane.
g. Accept all the changes in the document, then save it as **IL_WD_8_CallahanMarketingOverview_Final**.
h. Return the tracking option to the default setting: Strikethrough for deletions.
i. The completed document with all changes incorporated appears as shown in **Figure 8-28**.
j. Submit all the documents you created in this Skills Review to your instructor, then close all open documents and exit Word.

Figure 8-28

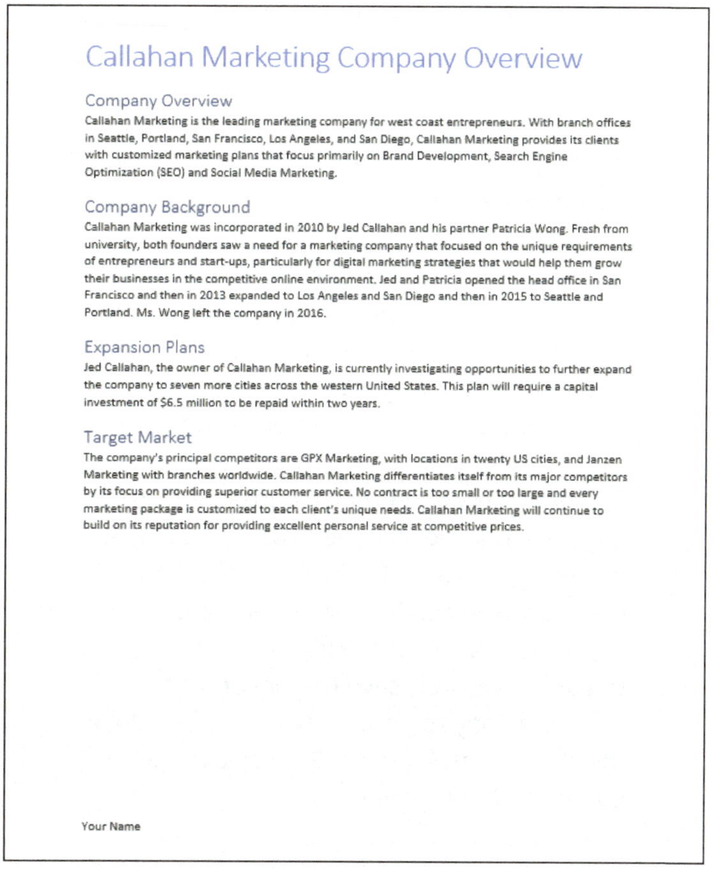

Callahan Marketing Company Overview

Company Overview

Callahan Marketing is the leading marketing company for west coast entrepreneurs. With branch offices in Seattle, Portland, San Francisco, Los Angeles, and San Diego, Callahan Marketing provides its clients with customized marketing plans that focus primarily on Brand Development, Search Engine Optimization (SEO) and Social Media Marketing.

Company Background

Callahan Marketing was incorporated in 2010 by Jed Callahan and his partner Patricia Wong. Fresh from university, both founders saw a need for a marketing company that focused on the unique requirements of entrepreneurs and start-ups, particularly for digital marketing strategies that would help them grow their businesses in the competitive online environment. Jed and Patricia opened the head office in San Francisco and then in 2013 expanded to Los Angeles and San Diego and then in 2015 to Seattle and Portland. Ms. Wong left the company in 2016.

Expansion Plans

Jed Callahan, the owner of Callahan Marketing, is currently investigating opportunities to further expand the company to seven more cities across the western United States. This plan will require a capital investment of $6.5 million to be repaid within two years.

Target Market

The company's principal competitors are GPX Marketing, with locations in twenty US cities, and Janzen Marketing with branches worldwide. Callahan Marketing differentiates itself from its major competitors by its focus on providing superior customer service. No contract is too small or too large and every marketing package is customized to each client's unique needs. Callahan Marketing will continue to build on its reputation for providing excellent personal service at competitive prices.

Your Name

Independent Challenge 1

You work for MTR Corporate Events, an event planning company based in Vancouver, Canada, that specializes in planning large corporate events. The company is organizing a seminar for local businesses called "Corporate Event Trends" to share the latest trends in planning and running effective corporate events. Two of your coworkers have been working on a preliminary outline for the seminar. They ask for your input.

a. Start Word, open the file IL_WD_8-9.docx from the drive and folder where you store your Data Files, then save it as **IL_WD_8_MTRSeminarOutline**.
b. Scroll through the document to read the comments and view the changes made by Inez Ramirez and Jamal Wilson.
c. Change the username to your name and initials if necessary. (**Hint**: Add a check mark to the Always use these values regardless of sign in to Office check box if you checked this box when you completed the lessons.)
d. Modify tracking options by changing the color of the inserted text to Blue.
e. In the 9:45 to 10:45 entry, select "Going Green", then insert a comment with the text **I suggest we change the name of this session to Building Eco-Friendly & Sustainable Events**.
f. Be sure the Track Changes feature is active, then apply Bold to the two instances of "Break: that are currently not bold.
g. Starting with the first comment, make all the suggested changes, including the change you suggested in your comment.
h. Accept all the changes, then delete all the comments in the document.
i. Type your name where indicated in the footer, then save and close the document.
j. Open IL_WD_8-10.docx, then save it as **IL_WD_8_MTRSeminarOutline_MurielKane**. The C.E.O. of MTR Corporate Events, Muriel Kane, changed "Hybrid Events – What They Are & Why They Are the Future" to "Hybrid Events are the Future" before turning on Track Changes. She also made two other changes, including changing the spelling of her last name from Kain to Kane.
k. With Track Changes turned on, change the username to your name and initials, change Sure-Fire to **Dynamite** in the 3:30 to 4:30 session, type your name where indicated in the footer, then save and close the document.
l. Compare the document IL_WD_8_MTRSeminarOutline.docx to IL_WD_8_MTRSeminarOutline_MurielKane. Display both of the source documents, close the Original and Revised documents, then accept all the changes in the compared document and save the document as **IL_WD_8_MTRSeminarOutline_Final**.
m. Restore the color setting for Insertions to "By author" and uncheck the Always use these values regardless of sign in to Office check box if you checked it in an earlier step.
n. Type your name where indicated in the document footer, save the document, submit a copy to your instructor, then close the document. **Figure 8-29** displays the completed document.

Figure 8-29

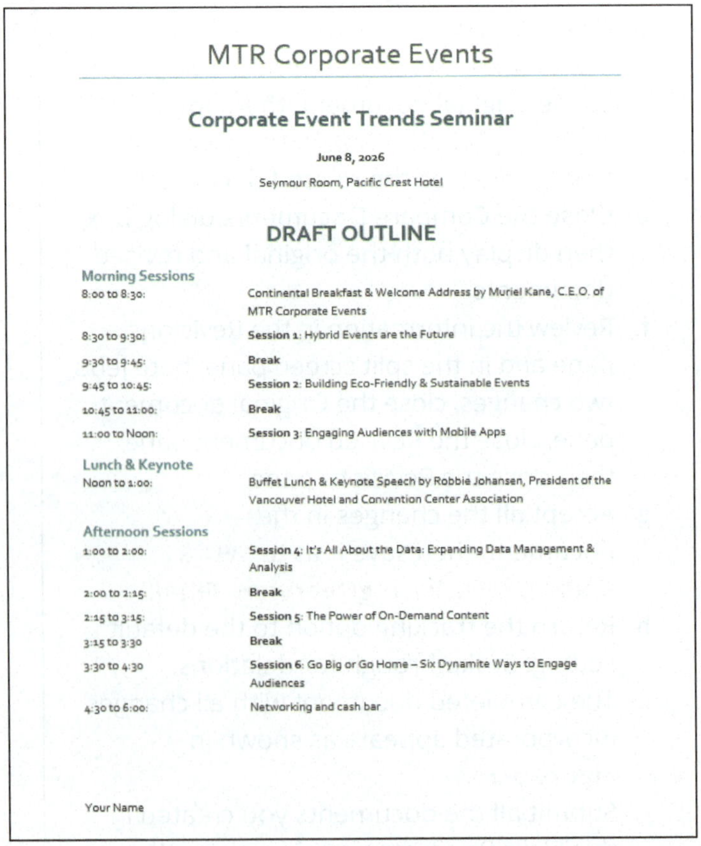
MTR Corporate Events

Corporate Event Trends Seminar

June 8, 2026

Seymour Room, Pacific Crest Hotel

DRAFT OUTLINE

Morning Sessions	
8:00 to 8:30:	Continental Breakfast & Welcome Address by Muriel Kane, C.E.O. of MTR Corporate Events
8:30 to 9:30:	**Session 1:** Hybrid Events are the Future
9:30 to 9:45:	**Break**
9:45 to 10:45:	**Session 2:** Building Eco-Friendly & Sustainable Events
10:45 to 11:00:	**Break**
11:00 to Noon:	**Session 3:** Engaging Audiences with Mobile Apps
Lunch & Keynote	
Noon to 1:00:	Buffet Lunch & Keynote Speech by Robbie Johansen, President of the Vancouver Hotel and Convention Center Association
Afternoon Sessions	
1:00 to 2:00:	**Session 4:** It's All About the Data: Expanding Data Management & Analysis
2:00 to 2:15:	**Break**
2:15 to 3:15:	**Session 5:** The Power of On-Demand Content
3:15 to 3:30	**Break**
3:30 to 4:30	**Session 6:** Go Big or Go Home – Six Dynamite Ways to Engage Audiences
4:30 to 6:00:	Networking and cash bar

Your Name

Independent Challenge 2

You've been hired to manage the office at the Crestview Bog Conservation Society, an environmentally significant conservation area in Michigan. To prepare for the upcoming Annual General Meeting of the Society's Board of Directors, you've been asked to prepare a report about the society's activities in the past year. The report includes information about a survey conducted of the society's many helpers and a summary of the society's funding sources. You open the report and complete it with objects inserted from Excel and PowerPoint, and charts you create in Word.

a. Start Word, open the file IL_WD_8-11.docx from the location where you store your Data Files, then save it as **IL_WD_8_CrestviewVolunteerReport**.
b. Insert an embedded PowerPoint slide above "Introduction" at the top of the document that includes **Crestview Bog Conservation Society Report** as the title and your name as the subtitle, then format the slide with the Berlin theme and the green variant (third variant from the left) and reduce its width to 2.48".
c. Move "Introduction" down one line.
d. Select and delete AGE PIE CHART but not the paragraph mark, then cut the table (contains Age Range and Number) and use the data to create a pie chart.
e. Edit the pie chart as follows: Enter **Volunteer Ages** as the chart title, apply the Style 12 chart style, change the colors to Colorful Palette 2, then add data labels that indicate percentages instead of values and with the labels in the Outside End position.
f. Change the position of the legend so it appears to the right of the pie chart, then enclose the pie chart in a Brown, Text 2, 1 pt border.
g. Select and delete REASONS TABLE but not the paragraph mark, then insert a Quick Table using the Tabular List format. Enter the data shown in **Figure 8-30** into the table, right-align the data in column 2, then delete any unused rows.
h. In the Seasonal Work section, cut the table, then use the data to create a bar chart.
i. Change the bar chart to a column chart, then switch the rows and columns.
j. Add **Number of Helpers** as the horizontal axis title to the chart and change the chart title to **Helper Hours by Season**, then enclose the column chart in a Brown, Text 2, 1 pt border.
k. Select and delete HOURS CHART but not the paragraph mark, open Support_WD_8-7.xlsx from File Explorer, then save it in Excel as **Support_WD_8_HelperHours**.
l. Copy the pie chart, then paste it into Word using the Keep Source Formatting & Link Data (F) paste option.
m. Note that the blue slice representing 11 to 20 hours accounts for 50% of the helpers who give between 11 and 20 hours a month of their time to working at the Crestview Bog. Return to Excel, change the value in cell B2 to **45** and the value in cell B3 to **80**, then verify the value of the 11 to 20 hours slice (40%).
n. Return to Word and verify that the blue slice is now 40%. Change 37% to **40%** in the text above the chart.
o. Enclose the pie chart in a Brown, Text 2, 1 pt border, then change the Height to 3.3" and the width to 6".
p. Scroll to and delete POWERPOINT SLIDE, but not the paragraph mark, open Support_WD_8-8.pptx from File Explorer, then save it in PowerPoint as **Support_WD_8_CrestviewHelper**.
q. Go to Slide Sorter view in PowerPoint, copy the slide, then paste the PowerPoint Slide Object in Word as a link.
r. In PowerPoint, delete the yellow text box, then switch to Word and update the linked slide to reflect the change.

Figure 8-30

Reason	Volunteers
Meet people	70
Preserve the environment	60
Build new skills & experience	40
Spend time outdoors	30

Independent Challenge 2 (Continued)

s. Change the height of the PowerPoint slide in Word to 3".
t. Delete the placeholder text FUNDING WORKSHEET but not the paragraph mark, then insert the file **Support_WD_8-9.xlsx** as an embedded object into the Word document.
u. Edit the worksheet object by changing the value in cell B3 to **95,000**, apply the Berlin theme to the Excel workbook, then click cell A1 before returning to Word.
v. Save the document.
w. Save the document again as **IL_WD_8_CrestviewVolunteerReport_Distribution**.
x. Open the Links dialog box, then break the link to the PowerPoint slide and the chart.
y. View the five pages of the document in Multiple Pages view, compare it to **Figure 8-31**, save the document, submit all files to your instructor, close the document, then exit Word and any other open applications.

Figure 8-31

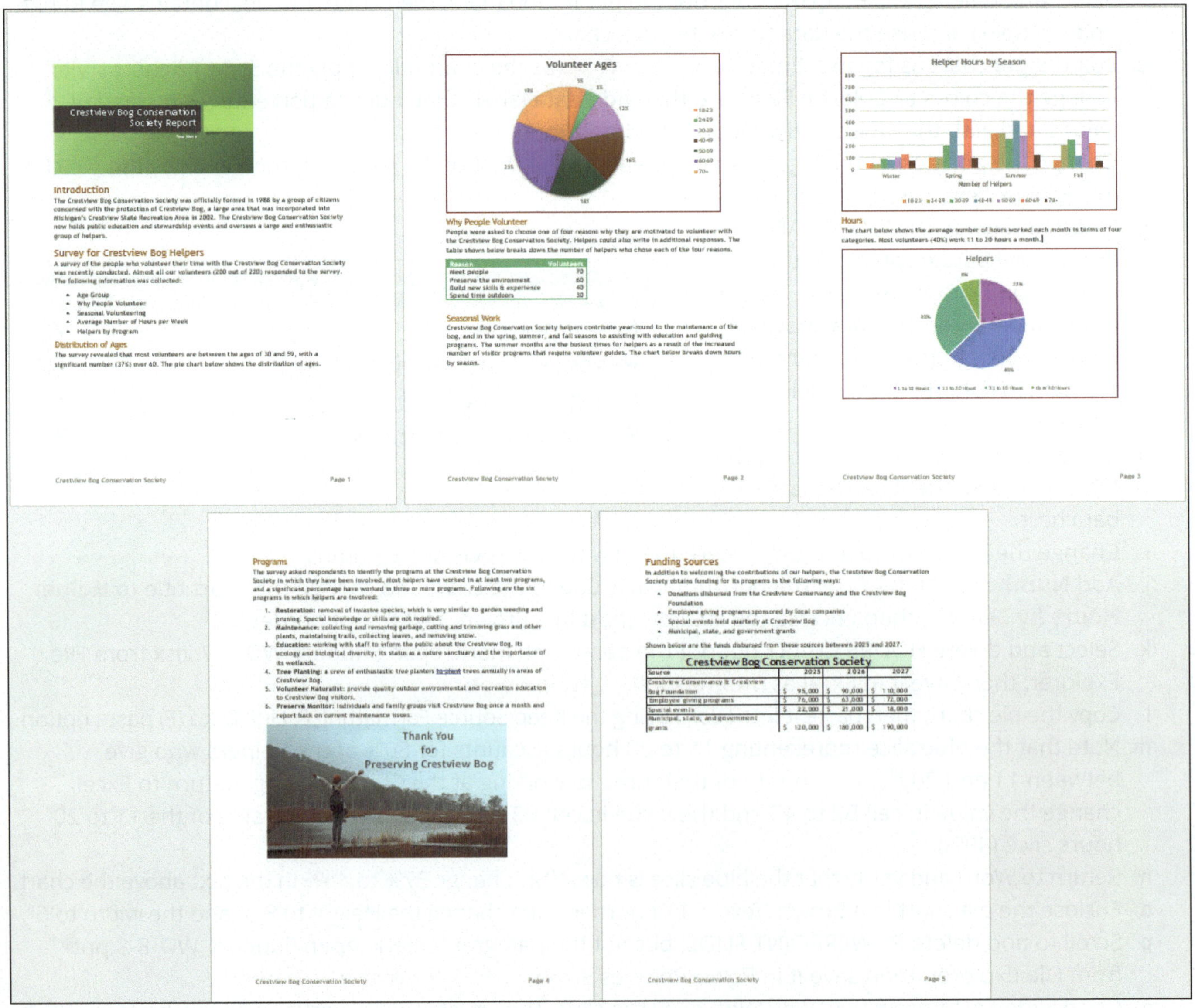

Han Sen/Pexels

Visual Workshop

Start a new document in Word, select the Facet theme (or a different theme if the Facet theme is not available), open the PowerPoint slide **Support_WD_8-10.pptx**, copy the slide, paste the slide as a Microsoft PowerPoint Object into Word (but *not* as a link), then edit the slide from Word to change the height to 2.98" and the width to 5.33", and add your name to the subtitle. Below the slide in Word, add the text **The worksheet and pie chart shown below summarize Quarter 2 real estate sales at Meadowbrook Realtors**. Embed the Excel worksheet from **Support_WD_8-11.xlsx**, then change the number of properties sold by Bailey Crawford to **32** and apply the Facet theme (or the same theme you applied to the Word document). Below the worksheet object, create the pie chart using data from the worksheet. Format the chart as shown in **Figure 8-32**: modify the title, apply Chart Style 5 and the Monochromatic Palette 2 color scheme, move the legend to the right, and display the values as percentages with data labels positioned Outside End. Add a 3 pt border with the color Dark Green, Accent 2. Change the height of the chart to 3.3" and the width of the chart to 5.5". Save the document as **IL_WD_8_MeadowbrookRealtorsQuarter2Sales**, submit the file to your instructor, close the document, close the presentation in PowerPoint and the workbook in Excel, then exit all programs.

Figure 8-32

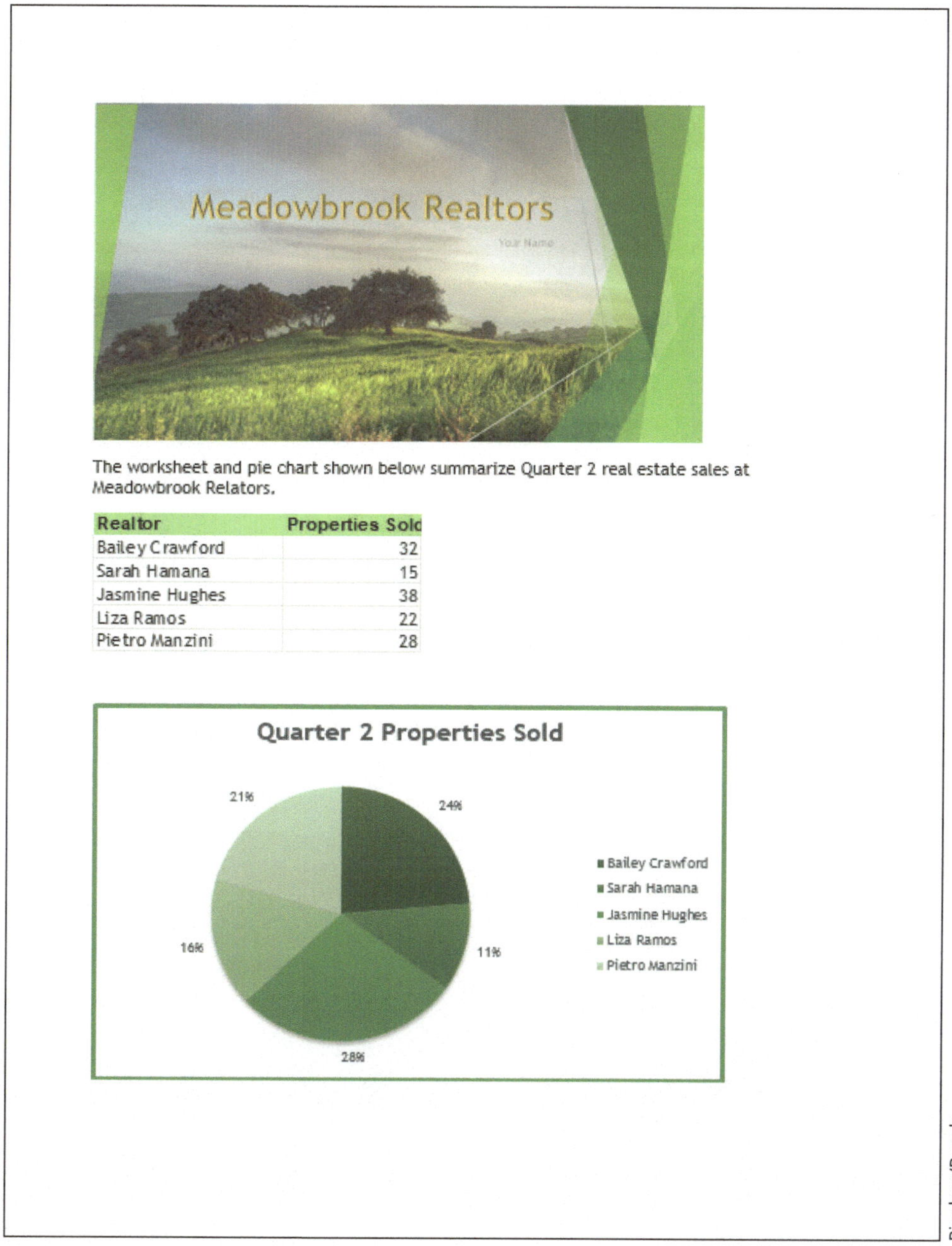

The worksheet and pie chart shown below summarize Quarter 2 real estate sales at Meadowbrook Relators.

Realtor	Properties Sold
Bailey Crawford	32
Sarah Hamana	15
Jasmine Hughes	38
Liza Ramos	22
Pietro Manzini	28

Pixabay/Pexels

Developing Multi-Page Documents

Case

As part of your work in the Office for International Students at Mountain Springs Institute of Technology (MSIT) in Denver, Colorado, you have been asked to edit and format a guide to help international students settle into their studies at MSIT. You start by working in Outline view to revise the structure for the guide, and then you use several advanced Word features to format the document for publication.

Module Objectives

After completing this module, you will be able to:

- Build a document in Outline view
- Work in Outline view
- Navigate a document
- Insert and modify screenshots
- Use advanced find and replace options
- Add and modify captions
- Insert a table of contents
- Mark text for an index
- Generate an index
- Insert footers in multiple sections
- Insert headers in multiple sections
- Finalize a multi-page document
- Insert and format with equations
- Insert master documents and subdocuments

Files You Will Need

IL_WD_9-1.docx
Support_WD_9_StudentGuideImages.docx
IL_WD_9-2.docx
Support_WD_9_OrientationEvents.docx
IL_WD_9-3.docx
IL_WD_9-4.docx
Support_WD_9_Images.docx
IL_WD_9-5.docx
Support_WD_9_WesternFinance.docx
IL_WD_9-6.docx
IL_WD_9-7.docx
Support_WD_9_EventOrganization.docx
IL_WD_9-8.docx
Support_WD_9_CommunityImages.docx
Support_WD_9_Parks.docx
Support_WD_9_RecreationPolicies.docx
IL_WD_9-9.docx
Support_WD_9_Graphic.docx

Build a Document in Outline View

Case You work in Outline view to develop the structure of the student guide.

Objectives
- Open Outline view
- Demote and promote headings

You work in Outline view to organize the headings and subheadings that identify topics and subtopics in multi-page documents. In Outline view, each heading is assigned a level from 1 to 9, with Level 1 being the highest level and Level 9 being the lowest level. In addition, you can assign the Body Text level to each paragraph of text that appears below a document heading. Each level is formatted with one of Word's predefined styles. For example, Level 1 is formatted with the Heading 1 style, and the Body Text level is formatted with the Normal style.

Steps

Trouble
If the headings do not appear blue and bold, click the Show Text Formatting check box in the Outline Tools group to select it.

1. **Start Word, create a new blank document, click the Show/Hide button ¶ in the Paragraph group to show paragraph marks if necessary, click the View tab, then click the Outline button in the Views group**
   In Outline view, the Outlining tab is active. **Table 9-1** describes the buttons on the Outlining tab.
2. **Type International Student Guide**
   Figure 9-1 shows the text in Outline view. By default, the text appears at the left margin, is designated as Level 1, and is formatted with the Heading 1 style.
3. **Press ENTER, click the Demote button → in the Outline Tools group to move to Level 2, then type Welcome**
   The text is indented, designated as Level 2, and formatted with the Heading 2 style.
4. **Press ENTER, then click the Demote to Body Text button » in the Outline Tools group**
5. **Type the following text: Three topics are included in this guide: Pre-Arrival Checklist, Academic Support, and Wellness Guide.**
   The text is indented, designated as Body Text level, and formatted with the Normal style. Notice that both the Level 1 and Level 2 text are preceded by a plus symbol ⊕. This symbol indicates that the heading includes subtext, which could be another subheading or a paragraph of body text.
6. **Press ENTER, then click the Promote to Heading 1 button « in the Outline Tools group**
   The insertion point returns to the left margin and the Level 1 position.

Quick Tip
Press TAB to move from a higher level to a lower level, and press SHIFT+TAB to move from a lower level to a higher level.

7. **Type Pre-Arrival Checklist, press ENTER, then save the document as IL_WD_9_InternationalStudentGuide_Outline where you store your Data Files**
   When you create a long document, you often enter all the headings and subheadings first to establish the overall structure of your document.
8. **Use the Promote ←, Demote →, and Promote to Heading 1 « buttons to complete the outline shown in Figure 9-2**
9. **Place the insertion point after International Student Guide at the top of the page, press ENTER, click the Demote to Body text button », then type Prepared by followed by your name**
   In addition to Outline view, you can display a document in Draft view.
10. **Click the Close Outline View button in the Close group, click the View tab, click Draft view, then save and close the document**

Figure 9-1: Text in Outline view

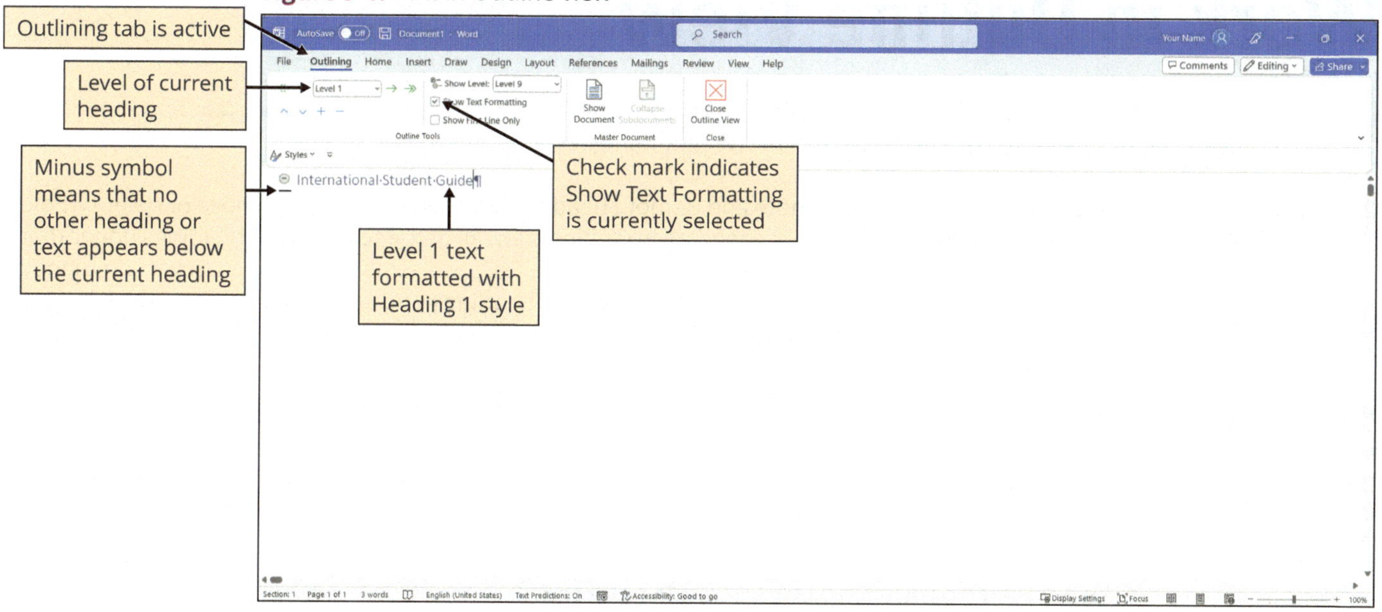

Figure 9-2: Completed outline

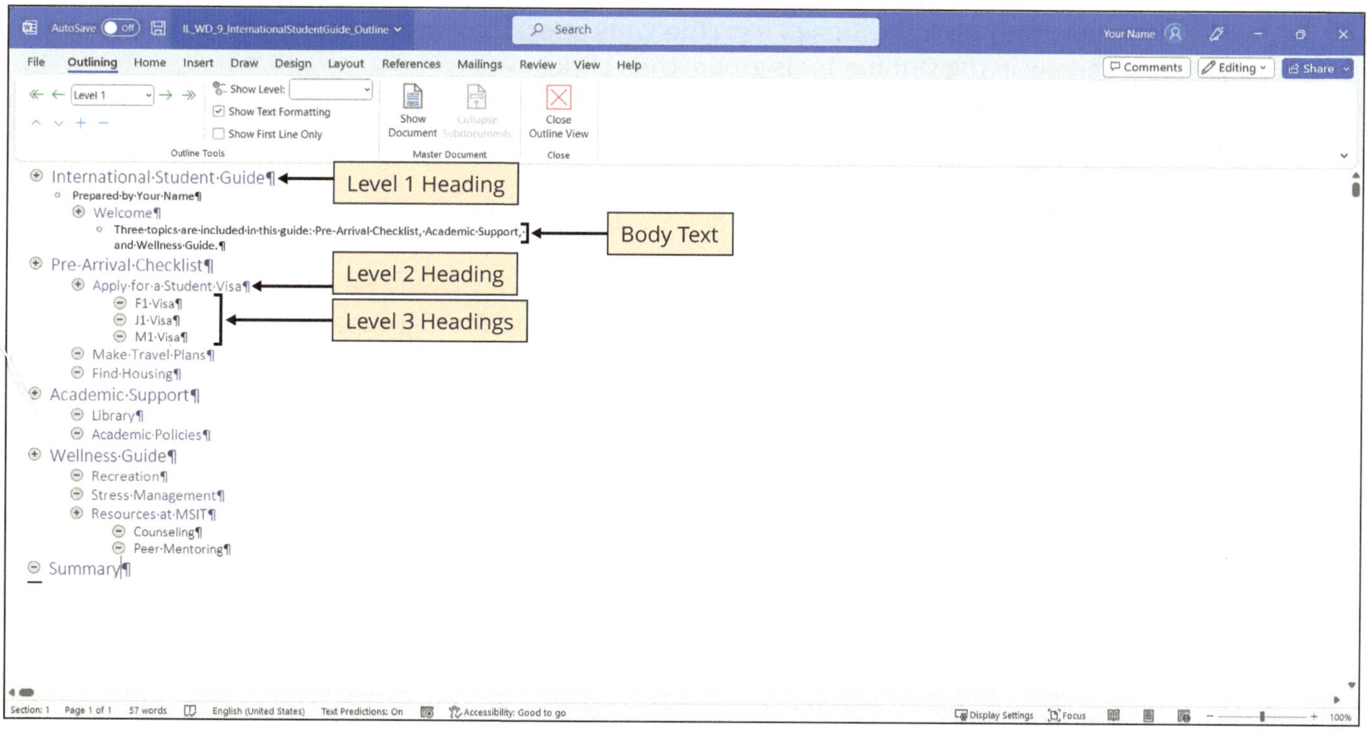

Table 9-1: Frequently used buttons in the Outline Tools group on the Outlining tab

button	use to	button	use to
	Promote text to Heading 1		Move a heading and its text up one line
	Promote text one level		Move a heading and its text down one line
	Demote text one level		Expand text
	Demote to body text		Collapse text

Work in Outline View

Case You work in Outline view to develop a draft of the guide for international students. In Outline view, each heading is formatted with a heading style based on its corresponding level.

Objectives
- Collapse/expand headings in Outline view
- Move headings and show levels

In Outline view, you can promote and demote headings and subheadings and move or delete whole blocks of text. When you move a heading in Outline view, all of the text and subheadings under that heading move with the heading. You also can use the Collapse, Expand, and Show Level commands on the Outlining tab to view all or just some of the headings and subheadings. For example, you can choose to view just the headings assigned to Level 1 so that you can quickly evaluate the main topics of your document.

Steps

Quick Tip
The pictures and the pie chart are not visible in Outline view.

Quick Tip
The selected heading will be gray to indicate it is selected.

1. **sam Open the file IL_WD_9-1.docx from the location where you store your Data Files, then save the document as IL_WD_9_InternationalStudentGuide**
2. **Click the View tab, click the Outline button in the Views group, then verify that the Show Text Formatting check box is selected**
   The document changes to Outline view, and the Outlining tab opens.
3. **Click the Show First Line Only check box to select it, scroll to display every heading and sub-heading and the first line of each paragraph (note spaces where images are inserted), click the Show First Line Only check box to deselect it, click the Show Level arrow in the Outline Tools group, then click Level 1**
   All the headings assigned to Level 1 are formatted with the Heading 1 style. The title of the document "International Student Guide" does not appear because the title text is not formatted as Level 1.
4. **Click the plus button ⊕ to the left of Find Housing to select the heading and all its subtext**
5. **Press and hold SHIFT, click the heading Enroll in Orientation Events, release SHIFT, then click the Demote button → in the Outline Tools group**
   The headings are demoted one level to Level 2, as shown in **Figure 9-3**.
6. **Press CTRL+A to select all the headings, then click the Expand button + in the Outline Tools group**
   The outline expands to show all the subheadings and body text associated with each of the selected headings along with the document title. You can expand a single heading by selecting only that heading and then clicking the Expand button.
7. **Scroll down and click the Wellness Guide plus button ⊕ so only Wellness Guide and its associated subheadings and text are selected, click the Collapse button − in the Outline Tools group to collapse all the subheadings and text associated with each subheading, click the Academic Support plus button ⊕, then click the Collapse button −**
8. **Click the Move Up button ^ in the Outline Tools group once, then double-click the Academic Support plus button ⊕**
   When you move a heading in Outline view, all subheadings and their associated text also move.
9. **Click the Show Level arrow, click Level 3, double-click the Advocacy plus button ⊕, click the Disputing a Mark plus button ⊕, press DELETE, scroll up so the whole outline fills the screen, then compare the revised outline to Figure 9-4**
10. **Click the Close Outline View button in the Close group, then save the document**

Figure 9-3: Headings demoted to Level 2

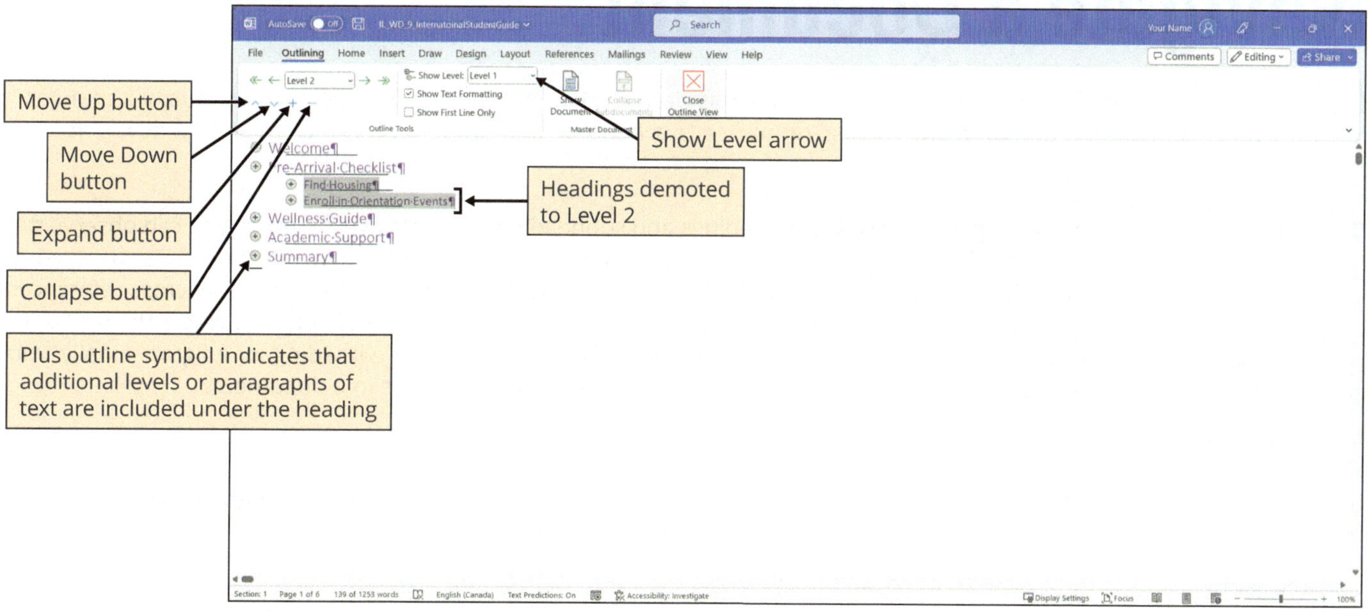

Figure 9-4: Revised outline

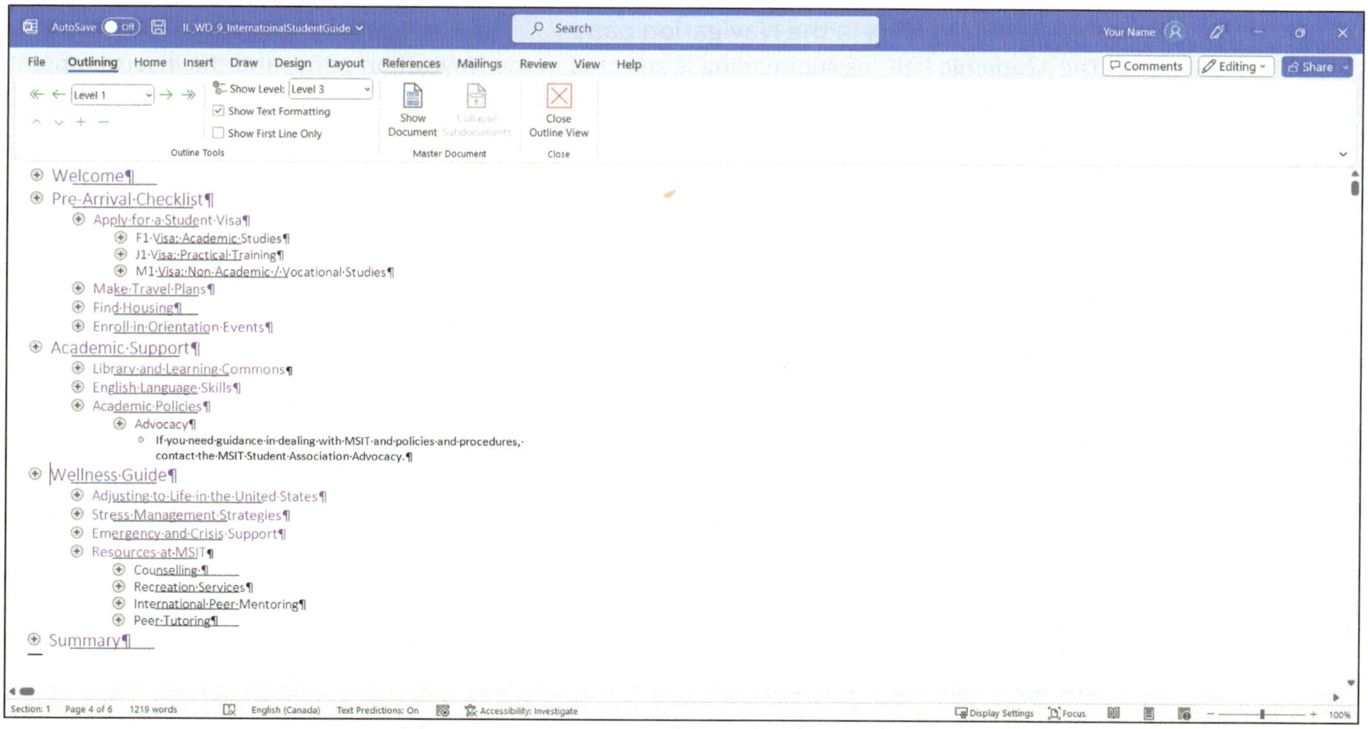

Navigate a Document

Case You expand and collapse headings in Print Layout view, work in the Navigation pane to make further changes to the document, and then add a cross-reference to a heading that students can click to go to a new place in the document.

Objectives
- Collapse/expand headings
- Move headings in the Navigation pane
- Create a hyperlink and cross-reference

You can expand and collapse headings and subheadings in Print Layout view so you can observe the structure of your document. You can also adjust the document structure in the **Navigation pane**, which shows all the headings and subheadings in the document, and you can create cross-references and hyperlinks in your document. A **cross-reference** is text that electronically refers the reader to another part of the document, such as a numbered paragraph, a heading, or a figure. Finally, you can insert a **hyperlink** to move from one place to another place in a document.

Steps

Quick Tip
You can click the Expand arrow to expand the heading again so you can read the text associated with that heading.

1. **Press CTRL+HOME, click Welcome, move the mouse slightly to the left to show the Collapse icon, then click the Collapse icon**
   The paragraph under the Welcome heading is hidden.
2. **Right-click Welcome, point to Expand/Collapse, click Collapse All Headings so only Level 1 headings are visible, right-click Welcome, point to Expand/Collapse, then click Expand All Headings**
   All headings and their associated text are visible again.
3. **Click the View tab, click the Navigation Pane check box in the Show group, click Headings at the top of the Navigation pane if it is not already selected, then click Academic Policies in the Navigation pane**
   The Academic Policies subheading is selected in the Navigation pane, and the insertion point moves to the Academic Policies subheading in the document.
4. **In the Navigation pane, drag Academic Policies up so that it appears above Library and Learning Commons as shown in Figure 9-5**
   From the Navigation pane, you can also right-click a heading to promote, demote, expand, and collapse headings, as well as delete headings and the text associated with them.

Quick Tip
If you create a cross-reference to an equation, you must ensure that the equation was created using the Equation Editor.

5. **Click Pages at the top of the Navigation pane, scroll up the Navigation pane, click the page 1 thumbnail, then select the word summary in the first line of paragraph 2 in the Welcome section**

Quick Tip
The selected text takes on the formatting of the text it is being linked to, so in this example "summary" changes to "Summary".

6. **Click the Insert tab, click the Links arrow to show the Links group if necessary, click the Cross-reference button in the Links group, click the Reference type arrow, click Heading, then scroll to and click Summary as shown in Figure 9-6**
   In the Cross-reference dialog box, you can create a cross-reference to a numbered item, a bookmark, a footnote or an endnote, an equation, and a table, as well as a figure such as a chart, a picture, or a diagram.
7. **Click Insert, click Close, then press SPACEBAR to insert a space after Summary, if necessary**
   The word "Summary" is now a hyperlink to the Summary heading at the end of the document.

Quick Tip
Text you specify as a hyperlink is underlined and shown in a different color.

8. **Click Summary, move the pointer over Summary to show the Click message, press and hold CTRL to show the Hand icon, then click Summary to move directly to the Summary heading**
9. **Press CTRL+HOME, select Wellness Guide at the end of paragraph 1, click the Link button in the Links group, click Place in This Document, click Wellness Guide (scroll if necessary), click OK, press and hold CTRL, click the underlined text Wellness Guide, then save the document**
   The insertion point goes directly to the "Wellness Guide" heading in the document.

Figure 9-5: Changing the order of a subheading in the Navigation pane

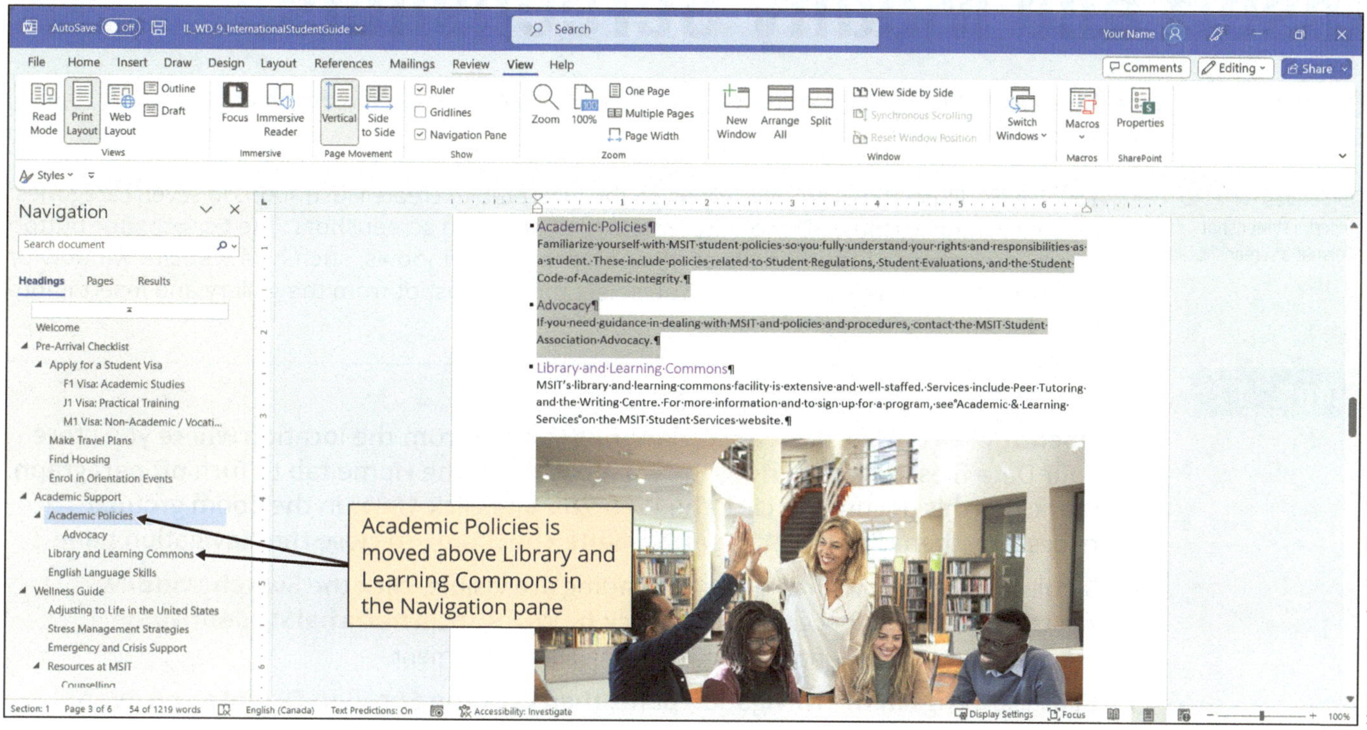

Kampus Production/Pexels

Figure 9-6: Cross-reference dialog box

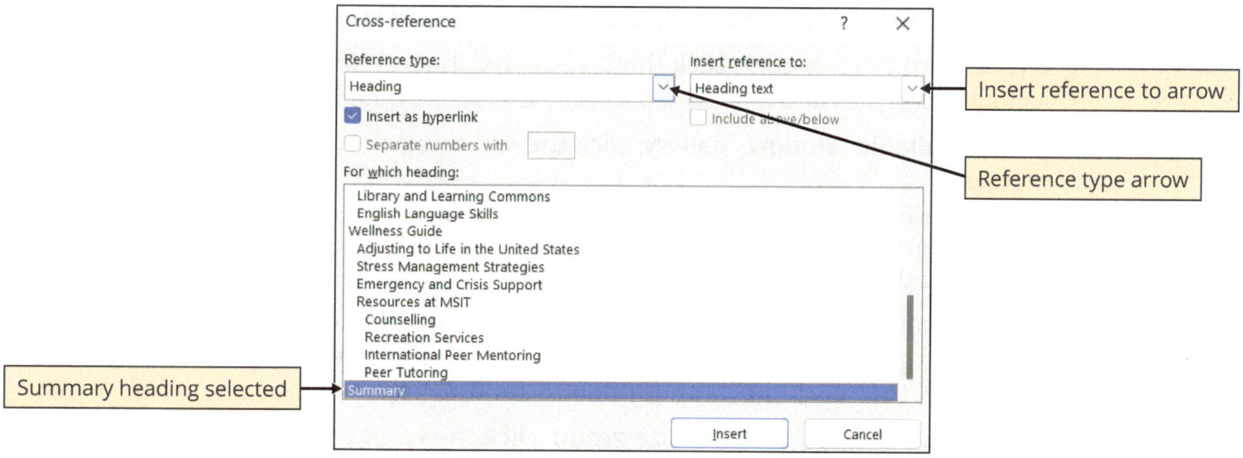

Using bookmarks

A **bookmark** identifies a location or a selection of text in a document. To create a bookmark, you first move the insertion point to the location in the text that you want to reference. This location can be a word, the beginning of a paragraph, or a heading. Click the Insert tab, then click the Bookmark button in the Links group to open the Bookmark dialog box. In this dialog box, you type a name (which cannot contain spaces) for the bookmark, then click Add. To find a bookmark, press CTRL+G to open the Find and Replace dialog box with the Go To tab active, click Bookmark in the Go to what box, click the Enter bookmark name arrow to access the list of bookmarks in the document, select the bookmark you want to go to, click Go To, then close the Find and Replace dialog box. To delete a bookmark you no longer need, click the Bookmark in the Links group, click the bookmark button you want to remove, then click Delete in the Bookmark dialog box. You can also create a hyperlink to a bookmark. Click the Insert tab, click the Link button in the Links group, click Place in This Document, click Bookmarks, click the bookmark you want the hyperlink to go to, then click OK.

Insert and Modify Screenshots

Case You enhance the appeal of the guide for students by including a screenshot of a document containing three images of students at orientation events.

Objectives
- Insert a screenshot
- Format a screenshot

You use the Illustrations group buttons on the Insert tab to create illustrations in seven categories: pictures, shapes, icons, 3D models, SmartArt, charts, and screenshots. The **Screenshot** button displays a gallery of thumbnails of all open program windows, such as a website window or another Office application window. You select the screenshot from the gallery and insert it into your document as a graphic object.

Steps

1. Open **Support_WD_9_StudentGuideImages.docx** from the location where you store your Data files, click the **Show/Hide button** ¶ on the Home tab to turn off paragraph marks for this document, click the **View tab** and click **100%** in the Zoom group if necessary, then click the **Navigation pane check box** to close the Navigation pane
2. Scroll so all three pictures and the heading are visible, click the **Switch Windows button** in the Window group, then click **IL_WD_9_InternationalStudentGuide**
   You are returned to the International Student Guide document.
3. Click **Headings** in the Navigation pane, then click the **Enroll in Orientation Events heading**
4. Delete the text **ORIENTATION SCREENSHOTS** in the document but not the paragraph mark
   Your insertion point is positioned where you want to insert the screenshot.
5. Click the **Insert tab**, then click the **Screenshot button** in the Illustrations group
   A thumbnail of the Word window appears in the Available Windows gallery, as shown in **Figure 9-7**.
6. In the Available Windows gallery, click the **Word window thumbnail** containing the pictures
   The screenshot of the Word window is inserted in the Word document as a graphic object. You can crop, resize, position, and format the object just as you would any graphic object, such as a picture or a chart.
7. Click the **screenshot**, click the **Picture Format tab**, if necessary, click the **Crop button** in the Size group on the Picture Format tab, crop the screenshot as shown in **Figure 9-8**, then click the **Crop button** to set the crop
8. Click the **Launcher** in the Size group, click the **Lock aspect ratio check box** to deselect it, set the Absolute Height at **4** and the Absolute Width at **6**, then click **OK**
9. Click the **Picture Border arrow** in the Picture Styles group, click the **Black, Text 1 color box**, click the **Home tab**, click the **Center button** in the Paragraph group, click away from the screenshot to deselect it, save the document, then continue to the next lesson to add a screen clipping

Figure 9-7: Thumbnail of a window available for screenshot

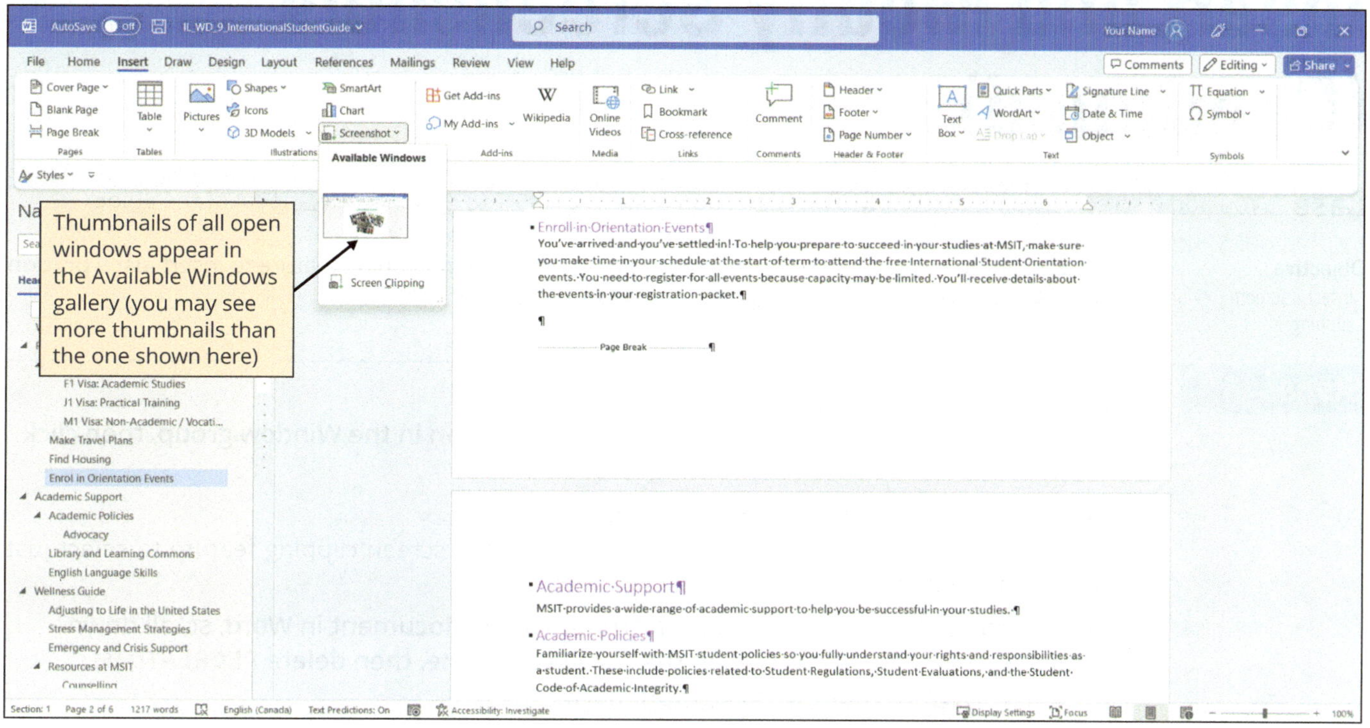

Figure 9-8: Screenshot cropped

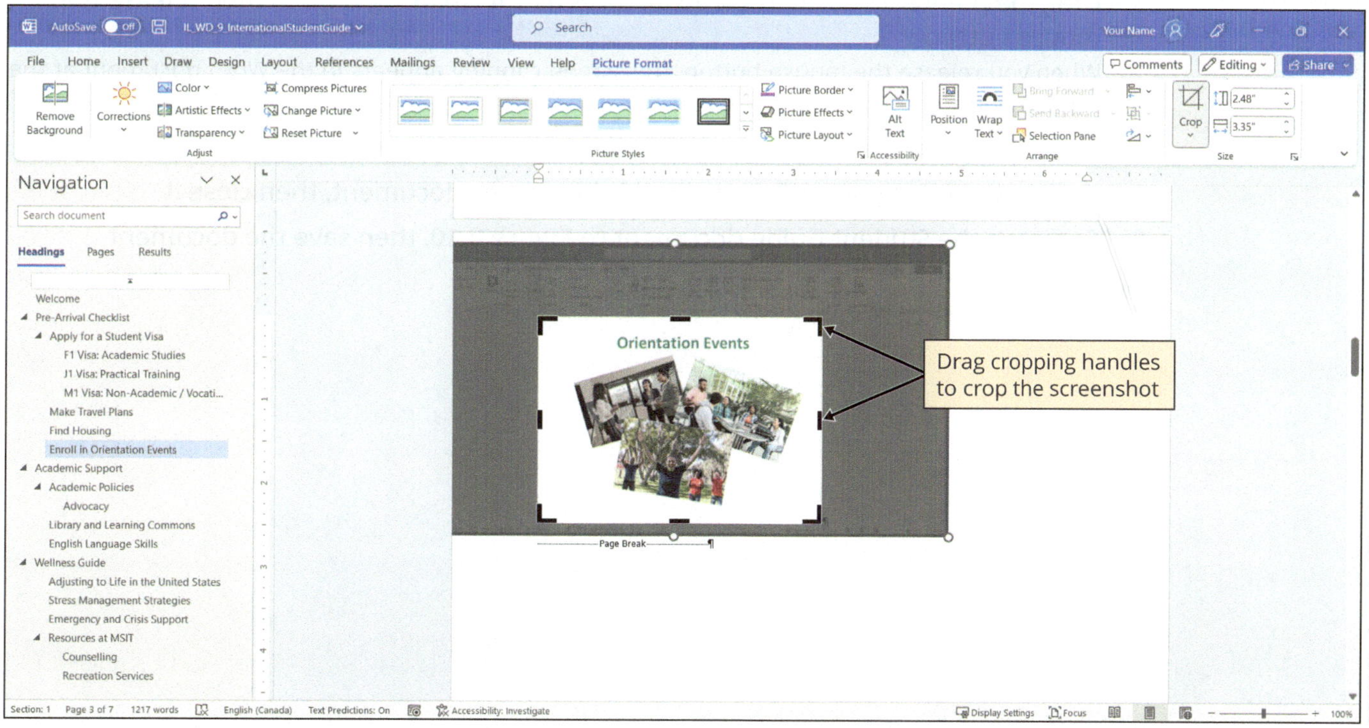

RDNE Stock project/Pexels

Insert and Modify Screenshots (Continued)

Case You add a screen clipping that shows two recreation options at MSIT to enhance the appeal of the guide.

Objective
- Insert a screen clipping

In addition to inserting a screenshot, you can use the Screen Clipping feature to insert just a portion of a window as a graphic object into your Word document.

Steps

1. **Click the View tab, click the Switch Windows button in the Window group, then click Support_WD_9_StudentGuideImages.docx**
2. **Scroll down to view the two pictures on page 2**
   In addition to cropping a screenshot, you can use the screen clipping feature to select just a portion of a screenshot.
3. **Return to the IL_WD_9_InternationalStudentGuide document in Word, scroll down and click Recreation Services in the Navigation pane, then delete RECREATION SCREENSHOT but not the paragraph mark**
4. **Click the Insert tab, click the Screenshot button in the Illustrations group, then click Screen Clipping**
   The Support_WD_9_StudentGuideImages Word window appears on screen and is dimmed.
5. **Drag the pointer to select the two pictures as shown in Figure 9-9, then release the mouse button**
   When you release the mouse button, the screen clipping appears in the Word document at the selected location.
6. **Deselect the image**
7. **Switch to the Support_WD_9_StudentGuideImages document, then close it**
8. **Compare the Student Guide document to Figure 9-10, then save the document**

Trouble
If you do not like the appearance of the clipped screen, click the Undo button, then repeat Steps 4 and 5.

Figure 9-9: Selecting a screen clipping

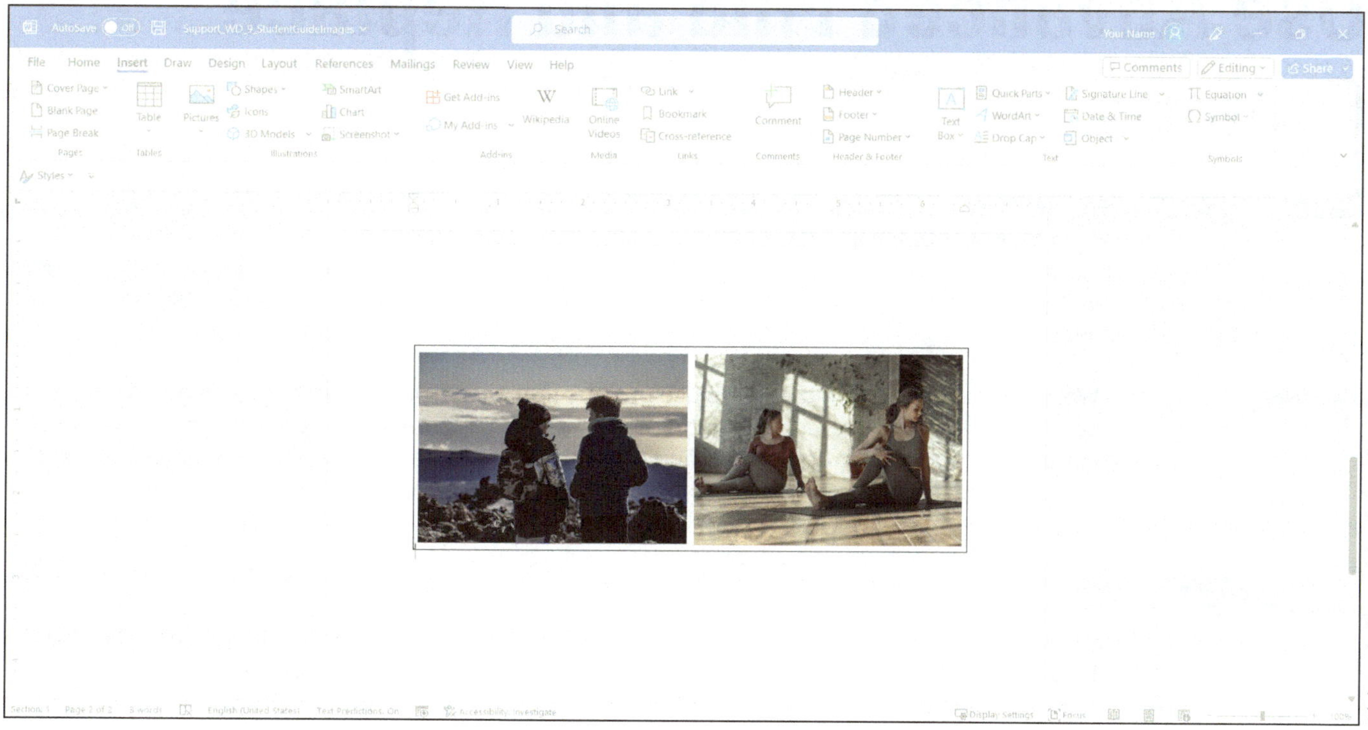

Oleksandr Canary Islands/Pexels; Cliff Booth/Pexels

Figure 9-10: Screen clipping inserted in the document

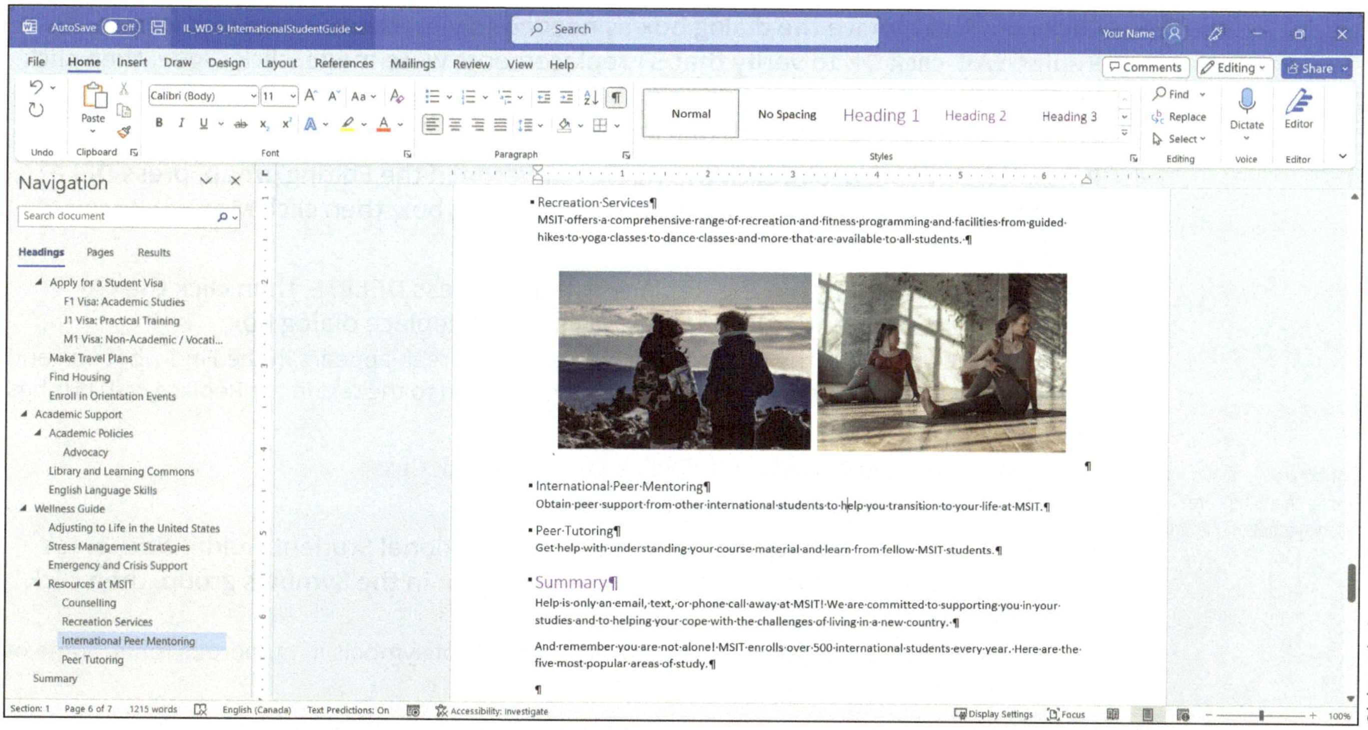

Oleksandr Canary Islands/Pexels; Cliff Booth/Pexels

Use Advanced Find and Replace Options

Case You use Find and Replace to find every instance of MSIT, then replace it with MSIT formatted in bold. You also notice that the document contains page breaks. You know that as a result of reorganizing the headings and adding graphics, the page breaks are no longer correct. You use Find and Replace to replace manual page breaks with nothing so the page breaks are removed. Finally, you insert a symbol from the Symbols dialog box into the document.

Objectives
- Find and replace formatting
- Find and replace special characters
- Insert a symbol

Word offers advanced find and replace options that allow you to search for and replace formats, special characters, and even nonprinting elements such as paragraph marks (¶) and section breaks. For example, you can direct Word to find every occurrence of a word or phrase of unformatted text, and then replace it with the same text formatted in a different font style and font size.

Steps

1. **Press CTRL+HOME, click the Home tab, click the Replace button in the Editing group to open the Find and Replace dialog box, type MSIT in the Find what box, press TAB, type MSIT, then click More if the Find and Replace dialog box is not already expanded**
   The Find and Replace dialog box expands, and a selection of Search Options appears.
2. **Click the Format button at the bottom of the Find and Replace dialog box, click Font to open the Replace Font dialog box, click Bold in the Font style list, then click OK**
   The format settings for the replacement text "MSIT" appear in the Find and Replace dialog box, as shown in **Figure 9-11**.
3. **Click Find Next, move the dialog box as needed to view the selected text, click Replace All, click OK to verify that 31 replacements were made, click Close, then click in the text**
   Every instance of MSIT is replaced with **MSIT**.
4. **Press CTRL+HOME again, click the Replace button in the Editing group, press DELETE, click the Special button at the bottom of the dialog box, then click Manual Page Break**
5. **Press TAB to select MSIT in the Replace with box, press DELETE, then click the No Formatting button at the bottom of the Find and Replace dialog box**
   As shown in **Figure 9-12**, the code for the manual page break appears in the Find what box and the Replace with box is empty, and the formatting assigned to the text in the Replace with box has been removed.

Quick Tip
Special characters are called symbols.

6. **Click Find Next, click Replace All, click OK, then click Close**
   Two hard page breaks are replaced with a blank line.
7. **Press CTRL+HOME, click to the right of the "International Student Guide" title, press ENTER, click the Insert tab, click the Symbol button in the Symbols group, then click More Symbols**
   In the Symbol dialog box, you can select from hundreds of symbols in numerous fonts. Some of the symbols are like small pictures.
8. **Click the Font arrow, scroll the alphabetical list of fonts to Wingdings, click Wingdings, click the happy face symbol shown in Figure 9-13, then click Insert**
9. **Click Insert two more times, click Close, then save the document**
   Three happy face symbols are inserted below the document title.

Figure 9-11: Find and Replace dialog box

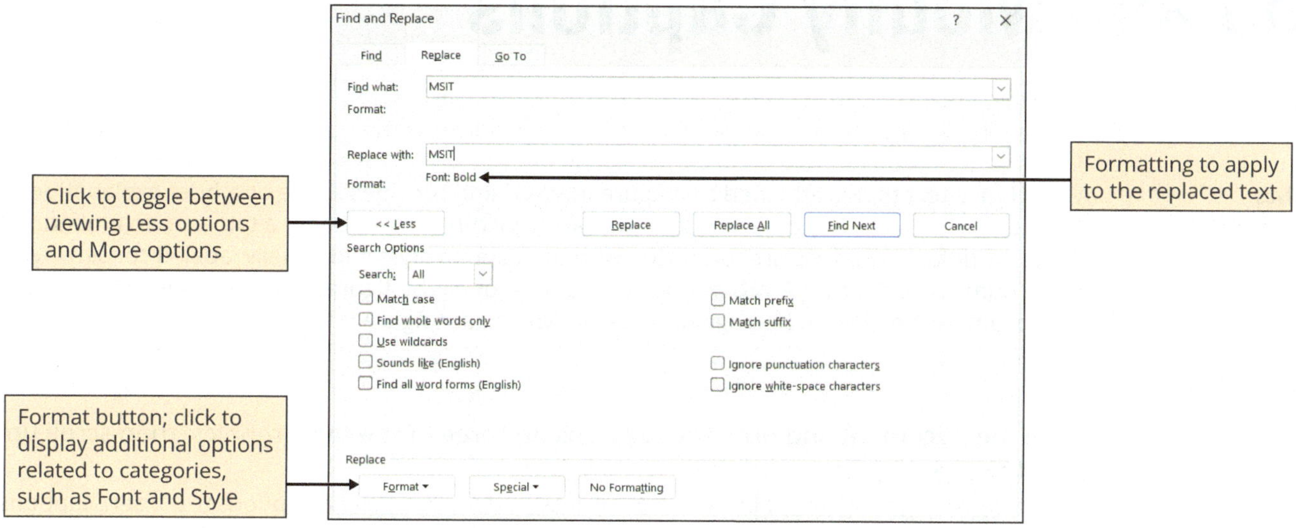

Figure 9-12: Find and Replace dialog box

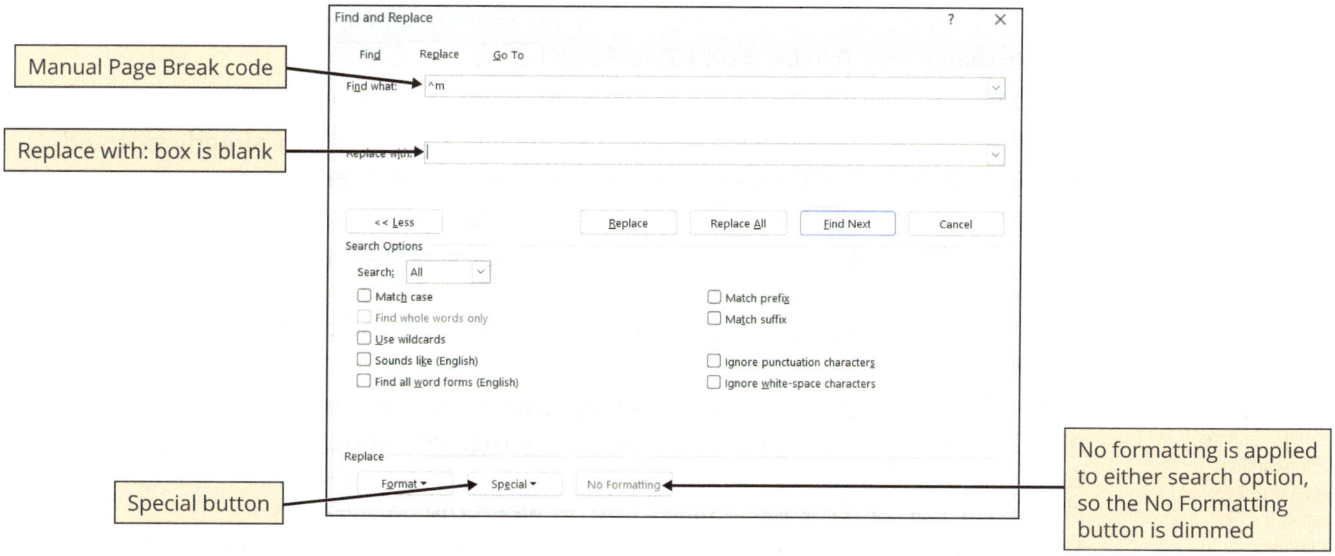

Figure 9-13: Symbol selected in the Symbol dialog box

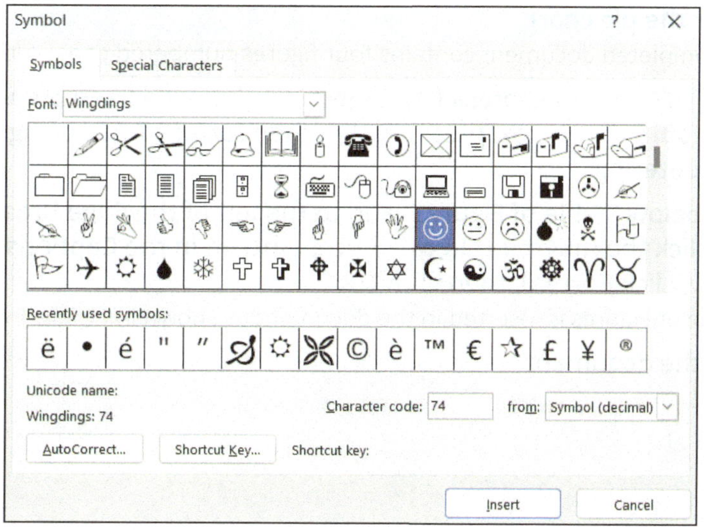

Add and Modify Captions

Case You add a caption to the screenshots in the current document, then remove the label from one of the captions and update the caption labels. Finally, you generate a table of figures that lists all the graphics included in the guide.

Objectives
- Insert and update captions
- Insert a table of figures

A **caption** is text that is attached to a figure in Word and provides a title or a brief explanation of the figure. A **figure** is any object such as a chart, a picture, an equation, a table, or an embedded object. By default, captions are formatted with the Caption style and usually labeled consecutively with a number or a letter. A **table of figures** is a list of all the figures with captions that are used in a document along with the page number on which each figure is found.

Steps

1. **Scroll the document and note the captions on three of the five graphics, then scroll up and click the orientation events screenshot**
   This screenshot you inserted in the previous lesson does not have a caption. You insert captions from the References tab.
2. **Click the References tab, then click the Insert Caption button in the Captions group**
   In the Caption dialog box, you can choose to position the caption above or below the selected item (the default). You can choose to exclude the caption number or letter, and you can select how the captions are numbered or lettered.
3. **Type a colon (:), press SPACEBAR, then type Orientation event images**
4. **Click Numbering, click the Format arrow, click 1, 2, 3,... if it isn't already selected, click OK, compare the Caption dialog box to Figure 9-14, then click OK**
   The figure is captioned Figure 2: Orientation event images.
5. **Scroll to and click the screen clipping of the two recreation images on page 6, click the Insert Caption button, type a colon (:), press SPACEBAR, type Some recreation options at MSIT, click OK, then press CTRL+E to center the caption under the screenshot**

Quick Tip
Press **F9** to update selected caption labels if your keyboard supports the F9 function key.

6. **Scroll up and click the picture of the four students in a kitchen (Figure 1), press DELETE, press DELETE again to remove the paragraph mark, then select and delete Figure 1: An off-campus co-housing situation with other students may be a good option for you and the extra blank line between the paragraphs**
   After you delete a caption, you need to update the numbering of the remaining captions.
7. **Scroll to the Figure 2 caption, right-click 2, click Update Field, then scroll to and update the Figure numbers for the remaining three captions, including the caption under the pie chart**
   The completed document contains four figures numbered consecutively.
8. **Press CTRL+HOME, press CTRL+ENTER to insert a page break, press CTRL+HOME, type Table of Figures, press ENTER, then format Table of Figures using 24 point, bold, and centering**
9. **Click below "Table of Figures" and to the left of the Page Break, click the References tab, click the Insert Table of Figures button in the Captions group, click the Formats arrow, click Formal, then click OK**
   A Table of Figures is inserted in the document as shown in **Figure 9-15**.
10. **Save the document**

Figure 9-14: Caption dialog box

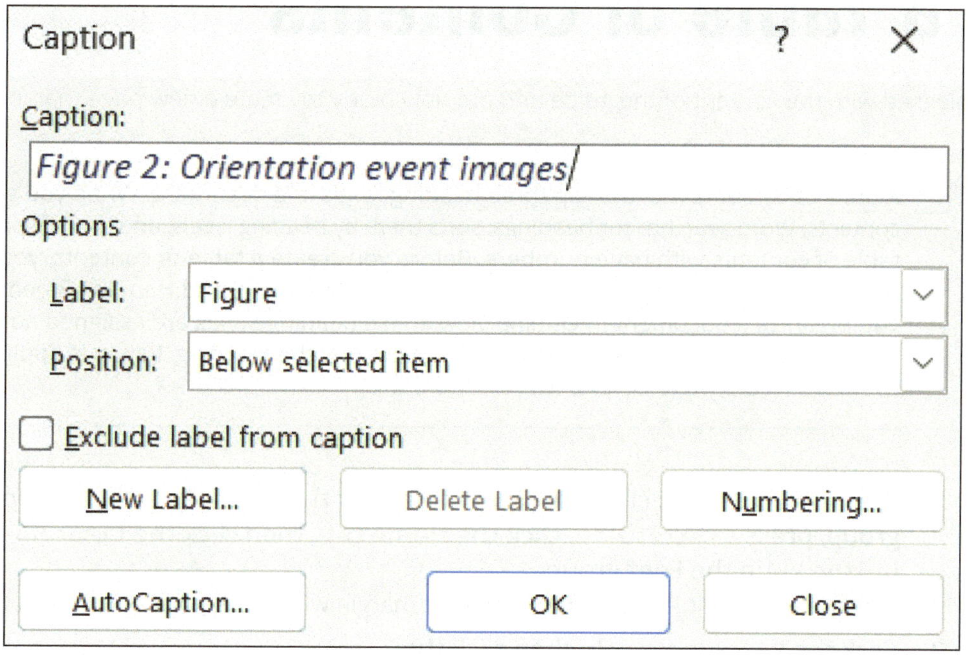

Figure 9-15: Table of figures

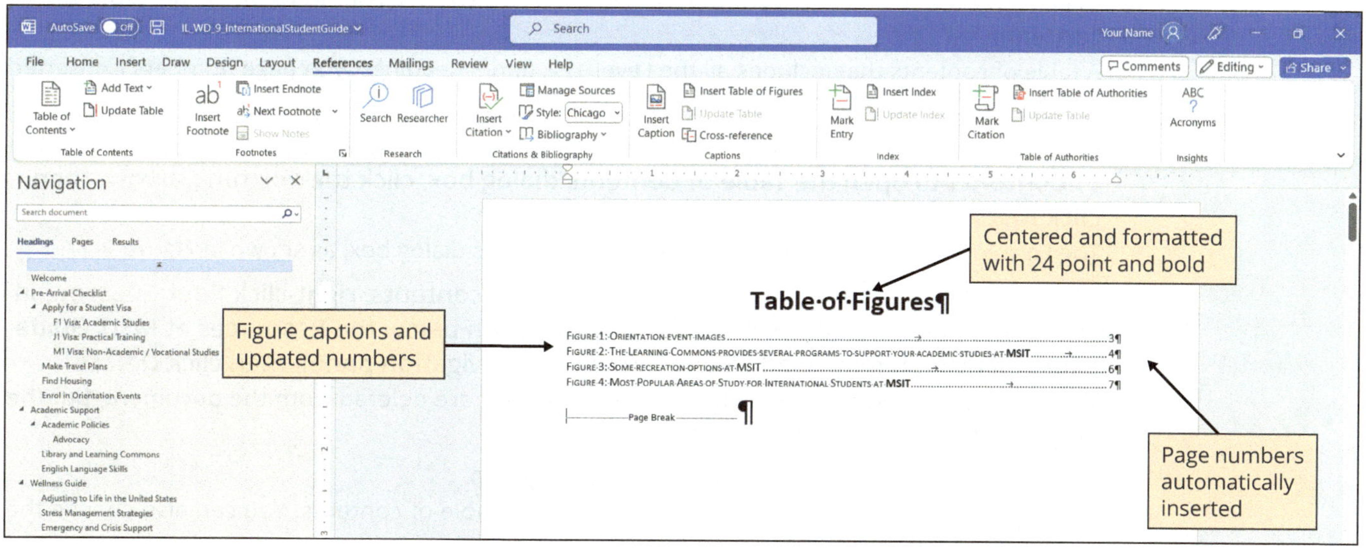

Table of Authorities

A table of authorities lists all the cases, statutes, rules, and other legal references included in a legal document, along with the page on which each reference appears. To create a table of authorities, click the References tab, go to the first reference (called a citation) that you wish to include in the table of authorities, then click the Mark Citation button in the Table of Authorities group. After you have marked all the citations in the document, click the Insert Table of Authorities button in the Table of Authorities group to build the table of authorities. Word organizes and then displays each citation you marked by category.

Insert a Table of Contents

Case You are pleased with the content of the guide and are now ready to create a new page that includes a table of contents.

Objectives
- Insert a table of contents
- Update a table of contents

A table of contents lists the top three heading levels in a document. When you generate a table of contents, Word searches for headings, sorts them by heading levels, and then displays the completed table of contents with page numbers. Before you create a table of contents, you must format the headings and subheadings with the Heading 1, Heading 2, and Heading 3 heading styles. When you organize a document in Outline view, these heading styles are assigned automatically to text based on the outline level of the text. For example, the Heading 1 style is applied to Level 1 text, the Heading 2 style to Level 2 text, and so on.

Steps

1. **Press CTRL+HOME, click the Insert tab, click the Blank Page button in the Pages group, press CTRL+HOME, click the Home tab, then click the Clear All Formatting button in the Font group**
   The insertion point is positioned at the left margin where the table of contents will begin.
2. **Click the References tab, then click the Table of Contents button in the Table of Contents group**
   A gallery of predefined styles for a table of contents opens.
3. **Click Automatic Table 2 as shown in Figure 9-16, then scroll up to view the table of contents**
   A table of contents that includes all the Level 1, 2, and 3 headings with page numbers is inserted on page 1.
4. **Click the Table of Contents button in the Table of Contents group, click Custom Table of Contents to open the Table of Contents dialog box, click the Formats arrow, then click Distinctive**
   The Formats setting is modified in the Table of Contents dialog box, as shown in **Figure 9-17**.
5. **Click OK, click Yes to replace the current table of contents, right-click Peer Tutoring in the Navigation pane in the Wellness Guide section below the Resources at MSIT Guide subheading (you may need to scroll down the Navigation pane), then click Delete**
   The Peer Tutoring subheading and its related subtext are deleted from the document, but the heading is not yet deleted from the table of contents.
6. **Click Update Table in the Table of Contents group**
   The Peer Tutoring subheading is removed from the table of contents. You can also change the appearance of the table of contents.
7. **Click the Table of Contents button in the Table of Contents group, click Custom Table of Contents, click the Tab leader arrow, click the dotted line tab leader style (top selection) below None, click OK, click Yes, then scroll up to view "Table of Contents"**
   Figure 9-18 displays the updated Table of Contents.
8. **Move the pointer over the heading Recreation Services in the Table of Contents (scroll down if necessary), press and hold CTRL, then click Recreation Services**
   The insertion point moves to the Recreation Services heading in the document.
9. **Save the document**

Quick Tip
To remove a table of contents, click the table of contents in the document, click the References tab, click the Table of Contents button in the Table of Contents group, then click Remove Table of Contents.

Figure 9-16: Inserting an automatic table of contents

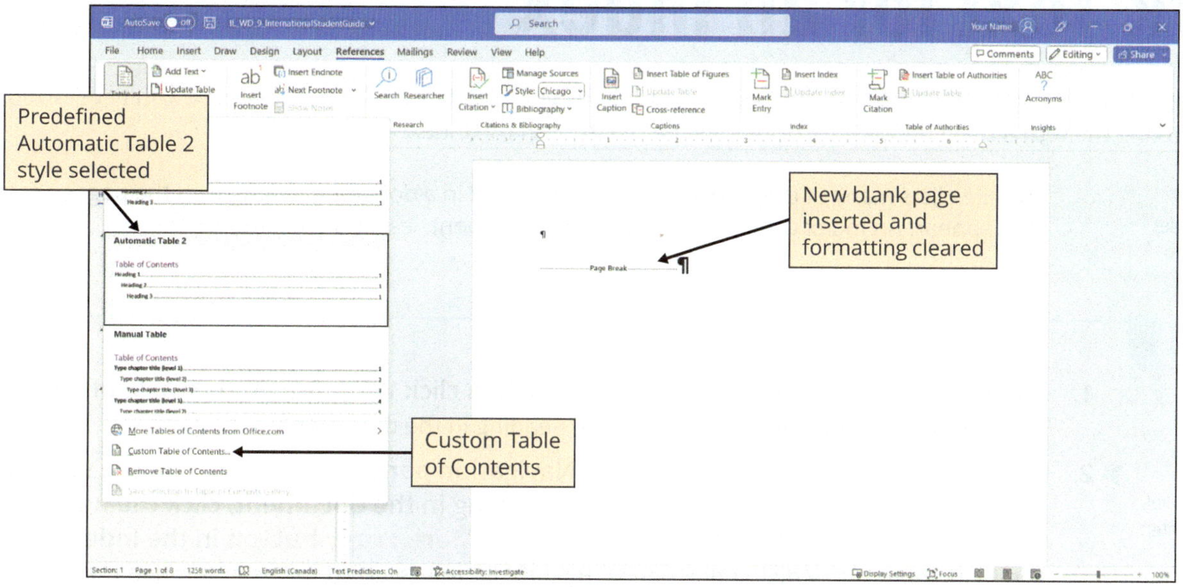

Figure 9-17: Table of Contents dialog box

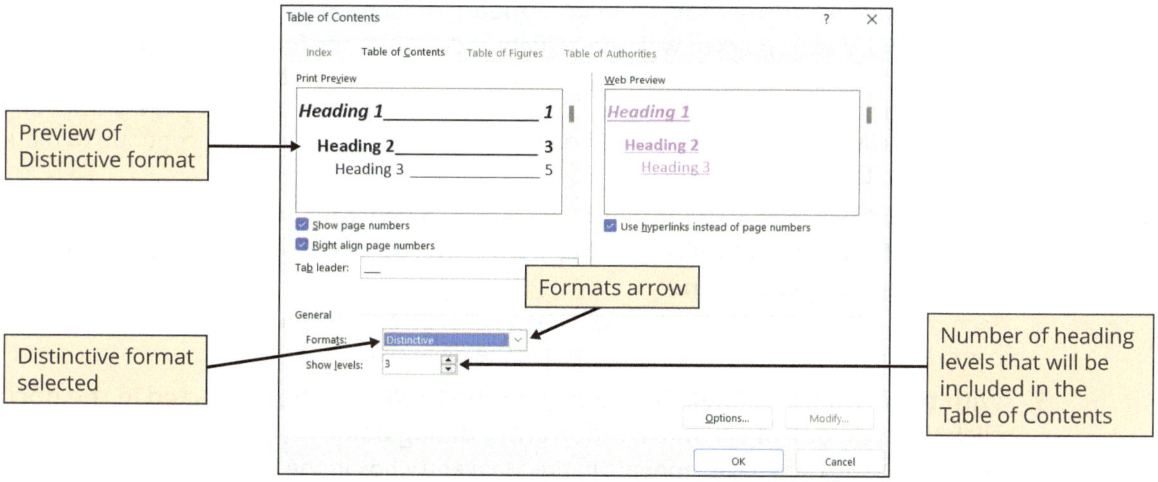

Figure 9-18: Formatted and updated table of contents

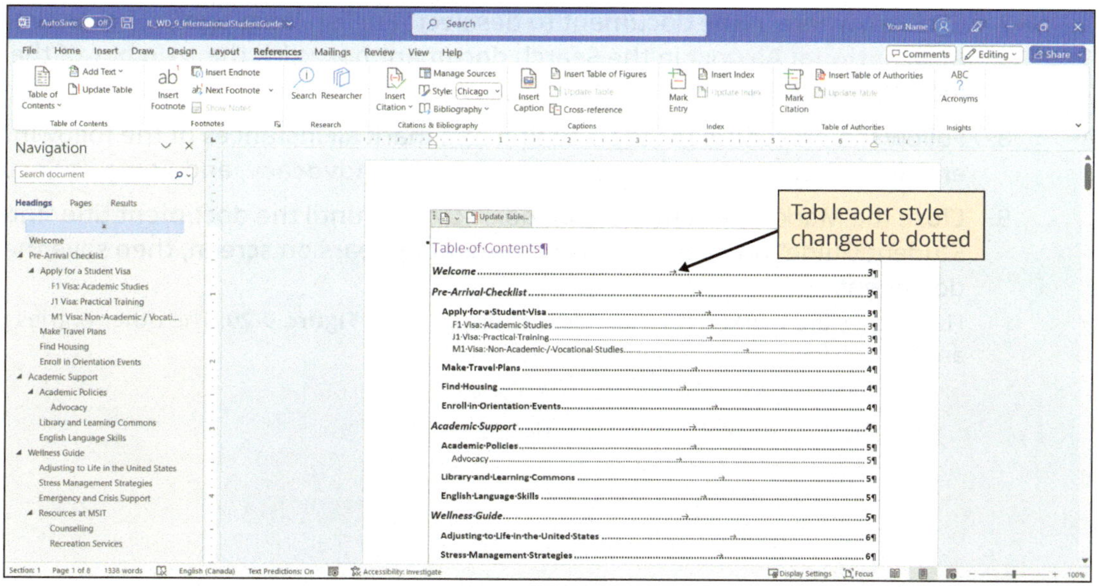

Mark Text for an Index

Case To help students quickly find main concepts in the guide, you decide to generate an index. You get started by marking the terms that you want to include as main entries in the index.

Objectives
- Mark index entries
- Search for text to index

An **index** lists many of the terms and topics included in a document, along with the pages on which they appear. An index can include main entries, subentries, and cross-references.

Steps

1. **Press CTRL+HOME, press and hold CTRL, then click Welcome in the table of contents**
   The insertion point moves to the Welcome heading in the document.

Quick Tip
Hidden codes do not appear in the printed document.

2. **Click Apply for a Student Visa in the Navigation pane, select F1 Visa in the second line under the Apply for a Student Visa heading in the document, click the References tab if it is not already selected, then click the Mark Entry button in the Index group**
   The Mark Index Entry dialog box opens. By default, the selected text is entered in the Main entry box and is treated as a main entry in the index.
3. **Click Mark All, click the Mark Index Entry dialog box title bar, move the dialog box if necessary, then verify that "F1 Visa" appears on screen as shown in Figure 9-19**
   The term "F1 Visa" is marked with the XE field code. XE stands for Index Entry. When you mark an entry for the index, the paragraph marks are turned on automatically if they were not already on so that you can view hidden codes such as paragraph marks, field codes, page breaks, and section breaks. The Mark Index Entry dialog box remains open so that you can continue to mark text for inclusion in the index.
4. **Click anywhere in the document to deselect the current index entry, click Results at the top of the Navigation pane, then type English language in the Search document box in the Navigation pane**
   Each occurrence of the term "English language" is listed in context and in bold in the Navigation pane, and each occurrence is highlighted in the document.
5. **With the instance of English language in the F1 Visa section selected in the document, click the title bar of the Mark Index Entry dialog box**
   The text "English language" appears in the Main entry box in the Mark Index Entry dialog box.
6. **Click Mark All**
   All instances of "English language" in the document are marked for inclusion in the index.

Quick Tip
Make sure you click in the document to deselect the currently selected text before you enter another search term.

7. **Click anywhere in the document to deselect "English language", type Denver International Airport in the Search document box, click the title bar of the Mark Index Entry dialog box, then click Mark All**
8. **Follow the procedure in Step 7 to find and mark all instances of the following main entries: J1 Visa, M1 Visa, Student Association Advocacy, and Campus Security**
9. **Close the Mark Index Entry dialog box, scroll up until the document title "International Student Guide" on page 3 of the document appears on screen, then save the document**
   Five entries are marked for the index, as displayed in Figure 9-20. The other entries you marked are further down the document.

Figure 9-19: Selected text in the Mark Index Entry dialog box

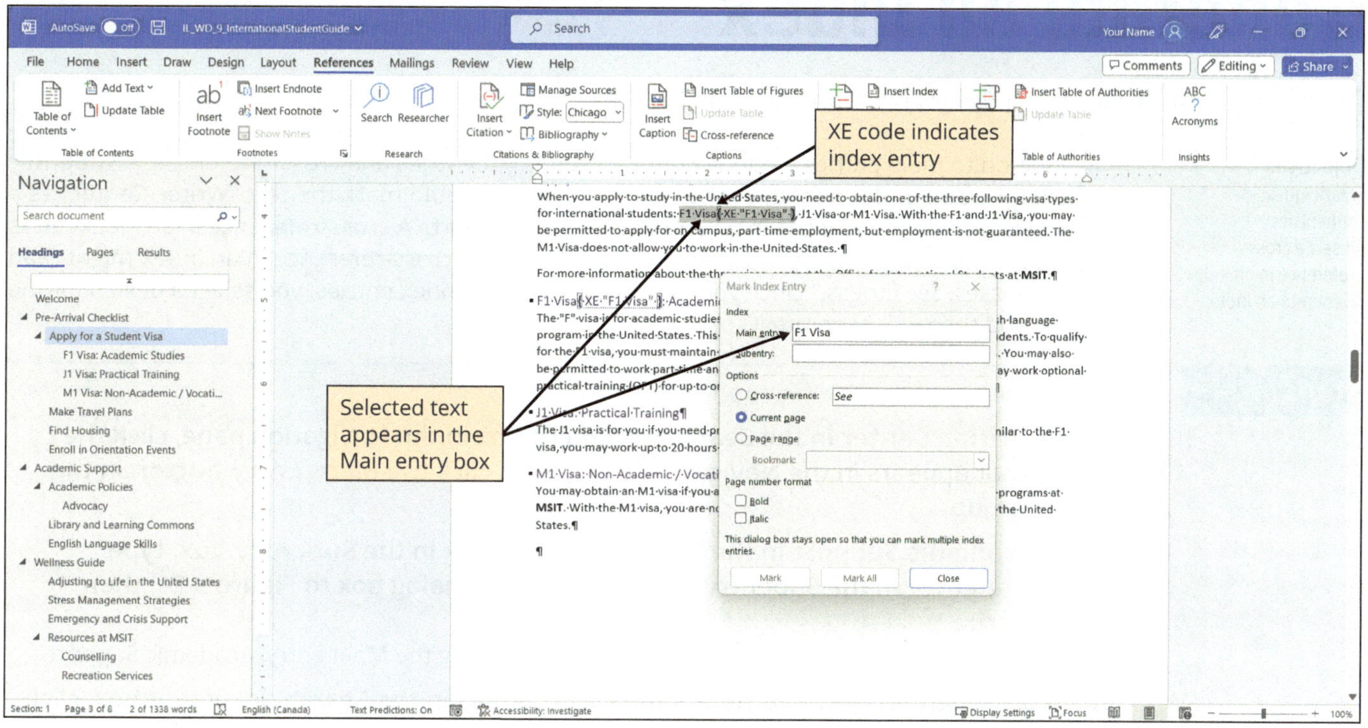

Figure 9-20: Index entries on the first page of the document

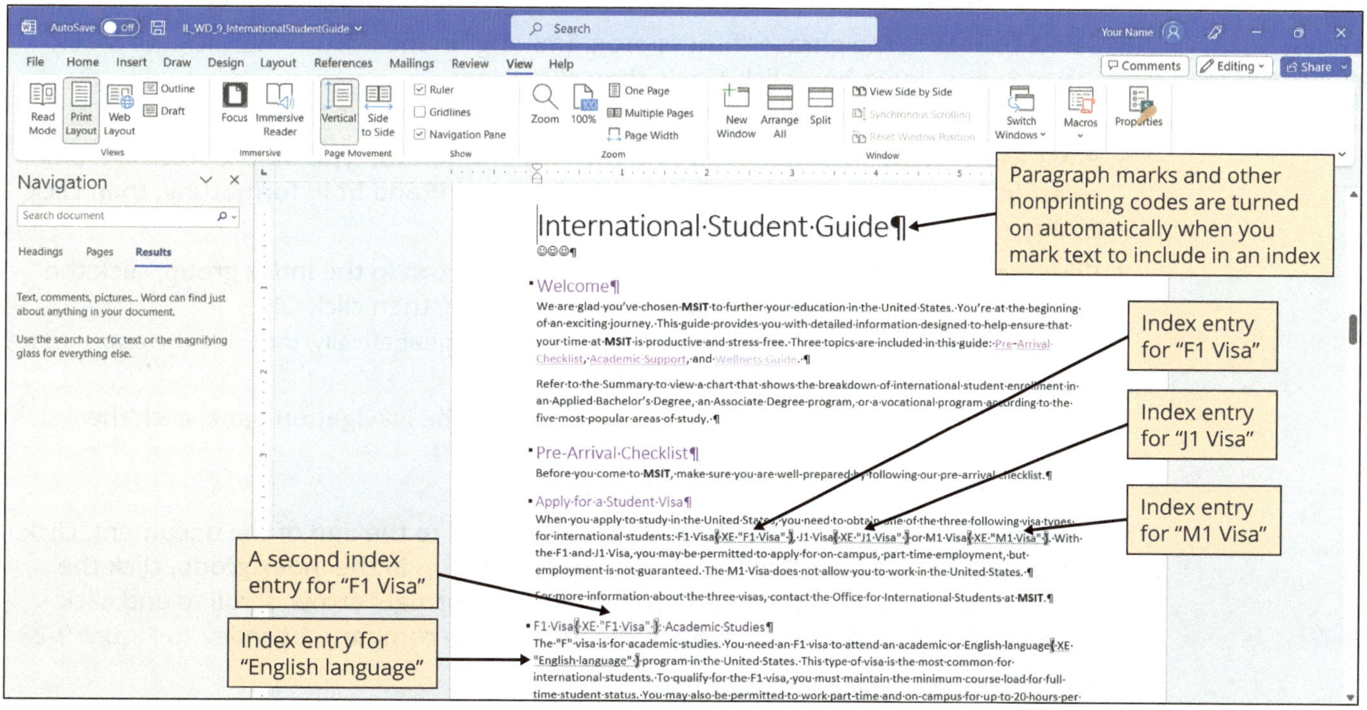

Generate an Index

Case You mark a subentry and cross-reference for the index, and then generate the index on a new last page.

Objectives
- Mark index subentries
- Insert a cross-reference in an index
- Generate an index

In addition to main entries, an index often includes subentries and cross-references. A **subentry** is text included under a main entry. For example, you could mark the text "Writer Center" as a subentry to appear under the main entry "Academic Support." A **cross-reference** in an index refers the reader to another entry in the index. For example, a cross-reference in an index might read "yoga classes. *See* fitness." Once you have marked all the index entries, you select a design for the index, and then you generate it.

Steps

1. Type **Writing Center** in the Search document box in the Navigation pane, click the entry that appears in the Navigation pane, then click the **Mark Entry button** in the Index group
2. Type **Academic Support** in the Main entry box, click in the **Subentry box**, type **Writing Center** in the Subentry box, compare the dialog box to **Figure 9-21**, then click **Mark**
   The text "Writing Center" is marked as a subentry following the Main entry, Academic Support.
3. Click anywhere in the document, type **yoga** classes in the Search document box, click the **Cross-reference option button** in the Mark Index Entry dialog box, click after **See**, type **fitness** as entered in **Figure 9-22**, then click **Mark**
   You also need to mark "fitness" so the Index lists the page number for "fitness."
4. Click in the document, type **fitness** in the Search document box, then click the **first entry** in the Navigation pane containing the text "fitness programming"
5. Select **fitness** in the phrase "fitness programming" in the document, click the **Mark Index Entry dialog box**, click **Mark**, then click **Close**
   The term "yoga classes" is cross-referenced with the term "fitness" in the same paragraph.
6. Press **CTRL+END**, press **CTRL+ENTER**, click the **Home tab**, type **Index**, press **ENTER**, select **Index**, apply **center alignment**, apply **18 point** and **bold** formatting, then click at the **left margin** below Index
7. Click the **References tab**, click the **Insert Index button** in the Index group, click the **Formats arrow** in the Index dialog box, click **Classic**, then click **OK**
   Word has collected all the index entries, sorted them alphabetically, included the appropriate page numbers, and removed duplicate entries.
8. Search for **Housing Guide**, click **Housing Guide** in the Navigation pane, click the **Mark Entry button** in the Index Group, then click **Mark All**
   The index now includes an entry for Housing Guide.
9. Close the dialog box and the Navigation pane, scroll to the end of the document, click anywhere in the index, click the **Update Index button** in the Index group, click the **Insert Index button** in the Index group, click the Formats arrow, scroll to and click **Formal**, click **OK**, click **OK** to replace the index, then compare the index to **Figure 9-23**
10. sam Save and close the document

Quick Tip
If necessary, drag the Mark Index Entry dialog box out of the way as needed to view the selected phrase.

Figure 9-21: Subentry in the Mark Index entry dialog box

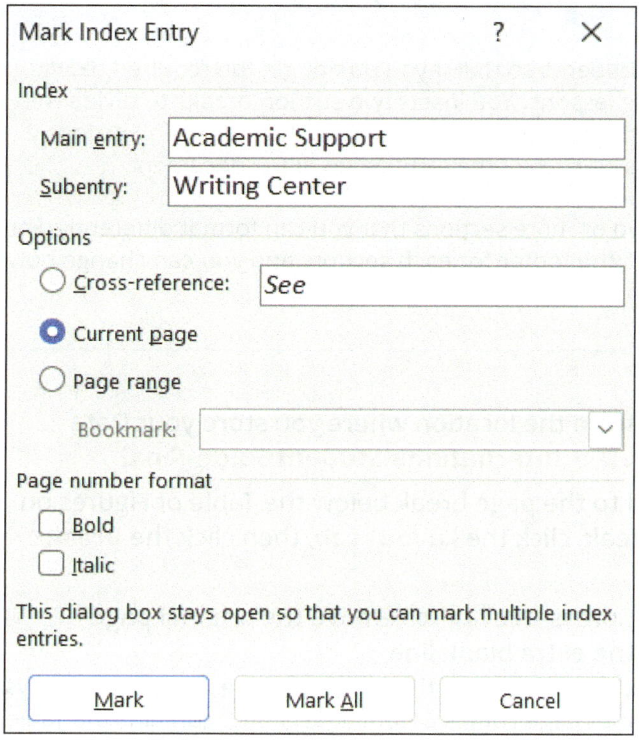

Figure 9-22: Cross-reference in the Mark Index entry dialog box

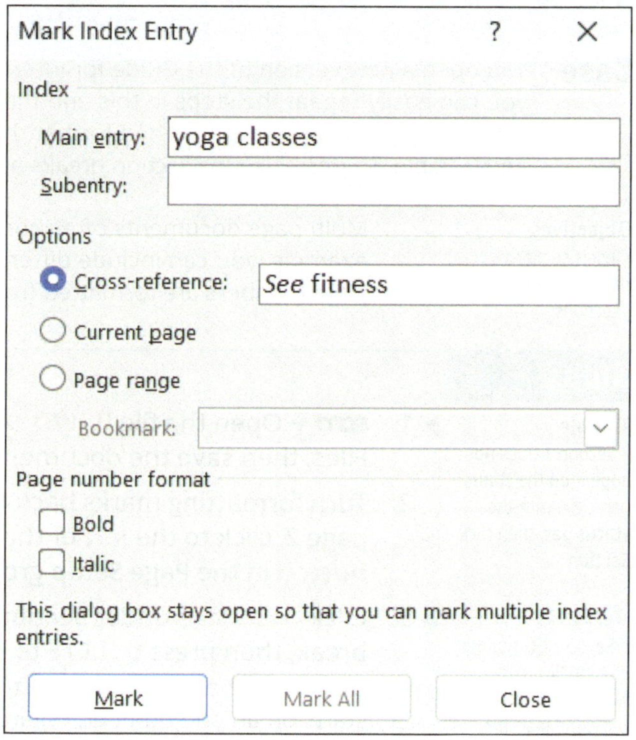

Figure 9-23: Completed index

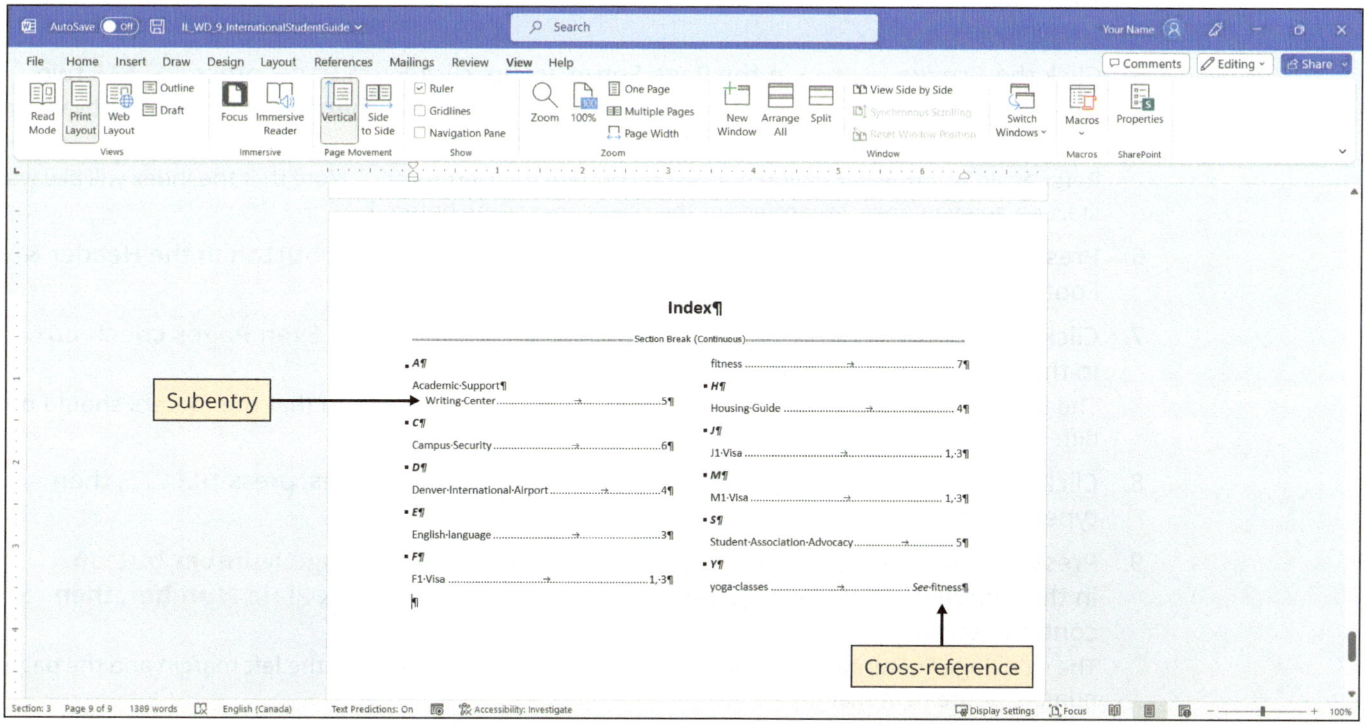

Insert Footers in Multiple Sections

Case You open a new version of the Guide for International Students so that if you do not get the required results, you can easily repeat the steps in this and the following lessons. You insert two section breaks to divide the report into three sections, and then format the footer differently in Section 1 from the footers in Sections 2 and 3. Table 9-2 describes the section breaks and footers on each of the eight pages in the document.

Objectives
- Insert sections
- Insert footers in sections

Multi-page documents often consist of two or more sections that you can format differently. For example, you can include different text in the footer for each section, and you can change how page numbers are formatted from section to section.

Steps

Trouble
If Section 1 does not appear on the status bar, right-click the **status bar**, then click **Section**.

Quick Tip
If Section 1 contained 3 pages, Word would insert a blank page and start the Introduction in Section 2 on the fifth page of the document because that is the first odd page after Section 1.

1. **sam Open the file IL_WD_9-2.docx from the location where you store your Data Files, then save the document as IL_WD_9_InternationalStudentGuide_Final**
2. **Turn formatting marks back on, scroll to the page break below the Table of Figures on page 2, click to the left of the page break, click the Layout tab, then click the Breaks button in the Page Setup group**
3. **Click Odd Page under Section Breaks, press DELETE to remove the original page break, then press DELETE to remove the extra blank line**
   By inserting an Odd Page section break, you guarantee that page 1 of the document always starts on an odd number, regardless of what page comes before it. Section 1 contains the Table of Contents, and the Table of Figures, and Section 2 contains the body of the document and the index.
4. **Scroll to page 8, click to the left of the page break on page 8 (below the pie chart), then press ENTER once**
   You've positioned the insertion point at the location where you want to insert an Even Page section break.
5. **Click the Breaks button in the Page Setup group, click Even Page, press DELETE two times to remove the page break and the extra blank line, then scroll up slightly to view the Even Page Section Break as shown in Figure 9-24**
   Refer again to **Table 9-2** so you understand where to insert footers. Note that the index will always start on an even page, regardless of the pages that come before it.
6. **Press CTRL+HOME, click the Insert tab, then click the Footer button in the Header & Footer group**
7. **Click Blank (Three Columns), then click the Different Odd & Even Pages check box in the Options group to select it**
   The Blank (Three Columns) format is selected, and you've specified that the footers should be different on the odd and even pages.
8. **Click to the left of the placeholder text to select all three items, press DELETE, then type your name**
9. **Press TAB two times, type Page, press SPACEBAR, click the Page Number button in the Header & Footer group, point to Current Position, click Plain Number, then continue to the next lesson to finish inserting footers**
   The Odd Page Footer for the entire document contains your name at the left margin and the page number at the right margin.

Figure 9-24: Even page section break on page 8

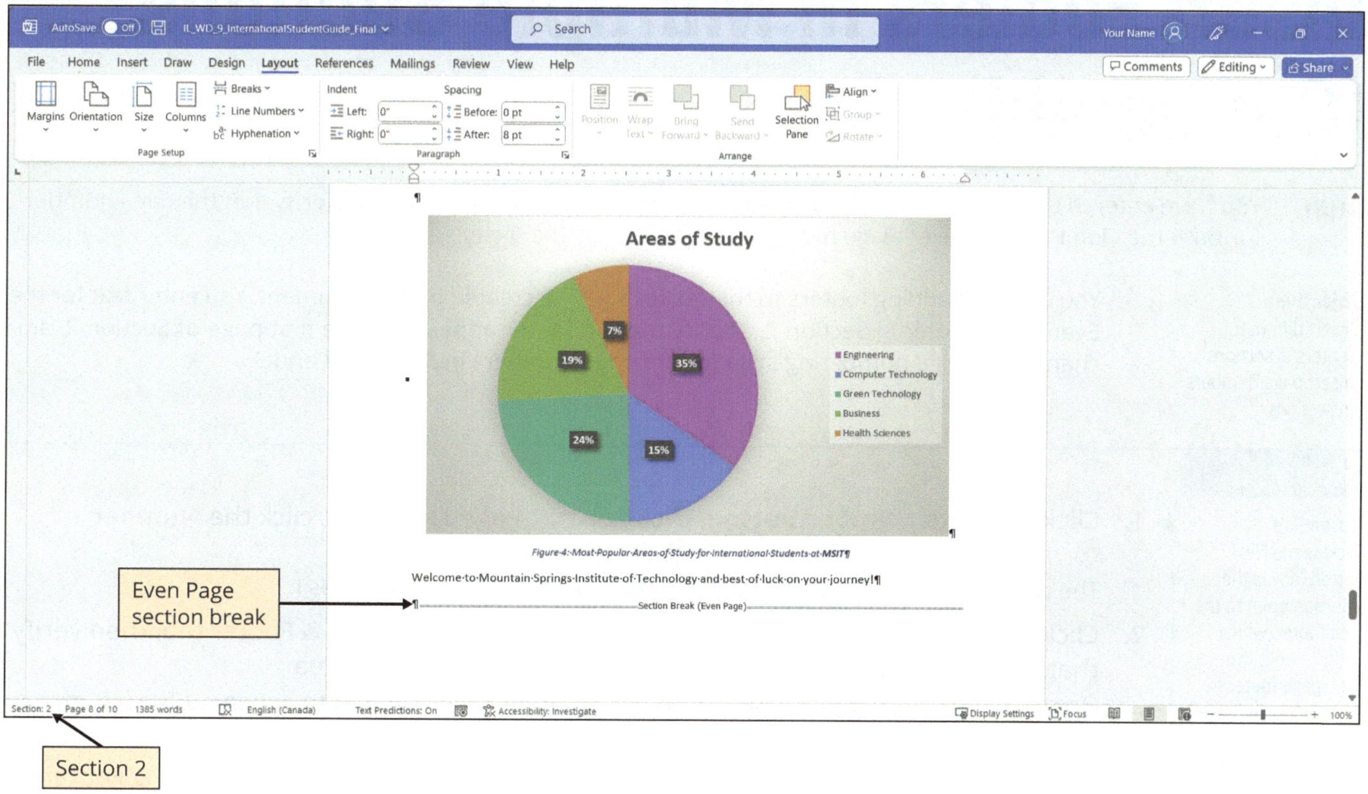

Table 9-2: Description of document sections and footers

Section	Page	Footer
Section 1	Table of Contents – Page i	Odd page footer with Your Name at the left margin and the "i" style page number at the right margin
Section 1	Table of Figures – Page ii	Even page footer with the "i" style page number at the left margin and Your Name at the right margin
Section 2 – Must start on an Odd Page	First page of the document ("Introduction")	No footer: specified that the first page footer for Section 2 is different from the other footers
Section 2	Second page of the document	Even page footer with the "1" style page number at the left margin and Your Name at the right margin
Section 2	Third page of the document	Odd page footer with Your Name at the left margin and the "1" style page number at the right margin
Section 2	Fourth page of the document	Even page footer
Section 2	Fifth page of the document	Odd page footer
Section 3 – Must start on an even page	Eighth page of the document	Even page footer

Insert Footers in Multiple Sections (Continued)

Case You have entered the text for the Odd Page Footer for Section 1. Now you want to specify that the page number for both the Odd Page and Even Page footers in Section 1 use the "i" style.

Objectives
- Insert different footers in sections
- Insert page numbers in sections

You continue adding footers to the sections you've created in the document. You enter text for the Even Page Footer in Section 2, specify that no footer appears on the first page of Section 2, and change the page numbering style for the page numbers in Sections 2 and 3.

Steps

Quick Tip
Clicking the Next button moves the insertion point to the next footer, which in this case is the even page footer for Section 1 as indicated by the section number in the status bar and on the Footer tab.

1. **Click the Page Number button, click Format Page Numbers, click the Number format arrow, click i, ii, iii, then click OK**
   The page number for the Odd Page Footer in Section 1 is formatted as i.
2. **Click the Next button in the Navigation group on the Header & Footer tab, then verify that Even Page Footer -Section 1- appears above the footer area**
   On the Even Page Footer for Section 1, you want the page number to appear at the left margin and your name to appear at the right margin.
3. **Type Page, press SPACEBAR, click the Page Number button in the Header & Footer group, point to Current Position, click Plain Number, press TAB two times, then type your name**
4. **Click the Next button in the Navigation group to go to the Odd Page Footer for Section 2, then click the Different First Page check box in the Options group to select it**
5. **Click the Link to Previous button in the Navigation group to deselect it**
   The Link to Previous button is deselected when it is no longer shaded gray. Deselecting the Link to Previous button is a crucial step when you want to make sure that the contents of the current footer (in this case, no text) are different from the contents in the previous footer, which includes your name and a page number.
6. **Click the Page Number button in the Header & Footer group, click Format Page Numbers, click the Start at option button, verify that 1 appears, then click OK**
7. **Click the Next button in the Navigation group, verify that Page 2 appears at the left margin and your name at the right margin as shown in Figure 9-25, click the Next button, verify that your name appears at the left margin and Page 3 appears at the right margin, then click the Next button to go to Section 3, which is Page 8 (the Index page)**
   You do not need to deselect Link to Previous for the Even Page Footer for Section 3 because you want it to display the page number and your name the same way as for the other pages of the document.
8. **Click the Close Header and Footer button, verify you are returned to page i, the Table of Contents page, then save the document**

Figure 9-25: Even Page footer in Section 2

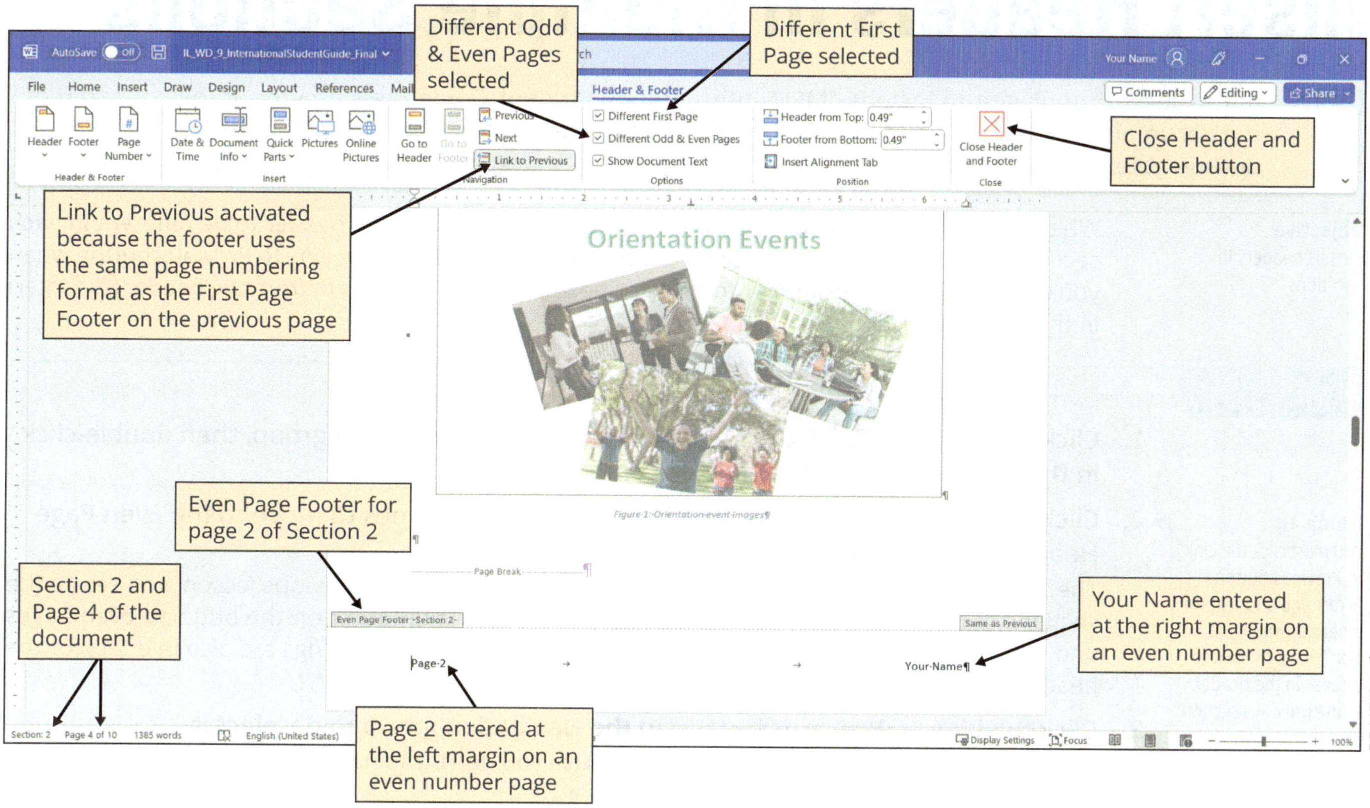

RDNE Stock project/Pexels

Using text flow options

You adjust text flow options to control how text in a multi-page document breaks across pages. To change text flow options, you use the Paragraph dialog box. To open the Paragraph dialog box, click the Launcher in the Paragraph group on the Home tab, and then select the Line and Page Breaks tab. In the Pagination section, you can choose to select or deselect four text flow options. For example, you select the Widow/Orphan control option to prevent the last line of a paragraph from printing at the top of a page (a widow) or the first line of a paragraph from printing at the bottom of a page (an orphan). By default, Widow/Orphan control is active. You can also select the Keep lines together check box to keep a paragraph from breaking across two pages.

Insert Headers in Multiple Sections

Case In this lesson, you want to include "MSIT International Student Guide" as a header on pages 2 to 6 of the document text, but not on the table of contents page, the table of figures page, or the first page of the document text.

Objective
- Insert headers in sections

When you divide your document into sections, you can modify the header to be different in each section. As you learned in the previous lesson, you must deselect the Link to Previous button when you want the text of a header (or footer) in a new section to be different from the header (or footer) in the previous section.

Steps

Quick Tip
You *must* click the Link to Previous button *before* you add text to a header when you don't want the text to appear in the header in the previous section.

Trouble
If the headers and footers do not appear as described, close the document, then return to the lesson "Inserting Footers in Multiple Sections" and repeat the steps.

1. **Click the View tab, click the Page Width button in the Zoom group, then double-click in the header area above Table of Contents**
2. **Click the Next button in the Navigation group three times to move to the Even Page Header for Section 2**
   The "Make Travel Plans" heading is at the top of the page. In the previous lesson, you set up the sections of the document and specified that the footer is different on the odd and even pages and that no footer appears on the first page of Section 2. These settings are also in effect for the header.
3. **Click the Link to Previous button in the Navigation group to deselect it**
   You deselect the Link to Previous button because you don't want the header text to appear on the even page header in Section 1 of the document.
4. **Type Mountain Springs Institute of Technology, select the text you just typed, including the paragraph mark, click the Home tab, increase the font size to 14 point, apply bold, then center the text as shown in Figure 9-26**
5. **Click the Copy button in the Clipboard group**
6. **Click the Header & Footer tab, then click the Next button in the Navigation group**
   The insertion point moves to the left margin of the Odd Page Header for Section 2.
7. **Click the Link to Previous button to deselect it so the header doesn't appear on page i of Section 1 (the Table of Contents page), press CTRL+V to paste the text, click the Close Header and Footer button in the Close group, press CTRL+HOME, then scroll through the document to verify the headers and footers are inserted correctly**
   No header text appears on the Table of Contents and Table of Figures pages in Section 1. No header and no footer appear on the first page of Section 2 (the first page of the document text). The text ("Mountain Springs Institute of Technology") appears in both the odd and even headers for Sections 2 and 3. The status bar displays the total number of pages in the document. The page numbers reflect the pagination you specified in the footers.
8. **Press CTRL+HOME, change the Zoom to 100%, update the entire table of contents, compare the updated table of contents to Figure 9-27, save the document, then continue to the next lesson to adjust the page layout**

Figure 9-26: Header text entered on the Even Page Header for Section 2

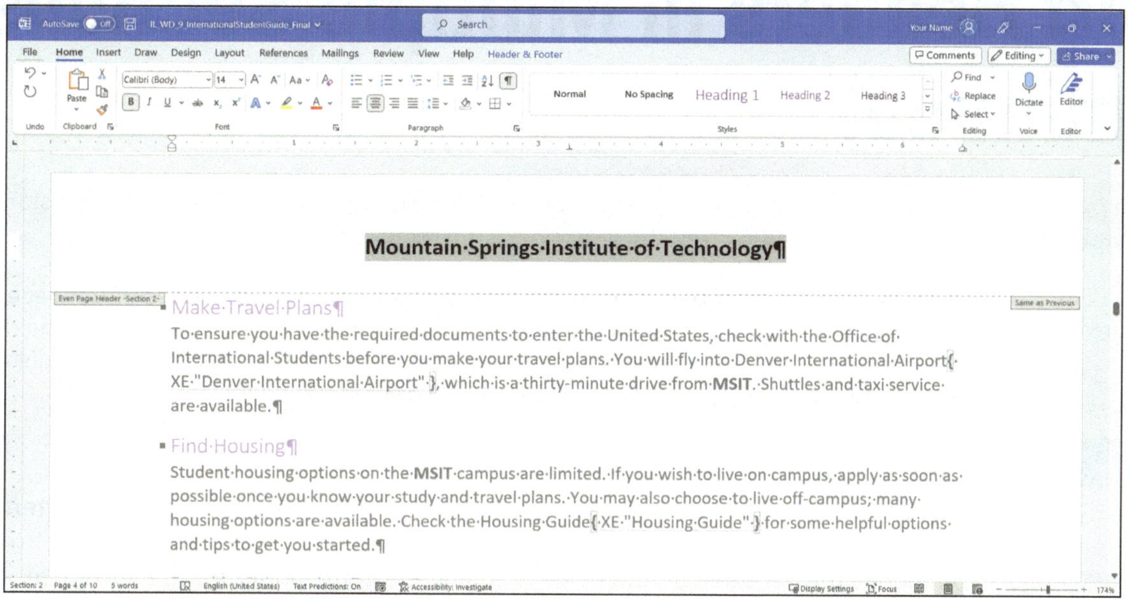

Figure 9-27: Updated table of contents

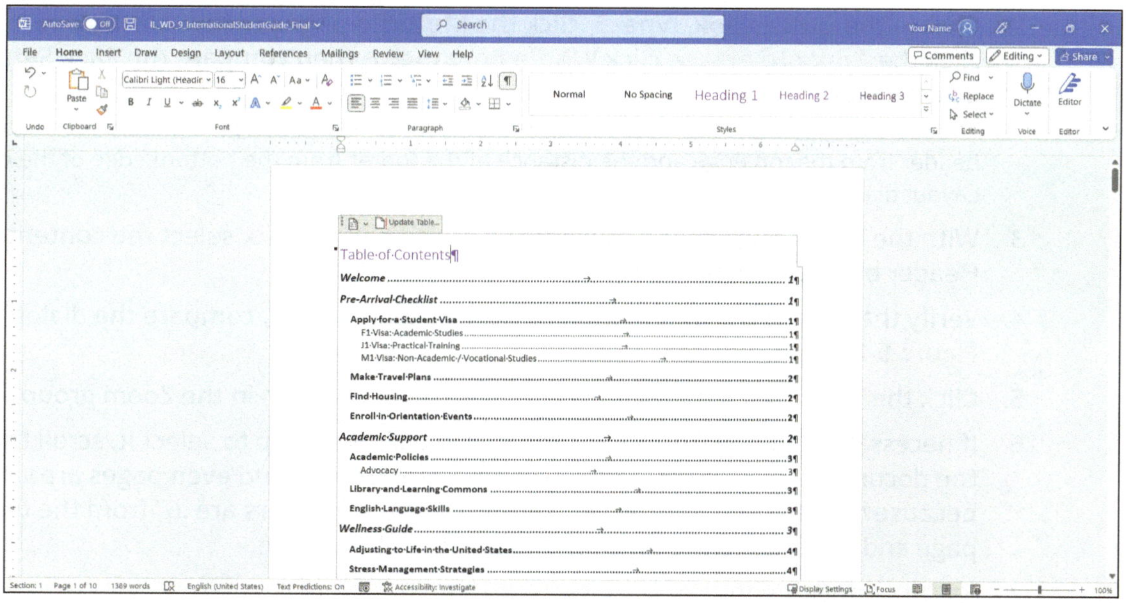

Understanding headers, footers, and sections

One reason you divide a document into sections is so that you can modify the page layout and the headers and footers differently in different sections. You can even modify the header and footer within a section because each section consists of two parts. The first part of a section is the first page, and the second part of the section is the remaining pages in the section. This section structure allows you to omit the header and footer on the first page of a section, and then include the header and footer on all subsequent pages in the same section. To do this, place the insertion point in the section you want to modify, then click the Different First Page check box in the Options group to specify that you wish to include a different header and/or footer (or no header and footer at all) on the first page of a section. In addition, you can also choose to format odd and even pages in a document in different ways by clicking the Different Odd & Even Pages check box in the Options group. For example, you can choose to right-align the document title on odd-numbered pages and left-align the chapter indicator on even-numbered pages.

Insert Headers in Multiple Sections (Continued)

Case To print the guide for binding, you change the gutter width for the document and change the distance of the header from the top edge of the page and the footer from the bottom edge of the page.

Objective
- Set a gutter margin

When you print a multi-page document that will be printed on two sides of the page, you need to set a gutter margin. When you set a gutter margin, Word adds extra space to the document's existing margins to allow space for binding the document. You can also modify the distance of the header and the footer from the top and bottom edges of the page.

Steps

1. **Click the Layout tab, click the Margins button in the Page Setup group, then click Custom Margins**

   You modify the page setup options by changing the gutter width for the document. A **gutter** is the blank space on the inside of each page, where the pages are bound together. You generally want to set a gutter width that adds to the inside margin and is wider than the outside margin to allow room for binding.

2. **Click in the Gutter box, type .5, click the Multiple pages arrow, click Mirror margins, click the Apply to arrow, click Whole document, then compare the Page Setup dialog box to Figure 9-28**

   The settings are applied to every page in the document. You can also modify the distance of the header from the top edge and the distance of the footer from the bottom edge of the page in the Layout dialog box.

3. **With the Page Setup dialog still open, click the Layout tab, select the contents of the Header box, type .6, press TAB, then type .6**

4. **Verify that Whole document appears in the Apply to box, compare the dialog box to Figure 9-29, then click OK**

5. **Click the View tab, then click the Multiple Pages button in the Zoom group**

6. **If necessary, click the Ruler check box in the Show group to select it, scroll through the document to verify that the inside margins on odd and even pages are wider because of the gutter widths you set and that the headers are .6" from the top of the page and the footers are .6" from the bottom of the page.**

7. **Save the document**

Figure 9-28: Setting the gutter width in the Page Setup dialog box

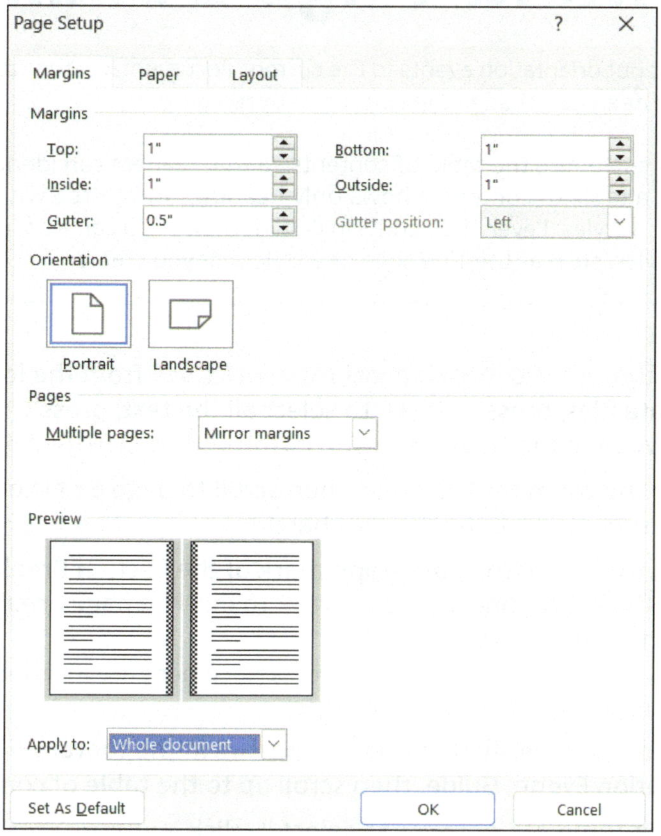

Figure 9-29: Setting the header and footer margin

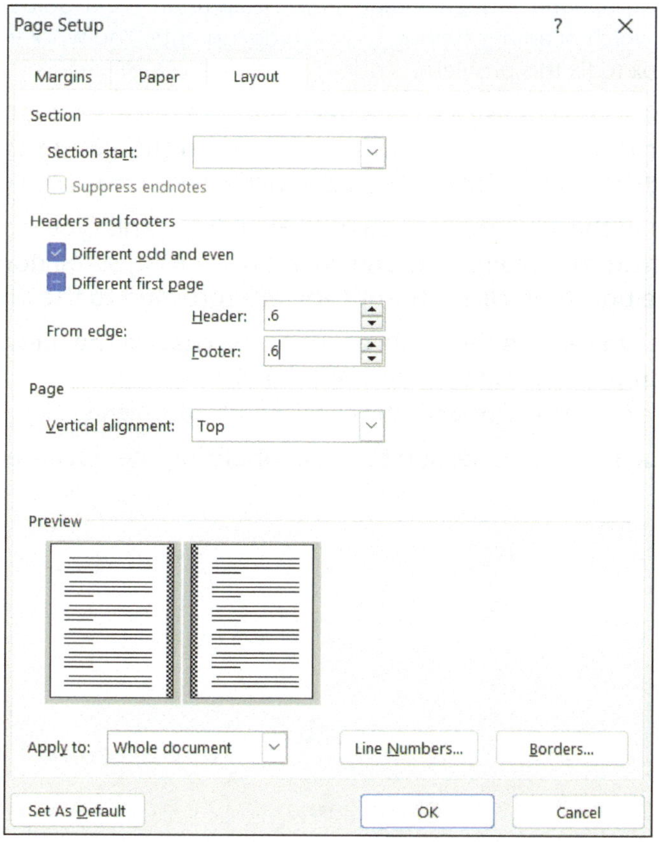

Finalize a Multi-Page Document

Case You add a document about orientation events to the current document, customize the table of contents to show four levels instead of three, then change the spacing between entries.

Objective
- Customize a table of contents

You can customize the table of contents so that readers can identify the document structure. By default, a table of contents shows only headings formatted with the Heading 1, Heading 2, or Heading 3 styles (Levels 1, 2, and 3 in Outline view). You can also include headings formatted with other styles, such as the Title style or a style that you create.

Steps

1. **Open Support_WD_9_OrientationEvents.docx from the location where you store your data files, press CTRL+A to select all the text, press CTRL+C to copy all the text, then switch to the IL_WD_9_InternationalStudentGuide_Final document**
2. **Reduce the zoom to One Page, then scroll to page 6 of the document text (page 8 of the document; contains the pie chart)**
3. **Click to the left of the paragraph mark of the Section Break at the bottom of page 6 (below the chart), press CTRL+ENTER to insert a page break, then press CTRL+V to paste the copied text**
   The two pages of the Orientation Events document are inserted into Section 2 and the entire document should now contain 12 pages.
4. **Zoom to 100%, verify that Page 8 appears in the footer on the second page of the Orientation Events Guide, then scroll up to the table of contents page**
5. **Click the Table of Contents to select it, click Update Table, click the Update entire table option button, click OK, then scroll to view the table of contents**
   The headings from each document are included in the table of contents but not the document titles ("International Student Guide" and "Orientation Event Guide"). As a result, you cannot easily identify which headings belong to which documents. You work in the Custom Table of Contents dialog box to fix this problem.
6. **Click the References tab, click the Table of Contents button in the Table of Contents group, click Custom Table of Contents, then click Options**
   Specify that the two headings formatted with the Title style are included in the table of contents.
7. **Select 1 in the TOC level box next to Heading 1 and type 2, type 3 next to Heading 2, type 4 next to Heading 3 as shown in Figure 9-30, scroll down to the Title box, type 1 in the Title box, then click OK until you are returned to the document**
8. **Click Yes to replace this table of contents, change the View to One Page, scroll up, then compare the table of contents to Figure 9-31**
   The table of contents includes the titles of both documents.
9. **Continue to the next lesson to finish finalizing the document**

Figure 9-30: Table of Contents Options dialog box

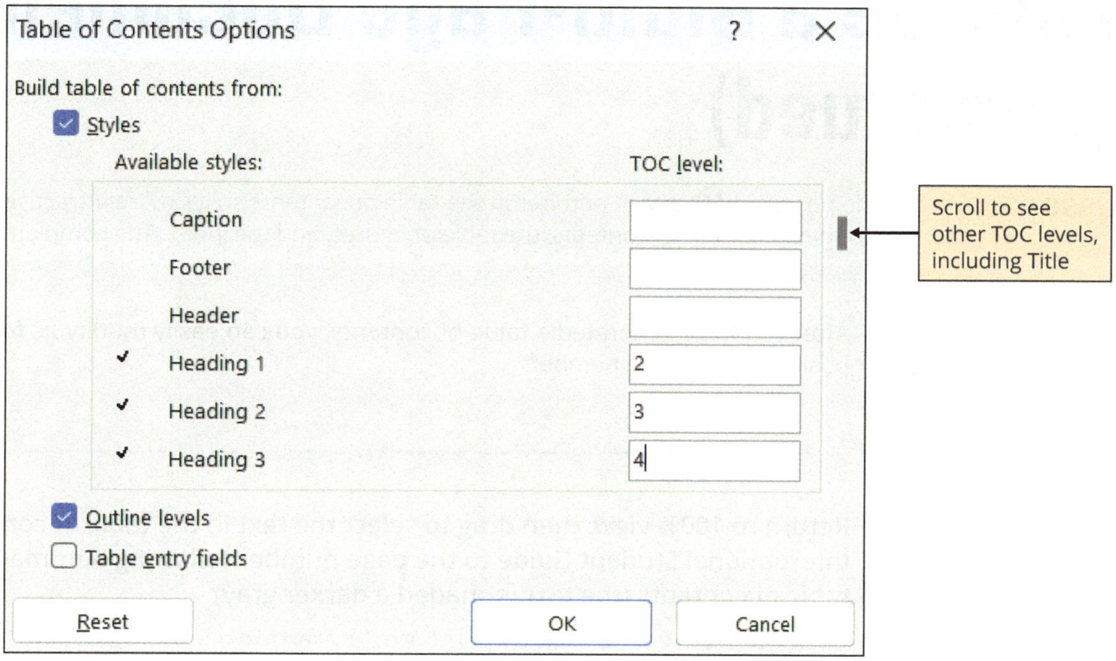

Figure 9-31: Revised table of contents

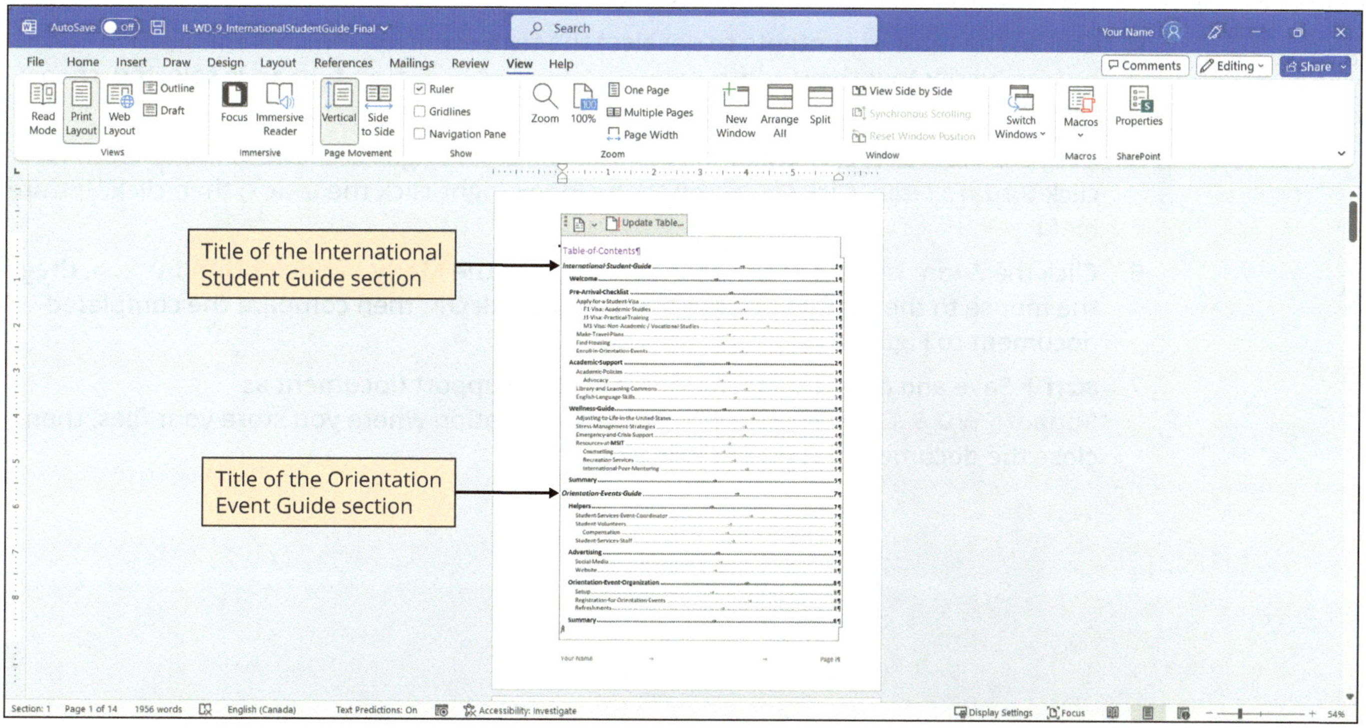

Finalize a Multi-Page Document (Continued)

Case You modify the position of the page number in the table of contents so it's more attractively aligned and easier to read, then update the table of contents, the table of figures, and the index. The completed document consists of a total of 10 pages.

Objective
- Modify table of contents page numbers

After you have generated a table of contents, you can easily modify its format and change the position of the page numbers.

Steps

Quick Tip
After you modify the formatting of a table of contents, you update page numbers only instead of updating the entire table. If you update the entire table, you lose the formatting.

1. **Return to 100% view, then drag to select the text in the table of contents from International Student Guide to the page number following Summary at the end of the table of contents (the text is shaded a darker gray)**
2. **Click the Home tab, click the Line and Paragraph Spacing arrow in the Paragraph group, then click Remove Space Before Paragraph**
3. **With the table of contents text still selected, click the Launcher in the Paragraph group, click Tabs, type 5.5 in the Tab stop position box, click the 3 option button in the Leader area, click Set, then click OK**
   The position of the page numbers is adjusted.
4. **Click in the table of contents to deselect the text, scroll up and click the Update Table button, verify that the Update page numbers only option button is selected, then click OK**
5. **Click the View tab, click the Multiple Pages button, right-click the Table of Figures, click Update Field, click OK, scroll to the Index, right-click the Index, then click Update Field**
6. **Click the Zoom button in the Zoom group, click the Many pages option button, drag the mouse to the right to select 2 × 6 pages, click OK, then compare the completed document to Figure 9-32**
7. **sam Save and close the document, save the Support document as Support_WD_9_OrientationEvents_2 to the location where you store your files, then close the document but do not exit Word**

Figure 9-32: The 11 pages of the completed document

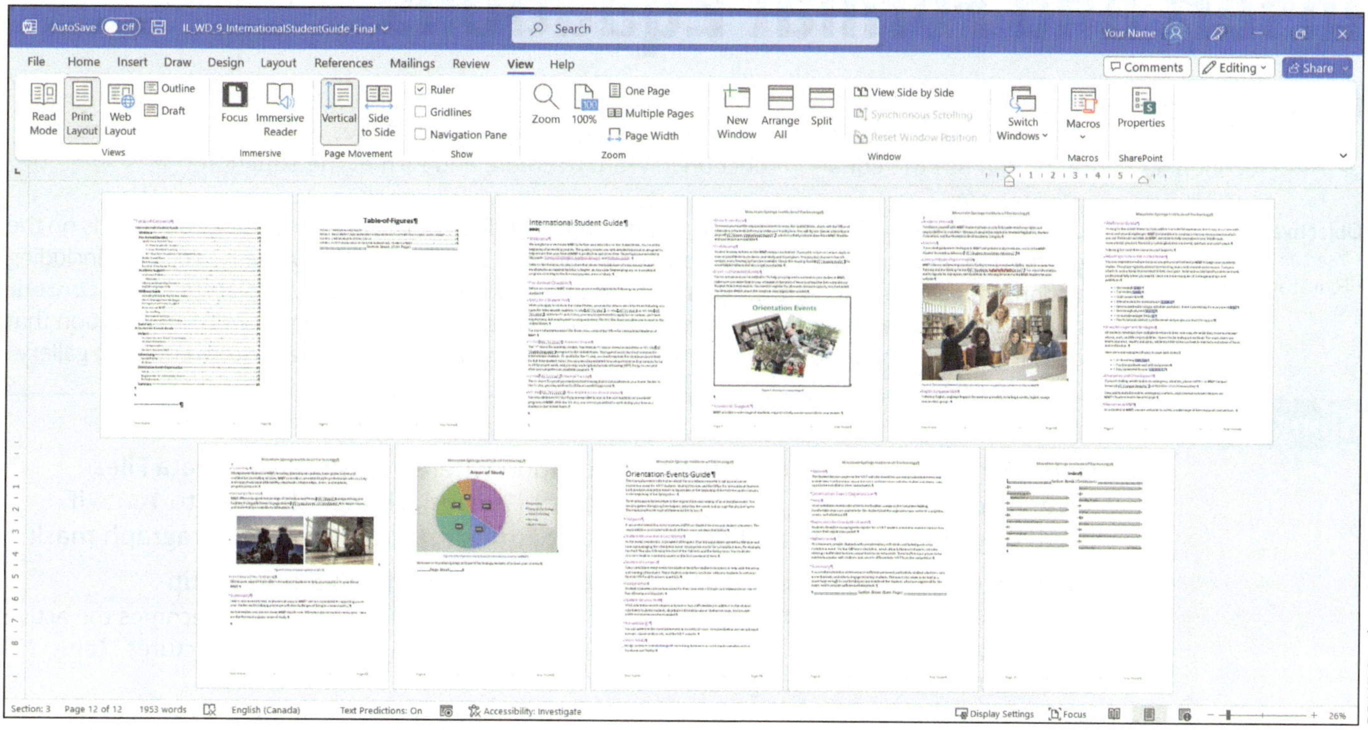

RDNE Stock project/Pexels; Kampus Production/Pexels; Cliff Booth/Pexels

Using Advanced Print Options

With Word, you can scale a document to fit a different paper size, and you can choose to print pages from specific sections or a series of sections, even when the page numbering restarts in each section. To scale a document, click the File tab, click Print, click the 1 Page Per Sheet arrow, then point to Scale to Paper Size and view the list of paper sizes available. You can also choose to print a multiple-page document on fewer sheets; for example, you can print the document on two pages per sheet up to 16 pages per sheet. In the Print screen, you can also specify how to print the pages of a multiple-section document that uses different page numbering in each section. You need to enter both the page number and the section number for the range of pages you wish to print. The syntax required is: PageNumberSectionNumber-PageNumberSectionNumber, which is shortened to p#s#-p#s#. For example, if you want to print from page 1 of Section 1 to page 4 of Section 3, you enter p1s1-p4s3 in the Pages box in the Settings area and then click Print.

Insert and Format Equations

Case A colleague has prepared a document that uses the economic concept of elasticity to describe the result of raising the price of the International Student tuition from $20,000 to $23,000 and includes an equation to express the economics concepts. You use the equation function in Word to create and format the equation.

Objectives
- Insert an equation
- Format an equation

You use the Equation feature to insert mathematical and scientific equations using commands on the Equation tab. You can also create your own equations that use a wide range of math structures, including fractions, radicals, and integrals. When you select a structure, Word inserts a placeholder, a **content control**, that you can then populate with symbols, values, or even text. If you write an equation that you want to use again, you can save the equation and then access it from a custom equation gallery.

Steps

1. **Open the file IL_WD_9-3.docx from the location where you store your Data Files, save the document as IL_WD_9_InternationalTuition, change the view to 100% if necessary, then scroll to and delete the text Equation 1, but not the paragraph mark**

2. **Click the Insert tab, then click the Equation button in the Symbols group**
   An equation content control is inserted in the document and the Equation tab becomes the active tab. This tab is divided into four groups: Tools, Conversions, Symbols, and Structures. **Table 9-3** describes the content of each group.

3. **Click the Fraction button in the Structures group to show a selection of fraction structures, click the Stacked Fraction structure (the first structure in the top row), then increase the zoom to 180%**
   Increasing the zoom helps you view the components of the equation.

4. **Click in the top half of the fraction (the numerator)**
   The box is shaded to indicate it is selected.

Trouble
Follow Step 3 to insert the fraction structure each time; use the keyboard arrow keys to move to different parts of the equation. If your insertion point moves outside the equation, click in the equation again.

5. **Click the More button in the Symbols group to expand the Symbols gallery, click the Basic Math arrow on the title bar, click Greek Letters, then click the Delta symbol (Δ) as shown in Figure 9-33**
   You can select commonly used math symbols from eight galleries as follows: Basic Math, Greek Letters, Letter-Like Symbols, Operators, Arrows, Negated Relations, Scripts, and Geometry.

6. **Type Q, press [↓] to move to the bottom half of the fraction (the denominator), type Q, press [→], type an equal sign (=), then complete the equation as shown in Figure 9-34, making sure to insert fraction structures as needed**

7. **Click the section handle (a portion of the equation is shaded), click the Home tab, change the Font size to 14 point, click the Shading arrow in the Paragraph group, click the Gold, Accent 4, Lighter 80% color box, then click away from the equation**

8. **Save and close the document, but do not exit Word**

Table 9-3: Contents of the Equation tab

Tools	• Use the Equation button to select a built-in equation • Select the equation style: Professional, Linear, or Normal Text
Conversions	• Convert equations to various formats; for example, you can convert an existing equation to a linear format • Click the Launcher to access the Equation Options dialog box where you can specify equation settings and access the Math AutoCorrect list of symbols
Symbols	• Select commonly used mathematical symbols such as (±) and (∞) • Click the More button to show a gallery of symbols • Click the arrow in the gallery to select the group for which you would like to view symbols
Structures	• Select common math structures, such as fractions and radicals • Click a structure button (such as the Fraction button) to select a specific format to insert in the equation for that structure

Figure 9-33: Selecting a symbol

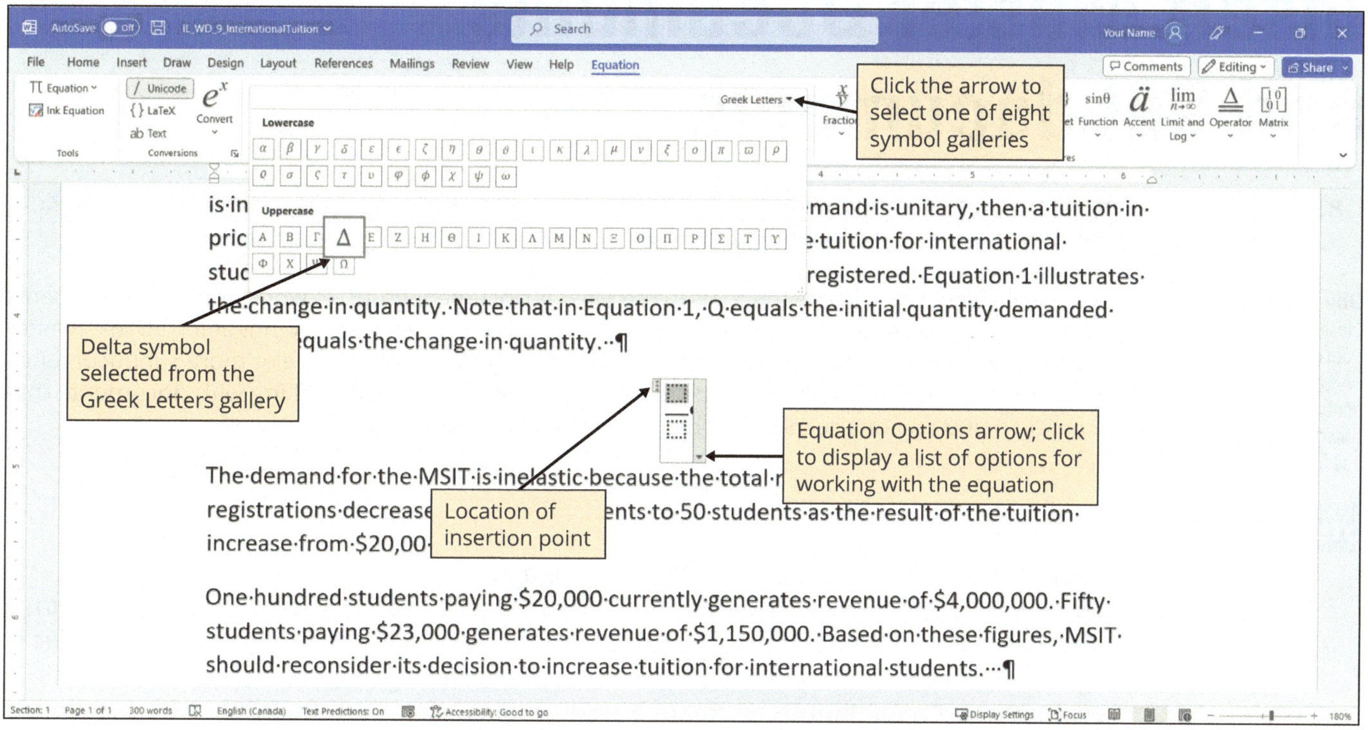

Figure 9-34: Completed Equation 1

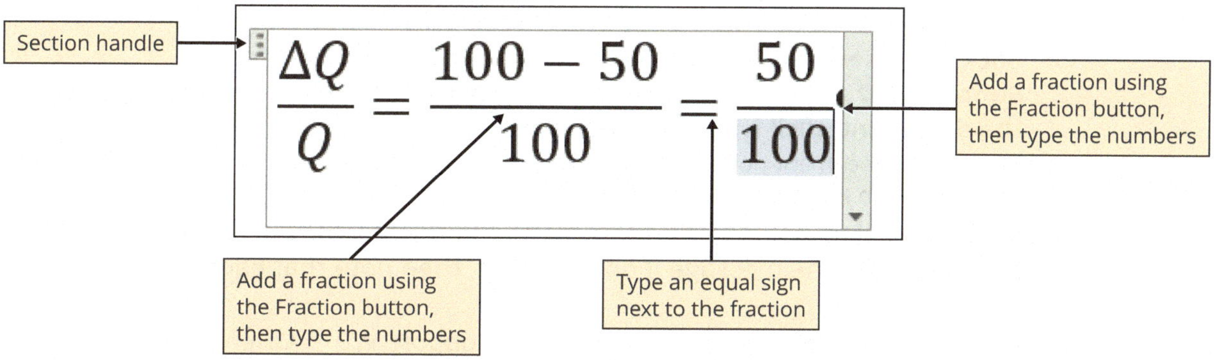

More equation options

From the Equation tab, you can click the Ink Equation button to write an equation using a digital pen or other pointing device. Word converts the written symbols into typed symbols.

From the Shapes button menu on the Insert tab, you can select one of the six equation shapes shown in **Figure 9-35**. You modify these shapes in the same way you modify any drawing shape.

Figure 9-35

Insert Master Documents and Subdocuments

Case You create a master document that contains two subdocuments, work with the options in the Master Document group in Outline view, then mark the document as Final.

Objectives
- Insert a master document
- Add and work with subdocuments
- Mark a document as final

In Outline view, you can use the tools in the Master Document group to work with large documents that consist of several subdocuments. A **subdocument** is a separate document linked to a master document. A **master document** is a document that contains links to one or more subdocuments. You create a master document and subdocuments when you are working with documents that contain many sections such as a book that includes multiple chapters.

Steps

1. **Open a new blank document in Word, save it as IL_WD_9_InternationalStudentGuide_Master, click the View tab and click 100% in the Zoom group if necessary, click the Outline button in the Views group, then click the Show Document button in the Master Document group**
   You use the Create button to create a new subdocument and the Insert button to insert an existing document. Both of the subdocuments you want to include in the master document are existing documents.
2. **Click the Insert button in the Master Document group, navigate to the location where you saved the document IL_WD_9_InternationalTuition, double-click IL_WD_9_InternationalTuition, then click No to All**
3. **Click the Insert button in the Master Document group, insert Support_WD_9_OrientationEvents_2.docx from the location where you saved the document, click No to All, then press CTRL+HOME**
   The master document now consists of two subdocuments, with the first subdocument on screen as displayed in **Figure 9-36**.

Quick Tip
You keep subdocuments as links to a master document when you want to reduce the file size of a master document.

4. **Click the Collapse Subdocuments button in the Master Document group, click OK in response to the message if one appears, then note that each document is now a hyperlink**
5. **Press CTRL and click the hyperlink to the Support_WD_9_OrientationEvents_2 document, view the document, close it, then click the Expand Subdocuments button in the Master Document group**
   The two subdocuments are again displayed in Outline view. When the combined files are not large, you can choose to unlink the subdocuments so they become part of the master document.
6. **Scroll to the Orientation Events document and click the Selection button to the left of the document, as shown in Figure 9-37 to select the entire subdocument, then click Unlink button in the Master Document group**
   The Orientation Events document is no longer a subdocument and cannot be collapsed to a link.
7. **Scroll up and click the Increasing Tuition document Selection button, click the Lock Document button in the Master Document group, double click any word in the document, then try to type text**
   The subdocument is locked; you cannot make any changes. You can also protect the entire document from changes.
8. **Click the File tab, click Info, click Protect Document in the Info pane, view the protection options available, click Mark as Final, click OK, then click OK**
   When you open a document that has been marked as Final, a message appears telling you that the document was marked as final to discourage editing. If you wish to edit the document, click Edit Anyway.
9. **Save and close the document, submit the files to your instructor, then exit Word**

Figure 9-36: Subdocuments inserted in Outline view

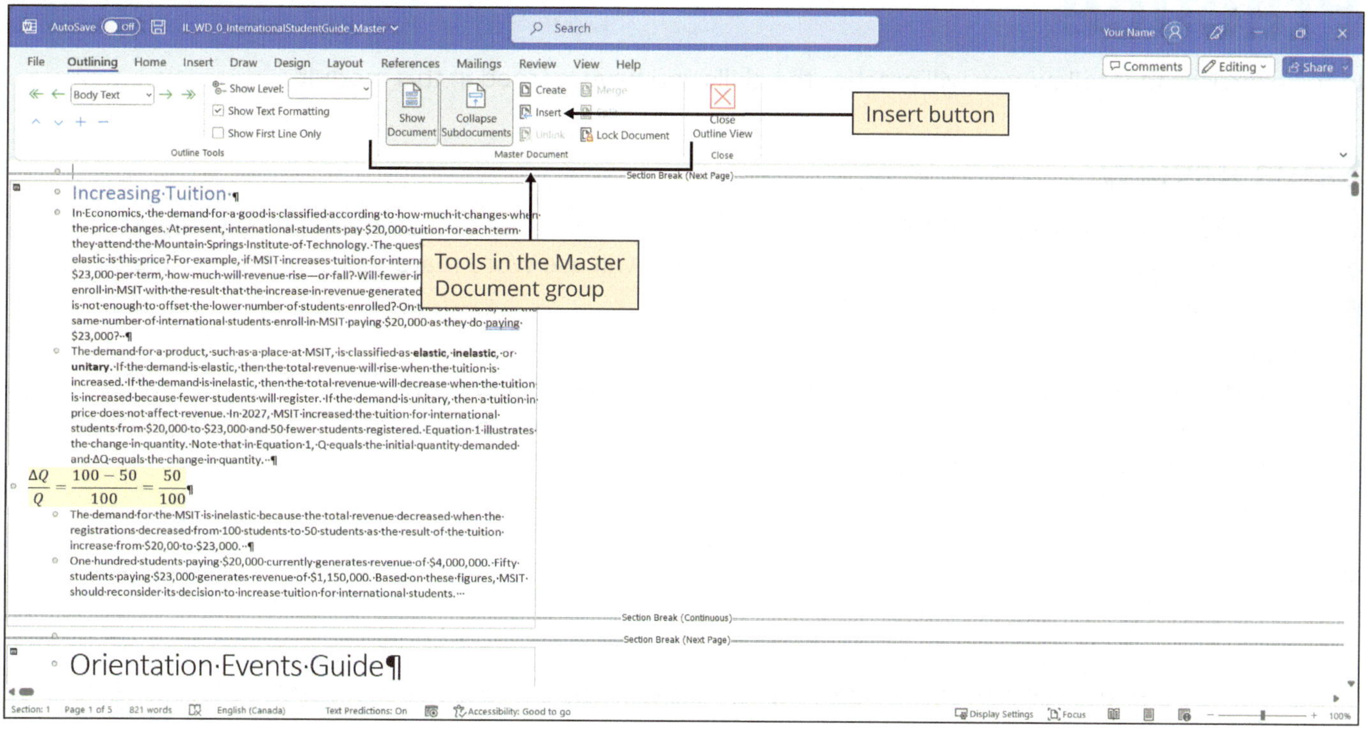

Figure 9-37: Subdocument selected in Outline view

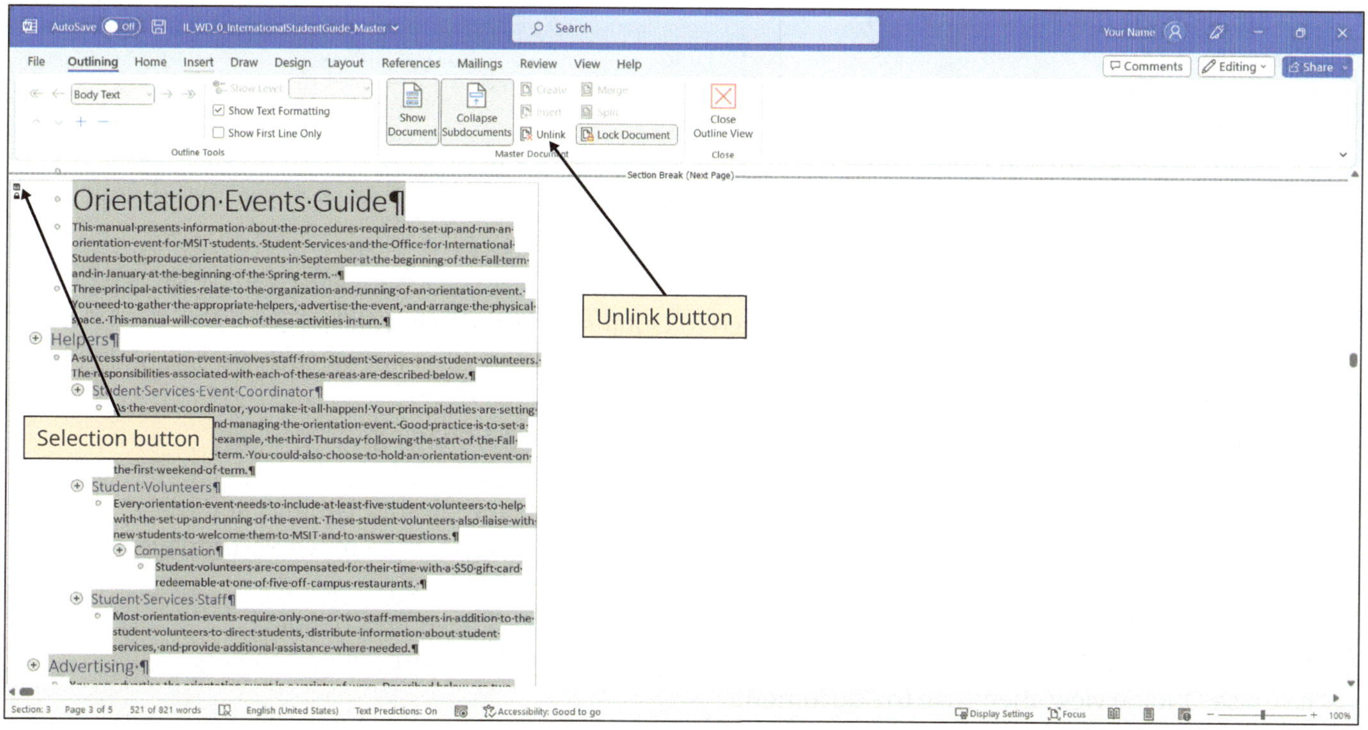

Inserting endnotes

Click the Insert Endnote button in the Footnotes group on the References tab to insert a note reference mark for an endnote. When you click the Insert Endnote button, the insertion point moves to the end of your document so that you can enter text for the endnote in the same way you enter text for a footnote. You click above the endnote separator to return to the text of your document. You work in the Footnote and Endnote dialog box to modify options for endnotes.

Practice

In the exercises that follow, you will practice the skills you have learned in this module.

Skills Review

You are assisting Evelyn George, C.E.O. of Mark One Accounting, to put together a multi-page report detailing a proposed partnership with Action Finance. You will use Word features from this module to help with this report.

1. **Build a document in Outline view.**
   a. Start Word, create a new blank document, then switch to Outline view.
   b. Type **Overview** and **by Your Name** as a Level 1 heading, press ENTER, type **Current Situation** as another Level 1 heading, then press ENTER.
   c. Type the text shown in **Figure 9-38** as body text under the Current Situation heading.
   d. Press ENTER after the body text, type **Advantages**, promote it to Level 1, then demote the heading to Level 2.
   e. Use the Promote, Demote, and Promote to Heading 1 buttons to complete the outline, as shown in **Figure 9-38**.
   f. Save the document as **IL_WD_9_PartnershipOutline** to the location where you store your Data Files, then close the document.

Figure 9-38

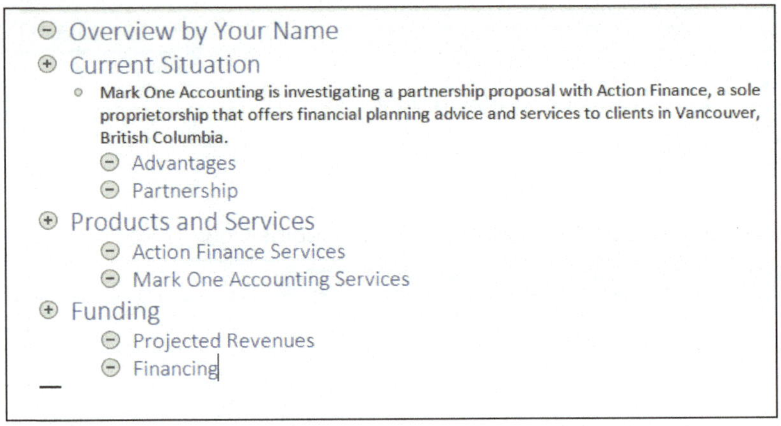
Overview by Your Name
Current Situation
Mark One Accounting is investigating a partnership proposal with Action Finance, a sole proprietorship that offers financial planning advice and services to clients in Vancouver, British Columbia.
Advantages
Partnership
Products and Services
Action Finance Services
Mark One Accounting Services
Funding
Projected Revenues
Financing

2. **Work in Outline view.**
   a. Open the file IL_WD_9-4.docx from the location where you store your Data Files, save it as **IL_WD_9_PartnershipConsiderations**, switch to Outline view, then show all levels.
   b. Show the first line only for each heading and subheading and the first line of each paragraph in the document.
   c. Deselect the Show First Line Only option, then show only Level 1 headings.
   d. Move the Products and Services heading above Funding.
   e. Select the Current Situation heading, expand the heading to show all subheadings and their corresponding body text, collapse Partnership, collapse Advantages, then move Partnership and its subtext below Advantages.
   f. Expand all levels of the outline, then collapse only the Projected Revenues heading.
   g. Show only Level 3 headings, then select and delete the Package Opportunities heading.
   h. Close Outline view, then save the document.

3. **Navigate a document.**
   a. Show paragraph marks if they are not already visible.
   b. Move to the top of the document and then in Print Layout view, collapse the Overview heading.
   c. Collapse all headings so only Level 1 headings are visible, then expand all headings.
   d. Open the Navigation pane, navigate to Financing, then change “eight months” to **two years** in the last line of the paragraph below the Financing Required heading.
   e. In the Navigation pane, move Mark One Accounting Services above Action Finance Services.

f. View the thumbnails of the document pages in the Navigation pane, click the second page, scroll to the Advantages heading, then select the text "Projected Revenues" at the end of the paragraph.
g. Create a cross-reference from the text "Projected Revenues" to the Projected Revenues heading.
h. Test the cross-reference.
i. Go to the top of the document, create a hyperlink from the text "Products and Services" in the list of factors (the other two factors are already hyperlinks) in the middle of paragraph 1 under "Overview," to the Products and Services heading, then test the hyperlink.
j. Save the document and keep the Navigation pane open.

4. **Create and modify screenshots.**
   a. Open **Support_WD_9_Images.docx** from the location where you save your Data files, turn off paragraph marks, then ensure the View is 100%.
   b. Switch to the IL_WD_9_PartnershipConsiderations document.
   c. Scroll to and delete the text VANCOUVER SCREENSHOT on page 2, but not the paragraph mark.
   d. Insert a screenshot of the Word window containing the support document showing the two pictures of Vancouver. Make sure the Navigation pane is closed and paragraph marks are not showing in the screenshot.
   e. Crop the screenshot to the edges of the document containing the "Beautiful Vancouver" heading and the two pictures.
   f. Change the width of the cropped screenshot to 4", apply a picture border using the Black, Text 1 color, then center the screenshot.
   g. Switch back to the Support_WD_9_Images document, then scroll to view the three pictures on page 2 of the document.
   h. Return to the main document in Word, navigate to the Mark One Accounting Services heading, delete SERVICES PICTURES but not the paragraph mark, then create a screen clipping that includes only the three pictures and the heading on page 2 of the Support document.
   i. Change the width of the screen clipping to 4", apply a picture border using the Black, Text 1 color, then center the screen clipping.
   j. Save the document, switch to the Support document, then close it.

5. **Use advanced find and replace options.**
   a. Go to the top of the document, then use Advanced Find and Replace to find every instance of **Mark One Accounting** and replace it with **Mark One Accounting** formatted in bold.
   b. In the Find and Replace dialog box, delete the text in the Find what and Replace what text boxes and remove the formatting.
   c. Use the list of Special characters from the Replace dialog box to find every instance of manual page break and replace it with nothing. You will make two replacements. Scroll to and remove the blank line after the first paragraph in the Current Situation section.
   d. Go to the top of the document, press ENTER after Finance in the document title, then insert three diamond shapes (Character Code 117) from the Wingdings font.
   e. Save the document.

6. **Add and modify captions.**
   a. Scroll through the document and note the captions on three of the five graphics, then navigate to the Current Situation heading and click the screenshot of the Vancouver images.
   b. Insert a caption that includes a colon after the figure number and the text. **Most clients are based in Vancouver**.
   c. Exit the Captions dialog box.
   d. Scroll to and click the screenshot of the three services images, then insert a caption that includes a colon (**:**) and the text **Mark One Accounting uses these images to promote its services**.
   e. Scroll up and then delete the picture and the caption of the people in a meeting, along with any extra blank lines.

Skills Review (Continued)

f. Update the numbering for all the remaining two captions in the document.
g. Go to the top of the document, insert a manual page break, press CTRL+HOME, then enter the text **Table of Figures** followed by a hard return at the top of the new blank page.
h. Center the text and format it with 24 point and bold.
i. Click after "Figures," press ENTER, then clear the formatting (**Hint**: Clear the Clear All Formatting button in the Font group on the Home tab).
j. Generate a table of figures using the Distinctive format.
k. Save the document.

7. Insert a table of contents.

a. Go to the top of the document.
b. Insert a page break, then return to the top of the document and clear all the formatting.
c. Insert a table of contents using the Automatic Table 2 predefined style.
d. Replace the table of contents with a custom table of contents using the Formal format.
e. Use CTRL+click from the table of contents to navigate to Pine Valley Finance in the document, view the document headings in the Navigation pane, then right-click and delete the Pine Valley Finance heading from the Navigation pane.
f. Update the table of contents, then save the document.

8. Mark text for an index.

a. Show the Results section of the Navigation pane, find the word **languages**, then mark all occurrences for inclusion in the index.
b. Find and mark only the first instance of each of the following main entries: **financial planning**, **wealth management**, **translation**, and **customized services**. (**Hint**: Click Mark instead of Mark All.)
c. Save the document.

9. Generate an index.

a. Find **multilingual financial advice**, click in the Mark Index Entry dialog box, select multilingual financial advice in the Main entry box, type **Action Finance** as the Main entry and **multilingual financial advice** as the Subentry, then click Mark All.
b. Repeat the process to insert **small business financing** as a subentry of Action Finance.
c. Find the first instance of the text **consultants**, then create a cross-reference in the Mark Index Entry dialog box to **languages**. Note that you already have an index entry for languages.
d. Close the Mark Index Entry dialog box.
e. Insert a new page at the end of the document, type **Index** at the top of the page, center the text, and format it with bold and 24 point.
f. Double-click below the index, clear any formatting and press BACKSPACE if necessary so the insertion point appears at the left margin, then insert an index using the Formal format.
g. Find the text **Vancouver**, click the second entry in the Navigation pane, open the Mark Index Entry dialog box, and click Mark All, then close the Mark Index Entry dialog box and the Navigation pane.
h. Scroll to the index page, update the index so it includes the new entry, then save and close the document.

10. Insert footers in multiple sections.

a. Open the file IL_WD_9-5.docx from the location where you store your Data Files, then save it as **IL_WD_9_PartnershipConsiderations_Final**.
b. At the top of the document, check that Section 1 appears on the status bar and that the document contains 7 pages.
c. Scroll to the page break below the Table of Figures on page 2, click to the left of the page break, then insert an Odd Page section break.
d. Press DELETE to remove the original page break, then press DELETE again to remove the extra blank line.

e. Scroll to the Index page, scroll up and click to the left of the page break on page 6, insert an Even Page section break, then delete the original page break and the extra blank line.
f. On the table of contents page, insert a footer using the Blank (Three Columns) format.
g. Select the Different Odd & Even Pages check box.
h. Click to the left of the placeholder text to select all three items, press DELETE, type your name, press TAB two times, type **Page**, press SPACEBAR, then insert a page number at the current position of the insertion point using the Plain Number page number.
i. Format the page numbers with the i, ii, iii style.
j. Click Next in the Navigation group to go to the Even Page Footer for Section 1, type **Page**, press SPACEBAR, insert a Plain Number page number at the current position of the insertion point, press TAB two times, then type your name.
k. Click Next in the Navigation group, select the Different First Page check box, then click the Link to Previous button to deselect it (the button is no longer gray).
l. Change the format of the page numbers to start at 1.
m. Click Next to go to the next footer (Even Page Footer -Section 2-), verify that Page 2 appears at the left margin and your name at the right margin, click Next, verify that your name appears at the left margin and Page 3 at the right margin, then click Next to go to Section 3, which is Page 6 (the Index page) and the Even Page Footer for Section 3. Note that Page 8 of 8 appears in the status bar because the entire document, including the table of contents and table of figures pages (Section 1) contains 8 pages.
n. Exit the footer area, then scroll through the document to verify that the footers appear correctly. Note that your name and Page i appears on the Table of Contents page, Page ii and your name appears on the Table of Figures page, no footer appears on the first page of the document text, Page 2 and your name appears on Page 2 of the document text and your name and Page 3 appears on Page 3 of the document text and so on to the end of the document.
o. Save the document.

11. **Insert headers in multiple sections.**
a. Press CTRL+HOME to go to the top of the document, change the View to Page Width, close the Navigation pane if necessary, insert a header using the blank format, then move to the Even Page Header for Section 2. Verify that Even Page Header -Section 2- appears, *not* First Page Header -Section 2-.
b. Deselect the Link to Previous button, then enter **Partnership Considerations** as the header text.
c. Format the header text with a font size to 14 point, apply bold, center the text, then copy the header text, including the paragraph mark.
d. Move to the Odd Page Header -Section 2-, deselect the Link to Previous button, paste the "Partnership Considerations" header text, then, if necessary, remove a paragraph mark so only one blank line appears between "Partnership Considerations Arrangement" and the document text.
e. Exit the header area, then return to the top of the document.
f. Scroll through the document to verify that no header text appears on the first three pages of the document. The header text appears only on pages 2 to 8 of the document text.
g. In the Page Setup dialog box, set the Gutter width for the whole document to .5, then mirror the margins.
h. Set the distance of the Header and Footer from the top and bottom of the page to .3 for the whole document.
i. View the entire document in Multiple Pages view, verify the headers and footers are correct, then save the document.

12. **Finalize a multi-page document.**
a. Open **Support_WD_9_WesternFinance.docx** from the location where you store your data files, select and copy all the text, then save it at Support_WD_9_WesternFinance_2.
b. Switch to the IL_WD_9_PartnershipConsiderations_Final document, return to Page Width, scroll to the bottom of page 4 (contains the Conclusion), click to the left of the section break, then insert a page break.

Skills Review (Continued)

c. Paste the copied text.
d. Update the entire table of contents.
e. Modify the table of contents options so that Heading 1 corresponds to TOC level 2 text, Heading 2 corresponds to TOC level 3 text, Heading 3 corresponds to TOC level 4 text, and Title text corresponds to TOC level 1 text.
f. Verify that the updated table of contents includes the titles of the two documents, select all the text in the table of contents, then remove the After Paragraph spacing.
g. Open the Tabs dialog from the Paragraph dialog box, then set a Right tab of 6 with the 3 Leader style.
h. Update the Table of Figures, then update the Index.
i. Display 2 × 5 pages in the Zoom dialog box, then compare the completed document to **Figure 9-39**. If you can't view 2 × 5 pages, display 2 × 4 pages.
j. Save and close the document, close the Support document, but do not exit Word.

Figure 9-39

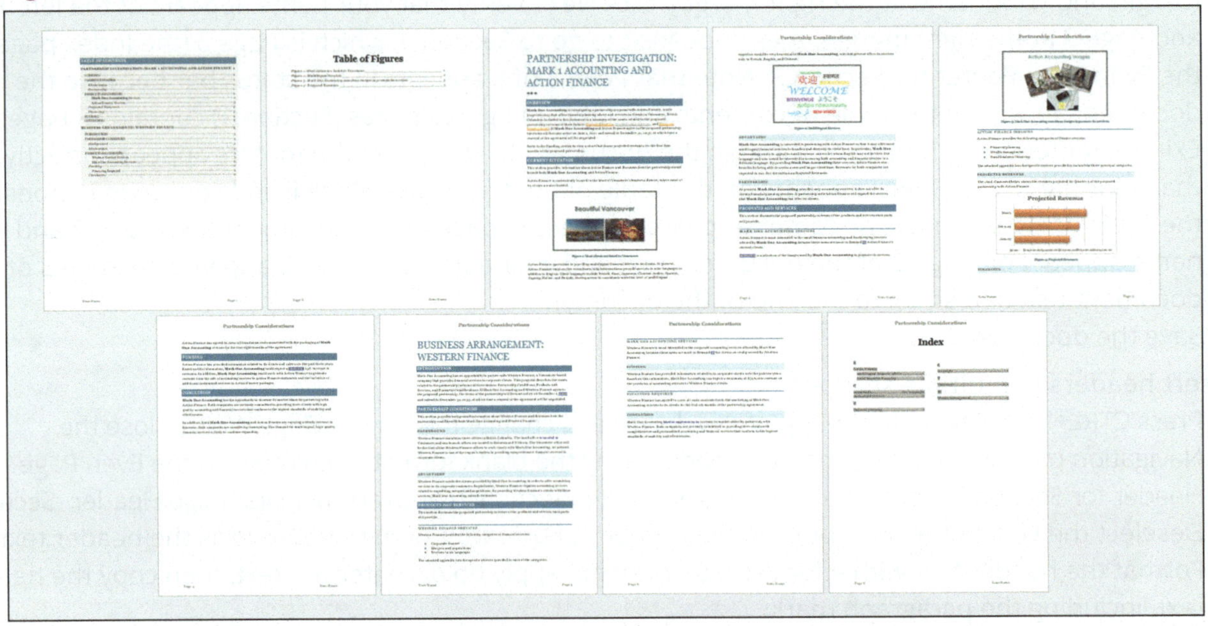

Adi K/Pexels; Tumisu/Pexels; Vlad Vasnetsov/Pexels; Nataliya Vaitkevich/Pexels; Tima Miroshnichenko/Pexels; Fauxels/Pexels

13. Work with equations

a. Open the file IL_WD_9-6.docx from the location where you store your Data Files, then save the document as **IL_WD_9_HourlyRate**.
b. Go to the [Equation1] placeholder, then replace it with an equation content control.
c. Increase the zoom to 180%, then create the equation shown in **Figure 9-40**.
d. Format the new equation by increasing its font size to 16 point, then shade it with Green, Accent 6, Lighter 80%. (**Hint**: Remember to select the equation content control before applying the shading).
e. Save and close the document, but do not exit Word.

Figure 9-40

$$\frac{\Delta Q}{Q} = \frac{100 - 40}{100} = \frac{60}{100}$$

14. Create master documents and subdocuments.

a. Open a new blank document in Word, save the document as **IL_WD_9_PartnershipConsiderations_Master**, then switch to Outline view.
b. Insert the document **IL_WD_9_HourlyRate.docx** you saved in the previous activity, clicking No to All if prompted.

c. Insert **Support_WD_9_WesternFinance_2.docx**, answering No to All if prompted.
d. Collapse the subdocuments, answering OK when prompted, click the hyperlink to the Support_WD_9_WesternFinance_2.docx file, view the document, then close it.
e. Expand the subdocuments.
f. Select and then unlink the IL_WD_9_HourlyRate.docx subdocument.
g. Collapse the Support_WD_9_WesternFinance_2.docx subdocument, then use the Lock Document button to lock it.
h. Exit Outline view, then mark the entire document as final.
i. Close the document, submit all the files you have created in this Skills Review to your instructor, then exit Word.

Independent Challenge 1

Patti Yun is the office manager at All Bright Event Planning, a corporate event planning service based in Chicago. She asks you to help her develop guidelines related to the company's office procedures, client relations, and billing protocols. Patti plans to use this document to create a manual for all the company's event planning consultants.

a. Start Word, open the file IL_WD_9-7.docx from the drive and folder where you store your Data Files, save it as **IL_WD_9_AllBrightEventPlanning**, then switch to Outline view.
b. Show only Level 1 headings, select the Applications and Manual Content headings, then demote them to Level 2.
c. Select and expand all the headings, collapse the Procedures Manual and Client Relations headings, then move the Client Relations heading above the Procedures Manual heading.
d. Show only Level 3 headings, select and delete the heading Manual Format and its associated subtext, then close Outline view.
e. Move to the top of the document, collapse the Introduction heading, collapse all headings, expand all headings, show the headings in the Navigation pane, then drag the Payment Process heading below the Payment Policy heading.
f. Display the thumbnails in the Navigation pane, scroll to and click the page 1 thumbnail, position the insertion point after "hours" in the last sentence in the paragraph below the Introduction heading (fifth line), insert a cross-reference to the chart (Figure 1), then select Above/below in the Insert reference to list.
g. Ensure a space appears before and after "below", then test that the cross-reference goes to the figure caption for the chart.
h. Move to the top of the document, insert a blank page, move to the top of the document again, press ENTER, press the Up arrow, insert a table of contents using the Automatic Table 2 option, then replace the table of contents with a custom table of contents using the Formal format.
i. Use the Navigation pane to navigate to the Timeline subheading, delete the subheading and its associated text, then update the table of contents.
j. Show Results in the Navigation pane, search for **Office Manager**, click the second instance in the Navigation pane, open the Mark Entry dialog box, then mark all instances of "Office Manager" for inclusion in the index.
k. Starting from the top of the document, find and mark all instances of the following main entries: **logistics**, **catering**, **timeline**, and **contingency plan**.
l. Search for **invoices**, then enter **payment** in the Main entry box and **invoices** in the Subentry box. Mark one instance.
m. Search for **credit card**, then create a cross-reference for credit card supplies to payment.
n. Go to the end of the document, insert an index using the Formal format, search for **program topics**, mark it for inclusion in the index, then update the index.

Independent Challenge 1 (Continued)

o. Move to the top of the document, scroll to the page break below the table of contents, replace the page break with an Odd Page section break, then remove the page break and the extra hard return.

p. Move to the page break above the index, replace the page with an Even Page section break, then remove the page break and the extra hard return.

q. On page 1 of the document (Section 1), insert a footer using the Blank (Three Columns) format, then select Different Odd and Even pages.

r. Delete the placeholder text, type **Page** at the left margin followed by a space and a plain page number, press TAB two times, type your name at the right margin, then change the page number format to i, ii, iii.

s. Go to Odd Page Footer -Section 2-, then click the Link to Previous button to deselect it. Format the page numbers to start at 1.

t. Go to the Even Page Footer -Section 2-, enter your name at the left margin, press TAB twice to move to the right margin, type **Page** followed by the plain page number, then verify the page number format is 1, 2, 3.

u. Exit the footer area, save the document, then scroll to the chart, click after areas at the end of the caption for the chart, then add a page break to the left of the current Even Page section break.

v. Open **Support_WD_9_EventOrganization.docx**, select and then copy all the text, switch to the document IL_WD_9_AllBrightEventPlanning, then paste the copied text.

w. Scroll up to the table of contents, update the table of contents, open the Custom Table of Contents Options dialog box, then designate heading levels as follows: Heading 1: 2, Heading 2: 3, Heading 3: 4 and Title: 1.

x. Select all the text in the table of contents, change the Before and After Spacing to 0, set the right tab at 5.5", then select the 3 tab leader style.

y. Scroll to and update the index, then compare the revised table of contents and updated index to **Figure 9-41** and **Figure 9-42**

z. Save the document, submit the file to your instructor, then close all documents.

Figure 9-41

Table of Contents

Figure 9-42

Index

Independent Challenge 2

You work as an administrator for the municipality of Jonson Bridge in Washington state. The new mayor has asked you to put together a document containing information about the municipality's services related to parks and recreation, culture, and education. You modify an existing document containing information about the town's services, then make it a master document and insert two subdocuments, one containing information about the town's parks and the other containing information about the recreation policies.

a. Open IL_WD_9-8.docx, save it as **IL_WD_9_JonsonBridgeServices**, open **Support_WD_9_CommunityImages.docx**, then turn off paragraph marks if they are showing. Set the view at 100%, then switch back to IL_WD_9_JonsonBridgeServices.
b. Select and delete SCREEN CLIPPING on page 1 but leave a blank line, then insert a screen clipping of the picture of a person standing on a beach.
c. Crop the picture to remove as much white space as possible so only the oval picture is selected. Change the width of the screen clipping to 4", then center it.
d. In the Support_WD_9_CommunityImages file, scroll to the second page, return to the main document, select and delete RECREATIONSCREENSHOT on page 2, then insert a screenshot of the Word window containing the outdoor activity images on page 2.
e. Crop the screenshot in the main document so that only the pictures and heading are visible. Enclose the screenshot in a black border, center it, then change its width to 5".
f. Go to the top of the document, then use Advanced Find and Replace to find a section break and replace it with a manual page break.
g. Go to the top of the document, then use Advanced Find and Replace to find every instance of **Jonson Bridge** and replace it with **Jonson Bridge** formatted in bold and italic.
h. On the blank line below the document title "Municipality of Jonson Bridge", insert three symbols of a fancy star from Wingdings (symbol 173). Increase the font size of the three symbols to 18 point, then center them below the title.
i. Insert a caption on the oval picture with the text: **Stunning beaches are easily accessible from the Municipality of Jonson Bridge** using the 1, 2, 3 style.
j. Insert a caption on the picture of the recreation activities (kayaking and fishing): **Jonson Bridge residents enjoy outdoor activities year round.**
k. Scroll to the picture of the children in a library, then, if necessary, update the caption number
l. Scroll to and delete EQUATION 1 but not the paragraph mark.

Independent Challenge 2 (Continued)

m. Insert the equation shown in **Figure 9-43**, typing × for the multiplication sign.

n. Format the equation by changing the font size to 16 point and applying the Gold, Accent 3, Lighter 80% shading.

o. Go to the top of the document, insert a Next Page section break, then return to the top of the page, type **Table of Figures**, clear the formatting, format it with 16 point and bold, center it, then add a blank line following the title.

p. Insert a table of figures using the Distinctive format.

q. Insert a header in Section 1 using the Blank (Three Columns) format, delete the placeholder text, go to Section 2, deselect the Link to Previous button, type the text **Jonson Bridge Municipality** at the left margin, press TAB two times to move to the right margin, enter your name at the right margin, then exit the header area.

r. Go to the end of the document, switch to Outline view, then click the Show Document button in the Master Document group.

s. Open the file Support_WD_9_Parks.docx from the location where you store your Data Files, save it as **Support_WD_9_Parks2**, close it, then insert it as a subdocument, answering No to All if prompted.

t. Open the file Support_WD_9_RecreationPolicies.docx from the location where you store your Data Files, save it as **Support_WD_9_RecreationPolicies2**, close it, then insert it as a subdocument, answering No to All if prompted.

u. Collapse the subdocuments, click OK in response to any message, scroll down as needed to verify that the two subdocuments are now hyperlinks, press and hold CTRL and click the hyperlink to the Support_WD_9_RecreationPolicies2.docx file, view the document, then close it.

v. Expand all the Subdocuments, close Outline view, navigate to the picture of the two people walking in the forest in the parks document, verify that the figure is updated to Figure 4, or update it if necessary.

w. In the Master document, set the gutter width at .5" for the whole document and select Mirror Margins.

x. Update the table of figures, change the Zoom for the document to 2 × 4, then compare the completed document to **Figure 9-44**.

y. Save the document, close it and all open documents, then submit your files to your instructor.

Figure 9-43

$$\frac{1}{2} X \frac{3}{4} = \frac{3}{8}$$

Figure 9-44

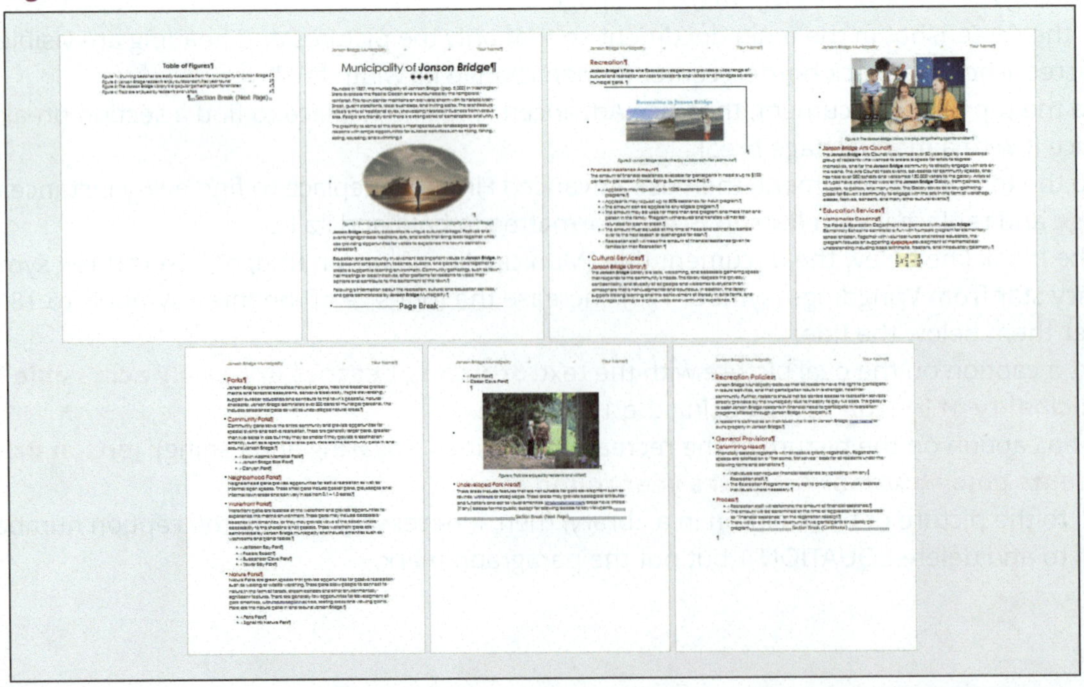

Vlada Karpovich/Pexels; Roman Pohorecki/PexelsMídia/Pexels; Anastasia Shuraeva/Pexels; Magda Ehlers/Pexels

Visual Workshop

Open the file IL_WD_9-9.docx from the drive and folder where you store your Data Files, then save it as **IL_WD_9_ForestviewExpansionPlan**. Switch to Outline view, then modify the outline so the headings and subheadings are in the same order as they appear in the table of contents of the first two pages of the completed document in **Figure 9-45**. Exit Outline view, add a Next Page section break at the beginning of the document, then on the new blank page, generate a custom table of contents using the Fancy format, Insert a page break before Financial Assessment in the text, then create a footer in Section 2 (remember to deselect Link to Previous *before* you type text) with your name at the left margin and a page number that starts with 1 at the right margin. Make sure no text appears in the footer in section 1. In Print Layout view, insert and crop the screen clipping included in the file Support_WD_9_Graphic.docx to the left of the page break. Refer to **Figure 9-45**. Change the width to 3", then add the caption **Expansion Leads to New Growth**. Update the table of contents. Save and close the document, then submit the file to your instructor.

Figure 9-45

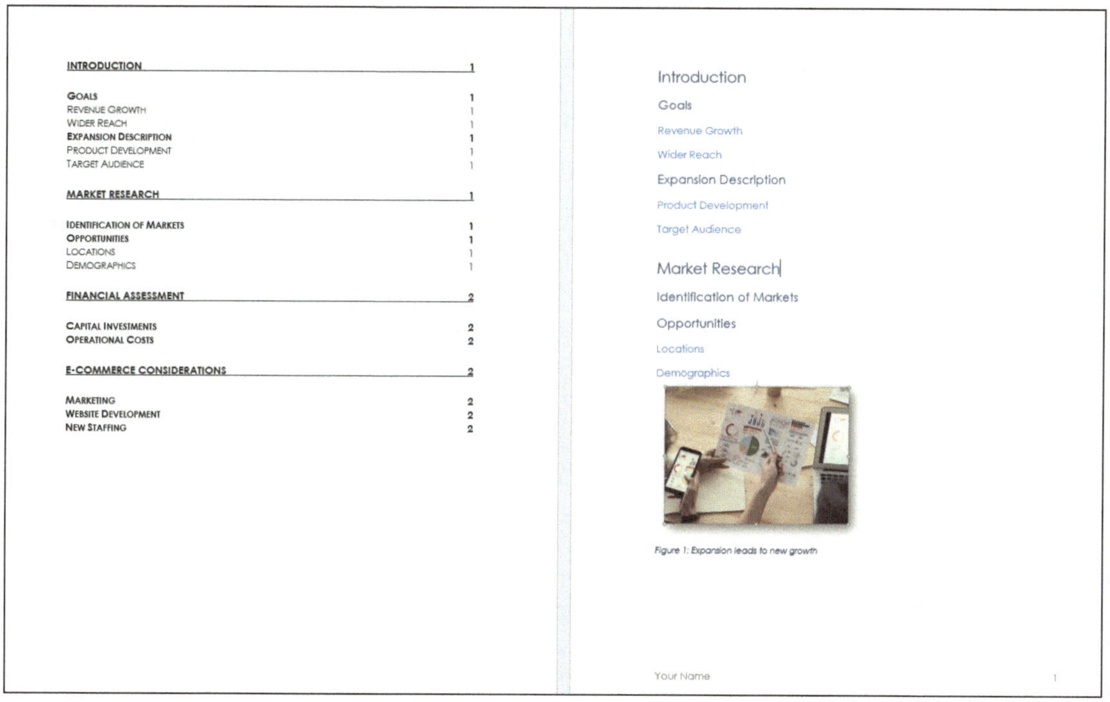

Fauxels/Pexels

Building Forms

Case

As part of your work in the Office for International Students at Mountain Springs Institute of Technology (MSIT) in Denver, Colorado, you have been asked to create a form to survey international students about their experiences attending MSIT. You start by creating the form template, then you add content controls, format and protect the form, and, finally, fill it in as a user.

Module Objectives

After completing this module, you will be able to:

- Convert tables and text
- Construct a form template
- Add Text content controls
- Add Date Picker and Picture content controls
- Add Repeating Section and Check Box content controls
- Add Building Block content controls
- Add Drop-Down content controls
- Insert Legacy Tools controls
- Format and Protect a form
- Edit a form
- Fill in a form as a user

Files You Will Need

IL_WD_10-1.docx
Support_WD_10_Instructor1.jpg
Support_WD_10_Instructor2.jpg
IL_WD_10-2.docx
Support_WD_10_Facilitator.jpg
IL_WD_10-3.docx
Support_WD_10_WindEnergy.jpg
IL_WD_10-4.docx
Support_WD_10_Balloons.jpg

Convert Tables and Text

Case You open a document containing much of the text needed for your form and convert a table containing the school's contact information into text and then convert the text required for the form into a table. You start by changing the page size.

Objectives
- Change the paper size
- Convert text to a table
- Convert a table to text

You can convert text that is separated by a tab, a comma, or another separator character, into a table. For example, to create a two-column table of last and first names, you could type the names as a list with a comma separating the last and first name in each line, and then convert the text to a table. The separator character—a comma in this example—indicates where you want to divide the table into columns, and a paragraph mark indicates where you want to begin a new row. Conversely, you can convert a table to text that is separated by tabs, commas, or some other character.

Steps

1. **sam Start Word, open the file IL_WD_10-1.docx from the location where you store your Data Files, save the document as IL_WD_10_StudentSurveySetup, then click the Show/Hide button ¶ in the Paragraph group to show paragraph marks, if necessary**
2. **Click the Layout tab, then click the Size button in the Page Setup group**
   A selection of page sizes appears. The Executive page size is currently selected.
3. **Click Letter**
4. **Click anywhere in the table under Mountain Springs Institute of Technology, then click the table move handle**
   You select the table so that you can then convert the table into a line of text.
5. **Click the Layout contextual tab for tables, then click the Convert to Text button in the Data group**
   When you convert a table into text, you can choose various ways in which you want to separate the text contained in each table cell. For this table, you want the text separated with the | symbol.
6. **Click the Other option button, type |, (refer to Figure 10-1), click OK, then click the Center button**
   The company contact information is displayed as a centered line of text with the sections separated by the | symbol.
7. **Select the text from Name to Top Courses**
   Notice the TAB characters between the text. You want each TAB character to convert into a table cell.
8. **Click the Insert tab, click the Table button in the Tables group, then click Convert Text to Table**
   The Convert Text to Table dialog box opens. In this dialog box, 4 is entered as the number of columns based on the number of TAB characters in the selected text (refer to **Figure 10-2**).
9. **Click OK, click below the table to deselect it, then save the document**
   Word converts the TAB characters and text into a table containing four columns. Refer to **Figure 10-3**.

Quick Tip
To enter the | symbol, press SHIFT and then the backslash (\) key.

Figure 10-1: Convert Table to Text dialog box

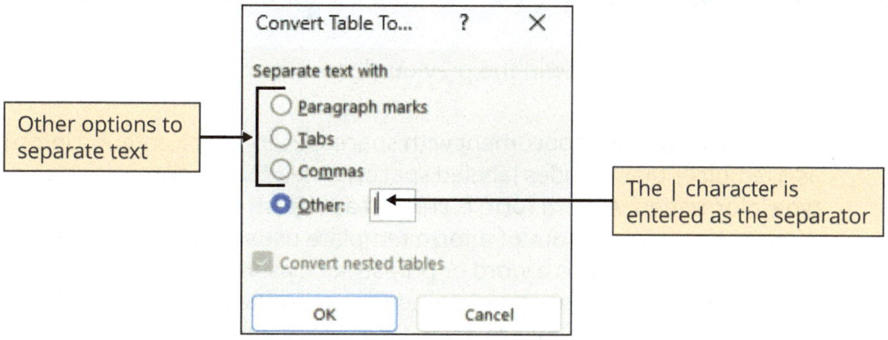

Figure 10-2: Convert Text to Table dialog box

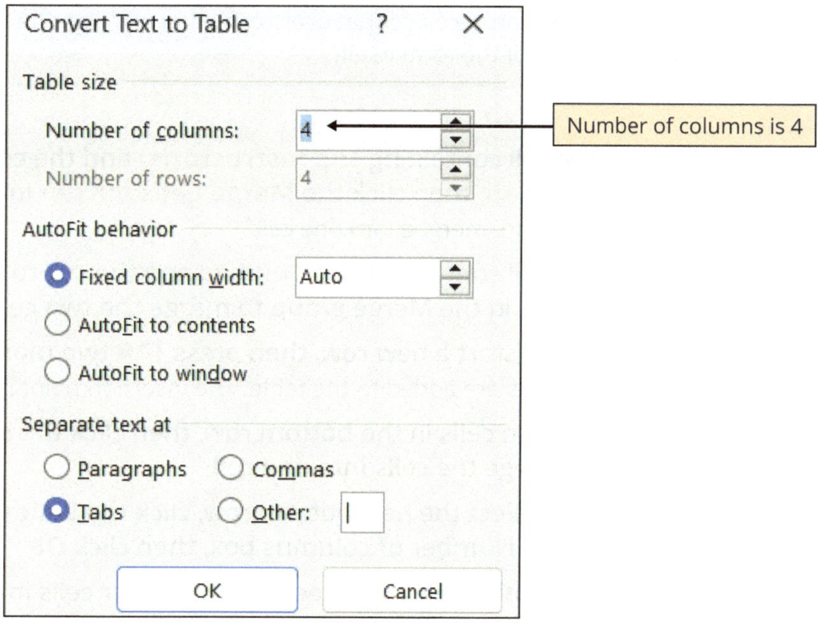

Figure 10-3: Table for the form

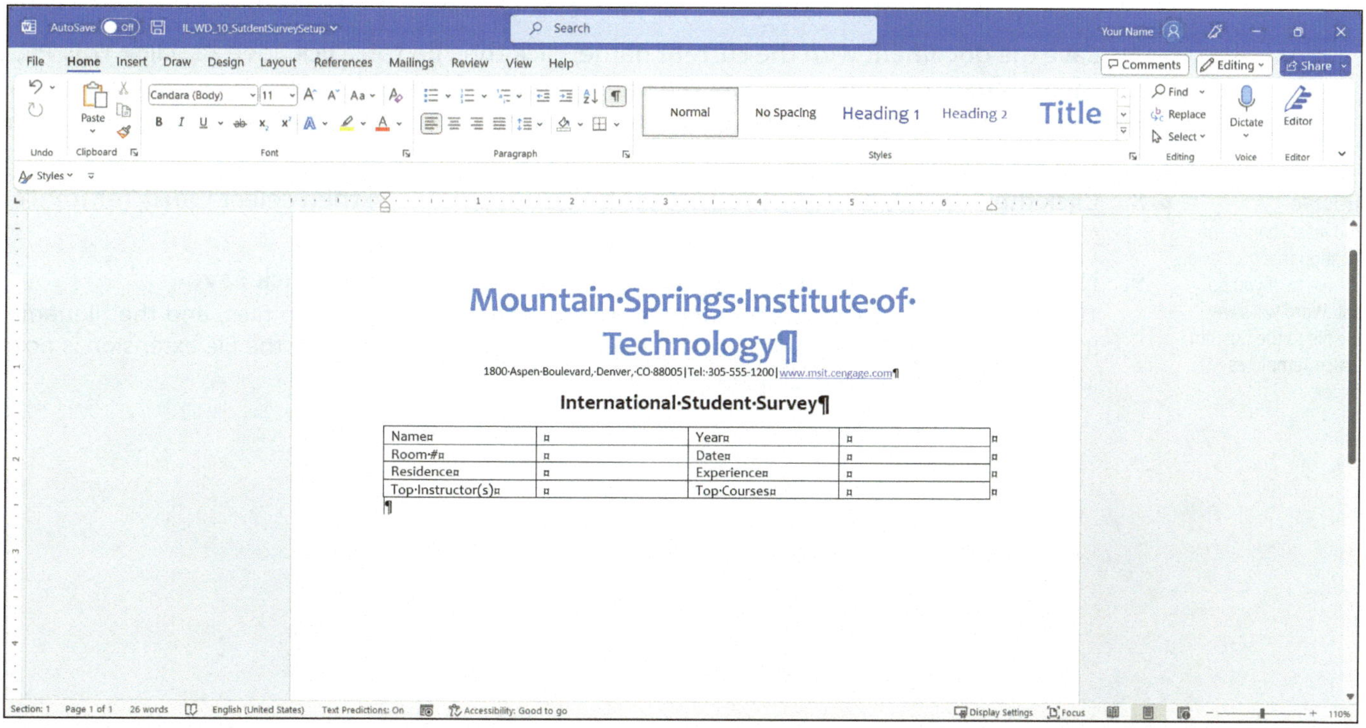

Construct a Form Template

Case You build on the table that you started in the previous lesson and then you save the document as a template.

Objective
- Save a form as a template

A **form** is a structured document with spaces reserved for entering information. You create a form as a template that includes labeled spaces, called **form controls**, which are **fields** into which users type information. A Word form is created as a **form template**, which contains all the components of the form. The structure of a form template usually consists of a table that contains labels and form controls. A **label** is a word or phrase such as "Name" or "Date" that tells people who fill in the form the kind of information required for a given field. A form control, often referred to simply as a control, is the placeholder that you, as the form developer, insert into the form. The type of form control you insert in a form depends on the type of data you want users to insert. **Figure 10-4** shows a completed form template containing several different types of controls. Once you have created a form, you can protect it so that users can enter information into the form, but they cannot change the structure of the form itself.

Steps

Quick Tip
To merge cells, the cells must be contiguous; that is, they must share a common border.

1. **Select the cell containing Top Instructor(s) and the cell to the right, click the Layout contextual tab, then click the Merge Cells button in the Merge group**
   The two cells are merged into one cell.
2. **Select the cell containing Top Courses and the cell to its right, then click the Merge Cells button in the Merge group to merge the two cells into one cell**
3. **Press TAB to start a new row, then press TAB two more times**
   Two blank rows are added to the table. The insertion point is in the first cell of the bottom row.
4. **Select the two cells in the bottom row, then click the Merge Cells button in the Merge group to merge the cells into one cell**

Quick Tip
Press **TAB** to move from cell to cell when entering text in a table.

5. **Press TAB, select the new bottom row, click the Split Cells button in the Merge group, type 4 in the Number of columns box, then click OK**
6. **Press TAB until there are three rows with four cells in each row at the bottom of the table, merge the last three cells in the last row, then refer to Figure 10-5 to enter text in the table**
   Once you have created the structure for your form, you can save it as a template.
7. **Save the document with the current name, click the File tab, click Save As, click This PC, then change the filename in the File name box to IL_WD_10_StudentSurveyForm**
   You need to specify that the file is saved as a template so you can use it as the basis for a form that users will fill out.

Trouble
You *must* change the location that you save the file to. If you do not, Word will save the file to the Custom Office Templates folder.

8. **Click the More options link, click the Save as type arrow, then select Word Template (*.dotx) from the list of file types**
9. **Navigate to the location where you store your Data Files, then click Save**
   The document is saved as a template to the location where you save files, and the filename IL_WD_10_StudentSurveyForm.dotx appears in the title bar. Notice that the file extension is now .dotx because the file is a template.

Figure 10-4: Form construction

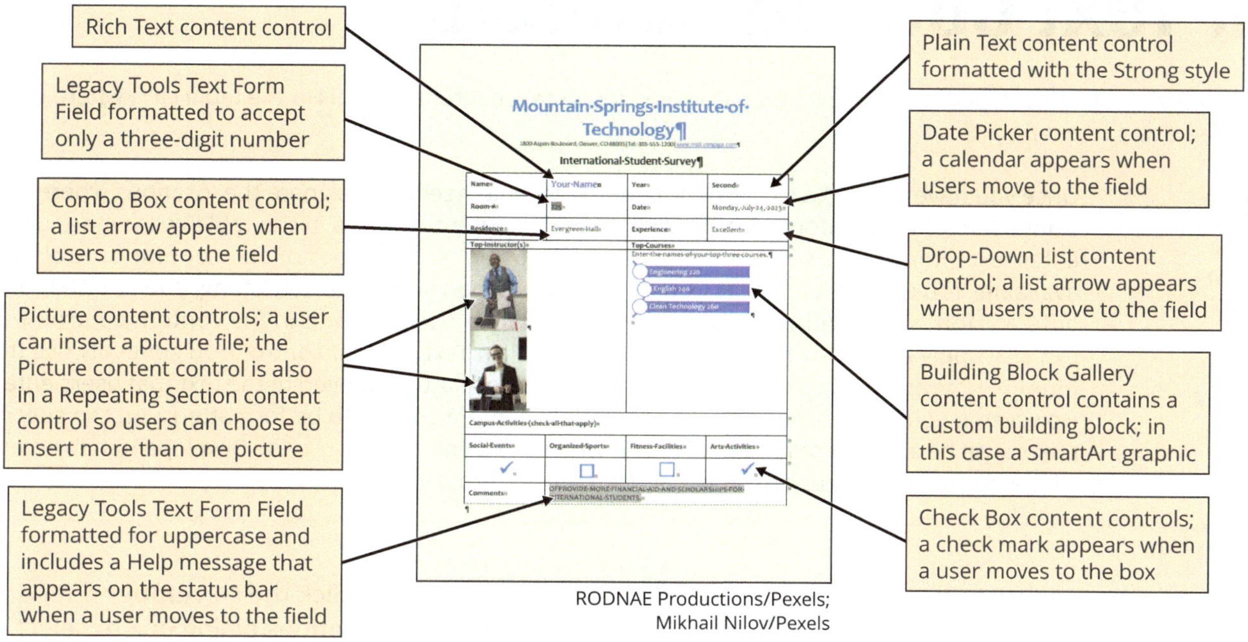

RODNAE Productions/Pexels;
Mikhail Nilov/Pexels

Figure 10-5: Table form with labels and merged cells

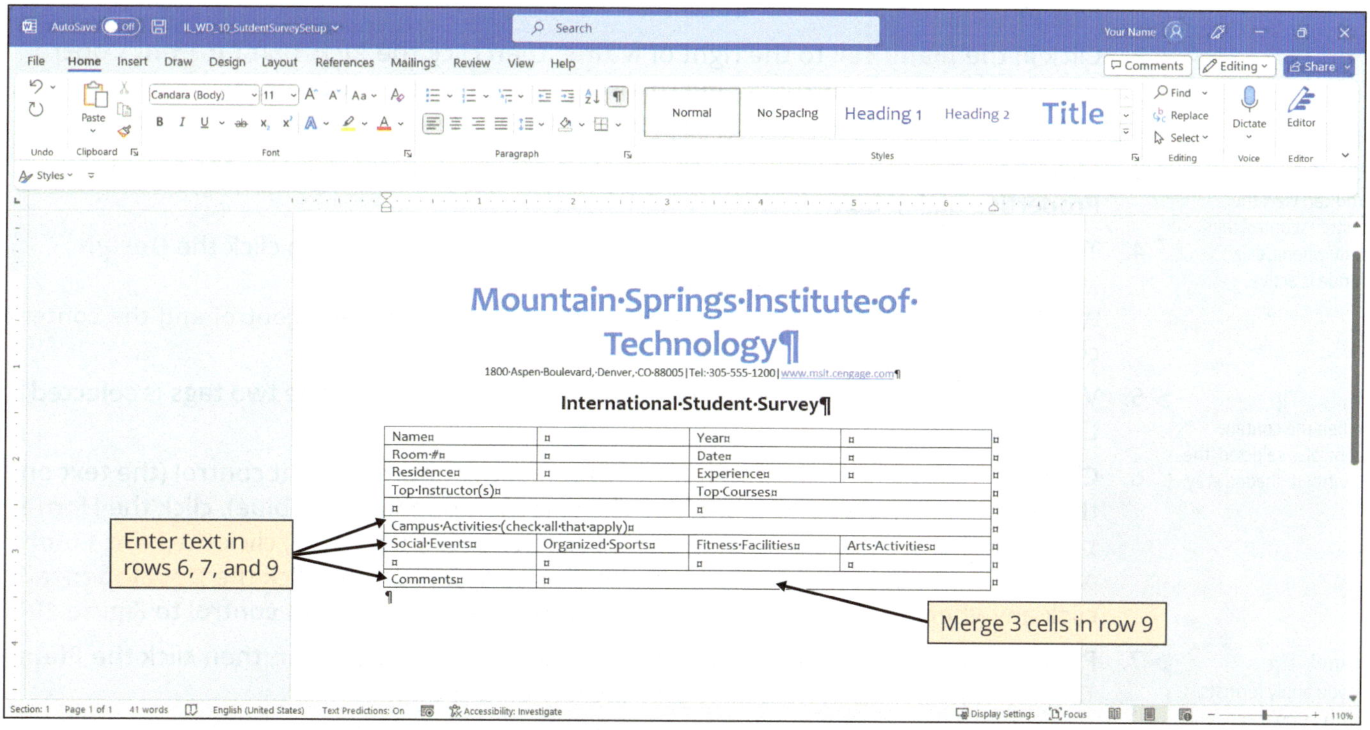

Editing a template

A template is not the same as a document. You need to use a specific set of steps to open a template when you want to edit it. If you choose not to complete all the lessons in this module in one sitting, you will need to use the following procedure to open the template file so you can continue working. Click the File tab, click Open, click Browse, navigate to the location where you store your files for this book, click IL_WD_10_StudentSurveyForm.dotx, then click Open. If you double-click the file, a new document opens. Close this document and use the procedure described to open the template file so that you can continue working with it.

Add Text Content Controls

Case You display the Developer tab on the Ribbon, then you insert text content controls in the table cells where you need users to enter text.

Objectives
- Add a Rich Text content control
- Add a Plain Text content control

Once you have created a structure for your form, you need to designate the locations where you want users to enter information. You insert text content controls in the table cells where users enter text information, such as their names or positions. Two types of text content controls are available. You use the **Rich Text content control** when you want formatting, such as bold or a different font size, automatically applied to text when users enter it in the content control. You can also apply a style, such as the Title style, to a Rich Text content control. You generally use the **Plain Text content control** when you do not need formatting applied to the text that users enter. However, if you want text entered in a Plain Text content control to be formatted, you can specify that a style be automatically applied to text when users enter it. You use the Developer tab to access all the commands you use to create and work with forms in Word.

Steps

1. Click the **File tab**, click **Options**, click **Customize Ribbon**, click the **Developer check box** in the list of main tabs on the right side of the Word Options dialog box to select it, if necessary, click **OK**, then click the **Developer tab** on the Ribbon
   The buttons used to create and modify a form are in the Controls group on the Developer tab; refer to **Table 10-1**.
2. Click in the **blank cell** to the right of **Name**, then click the **Rich Text Content Control button** Aa in the Controls group to insert a Rich Text content control
   When completing the form, the user will be able to enter text into this content control.
3. Click the **Properties button** in the Controls group to open the Content Control Properties dialog box
4. Type **Full Name** as the title of the content control, click **OK**, then click the **Design Mode button** in the Controls group
   Word automatically assigns Full Name to the title of the content control and the content control tags.
5. Verify that the text **Click or tap here to enter text.** between the two tags is selected, then type **Enter your full name here.**
6. Click the **Full Name selection handle** to select the entire content control (the text on the selection handle turns white and the selection handle turns blue), click the **Home tab**, click the **Font Size arrow**, click **14**, click the **Bold button** B, click the **Font Color arrow** A, select **Blue, Accent 1** in the Theme Colors group, click the **Developer tab**, click anywhere in the content control, then compare the content control to **Figure 10-6**
7. Press **TAB** two times to move to the blank cell to the right of **Year**, then click the **Plain Text Content Control button** Aa in the Controls group
8. Click the **Properties button**, type **Year** in the Title box, click the **Use a style to format text typed into the empty control check box**, click the **Style arrow**, select **Strong** (refer to **Figure 10-7**), then click **OK**
   If you want text entered in a Plain Text content control to appear formatted when the user fills in the form, you must apply a paragraph style. The Strong paragraph style that you applied to the Plain Text content control will show when you fill in the form as a user.
9. Select the **Click or tap here to enter text.** text between the two Year tags, type **Enter First, Second, or Third year**, click outside the table, then click the **Save button** on the Quick Access toolbar to save the template

Quick Tip
You can view the content control tags only when Design Mode is active.

Quick Tip
When the content control is selected, the control is shaded gray.

Quick Tip
If you apply formats, such as bold and font size, to the Plain Text content control, the formatting will be lost when the form is opened and filled in by a user. You can format both Rich Text and Plain Text content controls with a paragraph style.

Figure 10-6: Rich Text content control

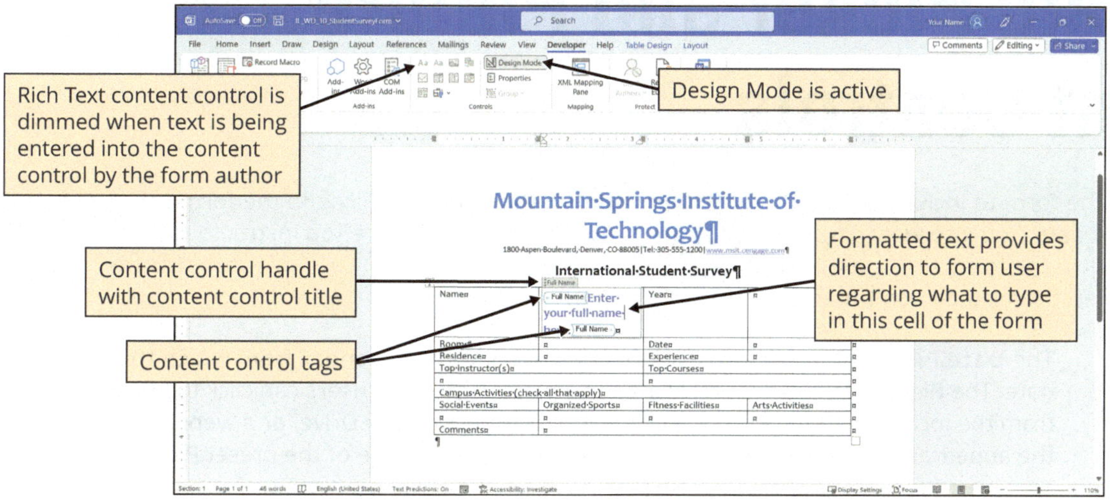

Figure 10-7: Content Control Properties dialog box

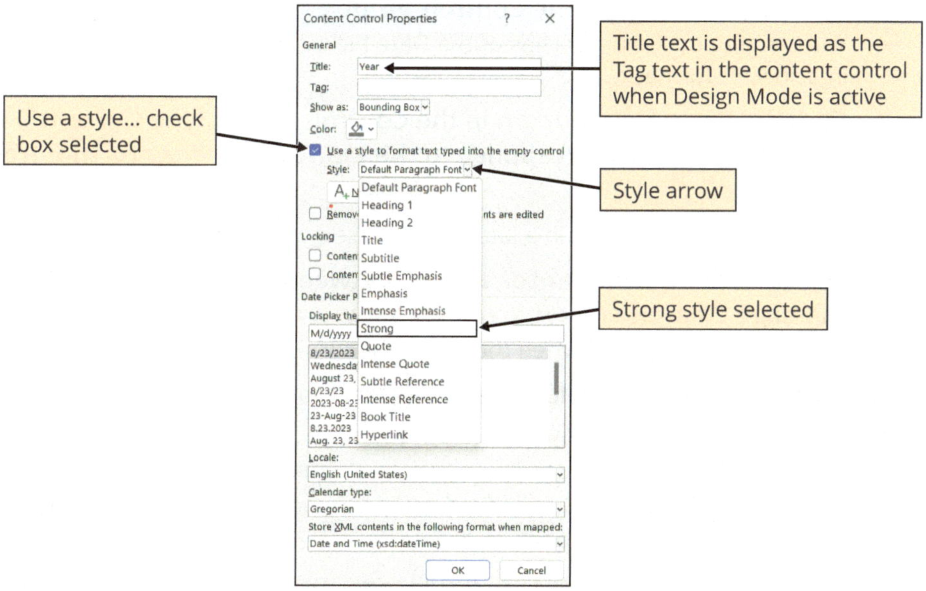

Table 10-1: Buttons in the Controls group

button	use to insert a
Aa	Rich Text content control when you want to apply formatting, such as bold, to text that users type
Aa	Plain Text content control when you want the text that users type to display as plain, unformatted text
	Picture content control when you want users to be able to insert a picture file
	Building Block Gallery content control when you want to insert a custom building block, such as a cover page
	Check Box content control when you want to insert a check box that users can click to indicate a selection
	Combo Box content control when you want users to select from a list or be able to add a new item
	Drop-Down List content control when you want to provide users with a list of restricted choices
	Date Picker content control when you want to include a calendar control that users can use to select a specific date
	Repeating Section content control when you want to repeat content, including other content controls
	Control from the Legacy Tools options when you want additional control over the content that can be entered into a control; if you have programming experience, you can insert ActiveX Controls into forms using the Legacy Tools button

Add Date Picker and Picture Content Controls

Case You want the form to include a Date Picker content control that students filling in the form can click to enter the current date. You also want to include a Picture content control under the Top Instructor(s) table cell. When students fill in the form, they click the Picture content control and select a picture file stored at the location of their choice, such as their computer or OneDrive account.

Objectives
- Add a Date Picker content control
- Add a Picture content control

The **Date Picker content control** provides users with a calendar from which they can select a date. The **Picture content control** inserts a placeholder that users can click to insert a picture file from the location of their choice, such as their computer, OneDrive, or a website. You can modify the appearance of the Picture content control by applying one of the preset Picture styles.

Steps

1. **Click in the blank table cell to the right of Date, then click the Date Picker Content Control button in the Controls group**
   You can modify the properties of the Date Picker content control so the date users enter appears in a specific format.
2. **Click the Properties button in the Controls group, type Current Date as the title, then click the date that corresponds to the Month Day, Year format (refer to Figure 10-8)**
3. **Click OK**
   You will see the calendar in a later lesson when you complete the form as a user.
4. **Select Click or tap to enter a date. between the two Current Date tags, then type the message Click the down arrow to show a calendar and select the current date.**
   Users see this message when they fill in the form.
5. **Click the blank cell below the Top Instructor(s) label**
6. **Click the Picture Content Control button in the Controls group**
   A Picture content control is inserted in the table cell. When users fill in the form, they click the picture icon to insert a picture file from a location of their choice, such as their computer's hard drive, their OneDrive account, or a website.
7. **Click the Properties button, type Insert up to three pictures, then click OK**
   The title text advises users that they will be able to insert more than one picture.
8. **Click the Design Mode button in the Controls group to toggle out of Design mode, compare the table form to Figure 10-9, then save the template**
   You need to toggle out of Design mode so you can work with the Repeating Section content control in the next lesson.

Figure 10-8: Selecting a date format

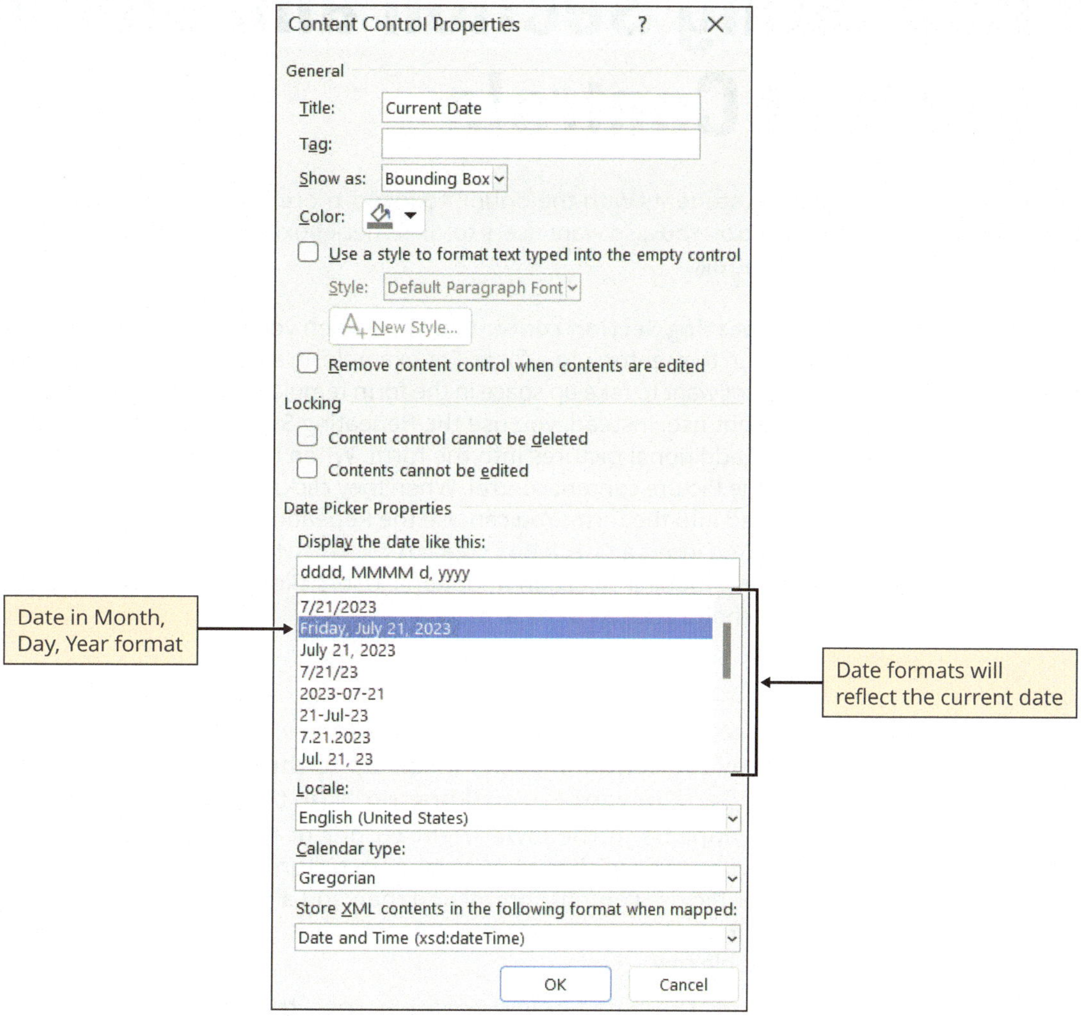

Figure 10-9: Picture content control

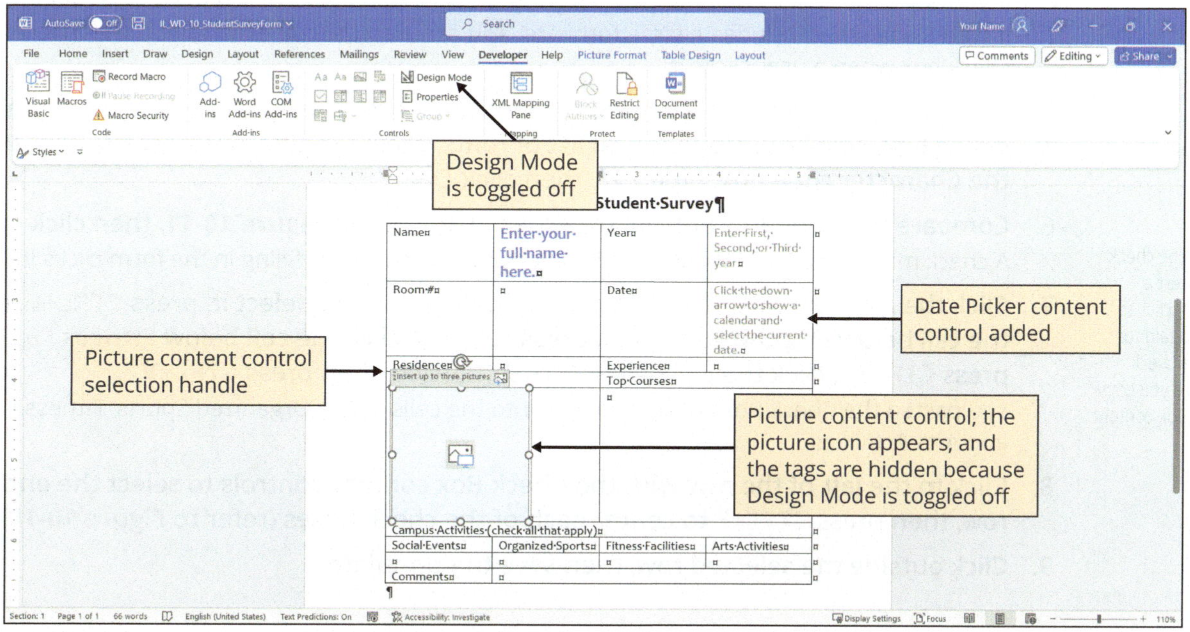

Add Repeating Section and Check Box Content Controls

Case You want the form to provide students with the option to insert more than one picture, so you include the Repeating Section content control. You also want users to click check boxes to indicate their preferences, so you include Check Box content controls.

Objectives
- Add the Repeating Section content control
- Add Check Box content controls

You insert a **Repeating Section content control** when you want to give users the option to add to the information they enter into a form. For example, in a form that includes one Picture content control, you do not want to take up space in the form template with multiple Picture content controls that users may not use. Instead, you use the Repeating Section content control to give users the option to insert additional pictures into the form. When users fill out the form, they see an Add button next to the Picture content control. When they click the Add button, another Picture content control is inserted into the form. You can use the Repeating Section content control to repeat any content control. You insert a **Check Box content control** when you want users to be able to indicate their preferences among a selection of options. Users click a check box to insert an X or another symbol of your choice such as a check mark.

Steps

Trouble
If the Repeating Section Content Control button is dimmed, click the Design Mode button to toggle it off.

1. **Click the Picture content control, click the Picture content control selection handle (the gray tab containing the "Insert up to three pictures" text), then click the Repeating Section Content Control button in the Controls group**
   An Add button appears in the lower-right corner of the Picture content control (refer to **Figure 10-10**). A user who wishes to include more pictures in the form can click the Add button to insert another Picture content control and then add a picture to that Picture content control. When adding a Repeating Section content control, it is good practice to keep the section that repeats to one table row.
2. **Click in the blank table cell below Social Events, then click the Check Box Content Control button in the Controls group**
3. **Click the Properties button, then type Activity**
4. **Click the Use a style... check box, click the Style arrow, then click Title**
   If you want the check box to appear larger than the default size in the form, you need to modify it with a style that includes a large font size. You can also choose which symbol is inserted in the check box when a user clicks it.
5. **Click Change next to the Checked symbol label, click the Font arrow in the Symbol dialog box, scroll the alphabetical list of fonts, click Wingdings, select the contents of the Character code box, type 252, then click OK**

Trouble
If you click the check box and insert a check mark, click the check box again to remove the check mark before you copy the Check Box content control.

6. **Compare the Content Control Properties dialog box to Figure 10-11, then click OK**
   A check mark symbol will appear in the check box when a user filling in the form clicks it.
7. **Click the Activity content control selection handle to select it, press CTRL+C, click the cell below Organized Sports, press CTRL+V, click the cell below Fitness Facilities, press CTRL+V, click the cell below Arts Activities, then press CTRL+V**
   You pasted the Check Box content control into the cells below Organized Sports, Fitness Facilities, and Arts Activities.
8. **Click to the left of the row with the Check Box content controls to select the entire row, then press CTRL+E to center each of the check boxes (refer to Figure 10-12)**
9. **Click outside the selected row, then save the template**

Figure 10-10: Add button for the Repeating Section content control

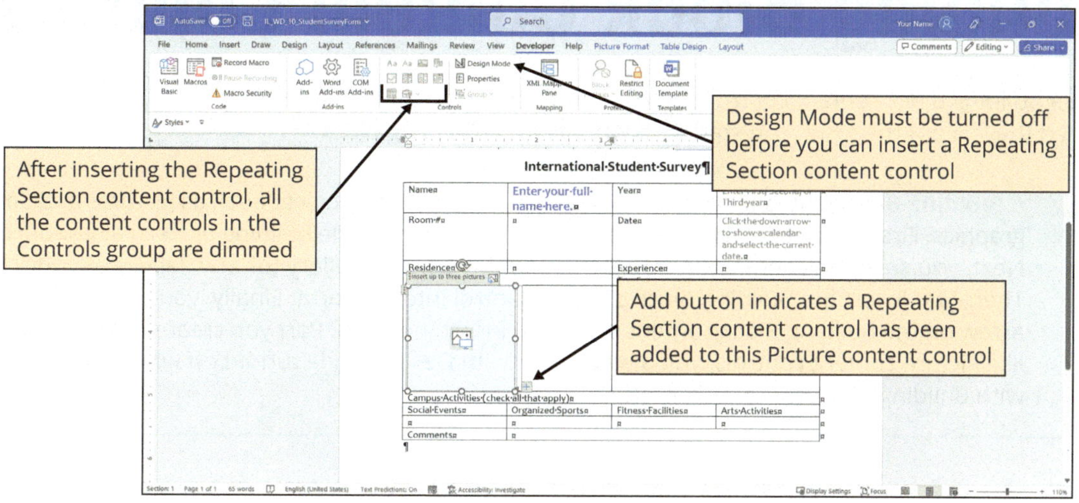

Figure 10-11: Check Box content control properties

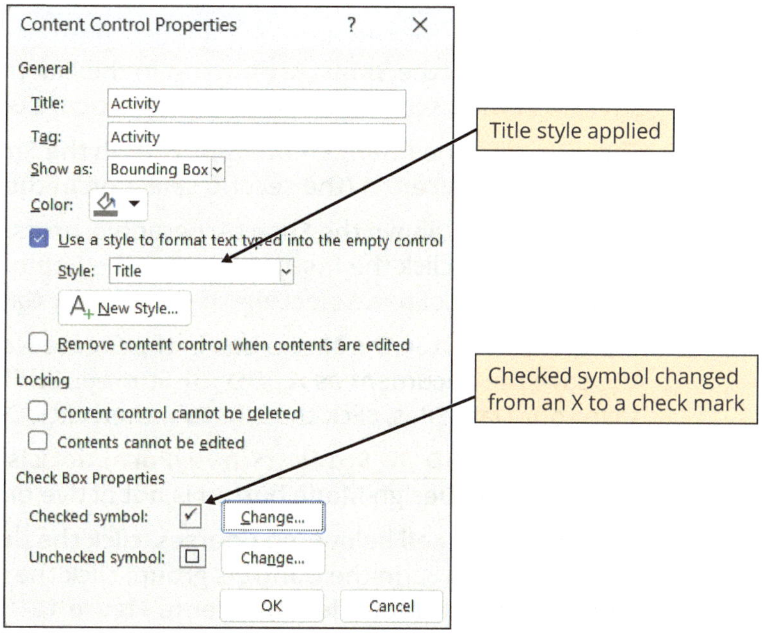

Figure 10-12: Table form with the Check Box content controls added

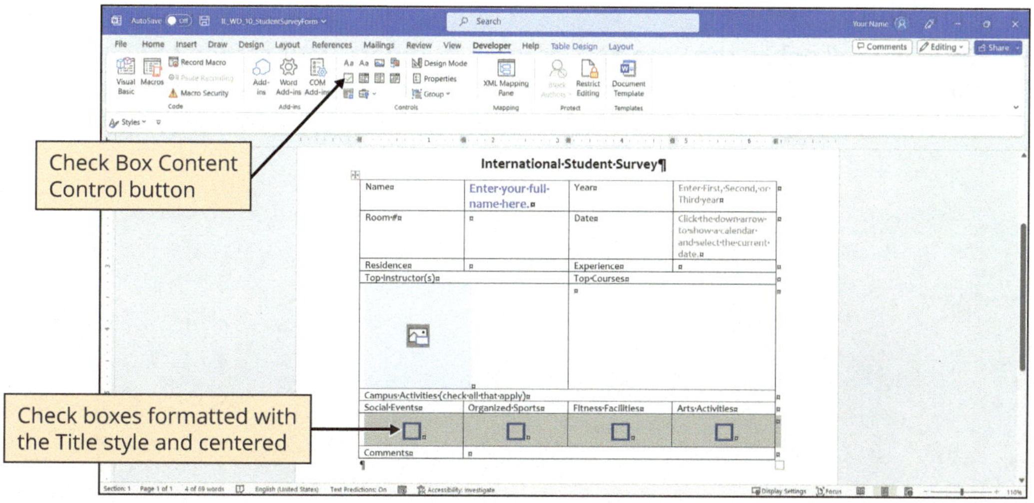

Add Building Block Content Controls

Case You create a Building Block content control that contains instructions and a SmartArt graphic that students can modify when they fill out the form. You start by creating a new Building Block.

Objectives
- Insert a Quick Part
- Add a Building Block content control

A **Building Block content control** can contain both text and objects, such as pictures and SmartArt graphics. First, you create the content you want to appear in the building block in a new document. Next, you save the content as a Quick Part to the General gallery (or any gallery of your choice). Then, you insert the Building Block content control into the form. Finally, you use the Quick Parts arrow on the Building Block content control to insert the Quick Part you created into the form. Just like Picture content controls, you always work with Design Mode turned off when you are working with Building Block content controls.

Steps

1. Click the **File tab**, click **New**, then click **Blank document**
   You create a new blank document that will contain the new building block you want to appear in the form.
2. Type the text **Enter the names of your top three courses.**, press **ENTER**, click the **Insert tab**, click the **SmartArt button** in the Illustrations group, click **List** in the list of SmartArt types, scroll down, then click **Vertical Curved List** (ninth row, sixth column)
3. Click **OK**, click the **Change Colors button** in the SmartArt Styles group, then click **Colored Fill - Accent 1** (the second selection in the Accent 1 section)
4. Click in the text above the SmartArt graphic, press **CTRL+A** to select the contents of the document, click the **Insert tab**, click the **Explore Quick Parts button** in the Text group, then click **Save Selection to Quick Part Gallery**
5. Type **Course List** in the Name box in the Create New Building Block dialog box, click **OK**, save the document as **IL_WD_10_SurveyBuildingBlock** to the location where you save your Data Files, click the **File tab**, then click **Close**
6. Verify that **IL_WD_10_StudentSurveyForm.dotx** is again the active document, then verify that the Design Mode button is not active on the Developer tab
7. Click the **blank cell** below Top Courses, click the **Building Block Gallery Content Control button** in the Controls group, click the **Quick Parts arrow** on the Building Block content control title tab (refer to **Figure 10-13**), then click **Course List**
8. Click the **white area** above the top [Text] box to select the graphic, click the **Format tab**, click the **Size button**, then use the down arrows to reduce the Height to **1.2** and the Width to type **2.4**
9. Click any cell below the SmartArt graphic, compare your screen to **Figure 10-14**, then click the **Save button** on the Quick Access toolbar to save the template

Quick Tip
The default Office theme was applied when you created the SmartArt graphic in a new document.

Figure 10-13: Inserting a Building Block content control

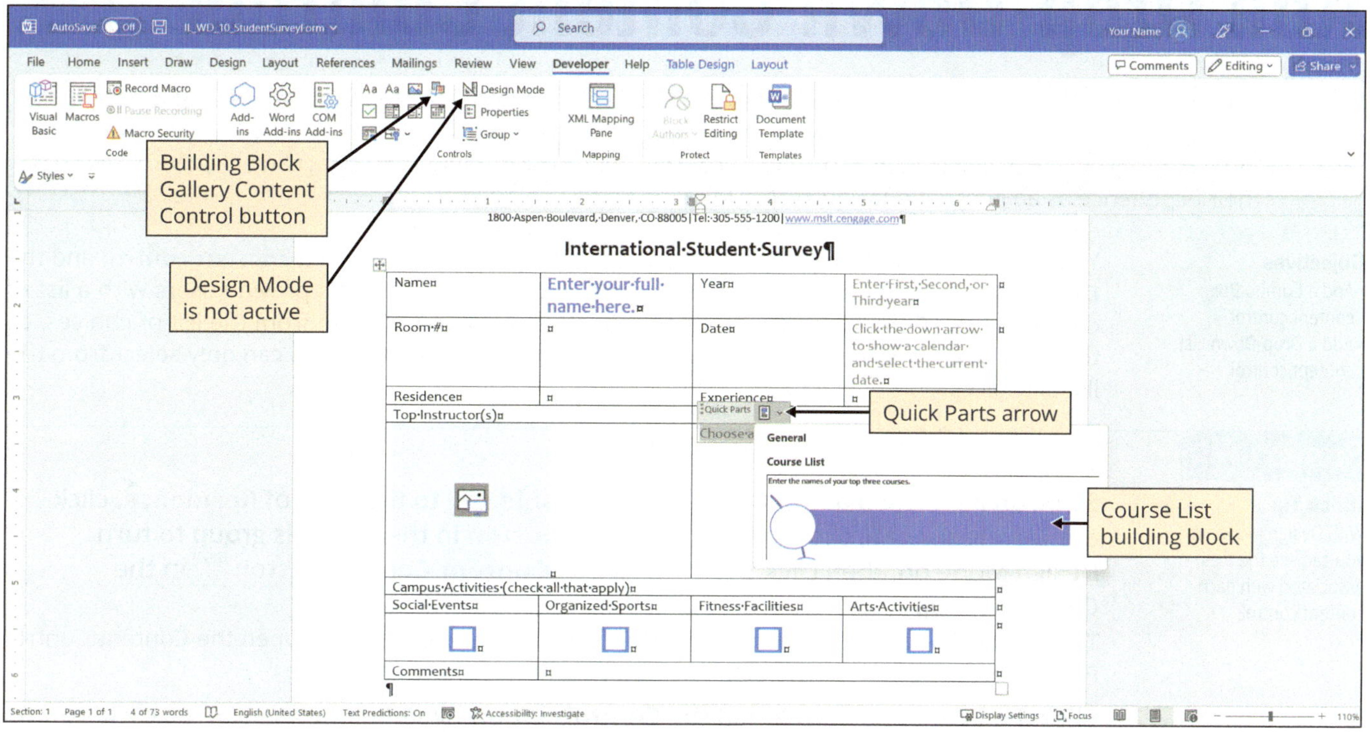

Figure 10-14: Completed Building Block content control

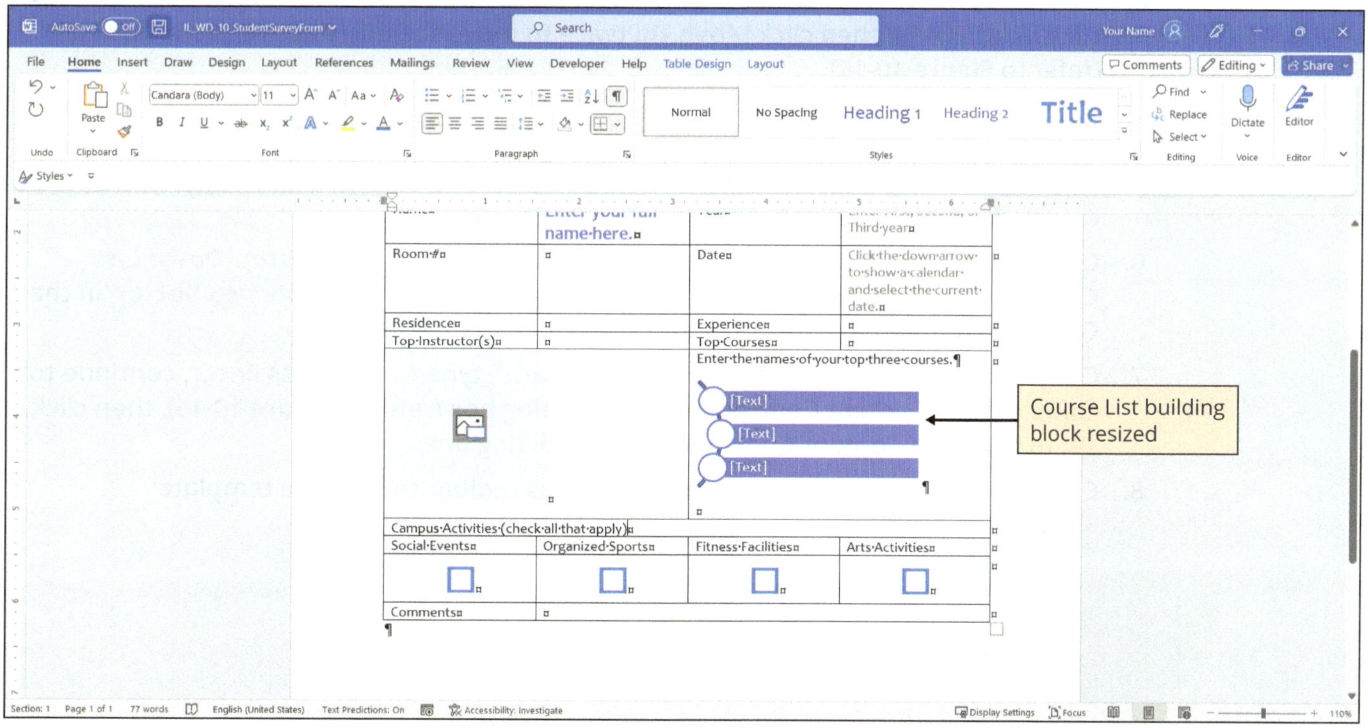

Add Drop-Down Content Controls

Case You insert a Combo Box content control next to the Residence table cell so students can select the location of their student residence if it is listed, or they can type the location of their residence if it is not listed (for example, "off-campus"). You then insert a Drop-Down List content control so students can select an adjective to describe their experience as an international student at MSIT.

Objectives
- Add a Combo Box content control
- Add a Drop-Down List content control

You can choose from two drop-down content controls: the **Combo Box content control** and the **Drop-Down List content control**. Both drop-down content controls provide users with a list of choices. In the Combo Box content control, users can select an item from the list of choices, or they can type a new item. In the Drop-Down List content control, users can only select from the list of choices.

Steps

Quick Tip
With Design Mode on, you can see the tags associated with each content control.

1. Scroll up as needed and click in the **blank table cell** to the right of **Residence**, click the **Developer tab**, click the **Design Mode button** in the Controls group to turn Design Mode on, then click the **Combo Box Content Control button** in the Controls group
   The Combo Box content control is inserted in the table cell. Next, you open the Content Control Properties dialog box to enter the items that users can select.
2. Click the **Properties button** in the Controls group, type **Residence Name**, click **Add** to open the Add Choice box, type **Evergreen Hall**, then click **OK**
3. Click **Add**, type **Mountain Place**, click **OK**, click **Add**, type **Acadia Hall**, then click **OK**
4. Click **Mountain Place**, click **Modify**, select **Mountain**, type **Mountainview**, click **OK**, click **Acadia Hall**, then click **Move Up** twice to move the entry above Evergreen Hall (refer to **Figure 10-15**)
   The list is now in alphabetical order.
5. Click **OK** to close the Content Controls dialog box
   When a student clicks the Residence content control, the list of options will be displayed. The user can select one of the options or type a different option in the box.
6. Click in the **blank table cell** to the right of Experience, click the **Drop-Down List Content Control button** in the Controls group, click the **Properties button** in the Controls group, then enter **College Experience** in the Title box
7. Click **Add**, type **Excellent**, press **Enter**, click **Add**, type **Good**, press **Enter**, continue to complete the Content Control Properties dialog box (refer to **Figure 10-16**), then click **OK** to close the Content Control Properties dialog box
8. Click the **Save button** on the Quick Access toolbar to save the template

Figure 10-15: Entries for the Combo Box content control

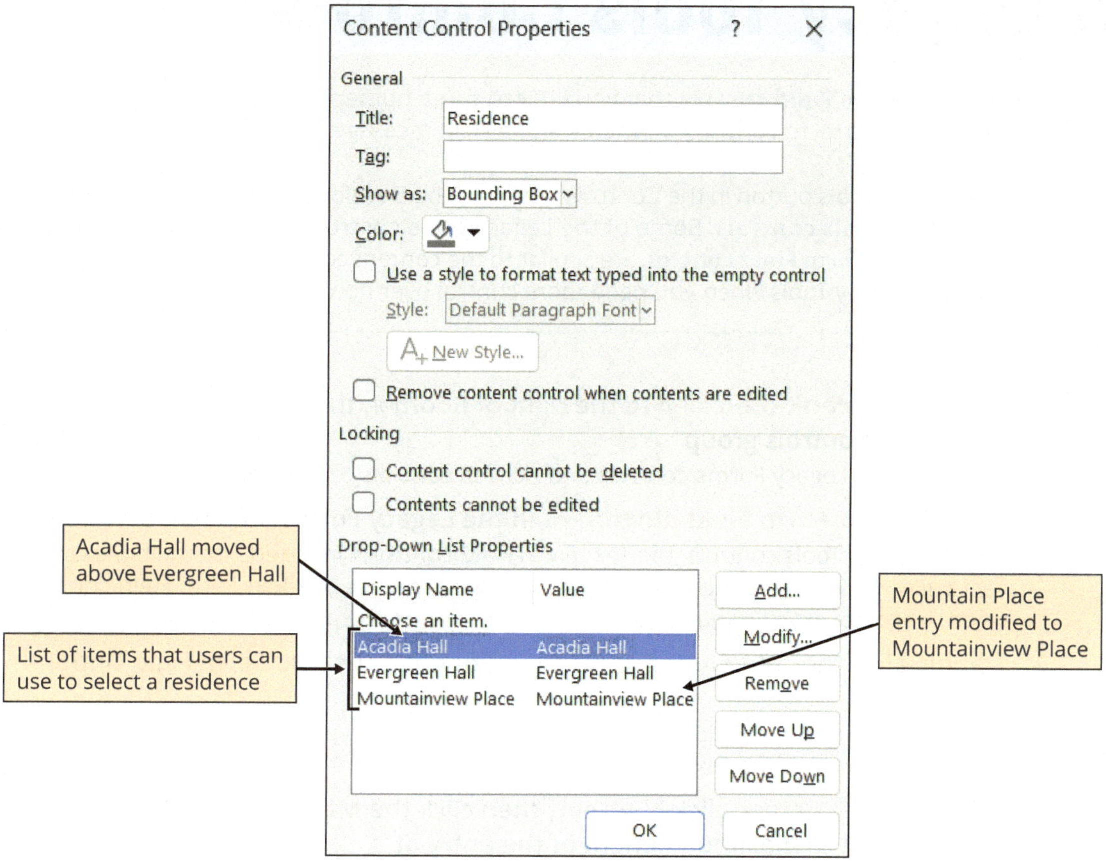

Figure 10-16: Entries for the Drop-Down List content control

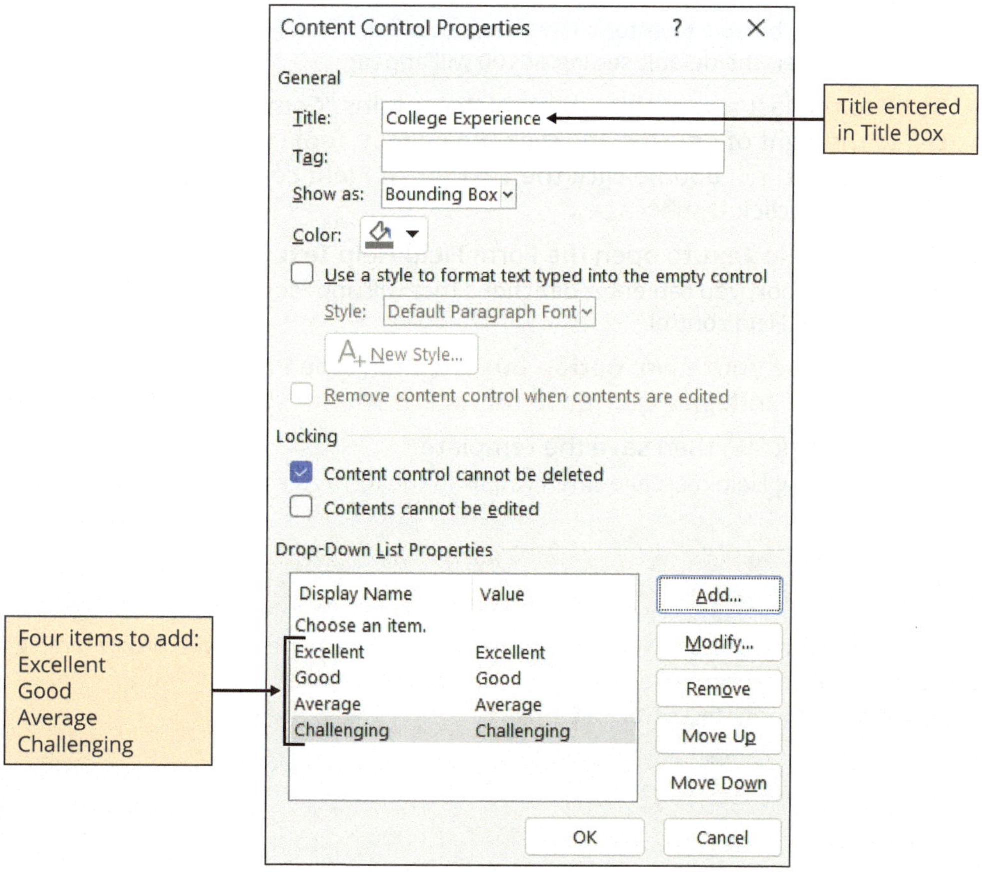

Insert Legacy Tools Controls

Case First, you insert a **Text Form Field control** that you limit to three numerical characters, and then you insert another Text Form Field control to contain comments and a Help message.

Objectives
- Insert a Text form field
- Insert Help text

The Legacy Tools button in the Controls group on the Developer tab provides access to a selection of **Legacy Tools controls**. Some of the Legacy Tools controls, such as the **Text control** and the **Drop-Down Form Field control**, are similar to the content controls you have already worked with. You use Legacy Tools when you need more control over how the content control is configured.

Steps

1. **Click in the blank table cell to the right of Room #, then click the Legacy Tools button in the Controls group**
   The gallery of Legacy Forms controls and ActiveX controls opens (refer to **Figure 10-17**).
2. **Click the Text Form Field button in the Legacy Forms area to insert a form field**
   Like all Legacy Tools controls, the Text Form Field control is inserted into the table cell as a shaded rectangle and does not include a title bar or tags. You use the Text Form Field control when you need to control exactly what data a user can enter into the placeholder.
3. **Double-click the Text Form Field control to open the Text Form Field Options dialog box**
   In the Text Form Field Options dialog box, you define the type and characteristics of the data that users can enter into the Text Form Field control.
4. **Click the Type arrow, click Number, then click the Maximum length up arrow three times to set the maximum length of the entry at 3**
5. **Click the Default number box, type 100, compare your Text Form Field Options dialog box to Figure 10-18, then click OK**
   Users will only be able to enter a three-digit number in the Text Form Field control. If users do not enter a number, the default setting of 100 will appear.
6. **Scroll to the last row of the table which contains "Comments", click in the blank table cell to the right of Comments, click the Legacy Tools button, click the Text Form Field button, double-click the Text Form Field control, click the Text format arrow, then click Uppercase**
7. **Click Add Help Text to open the Form Field Help Text dialog box**
   In this dialog box, you can enter directions that will appear on the status bar when users click in the Text Form Field control.
8. **Click the Type your own: option button, then type Provide suggestions to help us improve the college experience for international students. (refer to Figure 10-19)**
9. **Click OK, click OK, then save the template**
   You will see the Help message when you fill in the form as a user in a later lesson.

Using ActiveX controls

The Legacy Tools button also provides access to ActiveX controls that you can use to offer options to users or to run macros or scripts that automate specific tasks. You need to have some experience with programming to use most of the ActiveX controls.

Figure 10-17: Inserting a Text Form Field control

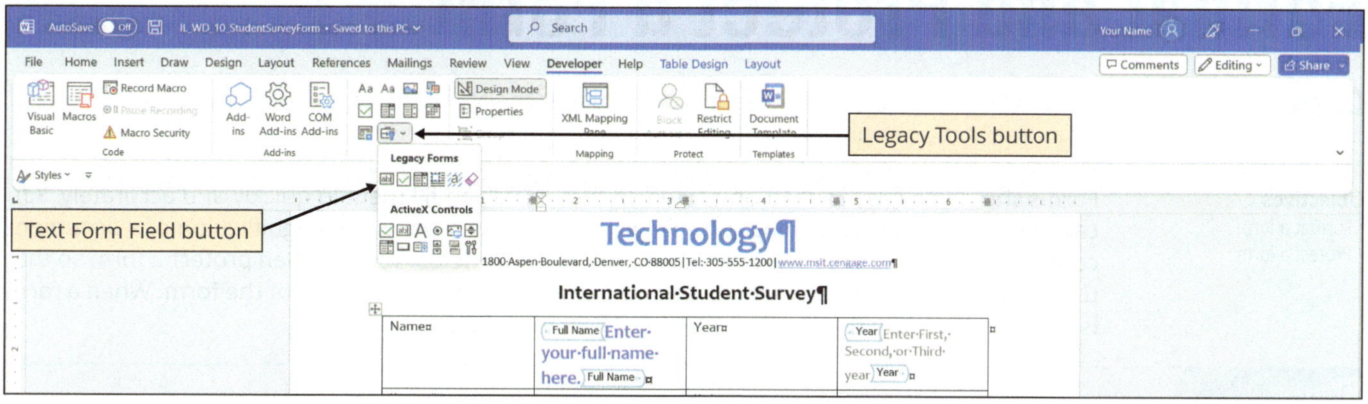

Figure 10-18: Text Form Field Options dialog box

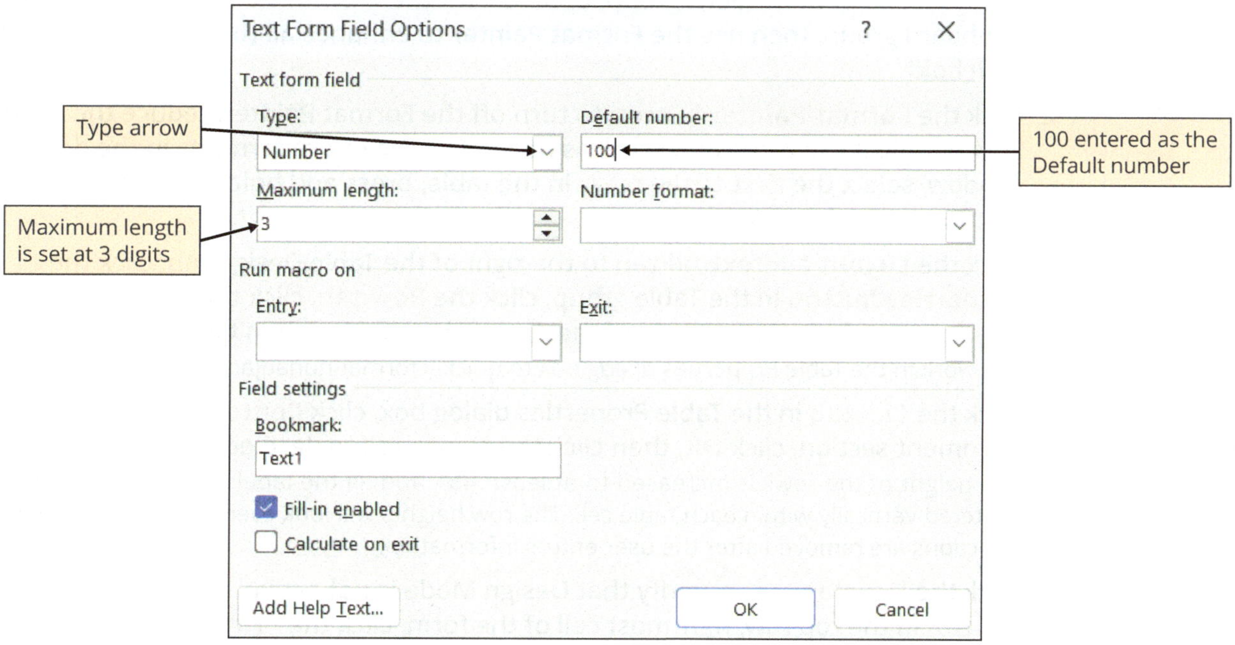

Figure 10-19: Adding Help text

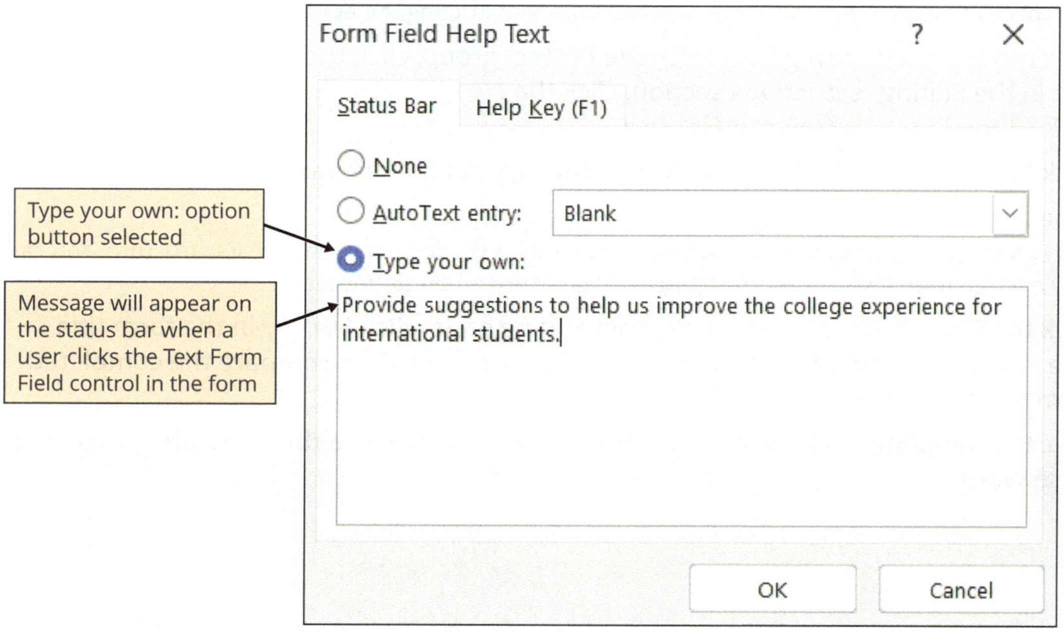

Format and Protect a Form

Case You enhance the field labels, modify the table form, specify that the Name content control cannot be deleted, and then protect and save the template.

Objectives
- Format a form
- Protect a form

Forms should be easy to read on-screen so that users can fill them in quickly and accurately. You can enhance a table containing form fields, and you can modify the magnification of a document containing a form so that users can easily see the form fields. You can then protect a form so that users can enter only the data required and cannot change the structure of the form. When a form is protected, information can be entered only in form fields.

Steps

Quick Tip
Instead of using the Format Painter, you can use the CTRL key to select each label, then click the Bold button.

Quick Tip
Before you protect a document, you must be sure Design Mode is turned off.

Trouble
If the passwords don't match, you will be prompted to reenter the password.

1. **Scroll up and select Name in the first cell of the table, click the Home tab, click the Bold button [B] in the Font group, double-click the Format Painter button in the Clipboard group, then use the Format Painter to enhance all the labels in the table with bold**
2. **Click the Format Painter button to turn off the Format Painter, reduce the zoom to 70% or adjust the zoom and scroll as needed so the entire form fits in the document window, select the first three rows in the table, press and hold CTRL, then select the last four rows in the table**
3. **Click the Layout contextual tab to the right of the Table Design tab, click the Properties button in the Table group, click the Row tab, click the Specify height check box, select the contents of the Specify height box, then type .45**
   You work in the Table Properties dialog box to quickly format nonadjacent rows in a table.
4. **Click the Cell tab in the Table Properties dialog box, click Center in the Vertical alignment section, click OK, then click the Name cell to deselect the rows**
   The height of the rows is increased to at least .45", and all the labels and content controls are centered vertically within each table cell. The row heights will look even when the content control directions are removed after the user enters information.
5. **Click the Developer tab, verify that Design Mode is not active, click the Year content control in the top row, rightmost cell of the form, click the Properties button in the Controls group, click the Content Control cannot be deleted check box to select it (refer to Figure 10-20), then click OK**
   You specify that a control cannot be deleted before restricting the editing of the entire form.
6. **Click the Restrict Editing button in the Protect group, click the Allow only...check box in the Editing restrictions section, click the No changes (Read only) arrow, then click Filling in forms (refer to Figure 10-21)**
7. **Click Yes, Start Enforcing Protection in the Restrict Editing pane**
8. **Type cengage, press TAB, type cengage, then click OK**
   You enter a password so that a user cannot unprotect the form and change its structure. You can only edit the form if you enter the "cengage" password when prompted.
9. **Click the Close button [X] in the Restrict Editing pane, click Survey in the form title (the Full Name content control appears to be selected), then compare the completed form template to Figure 10-22**
10. **Save the template, click the File tab, then click Close to close the template, but do not close Word**

Figure 10-20: Locking a content control

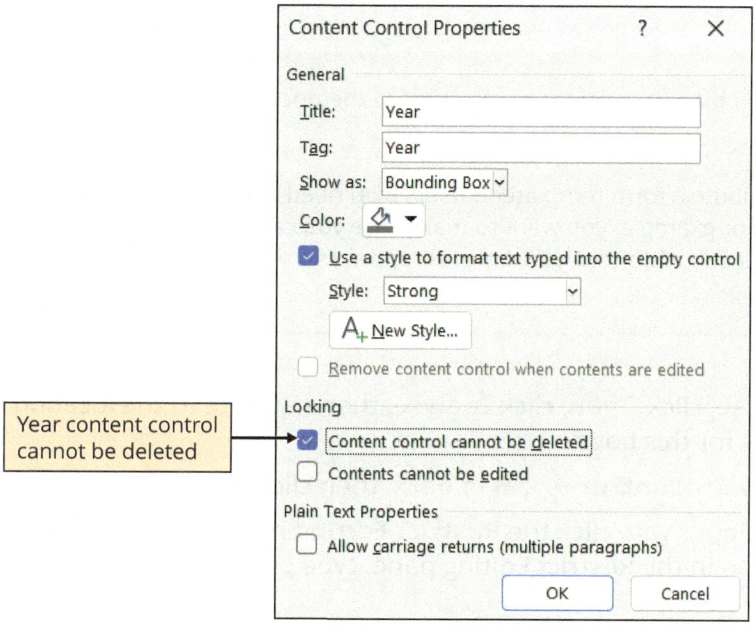

Figure 10-21: Protecting a form

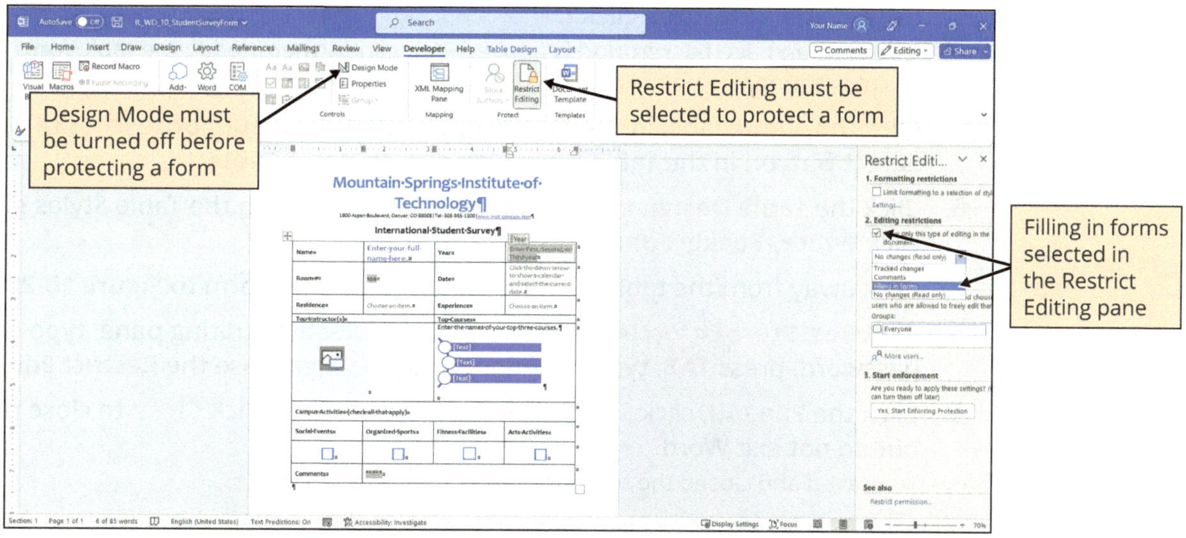

Figure 10-22: Completed form template

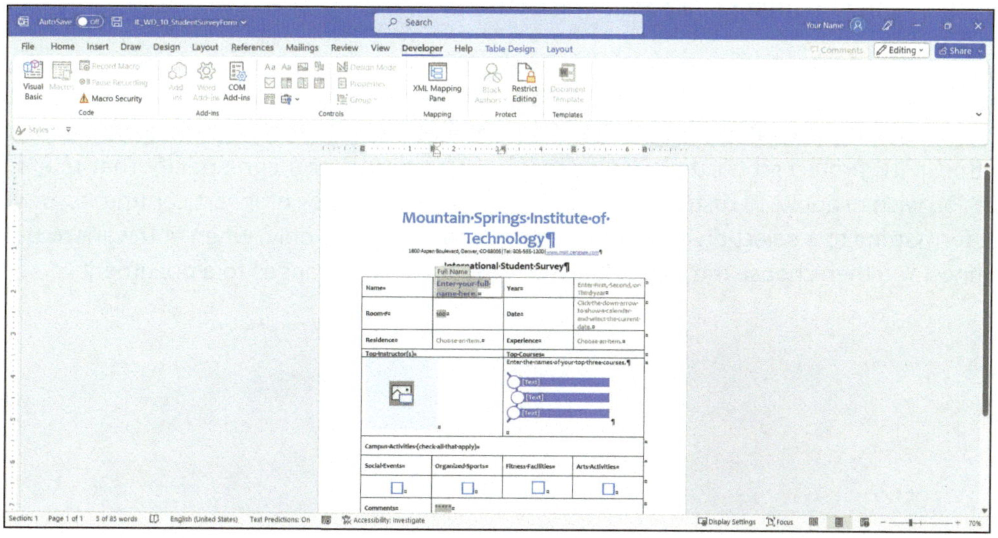

Edit a Form

Case You open and edit the form template by adding a page color to the document and removing the border from the table form.

Objectives
- Change the page color
- Edit a form

Before you distribute a form template to users, you need to test it to ensure that all the elements work correctly. For example, you want to make sure you can insert a picture in the Picture content control and that the Help text you entered appears in the status bar when you move to the Comments cell.

Steps

Trouble
Do *not* double-click the filename to open it. You must use the File, Open method to open the template file so that you can make changes to it.

Quick Tip
Before you can edit any part of the template, you need to stop protection.

1. Click the **File tab**, click **Open**, click **Browse**, then navigate to the location where you store your files for this book
2. Click **IL_WD_10_StudentSurveyForm.dotx**, then click **Open**
3. Click the **Developer tab**, click the **Restrict Editing button** in the Protect group, click **Stop Protection** in the Restrict Editing pane, type **cengage** (refer to **Figure 10-23**), then click **OK**
4. Click the **Design tab**, click the **Page Color button** in the Page Background group, click **More Colors**, click the **Custom tab**, refer to **Figure 10-24** to enter values for **Red**, **Green**, and **Blue**, then click **OK**
   A light green page background is applied. You can further modify the table form by changing the fill color and removing the outside table border.
5. Click the **Name** label in the table form, click the **Layout contextual tab**, click the **Select button** in the Table group, then click **Select Table**
6. Click the **Table Design tab**, click the **Shading arrow** in the Table Styles group, then click **White, Background 1**
7. Click away from the table, then compare the edited form to **Figure 10-25**
8. Click **Yes, Start Enforcing Protection** in the Restrict Editing pane, type **cengage** as the password, press **TAB**, type **cengage**, click **OK**, then close the Restrict Editing pane
9. Click the **File tab**, click **Save**, click the **File tab**, then click **Close** to close the template but do not exit Word
   You saved and closed the template but did not exit Word.

Protecting documents with formatting and editing restrictions

You protect a form so that users can enter data only in designated areas. You can also protect a document. To protect a document, click the Developer tab, click the Restrict Editing button in the Protect group, then choose the restriction settings you wish to apply. To restrict formatting, you click the Limit formatting to a selection of styles check box, then click Settings. You then choose the styles that you do not want users to use when formatting a document. For example, you can choose to prevent users from using the Heading 1 style or some of the table styles. For editing restrictions, you can specify that users may only make tracked changes or insert comments, or you can select No changes (read-only) when you want to prevent users from making any changes to a document.

Figure 10-23: Unprotecting the form

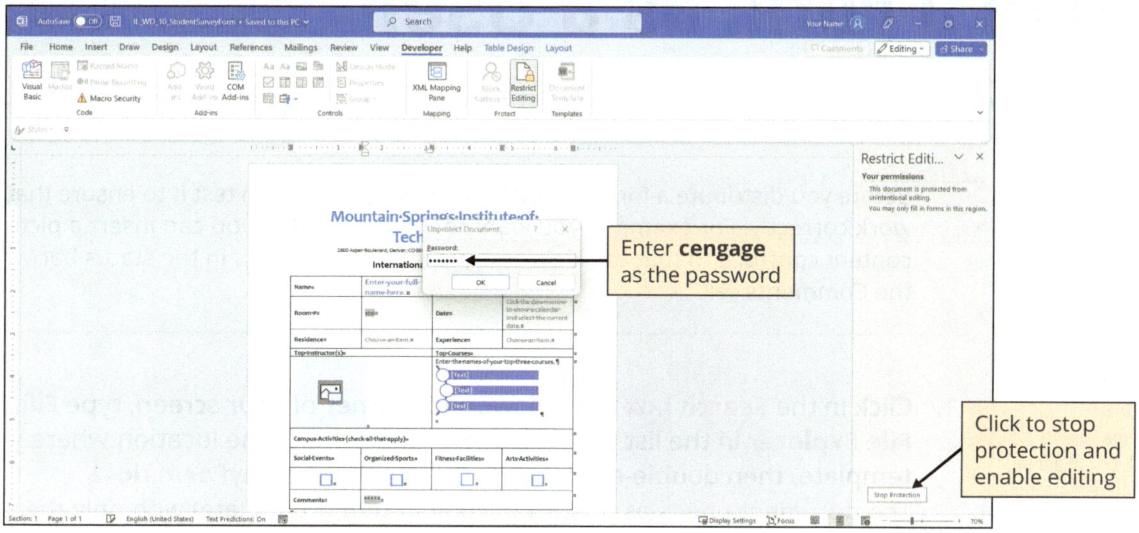

Figure 10-24: Page color settings

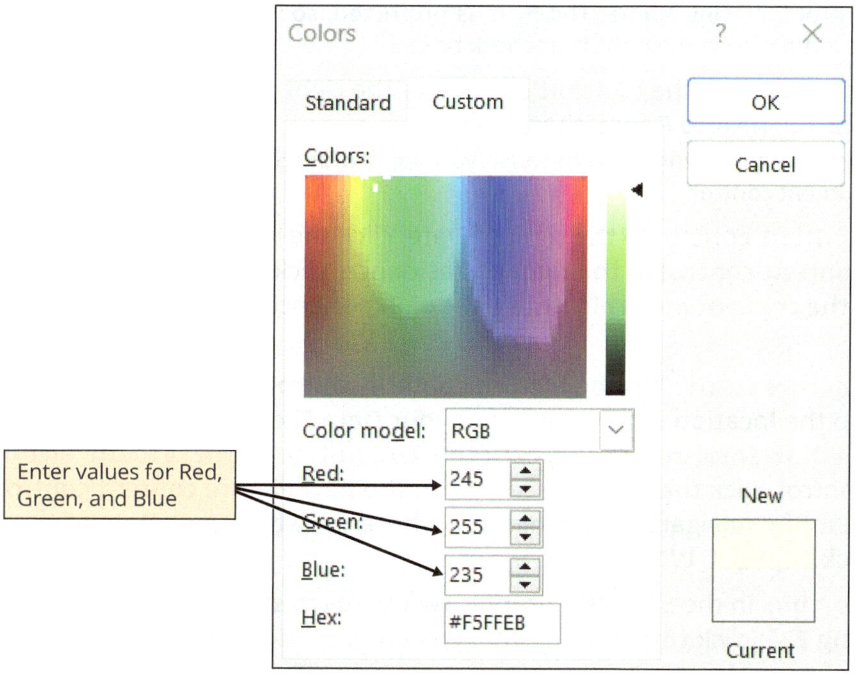

Figure 10-25: Formatted form

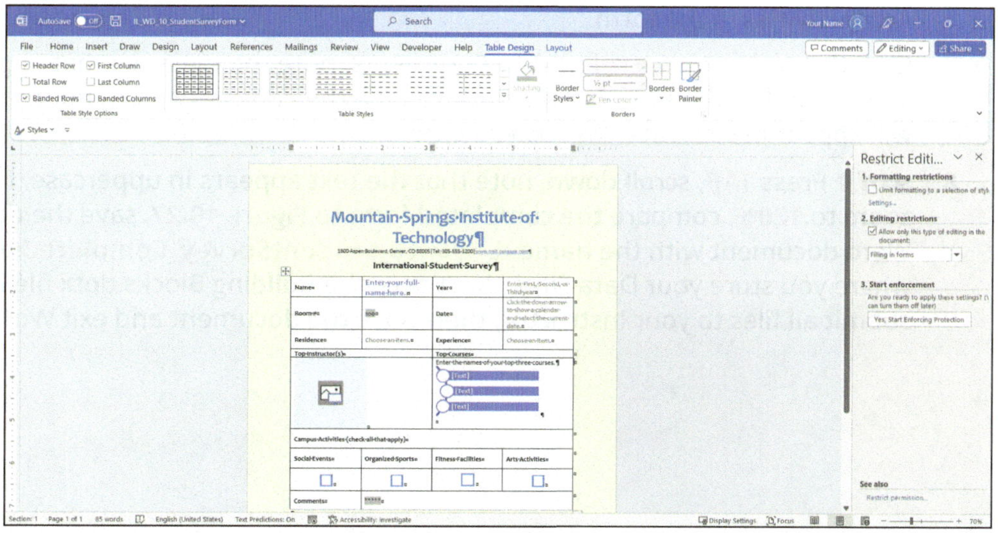

Fill in a Form as a User

Case You open a new document based on the template and fill in the form as if you were an international student at MSIT.

Objective
- Fill in a form

Before you distribute a form template to users, you need to test it to ensure that all the elements work correctly. For example, you want to make sure that you can insert a picture in the Picture content control and that the Help text you entered appears in the status bar when you move to the Comments cell.

Steps

Trouble
The Type here to search box might be in a different location, depending on where the taskbar is docked.

1. **Click in the Search box in the lower-left corner of your screen, type File Explorer, click File Explorer in the list of applications, navigate to the location where you stored the template, then double-click IL_WD_10_StudentSurveyForm.dotx**
   The document opens as a Word document (not a template) with only the content controls active. You will see Document2 – Word (or another document number depending on what other document you've been working on in Word) in the title bar. The insertion point highlights the content control following Name. The form is protected, so you can enter information only in spaces that contain content controls or check boxes.

Quick Tip
To enter a choice that is not listed in the Combo Box content control, select the text in the content control, then type the required text.

2. **Type your name, click the content control to the right of Year, type Second, double-click 100 next to Room, then type 225**
   Notice how the year appears bold because you applied the Strong style when you inserted the Plain Text content control.
3. **Click the content control to the right of Date, click the down arrow, click Today, click the content control to the right of Residence, click the arrow, click Evergreen Hall, click the content control to the right of Experience, click the arrow, then click Excellent**

Trouble
If the document extends to two pages (with the second page blank), reduce the height of the two pictures so that the document consists of just one page.

4. **Click the picture icon in the Picture content control, click From a file, navigate to the location where you store your Data Files, double-click Support_WD_10_Instructor1.jpg, click the Add button next to the Picture content control, click the picture icon in the new Picture content control, click From a file, navigate to the location where you store your Data Files, then double-click Support_WD_10_Instructor2.jpg**
5. **Click the top box in the SmartArt graphic two times to show the insertion point, type Engineering 220, click the middle box, type English 240, click the bottom box, then type Clean Technology 260**
6. **Click the check box below Social Events in the form, then click the check box below Arts Activities in the form**

Trouble
A form template that you open and fill in as a user and then save as a Word document will open in Read Mode. To fill in the form with additional information or to edit it, click View on the Ribbon, then click Edit Document.

7. **Click the content control next to Comments, note the message that appears on the status bar, then refer to Figure 10-26 to type the comment text, noting that the text will appear in sentence case as you type**
8. **Press TAB, scroll down, note that the text appears in uppercase, increase the zoom to 120%, compare the completed form to Figure 10-27, save the document as a Word document with the name IL_WD_10_StudentSurvey_Completed to the location where you store your Data Files, don't save the Building Blocks.dotx file if asked, submit all files to your instructor, then close the document and exit Word**

Figure 10-26: Comment entry

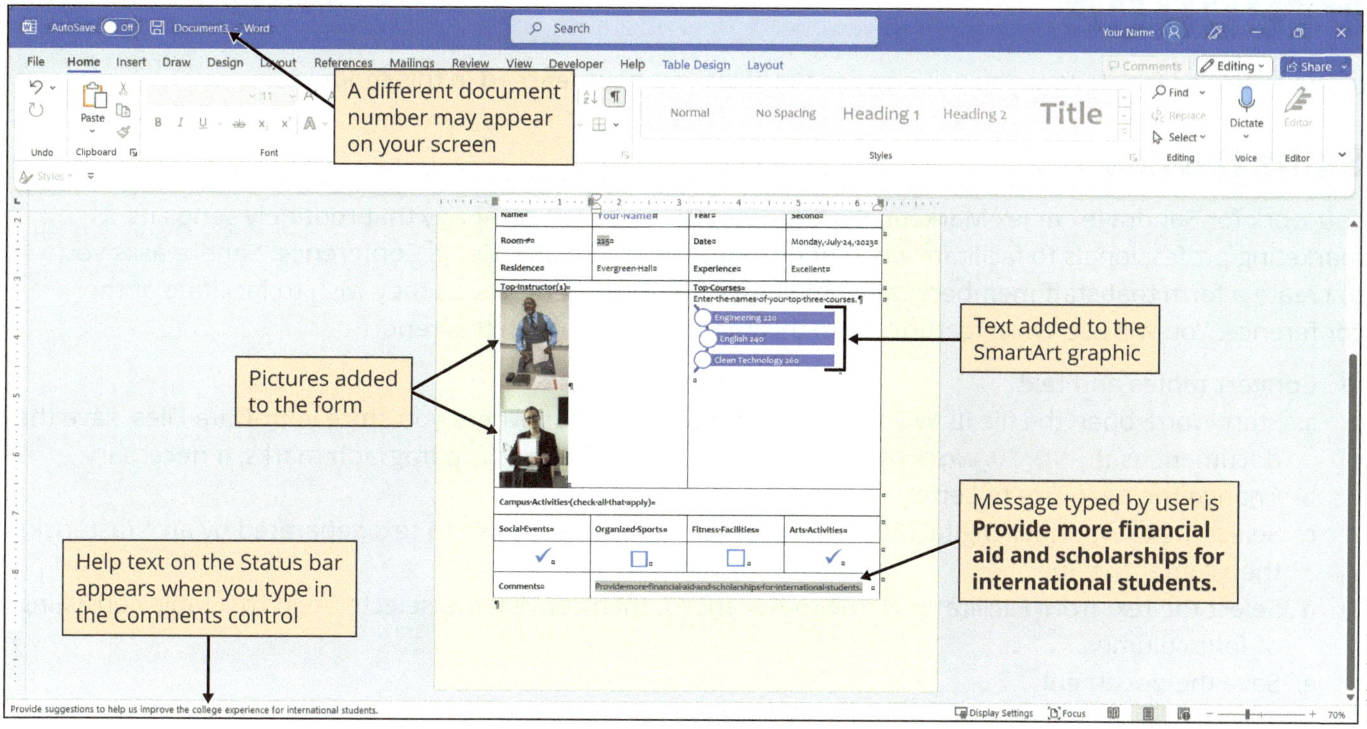

Mikhail Nilov/Pexels; RODNAE Productions/Pexels

Figure 10-27: Completed form

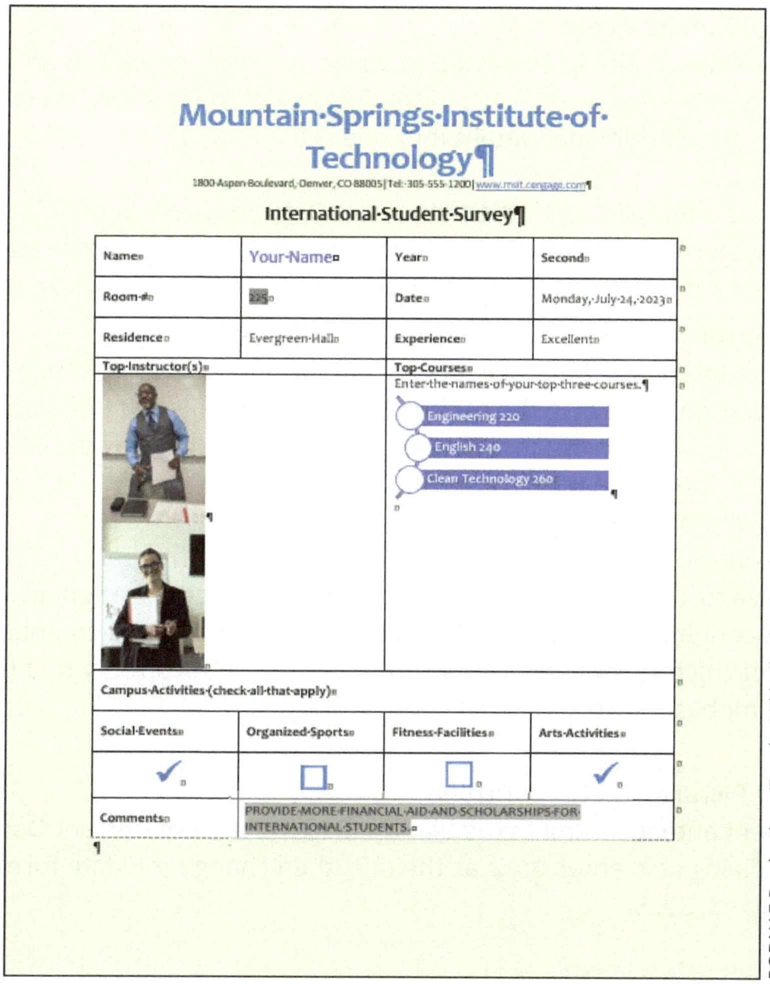

RODNAE Productions/Pexels; Mikhail Nilov/Pexels

Practice

In the exercises that follow, you will practice the skills you have learned in this module.

Skills Review

You work for Sandra Jex at Jex Marketing, a large San Diego-based company that routinely sends its marketing professionals to facilitate workshops at the annual Digital Media Conference. Sandra asks you to create a form that staff members can complete to select the workshops they wish to facilitate at the conference. You will use Word features from this module to help with this report.

1. **Convert tables and text.**
   a. Start Word, open the file IL_WD_10-2.docx from the location where you store your Data Files, save the document as **IL_WD_10_WorkshopApplicationSetup**, then show paragraph marks, if necessary.
   b. Change the page size to Letter.
   c. Select the table under Digital Media Conference, convert the table to text separated by an * (asterisk), then center the line.
   d. Select the text from Facilitator Name to Advanced, then convert the selected text to a table consisting of four columns.
   e. Save the document.
2. **Construct a form template.**
   a. Merge the first two cells in the second row (contains Facilitator Picture) into one cell, then merge the next two cells in the second row (contains Past Workshops) into one cell.
   b. Merge the first two cells in the third row into one cell, then merge the next two cells in the third row into one cell so row 3 matches row 2.
   c. Press TAB from the cell containing Advanced to start a new row, press TAB another four times to start another new row, type **Additional Details** in the first cell of the last row, press TAB, then merge the three cells to the right of Additional Details into one cell.
   d. Save the file.
   e. Save the file again as a template with the name **IL_WD_10_WorkshopApplicationForm.dotx** to the location where you store your Data Files. (Note: Make sure you specify the location where you save the template so that it is not saved to the Custom Templates Folder on your system.)
3. **Add Text content controls.**
   a. Show the Developer tab on the Ribbon if it is not already displayed, then turn on Design Mode.
   b. Insert a Rich Text content control in the table cell to the right of Facilitator Name.
   c. In the Properties dialog box for the content control, type **Full Name** as the title, exit the Properties dialog box, then click the Home tab.
   d. Between the two Full Name tags, enter **Type your full name.**
   e. Select the entire control, verify the control handle is blue with white text to indicate it is selected, change the font size to 14 point and the font color to Plum, Accent 2, then apply bold.
   f. Insert a Plain Text content control in the blank cell to the right of Department.
   g. In the Properties dialog box, enter **Department** as the title, then specify that the text be formatted with the Intense Emphasis style.
   h. Save the template.
4. **Add Date Picker and Picture content controls.**
   a. Insert a Date Picker content control in the blank cell to the right of Current Date.
   b. In the Properties dialog box, enter **Date** as the title, then change the date format to the format that corresponds to June 3, 2028.

c. Between the two Date tags, type the message **Click the down arrow to show a calendar, then select Today.**
d. In the blank cell below Facilitator Picture, insert a Picture content control.
e. Save the template.

5. **Add Repeating Section and Check Box content controls.**
   a. Select the blank row below the Workshop Name, Category Code, Introductory, and Advanced labels, insert a Repeating Section content control, then turn off Design Mode to view the Add button. You will add controls to this row in a later step.
   b. Turn on Design Mode, then insert a Check Box content control in the cell below Introductory.
   c. In the Content Control Properties dialog box, name the control **Code**, apply the Heading 2 style to the Check Box content control, then change the Checked symbol to Character code **251** (a stylized x) from the Wingdings font.
   d. Select the Code Check Box content control, copy it, then paste it in the cell below Advanced.
   e. Save the template.

6. **Add Building Blocks content controls.**
   a. Start a new blank document, then type the text **Enter up to three of your most recent workshops.**
   b. Press ENTER, then insert a SmartArt graphic using the Vertical Box List type in the List category.
   c. Apply Colored Fill - Accent 6 to the SmartArt graphic, then click away from the graphic to deselect it.
   d. Press CTRL+A to select the contents of the document, then save the selection to the Quick Part Gallery using the name **Workshop List** as the building block name.
   e. Save the document as **IL_WD_10_WorkshopBuildingBlock** to the location where you store your Data Files, then close the document.
   f. Verify that IL_WD_10_WorkshopApplicationForm.dotx is again the active document, then verify that the Design Mode button on the Developer tab is not active.
   g. Click the blank cell below Past Workshops, then insert the Workshop List building block content control by clicking the Building Block Gallery Content Control button in the Controls group.
   h. Select the graphic, then change the height to **1.4"** and the width to **3"**. (Hint: Use the down arrows to change the height and width.)
   i. Save the template.

7. **Add Drop-Down content controls.**
   a. Click in the cell below Workshop Name, then insert a Combo Box content control.
   b. In the Content Control Properties dialog box, enter **Workshop Name** as the title.
   c. Add the following entries: **Content**, **Email Marketing**, **Video Production & Editing**, and **Influencer Marketing**.
   d. Change Content to **Content Marketing**, then move Influencer Marketing up so it appears immediately after Email Marketing.
   e. Click in the cell below Category Code, then insert a Drop-Down List content control.
   f. In the Content Control Properties dialog box, enter **Category Code** as the title, then add the following entries: **150**, **175**, **200**, and **225**.
   g. Save the template.

8. **Insert Legacy Tools controls.**
   a. Insert a Text Form Field control from the Legacy Tools gallery in the blank cell to the right of Office Local.
   b. Double-click the control to open the Text Form Field Options dialog box, change the Type to Number, change the Maximum length to **4**, then enter **1234** as the default.
   c. Insert a Text Form Field control from the Legacy Tools gallery in the blank cell to the right of Additional Details.
   d. Specify that the text format should be uppercase, add the help text: **Provide additional details about your experience.**, then save the template.

Skills Review (Continued)

9. Format and protect a form.

a. Verify that Design Mode is off, then apply bold to all the labels in the form template.

b. Change the view to 90%, select the table, then change the row height to at least **.3"**.

c. Vertically center align the text in all the cells. (**Hint**: Use the Cell tab in the Table Properties dialog box.)

d. Protect the document for users filling in forms using the password **skills**, then save and close the template but do not exit Word. (Note: If you turned Design Mode on, it must be turned off to protect the document.)

10. Edit a form.

a. From Word, open the template IL_WD_WorkshopApplicationForm.dotx (remember *not* to double-click it to open it), then stop protection using the **skills** password.

b. Change the page color to the custom color Red: 255, Green: 250, Blue: 250

c. Fill the table form with the White, Background 1 shading color.

d. Click below the table, press ENTER, then type your name.

e. Protect the form again using the **skills** password.

f. Save and close the template but do not exit Word.

11. Fill in a form as a user.

a. Open File Explorer, navigate to the Workshop Application Form template, then double-click it to start a new document.

b. Refer to **Figure 10-28** to complete the form. Insert Support_WD_10_Facilitator.jpg in the Picture content control and **623** for the Office Local.

c. Select the current date, select the information for the first course (Blogging for Business), then click the Repeating Section content control and enter the information for the second course (Event Planning). The comment text is: **I've presented at the last three conferences and received excellent reviews.**

d. Save the document as **IL_WD_10_WorkshopApplication_Completed** to the location where you store your Data Files, answer no to save the Building Blocks.dotx file, submit the file to your instructor, then close the document and exit Word.

Figure 10-28

Digital Media Conference

450 Pacific Way, San Diego, CA 92014 • Tel: 707-555-1900 • www.dmconference.cengage.com

Workshop Application Form

Facilitator Name	Selina Harris	Department	Social Media
Facilitator Picture		Past Workshops Enter up to three of your most recent workshops. Tik Tok Tips Social Media for Beginners Social Media Strategy	
Current Date	7/24/2023	Office Local	623
Workshop Name	Category Code	Introductory	Advanced
Content Marketing	175	x	☐
Influencer Marketing	225	☐	x
Additional Details	I'VE PRESENTED AT THE LAST THREE CONFERENCES AND RECEIVED EXCELLENT REVIEWS.		

Your Name

Kampus Production/Pexels

Independent Challenge 1

You work in the Finance Department at Azure Skies Technology, based in Vancouver, BC. Climate consultants employed by the company frequently travel to countries around the world to oversee clean technology projects. Your supervisor asks you to create a travel form that the consultants can complete online to help them keep track of their travel details.

a. Start Word and open the file IL_WD_10-3.docx from the drive and folder where you store your Data Files. Save it as **IL_WD_10_TravelFormSetup**.
b. Turn on paragraph marks, if necessary, then convert the table containing the contact information for Azure Skies Technology into text separated by the | character.
c. Select the text from Name to the paragraph mark following Picture of Project, then convert the selected text into a table consisting of four columns and rows.
d. Add two more rows with four columns each at the end of the table.
e. Merge the three cells to the right of Travel Purpose into one cell, then merge the three cells to the right of Picture of Project into one cell.
f. In the next row containing four columns, enter the following four labels: **Date**, **Location**, **Category**, **Contact**.
g. From the Developer tab, make the Design Mode active, then insert a Rich Text content control in the blank cell to the right of the Name label. Enter **Full Name** as the title, then format the control with 14 pt and bold.
h. Insert a Date Picker control in the blank cell to the right of Current Date. Enter **Current Date** as the title, then select the date format that corresponds with 6-Feb-28.
i. Insert a Drop-Down List content control in the blank cell to the right of Department. Enter **Department** as the title, then add **Research**, **Production**, **Marketing**, and **Finance**, and put the entries in alphabetical order.
j. Insert a Text Form Field control from the Legacy Tools gallery in the blank cell to the right of Extension. Specify the type as Number, a Maximum length of **3**, and **100** as the Default number.
k. Insert a Plain Text content control in the cell to the right of Travel Purpose. Enter **Travel Purpose** for the title, then apply the Emphasis style.
l. Copy the Date Picker content control you inserted next to Current Date, then paste it in the cell below Date.
m. Insert a Combo Box content control in the cell below Location. Enter **Location** as the title, then add five selections: **China**, **United States**, **Sweden**, **New Zealand**, and **Germany,** and put them in alphabetical order. Enter the text **Select a country or type a new one.** between the two tags.
n. Insert a Drop-Down List Box content control in the cell below Category. Enter **Category** as the title, then add four selections: **Wind**, **Solar**, **Hydro**, and **Biomass**, and put them in alphabetical order.
o. Insert a Rich Text content control in the cell below Contact. Enter the text **Click the Add button for more rows.** between the tags, then open the Content Control Properties dialog box, enter **Contact** as the title, and select the Dark Red color for the control.
p. Select the last row in the form (contains the four content controls you just created), then click the Repeating Section Content Control button. If the plus sign is not visible, turn off Design Mode. When users fill in the form, they can click the plus sign to add more rows to supply details about additional trips.
q. Insert a Picture content control in the blank cell to the right of Picture of Project. Click the Picture content control, then drag the middle-right sizing handle to the right to increase the width of the control so it almost fills the table cell.
r. Apply bold to all the form labels.
s. Enter your name where indicated below the form, then save the document.
t. Save the document again as a template with the name **IL_WD_10_TravelForm.dotx** to the location where you store your Data Files.

Independent Challenge 1 (Continued)

u. Protect the form using the Filling in forms selection, enter **ic1** as the password, then save and close the template but do not exit Word.

v. Start a new document by double-clicking the IL_WD_10_TravelForm.dotx template file in File Explorer (verify that Document1 or another number appears in the title bar), enter your name and the current date in row 1, then enter **Production** as the Department, **380** as the Extension, and **Touring energy projects in Europe.** as the Travel Purpose.

w. Insert Support_WD_10_WindEnergy.jpg in the Picture content control.

x. Enter itinerary information as shown in **Table 10-2**, clicking the Add button after you've entered data for each row for a total of four rows. Note that you will need to type the Location information ("Norway" and "Denmark") in the Combo Box control.

Table 10-2

date	location	category	contact
5-May-28	Norway	Wind	Boris Bense
8-May-28	Sweden	Wind	Maya Johansen
22-May-28	Denmark	Wind	Henrik Andersen
29-May-28	Germany	Biomass	Helga Schmidt

y. Compare the completed form to **Figure 10-29**, save the form as **IL_WD_10_TravelForm_Completed**, submit a copy to your instructor, then close the document and exit Word.

Figure 10-29

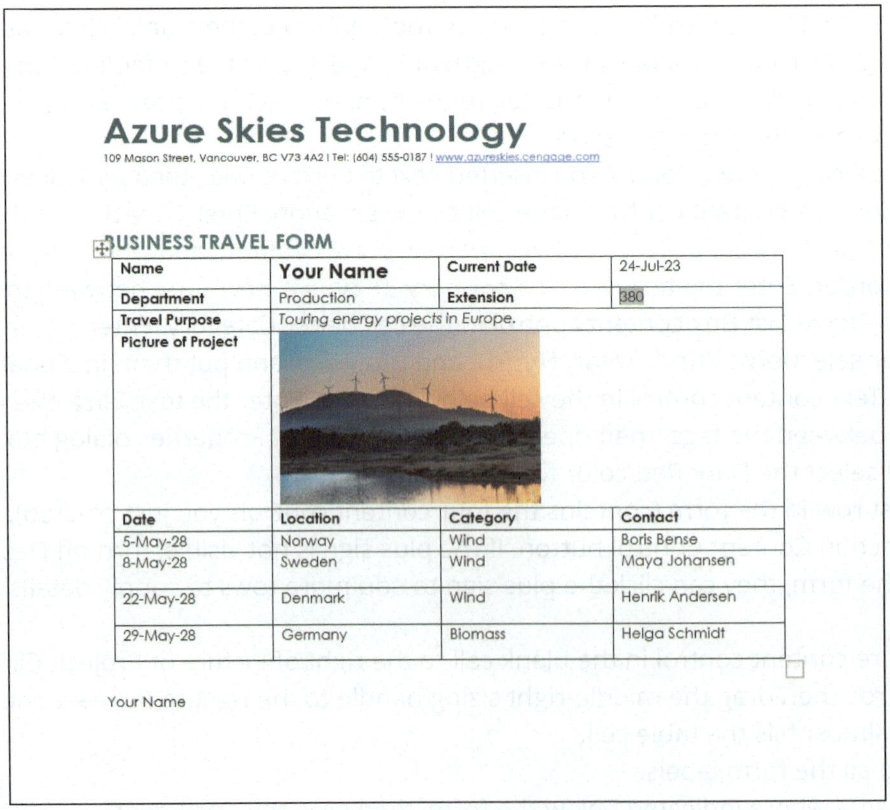

Azure Skies Technology

109 Mason Street, Vancouver, BC V73 4A2 | Tel: (604) 555-0187 | www.azureskies.cengage.com

BUSINESS TRAVEL FORM

Name	Your Name	Current Date	24-Jul-23
Department	Production	Extension	380
Travel Purpose	Touring energy projects in Europe.		
Picture of Project			

Date	Location	Category	Contact
5-May-28	Norway	Wind	Boris Bense
8-May-28	Sweden	Wind	Maya Johansen
22-May-28	Denmark	Wind	Henrik Andersen
29-May-28	Germany	Biomass	Helga Schmidt

Your Name

Nitin Sharma/Pexels

Independent Challenge 2

You run the office for KVC Real Estate, a small real estate company based in Honolulu, HI, that sells condos, townhouses, and houses on four of the Hawaiian Islands: Oahu, Maui, Kauai, and Hawaii. The owner of the company, Kaye V. Calhoun, asks you to create a form that the four agents who work for the company can complete to list their sales at the end of each month.

a. Start Word and open the file IL_WD_10-4.docx from the location where your Data Files are located. Save it as a template with the name **IL_WD_10_RealEstateForm** to the location where you store your Data Files.
b. Change the page size to Letter.
c. From the Developer tab, switch to Design Mode, then insert and format controls as described in **Table 10-3**:

Table 10-3

location	content control	title	properties
Name	Rich Text content control	**Full Name**	Format with Heading 1
Current Date	Date Picker content control	**Date**	Format with the 10.25.2028 date format.
Agent	Drop-Down List content control	**Agent**	Add the names of four agents: **Kaye Calhoun**, **Terry Lin**, **Sara Barton**, **Wim James**, and **Gary Kamaka,** and put them in alphabetical order by last name.
Island	Drop-Down List content control	**Island**	Add entries for four islands in alphabetical order: **Oahu, Kauai**, **Maui**, and **Hawaii**; type the text **Select the island you're based on.** between the form tags as a direction to users.
Property Address	Text Form Field control from Legacy Tools		Enter the Help text **Click the Add button to insert up to three more properties**.
Property Types	Check Box content control in each of the 4 blank cells for the property type (e.g., Condo, Townhouse, etc.)	**Type**	Format with the Heading 1 style and the Wingdings **252** check mark character (Hint: Insert and modify the first check box content control, then copy and paste it to the remaining table cells.)

d. Select the row containing the Text Form Field and Check Box content controls and make the row a Repeating Section. Turn off Design Mode and verify that the Add button appears to the right of the last cell in the row.
e. Save the template, then create a new blank document.
f. Turn on bold, then type the text: **Type three words that summarize the client experience**.
g. Press ENTER, then insert the Basic Venn graphic from the Relationship category.
h. Apply the Colorful– Accent Colors color scheme.
i. Select all the text and the SmartArt graphic, then save it as a building block with the name **Experience** in the Quick Parts gallery.
j. Save the document as **IL_WD_10_ExperienceBuildingBlock** to the location where you store your Data Files, then close it.
k. In the form template, verify that Design Mode is off, then insert the Experience building block into the last row of the table. Resize the graphic to 2" high and 4" wide so the entire form fits on one page.
l. Click away from the table, then change the page color for the document to Red: 245, Green: 235, and Blue: 250. Change the fill color of the table form to White, Background 1.

Independent Challenge 2 (Continued)

m. Protect the form for filling in forms, click OK to bypass password protection when prompted, then save and close the template but do not exit Word.

n. Open the template IL_WD_10_RealEstateForm.dotx and unprotect it, then remove Wim James from the list of the agents in the Drop-Down List content control so the list includes only four agents.

o. Protect the form again, then save and close the template but do not exit Word.

p. Start a new document by double-clicking IL_WD_10_RealEstateForm.dotx in File Explorer, enter your name in the Name cell and the current date in the Current Date cell, select Gary Kamaka as the agent, then type **Kauai** in the List Box content control to the right of Island.

q. In the content control below Property Address, type **16 Palm Drive**, then click the check box under House.

r. Use the Add button to add another row. (Note: 16 Palm Drive is entered, but you can type over it.) Enter **200 Pacific View Crescent** as the address and click the check box under Townhouse, then add another row and enter **500 Sunset Drive** as the address and House as the property type.

s. Type these three words in the three boxes of the SmartArt graphic: **Efficient, Supportive**, **Friendly**.

t. Save the document as **IL_WD_10_RealEstateForm_Completed** to the location where you store the files for this book, don't save the Building Blocks.dotx file, compare the completed form to **Figure 10-30**, submit the form document to your instructor, then close the document and exit Word.

Figure 10-30

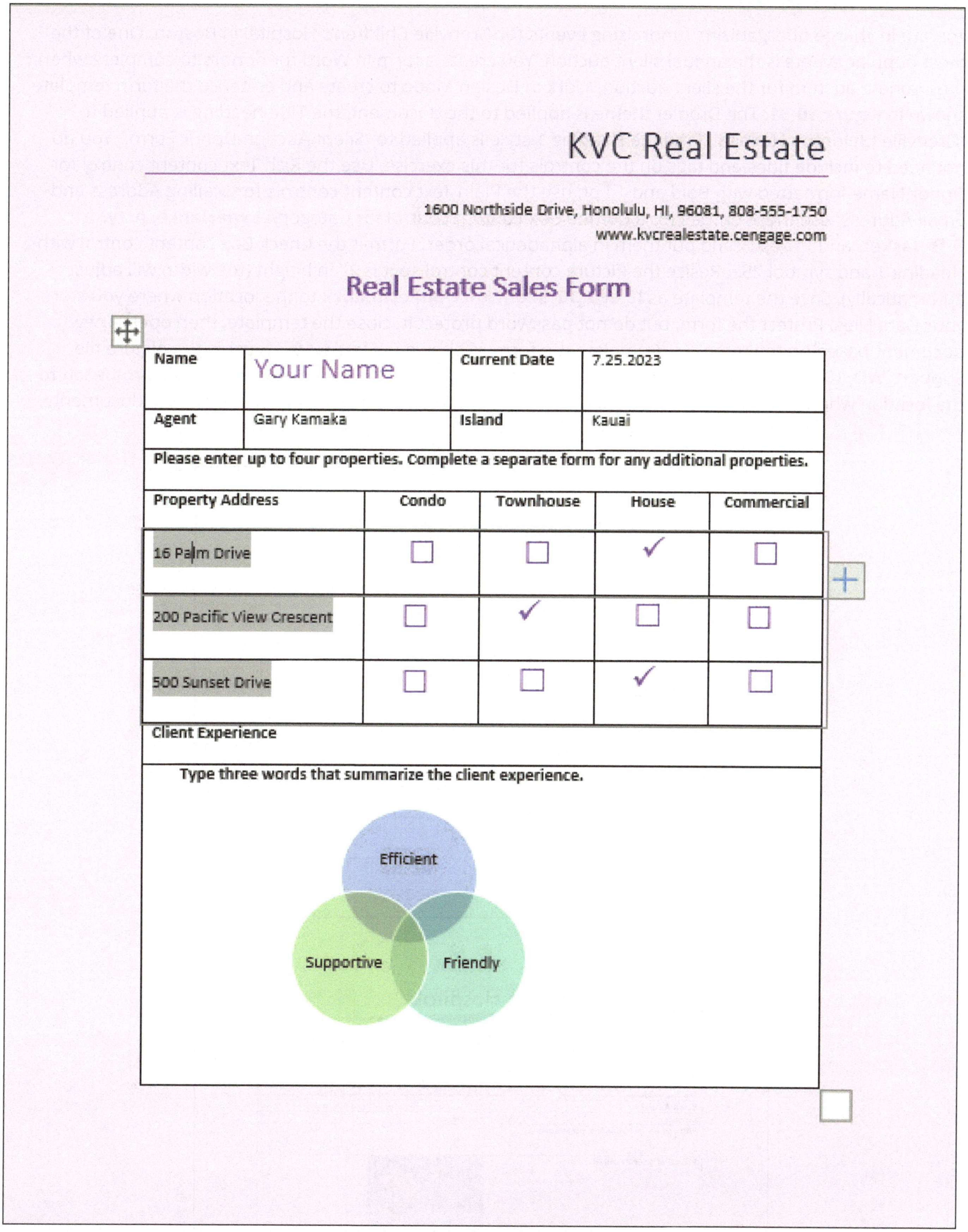

KVC Real Estate

1600 Northside Drive, Honolulu, HI, 96081, 808-555-1750
www.kvcrealestate.cengage.com

Real Estate Sales Form

Name	Your Name		Current Date	7.25.2023
Agent	Gary Kamaka		Island	Kauai
Please enter up to four properties. Complete a separate form for any additional properties.				
Property Address	Condo	Townhouse	House	Commercial
16 Palm Drive	☐	☐	✓	☐
200 Pacific View Crescent	☐	✓	☐	☐
500 Sunset Drive	☐	☐	✓	☐
Client Experience				
Type three words that summarize the client experience.				

Visual Workshop

You are in charge of organizing fundraising events for Grenville Children's Hospital in Boston. One of the most popular events is the annual silent auction. You create a form in Word for donors to complete when they donate an item for the silent auction. Work in Design Mode to create and enhance the form template shown in **Figure 10-31**. The Droplet theme is applied to the document, the Title heading is applied to "Grenville Children's Hospital," and the Heading 1 style is applied to "Silent Auction Donor Form." You do not need to include titles and tags on the controls for this exercise. Use the Rich Text content control for Donor Name formatted with Bold and 14 pt; use the Plain Text content controls for Mailing Address and Email Address; use these entries for a Combo Box content control for Category: **Experience**, **Artwork**, **Gift Basket**, and **Product** and put them in alphabetical order. Format the Check Box content control with Heading 1 and symbol 252. Resize the Picture content control so it is **2"** in height (the width will adjust automatically). Save the template as **IL_WD_10_SilentAuctionForm.dotx** to the location where you store your Data Files. Protect the form, but do not password protect it, close the template, then open a new document based on the template. Complete the form as shown in **Figure 10-32**, using the picture file Support_WD_10_Balloons.jpg. Save the completed form as **IL_WD_10_SilentAuctionForm_Completed** to the location where you store your Data Files, submit a copy to your instructor, then close the document.

Figure 10-31

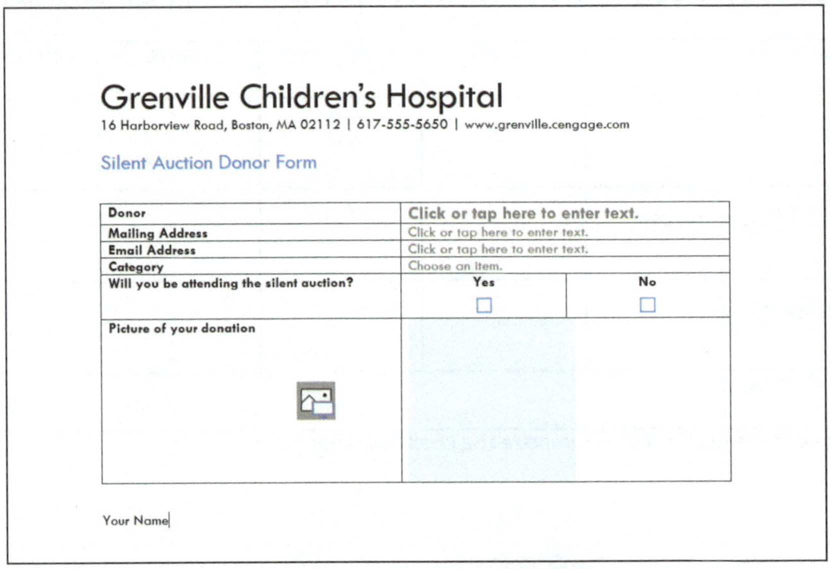
Grenville Children's Hospital

16 Harborview Road, Boston, MA 02112 | 617-555-5650 | www.grenville.cengage.com

Silent Auction Donor Form

Donor	Click or tap here to enter text.	
Mailing Address	Click or tap here to enter text.	
Email Address	Click or tap here to enter text.	
Category	Choose an item.	
Will you be attending the silent auction?	Yes ☐	No ☐
Picture of your donation		

Your Name

Figure 10-32

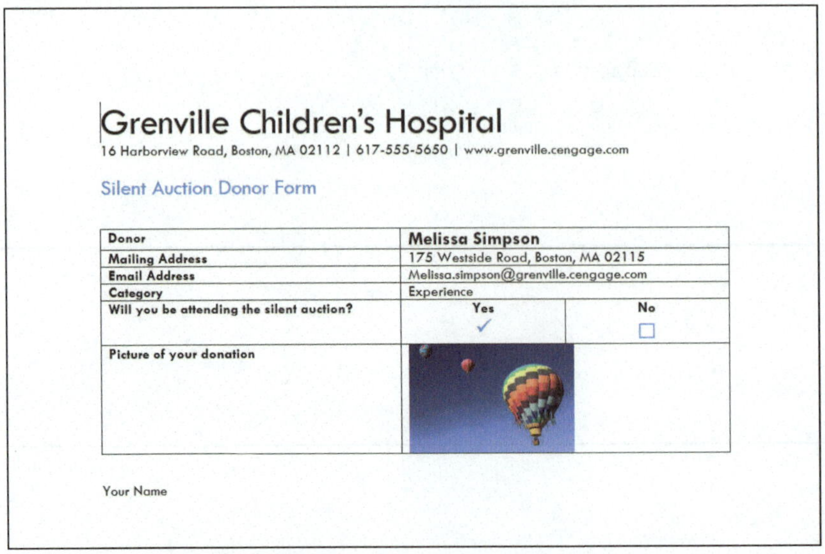
Grenville Children's Hospital

16 Harborview Road, Boston, MA 02112 | 617-555-5650 | www.grenville.cengage.com

Silent Auction Donor Form

Donor	Melissa Simpson	
Mailing Address	175 Westside Road, Boston, MA 02115	
Email Address	Melissa.simpson@grenville.cengage.com	
Category	Experience	
Will you be attending the silent auction?	Yes ✓	No ☐
Picture of your donation		

Your Name

Donna Hamlet/Pexels

Automating and Customizing Word

Case

You work in the Office for International Students, which is part of Student Services at Mountain Springs Institute of Technology (MSIT) in Denver, Colorado. To help promote MSIT to students who may wish to come from other countries to study, you have interviewed two of MSIT's international students. After formatting the interviews, you'll feature them in marketing materials and on the MSIT website. You also format a series of personal stories written by other international students for the website. You start by formatting paragraphs and graphics and creating styles for an interview with Akiko Matsuda, who has come from Japan to study at MSIT. You then create a macro to automate formatting tasks for the student stories, check the accessibility of a document, and use the dictation tool. To finish up, you customize Word options and add a digital signature to a document.

Module Objectives

After completing this module, you will be able to:

- Use pagination settings
- Edit pictures
- Apply layering options
- Arrange and compress pictures
- Create character styles
- Manage styles
- Plan a macro
- Record macro steps
- Run a macro
- Edit a macro in Visual Basic
- Use Accessibility tools
- Use the Dictate Tool
- Customize Word
- Sign a document digitally

Files You Will Need

IL_WD_11-1.docx
Support_WD_11_Akiko.jpg
IL_WD_11-2.docx
IL_WD_11-3.docx
IL_WD_11-4.docx
IL_WD_11-5.docx
IL_WD_11-6.docx
Support_WD_11_WestCoast.jpg
IL_WD_11-7.docx
IL_WD_11-8.docx
IL_WD_11-9.docx
IL_WD_11-10.docx
IL_WD_11-11.docx
Support_WD_11_Trucks.jpg
Support_WD_11_LMWEnvironmentalPolicy.docx
IL_WD_11-12.docx
IL_WD_11-13.docx
IL_WD_11-14.docx

Use Pagination Settings

Case You open a document containing an interview with Akiko Matsuda, modify how the paragraphs break across pages, and then designate selected text as hidden.

Objectives
- Set paragraph pagination options
- Format text as hidden

You apply pagination settings to control the flow of text between pages or between columns in a document. These settings specify where Word positions automatic page breaks. Choose the Keep with next option when you want a paragraph to appear together with the next paragraph on the same page. Choose the Keep lines together option to keep all the lines in a selected paragraph together on a page. To add an automatic page break before a specific paragraph, choose the Page break before option. You can set Widow/Orphan control options to control the number of lines appearing at the top or bottom of a page. Turned on by default, **Widow/Orphan control** ensures that at least two lines of a paragraph appear at the top and bottom of every page or column. You can also designate selected text in a document as hidden text.

Steps

Trouble
Click the **Show/Hide button** ¶ in the Paragraph group to show paragraph marks, if necessary.

1. **sam Start Word, open the file IL_WD_11-1.docx from the location where you store your Data Files, verify paragraph marks are showing, then save the document as IL_WD_11_AkikoMatsudaInterview**

2. **Scroll down and click in the Keep Fit heading at the bottom of page 2, click the Launcher in the Paragraph group, then click the Line and Page Breaks tab**
   The Line and Page Breaks tab in the Paragraph dialog box opens (refer to **Figure 11-1**). By default, the Heading 1 style applied to the heading includes three settings: Widow/Orphan control, Keep with next, and Keep lines together. If a paragraph in a document is breaking in an unexpected way, you can check the Line and Page Breaks tab to determine if another person who worked on the document chose different selections.

3. **Click OK, click in the line that starts with I was astonished..., click the Launcher in the Paragraph group, click the Keep lines together check box, then click OK**
   All six lines of the paragraph along with the heading move to the top of Page 3.

4. **Scroll down page 3, click in the heading Stay In Contact with Family Back Home, click the Launcher in the Paragraph group, click the Page break before check box, then click OK**
   The heading and the text that relates to it move to the top of Page 4.

5. **Scroll up to the top of page 2**
   The last two words in a paragraph appear alone at the top of the page. This line is a widow. A **widow** is the last line of a paragraph appearing alone at the top of a page. An **orphan** is the first line of a paragraph appearing alone at the bottom of a page.

Trouble
If you select the paragraph mark and then hide the text, the blank line between the two paragraphs will be removed when the document is printed.

6. **Scroll up slightly to the bottom of page 1, click in the paragraph under the What are your top three favorite courses so far? heading, click the Launcher in the Paragraph group, click the Widow/Orphan control check box, then click OK**
   The entire paragraph moves to the top of page 2 along with the heading because it was formatted with the Keep with next option.

7. **Press CTRL+HOME, then select the line at the end of paragraph 2 that begins Akiko loves her courses..., but *not* the paragraph mark (refer to Figure 11-2)**

8. **Click the Launcher in the Font group, click the Hidden check box as shown in Figure 11-3, click OK, then click away from the selected text**
   A dotted line appears under the text. This text will not appear in the printed document.

9. **Click the File tab, click Print, note that the sentence does not appear in the second paragraph in the Print Preview screen, click the Back button to return to the document, then save the document**

Figure 11-1: Paragraph dialog box

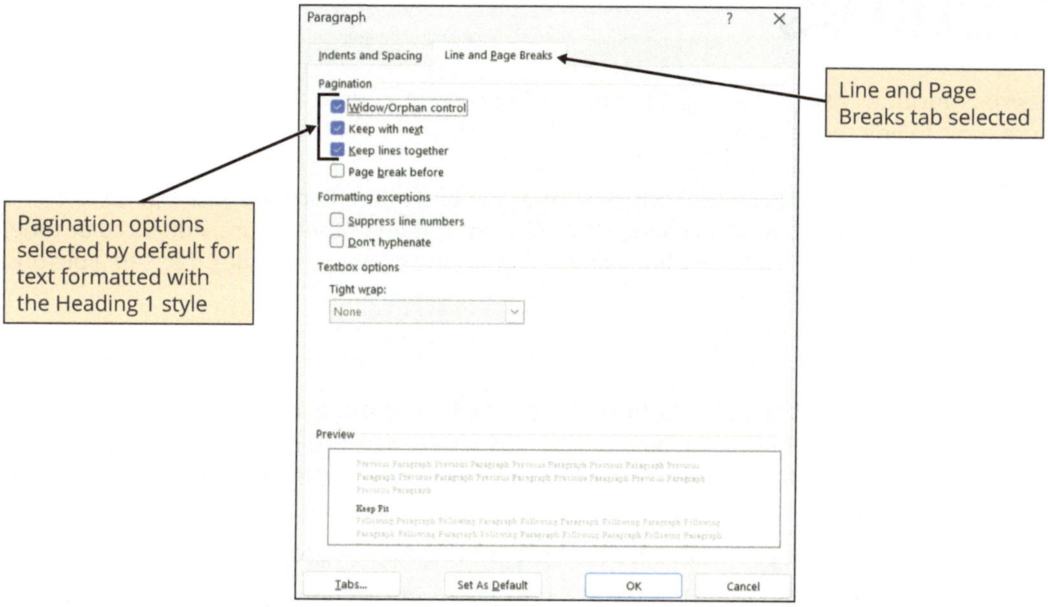

Figure 11-2: Text selected to make hidden

George Pak/Pexels

Figure 11-3: Hidden effect selected

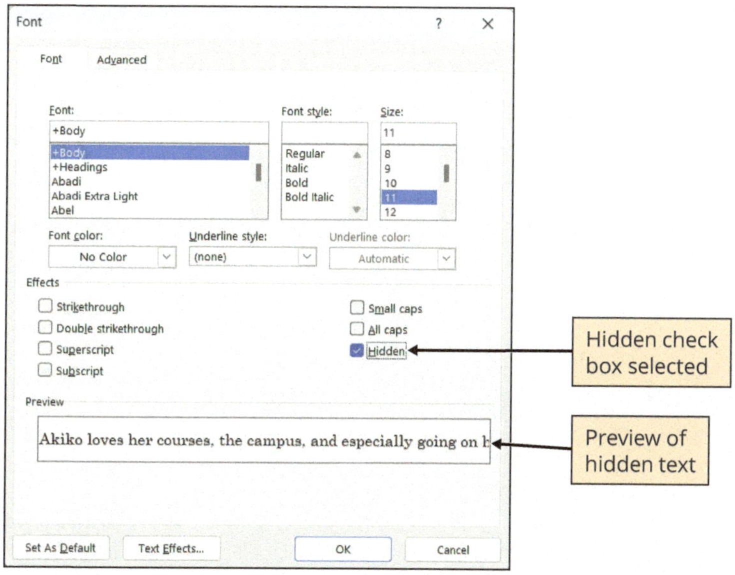

Edit Pictures

Case The document includes Akiko's picture. You change the current picture to another picture of Akiko, then use the picture tools to edit the picture.

Objective
- Apply artistic and picture effects

You use the tools on the Picture Format tab and in the Format Picture pane to edit a picture in a variety of ways. You can change the color saturation of the picture, edit its color tone, and modify its sharpness or softness. You can also apply one of the 23 artistic effects to a picture or swap out a picture by selecting a new picture.

Steps

Quick Tip
ScreenTips appears to help you select the correct saturation or color tone effects.

Quick Tip
To change the sharpness and contrast of a picture, click the **Corrections button** in the Adjust group.

1. **Double-click the picture of Akiko at the top of page 1**
   When you double-click a picture, the Picture Format tab appears on the Ribbon and becomes the active tab. In addition, the Layout Options button appears outside the top-right corner of the picture.
2. **Click the Change Picture button in the Adjust group, then click This Device**
3. **Navigate to the location where you store your Data Files, then double-click Support_WD_11_Akiko.jpg**
   A different picture of Akiko is inserted. You also can adjust the appearance of the picture using the Adjust group on the Picture Format tab.
4. **Click the Color button in the Adjust group**
5. **Click Saturation: 200% in the Color Saturation row (refer to Figure 11-4)**
   Use the Color button in the Adjust group to change the saturation and color tone of a picture, or to recolor it. Click Picture Color Options to open the Format Picture pane for additional options to modify the picture.
6. **Click the Color arrow in the Adjust group, then select Temperature: 5900 K color tone in the Color Tone row**
   The color saturation and color tone of the picture are modified. You can also use Artistic Effects to apply a selection of preset effects to a picture.
7. **Scroll to the bottom of the document, click the picture of the person with a camera, then click the Artistic Effects button in the Adjust group**
   The selection of artistic effects opens.
8. **Move the pointer over each of the artistic effects to preview how the picture changes, then click the Film Grain artistic effect (refer to Figure 11-5)**
9. **Save the document**

Figure 11-4: Selecting color saturation

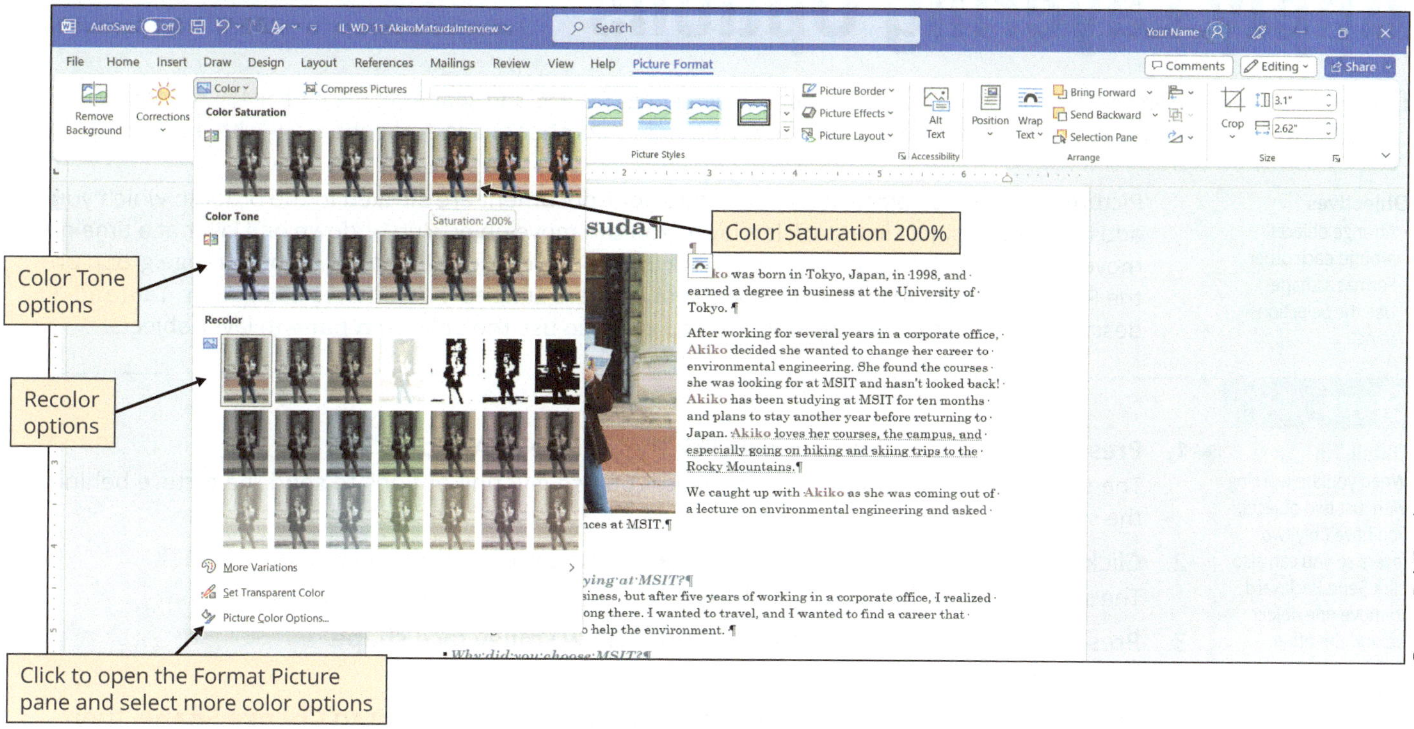

George Pak/Pexels

Figure 11-5: Applying an artistic effect to a picture

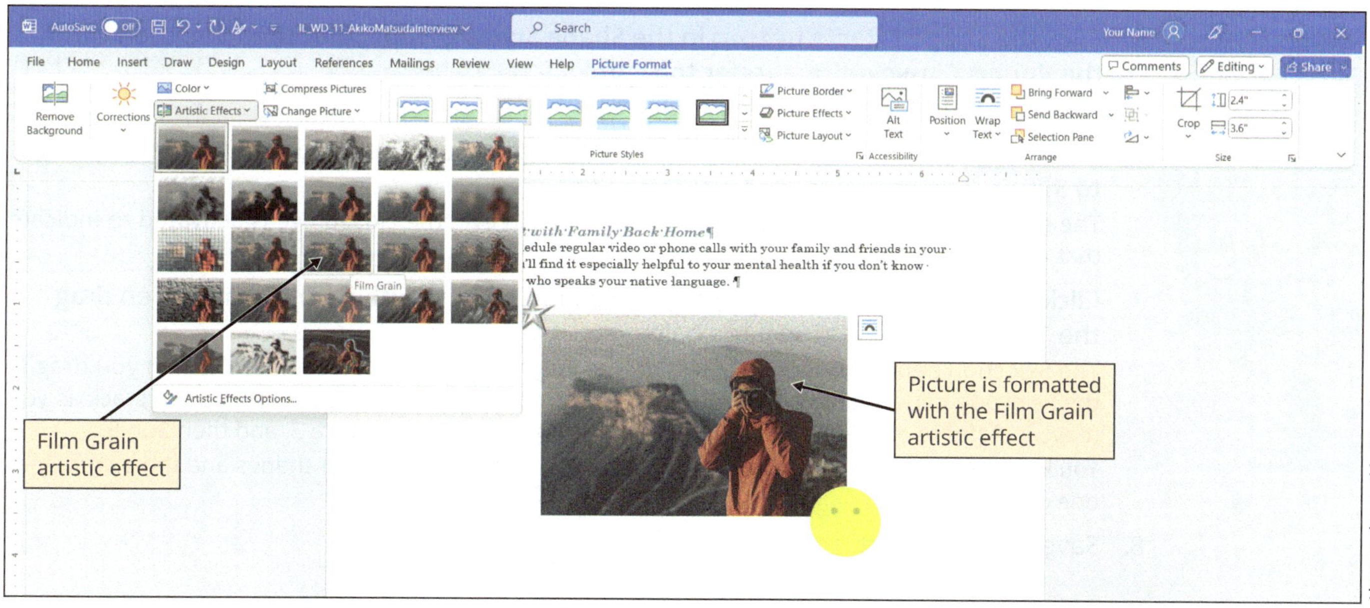

Alessandro Avilés/Pexels

Applying 3-D and 3-D Rotation effects to a picture

You can enhance a picture with a variety of picture effects including reflection, shadow, glow, soft edges, and bevel. The bevel picture effect applies a 3-D effect to the selected picture. To add a 3-D bevel effect, click the Picture Effects button on the Picture Format tab, point to Bevel, then select a preset bevel effect. To further modify a bevel effect, click 3-D Options below the selection of bevel effects to open the 3-D Format section of the Format Picture pane. Here, you can specify the width and height of the top and bottom bevels, and specify a color, depth, contour, material, and lighting for the 3-D effect. You can achieve a wide variety of interesting 3-D effects by selecting different options in the Format Picture pane. Another 3-D effect you can apply to a picture is a 3-D Rotation effect. Click Picture Effects in the Picture Styles group, point to 3-D Rotation, then select a 3-D rotation effect from one of three categories: Parallel, Perspective, and Oblique.

Apply Layering Options

Case You use layering options and the Selection pane to arrange the pictures and shapes at the end of Akiko's interview. You also change one of the drawn shapes in the document to another shape and enhance it with a 3-D effect.

Objectives
- Arrange objects around each other
- Format a shape
- Use the Selection pane

Pictures or graphic objects that you add to your document are stacked in the order in which you add them. Each object in a stack is a layer. You can move objects up or down one layer at a time or move them to the top or bottom of a stack in one move. You use options in the Arrange group on the Picture Format tab to specify how the objects are stacked in relation to each other. **Table 11-1** describes each of the layering options. You can also use the **Selection pane** to layer objects.

Steps

Quick Tip When you are working with just two objects, you have only two layers so you can also click Send Backward to move one object behind the other.

Quick Tip You can further enhance the 3-D effect by clicking 3-D Options to open the Format pane.

1. **Press CTRL+HOME, then double-click the picture of Akiko**
   The picture is partially hiding a star shape. You use layering options to send the picture behind the star.
2. **Click the Send Backward arrow in the Arrange group, then click Send to Back**
   The star now overlaps part of the picture.
3. **Press CTRL+END, then double-click the yellow smiley face shape**
   The Shape Format tab is active.
4. **Click the Edit Shape button in the Insert Shapes group, point to Change Shape, then click the Sun shape in the Basic Shapes section as shown in Figure 11-6**
   The smiley face shape is now a sun shape, and it is selected.
5. **Click the Shape Effects button in the Shape Styles group, point to Bevel, then click the Round Convex effect (refer to Figure 11-7)**
   You've applied a 3-D effect to the sun shape.
6. **Click the Selection Pane button in the Arrange group, then click the open eye next to Sun 5**
   The eye button is a toggle. When you click the open eye, the closed eye is activated to indicate that the object is hidden.
7. **Click the closed eye for Sun 5 in the Selection pane to unhide the shape, then drag the Sun 5 in the Selection pane below Picture 3**
   The Selection pane shows the objects on the current page of the document. When you drag in the Selection pane, a blue horizontal bar shows you the location of the object in the stack as you move it. Refer to **Figure 11-8**. The order is now Star: 5 Points 4, Picture 3, and then Sun 5.
   You keep the Selection pane open so that you can next group the two shapes and the picture into one object.
8. **Save the document**

Table 11-1: Layering Options

layering option	to move an object	layering option	to move an object
Bring Forward	up one layer	Send Backward	down one layer
Bring to Front	to the top of a stack of objects	Send to Back	to the bottom of a stack of objects
Bring in Front of Text	in front of text	Send Behind Text	behind text

Figure 11-6: Changing a shape to another shape

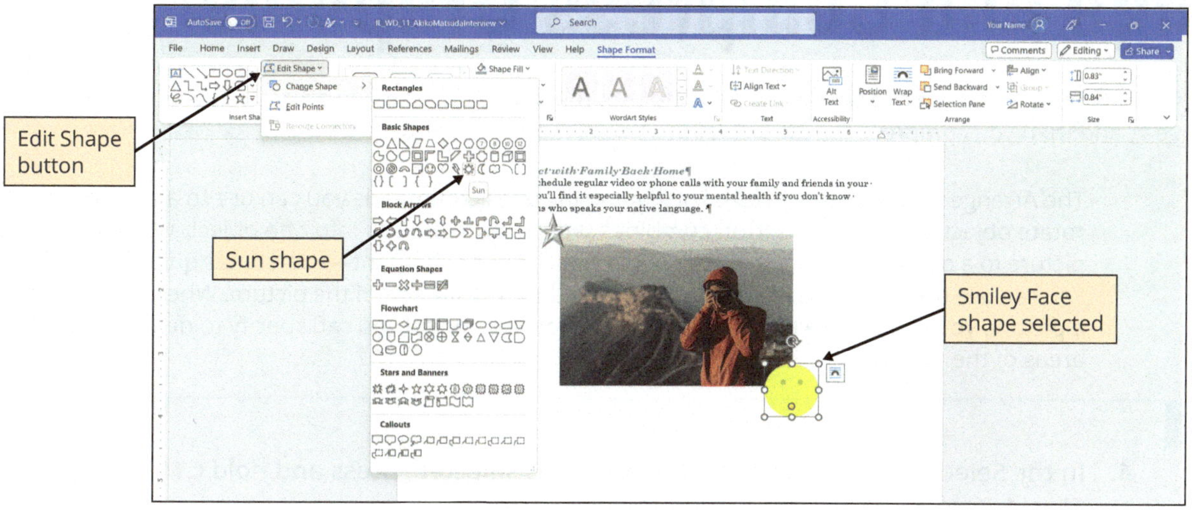

Alessandro Avilés/Pexels

Figure 11-7: Applying a Bevel 3-D effect

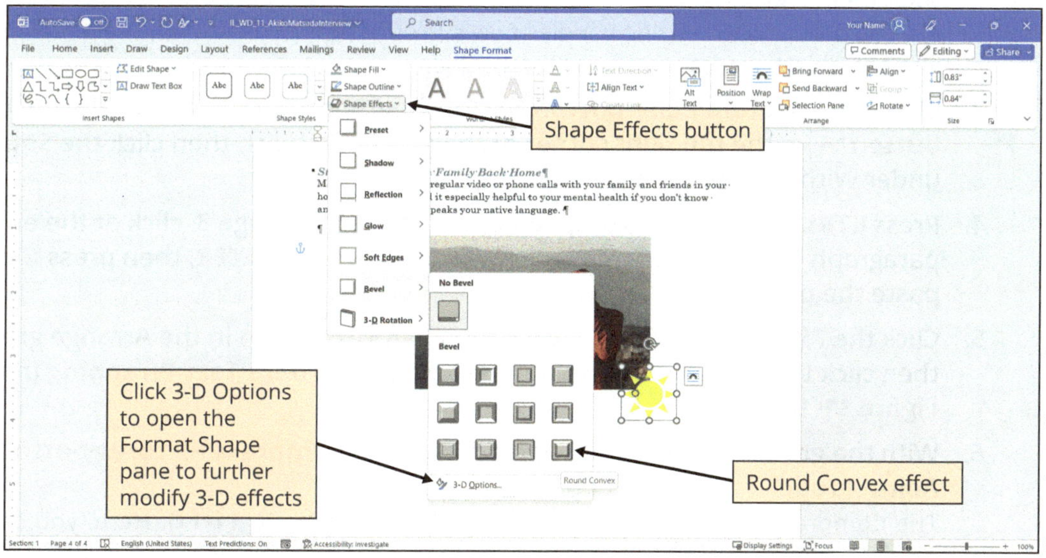

Alessandro Avilés/Pexels

Figure 11-8: Moving an object in the Selection pane

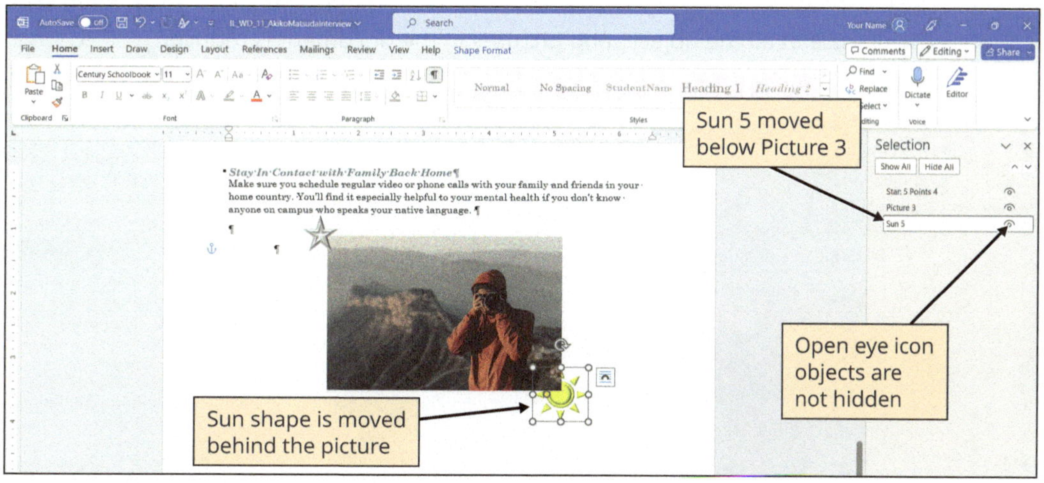

Alessandro Avilés/Pexels

Arrange and Compress Graphics

Case You group the picture and the two shapes at the bottom of the document into one object that you then position on page 2, and then you compress the file size of the two pictures in the document.

Objectives
- Group objects
- Compress a picture

The Arrange group on the Picture Format tab includes commands you can use to align, group, and rotate objects. The Group button combines two or more objects into one object. When you add a picture to a document, you increase the file size of your document—sometimes quite dramatically. You can use the Compress Pictures button to reduce the file size of the picture. When you compress a picture, you can choose to reduce the image resolution and you can specify to delete all cropped areas of the picture.

Steps

1. **In the Selection pane, verify that Picture 3 is selected, press and hold CTRL, click Star: 5 Points 4, click Sun 5, then release CTRL**
   All three objects are selected.

Quick Tip
In the Selection pane, the three objects are listed under Group 1 to show they are all included in one group.

2. **Click the Picture Format tab, click the Group Objects button (refer to Figure 11-9), then click Group**
   A single border with resizing handles now surrounds the objects. With the three objects grouped into one object, you can more easily reposition it.

Quick Tip
To ungroup the object, click the **Group Objects button**, then click **Ungroup**.

3. **Click the Selection Pane button to close the Selection pane, click the Layout Options button in the top right corner of the grouped object, then click the Square button under With Text Wrapping**
4. **Press CTRL+X to cut the grouped object, scroll up to page 3, click at the end of the last paragraph (ends "and scarves to stay warm."), press ENTER, then press CTRL+V to paste the object**
5. **Click the Picture Format tab, click the Position button in the Arrange group, then click the Position in Bottom Center with Square Text Wrapping (refer to Figure 11-10)**
6. **With the grouped object still selected, click the Compress Pictures button in the Adjust group**
   The Compress Pictures dialog box opens (refer to **Figure 11-11**). Here, you can specify the resolution that you want to use. If you have more than one picture in a document, you can specify that you wish to apply the same compression options to every picture.

Quick Tip
Choose 220 ppi (pixels per inch) for pictures that you want to print and 96 ppi for pictures that you want to send via email.

7. **Click the Apply only to this picture check box to deselect it**
8. **Click the Web (150 ppi) option button to select it, click OK, then save the document**
   The file size of all the objects and pictures in the document is reduced.

Figure 11-9: Grouping objects

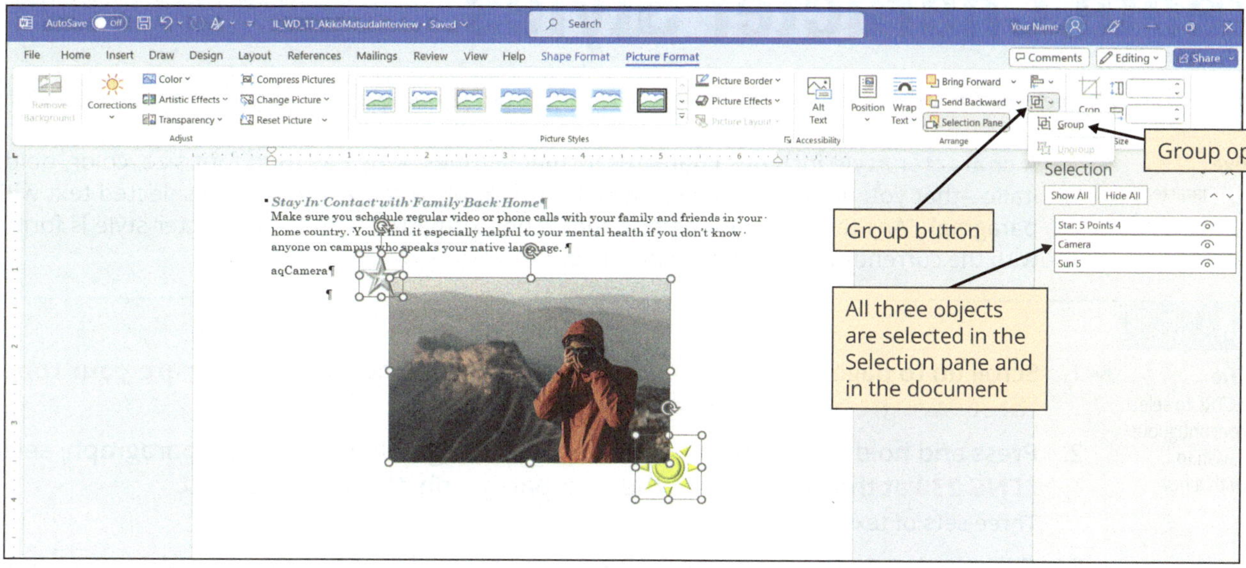

Alessandro Avilés/Pexels

Figure 11-10: Positioning the grouped object

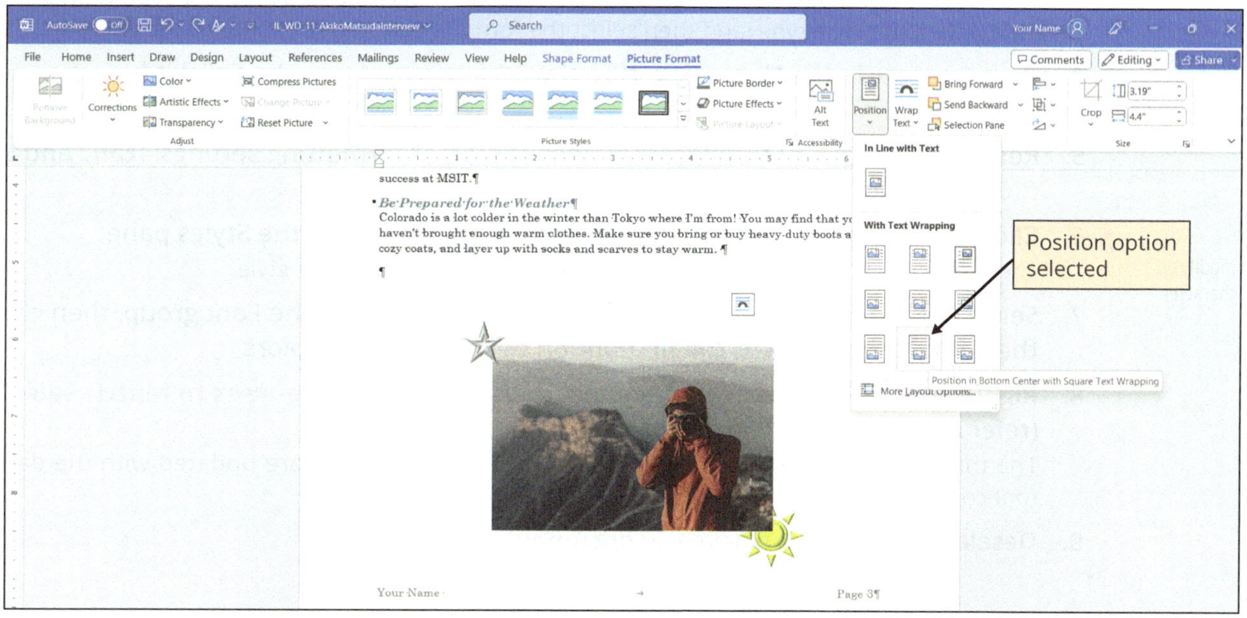

Alessandro Avilés/Pexels

Figure 11-11: Compress Pictures dialog box

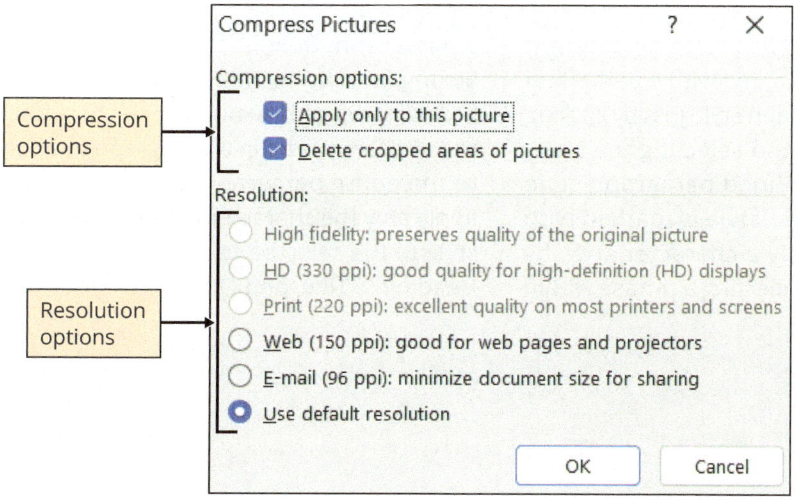

Create Character Styles

Case You create a character style called Courses to apply to each Course name in the list of Akiko's favorite courses.

Objective
- Create a character style

A **character style** includes character format settings—such as font, font size, color, bold, and italic—that you name and save as a style. You apply a character style to selected text within a paragraph. Any text in the paragraph that is not formatted with the character style is formatted with the currently applied paragraph style.

Steps

Quick Tip
You use CTRL to select all the noncontiguous text you wish to format with a new style.

1. **Scroll up to page 2, select EENG 101 in the first line below the What are your top three favorite courses so far? heading**
2. **Press and hold CTRL, select EENG 200 at the beginning of the next paragraph, select EENG 230 at the beginning of the next paragraph, then release CTRL**
   Three sets of text are selected.
3. **Click the Launcher in the Styles group, then click the New Style button at the bottom of the Styles pane**
   The Create New Style from Formatting dialog box opens. In this dialog box, you name the new style, select the style type, and then select the formats you want to enhance the text.
4. **Type Courses in the Name box, click the Style type arrow, then click Character as the style type**
5. **Refer to Figure 11-12 to select the other character formatting settings: Italic and the Blue font color in the Standard Colors section**

Quick Tip
You can modify an existing character style.

6. **Click OK, click away from the text to deselect it, then close the Styles pane**
   The text you selected is formatted with the new Courses character style.
7. **Select EENG 101 again, click the Font Color arrow in the Font group, then click the Dark Red color box, the first option below Standard Colors**
8. **Right-click Courses in the Styles pane, then click Update Courses to Match Selection (refer to Figure 11-13)**
   The three courses formatted with the Courses character style are updated with the dark red font color.
9. **Deselect the text, then save the document**

Identifying paragraph, character, and linked styles

Style types are identified in the Styles pane by different symbols. Each paragraph style is marked with a paragraph symbol: ¶a. You can apply a paragraph style just by clicking on any paragraph or line of text and selecting the style. The most commonly used predefined paragraph style is the Normal style. Each character style is marked with a character symbol: a. You apply a character style by clicking anywhere in a word or by selecting a phrase within a paragraph. Built-in character styles include Emphasis, Strong, and Book Title. Each linked style is marked with both a paragraph symbol and a character symbol: ¶a. You can click anywhere in a paragraph to apply the linked style to the entire paragraph, or you can select text and then apply only the character formats associated with the linked style to the selected text. Predefined linked styles include Heading 1, Title, and Quote.

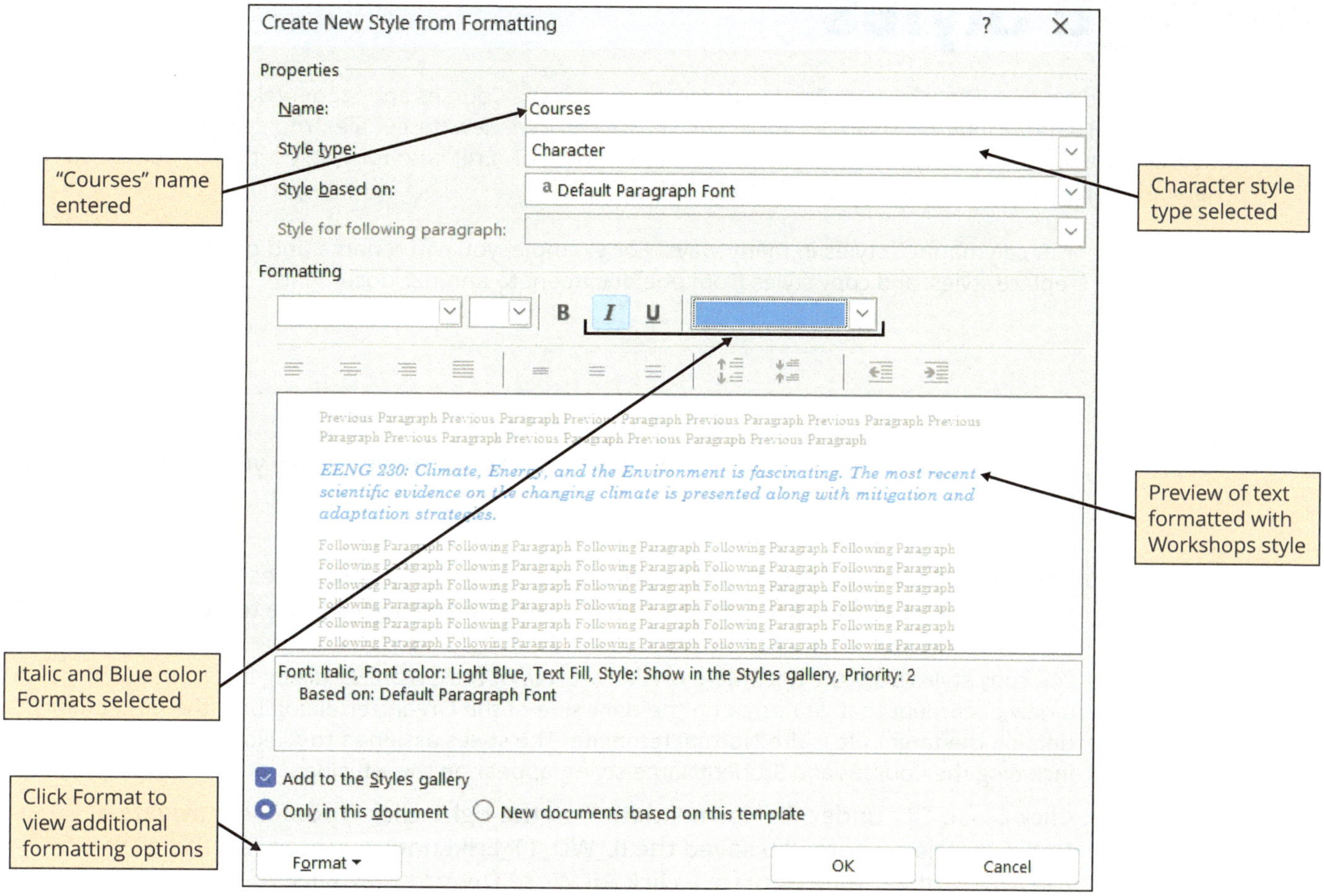

Figure 11-12: Create New Style from Formatting dialog box

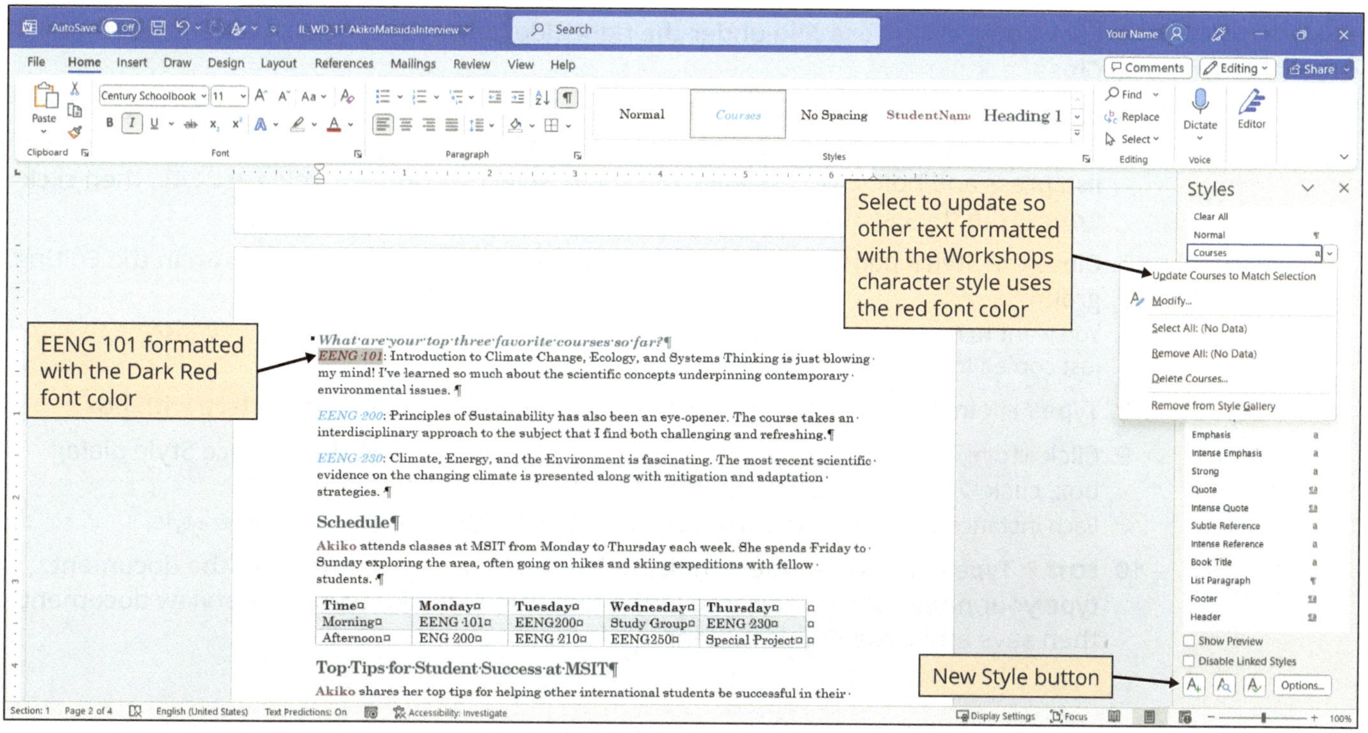

Figure 11-13: Updating the Courses character style

Manage Styles

Case You open and save an interview with Erik Lundgren, then copy the Courses and StudentName character styles from Akiko Matsuda's interview (source file) to Erik Lundgren's interview (target file). You then apply the copied Courses style to Erik's courses. Finally, you find every instance of "Erik" and format it with the StudentName character style.

Objectives
- Copy styles between documents
- Find and replace styles

You can manage styles in many ways. For example, you can rename and delete styles, find and replace styles, and copy styles from one document to another document.

Steps

1. **Open the file IL_WD_11-2.docx from the location where you store your Data Files, save the document as IL_WD_11_ErikLundgrenInterview, then close it**
   Akiko's interview is again the active document.

Trouble
Word documents are not listed because, by default, Word lists only templates.

2. **Verify the Home tab is selected, click the Launcher in the Styles group to open the Styles pane, click the Manage Styles button in the Styles pane to open the Manage Styles dialog box, then click Import/Export**
   You copy styles from the document on the left side of the Organizer dialog box (the source file) to a new document that you open on the right side of the Organizer dialog box (the target file). By default, the target file is the Normal template. The styles assigned to Akiko Matsuda's interview, including the Courses and StudentName styles, appear on the left side.
3. **Click Close File under "in Normal.dotm" on the right, click Open File, navigate to the location where you saved the IL_WD_11_ErikLundgrenInterview file, click the All Word Templates arrow, click All Word Documents, click IL_WD_11_ErikLundgrenInterview.docx, then click Open**

Quick Tip
Scroll down the right list to verify that the styles have been copied over to that file.

4. **Scroll the list of styles on the left side of the Organizer dialog box, click Courses, press and hold CTRL, scroll down, click StudentName to select both styles, then release CTRL (refer to Figure 11-14)**

Trouble
Do not select the text in the table.

5. **Click Copy, click Close File under the right side (Erik's document), click Save, then click Close**
6. **Click File, click Open, click IL_WD_11_ErikLundgrenInterview.docx, scroll to the list of favorite courses in the document, open the Styles pane again, select DMAA 150 in the list, press and hold CTRL, select DMAA 170, select DMAA 180, release CTRL, then click Courses in the list of styles in the Styles pane (refer to Figure 11-15)**
7. **Close the Styles pane, press CTRL+HOME, then click the Replace button in the Editing group**
   You want to replace every instance of "Erik" with "Erik" formatted with the StudentName style you just copied from Akiko's profile.
8. **Type Erik in the Find what box, press TAB, then type Erik in the Replace with box**
9. **Click More, click Format, click Style, click StudentName in the Replace Style dialog box, click OK, click Replace All, click OK, then click Close**
   Each instance of Erik's name is now formatted with the StudentName character style.
10. **sam Type your name where indicated in the footer, save and close the document, type your name where indicated in the footer in Akiko Matsuda's interview document, then save and close the document**

Figure 11-14: Managing styles using the Organizer dialog box

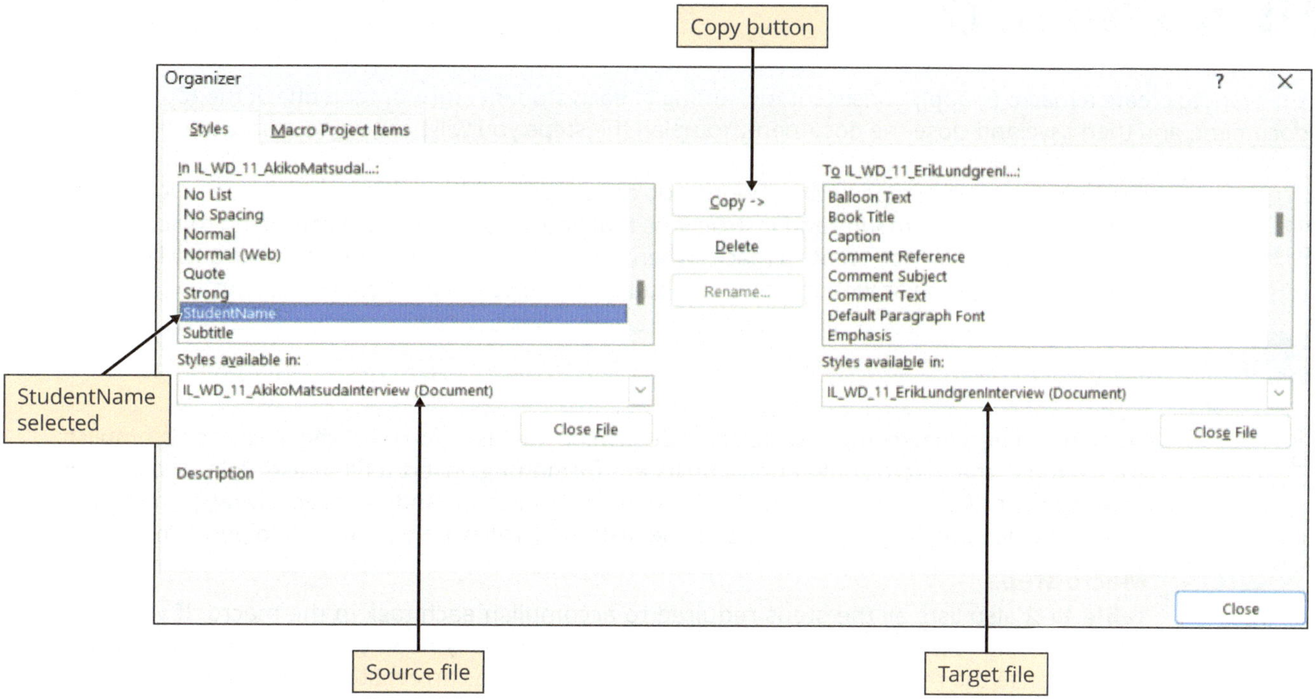

Figure 11-15: Applying the Courses style

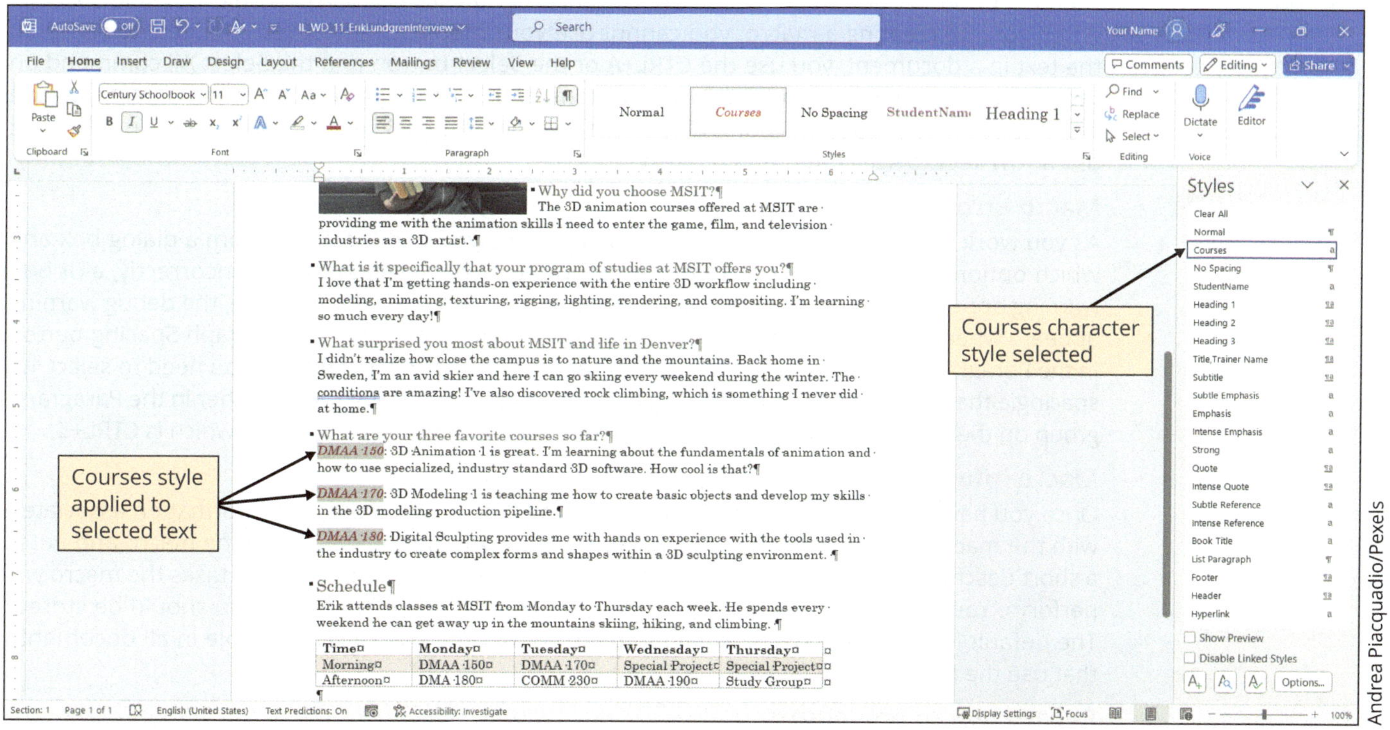

More ways to manage styles

To rename a style, right-click it in the Styles pane, click Modify, type a new name, then press ENTER. To delete a style, right-click the style, then click Delete [Style name]. The style is deleted from the Styles pane, but it is not deleted from your computer. Click the Manage Styles button at the bottom of the Styles pane, select the style to delete, click Delete, then click OK to close the Manage Styles dialog box.

Plan a Macro

Case You want to create a macro to apply consistent formatting to each student story, enter a title at the top of each document, and then save and close the document. You plan the steps you will perform to create the macro.

Objectives
- Define macros
- Identify macro steps

If you perform a task repeatedly in Word, you can automate the task by using a macro. A **macro** is a series of Word commands and instructions that you group as a single command to accomplish a task automatically. You create a macro when you want to perform multiple tasks quickly, usually in just one step, such as with the click of a button or the use of a keyboard shortcut.

Details

Quick Tip
You plan and practice the macro steps before you create a macro so you can perform the steps without error when you create the macro.

Trouble
If a debug warning appears, you need to click End and then record the macro steps again.

- **Macro tasks**
  When planning a macro, the first step is to determine the tasks you want the macro to accomplish. For example, the macro could apply consistent formatting, insert a fill-in text field so users can enter text specific to each document, and then perform commands such as saving, printing, and closing the document. **Table 11-2** lists all the tasks that you want your macro to perform.

- **Macro steps**
  Table 11-2 also lists all the steps required to accomplish each task in the macro. If you make an error while recording the steps in the macro, you usually need to stop recording and start over because the recorded macro will include not only the correct steps but also the errors. By rehearsing the steps required before recording the macro, you ensure accuracy. While recording a macro, you can use the mouse to select options from drop-down lists and dialog boxes available via the Ribbon or you can use keystroke commands, such as CTRL+2 to turn on double spacing. When you are creating a macro, you cannot use your mouse to select text. Instead, to select all the text in a document, you use the CTRL+A or the Select button and the Select All command on the Select menu in the Editing group on the Home tab. Or, to select just a portion of text, you use arrow keys to move the insertion point to the text, press the F8 key to turn on select mode, then use arrow keys to select the required text.

- **Macro Errors**
  As you work with macros, you discover which options you need to select from a dialog box and which options you can select from the Ribbon. When you select an option incorrectly, a **debug** warning appears when you run the macro (refer to **Figure 11-16**). For example, the debug warning appears when you set line spacing by selecting 1.5 using the Line and Paragraph Spacing button in the Paragraph group on the Home tab. To set the line spacing in a macro, you need to select 1.5 spacing either from the Paragraph dialog box, which you open using the Launcher in the Paragraph group on the Home tab, or by pressing the keyboard shortcut for 1.5 spacing, which is CTRL+5.

- **Macro information**
  Once you have practiced the steps required for the macro, you create the information associated with the macro. You open the Record Macro dialog box and then you name the macro and enter a short description of the macro. This description is usually a summary of the tasks the macro will perform. You also use this dialog box to assign the location where the macro should be stored. The default location is in the Normal template so that the macro is accessible in all documents that use the Normal template.

- **Record macro procedure**
  When you click OK after completing the Record Macro dialog box, the Macro Recorder pointer is the active pointer, indicating that you are ready to start recording the macro. In addition, the Stop Recording button and the Pause Recording button appear in the Code group on the Developer tab as shown in **Figure 11-17**. These buttons are toggle buttons. You click the Pause Recording button if, for example, you want to pause recording to perform steps not included in the macro. For example, you may need to pause to check information in another document or even attend to an email. You click the Stop Recording button when you have completed all the steps required for the macro, or when you have made a mistake and want to start over.

Figure 11-16: "Debug" warning that appears when the macro does not recognize a step

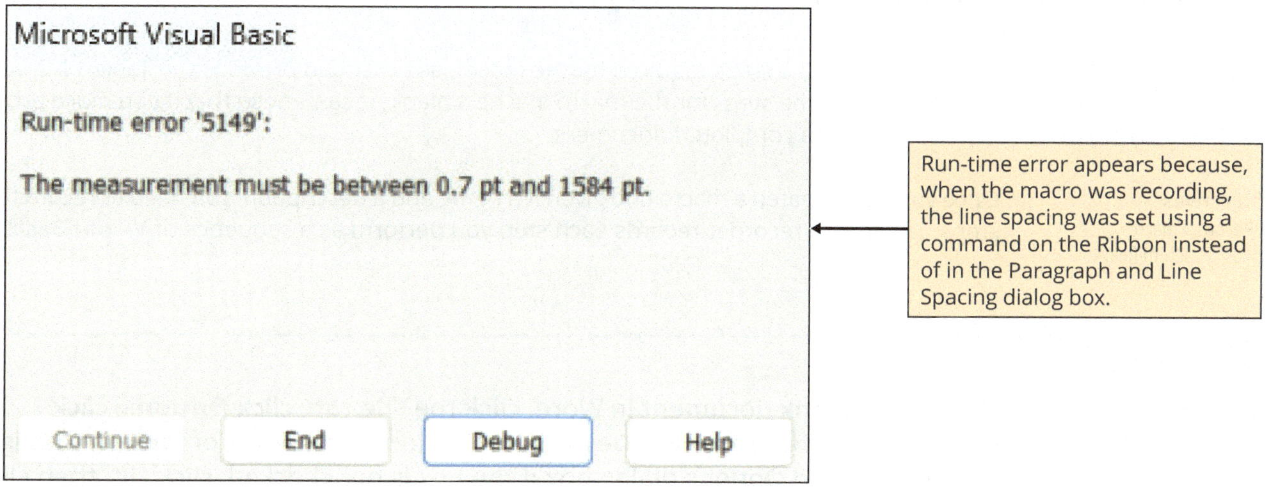

Figure 11-17: Recording a macro

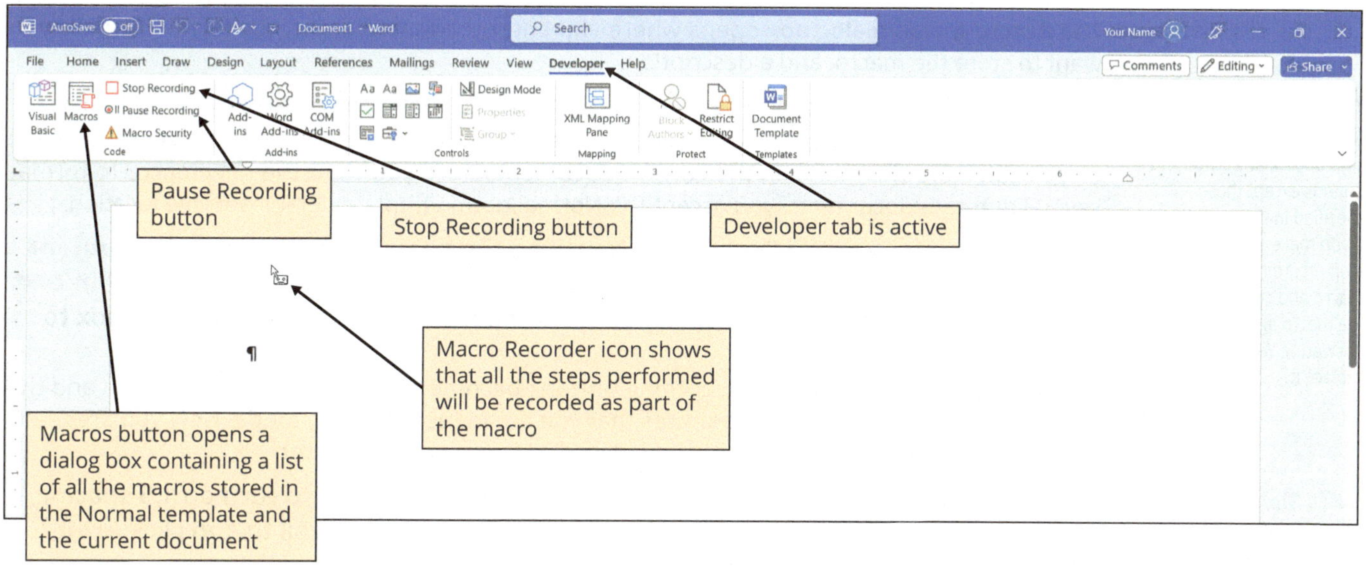

Table 11-2: Macro tasks and steps to complete the tasks

task to complete	steps to create macro
Select all the text	Press **CTRL+A**
Change the line spacing to 1.5	Press **CTRL+5**
Select the Arial font	Click the **Font arrow** in the Font group, then click **Arial**
Select 14 pt	Click the **Font Size arrow**, then click **14**
Insert a fill-in field text box	Press the Up Arrow once to deselect the text and move to the top of the document, click the **Insert tab**, click the **Quick Parts button**, click **Field**, scroll down the list of Field names, click **Fill-in**, click **OK**, then click **OK**
Add a blank line	Press **ENTER**
Save the document	Click the **Save button** on the Quick Access toolbar
Close the document	Click the **File tab**, then click **Close**

Record Macro Steps

Case Now that you have determined the steps required for the macro, as described previously in Table 11-2, you need to record the steps. You record the steps for the macro in a new blank document so that if you make errors, you do not affect the formatting of a completed document.

Objectives
- Record a macro
- Add a custom field

Once you have created a macro and given it a name and a description, you need to record the macro steps. The macro recorder records each step you perform as a sequence of **Visual Basic** codes.

Steps

Quick Tip The Code group on the Developer tab contains the buttons you use to create and modify a macro.

Quick Tip A macro name cannot contain any spaces.

Trouble DO NOT press any keys or click any other options except those specified in the steps. If you make a mistake, stop recording the macro and create the macro again, answering Yes to replace it.

Quick Tip When you are recording a macro, you must use keystrokes to move around a document. You cannot use the mouse to position the insertion point.

1. **Start a new blank document in Word, click the File tab, click Options, click Customize Ribbon, click the Developer check box in the list of tabs on the right side of the Word Options dialog box if the box is not checked, click OK, then click the Developer tab**
2. **Save the blank document as IL_WD_11_StoriesMacroSetup to the location where you store your Data Files, press ENTER three times, then click the Record Macro button in the Code group**

   The Record Macro dialog box opens where you enter the macro name, the location where you want to store the macro, and a description.
3. **Type FormatStories, then press TAB three times to move to the Store macro in list**

   You can store the macro in the Normal.dotm template so that it is available to all new documents or you can store the macro in the current document. Since you want the new macro to format several different documents, you accept the Normal.dotm template default storage location.
4. **Press TAB to move to the Description box, type the description Select the document, change the line spacing to 1.5, format text with Arial and 14 pt, insert a fill-in text box, then save and close the document., compare the Record Macro dialog box to Figure 11-18, then click OK**

   The Stop Recording and Pause Recording buttons become available in the Code group and the pointer changes to [icon]. This icon indicates that you are in record macro mode. Now you are ready to record the steps in the macro that you identified in the previous lesson.
5. **Press CTRL+A to select all the paragraph marks, press CTRL+5 to turn on 1.5 spacing, click the Home tab, click the Font arrow in the Font group, scroll to and click Arial, click the Font Size arrow in the Font group, then click 14**
6. **Press UP ARROW once to move to the top of the document, click the Insert tab, click the Explore Quick Parts button [icon] in the Text group, click Field, scroll down and click Fill-in from the list of Field names (refer to Figure 11-19), then click OK**

   When you run the macro, you will enter text in the fill-in field text box that appears as shown in **Figure 11-20**.
7. **Click OK, press ENTER, click the Save button [icon] on the Quick Access toolbar, click the File tab, then click Close**
8. **Click the Developer tab, then click the Stop Recording button in the Code group**

   The file is saved and closed. The macro steps are completed, the Stop Recording button no longer appears in the Code group, and the Pause Recording button is dimmed.
9. **Open IL_WD_11_StoriesMacroSetup, type your name on the first line, then save and close the document**

Figure 11-18: Record Macro dialog box

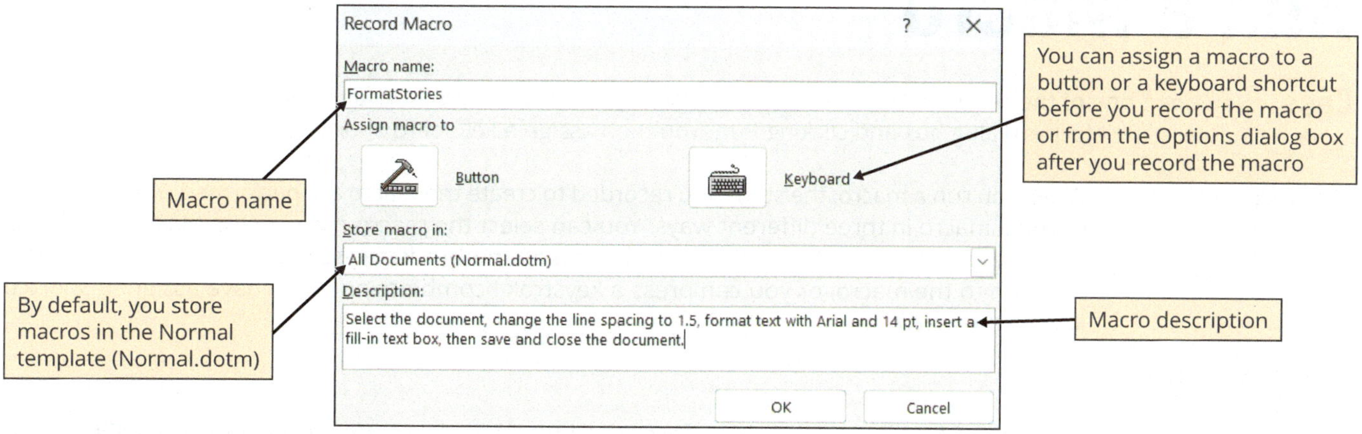

Figure 11-19: Field dialog box

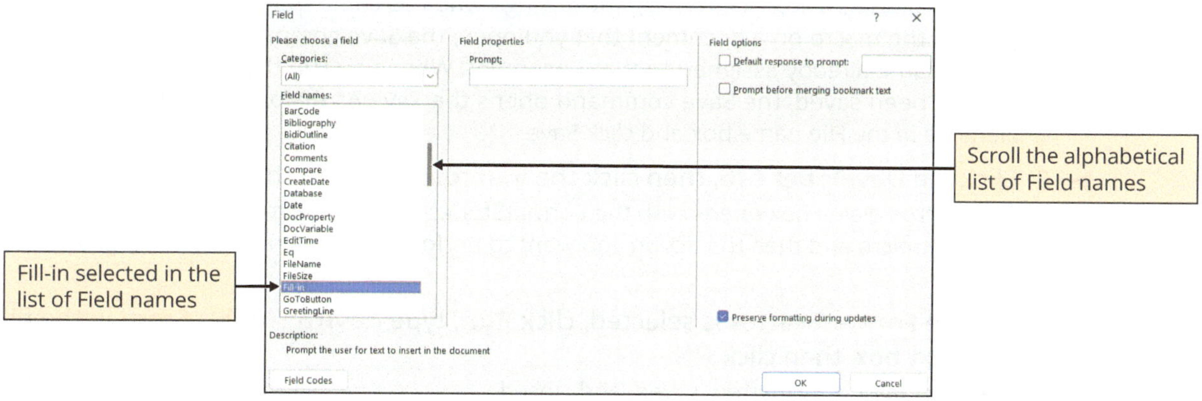

Figure 11-20: Inserting the Fill-in text box

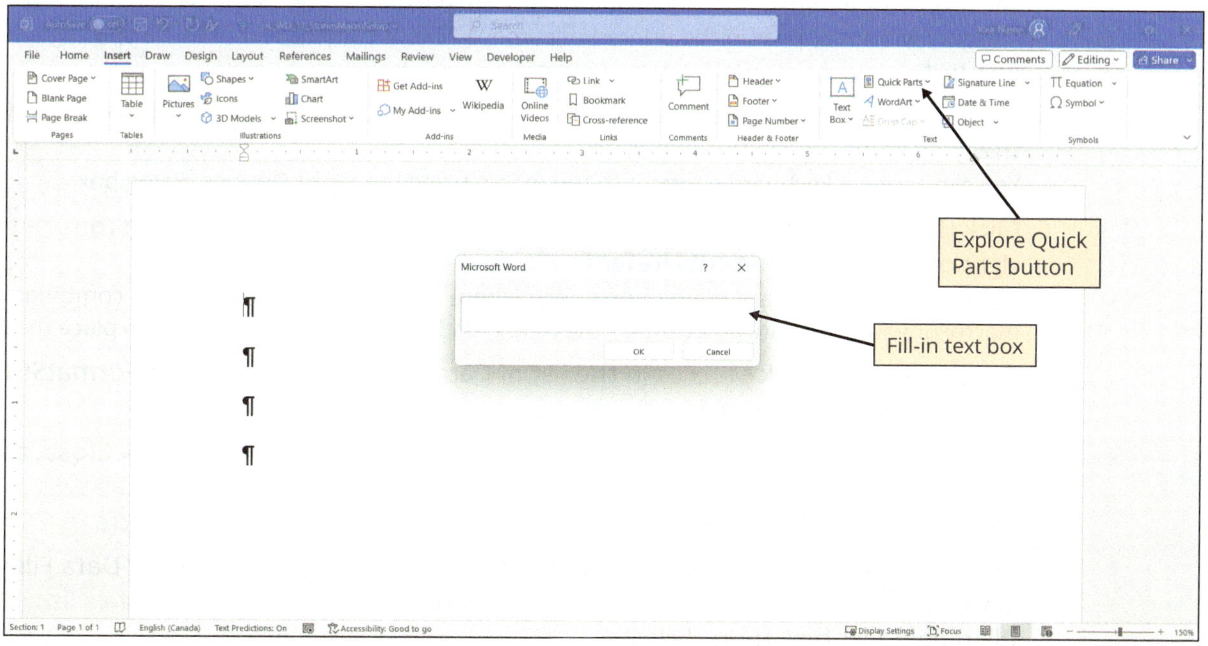

Pausing when recording a macro

If you need to interrupt the macro recording to perform other work such as checking an email or working on a different Word document, you can pause the recording. Click the Pause Recording button in the Code group on the Developer tab. When you want to resume recording the macro steps, press the Pause Recording button again.

Run a Macro

Case You open one of the documents you want to format and run the FormatStories macro by selecting the macro name in the Macros dialog box and clicking Run. You then assign a keyboard shortcut to the macro.

Objectives
- Run a macro
- Assign a keyboard shortcut to a macro

When you run a macro, the steps you recorded to create the macro are performed. You can choose to run a macro in three different ways. You can select the macro name in the Macros dialog box and click the Run button, you can click a button on the Quick Access toolbar if you have assigned a button to the macro, or you can press a keystroke combination if you have assigned shortcut keys to the macro.

Steps

Trouble
If a run-time error appears when you run the macro, delete the macro, and repeat the previous lesson to record the macro again.

1. **Open the file IL_WD_11-3.docx from the location where you store your Data Files, then save it as IL_WD_11_KavitaSinghStory**
   The file contains a story written by Kavita Singh who has come from India to study at MSIT. When you run the macro on a document that you open, the Save command saves the document with the filename already assigned to that document. When you run the macro on a document that has not been saved, the Save command opens the Save As dialog box so that you can enter a filename in the File name box and click Save.
2. **Click the Developer tab, then click the Macros button in the Code group**
   The Macros dialog box opens with the FormatStories macro selected in the Macro name box. You select a macro and then the action you want to perform, such as running, editing, or deleting the macro.
3. **Be sure FormatStories is selected, click Run, type Kavita Singh's Story in the fill-in field text box, then click OK**
   The document is formatted, saved, and closed.
4. **Open IL_WD_11_KavitaSinghStory**
   The text you entered in the fill-in field text box appears at the top of the page highlighted in gray. The gray will not appear in the printed document. The document text uses 1.5 spacing and 14 pt, Arial text.
5. **Enter your name where indicated at the bottom of the document, then save and close the document but do not exit Word**
   You can assign a keyboard shortcut to the macro using the Word Options dialog box.
6. **Click the File tab, click Options, click Customize Ribbon, then click Customize to the right of Keyboard shortcuts (refer to Figure 11-21)**
   The Customize Keyboard dialog box opens where you can assign a keystroke combination to a macro, or you can create a button for the macro and identify on which toolbar to place the button.
7. **Scroll down and click Macros in the list of Categories, then verify that FormatStories is selected (refer to Figure 11-22)**
8. **Click in the Press new shortcut key box, press Alt+S, click Assign, click Close, then click OK**
   When the keyboard shortcut Alt+S is pressed, it will run the FormatStories macro.
9. **Open the file IL_WD_11-4.docx from the location where you store your Data Files, save the file as IL_WD_11_DiegoSilvaStory, press Alt+S, type Diego Silva's Story in the fill-in field text box, then click OK**
   The macro formats, saves, and closes the document.
10. **Open the file IL_WD_11_DiegoSilvaStory.docx to verify that the macro has been applied, then close the file but do not exit Word**

Figure 11-21: Word Options dialog box

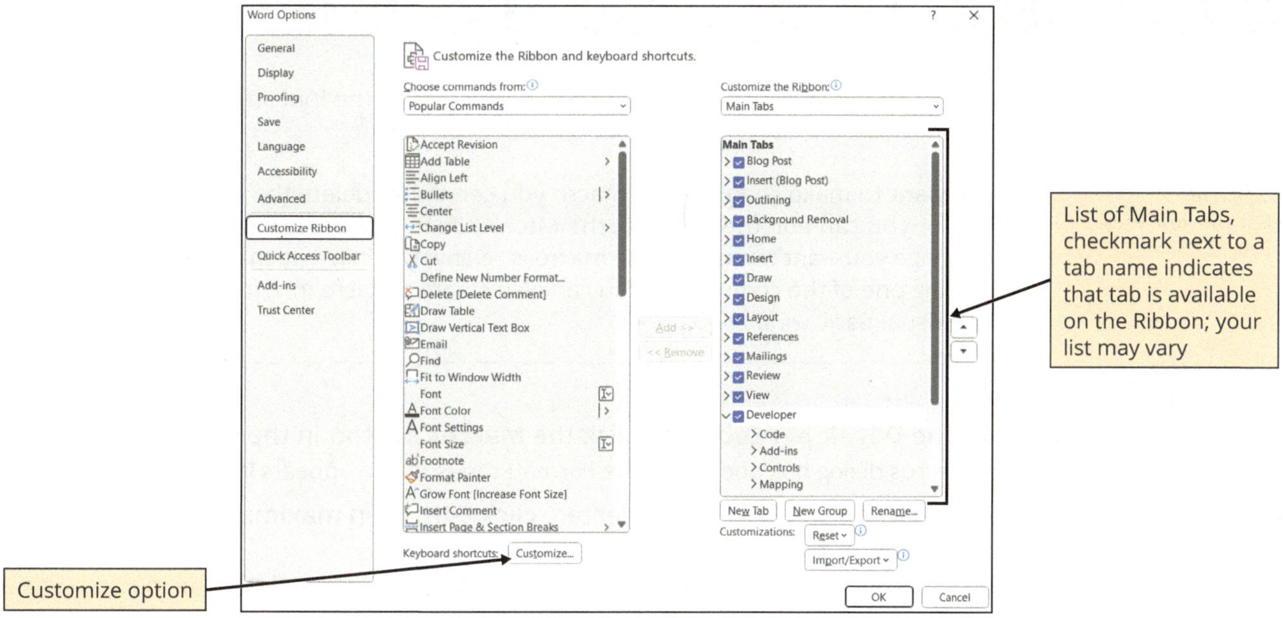

Figure 11-22: Customize Keyboard dialog box

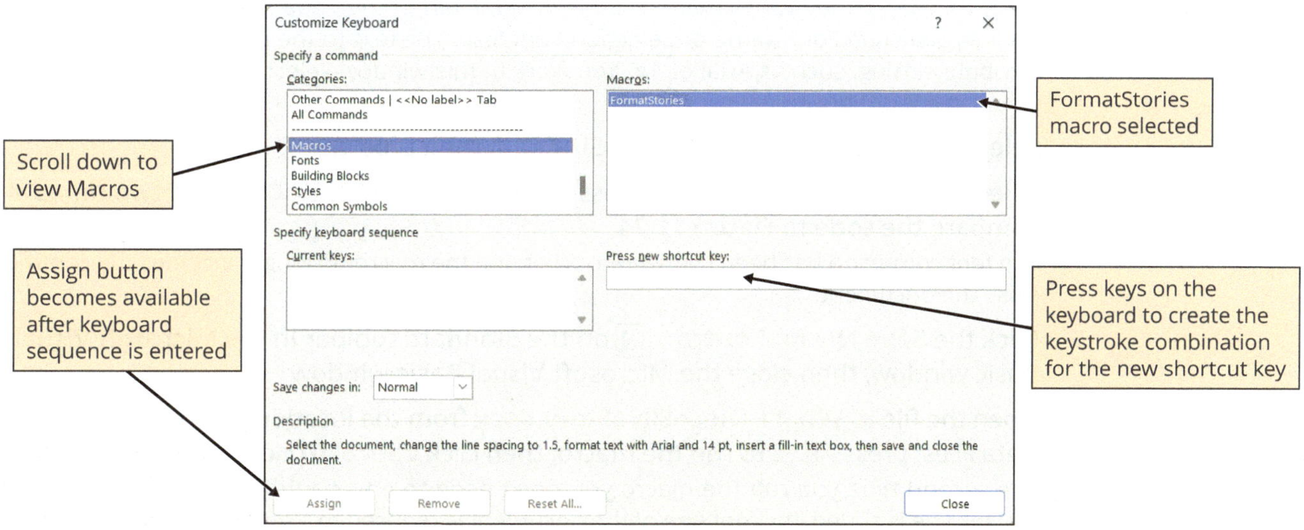

Finding keyboard shortcuts

Word includes hundreds of keyboard shortcuts that you can use to streamline document formatting tasks and to help you work efficiently in Word. You access the list of Word's keyboard shortcuts from Help. Click in the Search box on the title bar, type "keyboard shortcuts", then click "keyboard shortcuts" in the Get Help on section of the menu that opens. In the Help pane that opens, click links to articles to read more about keyboard shortcuts. You can also create your own keyboard shortcuts for procedures you use frequently. **Table 11-3** shows some common keyboard shortcuts.

Table 11-3: Some common keyboard shortcuts

function	keyboard shortcut	function	keyboard shortcut
Bold text	CTRL+B	Print a document	CTRL+P
Center text	CTRL+E	Redo or repeat an action	CTRL+Y
Copy text	CTRL+C	Save a document	CTRL+S
Cut text	CTRL+X	Select all text	CTRL+A
Open a document	CTRL+O	Turn on double spacing	CTRL+2
Paste text	CTRL+V	Undo an action	CTRL+Z

Edit a Macro in Visual Basic

Case You work in Visual Basic to edit the FormatStories macro by decreasing the font size that the macro applies to text from 14 pt to 12 pt and then removing the close document command.

Objective
- Edit a macro in Visual Basic

If you want to make changes to a macro you can either delete the macro and record the steps again, or you can edit the macro in the **Microsoft Visual Basic window**. Edit the macro when the change you want to make to the macro is relatively minor—such as changing the font style or removing one of the commands. You can also create a macro in Visual Basic by typing the codes in the Visual Basic window.

Steps

1. **Click the Developer tab, then click the Macros button in the Code group**
   The Macros dialog box opens and the FormatStories macro appears in the list of available macros.
2. **Verify that FormatStories is selected, click Edit, then maximize the Microsoft Visual Basic window, if necessary**
   The Microsoft Visual Basic window opens as shown in **Figure 11-23**. The macro name and the description you entered when you created the macro appear in green text. Command codes, a Basic program, appear below the description. This program was created as you recorded the steps for the FormatStories macro. The text to the left of the equal sign is the specific attribute, such as Selection.Font.Name or Selection.Font.Size. The text to the right of the equal sign is the attribute setting, such as Arial or 14. You work in this window selecting and deleting text as you would in a Word document.
3. **Select 14 in the line Selection.Font.Size = 14, then type 12**
4. **Select ActiveDocument.Close, press DELETE, then press BACKSPACE two times and compare the code to Figure 11-24**
   The font command has been changed to 12 pt and the macro no longer includes the command to close the document.
5. **Click the Save Normal button on the Standard toolbar in the Microsoft Visual Basic window, then close the Microsoft Visual Basic window**
6. **Open the file IL_WD_11_DiegoSilvaStory.docx from the location where you store your Data Files, press Alt+S to run the macro, then click Cancel to close the fill-in field text box**
   The second time you run the macro you don't need to enter a title in the fill-in field text box. A blank line is added, the font size of the document is reduced to 12 pt and the document is saved but not closed.
7. **Type your name where indicated at the bottom of the document, then save and close the document**
8. **Click the Developer tab, click the Visual Basic button in the Code group, press CTRL+A to select all the FormatStories macro code in the Visual Basic window, press CTRL+C to copy the code to the Clipboard, then close the Microsoft Visual Basic window**
9. **Press CTRL+N to open a new blank Word document, press CTRL+V, press ENTER, type Created by followed by your name, save the document as IL_WD_11_MacroCodes, then close the document**

Quick Tip
You save a copy of your macro code so you have a reference to verify the macro steps you performed.

Figure 11-23: Visual Basic window

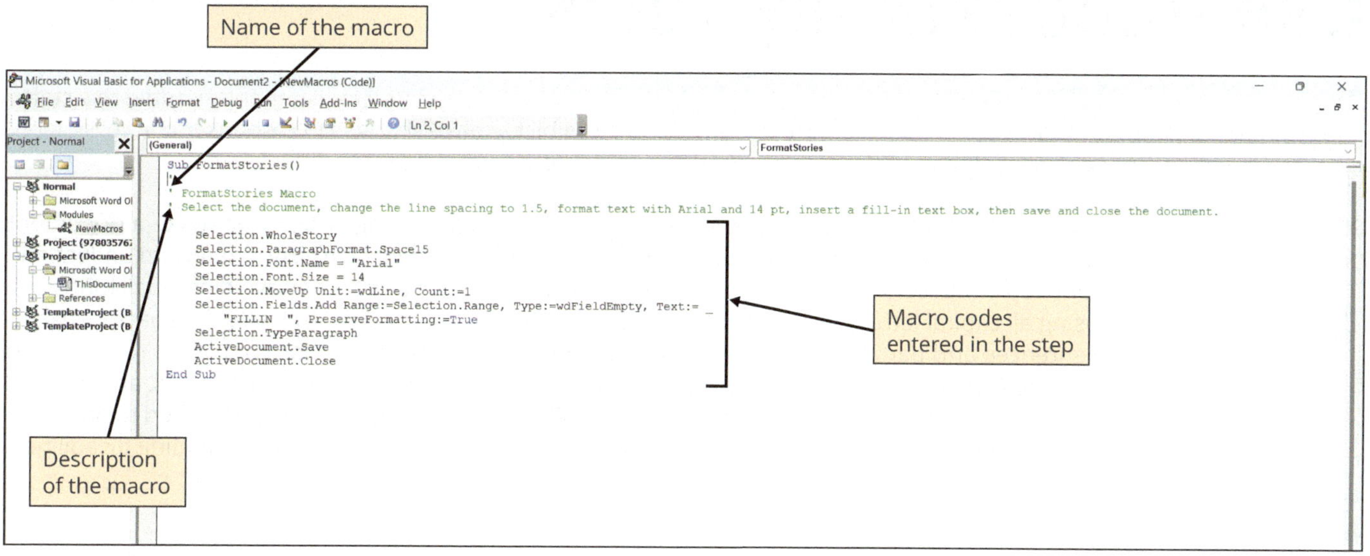

Figure 11-24: Edited macro

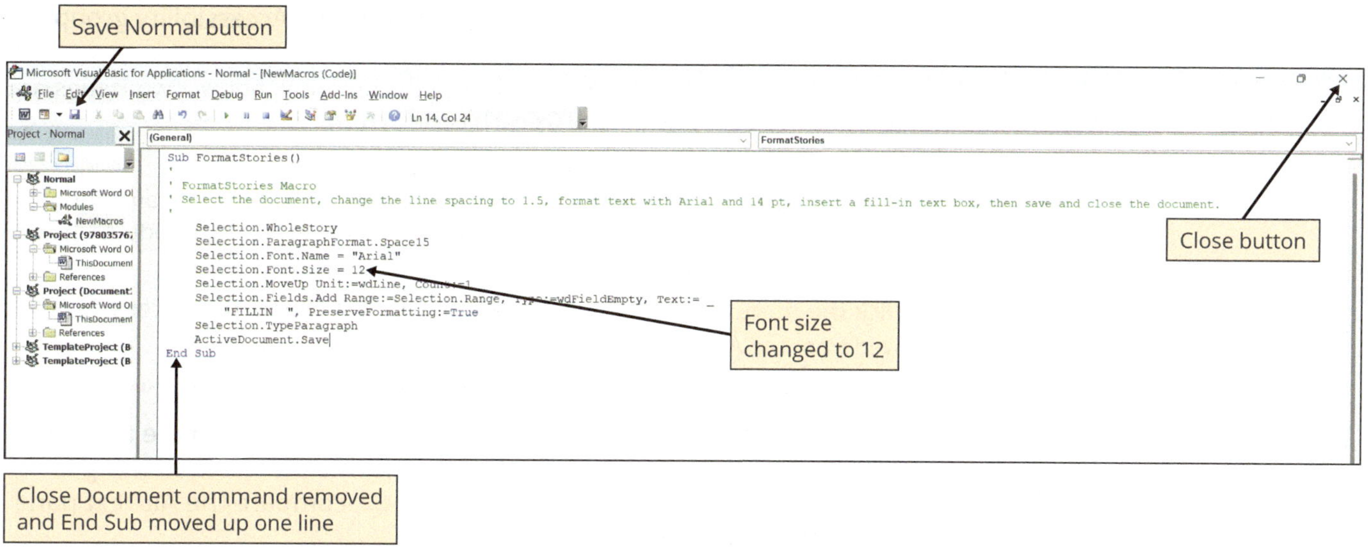

Creating a macro in Visual Basic

You can create a macro by entering codes into Visual Basic. From the Developer tab, click the Macros button in the Code group, type a macro name, select the template or document in which to store the macro, and then click Create to open the Visual Basic Editor. You can paste code from an existing macro or you can enter codes for the macro. To find a list of codes and information about working with Visual Basic, press F1 to open the Microsoft Visual Basic Help menu or click Help on the menu bar, then click Microsoft Visual Basic for Applications Help.

Copying a macro to another document

You can copy a macro that you saved in a document instead of in the Normal template to another document. You use the same procedure to copy a macro from one document to another document as you used to copy a style or selection of styles from one document to another document. Click the Launcher in the Styles group on the Home tab, click the Manage Styles button at the bottom of the Styles pane, then click Import/Export. In the Organizer dialog box, click the Macro Projects Items tab, open the file containing the macro you want to copy (the source file), open the file you want to copy the macro to (the destination file), select the macro in the source file, then click Copy.

Use Accessibility Tools

Case You want to email the interview document for Akiko Matsuda that you completed earlier in this module to a staff member who has low vision. You check the document's accessibility, make changes in response to accessibility issues including adding alt text to the pictures, and then view accessibility options.

Objectives
- Check Accessibility
- Add Alt text to a table
- Modify Accessibility Options

You use the Accessibility Checker in Word to highlight formatting issues that make a document difficult to read so you can make changes to ensure your documents are easy to read and understand for people with certain disabilities. You can minimize accessibility issues by avoiding small font sizes, using all capital letters or excessive italics and underlining, including ample white space between sentences and paragraphs, and choosing easy-to-read colors and color contrasts. You can also provide Alternative text (Alt text) for all objects such as pictures, drawings, and tables, and you can choose how Word checks a document's accessibility. **Alt text** is descriptive text added to an object that improves the accessibility of the document for people who have vision or reading disabilities.

Steps

1. **Open the file IL_WD_11-5.docx from the location where you store your Data Files, then save it as IL_WD_11_AkikoMatsudaAccessible**
2. **Click the Review tab, click the Check Accessibility arrow in the Accessibility group, then click Check Accessibility**
   The Accessibility pane opens along the right side of the document window. Two issues are highlighted: refer to **Figure 11-25**. You view and fix each issue in turn.
3. **Click Missing Object Description (3) in the Accessibility pane**
   Three objects needing an object description are listed: Star: 5 Points 1, Picture 2, and Group 1, which refers to the grouped object on page 2. You can choose to remove an object, add Alt Text to an object so the description can be read by a screen reader, or make it decorative.
4. **Scroll to page 2, click the picture grouped with the star and sun shape, then press DELETE**
   The object is removed from the Accessibility pane.
5. **Click Star: 5 Points 1 in the Accessibility pane, then click Mark as Decorative**
6. **Click Picture 2 in the Accessibility pane, click Add a Description, click in the text box in the Alt Text pane, if necessary, type A photograph of Akiko Matsuda holding a textbook and standing in front of a building on campus, compare the Alt Text pane to Figure 11-26, then close the Alt Text pane**
   The second error refers to the positioning of the picture.
7. **Click Image or Object Not Inline in the Accessibility pane, click Picture 2, read the "Why Fix" description in the Accessibility task pane, right-click the picture in the document, click Wrap Text, then click In Line with Text**
   The picture now appears on its own line above the text. All Accessibility issues have been resolved and the Accessibility pane displays the message "No accessibility issues found."
8. **Close the Accessibility pane, click the Review tab, click Check the Accessibility arrow, click Options: Accessibility, view the options you can change (refer to Figure 11-27), click OK, then save the document**

Figure 11-25: Accessibility issues listed in the Accessibility pane

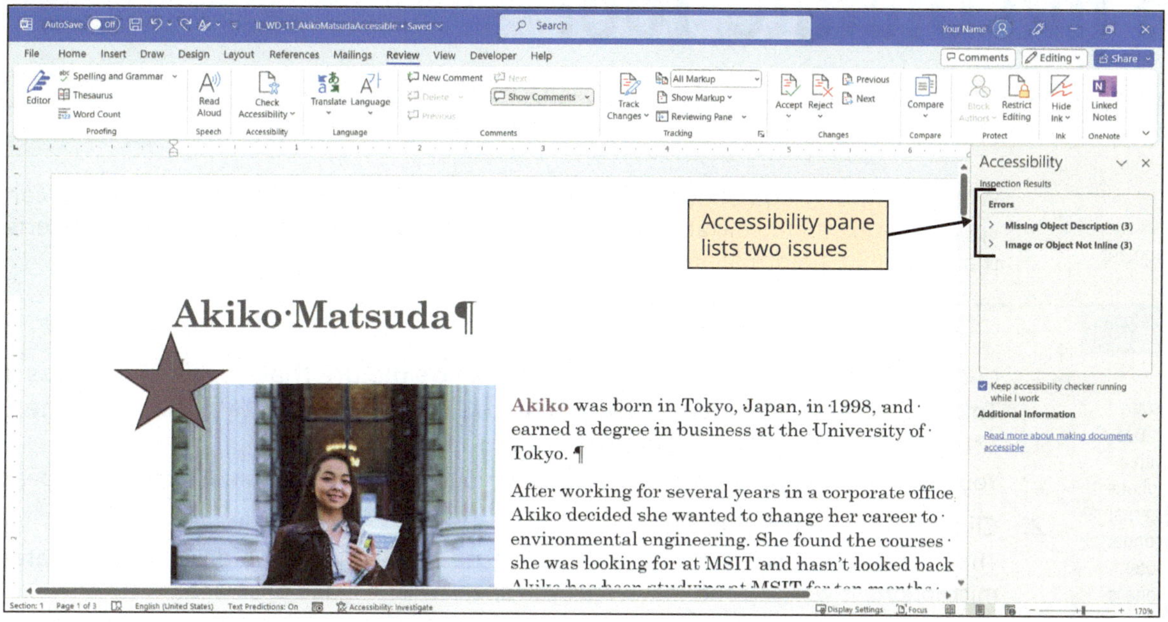

George Pak/Pexels

Figure 11-26: Description entered in the Alt Text pane

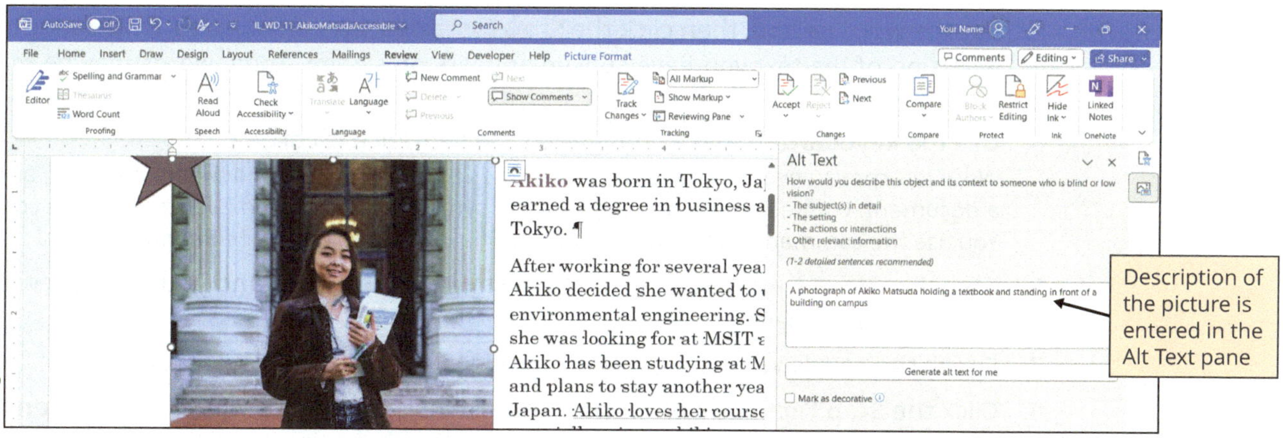

George Pak/Pexels

Figure 11-27: Accessibility options available

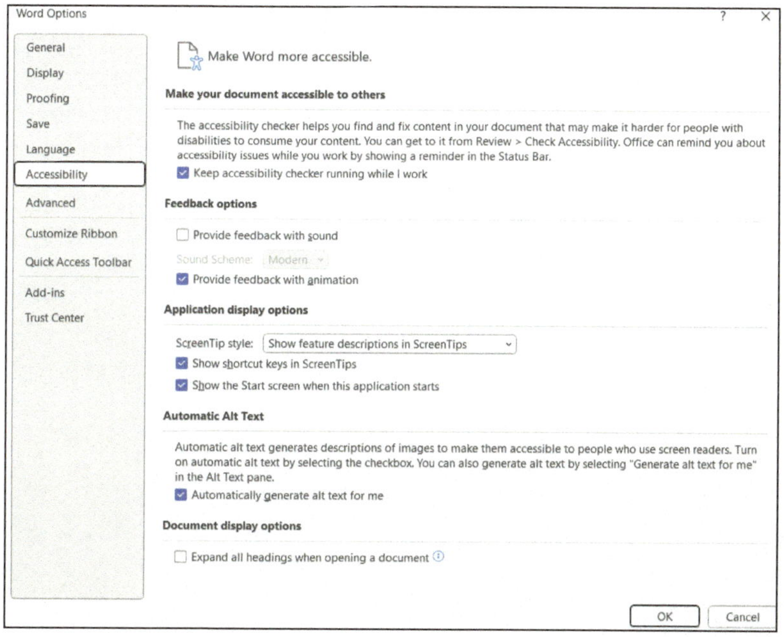

Use the Dictate Tool

Case You use the Dictate tool to add a line of text at the end of Akiko's document in Word and then you use it to insert a comment.

Objectives
- Dictate text
- Dictate a comment

With a computer equipped with a microphone and an Internet connection, you can use the speech-to-text tool to dictate text and comments in Word. Your speech will be converted to text that you can then format and change.

Steps

Trouble
To use the Dictate tool, you must use a computer with a built-in microphone or have an external microphone connected to your computer. If no microphone is connected, the Dictate tool will not function.

1. **Click to the left of the paragraph under Akiko's picture that begins "Akiko was born in Tokyo...", press ENTER, press the Up Arrow, click the Home tab, then click the Clear All Formatting button in the Font group**
   You've positioned your insertion point where you want the text you will dictate to appear.
2. **Click Dictate in the Voice group**
   The Dictation toolbar is activated (refer to **Figure 11-28**) and the word Listening indicates that the microphone is working and that words you speak will be typed onscreen.
3. **Say the words Akiko is an international student at MSIT**
   The text appears on the screen as you type. You can say punctuation marks.
4. **Say the word period, then click the Stop Dictation button to turn off dictation mode**
   A version of the text you have spoken appears on screen. Some words may be missing or incomplete.
5. **Use the keyboard to make changes so the sentence is correct**
   Word interprets several phrases as commands to insert punctuation; edit, navigate, and format a document; create lists and tables; and add symbols. Word also recognizes several commands. You use the command Add Comment to insert a comment in the document.
6. **Click the Office Dictation button, then say Add Comment and pause for a few seconds**
   A comment box opens.
7. **Speak the words We interviewed her in March and then say period**
8. **Click the Stop Dictation button to turn off dictation, compare your screen to Figure 11-29, post the comment, then save the document**

Figure 11-28: Dictation toolbar activated

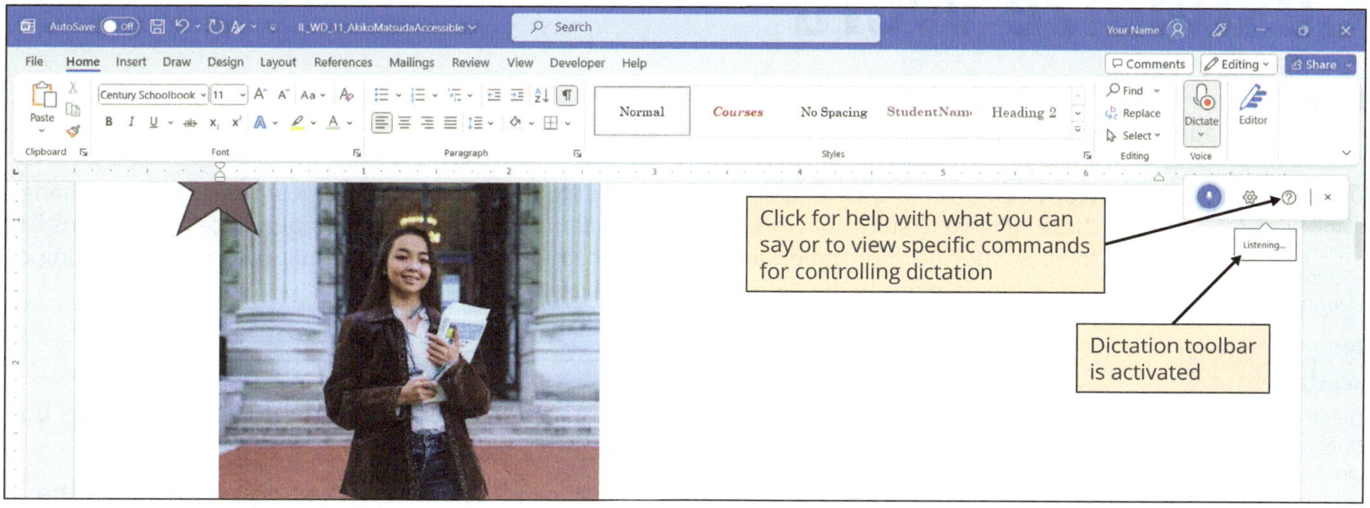

George Pak/Pexels

Figure 11-29: Dictated comment inserted in Word

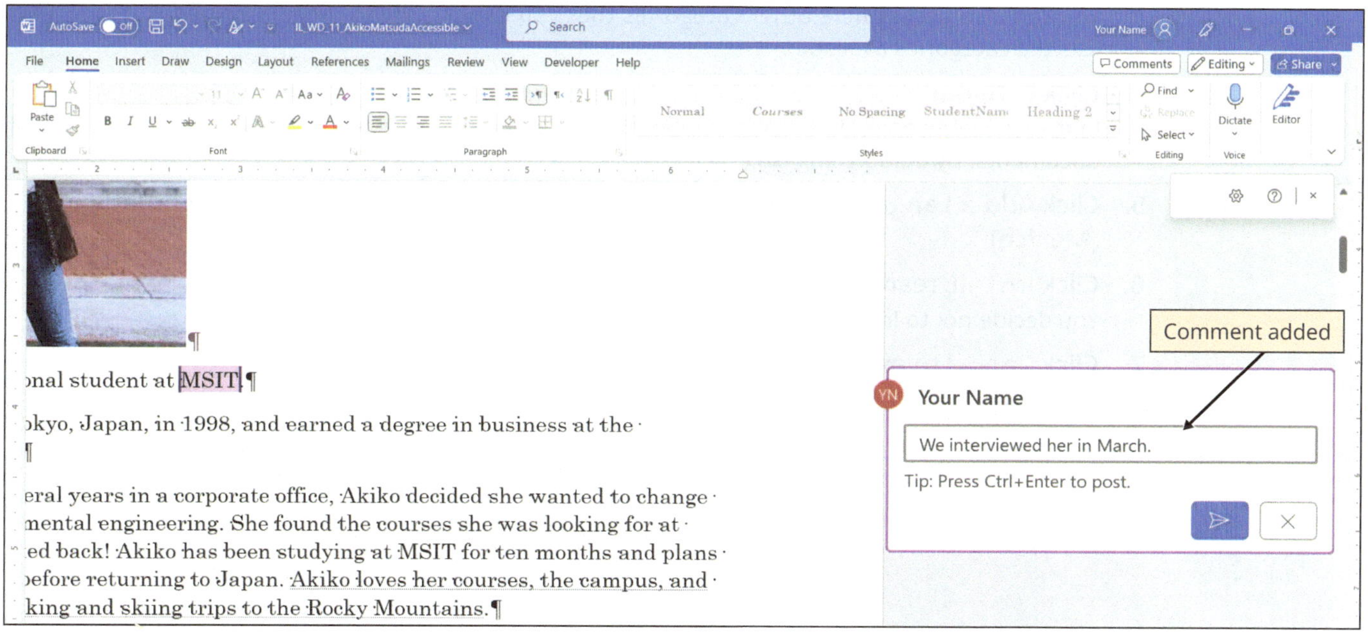

George Pak/Pexels

Customize Word

Case To match the standard way that Word has been set up in the Office for International Students, you customize the appearance of the status bar and set a new proofing language.

Objectives
- Customize the status bar
- Set the proofing language

Word includes many default settings designed to meet the needs of most users. You can change these settings to suit your working style. You can also customize the appearance of the status bar to show specific information about your document. You modify default settings by selecting or deselecting options in the Word Options dialog box.

Steps

Quick Tip
To restore items, right-click the status bar, then click the items again.

1. **Press CTRL+HOME to move to the top of the document, then right-click the status bar**
   A selection of options is displayed (refer to **Figure 11-30**)
2. **Click Section to deselect it, click Word Count to deselect it, then click away from the options to hide them**
   These two options are now removed from the status bar.
3. **Click the File tab, scroll down, if necessary, then click Options**
   From the Word Options dialog box, you can customize the Ribbon and the Quick Access toolbar. You can also access nine other categories that you can modify to meet your needs. **Table 11-4** lists the categories available.
4. **Click Language**
   In the Language pane of the Word Options dialog box, you can select the languages used to proof documents. By default, English is selected.
5. **Click Add a Language, scroll the alphabetical list of languages, then click Spanish (Mexico)**
6. **Click Install, read the message that appears, then click Cancel**
   You decide not to install the language at this time.
7. **Click Cancel to exit the dialog box, then save the document**

Figure 11-30: Customize the status bar options

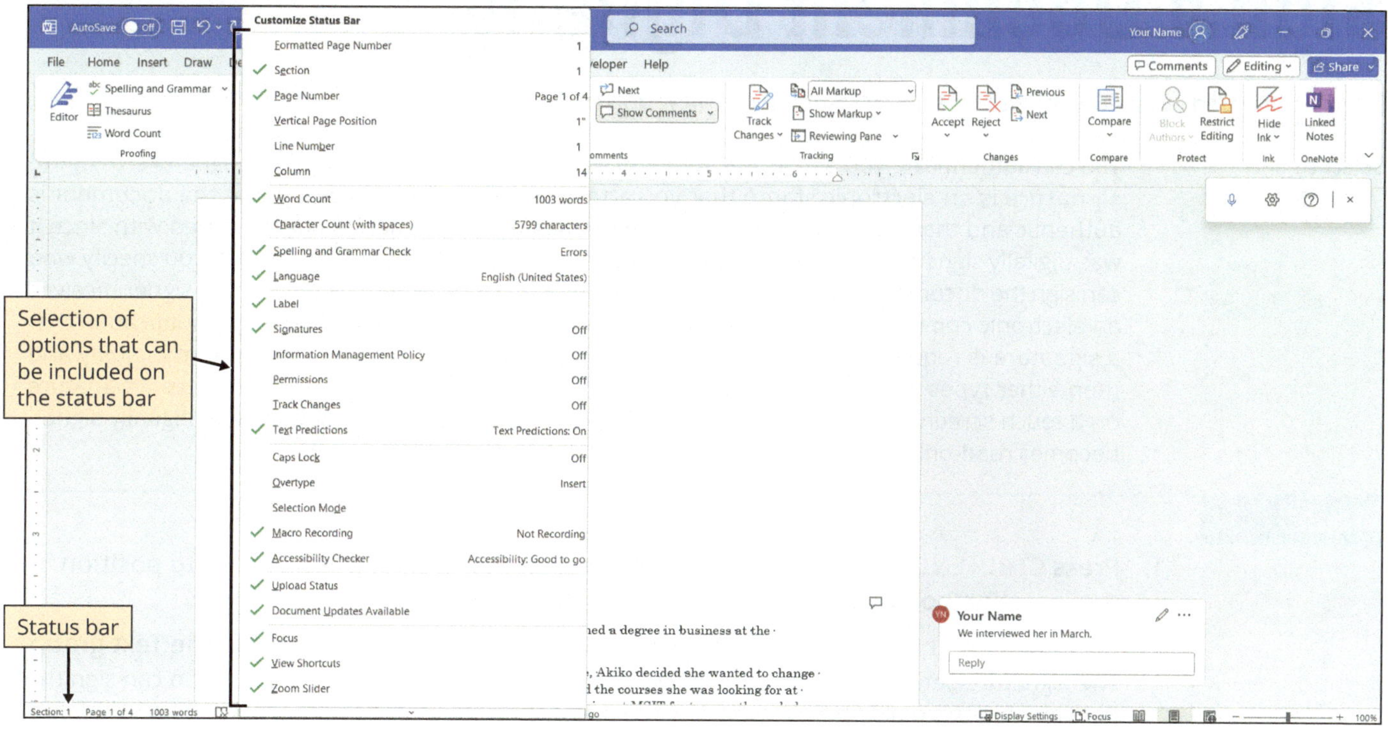

Table 11-4: Categories in the Word Options dialog box

category	description
General	Options include those used to modify the user interface, personalize Office, and modify collaboration options
Display	Change the page display, formatting options, and printing options
Proofing	Modify AutoCorrect and spelling and grammar options and exceptions
Save	Modify options related to saving documents and editing them offline
Language	Select editing, display, and Help languages
Ease of Access	Select feedback options, application and document display options, and automatic alt text
Advanced	Modify options related to editing, images, document display, saving, and printing, layout, and document compatibility
Add-ins	Includes the list of programs included with or added to Word
Trust Center	Access security options and the Microsoft Word Trust Center

Sign a Document Digitally

Case You add a digital signature to Akiko Matsuda's interview document.

Objective
- Add a digital signature

You can authenticate yourself as the author of a document by inserting a digital signature. A **digital signature** is an electronic stamp that you attach to a document to verify that the document is authentic and that the content of the document has not been changed or tampered with since it was digitally signed. When you insert a digital signature line into a Word document, you specify who can sign the document and include instructions for the signer. When the designated signer receives an electronic copy of the document, they will notice a signature line and receive a notification that a signature is requested. The signer clicks the signature line to sign the document digitally and then either types a signature, selects a digital image of his or her signature, or writes a signature on a touch screen such as those used with Tablet PCs. A document that has been digitally signed becomes read-only so that no one else can make changes to the content.

Steps

Trouble
If the message does not appear after double-clicking the signature line, type your name, click **Sign**, read the message that appears, then click **No**. In Step 6, Click **Cancel**, then save the document.

1. **Press CTRL+END to move to the end of the document, then press ENTER to position the insertion point where want to add the signature line**
2. **Click the Insert tab, then click the Add a Signature Line button in the Text group**
   The Signature Setup dialog box opens. You enter information about the person who can sign the document in this dialog box.
3. **Type your name in the Suggested signer box in the Signature Setup dialog box (refer to Figure 11-31)**
4. **Click OK**
   A space for your signature, with an X and your name below a horizontal line appears at the position of the insertion point.
5. **Double-click the signature line, type your name, click Sign, read the message that appears, then click No**
   If you click in the line and then click Yes, you are taken to a page on the Microsoft website that lists Microsoft partners that supply digital IDs. Once you have obtained a Digital ID, you can enter it in the signature line. However, you will not be obtaining a Digital ID, so the signature line will remain blank.
6. **Click Cancel, then save the document**
7. **Submit a copy of all the files you created in this module to your instructor, then exit Word**

Figure 11-31: Signature Setup dialog box

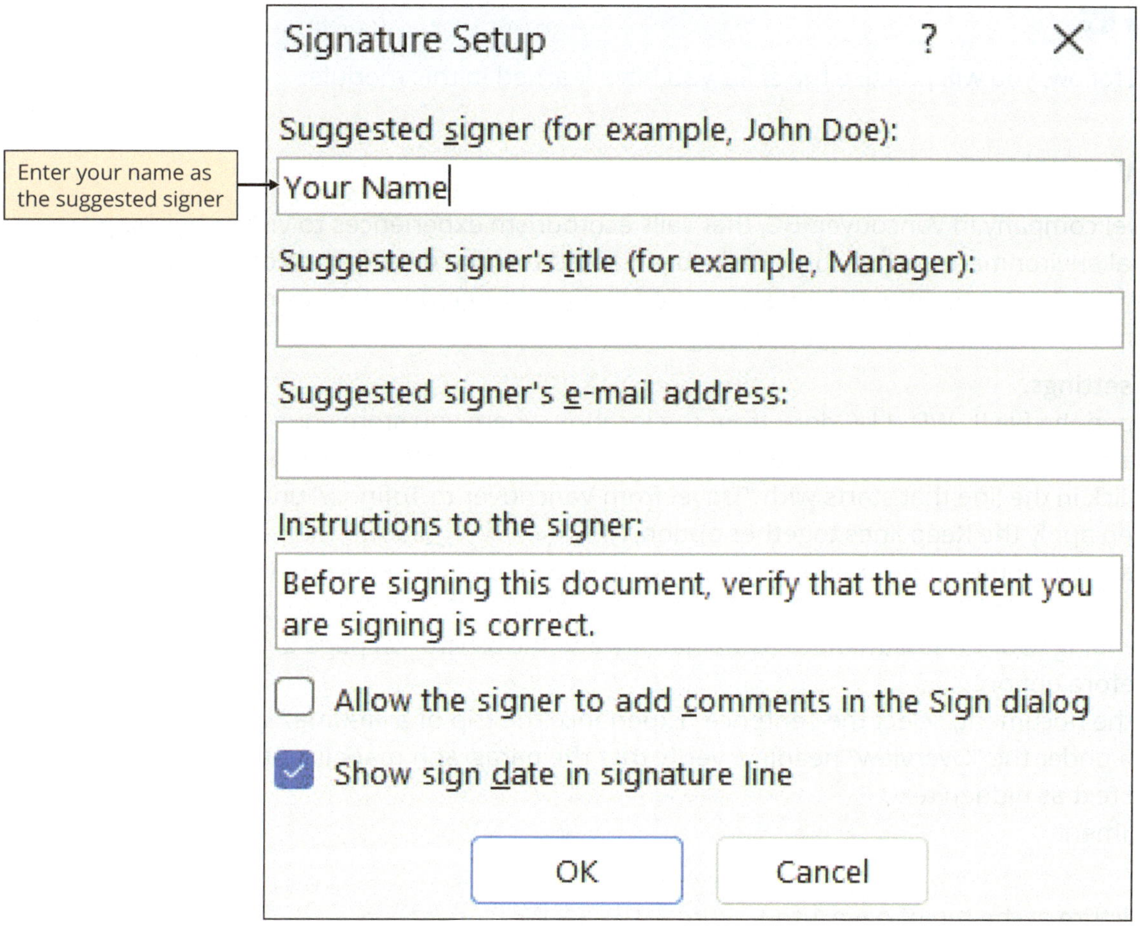

Customizing the Quick Access toolbar

To customize the Quick Access toolbar, click the File tab, click Options, then click Quick Access toolbar. The buttons included by default on the Quick Access toolbar appear in the list on the right. These buttons are AutoSave, Save, Undo, and Redo. To add a new command to the Quick Access toolbar, select the command from the list on the left, then click Add. To remove a button from the Quick Access toolbar, select the command in the list on the right, then click Remove.

Acquiring a digital ID

You acquire a **digital ID** by purchasing one from a Microsoft partner. When you click Yes to acquire a digital ID, you are taken to a page with links to Microsoft partners. You can click on one of the links and purchase a digital ID. Other people can use the digital ID to verify that your digital signature is authentic. The Microsoft partner that issues the digital ID ensures the authenticity of the person or organization that acquires the digital ID.

Practice

In the exercises that follow, you will practice the skills you have learned in this module.

Skills Review

You work with a travel company in Vancouver, BC, that sells ecotourism experiences to visitors wishing to explore the natural environment sustainably. You've been asked to write descriptions of two of the company's tours for distribution to potential guests and to format first-person accounts of two tour experiences you want to feature on the company's blog.

1. **Use pagination settings.**
   a. Start Word, open the file IL_WD_11-6.docx from the location where you store your Data Files, verify paragraph marks are showing, then save the document as **IL_WD_11_WestCoastAdventureTour**.
   b. Scroll down, click in the line that starts with "Travel from Vancouver to Tofino..." under the heading "Itinerary", then apply the Keep lines together option.
   c. Scroll to the last line of the final paragraph (a widow), then turn on Widow/Orphan control for the paragraph.
   d. Click in the heading "Our Commitment to Sustainability and Inclusivity" on page 2, then apply the Page break before option.
   e. At the top of the document, select the sentence "Experience the trip of a lifetime." at the end of the paragraph under the "Overview" heading, verify that the paragraph mark is not selected, then designate the text as hidden text.
   f. Save the document.
2. **Edit pictures.**
   a. Change the picture at the top of page 1 to **Support_WD_11_WestCoast.jpg**.
   b. Change the color saturation to 66%.
   c. Change the color tone to Temperature: 7200 K.
   d. Scroll to the bottom of the document, click the picture, then apply the Paint Brush artistic effect.
   e. Save the document.
3. **Apply layering options.**
   a. Go to the top of page 1, then send the picture of the beach behind the star shape.
   b. Go to the end of the document, then change the lightning bolt shape to a cloud shape.
   c. Apply the Slant bevel effect to the cloud shape.
   d. Open the Selection pane, hide the picture of the cloud shape, then show the picture again.
   e. Drag the picture of the cloud shape below Picture2 in the Selection pane.
   f. Save the document.
4. **Arrange and compress pictures.**
   a. In the Selection pane, use CTRL to select all three objects starting with Cloud 1, then Picture2, then Star: 10 Points 7.
   b. Group the three objects into one object.
   c. Change the wrapping of the grouped object to Square.
   d. Cut the grouped object, paste it at the top of page 1, change the Height to 2.3" and Width to 3.7", then position it below the "Getting Here Is Half the Fun" heading as shown in the completed document in **Figure 11-32**.
   e. Compress all the pictures in the document using the Web (150 ppi) option.
   f. Close the Selection pane, then save the document.

5. **Create character styles.**
   a. On page 2, select the text "Kayaking Tour" in the first bulleted point below the Itinerary heading, then use CTRL to select "Hiking Trip" and "Wildlife Boat Cruise" so all three phrases are selected.
   b. Create a new style called **Activity**, then designate it as a Character style.
   c. Select these character formatting settings: a font size of 14 pt, Bold, Italic, and the Green font color in the Standard Colors section.
   d. Select just "Kayaking Tour", change the font color to Dark Red, Accent 1 in the top row of the Theme Colors palette, then update the Activity character style to match the selection.
   e. Close the Styles pane, then save the document, but do not close it.

6. **Manage styles.**
   a. Open the file **IL_WD_11-7.docx** from the location where you store your Data Files, save the document as **IL_WD_11_BackCountryRanchExperience**, then close it.
   b. Open the Organizer dialog box from the Styles pane.
   c. Verify that the source file is IL_WD_11_WestCoastAdventureTour.docx.
   d. Open IL_WD_11_BackCountryRanchExperience.docx as the destination file. Remember to select All Word Documents to view the Word document.
   e. Copy the styles **Activity** and **Tour** from the source file to the destination file.
   f. Close and save the destination file, then close the Organizer dialog box.
   g. Open IL_WD_11_BackCountryRanchExperience.docx, use CTRL to select the three adventure tours "Horseback Riding", "Backcountry Hiking", and "Canoeing", then apply the Activity character style.
   h. Go to the top of the document, then use the Replace feature to find every instance of **Mirror Lake Ranch** and replace it with "Mirror Lake Ranch" formatted with the Tour character style you just copied from the West Coast Adventure Tour document.
   i. Type your name where indicated in the footer, save and close the document, type your name where indicated in the footer in the West Coast Adventure Tour document, compare the completed West Coast Adventure Tour document to **Figure 11-32**, then save and close the document.

Figure 11-32

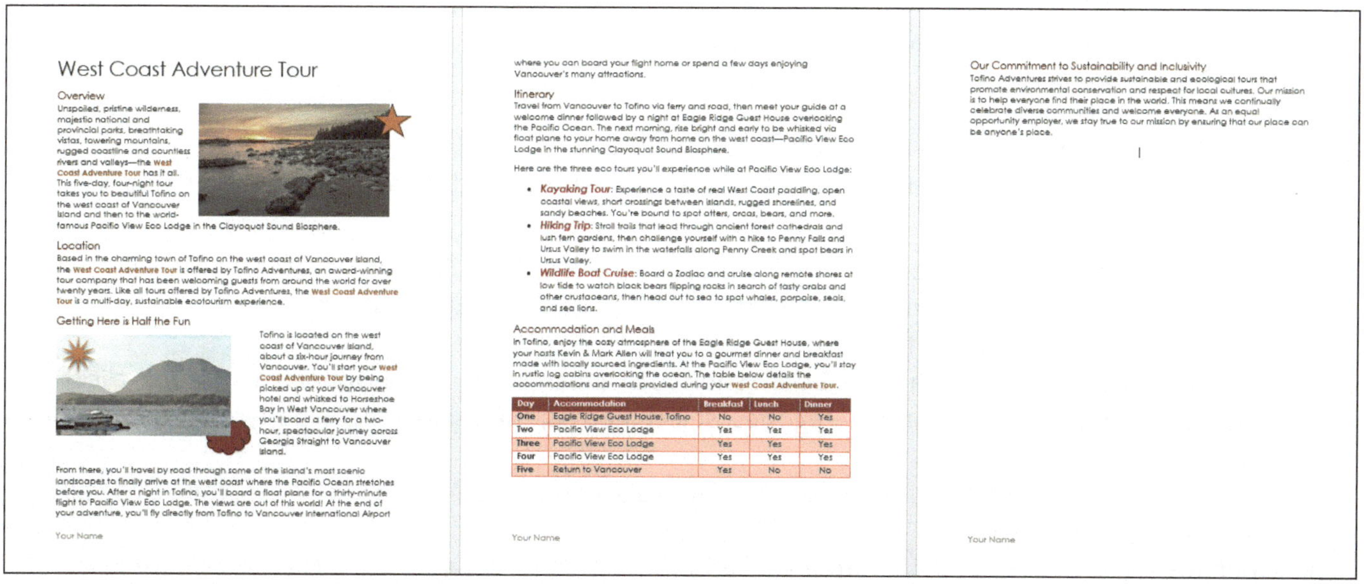
West Coast Adventure Tour

Overview

Unspoiled, pristine wilderness, majestic national and provincial parks, breathtaking vistas, towering mountains, rugged coastline and countless rivers and valleys—the West Coast Adventure Tour has it all. This five-day, four-night tour takes you to beautiful Tofino on the west coast of Vancouver Island and then to the world-famous Pacific View Eco Lodge in the Clayoquot Sound Biosphere.

Location

Based in the charming town of Tofino on the west coast of Vancouver Island, the West Coast Adventure Tour is offered by Tofino Adventures, an award-winning tour company that has been welcoming guests from around the world for over twenty years. Like all tours offered by Tofino Adventures, the West Coast Adventure Tour is a multi-day, sustainable ecotourism experience.

Getting Here is Half the Fun

Tofino is located on the west coast of Vancouver Island, about a six-hour journey from Vancouver. You'll start your West Coast Adventure Tour by being picked up at your Vancouver hotel and whisked to Horseshoe Bay in West Vancouver where you'll board a ferry for a two-hour, spectacular journey across Georgia Straight to Vancouver Island.

From there, you'll travel by road through some of the island's most scenic landscapes to finally arrive at the west coast where the Pacific Ocean stretches before you. After a night in Tofino, you'll board a float plane for a thirty-minute flight to Pacific View Eco Lodge. The views are out of this world! At the end of your adventure, you'll fly directly from Tofino to Vancouver International Airport

Your Name

where you can board your flight home or spend a few days enjoying Vancouver's many attractions.

Itinerary

Travel from Vancouver to Tofino via ferry and road, then meet your guide at a welcome dinner followed by a night at Eagle Ridge Guest House overlooking the Pacific Ocean. The next morning, rise bright and early to be whisked via float plane to your home away from home on the west coast—Pacific View Eco Lodge in the stunning Clayoquot Sound Biosphere.

Here are the three eco tours you'll experience while at Pacific View Eco Lodge:

- ***Kayaking Tour***: Experience a taste of real West Coast paddling, open coastal views, short crossings between islands, rugged shorelines, and sandy beaches. You're bound to spot otters, orcas, bears, and more.
- ***Hiking Trip***: Stroll trails that lead through ancient forest cathedrals and lush fern gardens, then challenge yourself with a hike to Penny Falls and Ursus Valley to swim in the waterfalls along Penny Creek and spot bears in Ursus Valley.
- ***Wildlife Boat Cruise***: Board a Zodiac and cruise along remote shores at low tide to watch black bears flipping rocks in search of tasty crabs and other crustaceans, then head out to sea to spot whales, porpoise, seals, and sea lions.

Accommodation and Meals

In Tofino, enjoy the cozy atmosphere of the Eagle Ridge Guest House, where your hosts Kevin & Mark Allen will treat you to a gourmet dinner and breakfast made with locally sourced ingredients. At the Pacific View Eco Lodge, you'll stay in rustic log cabins overlooking the ocean. The table below details the accommodations and meals provided during your West Coast Adventure Tour.

Day	Accommodation	Breakfast	Lunch	Dinner
One	Eagle Ridge Guest House, Tofino	No	No	Yes
Two	Pacific View Eco Lodge	Yes	Yes	Yes
Three	Pacific View Eco Lodge	Yes	Yes	Yes
Four	Pacific View Eco Lodge	Yes	Yes	Yes
Five	Return to Vancouver	Yes	No	No

Your Name

Our Commitment to Sustainability and Inclusivity

Tofino Adventures strives to provide sustainable and ecological tours that promote environmental conservation and respect for local cultures. Our mission is to help everyone find their place in the world. This means we continually celebrate diverse communities and welcome everyone. As an equal opportunity employer, we stay true to our mission by ensuring that our place can be anyone's place.

Your Name

James Wheeler/Pexels; Ventiil8 Productions/Pexels

Skills Review (Continued)

7. **Plan a macro.**
   a. Refer to **Table 11-5** to review the steps required for the macro you will create in the next step:

Table 11-5: Macro tasks plan

Macro tasks	Steps to complete the tasks
Select all the text	Press **CTRL+A**
Change the line spacing to double	Press **CTRL+2**
Select the Arial Black font	Click the **Font arrow** in the Font group, then click **Arial**
Select 18 pt	Click the **Font Size arrow**, then click **16**
Insert a fill-in field text box	Press the up arrow once to deselect the text and move to the top of the document, click the **Insert tab,** click the **Explore Quick Parts button**, click **Field**, scroll down the list of Field names, click **Fill-in**, click **OK**, then click **OK**
Add a blank line	Press **ENTER**
Save the document	Click the **Save button** on the Quick Access toolbar

8. **Record macro steps.**
   a. Start a new blank document, show the Developer tab if it is not already displayed on the Ribbon, then show the paragraph marks, if necessary.
   b. Press ENTER three times, then save the blank document as **IL_WD_11_ExperienceMacroSetup**.
   c. Make the Developer tab the active tab, open the Record Macro dialog box, then type **Experience** as the macro name.
   d. Enter the following description in the Description box: **Select all the text, change the line spacing to double, change the font to Arial and 16 pt, insert a fill-in text box, then save the document.**
   e. Exit the Record Macro dialog box, then perform the macro steps as follows:
      1. Press CTRL+A to select all the text.
      2. Press CTRL+2 to turn on double spacing.
      3. Select the Arial font.
      4. Change the font size to 16 pt.
      5. Press the up arrow once.
      6. Insert a Fill-in box and click OK.
      7. Press ENTER.
      8. Save the document.
   f. From the Developer tab, stop the macro recording.
   g. Type your name at the top of the document, then save and close the document but do not exit Word.

9. **Run a macro.**
   a. Open the file IL_WD_11-8.docx from the location where your Data Files are located, save it as **IL_WD_11_RickDavis**, then from the Macros dialog box, run the Experience macro.
   b. Enter **Rick Davis** in the Fill-in text box.
   c. Open the Customize Ribbon and keyboard shortcuts screen in the Word Options dialog box, click Customize, scroll down the list of Categories, select Macros, then select the Experience macro in the Macros list.
   d. In the Press new shortcut key box, enter the keystroke command **Alt+F**, click Assign, then close all open dialog boxes.
   e. Open the file **IL_WD_11-9.docx** from the location where you store your Data Files, then save it as **IL_WD_11_EllenChung**.
   f. Use the Alt+F macro to format the document, entering **Ellen Chung** in the fill-in text box.

10. Edit a macro in Visual Basic.

a. Open the Macros dialog box, select the Experience macro, then click Edit. (**Note**: Two macros are listed—the FormatStories macro you created in the lessons and the Experience macro you just created. In the steps that follow, you make corrections to the Experience macro.)

b. Find Selection.Font.Name = "Arial", change the font to **Calibri** and keep the quotation marks around Calibri, then change Selection.Font.Size = 16 to **14**.

c. Save the macro, select only the components of the Experience macro in the Visual Basic window, copy them, close the Visual Basic window, press CTRL+N to open a new blank Word document, paste the code into the blank document, type **Created by** followed by your name below the last line, save the document as **IL_WD_11_ExperienceMacroCodes** to the location where you store your files for this book, then close it and close the Visual Basic window.

d. Verify that IL_WD_11_EllenChung is the active document, then use the Alt+F keystrokes to run the revised macro. Remember to press Cancel to bypass the Fill-in box.

e. Verify that the font style of the document title is now Calibri and the font size is 14 pt, remove the blank line at the top of the document, type your name where indicated at the end of the document, then save and close the document.

f. Run the Experience macro on the Rick Davis story, then remove the extra blank line at the time, add your name where indicated, then save and close the document.

g. Save and close the ExperienceMacroSetup document.

11. Use Accessibility Tools.

a. Open the file IL_WD_11-10.docx from the location where you store your Data Files, then save it as **IL_WD_11_WestCoastAdventureTourAccessible**.

b. Check the accessibility of the document, then in response to the Missing Object Description issues listed in the Accessibility pane, delete the grouped picture and mark Star: 5 Points 1 as Decorative.

c. For the picture, click add the description **A photograph of a rocky beach at sunset**.

d. Change the wrapping of the picture to Inline with Text, then save the document.

12. Use the Dictate Tool

a. Go to the top of the document, click at the end of the Overview paragraph, press ENTER, turn on Dictation, say the words **The West Coast Adventure Tour is very highly rated**, then say the word **period** and turn off dictation.

b. Use the keyboard to make changes so the sentence is correct.

c. Click at the end of the paragraph under the Location heading, then use the Office Dictation tool to add the comment **Full week adventure tours are also available** followed by a period.

d. Post the comment, then save the document.

13. Customize Word.

a. Customize the status bar so that Section and Word Count are both selected.

b. In the Language section of the Options dialog box, Add French (Canada) as a proofing language.

c. Remove French (Canada) as a proofing language, then save the document.

14. Sign a document digitally.

a. Delete your name in the footer of the current document, then go to the end of the document to position the insertion point where you want to add a signature line.

b. Insert a signature line that includes your name.

c. Save and close the document, then save and close all files.

d. Submit a copy of all the files you created in this module to your instructor, then exit Word.

Independent Challenge 1

You work in the Human Resources department at LMW Transport, a transportation company based in Columbus, Ohio, that manages a large fleet of trucks and employs over 200 people. You've been asked to format a document outlining the company's new Health & Safety Policy. You open a draft of the policy and set paragraph pagination options, edit pictures, and create and then modify a character style. Finally, you copy a character style from another policy document and apply it to the selected text.

a. Start Word, open the file IL_WD_11-11.docx from the location where you store your Data Files, save it as **IL_WD_11_LMWSafetyPolicy**, then show formatting marks if necessary.
b. Turn on Widow/Orphan control for the paragraph that begins "Health and safety performance in all areas..." under the Review heading at the bottom of page 1, then apply the Keep with Next option to the Review heading so it is moved to the next page and stays with the paragraph it relates to.
c. Format the text "We put safety first!" at the end of the first paragraph as hidden.
d. Change the picture on page 1 to the picture **Support_WD_11_Trucks.jpg**.
e. Apply the Texturizer artistic effect to the picture, then set the color saturation at 33% and the color tone at 7200 K.
f. Use the Selection pane to move the picture below the lightning bolt shape, then modify the lightning bolt shape so it uses the Divot bevel effect.
g. Group the lightning bolt shape and the picture into one object. Change the wrapping to In Line with Text, cut the grouped object, then paste it below "Introduction" as shown in the completed document in **Figure 11-33**, adding a hard return as needed.
h. Select the words "Prevention", "Improvement," and "Commitment" in the bulleted list, then create a character style called **Goals** that uses the following formats: Bold, Italic, and the Gold, Accent 1 font color.
i. Select "Prevention" and remove italics and change the Font color to Dark Blue in the selection of Standard Colors, then update the Goals character style to match the selection.
j. Check the accessibility of the document and make changes: mark the picture used as a logo in the header as Decorative, add the description **White trucks driving on a road with a lightning bolt shape in the top left corner** to the grouped object, then make the grouped object an inline graphic. Press ENTER to the left of "LMW Transport is committed to..." next to the picture to move the paragraph down.
k. Go to the paragraph under the Managers heading, then use the dictation tool to add the text **All employees are involved in our health and safety management system** as a new sentence that includes a period.
l. Save the document, then close it.
m. From a blank Word document, open the Organizer dialog box from the Styles pane. Close the file on the left (the current blank document), then open the file **Support_WD_11_LMWEnvironmentalPolicy.docx** from the location where you save your files. This is the source file.
n. Close the file on the right, then open the file **IL_WD_11_LMWSafetyPolicy.docx**. This is the destination file.
o. Copy the Company character style from the Environmental Policy document on the left to the Safety Policy document on the right.
p. Close and save the Safety Policy document, then close the Organizer dialog box.
q. Open **IL_WD_11_LMWSafetyPolicy** and use Find and Replace to find every instance of "LMW Transport" and replace it with **LMW Transport** formatted with the Company style.
r. Type your name where indicated in the footer on the second page, save the document, then close it and any other open documents. The completed document is illustrated in **Figure 11-33**.

Figure 11-33

Suite 870 – Grandview Way, Columbus, OH 43007
www.lmwtransport.cengage.com

Health & Safety Policy

Introduction

LMW Transport is committed to the protection of the health and safety of our employees, our customer's employees, and the general public. We believe that incidents and injuries are preventable, and that a job is only well done if it is done safely. We have documented Health, Safety and Environmental policies in place, and have a Safety Management System in operation.

Health & Safety Goals

We are committed to the following goals:

- **Prevention:** Policies are in place to prevent workplace incidents and injuries.
- **Improvement:** We work to continually improve our health and safety performance.
- **Commitment:** We foster a culture in which all employees, partners, contractors and subcontractors share our commitment to health and safety and the environment.

Best Practices

At *LMW Transport*, we've assembled a Health & Safety team that reports to the Vice President of Human Resources.

Operators

The team has compiled materials for all our operators to ensure they manage operations in the safest manner, by recognizing and assessing hazards and applying effective controls. In addition, safe conduct has been made a condition of employment, and all employees are expected to comply with health and safety legislation and guidelines.

Managers

Managers and supervisors are provided with the tools, supervision, training, and resources needed to ensure that all employees work safely on *LMW Transport* worksites and elsewhere. All employees are involved in our health and safety management system. All employees are involved in our health and safety management system.

Review

Health and safety performance in all areas of the company are regularly evaluated and performance information communicated in a timely manner. *LMW Transport* and the Health & Safety Team are committed to learning from our experiences to prevent future incidents.

Employee Interaction

The Health & Safety team welcomes feedback from all employees regarding health and safety issues. In particular, we are always interested in learning new ways in which we can prevent accidents. Employees are encouraged to email Mick Olivent, Team Leader, with suggestions and recommendations.

Accident Statistics

LMW Transport can be justifiably proud of its sterling record. Since 2023, the number of accidents reported by *LMW Transport* employees has steadily declined. Of these accidents, 85% are considered minor with no physical injuries reported.

Accident Type	2023	2024	2025	2026	2027
Fender bender	30	28	21	19	15
Rear-end collision	13	9	8	6	5
Head-on collision	7	6	4	3	2
T-bone accident	3	1	0	2	0
Rollover accident	2	1	1	0	0

Your Name

Quintin Gellar/Pexels

Independent Challenge 2

You work for Simply Franchises, a web-based company that showcases leading franchises available across the United States and Canada. The company helps people start their own franchise business using the helpful franchise resources available. To help market the company's services, you're collecting information about how people have launched successful franchises. You create a macro that standardizes the formatting and then you apply it to format two descriptions.

a. Start a new blank document, show the Developer tab if it is not already displayed on the Ribbon, press ENTER three times, then save the blank document as **IL_WD_11_FranchiseMacroSetup**.

b. Open the Record Macro dialog box, then enter **Franchise** as the macro name.

c. Enter the following description in the Description box: **Select all the text, change the line spacing to double, change the font to Times New Roman and 12 pt, apply italics, insert a fill-in text box, then save the document.**

d. Exit the Record Macro dialog box, then perform the macro steps as follows:
   1. Press CTRL+A to select all the text.
   2. Press CTRL+2 to turn on double spacing.
   3. Select the Times New Roman font.
   4. Change the font size to 12 pt.
   5. Press Ctrl+I to apply italics.
   6. Press the up arrow once.
   7. Insert a Fill-in text box and click OK.
   8. Press ENTER.
   9. Save the document.

e. From the Developer tab, stop the macro recording.

f. Type your name at the top of the document, then save and close the document but do not exit Word.

g. Open the file **IL_WD_11-12.docx**, then save it as **IL_WD_11_Franchise1**.

h. From the Macros dialog box, run the Franchise macro, entering **Wandering Families Franchise** in the Fill-in text box.

Independent Challenge 2 (Continued)

i. Open the Customize the Ribbon and keyboard shortcuts screen in the Word Options dialog box, click Customize, scroll down the list of Categories, select Macros, then select the Franchise macro in the Macros list.

j. In the Press new shortcut key box, enter the command Alt+T, click Assign, then close all dialog boxes.

k. Open the file **IL_WD_11-13.docx** from the location where you store your Data Files, then save it as **IL_WD_11_Franchise2**.

l. Use the Alt+T macro to format the document, entering **Math Kids Franchise** in the fill-in text box.

m. Open the Macros dialog box, select the Franchise macro, then click Edit.

n. Find Selection.Font.Name = "Times New Roman", change the font to **Calibri** and keep the quotation marks around Calibri, then change Selection.Font.Size = 12 to **13**.

o. Save the macro, select all the components of the Franchise macro in the Visual Basic window, copy them, close the Visual Basic window, press CTRL+N to open a new blank Word document, paste the code into the blank document, type **Created by** followed by your name below the last line, save the document as **IL_WD_11_FranchiseMacroCodes**, then close it.

p. Verify that IL_WD_11_Franchise2 is the active document, then use the Alt+T keystrokes to run the revised macro. Remember to press Cancel to bypass the Fill-in text box.

q. Verify that the font style of the document title is now Calibri and the font size is 13 pt.

r. Customize the status bar so that the language is selected.

s. In the Language section of the Options dialog box, add English (Canada) as a proofing language, if necessary.

t. On a blank line at the end of the document, insert a signature line that includes your name. Do not sign the document.

u. Save and close the document, then save and close the Franchise1 document. Remove English (Canada) as a proofing language.

v. Submit a copy of all the files you created for Independent Challenge 2 to your instructor, then exit Word. The document showing the macro codes for the Franchise macro is illustrated in **Figure 11-34**.

Figure 11-34

```
Sub Franchise()
'
' Franchise Macro
' Select all the text, change the line spacing to double, change the font to Times New Roman and 12 pt,
apply italics, insert a fill-in text box, then save the document.
'
    Selection.WholeStory
    Selection.ParagraphFormat.Space2
    Selection.Font.Name = "Calibri"
    Selection.Font.Size = 13
    Selection.Font.Italic = wdToggle
    Selection.MoveUp Unit:=wdLine, Count:=1
    Selection.Fields.Add Range:=Selection.Range, Type:=wdFieldEmpty, Text:= _
        "FILLIN ", PreserveFormatting:=True
    Selection.TypeParagraph
    ActiveDocument.Save
End Sub
Created by Your Name
```

Visual Workshop

You work for Lemieux Realty in Burlington, Vermont. The owner of the company, Antoine Lemieux, regularly holds seminars to teach first-time home buyers all about how to purchase a home. Antoine asks you to create a flyer to distribute around town and on social media. Open IL_WD_11-14.docx from the location where you store your Data Files, then save it as **IL_WD_11_LemieuxRealtyFlyer**. Select THURSDAY, May 11, 2028 (but not the paragraph mark following), then create a character style called **Flyer** that uses these formats: Bold, Italic, 18 pt, and the Light Blue font color. Apply the Flyer character style to First Time Home Buyer. Modify the character style by changing the font size to 24 pt and the color to Blue. Format, arrange, and group the three graphic objects so the completed flyer appears as shown in **Figure 11-35**. You will need to apply the Convex bevel effect to the sun shape, the Cutout artistic effect to the picture of the Sold sign, and the 8800 K color tone to the oval picture of the couple holding a set of keys. Compress all the pictures in the document to 150 ppi. Enter your name where indicated in the footer, save the document, submit a copy to your instructor, then close the document.

Figure 11-35

First Time Home Buyer

Seminar

Hosted by Antoine Lemieux

THURSDAY, May 11, 2028

Lemieux Realty
56 Garden Drive, Burlington, VT 05401
802-555-2232

Your Name

Thirdman/Pexels; RDNE Stock project/Pexels

Index

D

E